Professional Economics Ltd.

Infrastructure and Utility Economics: the economics of sunk costs
(Second edition)

An introduction to the innate economics of electricity, gas, water, wastewater, rail and all industries requiring significant sunk costs
(formerly Basic Network Utility Economics)

By Mark Hull

Copyright © Mark Hull 2017

All rights reserved. No reproduction, copy or transmission of this publication may be made without written permission.

No portion of this publication may be reproduced, copied or transmitted save with written permission or in accordance with the provisions of the Copyright, Designs and Patent Act 1988, or under the terms of any licence permitting limited copying issued by the Copyright Licensing Agency, Saffron House, 6-10 Kirby Street, London EC1N 8TS. In the United States of America Sections 107 and 108 of the 1976 United States Copyright Act apply.

Any person who does any unauthorized act in relation to this publication may be liable to criminal prosecution and civil claims for damages.

Limit of liability / Disclaimer of Warranty: while the publisher and author have used their best efforts in preparing this book, they make no representation or warranties with respect to the accuracy or completeness of the contents of this book and specifically disclaim any implied warranties of merchantability or fitness for a specific purpose. No warranty may be created or extended by sales representatives or written sales material. The advice and strategies contained herein are intended for a general global readership, and may not be suitable for your situation; where appropriate you should consult a professional experienced in your field. Neither the publisher nor the author shall be liable for any loss of profit or any other commercial damages, including but not limited to special, incidental, consequential or other damages.

The Author has asserted his right to be identified as the author of this work in accordance with the Copyright, Designs and Patent Act 1988.

This edition published 2017 by Professional Economics Limited, Registered Office 20-22 Wenlock Road, London England N1 7GU. Previous editions were published in 2013 (Review edition) and 2014 (First edition) under the title Basic Network Utility Economics by the same author.

For details of this and other books published by Professional Economics Limited visit www.professionaleconomics.net

ISBN: 978-0-9576990-1-4

Printed by PrintOnDemand-Worldwide.com, Peterborough, UK

Explain this using neoclassical economics

Copyright image untraceable; the publisher donates ¢10 to UNESCO for every copy sold

"If you find from your own experience that something is a fact and it contradicts what some authority has written down, then you must abandon the authority and base your reasoning on your own findings."

Leonardo da Vinci Notebooks circa 1510

This book is dedicated to the following inspiring teachers who taught me at the Economics Faculty in the University of Bristol 1974-1977: Anup Shah, Tony Brewer, Miles Fleming, Chris Gilbert, Bryn Giles, Martin Slater, David Demery, Richard Lecomber, Alan Armstrong, Malcolm Clarke and Nigel Duck.

And to the following inspirational teachers at London Business School 1986-88: Peter Williamson, John Bateson, Rob Goffey, Roy Westbrook, Elroy Dimson, Derek Bunn, and Michael Hay.

And, of course, to the following inspired statisticians and economists: MJ Farrell, Harvey Liebenstein, Ralph Turvey, Andre Shleifer, Michael Beesley, Stephen Littlechild, and Ian Byatt.

Introduction

I once read an article by an academic economist with a title something like "32 Kinds Of General Barrier To Entering an Industry"[1]. If this seems a perfectly reasonable kind of thing for an economist to write about, I suggest you put this book down right now and find a really good book to read.

If, on the other hand, you share my incredulity that someone could want to write such a useless article then this book may be for you. My reaction to that article was disbelief, which was why I continued skimming it: Why would anyone want a list of thirty-two kinds of barrier to entry? Who was this person who could not understand the general idea of a barrier to entry, or assumed their readers could not? Surely, the author could apply themselves, and think of a thirty-third kind of entry barrier? Who would ever commission such a useless article? As a person who uses economics for practical purposes, I cannot bear to read applied economics which cannot be applied. There is very little economics that is more pragmatic than infrastructure economics, and yet you will find it raises intriguing theoretical issues of wide application to micro- and even macro-economics.

Who this book is for

The prime target for this book is intelligent people who have the misfortune to be studying infrastructure or utility economics, and want to get it over and done with as fast as possible. Having practised this subject professionally for many years, and having worked in competitive industries, I know a lot of useless stuff has been written about utility economics. The good news is that none of it appears in these pages, except an Appendix at the back of this book, which is included solely to show the uselessness of comparative static welfare economics. So if you have burning questions such as 'Why is there one electricity grid and two broadband grids in my home town, but a dozen broadband cables in a big city centre?', or 'What is water really used for in a modern economy?' or 'Will the Earth run out of energy one day?' then this book offers some insightful answers. I can't guarantee the answers are correct, but they might be right, and you won't find them anywhere else. After all, a useful theory must help you create predictions you could not make using just common sense, and neither common sense nor conventional textbooks will give you proper answers to those three questions.

But to speak a little more generally, this book is aimed at economists who have passed Economics 101, understand the time value of money (discounted cash flows – as well as understanding the opportunity cost of your own time) and who want to

- deepen your knowledge of real business economics, including the economics of sunk costs when technologies change (you guys should focus mainly on Chapters 3 and 4)

---

[1] This is where I am supposed to put an academic reference to this article. For reasons that will soon become apparent I am not going to.

- begin studies on industrial or regulation economics (it's the whole book for you), or
- professionals who have been given their first assignment in infrastructure or utility economics (ditto – but get the firm to buy the book; the largest cost will be your time).

To all of you, welcome! Even if this subject was not your first choice, put that behind you. Building infrastructure and running network utilities account for a good tenth of most countries' GDP, so someone has to study them properly, and it might as well be you. Let's do this properly, and make it as painless as possible.

A note on style
The style of this book is straightforward, simple, and graphic, because I believe people studying economics generally have stronger visual than verbal memories. If economists really had stronger aural recall than visual recall good textbooks would be written with 'Welfare losses from Monopoly' as a ballad, or 'Axioms of the general sequential model' as a rap. Indeed, if you have a strong aural memory you have probably already written a handful of limericks yourself on The Inutility of Giffen Goods, or set The Limits To The Hecksher-Ohlin Theorem to a tune by Dolly Parton. Good! Keep writing, and play it to any students who will listen. The spread of economics needs more people like you.

What this book covers
This book describes the fundamental economics of all industries which require investors to sink significant funds into dedicated assets which have few alternative uses if the main 'hoped-for scenario' commercially fails. A physical distribution grid, such as is used in the energy or water industries, would be a classic example, but so is most of a country's physical infrastructure, as well as the very specific technologies developed by the makers of aircraft, cars, software, entertainment products and much capital equipment.

So, this book is of wide application to industries with heavy sunk costs in specific technologies or sites. It is of no help in understanding the economics of shipping on the Great Lakes, because the Lakes were built by nature, gifted free to mankind, and leave thousands of potential routes for ships to take. But the book can be directly applied to that industry's man-made rival – the canal network of North America – because investors paid for this canal grid to be created and the owners can charge ships for using each section of canal. So there is little question of any concentration of economic power in Great Lakes shipping, unless it is in the shipping business itself, while unique canals are inevitably monopolies which can absorb all the economic rent in a value chain. The fact that canal networks do not nowadays make vast profits is due to the presence of superior technologies: road and rail. Two hundred years ago, when these canals were created, canals had no substitutes for heavy transport and so could be very profitable monopolies – unless or until someone built a second, rival, canal.

This book therefore covers the innate economics of grid industries such as canals, rail, road, water, sewers, gas, electricity, fixed-line telecoms and cable, and oil pipelines, as well as other industries that require a spatial network to be built up, such as mobile phone mast networks, mail systems, parcel delivery networks, on-the-spot news coverage, and all other industrial or commercial distribution and collection networks. The final four chapters assess some of the experiences of governments around the world who restructured and privatised their state-owned utilities.

Infrastructure economics or regulatory economics?
Covering the utilities, this book appears to deal with the same industries as regulatory economists write about, and yet it is obviously not focused on regulatory economics. How can there be two types of economics written about the same industry? One answer is that these really are different subjects. This book is one of the few that discusses the economics of the series of decisions that needs to be made when building physical infrastructure, and how to maintain and operate these efficiently once running. It explicitly allows for technological progress changing the possibilities that successive entrants face, and handles the serious asset valuation and benchmarking problems that practical economic regulators face when making the most important assessments. Regulation theory tends to assume these problems away, and that the utility operating the asset is profitable, but this is often untrue; most of the world's rail industries, as well as many transport, water, wastewater, gas and electricity utilities make operating losses. A second, allied, point is that regulatory textbooks tend to be written by economists with little direct experience of the real problems innate in these industries.

The third, and deepest, answer is that this book is designed to *complement* regulatory theory courses by providing you with a solid grounding in the real 'natural' economics of the infrastructure and utility network industries *before the regulators or politicians get to work*. It is therefore globally applicable, and based on global experiences, rather than reflecting the politics and laws constraining the regulator in one particular country or State. So this book makes economic comparisons between industries, and across the world. It is the general textbook on infrastructure economics before we consider detailed regulatory issues, which inevitably vary by State and industry; if you are studying regulatory economics it is essential if you want to test the practical relevance of your tutor's theories.

What this book does not do
As we have just said, this book is not a specialist text on regulation. Although there are brief introductions to energy economics, water economics, natural resource marginal economics, transport economics, and posts/mail economics, this book is not a specialist textbook on any of these subjects. Rather, it attempts to bring together the common features of all these utilities, so that you can compare and contrast, before diving deeply into the one you happen to be engaged with first. Lastly, you already know that this book contains no poems or sheet music, and have correctly appraised that it cannot prop up a door off its

hinges or placate a large angry dog. Readers needing to stave off attacks from dogs are referred to the publisher's text on applied econometrics.

Why this book exists

This book grew out of a series of lectures given at Oxford Brookes University Business School between 2006 and 2012, which in turn reflected my experiences as a professional utility economist. At Brookes I sought basic modern textbooks for my students online, in University libraries, and in academic bookshops, but was disappointed to find nothing that was both correct and written at the level of a basic guide to infrastructure and utility economics.

How can this be? Surely this is all a well-known part of microeconomics? Well, it is true that modern general economics textbooks contain standard chapters on the "natural monopolies" that have not changed much since the 1930s. But the problem is that those books are generally written by economists with little direct experience of the utility industries. The authors just assume that network utilities have strong economies of scale, and therefore fit into an economic model of an industry with roots that go back to a theory by John Stuart Mill in 1848[2].

The problem is that modern professional utility economists know that
1. The neoclassical model of static demand and cost curves is rarely the most useful way to analyse a market in the twenty first century
2. The evidence for strong economies of scale in the classic natural monopolies (electricity, gas or water) is weak beyond a point that is far smaller than most of today's utilities. The balance of evidence seems to suggest now that fully-costed grid long run cost curves are rather flat, not downward-sloping, as Mill and co. believed in the nineteenth century
3. The distinguishing feature of most infrastructure and physical networks is their *sunk costs* and their embodiment of the state of technology at the time they were built. Sunk costs do not fit into neoclassical economics because they are an asymmetry in time, and time as an irreversible arrow simply does not feature in the neoclassical paradigm. In the neoclassical world resources are time-symmetric, homogenous, and available to all. In the real world the future is unknowable, technology improves apparently randomly, and there is no guarantee that a new technology will have the same sort of shape of cost curve or production function as the old technology, so if technological shifts are admitted any justification for applying the calculus (the rationale of the neoclassicals) disappears.

Consequently, economists need some radically different theories to explain infrastructure economics, and why heavy utilities are so strongly monopolised. In fact, the theories are not difficult to grasp, but they lie outside what is currently

---

[2] Principles of Political Economy Book 2, Chapter 15. However, by Book 5 Chapter 11 Mill calls them "practical monopolies", implicitly acknowledging that there is little that is 'natural' about a man-made canal, water, or gas grid (there were no electricity grids in 1848).

accepted as economic theory – even though practising utility economists need to know them! Several times the author has been told that these theories may work but they should be seen as business strategy rather than economics. No! Wrong! It is economics. Or what economics should be.

My reaction is 'The world is as it is, and economics needs theories that fit the world, not to squeeze the world into theories based on assumptions that were valid a hundred years ago.' I believe that intelligent, inquisitive readers should have the general theories explained in full, so that you are able to come to informed conclusions on your own. And, since I could not find such a book, I have had to write it myself.

Preface to the Second Edition

This book was first published in 2013 as Basic Network Utility Economics. I changed the title in this second edition because of the growing recognition of the importance of infrastructure in enabling modern economies to grow sustainably. This is the only economics text that explains the sequence of decisions that should be made before a piece of infrastructure is rationally built, and the economics of utilities that use the infrastructure, once built.

Of course this same explicit analysis of sunk costs applies to a decision by a firm considering *any* market entry or expansion, as all entry decisions involve some degree of sunk costs in practice. It is also essential to link the economics of creating the infrastructure of the classic utilities to their role as irretrievably sunk costs, and hence their prominence as innate natural monopolies. Many textbooks on utility regulation simply assume utilities have infrastructure and that utilities are monopolies, as if the two are unrelated – which of course they will be, if your economic models fail to take account of changes in technology, and fail to treat sunk costs as an asymmetry in time. Some textbooks hide behind the neoclassical façade that all utilities have very high fixed costs, but the modern evidence (see Chapter 2) does not support this. Others concede that the natural monopolies are caused by sunk costs, but do not follow this up with a coherent analysis of sunk costs through time. This textbook is the only one of which the author is aware that takes a strictly sequential approach to modelling the sequence of sunk cost investment and operating decisions that create natural utility monopolies. If the sunk cost assumptions are varied appropriately, the same theory, outlined in Chapter 3, and more fully developed in Chapter 4, accurately predicts zero entrants to a market, monopolies, duopolies, oligopoly, monopolistic (or imperfect) competition, and perfect competition without the need to assume any production or cost functions (see Figure 48 on page 116). It is a truly general model explaining the evolution of the main market structures recognised in textbooks today.

The main changes since the First Edition are that the old Chapter 1 has been relegated to an Appendix in the book, so that we begin by introducing the industry's basic terms and concepts, briefly review the evidence for the traditional theory in Chapter Two, and then explain sunk costs and the general sequential model in Chapter Three. A new Chapter Four fleshes out the general sequential theory into more formal models of decision-making sequences and dynamic business systems involving three key stakeholders: investors, managers and customers. Chapters Five and onwards follow the First edition: inevitably some errors were brought to my attention (particularly in Chapter Eight), and some chapters needed to be updated after three years. I particularly wish to thank Stephen Littlechild for his efforts to correct and improve sections of the text, and Kim Warren for his considerable help in formulating the systems models in Chapter 4. Naturally, all remaining errors are my own.

Mark Hull
Oxford June 2017

List of Chapters

Introduction	v
Chapter 1: Basic utility industry concepts, value chains, and grids	1
Chapter 2: Economies of scale and scope – theory and evidence	36
Chapter 3: Sunk costs and a general sequence model	59
Chapter 4: Applying the general sequence model to markets with significant sunk costs	84
Chapter 5: Calculating forward-looking long run marginal costs of a network utility (LRICs)	132
Chapter 6: Measuring utility outputs properly, and the evolution of utility value chains	142
Chapter 7: Measuring the efficiency of utilities	166
Chapter 8: Competition, concessions and regulation: the main options in practice	225
Chapter 9: Electricity restructuring and privatisation lessons	274
Chapter 10: Gas restructuring and privatisation	306
Chapter 11: Water privatisations, concessions and trading	330
Chapter 12: Restructuring of rail	363
Chapter 13: Some overall conclusions	391
Appendix: Neoclassical theory of monopoly welfare losses	397
Index	419

Detailed Table of Contents

Introduction	v
Who this book is for	v
A note on style	vi
What this book covers	vi
Infrastructure economics or regulatory economics?	vii
What this book does not do	vii
Why this book exists	viii
Preface to the Second Edition	x
Acknowledgements	xxvii
Chapter 1: Basic utility industry concepts, value chains, and grids.	1
Basic definitions of market structure	1
Industry value chains:	1
The core idea	1
Value added definitions	2
A specific example: bread	3
Bread in an urban economy	3
The energy and water industries' value chains	7
Electricity	8
Gas	10
Water	11
Waste water	13
Of grids and dendritic networks	14
Transmission grids	14
Distribution and Collection networks	14
Comparison of utility value chains with bread or milk	17
General policy implications of the utilities' value chains	18
Energy economics – in four pages	19
Energy flows in a real economy	19
Has the world got enough energy? Will future generations face serious energy shortages?	21
When will the world run out of fossil fuels?	23
Demand characteristics of the classic utilities	23
Electricity	24
Gas	25
Water economics	26
Water demand	26
Domestic water demand	27
Waste water demand	28
Transport economics	29
Innate transport demand	29
Maritime transport economics	30
Economics of wheeled transport	30
Road economics	31
Air transport	33
Postal services, and other 'intermittent grids'	33

Appendix 1: The intellectual origins of value added chains 35
Chapter 2: Economies of scale and scope – theory and evidence 36
   The simple neo-classical theory of network monopolies 36
      Immediate objections 37
   Better-formulated hypotheses on scale and scope economies 39
      Economies of scope 39
      Governance and efficiency 47
   Empirical evidence of scale and scope economies 47
      Evidence from electricity 48
      From gas 50
      From water 52
      Evidence of economies of scope 52
      Overall evidence on economies of scale and scope in grids 54
      The telecoms paradox 54
   Generic limitations of static neo-classical economic theories 55
      Industries with strong economies of scale 55
      Technological progress 56
      Industries without technological progress? 57
      Growing incomes 57
Chapter 3: Sunk costs and a general sequence model 59
   Sunk costs 59
      Sunk cost concepts & definitions – some refinements 59
      Examples of sunk costs in practice 60
      The elapsed life of a sunk cost asset 64
      The financial performance of enduring utility industries 66
   A general sequence model 67
      Axioms of a general sequence theory 68
      The number of players in a market 68
      The business environment of an industry or firm 69
      Entry and exit decision rules for the firm 70
      Entry barriers and sunk costs: are they the same? 74
      The economics of small sunk expenditures 75
   The economics of large sunk costs 75
      Lumpy investments 76
      Sequential discrete investments 76
      The different perceptions of investors and managers 78
      Railways as an example 78
   *Appendix 1: A financial ratio comparison of enduring utilities with
   other businesses* 82
Chapter 4: Applying the general sequence model to markets with
significant sunk costs 84
   The general sequence model of entries with significant sunk costs 84
      Zero entrants 84
      First mover entry – monopoly 85
      Sequential entry of a second player 87
      Dynamic market entry concepts 90
      Systems modelling of one and two player games through time 94

"Scooping the market" 98
Full systems modelling games of twin entrants 100
Simultaneous entry of a second player 101
Two player entries: conclusions 107
Middle-games and end-games 107
A third entrant 108
Simultaneous entry of three or more players 111
General conclusions on sequential or simultaneous entry conditions 113
Competitive strategies for middle-games 113
A transformed business environment 114
End-games 116
The model applied to non-grid utilities 117
Posts 117
Telecommunications 118
Buses 118
Radio & TV networks 119
Wider applications of the general sequence model 120
Appendix 1: Hotelling's linear positioning model 122
An ice cream seller on the beach – monopoly 122
Two ice cream sellers – duopoly 123
A third ice cream seller – tri-opoly 124
Specific conclusions from the Hotelling model 125
General conclusions from the linear positioning model 126
Appendix 2: The intellectual derivation of the sequence model 127
JS Mill's theory of natural monopolies 127
Baumol's contestability and the fixed cost/sunk cost thought-experiment 127
The sequence model of sunk costs 129

Chapter 5: Calculating forward-looking long run marginal costs of a network utility (LRICs) 132
LRMC in a growing economy: Long Run Incremental Costs 132
How to calculate LRIC for a firm or industry 132
Calculating the Long Run Incremental Cost of a piped water system ... 133
The Long Run Incremental Cost of bulk treated water 133
The LRIC for water transmission and distribution grids 135
LRIC of water retailing and testing 139
Summary LRIC for drinking water 140

Chapter 6: Measuring utility outputs properly, and the evolution of utility value chains 142
Bulk production 143
Energy bulk production 143
Water and wastewater bulk treatment 143
Plant economies of scale in the water industry 145
Grids 147
Population clustering 147
Connections per person 148

- The default measures of scale for a utility grid: mains length and number of connections ... 148
  - Hilliness as a driver of water distribution costs ... 149
- *Retail* ... 151
- *Growth of energy value chains in the long term* ... 151
  - Delivered energy value chains ... 151
- *The long run evolution of water and wastewater value chains* ... 152
  - Water and wastewater provision in poor countries ... 152
  - Growth of the water and wastewater value chains in richer countries ... 155
  - The clean water value chain in rich countries ... 155
  - The wastewater value chain in rich countries ... 157
  - Stewardship of the planet – and its costs ... 164
- Chapter 7: Measuring the efficiency of utilities ... 166
  - *The core concepts of productivity and efficiency* ... 166
  - *Measuring inputs: first, the pragmatic approach* ... 167
  - *The theoretical approach: allocative efficiency or productive efficiency?* ... 169
    - Productive or technical efficiency ... 170
    - Allocative efficiency ... 171
    - Productive or technical inefficiency and X-inefficiency: same idea, new words ... 172
    - Allocative or productive efficiency? ... 173
  - *Unit cost comparisons* ... 174
    - Bulk energy generation ... 174
    - Utility retailing ... 175
  - *Regression measures of efficiency – including multiple outputs* ... 175
    - Water and wastewater treatment – a simple regression ... 175
    - Twin outputs – for a grid ... 179
    - Cross-sectional econometrics ... 180
    - Using regression techniques to measure inefficiency ... 181
  - *Data Envelopment Analysis (DEA)* ... 182
    - Expanding the sample efficiency frontier ... 187
  - *Different definitions of the productivity frontier* ... 189
  - *Patterns of industry inefficiency: potential distributions inside the production set* ... 191
  - *Theories, facts and Bayes* ... 193
    - Rationalism, empiricism and Kant's synthesis ... 193
    - Positive and normative economics ... 197
    - Bayesian approaches ... 198
    - Bayesian handling of useless data ... 200
    - Applying Bayesian methods in economics ... 201
    - Bayes and the parametric vs non-parametric debate ... 202
    - Cross-sectional comparisons – a suggested approach ... 204
    - Use significance levels below 95% when testing down ... 204
    - Stochastic Frontiers Analysis ... 205
    - Problems with using stochastic frontiers in utilities ... 207

Non-traditional assumptions of inefficiency distributions
in utilities 207
Total Factor Productivity (TFP) 211
Malmquist measures 213
    Malmquist measures – when the industry average does
    not move 213
    Malmquist measures – the general case 215
    Possible Malmquist frontiers when technology is forgotten 217
    Stochastic Malmquist frontiers 218
    Malmquist indices allowing for economies of scale or scope? 218
Panel data 219
The importance of good quality data 220
Appendix 1: the intellectual development of Malmquist indices 221
Appendix 2: panel data inadequacies 223

Chapter 8: Competition, concessions and regulation: the main options in practice 225
General competition policies to rebalance consumers' interests 225
Competition policy in the USA 226
    Trusts and anti-trust law 226
Competition policy in Europe 228
    Article 101 229
    Article 102 229
    Summary of EU competition policy 230
Overall goals for injecting competition into utility monopolies 231
    Restructuring an industry to promote as much
    competition as possible 231
Monopoly concessions or outsourcing 233
    The main concession possibilities 233
    Common utility concession problems 235
    Concession and outsourcing conclusions 238
    Policy conclusions on promoting competition in utilities 238
The basic idea of regulating a monopoly 239
    Regulation methods 239
Principal Agent theory 241
    General criticisms of Principal Agent theory 241
    Specific criticisms of Principal Agent theory 241
Incentivisation under more holistic management theories 243
    Running cost incentives 244
    Capital incentives 245
    Revenue control or price controls? 246
Rate of Return (or Cost of Service) regulation 247
    Cost of Service model – and the over-bidding game 248
    The Gain Sharing model 249
    General incentives under Rate of Return regulation (in practice) . . . 251
Yardstick regulation 252
    Shleifer's vision 252
    America's reluctance to implement Shleifer 254

The emergence of price cap regulation 255
    Littlechild's 1983 price cap 256
    Indexing for inflation: the RPI – X formula 258
    Littlechild's 1986 report on the water industry 260
    Pure price-cap or pure rate of return, and ex ante or ex
    post price setting 264
Yardsticking in practice 265
    The regulatory period & the optimal time for keeping
    efficiencies 266
    The Cost of Capital 269
    Valuing past sunk costs and Infrastructure Renewals Accounting.... 270
Chapter 9: Electricity restructuring and privatisation lessons 274
Introduction – general papers 274
The Scandinavian electricity market 274
    Nord Pool 274
    The significance of the Nordic electricity market today 276
    Nordic exchange, PJM and similar models of centralised
    trading 277
Chile and Argentina 278
    Chile 278
    Argentina 280
*The UK after 1990: continual reform eventually produces
competition* 281
    Wholesale electricity markets - the Pool and its successors 282
    Generation and transmission 284
    Electricity distribution and supply 287
    Summary evaluations of benefits of competition 290
Texas and California: contrasting approaches, different results 291
    Progressive reform in Texas 291
    California: the starting position 293
    California's restructuring & reforms 294
    The 2000 – 2001 California meltdown 296
    California trading and gaming 296
    California: the immediate lessons 299
    A longer-term comparison of the electricity reforms
    in California and Texas 300
Some international conclusions about electricity industry reform 301
Appendix: answers to questions about the UK's privatisation 305
Chapter 10: Gas restructuring and privatisation 306
Introduction 306
The sources of natural gas 306
The North American gas industry 308
    History of the North American gas industry 308
    Geography of the North American gas industry 309
    Growth of the North American gas grid 310
    Fundamental competition issues of North American gas
    markets 312

  Deregulation of the retail gas monopolies 312
  Other concentrations of market power in American gas markets 314
  North American gas market conclusions 318
 The UK: exploding a vertically integrated monopoly
 AFTER privatisation 318
  Background 318
  How to abuse your market position / play to your
  strategic strengths 320
  Breaking-up British Gas 1994-1998 320
  Legal separation of the gas businesses 321
  Levelling the playing field 323
  Post 1998 reforms to promote upstream competition 323
  Downstream competition and regulation within the UK
  since 1998 324
  Other gas examples – Japan 326
 Appendix: Answers to the Japanese gas company quiz 328
Chapter 11: Water privatisations, concessions and trading 330
 Water industry theory 330
  Competition, concessions and regulation: the general prospects . . . 332
 The UK's experience since 1989: consolidation but no vertical
 separation 333
  Background 333
  The 1989 framework for regulating private water monopolies 334
  The 1989 privatisation 336
  Privatisation – the short term results 1989-94 336
  Privatisation – the long term results 337
  The experience of regulation since 1989 340
  Introduction of competition? 342
  Overall conclusions 343
 Chile 1988- 2008 343
 Water concessions or franchises 345
  Colombia – Cartagena 1994 345
  Bolivia – Cochabamba 2000! 346
  Comparing Carthagena and Cochabamba 347
  Argentina – Buenos Aires 1993-2006 348
  Some general conclusions about water or wastewater
  regulation and concessions 350
 Water trading 350
  Alternative theoretical concepts 350
  Direct trading of water 351
  Physical trading of water in practice 352
  Trading water rights – the theoretical debate 354
  Chilean water trading 356
  Trading water in the western USA 357
  Australia: successful trading of water rights 359
  Lessons from Chilean, American and Australian water
  rights trading 361

Chapter 12: Restructuring of rail 363
   Total transport demand and modal demands 363
      Patterns of intermodal transport demand 363
   Fundamental economic characteristics of surface transport 366
   Rail's general characteristics 367
      The proportion of revenues from customers vs non-customers 369
   US freight – profitable, competitive & de-regulated 369
      Sunshine regulation 369
      The emergence of Rate of Return Regulation 370
      The Interstate Commerce Commission 1887-1980 371
      Deregulation of rail 1976-1980 372
      Competitive rail freight since 1980 372
      US rail conclusions 373
   Sweden's slow progressive reforms 373
      Background 373
      The reforms of the 1980s and 90s 374
      Effects of the twentieth century reforms 375
      21st century problems and reforms 375
   Britain's restructuring and privatisation 377
      Background 377
      Privatisation 1994-1997 379
      The rolling stock 380
      The operating companies' franchises 381
      Infrastructure provision: Railtrack then Network Rail 382
   Conclusions about rail sector reforms 384
      The inter-relationship of new track and rolling stock assets 388
   Appendix to Chapter 12 389
      Answers to the Quick Quiz 389
Chapter 13: Some overall conclusions 391
   Economic theory 391
   Measuring efficiency 391
   Competition, concessions and regulation 392
   Professional texts 392
   Restructurings in practice 394
      The main results from successful utility reforms 395
      Appendix: suggestions for further reading 396
      Professional texts 396
      Textbooks 396
   Appendix 1: Neoclassical theory of monopoly welfare losses 397
   Demand curves and consumer surplus 397
   Monopolies 399
      A real example 400
      Origins of monopolies 401
   The neoclassical monopoly model 403
   Monopolistic ('imperfect') competition due to product differentiation 407
      Brand example 408

> Comparison of monopolistic competition with monopoly 408
> *Welfare losses from monopoly* 409
> > A general monopoly with conventional rising costs 409
> > Natural monopolies with never-ending economies of scale 412
> > Where monopoly creates inefficiency 415
> *Realism of theoretical welfare losses* 416
> > The usual textbook answer 416
> > An alternative view 416

Index 419

List of figures

Figure 1: The wheat-to-bread value chain in the UK 6
Figure 2: The value chain for fresh milk in the UK 7
Figure 3: The electricity industry value chain 8
Figure 4: An electricity sub-station hard at work 8
Figure 5: Electricity distribution wires to a farm 9
Figure 6: A 'dendritic' pattern: a hornbeam tree in winter 15
Figure 7: A beech tree busy both collecting and distributing nutrients 16
Figure 8: Value chains of UK utilities compared with 'normal'
  industry value chains for bread and milk 17
Figure 9: The main commercial energy flows in the UK (in million
tonnes of oil equivalent) 20
Figure 10: Maslow's hierarchy of needs - applied to water services 28
Figure 11: The speed-flow curve of a given road 31
Figure 12: Effects of congestion on equilibrium road traffic levels 32
Figure 13: Conventional textbook explanation of grid monopolies 36
Figure 14: Economies of scope 40
Figure 15: Maintaining utility distribution assets – find the
  economies of scope in this 44
Figure 16: Laying new telecoms cables directly on top of old 55
Figure 17: A clear sunk cost 61
Figure 18: How much of this communications tower is a sunk cost? 61
Figure 19: A sunk cost? 63
Figure 20: Sinking the asset 64
Figure 21: A modern sunk cost: the Millau viaduct in France 64
Figure 22: A classic utility asset – and sunk cost – constructed
  two thousand years ago 65
Figure 23: The water conduit inside the Pont du Gard 65
Figure 24: The general expected cash flow of a firm considering
  entering and exiting a new market 70
Figure 25: The sunk costs of entering a market 72
Figure 26: The general entry decision for any firm considering
  entering a market 73
Figure 27: The stylised annual cash flow of a large lumpy investment 76
Figure 28: The stylised decision sequence & annual cash flow of
  a general infrastructure asset 77
Figure 29: The sequence of entry decisions for the first mover
  in a utility market 86
Figure 30: Entry of player Number Two can be simultaneous
  or sequential 88
Figure 31: The First Mover's perspective at its key Go Ahead decision 88
Figure 32: Mover One's perspective one year after launching 89
Figure 33: Mover One's perspective after it discovers Mover
  Two's impending entry 89
Figure 34: The growth of a monopoly utility's infrastructure and
  customer base 90

Figure 35: The extent of competition: cities within a country 91
Figure 36: Possible patterns of competition between distribution
zones in a city 92
Figure 37: The general evolution of two utilities entering a
geographically-segmented market 94
Figure 38: A business dynamics model of a developing monopoly
utility's resources and capabilities 95
Figure 39: Screen shot from a systems model of Mover 1's
profitable monopoly game 97
Figure 40: Simplified dynamic model of two competing
utilities where Firm One launched first 98
Figure 41: Mover Two's business model if Mover One has
scooped the market 99
Figure 42: Screen shot of a systems model where Mover One
has scooped the market 100
Figure 43: Enter Player Three: the decision sequence 108
Figure 44: Possible distributions of investors' estimates of
the ultimate size of a fast-growing market 109
Figure 45: The time-adjustment paths of 1) technology adoption,
2) capital markets, and 3) sales of a new product 110
Figure 46: Porter's mid-game competitive strategies in a
stable business environment 114
Figure 47: Utility competition-in-the-market: a 'green sheen'
of new telecoms cables laid right on top of old ones 116
Figure 48: The standard end game market structures, and how
they are reached 116
Figure 49: A hot beach with a uniform distribution of consumers
along it 122
Figure 50: Where will two ice cream sellers position themselves? 123
Figure 51: What is the Nash equilibrium with three sellers? 124
Figure 52: Average lifetime costs for each long term supply solution 134
Figure 53: Step 2 – calculate the optimal investment path for a
firm by ranking schemes by cost 134
Figure 54: Step 3 – the LRIC of abstracting, storing and treating
piped water in bulk 135
Figure 55: The lifetime costs of a grid's IT system for small,
medium and large grids 136
Figure 56: The Long Run Incremental Costs of all the main
cost drivers in a water grid 137
Figure 57: Step 4: The LRIC of a water distribution grid 138
Figure 58: Step 5: The LRIC of retailing water 139
Figure 59: Step 6: Add all the LRICs together 140
Figure 60: step 7: Summary: the Long Run Incremental
Cost of piped water 140
Figure 61: The 'output' of three different water treatment
works A, B and C 144
Figure 62: Comparing the outputs of three different

sewage treatment works	145
Figure 63: House clustering reduces mains length and costs	147
Figure 64: Lifting water in a flat area	150
Figure 65: Lifting water in a hilly area	150
Figure 66: The world's wastewater challenges for 2030	154
Figure 67: The steadily rising outputs of the global drinking water value chain	155
Figure 68: The steadily rising outputs of the urban wastewater value chain	157
Figure 69: A simplified pattern of the sewers in an old town straddling a river	162
Figure 70: Designing interceptor sewers along a riverbank	163
Figure 71: Power creates responsibility in beings that are morally aware	164
Figure 72: The two types of economic inefficiency in a single-output twin input model	170
Figure 73: Firms D and E are more allocatively efficient (cheaper) than firms B and F	171
Figure 74: Scatter plot of ten water treatment companies' efficiencies	176
Figure 75: Simple regression of water treatment costs on treatment work for ten companies	177
Figure 76: Using a regression line to guesstimate the COLS efficiency frontier	178
Figure 77: Scatter plot of mains efficiency against connections efficiency for the 10 utilities	180
Figure 78: Using a simple regression to compare the efficiency of 10 utility grids	181
Figure 79: Estimating a production frontier using a regression	182
Figure 80: The regression slope has the wrong sign	183
Figure 81: DEA: the basic idea	185
Figure 82: Measuring efficiency using the DEA frontier	186
Figure 83: Expanding the DEA frontier	187
Figure 84: Expanding the production possibility frontier in general	188
Figure 85: Three theoretical definitions of the productivity frontier	189
Figure 86: Possible distributions of inefficiency in some selected industries	192
Figure 87: Distributions of inefficiency typically assumed in Stochastic Frontiers	206
Figure 88: Possible patterns of inefficiency: the standard half-normal distribution	209
Figure 89: A uniform distribution of inefficiency within the production set	209
Figure 90: The 'comfort zone' distribution of utility inefficiency	210
Figure 91: A Malmquist measure of utility grids' efficiencies and frontier shifts – the simple case	214
Figure 92: The general case of Malmquist efficiency indicators with two outputs	216

Figure 93: Twin output PPFs after a century 217
Figure 94: A world where technologies are forgotten 218
Figure 95: General value chains for heavy utilities 231
Figure 96: A product dimension map of utility outsourcing
    and concession 234
Figure 97: Regulating a monopoly: the basic idea 239
Figure 98: To grow profits in a utility regulators and investors
have to incentivise managers 244
Figure 99: American utilities at a glance 247
Figure 100: Management incentives under traditional US
    Gain Sharing regulation 250
Figure 101: Shleifer's benchmarking yardstick: the core idea 252
Figure 102: The change in a utility's revenue cap = RPI- X 262
Figure 103: A stylised version of the RPI-X revenue cap used in
    the water industry in England and Wales after privatisation 263
Figure 104: Circular logic 272
Figure 105: Setting regulatory asset values over time: the
    Byatt causal spiral 272
Figure 106: The evolution of Nord Pool in the 1990s 276
Figure 107: The UK electricity industry in 1989, prior to privatisation 281
Figure 108: Summary of the evolution of the privatised electricity
    industry in England and Wales 284
Figure 109: The five types of natural gas 307
Figure 110: The main sources of 'wet' and 'dry' natural gas
    in mainland USA 310
Figure 111: North American gas production since 1970 (Bcf pa) 311
Figure 112: The main gas transport routes of North America 311
Figure 113: States with Natural Gas Choice Programs in 2009 313
Figure 114: Privatisation of British Gas 319
Figure 115: Restructuring of the privatised UK gas industry 1995-2007 .. 322
Figure 116: The long run marginal cost of drinking water –
    again (for derivation see Chapter 5) 330
Figure 117: The sunk costs of water 331
Figure 118: The contestable parts of the modern water
    industry's value chains 332
Figure 119: Heavy duty regulation: the three regulators of a
    private water utility 334
Figure 120: Overwhelmed? The 6 main forces acting upon
    a private water utility 335
Figure 121: Average water charges in England and Wales since
    1989 in 2006-07 constant prices 338
Figure 122: The 17 exits from the water industry in England
    & Wales 1989-2012 341
Figure 123: The structure of the wastewater (sewage) industry
    in England and Wales 342
Figure 124: Evolution of the drinking water industry since
    privatisation 343

Figure 125: Modes of transport used by passengers in
    4 regions of the world 364
Figure 126: Modes of transport for freight around the world 365
Figure 127: Sources of modern rail revenues 366
Figure 128: The general economic structure of the rail industry 368
Figure 129: Sources of operating funds for two national rail systems 369
Figure 130: Swedish rail reforms in the late 20th century 375
Figure 131: Number of passenger journeys on British railways
    since 1921 377
Figure 132: The evolving structure of the British rail industry
    during and after privatisation 380
Figure 133: The two main sources of income for the British rail
    industry 1986-2013 in constant prices (2013-14 £m) 383
Figure 134: Strategic options for reforming the rail sector 385
Figure 135: The standard utility concession model 387
Figure 136: Product space map of train operators' routes 387
Figure 137: Marshall's basic 'X' of neo-classical supply and demand 398
Figure 138: A linear demand curve means the MR curve's slope
    is twice the AR curve's slope 404
Figure 139: (a) Unprofitable and (b) profitable monopolies 405
Figure 140: (a) Monopoly and (b) perfect competition in equilibrium 405
Figure 141: Comparison of monopoly with perfect competition
    (in equilibrium) 406
Figure 142: Monopolistic competition 408
Figure 143: Welfare losses from a monopoly with rising costs 410
Figure 144: Welfare losses from monopoly with rising costs
    (MC version) 411
Figure 145: Welfare losses with constant long run costs 413
Figure 146: Welfare losses from a monopoly with ever-falling
    unit costs 413
Figure 147: Welfare losses when monopoly leads to inefficiency 415

Acknowledgements

While obviously they do not necessarily agree with this book, and are certainly not responsible for any errors, the following people, as well as those formally cited in the references and the people listed in the Dedication, gave me useful experiences or taught me useful skills or knowledge which helped me hone economic ideas put forward here:

In the British Civil Service Patsy Harvey, Philip Hayes, Adrian Smith, Geoff Haley, Richard Herd, Martin Williamson, Peter Owen, Michael Stewart, John Barber, Graham Houston, Sid Price, Tim Tutton, Martin Smith, Richard Ireson, Tom Worsley, Tony Bottrill, Paula Diggle, Geoff Horton, Patricia Leahy, Tony Boote, Alistair Clark, Eric Price, and my Assistants at the Department of Energy Katherine and Phil;

At London Economics John Kay, Nick Morris, Sue Jaffer, Dan Elliott, David Ehrhardt, Andrew Sweet, Jeremy Leake, Ron Smith, Phil Burns, Danny Price, Chris Newton, Duncan Michie, Ian Alexander, Jonathan Davies, Rob Francis, David Harbord, Mike Webb, Robin Cohen, Nick Stern, and Richard Briant;

At Coopers & Lybrand/PricewaterhouseCoopers Charles Jenne, Wynne Jones, Steve Roberts, Chris Castles, David Storer, Nick Aked, Mike Lane, Sylvia Wenyon, Chris Smith, John Raftery, Robin Pratt, Paul Davies, Richard Laikin, Dick Dunmore, Alan Dion, Steve Smith, Robert Sale, David Noble; Sarah Deasley, Jason Mann, Dan Roberts, Frances Warburton, Trevor Sikorski, Suzanne Turner, John Gibbs, Alastair Campbell, Jean-Marc Simon, Graham Butler, Jonathan Letchfield, Mark Pearson, Chris Pleass and Helen Mounsey Baker;

At Indepen Ann Bishop, Phillipa Marks, John Hargreaves, Martin Silcock, Paul Sankey, John Smith, Brian Williamson, Matt Parr, Angela Whelan;

At centres of water industry excellence Tom Stephenson of Cranfield University, at Imperial College David Stuckey, at Leicester University Paul Herrington, and at WRc Martin Hall and Bill Kingdom;

At companies, Jean-Pierre Eymery, John Youngman, Mike Cockett, Gianrico Geissler Patrick Jarrosson, John Ley and Mike Hussey of Coates-Lorilleux Inks, Willie and John Alden, Robert Hay and Brian Winchester of the Alden Press, Mark Hannam at Heineken, at IBM Andy Stanford-Clark, at Thames Water Gordon Maxwell, Richard Oake, Steve Williams, Robin Clarke and Tony Rachwal, at Severn Trent Water Vic Cocker, and John Owen, at Welsh Water/Glas Cymru Nigel Annett and Paul Edwards, at Scottish Water Jim Brown and Ian Smith, at Bristol Water Alan Parsons and Mike King, at Mid Kent Water Malcom Bailey and Mike Clark, at East Surrey Water Phil Holder and Mike Hegarty, at Bournemouth Water Tony Cooke and Roger Harrington, at Cambridge Water Stephen Kay and Robert Burgin, at South East Water David Shore, and at Network Rail Gordon Dudman;

At regulators, Chris Bolt, Bill Emery, Tony Ballance, and Scott Reid of Ofwat, and at the Environment Agency Ronan Palmer;

And, finally, at teaching institutions Oxford Business College and Oxford Brookes University Business School Priscilla Clarke-Christopher, Tony Tooth, David Fogg, Nigel Brown, Eric Cassells, Paul Dudley, Paul Mantle, Judith Piggott, Maureen Pike, Andy Kilmister, David Horan, David Orr, Judith Thomas and Chris Harlow.

In addition, active help, comments and suggestions on this book came from

Stephen Littlechild, Fellow, Judge Business School, University of Cambridge, and Emeritus Professor, University of Birmingham

Kim Warren of Strategy Dynamics, formerly of London Business School

David Ehrhardt, Chief Executive Officer, Castalia, 1747 Pennsylvania Avenue NW Washington DC

Professor Michael Pollitt of the Judge Business School, Cambridge

Steve Smith at Ofgem,

Tom Worsley former Senior Economic Adviser Department for Transport,

Nick Aked of Frontier Economics,

Mike Lane of Edison Consulting Associates,

Tim Tutton former UK Director of Regulation at National Grid,

Verity Hull and Dom Smith of Oxford Brookes University Business School

Bob Breen, formerly of British Gas and Transco

Jo Hull of Dawn Foods and Bowman Ingredients

Tim Coelli and Chris O'Donnell from the Centre for Efficiency and Productivity Analysis at the University of Queensland

Val Harvey, David Demery and Nigel Duck of Bristol University Economics Department

And finally, of course, the love and support of my non-economist parents, Tony Hull and Jean Cockett, and my children Laura and Tom Hull, have made a massive implicit contribution to the book before you.

Chapter One

Basic utility industry concepts, value chains, and grids

Basic definitions of market structure
To begin, let's remind ourselves of some traditional, static, definitions:
- A market is a *monopoly* if there is just one firm (or 'agent') producing this good
- A market is a *duopoly* if there are just two firms ('players') in the industry, or game
- A market is a *triopoly* if there are three players in the game[3]
- A market is an *oligopoly* if there are a few large players
- A market is *competitive* if there are many firms and competition is strong
- An X-firm *concentration ratio* is the share of the market that the largest X firms have
  - e.g. a 5-firm concentration ratio of 80% means the 5 largest firms combined have 80% of the market

Now let's add some definitions which bring in a sense of time and motion:
- A market is said to be *contestable* if entry barriers are reasonably low, and a rational firm could choose to enter
- A market is said to be *un-contestable* if no rational firm would enter it given current conditions
- A normally competitive market is said to have *competition-in-the-market*
- Markets where firms compete for the right to have an exclusive monopoly are said to have *competition-for-the-market*
  - e.g. certain franchises, such as monopoly bus or train routes

Industry value chains:
The core idea
The concept of "Value Added" is at heart what retailers call "gross margin" – the

---

[3] Tri-opolies are rarely discussed but under the simple, quite feasible, assumptions of a Hotelling linear positioning game triopoly becomes the first true oligopoly – a fundamental shift from monopoly or duopoly. For a fuller explanation of this statement finish this chapter then see Chapter 4's Appendix One.

difference between a firm's sales revenue and the cost of its raw materials. In practice, for general use in all industries, the concept of "raw materials" has to be widened to include all purchases that are not factors of production:

Value added definitions
A _firm's_ value added is the difference between the "value of its goods sold" (its revenue) and its "value of goods purchased".

Note that value added includes wages, interest, taxes, depreciation, and other non-cash costs, as well as profits of all description.

An _industry_ value chain is the accumulation of value added through each stage in the production of a good, starting with a good in its natural state[4], as it enters mankind's economic system, and ending with its "final purchase" by a household or final consumer.

So the oil industry's value chain starts with crude oil in its thick black state, lying deep in the earth's crust under hundreds of metres of seawater, and finishes with you or I buying diesel for our cars, or buying a flight for which an airline will buy some jet fuel. The pencil value chain starts with trees growing in a wood and mineral graphite in the ground, and ends when we buy a pencil in the shop. A movie starts with a vision in someone's head, and ends when we have seen the movie in a cinema, bought the DVD, or downloaded it. We start with inputs valued at zero because we do not pay nature for her wonderful products – we only pay other humans. In the case of minerals, forests, and fishing, governments now often assume the place of Mother Nature and so mineral-extracting firms pay "royalties" to governments for the right to extract the minerals, in addition to all the other costs of extracting oil from under the sea. Of course governments do not pass this money on to Mother Nature, so it is in effect an extraction tax: for the extractor it is a necessary cost, while for many governments around the world it is a great source of revenue.

In passing we note that Value Added Tax (VAT) is a tax on each firm's value added. _To be an efficient tax the VAT rate should be held constant across most parts of the economy_, so there is no tax gain to be had from transferring profits or labour costs between one stage of production and the next, nor anything to be gained from introducing artificial buying and selling of goods between firms with the same owner. Its advantage over other forms of consumption tax is that all firms in the economy – not just retailers at the point of final sale – become tax collectors for the government, so an economy does not bypass the official retail sector or develop large hidden sectors behind the retailers which pay no tax. Obviously it is more complicated than a simple retail sales tax in concept, but once computer-based accounting systems became widely used by firms its implementation became relatively straightforward. In other words it could never

---

[4] For intellectual services which are sold commercially, such as books, music, movies, or games, we start with a (metaphorical) blank sheet of paper.

have become a widely adopted form of tax before the 1970s.

A specific example: bread
Let us take a basic good sold in shops the world over – bread – and break its value chain down. The first thing to note is that the industry value chain must vary according to the processes used in that economy. So in a very traditional part of the world, where cereals are grown by a householder, ground into flour, and baked daily into bread for their own consumption, we have a pure subsistence economy with no market-based value chain at all. If the economy is slightly market-based, and cereals are grown and then sold by farmers to households in the same village, who grind their flour and bake bread at home, the value chain starts with the farmer growing cereals, and ends when the farmer sells it to another household. In this case the 'bread' value chain is just a cereal-growing value chain.

As Adam Smith noticed two hundred years ago, in more complicated economies, each of the production stages and processes becomes specialised: each sells its contribution to the final output at a market-based price, which the next stage of production treats as its raw materials or inputs. So if the farmer sells her cereal to a professional miller nearly all her sales revenue is value added (ignoring the costs of any bought-in seed or fertilisers). This sale is the farmer's revenue but the miller's raw material cost. The miller adds value by grinding grains into flour which he sells for a higher price per kilogram. If this flour is now sold to final consumers – households – who bake their own bread the value chain ends, and we can now break down the value added into its two parts: the value added by the farmer, and the value added by the miller. Adding the two together should equal the sales price of flour to final consumers.

If we add a third commercial production stage – baking – into our value chain we can then explain the price of a loaf of bread as being the sum of the value added in each of the three stages of production: farming, milling and baking. We can now answer the question haunting classical theories of value – why does a house cost Z and not 17 x Z? *The sales price (the 'value' or 'worth') of a final good is the sum of the values added to it in every stage of production in the industry value chain.* Of course we now have to explain why just so much value is added at each stage of milling, baking etc., but this looks like a problem we can solve using all the familiar tools of factors of production, cost curves, industry structures, five forces etc. that the neo-classical economists and business strategists invented in the late 19th and 20th centuries. In passing we note that the final part of the theory of value conundrum – what determines the real wage rate? – is outside our scope here, and, to the extent that we have a satisfactory answer today, is found in modern growth theory.

Bread in an urban economy
Let's get real and put some numbers on these concepts. If we examine bread production in a modern economy like the UK, farmers grow wheat and sell it to millers at a price around £180 a tonne delivered to the mill[5]. It takes roughly

1½ tonnes of wheat, costing £270, to make a tonne of flour, but the miller sells the side-product (½ a tonne of chaff or bran) to farmers for pig food for around £40[6]. So, net of the chaff side-product, the miller pays roughly £270-£40 = £230 for the wheat to make a tonne of flour. The miller then sells the flour for a price of around £390 a tonne to bakers, who make bread. So, flour delivered to bakers is worth around £390 a tonne, of which the miller has had to pay about 60% (£230) for the raw material, wheat, while the other 40% represents the miller's value added. This is not all profit: out of this £160 the miller has to pay his staff and factory costs, his energy bills, his delivery costs, and fund working capital, as well as earning a decent operating profit on the capital employed in his business. In sum, at present world prices roughly a third of the value added in a tonne of flour comes from the miller and two thirds from the farmer.

In the next stage, bakers take the flour, add water, yeast, fat, salt and other ingredients, make dough, bake it, and then wrap it. For an 800g loaf that sells in the shops for 120-130p the baker will need around 440g of wheat flour, 40g of fat, yeast salt, etc. and 320g of water, so the baker needs 0.44/1000 x £390 or about 17 pence worth of flour for a loaf which he sells to wholesalers or supermarkets for a price around 51p. Table 1 shows this build-up of value added for a mass-produced 800g loaf of white bread:

Table 1: The value added components of a loaf of bread in a modern economy

Value Added Stage	Cost (p per loaf)		Function
	stage	cumulative	
Farmer	11	11	Grow wheat - natural raw material
Miller	6	17	Grind wheat into flour
Fat, salt, yeast & wrapper	4 ½	21 ½	Other raw materials kneaded to make dough
Energy (gas)	1 ½	23	Heat to bake dough
Baker	27 ½	50 ½	Make & wrap bread using capital, labour and land
Diesel	½	51	Fuel for transport to wholesaler & retailer

---

[5] Source: Bowman Ingredients and Dawn Foods Ltd, of Evesham Worcester, private communications from J Hull, European Technical Director, and colleagues.

[6] i.e. chaff is worth around £80 a tonne delivered to the pig food trader.

Table 1: The value added components of a loaf of bread in a modern economy - continued

Value Added Stage	Cost (p per loaf)		Function
	stage	cumulative	
Wholesaler	17	68	Store, break bulk, distribute, recycle waste
Retailer	57	125	Store, break bulk, retail attractively at customers' convenience, recycle waste
Retail sale price	125		Fresh loaf of bread at your convenience

Source: Bowman Ingredients and Dawn Foods Ltd., based on a world wheat price of £180 a tonne.

So, to take a typical stage in the middle of the industry value chain, the baking stage starts when the baker buys 17 pence worth of flour from a miller. The baker then adds around 33½p of value to a loaf by buying in about 4½ p of fat, salt, yeast etc., and 1½p of energy, and then adding a further 27½p as his own direct value added (labour, land and capital costs including depreciation, interest and profit) before selling the loaf for 51p (all these figures are in bulk of course) to a wholesaler. The wholesalers then 'break bulk', store, and rapidly transport bread to local shops (supermarkets carry out this wholesaling function internally). Finally, retailers (shops) sell the loaf directly to the public for a price that varies considerably with the retailers' gross margin, but centres around, say, 125p a loaf. Figure 1 illustrates the whole chain of value added from nature to the final consumer

Figure 1: The wheat-to-bread value chain in the UK

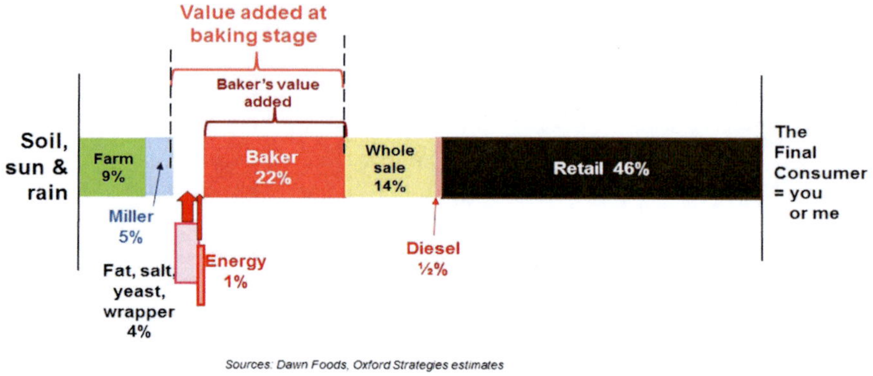

| Soil, sun & rain | Farm 9% | Baker 22% | Whole sale 14% | Retail 46% | The Final Consumer = you or me |

With inputs: Miller 5%; Fat, salt, yeast, wrapper 4%; Energy 1%; Diesel ½%. Value added at baking stage includes Baker's value added.

Sources: Dawn Foods, Oxford Strategies estimates

Please note that to simplify I have assumed that the baker, wholesaler and retailer generally own their own premises, instead of renting them, and that companies in general provide all functions themselves, rather than sub-contracting services in from specialist suppliers such as transport companies. From the economic point of view it makes no difference who owns the truck that transports the bread, or which firm pays the driver – the function is simply to transport and distribute the bread away from the centre of mass-production (the bakery), and it is an essential function whoever does it. However, the transporters will always have to buy in diesel, which comes from an entirely different value chain to bread.

Some readers may be surprised how much value added accrues to the retailer and wholesaler, who appear to do nothing to a loaf of bread except store it and move it. But in order to get the cost of manufacturing a loaf down to 51p we have had to centralise manufacturing to achieve considerable economies of scale. Demand, however, is widely dispersed. The essential other side of a concentrated manufacturing coin is a distribution function that requires staff, space and transport to get the goods out to customers across the country. In a modern economy gross retail margins are generally around 50% of the final retail sales prices, largely because of the cost of land and labour. Where land costs are lower – in rural areas, or North America (where population densities are lower, excluding the Eastern and Western seaboards) or in emerging economies – gross retail margins may be only 10-40%[7], depending, of course, on wastage rates and how fast the items sell (the stock turnover ratio). In the British bread industry it is thought that the prevalence of sell-by dates raised recycling and wastage rates to around 30% of all bakery output, until the major supermarkets put in significant efforts to reduce waste in their logistic chains in the 1990s. However, by implication, wastage rates in the rival distribution traditional chain involving traditional wholesalers and retailers may still be 30% overall. Whatever the true level, wastage rates for a perishable item like bread are nowhere near

---

[7] The author once had a student engaged in the Libyan wholesale date business, where gross retail margins for date sellers in the open air markets of Tripoli in peace time are 10-20%. Such low margins would be impossible if the retailer provides a shop lit by electricity, and totally inconceivable in Europe or North America.

zero, their cost is paid ultimately by the customer, and they are met within the distribution part of the value chain.

The neoclassical monopoly model
Figure 2 shows a value chain for the production and distribution of chilled fresh milk in a modern economy:

Figure 2: The value chain for fresh milk in the UK

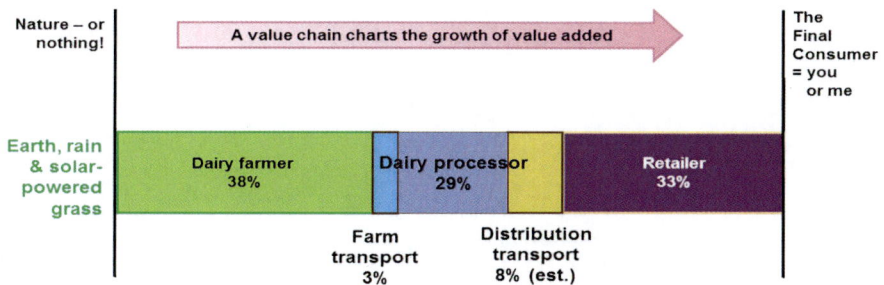

Sources: Dairy Supply Chain Margins 2011-12 by Agriculture & Horticulture Development Board on DairyCo website, Dairy Crest, Prices are for the average period 2005-2010 based on a farmgate average price of 24p per litre and an average retail price of 63 pence per litre

The dairy processor buys milk at the farm gate and delivers it to the retailer's shop[8]. Note that each sector's margins depend partly on competition in that sector – in the UK for example, the big chain retailers have a lot of power – but that even so margins can vary widely between chain retailers and independent (family-run) corner stores. Note also that because milk is heavier than bread, its transport and wastage costs may be higher, but if competition is strong and the stock turnover rate is higher than bread, retail margins in a competitive location should be lower than bread (in the UK market milk is a fiercely competitive 'foot-traffic generator' in convenience stores).

As economists reviewing the bread and milk industries, we notice that distribution, including the retailing function, seems to be taking up half the value chain, that all parts of these modern value added chains are in principle "contestable" and, in practice, some industries are very competitive – e.g. retailing, milling, baking, while the profitability of farming still follows well-known cycles and can still be heavily influenced by government agricultural policies.

The energy and water industries' value chains
Having examined industry value chains in general, we now turn to this book's main subject, utilities, and start by summarising each of the modern energy and water industries' value chains.

---

[8] See Dairyco website League Tables on www.dairyco.org.uk

Electricity

The electricity industry traditionally has the four main functions shown in Figure 3:

Figure 3: The electricity industry value chain

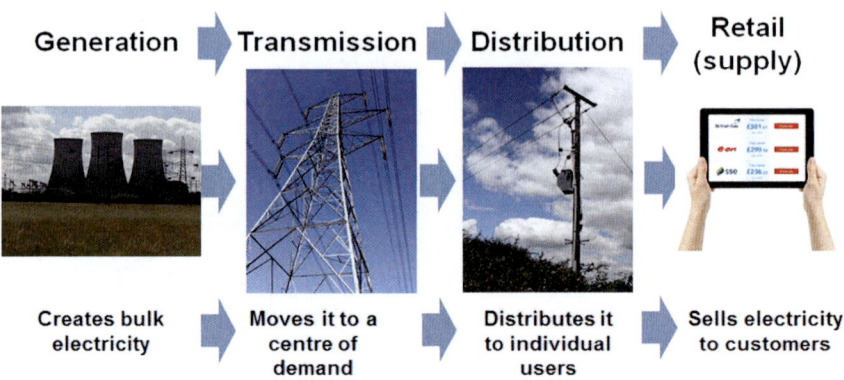

It is worth learning the four main functions of the electricity industry now, as we shall be using similar stages in the gas, water and wastewater industries.

In a conventional public electricity system electricity is generated in bulk by large power stations, and moved significant distances to the main markets across high voltage transmission wires. In most countries 'the national grid' refers to the grid of transmission towers (commonly known as pylons) and high voltage wires that transmit electricity in bulk to local centres of demand. Having arrived at each town the power is progressively stepped down to the lower voltage levels needed by most commercial or domestic customers – typically 240 or 120 Volts – using sub-stations like that shown in Figure 4.

Figure 4: An electricity sub-station hard at work

The lower voltage wires that distribute the electricity to individual premises around towns and across rural areas are called the distribution grid. In rural areas distribution wires are typically above ground; Figure 5 shows the distribution wires to a farm:

Figure 5: Electricity distribution wires to a farm

In towns, for safety and other reasons, utilities try to put distribution cables below ground, which is harder to show you in a photograph. Note that the total length of distribution grid wires in a country is far greater than the length of transmission grids because every connected street, road, or house has to have a distribution wire, while the transmission grids only need to connect the country's major centres of demand – towns and cities – with the major centres of supply – power stations or international 'inter-connectors'.

Once the electricity has been supplied to a house, office, or factory it is metered, and from this point on it is the owner's responsibility to distribute it safely around the building through their own private wiring system. However, there is then the question of paying for the electricity. This *retail, or 'supply' function* involves identifying customers at each premise, offering some kind of contract or tariff, obtaining the customer's agreement to a particular tariff, reading their electricity meters, invoicing them, and collecting the payment. There is also the socially messy business of disconnecting customers who do not pay their bills, and reconnecting new or disconnected customers. Because electricity can easily be switched off the balance of negotiating power between a customer and the electricity company can lie with the electricity supplier, especially if they are a monopoly. Consequently, many countries have laws about who may be disconnected, and in what circumstances. However, some customers have their own powerful negotiating tools. In a few countries the army or the police 'forget' to pay their electricity bills, on the understandable grounds that the government has not paid them recently, but the electricity company executives do not disconnect the army barracks or the police station – if they want to continue living, that is.

A complication to the structure of the electricity industry value chain is occurring in the 21st century: *distributed generation* has emerged and will become a lot more important. This is the generation of electricity from many small solar, wind or ground heat production units located near demand, or literally on top of it – on the roof of the customer's own premises. As technologies improve it is possible distributed generation will become more important than centrally-generated power by the mid-century, which might seem to undermine the need for national transmission grids. But such thinking is wrong: grids will still be needed to balance loads over the day (people want power at night, when there's no solar, and on days when there's no wind) or across a country, particularly if most renewable energy is generated by offshore wind, wave, or tidal power farms – i.e. a concentration of production, often nowhere near the consumers.

Grids are also essential for electricity trading between countries or continents. For instance, in principle[9], electricity can be moved along wires from Singapore in Asia through Malaysia, Thailand, Laos, Vietnam and China to Russia, and thence through Europe to Portugal and Ireland, while in the Americas, in principle, electricity can be moved from Alaska to Tierra del Fuego. But the fact that the wires are linked so that electricity can be traded between distant countries does not mean that in practice it is moved: actual trading depends on a host of political, economic, technical and commercial conditions being met, and is in fact much more likely to occur over short distances. For instance, although electricity grids are well-integrated across Europe, one company used to offer an electricity transport service from Spain to Norway, but in fact they provided excess power in Madrid, sold it there, and used the cash to buy bulk electricity in Oslo[10].

Gas

As already indicated, the structure of the gas value chain is very similar to the electricity value chain. Natural gas (methane) is produced from gas fields, which, like oil fields, occur on land and increasingly beneath the sea (70% of the earth's surface is sea). Most gas is moved initially through large diameter pipes to collection points on land where the gas is cleaned, compressed and transmitted long distances through a national or international gas pipeline grid. International trade in gas is very common; Russia developed a gas grid in the 1940s, Canada and the USA have had an integrated gas grid since the 1950s,

---

[9] In practice, such long distance flows would not occur due to technical limitations such as power losses, voltage drops and power system stability concerns.

[10] I am grateful to Nick Aked for this example.

which is now linked to the Mexican grid, while Europe has huge pipeline links from the North Sea, Russia, central Asia, and two from north Africa. Large diameter gas grids are spreading from the Middle East, central Asia, and Russia out to the new centres of demand in China, India and south east Asia, while Africa is starting to develop international gas transmission grids.

In addition, gas can be cooled to -162° Centigrade until it is a liquid, poured into specialised ships called Liquefied Natural Gas (LNG) tankers, and shipped in bulk across oceans. In the importing countries, terminals warm the liquid natural gas back into its gaseous state and pump it into the country's high pressure gas transmission pipes. Liquefying gas and putting it on ships enables countries such as Qatar, Indonesia or Nigeria, which have a lot of gas but are far from the main demand centres of Europe, Asia or America, to sell their gas in global markets. When gas was traded only through pipelines it was possible for gas prices to differ significantly between the continents (traditionally North America was cheaper than Europe or Asia), but with significant LNG trade and low intercontinental shipping costs, there is now a clear tendency for bulk gas prices, like the price of crude oil, to converge across the planet[11].

Once received in a gas consuming country, gas is moved around the country through the national gas transmission grid – which performs an identical function to the electricity transmission grid – until it reaches a centre of demand (a town or city). Just as an electricity sub-station reduces the voltage of the electricity closer to that needed by final consumers, so the pressure of the gas is reduced at Pressure Reduction Stations (PRSs or 'City Gates'), when the gas enters smaller diameter pipes for distribution around the city or surrounding rural areas. And, as with electricity, the length of distribution gas mains is far greater than the length of transmission mains, because, ultimately every street will have a gas pipe down it. The main difference between gas and electricity is that gas can be stored in bulk, while, at present, electricity cannot be stored in bulk directly (the main ways of storing gas are discussed on page 25).

Finally, and again just like electricity, there has to be a retail or 'supply' function involving exactly the same processes: customer identification, tariff offering, contract signing, meter reading, billing, debt collection, disconnection, reconnection, and new connections. And, since you ask, yes, where the government has not got its act together, gas executives do not disconnect army barracks or police stations in the winter.

Water
Raw water is extracted from nature either as surface water (lakes or rivers) or as ground water – water filtered through, and then embedded in, aquifers below

---

[11] The strong growth in 'fracking' natural gas in North America after 2005 created new supplies causing North American gas prices to fall well below levels in the rest of the world. After some years North America began to export LNG, rather than importing it. LNG is the main factor today making gas prices converge around the world.

the soil. In a few cities where water is very scarce seawater is desalinated from the sea or a brackish lagoon using either a distillation process or reverse osmosis, but these processes are very energy-intensive and so are limited to very dry locations (often islands) or places where the opportunity cost of the energy used (usually gas, but occasionally solar) is very low. As a source of raw water, ground water is surprisingly common and has several advantages over surface water: not only does the rock filter the water, so that it needs less treatment to be drinkable but the aquifer acts as a free natural storage device, while the land above the aquifer can be used for agricultural purposes, unlike a reservoir (the surface water equivalent) which requires a valley to be flooded and the agricultural land and homes on it to be lost. Many very poor villages around the world use wells partly because they provide year-round storage, partly because the water is naturally filtered, and partly because wells occupy little surface area and can be located near the centre of a village or town (literally at the centre of demand), where land is expensive. Surface water, on the other hand, may need to be stored in an expensive reservoir if the lake or river is unreliable, or if the water source is small relative to the demand for water (the 'population served').

The equivalent in the water industry of a power station or gas production field is the water treatment works. This stores water in bulk across seasons or through droughts, then treats it to pharmaceutical standards[12] and pumps it out through big pipes at high pressures. Around a town or city it is usual for the output of several large water treatment works to be linked together in a water grid akin to the electricity or gas transmission grids, except that water is usually moved around only 20-60km (10-30 miles) from production to consumption, rather than the thousands of kilometres of electricity or gas networks.

Water distribution networks tend to resemble the branches of a tree: they divide, and divide, gradually getting thinner in a *dendritic*[13] fashion. It is often not very clear exactly where a water transmission network ends and the distribution grid begins, as there are few standard break points between one level of network and another: they are generally *ad hoc* systems that have simply grown, and are expanded only when constraints in one part of the grid look like becoming binding. In general water networks rarely link up with large mains between one grid and a neighbour's, although in densely populated countries like England, Germany and the Netherlands, a skein of small distribution pipes often interconnects outlying villages and farms straddling the boundaries between companies.

Testing of supplies at each stage of production is essential in a modern water company. In a country with tens of millions of people, millions of water tests are done every day, from the raw surface- or ground-water sources through each

---

[12] European water is measured against more than 50 specific criteria, and impurities are measured in nanograms per litre – i.e. a billionth of a gram of impurity in a litre (a quart) of water.

[13] from the Greek dendros a tree

stage of treatment, transmission, storage and distribution, to the water flowing out of consumers' taps. National standards of drinking water are usually based on European or United Nations (World Health Organisation) recommended maximum levels of physical, chemical and biological pollutants. Because the tests and processes are completely standardised the testing process can be heavily automated. The tests do not have to be done by the water utility itself, but the testing processes must be frequently checked by a completely impartial external body, if they are to retain consumers' confidence.

Finally, and very similar to the energy utilities, water has a retail function, in that in most of the world's richer countries water is metered and bills are charged according to the amount consumed. Where water is very abundant and utilities are publicly-owned, charges for water services may be combined inside local property taxes, so the water is effectively provided free 'at the point of sale'. But privatisation of water utilities and rising demand for freshwater mean that this form of water charging is becoming scarce in the twenty first century. Other than this, water retailing has the same functions and problems faced by all utility retailers, including very strong political sensitivities about disconnecting households who have not paid their bills[14].

Waste water
Lastly we should explain the modern 'wastewater' value chain. This works in reverse from all the other network utilities – because it is a collection network, not a distribution network. So, after flushing the lavatory, sewage flows down sewer pipes by gravity until it is separated in a sewage treatment works, where liquids are cleaned and returned to rivers or the sea in a good condition – that is generally cleaner than the rivers or seas into which they are flowing using a collection of physical, chemical and biological processes. The solids are collected, further treated as sewage 'sludge', and then disposed of by incineration or returned as dry compost for agricultural land. Note that most sewer networks in the world are designed to drain down to a single point, a sewage treatment works, and these works are almost never connected to each other, so every treatment works serves a different collection of sewers. This means each works has an absolute monopoly of treating all the sewage in its district of sewers. Hence *sewage treatment works* cannot compete with each other: they *are innate local engineering monopolies*. Furthermore, *sludge treatment works* are usually located, quite sensibly, very near to the main sewage treatment works whose sludge they treat and, so they *too are usually innate local engineering monopolies*[15].

---

[14] In the 1990s the deputy CEO of an East European water utility admitted to me that they had a poor service record: water quality was poor and 'outages' (no water) occurred several times a year in that city. He conceded the utility also had a poor payment record from some customers, but overall he was cheery: "This is normal in eastern Europe. We pretend to provide a service; they pretend to pay."

[15] However, this is not the case for sludge treatment from some rural areas, where wet sludge is shipped by road from rural sewage treatment works to central sludge treatment

Just like the water industry, the wastewater industry (sewers, sewage treatment and sludge treatment) requires increasing amounts of automated testing, as the quality (but often not the quantity) of solids, liquids and gases returned to the natural environment is checked for compliance with standards set by that country or State's environmental regulators.

Of grids and dendritic networks

As they are a core feature of network utilities, we must discuss the nature of physical networks, and particularly the differences between transmission grids and collection or distribution networks. Most people, economists or not, instinctively feel that the grids that have to be physically constructed for our heavy network utilities are the core features that make them 'natural monopolies'; the very exemplar of a sunk cost[16], the grids seem to be the core reason why monopolies naturally arise in an area. So in this book we take the opportunity to examine grids and networks closely across all utilities. We start with some generalisations about transmission and distribution systems before applying these to our classic heavy utilities.

Transmission grids

The function of a transmission grid is very simple: it is to transport 'the product' (whatever it is) in bulk from one region of a country to another, and therefore to allow areas of excess supply to export product to areas of excess demand. One of the key measures of any transmission grid, therefore, must be its transmission capacity at selected 'choke points'.

Distribution and Collection networks

The function of a collection network is to collect 'product' from all the subscribing customers in one area and aggregate it into bulk 'product' so that it can be handled by the next stage in the bulk treatment process. By symmetry, the function of a distribution network is to 'break treated bulk product' and distribute it to those individual consumers who want it, *at the time they want it.*

If we think of the traditional postal system, or of branch- and main-line railways, or even of the bread and milk industries, there are clearly aspects of collection, transmission and distribution in all these public service industries. In our utilities, sewer networks are obviously collection networks which pass on the product to the next stage – sewage treatment plants. The energy and clean water networks are predominantly distribution networks, though for completeness we should add that aggregating several power stations into one electrical input point, or adding together dozens of gas field production pipes, or combining the inputs

---

works, often located next to a town's sewage treatment works. Once the sludge is taken out of a pipe and put aboard a road tanker (or occasionally a ship) it is possible for different sludge treatment centres to compete with each other, depending on their location and shipping costs.

[16] For a proper definition of sunk costs see Chapter 3, but for now think of it as a capital cost you can never recoup.

from several water treatment works, prior to transmitting their product around a region, is a collection function. So, properly speaking, a collection network feeds bulk product into a transmission grid, which transmits it to centres of demand, then point-feeds the product into distribution grids. However, because of its vast size in practice, the bulk of the network is the distribution function. Note, though, that in electricity if distributed generation becomes widespread then the nature of the 'distribution' grid will change, and it will become more like a transmission grid, balancing excess supplies and demand across a region.

As we will discuss more fully in Chapter 6, sewer and water networks (particularly water for irrigating crops) have been around for millennia. So mankind has been using these networks for thousands of years, and indeed the circulation of our own blood shows distribution and collection networks at work. So nature uses them too. But how? The classical Greek word for a tree *dendros* is the origin of our word 'dendritic'; dendritic describes the general pattern of static collection and distribution networks in which a large transmission grid (a trunk) splits into several large branches, each of which in turn splits into smaller and smaller branches, then twigs, and finally individual leaves. We see this shape in physical geography with river basins (a collection network) or blood vessels distributing blood into part of an animal's body. A dendritic pattern looks like Figure 6:

Figure 6: A 'dendritic' pattern: a hornbeam tree in winter

Photo: the author

One might think that a dendritic network must be either a collection network or a distribution network, but biology is far cleverer than that. Having invented a good thing like leaves, twigs, branches and a trunk, nature re-uses this costly structure not just as a system for collecting nutrients and energy during the Summer, but also as a distribution network to deliver water to the leaves all Summer, and to send nutrients to the twigs in Spring so that they can develop buds and grow. The beech tree in Figure 7 is pretty busy:

Figure 7: A beech tree busy both collecting and distributing nutrients

Photo by the author. The dendritic branches of this beech tree collect nutrients from its thousands of leaves, and distribute water and other nutrients absorbed by the roots to those leaves.

Manmade network utilities, by contrast, are far simpler: they consist of transmission grids that link the centres of supply and demand, and uni-directional dendritic collection or distribution grids. But just as a big tree invests a lot when it develops in one place – unlike, say, a plant like tumbleweed – so the classic utilities represent a heavy investment in sunk costs in one place. Transmission and dendritic networks are very specific investments: specific to the geography (they cannot be moved) and specific to the technology: when the technology of railways came along canal routes could not be used for the trains[17] and so the sunk costs of canals had to be written off. We return to this analysis in Chapter 3.

---

[17] Even after draining a canal the 'way' itself would usually have been too narrow and too curved, and the bridges too low, for tall trains travelling at speeds of 30 kph or more.

Comparison of utility value chains with bread or milk

Let's now look at reality. Figure 8 compares typical UK utility value chains with those for the modern bread and milk industries shown in Figure 1 and Figure 2:

Figure 8: Value chains of UK utilities compared with 'normal' industry value chains for bread and milk

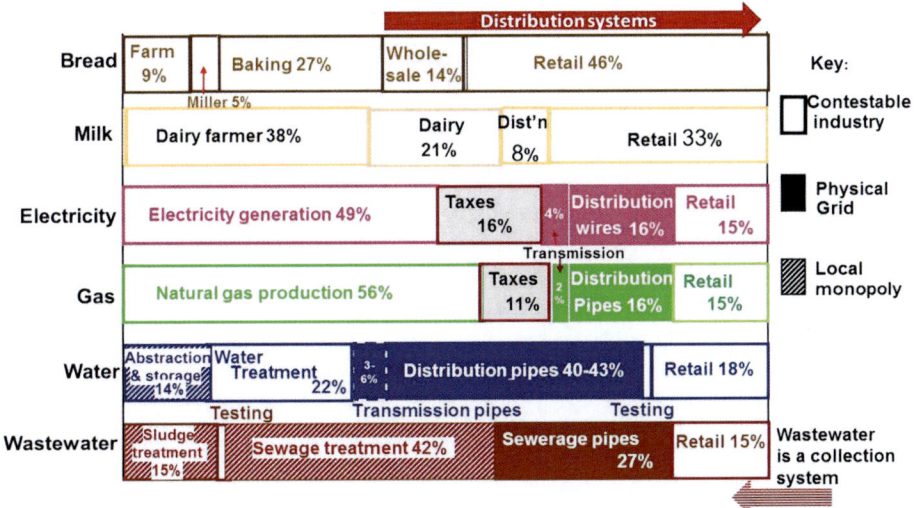

The first thing to note is that there is an element of tax (VAT plus carbon taxes) in the energy chains but not in food or water: in the UK, to help people on lower incomes, tap water and food consumed at home are zero rated for VAT – i.e. for social reasons.

Next, looking across all the utility value chains and comparing them with the bread and milk value chains, one immediate difference is that the pure retail function seems far smaller in the utilities than in bread or milk. This is partly because the physical transmission and distribution of the utilities' outputs has been separated and highlighted as a grid activity.

The third obvious difference is that the physical grids that transmit or distribute the utility services to every home and office are not 'contestable' industries. These grids are, in Mill's turn of phrase 'natural monopolies', in the sense that it would seem daft to build a second transmission or distribution grid on top of an existing grid. Yet this is precisely what would be required to achieve true competition-in-the-market for a transmission or distribution service. So grids are un-contestable stages of production, and they famously constitute a large part – but not all – of a utility's value chain.

Besides the innate monopolies of pipe or wire grids, we also have parts of utility value chains that are local monopolies because of scarcity of resources. To take the water industry example, London needs water for more than 10 million people. The only river in southern England of remotely suitable size to supply this amount of water is the River Thames, and there are only a few places where large enough quantities of raw water to supply 10 million people can be stored. So anyone who has control over rights to 'abstract' (extract) water from suitable parts of the River Thames and store it between seasons has a monopoly over this part of the water value chain. In fact, with the exception of a few water-plentiful countries such as Finland, Sweden, Canada, and Ireland, when we look at most urban and rural communities on planet Earth, there are usually only a very few suitable sites from which to abstract and store water for most towns, so these valued sites constitute highly-prized local natural monopolies, duopolies, or oligopolies. Often there is no other site suitable for storing water except the few obvious ones.

General policy implications of the utilities' value chains
Overall, what do we conclude from Figure 8? The first observation is that nearly all of the wastewater value chain consists of natural or innate monopoly services, and three fifths of the clean water value chain is 'naturally' monopolised due to grids or local monopolies. By contrast only about a fifth of the electricity or gas value chains is nowadays innately a 'natural monopoly'.

From the point of view of government policy, therefore, if the 'natural monopoly' utilities were state-owned, any attempt to privatise them should also reasonably try to restructure these industries vertically so that the efficiency-seeking forces of competition can be brought into the contestable parts of the value chain, while retaining the innate grid monopolies as privately-owned and managed regulated monopolies. And indeed, this is precisely what has happened in the UK's energy, rail, posts and telecoms sectors, over the last third of a century, where a government bent on privatising government-owned monopolies took a hard economic look at these value chains and attempted to introduce competition in all the contestable parts of the value chain. For the reasons just given about local and engineering monopolies, though, introducing competition into the water (and especially the wastewater) industry has proved practically impossible in the UK, although water value chains have been split up in a few cities or countries (see Chapter 11).

We shall look at privatisation and restructuring experiences in due course, but first we must return to those grids and ask exactly 'Why are they so often such strong monopolies?' To duplicate a grid seems evidently daft, but sometimes we find grids that are duplicated. Were the people who developed these second grids ignorant of the first grid, or completely mad, or wildly optimistic? This seems most unlikely, given that utility investors and managers are generally sober, well-informed citizens, with at least a normal aversion to risk. So, what is the rational explanation for developing a second or subsequent grid? We will return to this problem in Chapter 4.

Energy economics – in four pages
As stated in the introduction, this book is not a textbook in energy economics. However, knowledge of the basic concepts is essential before one can place

electricity and gas grids in their economic and industrial contexts.

The first thing to say about energy demand is obvious, namely that humans' demand for energy is a *derived demand*: we do not desire energy itself but the service that an appliance consuming energy can provide – light, heat, motion, the functionality of a computer, the entertainment provided by a screen, etc.

The second point is that in the twenty first century, *if cost is no object* nearly all forms of energy can technically be substituted for each other. The prevalence in practice of one particular form of energy over another is largely driven by the functional performance or convenience of the final energy consuming appliance, or its economics, as well as the overall economics of that particular value chain which gets the appliance and energy to the consumer at the right place and time. So, by contrast with, say the clothes industry, the local and global *economics* of energy pays a very large role in the selection of which energy fuels which appliance in each location. It is largely an economic decision which determines that aircraft are generally fuelled by jet fuel, rather than, say hydrogen, or that homes are heated by gas, kerosene, oil or electricity in your neighbourhood.

Energy flows in a real economy
The third fundamental point is that there is a general framework to describe the physical parts of the energy value chain from its naturally-occurring sources to the final end-consumer. This is shown in Figure 9 for a modern country – the UK.

We *start on the left* with production or imports of *primary energy*. Primary energy is the term used to describe all naturally-occurring energy. To use physics concepts, primary energy may be latent energy, kinetic energy, physical potential energy, and chemical or biological potential energy. No matter which, all the naturally-occurring fossil fuels – coal, lignite, oil, tar sands, natural gas liquids, and gas – are primary energy, as well as vegetation which is grown as a crop for energy – biofuels. Wood that is burned is a primary energy source too, as is brushwood, reeds, dried dung and other naturally growing plant-based matter. Animal power, also provides raw energy – e.g. oxen turning waterwheels, men pulling rickshaws, horses pulling ploughs, or elephants lifting tree trunks. In the UK these are negligible, but in the world they are not.

Primary energy is then converted into *secondary energy*; the two biggest converters shown in Figure 9 are power stations and oil refineries, so the main forms of secondary fuel are electricity and oil products. Although electricity itself is a secondary fuel, *nuclear* power is a primary source of energy, as are *hydroelectricity, wind, wave* and *all other forms of renewably-generated* electricity. In modern economies biofuels are mixed with oil products to create energetic liquids that fuel transport.

The *right hand side* of Figure 9 shows the end product: what we get from all this usable primary and secondary energy. Stand back a while and look at the overall picture: the UK produces or imports 315 million tonnes of oil equivalent (mtoe), exports 93, and sends 9 to non-energy uses (mainly oil products used for chemical and plastics). So its primary energy consumption is around 231 mtoe; in fact, because stock levels of coal, oil and gas increased in 2010, it was 228. This 228 was then used to create 159 mtoe of useful final energy, while 68 mtoe was wasted internally within the energy sector, eventually disappearing as heat which warmed the planet. And, so we're clear, when warming the planet, quite a bit of that 68 mtoe injected carbon products into the atmosphere.

Figure 9: The main commercial energy flows in the UK (in million tonnes of oil equivalent)

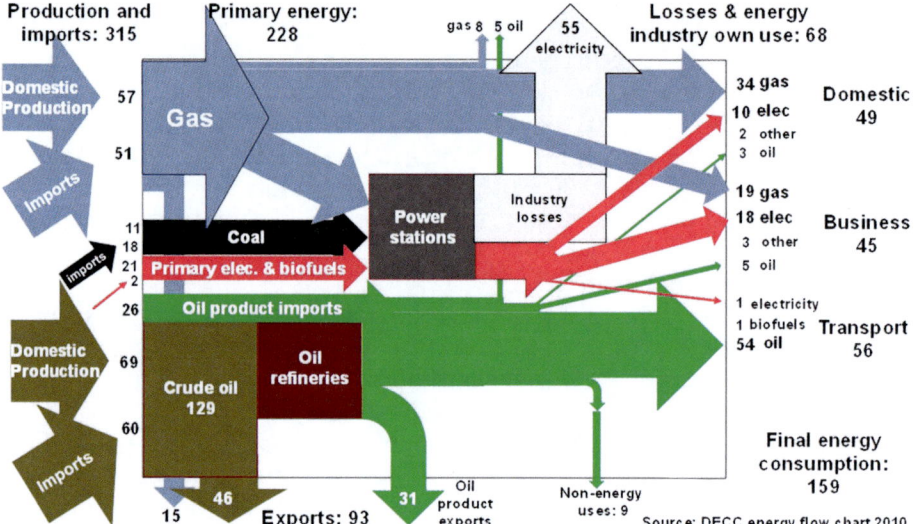

Source: Department of Energy and Climate Change Energy Flow Chart 2010, simplified by the author.

You may be horrified to see how much energy is wasted in modern energy transformation and distribution systems – and in a relatively efficient country like the UK. But did you really think gas grids and oil refineries run on thin air? No, very efficiently they burn some of their own fuel *in situ* – about 6½% in the case of oil and 8% for gas – and for that cost they move a natural mineral around the country, transform it into clean fuels we can use and distribute it to 98% of our homes and businesses (in the UK), or to a petrol station near you.

The biggest losses occur in the electricity sector. Just like the gas grid, there are transmission and distribution losses in running an electricity grid for a country the size of Britain, and these constitute about 14% of the gross electricity output from power stations. Seems like a lot, but the power stations themselves use a lot of electricity to start up, synchronise and vary loads by a factor of three or four over the course of a typical 24 hours. And, while running a grid on Alternating Current has huge advantages (you can switch voltages easily) it is bound to incur transmission losses (heat, which in wet climates you can hear fizzing off into the air).

However, the largest losses are undoubtedly in generating the raw electricity. Unless you are able to place a power station near a large town to reuse warmed cooling water in a combined-heat-and-power package, more than half the potential energy available is wasted. So even the best modern power stations are less than 50% efficient in practice. Old power stations are the worst, partly by design, and partly through parts which are wearing out. The UK's overall figure of 42% thermal efficiency is fairly typical for a modern economy.[18]

The *right hand side of the chart* shows that the useful energy delivered fuels the domestic sector (households), businesses, and the transport sector about equally. Given that oil has so many potential uses, and can therefore substitute for so many fuels, it is sometimes said that oil should be reserved for its 'premium' uses as a chemical feedstock or for 'premium transport', such as aircraft or light vehicles, because its unique molecular structure means that it can provide far more energy per kilogramme than any other fuel[19]. And this has happened. The author first looked at energy flow charts in the 1970s when less than 50% of oil products typically went to premium uses; nowadays in the UK, premium uses account for 85% of oil product end use. The biggest causes of this have been the growth of natural gas as a fuel in houses and businesses, combined with using more biofuels and renewable electricity.

Has the world got enough energy? Will future generations face serious energy shortages?

As an economist you may feel embarrassed to ask this apparently naive question, but it is a good question deserving a serious answer. The previous section introduced the raw concepts needed; with some key facts we can now apply these concepts globally.

World oil consumption was around 95 million barrels of oil a day (mbd[20]) in 2015[21]. Total primary energy consumption is currently almost three times this, around 260 mbd of oil equivalent (mbdoe), depending on estimates of biomass, animal power, and some critical conversion factors involving the assumed

---

[18] Electricity industry geeks debate the merits of different conversion systems to compare different methods of generation, and the International Energy Agency produces regular statistics on this kind of thing. The above 42% includes plant that transform coal into coke and gas, (a few) combined –heat-and-power plant etc., as well as power stations.

[19] Essentially, each carbon atom in an oil molecule carries many energy-bearing hydrogen atoms far more closely than those hydrogen atoms would be if paired as hydrogen molecules, even if you cooled the hydrogen to a liquid or solid.

[20] As a rough conversion factor there are around 50 million tonnes of oil equivalent a year to one million barrels a day.

[21] World energy consumption data in this section comes from the BP Statistical Review of World Energy, 2016, the Energy Information Administration (EIA) of the USA, NASA Science websites, Earth Radiation Budget/Environmental Science/Rutgers, the University of New Jersey, and United Nations Population Projections 2015.

thermal efficiency of various non-fossil fuel power stations. Global primary energy consumption is rising this century at about 2½ % a year due to rising incomes and population growth. To calculate an Orders-of-Magnitude "Worst case" peak world primary energy demand we note that American per capita primary energy demand has been fairly constant, around 7.25 tonnes of oil equivalent per person per year for the last forty years. If the world's population were to consume as much primary energy per head as the average American does now (a worst-case scenario), then global per capita primary energy consumption would rise four-fold from 1.8 to 7.25 t.o.e a year[22]. If we then assume the number of humans on the planet is expected to increase to around 10 billion people by 2050 (a plausible point in the United Nations' latest population projections) world primary energy demand could in the very worst case rise about six-fold to around 1500 mbdoe by around 2050-2075.

Could supply match this? Well, the truth is solar power received here on our planet already exceeds it a thousand times. NASA estimates that the upper atmosphere of the Earth receives about 170PW of solar energy, or about 15,033 X 10^{18} joules in a day. This is about 2.623 million mbdoe, so *total solar energy received by planet Earth from the sun is about ten thousand times bigger than current primary energy demand.*

Around 30% of the sun's radiation is reflected back into space, and about 20% warms the atmosphere, so that roughly half reaches the surface of our planet, where we live. Clearly we only need to find some relatively harmless way to tap into this biosphere heat to meet all our future energy needs forever. Figure 9 is carefully labelled as "commercial energy flows in the UK" because clouds, warm fronts, and the Gulf Stream daily blow massive quantities of energy into the UK quite naturally. We tap into a tiny proportion of this biosphere energy when we generate 'renewable' electricity from wind and waves.

Photovoltaic solar panels absorb solar energy on the earth's surface and convert it into electricity. It is possible to view them as even more "environmentally friendly" than wind and wave energy because their main effect[23] is to reduce the 787,000 mbdoe of radiation the Earth reflects quite uselessly back to space[24].

---

[22] According to the International Energy Agency global primary energy demand roughly doubled between 1973 and 2010, despite the massive growth in per capita incomes seen in Asia, the Americas, and some parts of Africa, so looking a similar distance ahead, a six-fold increase really is the worst case scenario.

[23] Besides slightly reducing the temperature of the air around them: no bad thing in the Sahara Desert, say, or generally in a world troubled by rising temperatures in the biosphere.

[24] A quick inter-planetary Environmental Impact Assessment of a policy to reduce energy radiated out to space from the Earth by 0.2% says it's negligible. The biggest effect would be on the moon, but a 0.2% reduction in reflected radiation from the Earth will always be dwarfed by variations in direct solar radiation from our sun – on any moon or planet in our solar system, or any other.

Clearly, thanks to our closeness to the sun, if we could find suitable materials to build enough solar panels and link them together with a global energy grid (a great deal of which already exists) there could be no shortage of primary energy on planet Earth. Of course there are absorption inefficiencies (the best photovoltaics are currently about 50% efficient) and transformer, transmission and distribution losses to include, but given the massive excess energy received by the Earth the real constraints are political, economic, and finding sufficient of the scarcer raw materials needed for the cells.

Does this mean we can stop worrying about fossil fuels causing global warming? No; that is an entirely separate argument altogether, about greenhouse gases changing the earth's atmosphere, and the effects of this on all our ecosystems: sea levels, ocean currents, climates, crops, flora, fauna, and natural habitats. We should not ignore some serious environmental thinking and action, but the issues are not driven by a shortage of primary energy on our planet. Indeed they never can be: one thing Einstein and the twentieth century physicists showed us most spectacularly is that energy and matter are interchangeable. With the knowledge we have today, and especially with likely future knowledge, one thing mankind should never have to worry about in the future is a shortage of primary energy. If it's daytime feel the heat of the sun; if it's night look out at the stars. Both are inconceivably vast potential sources of energy[25].

When will the world run out of fossil fuels?
The short answer is "in several hundred years". It is time to curtail this discussion and refer you to specialist recent publications and estimates, with the *caveat* to bear in mind that so-called "proven" figures of fossil fuel reserves are not the honest-but-conservative estimates of the amount of energy left in that part of the earth's crust that you might think they are. For instance, take, the longest run of well-defined reserve figures on the planet: in the lower 48 States of the USA American oil companies initially reported that they had 16 years worth of current production in "proven oil reserves" – in the year 1916. As we all know, US oil production did not cease in 1932, when the companies still reported 16 years worth of proven reserves at then-current production levels. This ratio of 16 years of current production, plus or minus 5 years, continues until today. However, do you really believe the lower 48 States will cease oil production by 2030? Whatever this ratio is telling us has nothing to do with the amount of crude oil lying in a certain part of the earth's crust, and a great deal to do with capital markets, and relationships between the CEO, the CFO, and the chief geologist of each oil company.

Demand characteristics of the classic utilities
We now consider the heavy utilities from the customers' point of view – the demand characteristics of secondary fuels, water, and transport of various kinds.

---

[25] The situation has been famously summarised in a remark attributed to former Saudi Arabian oil minister, Sheikh Ahmed Zaki Yamani: "The Stone Age didn't end because of a shortage of stones."

The first observation is the apparently minor one that, with the exception of some parts of transport, heavy utilities generally have homogenous outputs. What economists call a homogeneous good is called a 'commodity' by marketing folk. Unfortunately, marketing is still seen by many economists as a lightweight subject. By contrast, most business executives regard economics as a largely irrelevant subject, and marketing as much more useful, particularly when goods and services are "differentiated"[26]. Indeed, as a consultant working in a general consultancy for a decade, it seemed undeniable that the real reason economists were employed only in utilities and finance, and not any of the other consultancy markets, was that the products or services of most business sectors are differentiated, while utility and financial products are usually 'commodities'.

Electricity

As will be obvious from thinking about the energy balance chart for your own country, actual electricity demand changes significantly over time and between countries. So, in Canada and northern Europe the highest flow of delivered electricity in the year is driven by winter heating demand, while in Japan and most of the USA peak demand is in the summer, driven by air conditioning. Changes in the stock of electricity-using appliances largely drive long term changes in the pattern of demand. Technological progress means that completely new appliances emerge with their own electricity demands: I first studied energy economics around 1980, when there were no computers at home, or indeed in most small businesses, so the drivers of electricity demand at home were then cooking, heating, and the TV. Nearly forty years later portable devices, laptops and multi-media devices account for a significant part of domestic demand in most homes in the northern hemisphere.

Technological progress also has a huge effect on the efficiency of energy-using appliances. So although we welcome the invention of more energy-efficient light bulbs or Light Emitting Diodes, one has to factor in the efficiency of the entire appliance system: LEDs or solid state electronics may use only tiny amounts of electricity but often this is provided by converting mains 120/240V alternating current to 12 volt direct current electricity (and so on to far lower voltages within most devices), necessarily incurring (at present) significant energy losses as heat. While this heat may not be wasted in cold climates, in hot climates it simply adds to the demands on office or domestic air-conditioners; the efficiency of air conditioners *in situ* is of course well below 100%, particularly when viewed in terms of global warming, and the overall efficiency of the electricity generation and distribution system.

In most countries electricity demand is split about 50/50 between business users and households or "domestic" customers. The biggest overall determinant of this ratio is the country's state of economic development: pre-industrial

---

[26] Remember that most senior managers, and a high proportion of middle managers, have studied economics to roughly the Economics 101 level. However, many of these economics courses were poorly taught.

countries use more electricity domestically, especially in rural areas. Industrial countries such as China and India use more for manufacturing and heavy primary industries, while post-industrial countries may have a big demand from the commercial sector, but the characteristics of this "office" demand are very similar to domestic demand: lights, heating, PCs, printers and phones.

At the time of writing electricity cannot be stored economically in bulk, so the diurnal and seasonal variation in electricity demand instantaneously reflects the demands on that country's electrical appliances. Famously, British demand used to depend on whether the British were watching a football match on TV, or their favourite soap opera; the instant there was a break in the game or the episode ended millions of electric kettles were switched on for a cup of tea, and national electricity demand jolted upwards in a few seconds. With on-demand viewing and a wider variety of digital entertainments available this trend is blurring. However, electricity remains a relatively instantaneous demand.

Gas

Obviously gas, too, is a classic commodity product. Prior to concerns about greenhouse gas emissions from all fossil fuels, gas used to be regarded as the cleanest, neatest, fuel for general space and water heating demand, with very few undesirable by-products. It currently accounts for about a quarter of the planet's primary energy demand – around 70 mbdoe, or nearly twice OPEC's oil production. Of course some major gas producers are OPEC members – Iran, Qatar, Iraq, Saudi Arabia and the UAE for instance – but the three largest producers – Russia, the USA and Canada, who account for half of global gas production – are not.

Gas storage

Unlike electricity, from the demand point of view, gas can be stored in bulk, not just in depleted gas fields, natural underground caverns, or man-made tanks and gasometers (the large cylindrical storage structures seen in many cities), but also there is significant storage in the pipeline system itself. Ahead of a period of heavy demand, gas can be compressed, or 'packed', into thousands of kilometres of pipe, and stored in bulk relatively locally until end-user demand draws down the excess gas and causes the excess pressure to fall to the minimum level acceptable.

Because of its controllability, flexibility and cleanliness, gas is favoured by industry, especially when heavy industry needs bulk heat to melt solids such as metal ores, metals, or glass, or to cook or heat food, agricultural products, cement etc. When locally available it is also very popular in the domestic sector for space and water heating, and cooking. In poorer countries and rural areas "bottled gas" (in steel canisters) is generally a lot safer than kerosene for cooking. As already described, much of the *growth in global gas consumption over the last sixty years has been due to the quiet, steady expansion of gas distribution networks*. Oil and gas companies have always known the gas was there, but the problem has been developing the infrastructure to get it to the customers, particularly the local gas distribution grids for the domestic sector.

Being a clean, convenient fuel, but not, like oil, being widely used in transport, gas has a lower opportunity cost than oil, and so usually 'sells itself into' a market on price. In other words, sellers typically pick a target volume they wish to deliver, and then sell that volume for as high as price they can get. Because industry provides large chunks of demand at specific point destinations, gas is often first targeted at industry, with the result that in many developed economies more gas is demanded by industry than by commerce or the domestic sector. In the UK, because of de-industrialisation and a well-developed network of gas distribution grids, the domestic sector accounts for two thirds of final gas demand[27].

Water economics
Water economics has nothing directly to do with energy economics, although there are many parallels. The supply side is a branch of natural resource economics, and has much in common with the economics of finding minerals, particularly underground minerals if the source of water is also underground. However, one must bear in mind that water is a renewable mineral, and so has different economics to the non-renewable minerals, and also that it is a very low-value, heavy product, so transport costs in the transmission and distribution grids can dominate cost considerations. The economics of long run water supply are considered explicitly in Chapter 5, when we consider a forward-looking long run marginal costs curve of an entire water system.

Water demand
Water can be used for industrial, commercial, agricultural or domestic (household) reasons; the balance between them depends very much on a country or region's local geography. In a nutshell we may say that while physical geography determines water supply in an area, human geography (mostly) determines demand.

An exception to the latter clause is that in hot countries irrigation for agricultural production dominates water demand. Across the world as a whole 70% of humankind's water demand is for agriculture, and in many regions this figure reaches 80% or more[28]. Naturally in cooler countries, such as the UK, irrigation demand for water is much smaller, while in cool, wet countries like Ireland it is zero. Of course irrigation water does not have to be as high quality as drinking water and, like all water, it does get recycled, often quite locally. The real cause for environmental concern is that this demand can only be met in some countries by abstracting surface or particularly ground water (which is not visible to the public) faster than it is being replenished. Here, with falling water tables, rivers, or lakes, mankind is definitely living on borrowed time 'mining fossil water'.

---

[27] i.e. excluding from the denominator, gas to power stations, which is currently equal to domestic demand.

[28] Source: UN Millennium Development Goals Report 2009, page 44

Domestic water demand

While tap water is usually regarded as a commodity product, the first major difference between water demand and energy demand is that, rather than being a derived demand, water is absolutely needed by all living things on the planet. So, conceptually, this should mean that the demand elasticity for human water consumption ought to be zero, and the demand curve should be a vertical line. And, indeed there is anecdotal and empirical evidence that this price elasticity is very low.

We should not forget, though, that, depending on the climate, what we do and what else we drink or eat, humans only need a couple of litres of water a day to drink. In economic terms this means that unlike many other goods, *humans very soon reach their point of satiation in water consumption*, when no extra water is either needed or desired. This tends to reinforce the idea that the demand curve for drinking water in any given community is a vertical line – it will increase if there are more humans, or if the weather gets hotter, but our fundamental demand for water is not going to change if the price of water is halved or doubled: we will simply have to pay more or less. Water charges have therefore often been likened to a tax: they are a charge one has to pay for being a live human being.

This straightforward reasoning, however, has led some economists astray; they have forgotten the fact that the vast majority of water used in a household or office – 98% or so – is not directly drunk by humans, or our pet animals or plants, but is used by humans as an extremely handy fluid to move all kinds of "dirt" away from where we no longer want it. This 'dirt' may be dirt on your body (showers and baths), dirt in your clothes, dirt in your food, dirt on your dishes, dirt on your walls or floor, or human excrement[29]. Forget planet Earth for a moment, and consider designing a cleaning process for a space station or a colony on another planet where water is very scarce. Honestly, there is no single fluid that is anywhere near as good as water for all these gentle cleaning and transporting functions: you could *try* washing your clothes in liquid air, you could try washing your body in milk, you could try flushing the lavatory with cooking oil, you could try washing your cat in vinegar, but I doubt you'd be happy with the results. The cat certainly wouldn't be.

So the real reason domestic water demand is so price-insensitive has nothing to do with the tiny demand for drinking water – in a modern economy there are dozens of substitutes, many costing a thousand times as much per litre - and everything to do with the absence of a substitute all-purpose cleaning fluid.

Waste water demand

People often forget that there is a second water good, nowadays called wastewater, which consists of two separate social functions: sewerage – taking

---

[29] Modern water economists are indebted for this insight to David Kinnersley's seminal books, now unfortunately out of print "Troubled Water" (1989), or "Coming Clean" (1994).

water-and-dirt away from my house – and sewage treatment, which is processing that water-and-dirt so that it is safely recycled into the natural and man-made environments.

When we consider these twin services as economists we see that sewerage is a fairly normal good above a certain income level: very poor people do need water, but, quite reasonably given their education and income, choose not to spend their very scarce income on what the rest of us might call 'adequate sanitation'. But they also don't spend their precious money on many other things the rest of us regard as essential, like electricity or holidays. To use Maslow's hierarchy of needs (see Figure 10), clean water is a basic physiological need, piped clean water is safer and so meets our security needs, while sewerage also improves my family's security and comfort, but only after my water security needs have been met. But sewage treatment is a service no poor person would realistically consider: it is environmentally desirable, but I "need" it only in the sense that I achieve Maslow's highest need, self-fulfilment, by being environmentally responsible, and properly cleaning up behind myself.

Figure 10: Maslow's hierarchy of needs - applied to water services

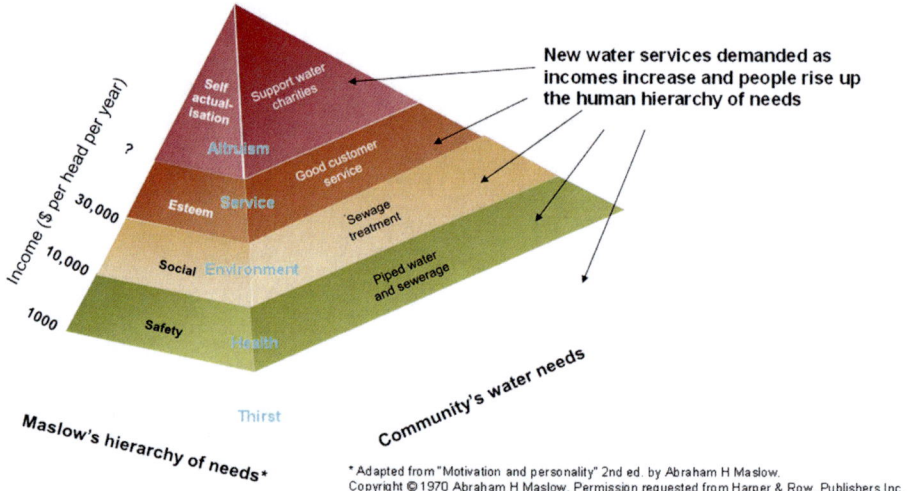

* Adapted from "Motivation and personality" 2nd ed. by Abraham H Maslow. Copyright © 1970 Abraham H Maslow. Permission requested from Harper & Row, Publishers Inc.

Sewage treatment, therefore, is not a normal good: I could argue that I get very little benefit out of my sewage being treated, but I derive benefit from *all* my community's sewage being treated. So in conventional economic terms it *is driven by positive externalities:* at its most basic humans will swim in their own urine but they don't want to swim in anyone else's. If even just five houses discharge untreated sewage into my local lake, river, or the sea, I probably do not want to go swimming in it, and the benefit of treating the sewage from the rest of the entire community is undone. It is therefore not a public good, like street lighting, in the economic sense of "if provided for one is available for all", but rather the opposite: "if it is provided it must include everyone." This is another reason why water and wastewater charges are likened to taxation or compulsory military service: "I don't want to pay for it, but if I have to, everyone must".

The provision of sewerage and sewage treatment at very low income levels is considered to have such important positive externalities in terms of the planet's health (human and environmental) that the term "sanitation" has been developed to describe this service. Basic sanitation was one of the United Nation's most important Millennium Goals, and huge progress was made up to 2015 and is being made now. It is a key part of the UN's Sustainable Development Goal 6 for 2030, which is assessed in the back part of Chapter 6. Why are these externalities so important? Not only does basic sanitation directly increase people's life expectancy, quality of life, and economic productivity, but also as a matter of public expenditure policy, it is such a good preventative policy that it is at least two – if not three – orders of magnitude cheaper to provide poor people with adequate sanitation and good drinking water than to wait for them to become ill before treating them with expensive drugs, doctors and nurses in hospitals. And on the environmental side, not polluting our rivers, lakes, and seas with tides of human excrement from our vast urban communities, preserves the natural biodiversity and productivity of all our surface waters, as well as making our water supplies cheaper, and smelling sweeter.

Transport economics

Innate transport demand

Like water, the demand for passenger transport is not derived, but is personally desired and personally experienced. Transport is a commodity product for short trips on buses, underground or commuter trains, or short flights – hence the growth of no-frills airlines – but a classically differentiated product if you are a first class passenger on a long rail, ship or airplane journey, where money can buy you space, privacy, your own bed, individual service, and a sense of position in society (a positional good).

With the exception of cruise holidays, nearly all journeys are very space- and time-specific, so that, unless the two locations or times are very close together, a journey to or from an alternative destination is not an adequate substitute. For business travellers an alternative time is usually a very inferior substitute, and in general most non-cruising travellers want to arrive as soon as possible. This desire to minimise time, and therefore maximise average speed, has naturally made the fastest forms of travel (air and high speed rail) the most desirable, and generally the most expensive. Transport economics accepts this as a first principle, and therefore values travellers' time as a cost of travel. Put another way, especially in congested systems, time taken to reach your destination is a second form of charging for the service. And if your decision whether to travel or not delays or affects others it should be valued as an externality, when calculating a social optimum.

Maritime transport economics

In my first week at University economics was defined to me as the study of the allocation and distribution of relatively scarce resources. Transport economics is the economics of industries that move people or cargo from one place to another. Given that canals have now largely been superseded by road and rail, transport economics now mostly covers the land and air modes of transport, with relatively little written about maritime economics, even though ocean shipping transports huge weights of freight around the planet. Perhaps the relative paucity of maritime economics is due to the fact that there is so much sea on our planet that space on the sea is not scarce, and so it does not really constrain operators; and of course no grid needs to be built, as would be needed for a canal. So, in a sense we have too much of this really useful resource – the sea – for it to be scarce, and so there is little economics of sea transport. Maybe, one day, energy economics will be like this.

Economics of wheeled transport

On land, excepting truly off-road vehicles, all wheeled vehicles need a flat surface or track on which to run. This means that someone must build and maintain the track, and since it would be wasteful to build this infrastructure for just one journey, person, or vehicle, the 'someone' who must build and maintain the track is often the public sector. This raises issues of charging private individuals to access the public infrastructure – access pricing – and possible charges per person.kilometre or tonne.kilometre for each journey.

If desired, the access charge can be further broken down into an *option* (a potential right) to access the track (I am purchasing the general right to use the track – i.e. "I am paying for the track to be built and maintained"), and an *'exercise' right* ("I want to access the track right now" – for a defined time and space). In Europe, for instance, where passenger train travel is more valuable than freight train transport, people use trains mainly to commute to large cities, and for fast intercity travel up to 500km. There is, though, considerable evidence that European citizens will pay to maintain the entire rail system even to remote places, which would otherwise be 'uneconomic' to serve without a cross-subsidy or government subsidy. In effect these people are saying "I am willing to pay for the option to travel by train to Aberystwyth[30], even if I personally have no immediate plans to do so. I believe it is right to maintain this infrastructure." Obviously not all citizens feel like this; strongly split feelings on this can lead to deep political divides. This split in society is analysed further in Chapter 12's analysis of the experience of rail restructurings.

Consequently, local tracks (roads) are nearly always built and maintained by a branch of local government, while railways and main roads are provided either by specialist government agencies or utilities that are structured like companies.

---

[30] Replace 'Aberystwyth' with some remote town in your own country that is reachable by train and ask yourself how you feel about it emotionally. You may be one of those who couldn't care two hoots, or you may suddenly think 'No: that's wrong'.

Even if these utilities are private they tend to be regarded not as *owning* the infrastructure but as *being stewards of it* – people trusted to take care of the community's valuable infrastructure. The utility may have built and maintained the track entirely with its own privately-raised capital – like Eurotunnel, or motorways in France – but after a few decades there is a feeling that the infrastructure they created really is public property and the owners are stewards of a public asset.

Road economics

All local roads may be said to fall into two categories: general 'linking' roads that join other roads at both ends, or 'radial' roads that join a linking road to one or more properties before petering out. If the radial road serves just one property it could be built and maintained by the property-owner, but in densely-populated areas such roads are very rare. In the more typical case a radial road serves more than one property, and there are potential externalities (my consumption affects you – imagine we are neighbours, you are a one-car household, and I run twenty trucks a day down 'our' road). So in general there are externalities with road economics which become stronger as population densities on our planet rise, more people can afford cars, and the extra demand causes congestion on our roads.

To analyse the externalities consider the following: a road of given surface and width has a defined capacity. Speed limits aside, if you are the only driver on it, you can drive on it as fast as you can, and reach your destination as quickly as possible. For most individuals this is the optimum: it cannot get any better than this. They are at the top of Figure 11:

Figure 11: the speed-flow curve of a given road

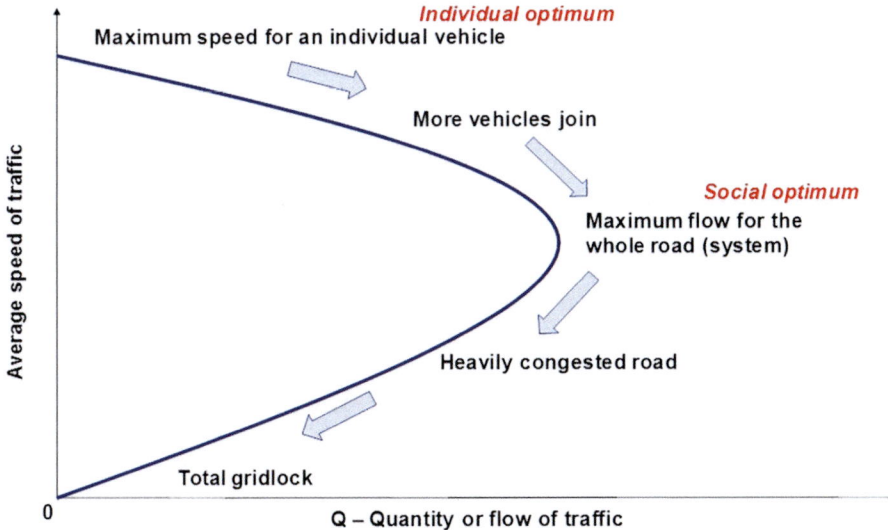

As more people join the road, traffic becomes more congested and drivers have to restrict their average speed until the whole road is working at maximum capacity. This is the social optimum for the system: it cannot contribute any more to the community's total output than working at this rate. If yet more vehicles join, average speeds decline still further, until we reach the self-defeating point of total gridlock, when the output of the road as a transport system is zero.

The economic consequences of this are shown in the well-known congestion externality diagram of Figure 12: which shows the different equilibria resulting from people considering only their own interests (the private costs of extra traffic), and the social optimum when all externalities are taken into account.

We assume that demand varies during a 24-hour day from very little in the middle of the night to a peak demand during the day – i.e. it varies between the two demand curves shown. The vertical axis depicts the unit costs incurred by drivers where we have *included and costed the drivers' and passengers' time*. The dashed curve shows the marginal private costs perceived by an individual driver or vehicle; these are constant as the total flow of traffic increases until we hit the congestion point, when we have to reduce our average speed, and the time and cost taken start to mount.

Figure 12: effects of congestion on equilibrium road traffic levels

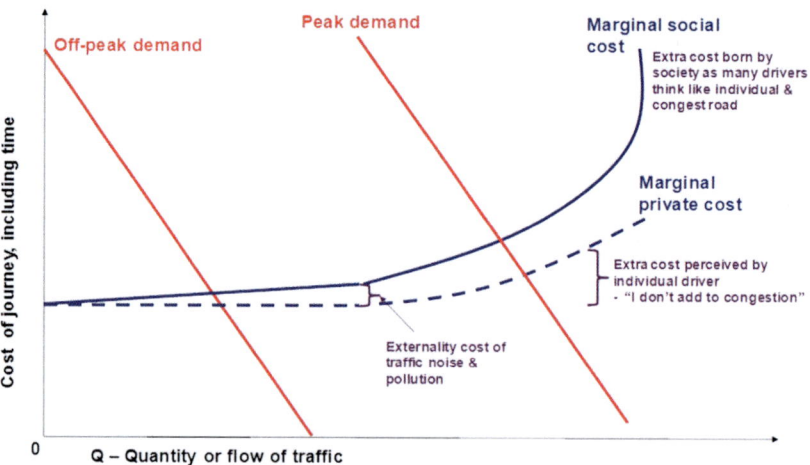

However the social cost of our road journey, including all externalities, is higher than this, because our journey imposes costs of traffic noise and pollution on society, which, inside our car, we tend to ignore. These external costs should rise in line with the volume of traffic. At the congestion point, however, the full costs of an extra car joining the road become obvious to a traffic camera monitoring traffic levels on the road. Inside the car, though, we tend to think that we do not add to congestion, and so ignore the congestion effects of our own vehicle on others. This leads to the two marginal cost curves shown in Figure 12: the dashed marginal private cost is what we perceive, while the solid marginal social cost curve is what we actually do to society. The social optimum is at a lower quantity and higher cost than the private outcome, suggesting that a congestion tax (in time or cost) would move the perceived private optimum closer to the social optimum. Traffic-dependent road taxing, known as time-of-day road pricing, was a transport economist's dream in the twentieth century, but is now a well-established reality in cities like London, Oslo and Singapore.

Although all of these systems have their critics (e.g. London does not charge by distance travelled within the Congestion Zone), congestion is a negative externality that is amenable to economic analysis. The general conclusion of transport economists is that road pricing is now economically feasible and can be superior to other forms of road rationing provided all 'congestable' roads are included in the pricing system[31]. That said, we have to admit that taxes on vehicle ownership and carbon in fuels used at the pump are remarkably easy ways of raising revenue, can be progressive taxes[32] in poor countries, and also provide vital databases for law enforcement.

Air transport
Because of its speed, demand for air travel has risen astronomically, particularly since the invention of the jet engine. The long term income elasticity for air travel may be one of the highest of any good observed, though to assess this properly requires multivariate analysis and good global data over the last two centuries, because the real cost of air travel has fallen dramatically at the same time as global incomes have risen massively. This has led to congestion in air travel in densely populated continents like Europe and Asia. For example, apart from congestion around airports on the ground, one in four flights in Britain currently experiences *air congestion* on take-off and landing. Although the chances of mid-air collisions or near-misses are very low, the consequences of just one incident are so frightening that producers and consumers alike readily concede huge powers to central regulators (air traffic controllers) to ration and allocate air space.

Postal services, and other 'intermittent grids'
The postal network is not an obvious grid because its 'nodes' (posting boxes, collecting, and sorting offices) are not physically connected to each other, as a gas or electricity grid is. However, it definitely shares some important grid characteristics, which we also see in other intermittent grids such as parcel and courier delivery services, distribution and delivery services for milk or any centrally-produced good, mobile phone masts, hub-and-spoke airline routes, and even news-gathering organisations. In each case:

---

[31] Taxing one road can have the effect of diverting traffic to alternative roads with higher marginal social costs.

[32] In poorer countries poor people can't afford cars, so they don't pay tax on owning a car or its fuel.

1. supply is centralised and demand is for a product or service at widely-spread locations (*distribution grids*), or
2. supply and demand must be linked through a grid (*communication networks*), or
3. supply comes from many geographically-distributed sources (*collection networks*).

Each of these grids or networks has similarities with a classic heavy utility grid:

- there are *high fixed costs* of operating the grid or network;
- the grid is *spread out geographically*, and has monopoly tendencies within its operational sphere;
- there *may be* some *sunk costs*: assets have been acquired with little alternative use.

I shall shortly argue that it is the size of the grid's sunk costs relative to its non-sunk costs that determines the strength of the grid's monopoly. But first, in Chapter 2, we look at the evidence for the traditional theory that natural monopolies have strong economies of scale.

Appendix 1: The intellectual origins of value added chains

The basic idea of an industry value chain is over two hundred years old and was a central preoccupation of the classical economists. The most famous today are Quesnay, Smith, Malthus, Ricardo, Walras, JS Mill and Karl Marx. These 18th and 19th century Europeans invented "theories of value" to explain how 'value' gets added to a (typically manufactured) good in a market or capitalist economy. In other words, although we know the physical processes involved, how do I explain why in a modern economy a brick sells for X, a brick wall of defined size costs Y, and an entire new house is worth Z? And how do we relate the cost of this house or its components to the income of the average person? What determines why these sums are X, Y and Z, and not 2X or 5Y or 17Z? Clearly it depends on the number of bricks in a wall, and walls in a house, but, given the differences we see around the world in the price of houses, how are the values of an economy put together to determine the real living standard of a typical person in this economy?

Sub-consciously, neo-classical economists essentially put this in the 'too difficult' box for a hundred and fifty years, and focussed on industry microeconomics. In the meantime Keynes started to view the whole economy as a circulating system of money and income, invented macroeconomic aggregates, and analysed the systematic inter-actions between households, firms, government, banks and the foreign sector, so inventing short-term macroeconomics. But after the Second World War economists returned to these central value problems. The results of neo-classical microeconomic theories were re-examined using the newer tools of input-output matrices[33], general equilibrium theory, and industrial economics to invent the first industry value chains, before being combined with firm-specific business strategy theories to determine the split between capital, labour and land in heterogeneous product and factor markets.

Intellectually more humble, yet in practice massively important, was the invention by the French tax authorities in 1954 of a completely new tax, Value Added Tax[34], and its subsequent adoption worldwide, which brought home to economists that these problems were both practical in the modern world and soluble. So, with hindsight, we can see that the neo-classicals were right to put this in the 'too difficult' box: despite the Herculean efforts of Marx and Mill[35], nineteenth century economists had neither the tools nor the experience necessary to crack this intricate web of problems.

---

[33] Leontieff's standardisation of Walras' input-output matrices finally solved the bricks-in-a-wall, walls-in-a-house, problem and deservedly earned him a Nobel prize. Fittingly, it became the central tool of the Soviet Union's economic planning system in the world's most truly centrally-planned economy. But intellectually, an input-output matrix solves only the quantity side of the conundrum, which is the easy part

[34] The first VAT (TVA in French) was introduced by Maurice Laure, Joint Director of the 'Direction generale des impots' as a way of spreading the process of tax-raising away from the point of retail sale, so as to reduce tax evasion.

[35] Do you really want to read all three volumes of Marx's "Capital" or five volumes of Mill's "Principles of Political Economy"?

Chapter Two

Economies of scale and scope – theory and evidence

The simple neo-classical theory of network monopolies

At its simplest the neo-classical textbook explanation of network grid monopolies is that if an industry exhibits continual economies of scale it is a 'natural monopoly'. The best examples of 'natural monopolies' are often held to be the water, gas, and electricity industries. A network utility's 'natural' economies of scale are said to come from operating a network or grid with high fixed costs and low variable costs. The high fixed costs are explained as being caused by central system costs, depreciation and simply maintenance of the grid or operating system; total costs do not appear to vary strongly with the load put through the system.

Combining these assumptions give us the classic textbook cost curves shown in Figure 13[36]:

Figure 13: Conventional textbook explanation of grid monopolies

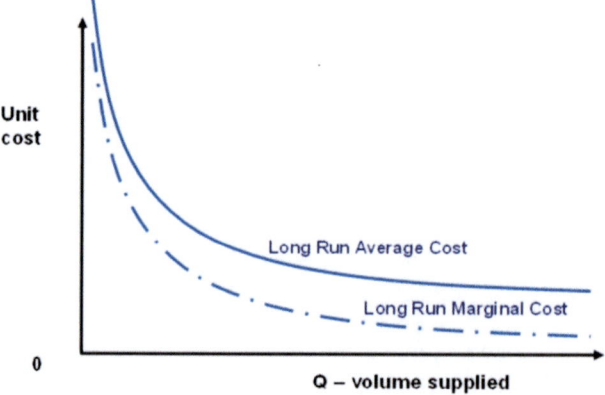

---

[36] Not only is this common in most elementary economics texts, but also in some professional texts specialising in regulation, e.g. Baldwin & Cave Understanding Regulation, OUP 1999, page 204

Thinking in this vein, a heuristic example might be to consider the cost of maintaining and servicing a city's electricity or gas distribution system. Ignore the costs of generating the energy in bulk and transmitting it to the city, and consider only the costs of distributing energy around the town. It could be argued, quite reasonably, that total costs should not vary proportionately with the amount of energy distributed each year, compared with, say, the year before, or the year after. For instance it should make almost no difference to this year's total distribution costs if the load or volume delivered (Q) rises by 10% above last year's load; the main determinant of total distribution costs will be the costs of maintaining and operating the grid, regardless of how much energy we deliver. So, in the long run, *marginal* and hence *average* costs should decline continually, as in Figure 13.

Immediate objections

Short run or long run?
The alert economist's first response to the above common sense example is that this is a logical argument, but it applies only in the short term – from one year to the next. In the life of a utility grid, seasonal or annual comparisons are short term fluctuations, not long term movements, so annual variations in output show moves along a *short* run marginal cost (SRMC) curve of currently-installed capacity, until capacity is exhausted and costs rise (the SRMC curves up again in a 'U'). At this point new capacity with a fresh SRMC should be created. The fact that each SRMC slopes downward after installation, before turning upwards, guarantees nothing about the shape of the enveloping LRMC. We cannot deduce that the enveloping LRMC will slope necessarily slope downwards or upwards. Or, it could be flat, before rising at some point in the future, when large firm diseconomies of scale set in.

The complex 'outputs' of a utility grid
The second major problem is that the heuristic theory over-simplifies the grid's 'outputs'. The proper definition of the output of an electrical distribution system is more complicated than just Terawatt hours of electricity delivered; it needs to be measured in several ways, or several 'dimensions', mathematically. For instance, if you listen to them (and as specified in the previous chapter), the management or customers of a utility will tell you that the true function of a distribution grid is *to be available* to distribute energy *when customers need it*, and then to deliver it at that time and place. Providing no service – called an 'outage' – is a serious failing; having your product available for only six hours a day is not what customers want, and making up the same volume (load) later in the day/week/month is no substitute if you want power at 9 in the morning and it is only available at 3 in the morning. Partial service, with outages, may be better than nothing; it may be what customers in many parts of the world resignedly accept as "normal in our city" or "typical for our country", but no outages is one of many dimensions of service that customers want, along with full voltage 24 hours a day in electricity, constant quality and full pressure in gas, constant pressure, temperature, quality and turbidity[37] in water etc.

As another example, consider the franchise question: imagine you were bidding to run the franchise for one of two similar city grids, each delivering the same amount of energy to its city, but one city's grid has 1 million connections and 10,000 km of mains while the other's has 2 million connections and 20,000 km of mains. Which would you expect to have the lower costs? Ask any utility engineer and they will tell you that every connection or hundred metres of main is not just an accounting asset, it is a piece of kit that can go wrong, and therefore needs either *pro-active planned maintenance* to pre-empt distribution problems, or *reactive maintenance* to fix problems after they have erupted. And, statistically, distribution problems *will* occur every year. So connections and km of mains are two of the main 'cost-drivers' of a network utility grid – probably far more so than the amount of energy or water carried.

So we could use the 'load' carried as one measure of output, but – and this argument applies to every network grid – our *outputs should include all measures of service levels (the 'quality of service'), the numbers of customers, their geographical dispersion[38], the number, size, and complexity of their connections,* etc. *and any other constraints imposed by local laws, geography, and history.*

Sounds complicated. Why include all this stuff as an 'output'? Surely energy distribution is a pretty simple business? Well, this list of legal, geographical and historical factors is effectively a set of constraints imposed by consumers (or layers of government on their behalf) that has to be met, and each constraint raises the costs of maintaining and operating a grid. If the grid operator does not meet these requirements it is not doing its job properly, and ultimately should lose its licence to operate, or, if publicly accountable, the top managers should be replaced. Also, recall that none of these 'outputs' is controlled by the managers of the utility: in general the managers do not choose how many people will live in their area, nor how many wish to be served, where those people will live, how many connections they will have, nor the pattern of their daily and seasonal demands. Yet all these factors can raise the total cost of operating the grid significantly.

As incomes rise, and customers become more socially and environmentally conscious, the set of constraints on a utility grows: not only must the utility deliver the load with no outages, maintain the grid, deal with earthquakes, ice storms[39] or frost-heave[40], and comply with national and local laws, but it must also sometimes repair roads to better standards than it found them, use engineering

---

[37] cloudiness of the water, due to tiny bubbles dissolved in it.

[38] All these factors are fully addressed in Chapter 6: 'Measuring utility outputs properly'.

[39] Ice storms cover electricity poles with ice and get blown down in severe winter weather, producing outages. They require the utility to re-string the wires as soon as possible, at considerable cost to some utilities but not to all.

[40] Frost-heave is the action of repeated freezing and thawing of ground around water and gas pipes which can cause the pipes to buckle and burst. Some utilities suffer more from this than others due to their different operating climates.

processes that are environmentally sustainable (rather than the cheapest), not disturb residents at night etc.. Simple comparisons of load delivered per unit cost between similar utilities in different countries or regions ignore all these extra different dimensions of output that a tightly-governed utility must deliver. The economic way of expressing this is to say that proper comparison of utility efficiencies requires us first to measure each utility's outputs properly – which we set about analysing seriously in Chapter 6 – and secondly to use a set of efficiency measurement techniques that fairly distinguishes between costs the managers of the utility could be expected to influence and those over which they are likely to have no control. We start tackling this set of problems in Chapter 7. However, it is worth saying right now that if we want to do this it will be essential to have a set of good quality data for quite a few utilities covering several years and using standardized data definitions – or we will simply be comparing the cost of one city's apples with another city's oranges.

To conclude, any decent comparison of the efficiency of one network with another should
1. use multi-dimensional measures of output, including some measures of service quality,
2. decide which of these are beyond management's ability to influence (which are 'exogenous cost-drivers') and
3. assume effectively that *management's job is to minimize the cost of inputs* subject to delivering all the (externally-determined) outputs.

Better-formulated hypotheses on scale and scope economies
So a proper testing of the neo-classical hypothesis applied to network utilities should specify several dimensions (a vector) of grid outputs and then examine the long run marginal cost curve, to see if it really is downward-sloping. In simple terms, because the X-axis (output) occurs in several dimensions, we cannot produce a series of charts of each industry's LRMC, but we can examine the evidence, do the maths, and draw some tentative conclusions.

Economies of scope
There is, however, a secondary theoretical argument that there are economies of scope in running network utilities. Economies of scope are the savings in costs that a firm achieves when producing and selling two or more goods, due to resources being shared in their production or marketing. Economies of scope are the economists' version of a wider and deeper general business strategy concept called product synergies, which ought to exist for any multi-product firm to exist. If we adopt the concepts of the 'Resource Based View' school of business strategy[41] then these synergies concern the development of a firm's capabilities, in that once a firm has developed the capabilities to create and market one product successfully, most firms look around to see if there is a

---

[41] John Kay made the definitive case for this in his 1999 article *Mastering Strategy: Resource Based Strategy* which is still available at http://www.johnkay.com/1999/09/27/mastering-strategy-resource-based-strategy

second or third product in which they can use the same capabilities to exploit their competitive advantage. So The Coca-Cola Company deploys its considerable marketing capabilities not just on Coca Cola but also on Sprite, Fanta and Dasani, while PepsiCo goes further by not just marketing drinks like Pepsi and Tropicana, but also foods such as FritoLay and Quaker Oats. Clearly there are few production synergies between PepsiCo's diverse range of products, yet the company has traded successfully for many decades in markets which are universally regarded as very competitive, so they must be extracting some significant marketing synergies from their unique product mix. To say the marketing synergies both companies have developed save costs, is to capture only a tiny part of the true multi-product synergies both these giant firms reap.

Still, as Chapter 2 showed, in marketing terms, utility outputs are nearly all commodities, and utilities do not have large marketing departments, so utility synergies could well be revealed as the economist's concept of economies of scope, shown in Figure 14:

Figure 14: Economies of scope

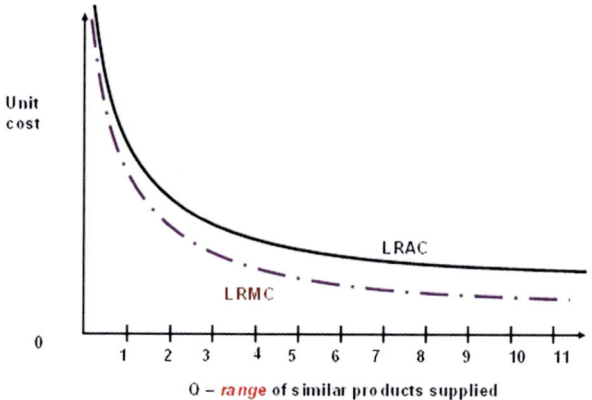

The only difference between economies of scale and scope is the horizontal axis label, which in scale economies says volume supplied and in scope economies specifies the number or range of products sold by the company for which these shared costs exist.

Following Coase's general line of argument from the contract theory of the firm, Teece in 1980[42] set out an important argument in principle against scope economies. He argued that synergies between businesses can be achieved without having to insist on common ownership of assets if the parties can specify and reach an agreement. So the owner of an orchard under which sheep graze (achieving synergies in fruit and sheep production – economies of scope) does not have to own the sheep, he can simply reach an agreement with a local

---

[42] Teece D, 1980, 'Economies of Scope and the Scope of Enterprise' *Journal of Economic Behaviour and Organisation* 1, 223-247

sheep farmer. The only constraints are the normal ones from contracting theory of the firm, that the two must be able to specify and monitor the contract, and that the synergies must exceed the transaction costs of the agreement.

Scope economies through vertical integration

So what might possible scope economies be in network utilities? Well, given that at the transmission and distribution stages at least, each utility is likely to be a local monopoly, we can either examine different utilities – preferably in the same region – undertaking similar functions, or we can consider different firms in the same industry merging to save costs: could there be economies of scope from vertical integration?

The most casual look around the world reveals that most utilities, whether privately or publicly owned, are vertically integrated to some degree. Power generation companies often own electricity transmission and distribution assets, gas producers own pipelines, energy retailers own generation plant, while water and wastewater utilities are nearly always totally vertically integrated, as well as often being merged across the two utilities. Vertical integration is particularly strong if the utilities are publicly owned. But is this vertical integration proof of economies of scope?

The first thing to note is that overwhelmingly this is due to historical reasons, and may not necessarily indicate any current economies of scope. In other words when these utilities were first established – often a century or more ago – the customers needed a vertically-integrated service, and there was usually a dearth of skilled people with the resources to deliver such diverse specialised functions, so utilities arose offering to guarantee a holistic service to customers.

Successful companies were rewarded with loyal customers supplying a guaranteed revenue stream. Once the managers of a utility had established a reliable service, and then a dominant position in the market, they could usually merge with any local rivals to create geographical monopolies, unless they were opposed by exceptionally active local politicians or pressure groups. Thus having established local vertical monopolies, privately-owned utilities were often allowed to merge horizontally. For instance, the number of privately owned water companies in England and Wales fell from several thousand around 1900 to a few hundred by 1945, and then to 39 by 1989. Facing identical pressures, publicly-owned utilities were also completely vertically integrated and then faced the same kind of pressures to merge horizontally, usually only being stopped by local political barriers. Life was comfortable and there were no incentives to change.

So what vertical economies of scope could there possibly be in today's utilities? Consider, first, potential synergies between bulk energy or water generation and bulk transmission. Other than minor managerial synergies such as saving Finance Directors or having similar large-project management skills, it is hard to see what synergies there really are between these two activities. Of course the whole system must be operated as one seamless network, usually from one control room, but utility grid control rooms in the 21st century are so automated that almost no-one is employed in them. It is an impressive experience to stand in the control room of a major energy or water utility and watch staff monitoring system developments as they happen, respond, and suddenly switch on valves, pumps or switchgear tens or hundreds of kilometres away. Obviously there are not zero people in the room, but it is such a small number that once a control room is up-and-running, and staffed by a constant rota of skilled people 24/7, this is not one of a utility's significant overall costs. Naturally maintenance of all the control room's functions is imperative, and gets the highest spending priority, but once commissioned and properly maintained this equipment should fail only rarely and so should not be a major cost-driver.

Between bulk energy transmission and distribution the synergies might also include similar capital management processes, as both require the managers to convince some external body (politicians or regulators) that capital must be spent to achieve one of the utility's stated goals. But even where the transporting technology is very similar between transmission and distribution (both use similar-sized wires or pipes) the core *cost-drivers* of each business unit (the factors which determine the bulk of costs) are different. Transmission's core cost-drivers are the need to match capacity to regional supply/demand imbalances while distribution's core cost-drivers are thousands of local problems caused by individual property developments, random asset failures, local capacity or quality issues, and interactions with other local utilities. *Transmission and distribution have fundamentally different cost-drivers, so one should expect few economies of scope.*

In water and wastewater there are close synergies between transmission and distribution because water and wastewater are not generally transmitted far (i.e. transport costs are a very high proportion of the value) and the transmission grid is not clearly defined separately from the distribution network. With a handful of exceptions around the world these two businesses are always vertically integrated in practice, and in costs, so there is nothing to test empirically here.

The last part of the vertical value chain is potential synergies between a utility's distribution business and its supply business. Given that this is providing the same utility to the same customers one would expect some strong synergies between these two businesses. Whether they show up in practice should be interesting, and now that quite a few utilities have separated distribution from retail, while many are still integrated one that we can test empirically.

The final vertical synergy concerns the possibility of linking the two ends of the utility value chain: retail or supply businesses with the generation businesses. Despite strenuous efforts to separate them vertically many utilities have re-combined energy generation and energy retail businesses because merging helps "close the firm's position" or "reduce its exposure" at lower cost than other methods.

The problem is this: a generator sells energy in wholesale markets and faces a perennial risk that the price of its output will fall and stay low. Similarly a retailer buys energy in the same energy markets and is perennially vulnerable to a sustained rise in energy prices. Both firms can "close off" their financial positions using financial techniques[43] but these financial markets have costs, which can mount up over many years, and in many cases the financial markets do not go out far enough into the future to reassure their investors – or at least, this is what the managers claim (see Chapter 8 for an analysis of shareholder/manager incentives). By merging a generator with a retailer the two businesses naturally complement each other for as far as anyone can see – provided that the customers and the generators are similar sized and good mirror images of each other. Again, given that there are many supply businesses around the world that are vertically integrated and ones that are not, this could be an interesting test.

Functional scope economies
Alternatively, if we compare *functional synergies between different utilities,* clearly the retailing function could be very similar if one were retailing more than one utility service. Stand-alone retailers each need an IT system, a call centre etc., but these can be added onto an existing system for only a small incremental cost, exactly as depicted by the LRMC curve above[44]. The savings would be particularly strong for overlapping geographical areas – i.e. if most customers in a city or region receive both services – as one could use the same database and add only a few additional fields to capture and measure the range of services each customer gets. So in principle there might be significant scope economies in retailing two or more utilities, such as electricity and gas, or water and sewerage, particularly if there is a strong geographical overlap of customers.

Can this apply to combining a gas and an electricity generation company, or water and gas transmission networks? Seems unlikely: we've hardly ever heard of companies alleging such synergies and it strikes one as improbable that any business can find significant synergies between operating several large power stations and operating several large gas fields. Regarding transmission, there are obvious parallels between gas and electricity networks – the process of capital planning, the regulatory cycle etc. – but there is a big difference between seeing broad *parallels* and *extracting significant daily synergies* as Coca-Cola or PepsiCo do when marketing one well-known drink after another. Even when companies do own both transmission networks in the same region (e.g. National Grid in the UK) they run each as almost entirely separate businesses. As we are about to see, there are huge differences between underground gas pipes and overground electricity cables.

What about distribution? Surely there can be significant cost savings from

---

[43] Such as long term contracts, or hedging one's position using forward or futures trading.

[44] It turns out this is not true: we examine incremental IT costs as part of marginal costs in Chapter 5, and find that the set-up hardware and software costs are only a small part of the total long run incremental costs of IT.

owning the same electricity wires, gas, water and sewage pipes in the same streets? It would be nice to think so, and we will shortly examine the empirical evidence either way, but before we do, consider some general theoretical issues, which can best be illustrated by looking into a typical hole in the road:

Figure 15: Maintaining utility distribution assets – find the economies of scope in this

Photo: from the author's extensive collection

We have a typical mess of utility networks that looks to the untrained eye like a rat's nest. But, of course, the skilled utility engineer who typically works on these soon discerns the old electricity cable starting at the bottom with a new black box around it, with a junction branching off to the right, just below the green telecoms cable, which also disappears off to the right. Beyond this, near the top of the picture, is a yellow gas pipe and some grey pipes containing other telecoms cables. Unseen, because it is covered by a thin layer of earth just below the yellow gas pipe, is a blue water pipe, which the workman showed me with his boot, and, of course, well hidden a metre or two below all this is the main street sewer – a pottery pipe at least 50cm in diameter.

Planned and reactive maintenance

Surely there must be synergies in serving all these utilities together? Can't we coordinate maintenance of all these pipes and cables so that we only dig up the street once?

Older readers who have spent years in cars stuck in traffic jams caused by utility repairs will sigh knowingly, and say "If only!" And, unfortunately, so will experienced utility engineers. The problem is core to all network utilities, and derives fundamentally from the fact that there are two kinds of maintenance:

- *Planned pro-active maintenance,* where an asset is scheduled to be repaired in advance, and
- *Reactive maintenance*, where an asset suffers an unscheduled breakdown and has to be repaired immediately in order to stop outages and hence restore service.

In non-utility industries most maintenance is planned. A firm cannot allow a key piece of capital equipment to decay to a state in which it becomes unreliable, so they schedule preventative or planned maintenance for some time when it will inconvenience operations the least, plan the whole procedure in detail, inform the operational staff, and, when given the "Go Ahead" signal, get on with it. Indeed this is precisely how most maintenance is done in a car factory, on an oil or gas production platform, or on the electricity pylons and cables of an electricity transmission network.

But *underground assets are different*. These are overwhelmingly serviced using reactive maintenance, where someone (often a householder – i.e. the consumer) reports a problem or outage, and the utility sends a team to identify the problem and fix it – to the best of the maintenance team's ability.

Clearly reactive maintenance is a second best solution. We've had to wait until a service failure occurs in a particular location – so by definition the customer is suffering – and we've turned up with a scratch team of generalists who try to cope with every possible type of failure the distribution network can throw at them. They may not have the right spare parts, or testing kit, or repair equipment, or the right specialist staff, and the immediate failure may have affected far more people than it needed to, compared to having planned this the day before as a scheduled repair. And inevitably it's pouring with rain at two o'clock in the morning, so the trench is filling up with water, the men are slipping around potentially causing more accidents, the utility is paying overtime, and the householders around are having their night's sleep disrupted. Everyone would prefer to maintain assets using planned maintenance. So why do we do it?

Consider the probabilities, costs and consequences involved in maintaining underground grids. In a well-run city with utilities that function adequately, at any moment in time 99% of all the distribution assets are working fine, but there may be a few problems, causing outages for, let's say, 1% of households (a horribly high figure for some utilities, but a dream state for many cities in the world). Let us suppose that the statistical failure rate for any metre of underground pipe or cable is, say, 1 in 10,000 per year, while each connection has a failure rate of say, 1 in 1000 per year. This means a city with say 500km of roads (= 500km of distribution network) and 100,000 connections will have 50 mains failures and 100 connection failures in an average year. "Fair enough", says the utility engineer for the city, "I'll keep a repair team on standby, and give them some planned maintenance work for the slack periods, such as adding new properties to the grid." Does he really have any choice? The problem is *he doesn't know which bit of his grid is going to fail, or when in the year it will fail.*

So if he tried to anticipate the failures, and plan maintenance he would end up having to dig up the entire grid, which is hugely expensive and might solve the failures for a few years, until even the new grid starts to have 1 in a million failures a year, at which point the whole second-best reactive maintenance cycle starts again. Reactive maintenance, like death and taxation, is a second-best solution in life, but also a certainty.

There is no point in quoting ratios of planned to reactive maintenance for each type of transmission or distribution grid as these vary hugely between cities or regions depending on the age of a grid, the climate and geology of the city, the materials and designs used, and particularly whether the systems has been "adequately" maintained in the past, or had almost no maintenance budget at all etc. As rough generalisations, in the author's experience we may say

- Sewers are almost always 100% reactive
- Water grids are generally 98% or more reactive
- Underground gas and electricity distribution grids *in steady state* are very hard to generalise; because the consequences of failure can be lethal – unlike water or sewerage – or cause an outage in the grid's performance across an entire city or region, there is a higher payoff to undertaking preventative maintenance, even if failures look unlikely or minor, so planned maintenance may be a much higher part of total maintenance spend.

However, even planned maintenance may not permit many economies of scope in practice: if we decide to re-lay an electricity main along most of 23rd Street what is the likelihood that this street is the highest priority in the whole city for the gas and water utilities? Many utilities gently nursing old distribution systems will also cite the old adage "If it ain't broke don't fix it." Which explains why most readers of this book over the age of thirty in most cities of the world will be able to reflect on their own personal experiences: they will be able to name the roads that were dug up for some length (equals planned maintenance) by one utility and reflect ruefully that within five years another utility (sometimes the same one!) dug up most of the same road.

Where does this leave economies of scope in distribution – which is the core monopoly here? Well, if most steady state distribution costs are maintenance, whether the maintenance is reactive or planned, we should not expect many economies of scope. In the reactive case the likelihood that the bit of gas pipe shown in Figure 15 fails in the same week as we happen to be repairing the water pipe or electricity cable shown in the same hole is 1 in a million – or less[45]. And due to changing demands and varying availability of maintenance funds, even planned maintenance is very hard to coordinate between utilities. We are

---

[45] Inevitably I am assuming the repair crews are competent, and don't actually create problems in one grid while fixing another grid in the same hole. In reality some crews are less than totally competent, but this problem is ultimately solved not by merging utilities, only by training and managing crews better.

left with small synergies indeed – unless there are wholesale plans to upgrade an entire region's infrastructure, in which case big savings could be achieved by merger – or simply by better coordination between separate utilities[46].

Governance and efficiency
Lastly we should reflect on the nature of the utility's 'governance' and its likely efficiency. In contestable markets we generally do not worry too much about whether firms in an industry are efficient or not, because competition sorts out the grossly inefficient. But utilities are usually monopolies so there is no competition, so if we observe costs in order to measure economies of scale or scope, we either have to assume each utility is 100% efficient, or make some explicit assumptions about rival utilities' efficiencies. This is why measuring the efficiency of utilities is a vital subject, which we address seriously in Chapters 6 and 7.

Finally, we must allow for differences in each utility's *governance*: the structures and processes by which chief executives are appointed and budgets set, the ways in which each utility's objectives are prioritised, and the main ways in which its performance is assessed. Plus, there can be big differences between the amount of money two utilities were allowed to spend *in the past* maintaining or enhancing their networks, which can lead one to have far lower costs than the other when we compare costs today. And because their governance structures may incentivise some utilities to be more efficient, while others are given wider social objectives, it would be wrong to cite some utilities' actual costs as necessary evidence of economies or diseconomies of scale or scope.

Empirical evidence of scale and scope economies
Testing apparently straightforward hypotheses in practice is always more difficult than you think, not least because one is forced to clarify relationships and specify assumptions that previously seemed trivial. In this case, the most basic question is "Are we considering economies of scale in a cross-sectional sense (comparing different sized utilities' average or marginal costs in the same industry in a given year), or are we considering them in a time-series sense (comparing one utility's unit costs over long periods of time, as demand rises)?" We reflect, and consider that the neo-classical cost curve represents the inverse of the production possibility frontier (PPF) with outputs and inputs each constrained to one dimension, so the PPF summarises production possibilities open to all producers at a moment in time. So it is the cross-sectional sense that matters most here. We will, though, return to how actual long run marginal costs are properly measured in a time-series sense in Chapter 5, and consider the evolution of the PPF and how to measure distances from it more generally in Chapter 7. Note in passing, though, that casual neo-classical analysis[47] assumes that a result in one sense will necessarily apply in the other sense.

---

[46] In the UK there is a body charged with doing just this: the National Joint Utilities Group.

[47] Of course this applies to none of the textbooks you will have read.

In addition there are dozens of practical difficulties such as agreeing on definitions of costs, cost allocations, and other terms between independent utilities that routinely plague efficiency comparisons of this kind. Notwithstanding the practical difficulties of governance, efficiency, and economies of scope, we need to come to a view of whether long run marginal costs really do slope downwards as assumed by neoclassical theory.

Evidence from electricity

Electricity distribution

The core grid monopoly function of electricity is distribution. Some of the most careful work here has been done by John Kwoka in the USA. Kwoka's 2005 study of electricity distributors found that economies of scale were minimised at 33.6 TWh of electricity distributed, or around 1½ million customers, but unit costs varied little over a considerable range, which suggests that underlying unit costs could well be largely flat over this range[48]. He also found cases where a poorly-performing utility had been permitted to take over smaller firms that had been performing better, and that the majority of mergers in the electricity industry had not led to cost reductions benefiting consumers. Kwoka's latter findings support wider merger studies across many industries which tend to show that mergers usually benefit the shareholders of companies being taken over, but there is no general evidence that mergers improve efficiency, and a considerable body of evidence that overall mergers have actually reduced shareholder value[49].

In Europe a thorough 2009 review of European electricity distributors by Growitsch, Jamasb and Pollitt[50] reported strong economies of scale in electricity distribution up to 20,000 customers, with rather smaller economies up to 100,000 customers. Beyond 100,000 customers they found economies were modest, and mixed up with issues of management efficiency and governance. Note that 20,000 *customers* means a population served of about 50,000 people, as a domestic 'customer' is typically one household, and an average household in Europe and America has around two and a half people in it (though this ratio is steadily falling as average family sizes shrink and the proportion of single person households rises)[51]. 100,000 customers (roughly a quarter of a million people served) is a small city, or a small county in a rural area, and is, you will note, far smaller than the average utility found around the world today.

---

[48] Kwoka, JE, "Electric Power Distribution: Economies of Scale, Mergers, and Restructuring," *Applied Economics*, November 2005.

[49] Reviews of the vast literature on this are found in most business strategy textbooks – e.g Grant 7th edition page 450, Johnson, Scholes and Whittington 8th edition page 359.

[50] Growitsch C, Jamasb T & Pollitt M, 2009. "Quality of service, efficiency and scale in network industries: an analysis of European electricity distribution," *Applied Economics*, Taylor and Francis Journals, vol. 41(20), pages 2555-2570

[51] However, matters get difficult if people live in apartment blocks and the block counts as one domestic customer.

Thus combining the US and European studies, we conclude that there seem to be strong economies of scale in electricity distribution up to 20,000 customers, but beyond 100,000 customers the evidence seems to be that unit costs are pretty flat. Modest potential economies of scale seem to be outweighed by issues of efficiency, governance and possible dis-economies of scale, as firms get too unwieldy to be managed tightly.

Electricity transmission
Most electricity transmission systems in the world do not evolve to some theoretically optimal size, as would happen in a contestable industry, but are sized to serve *political* units – typically whole countries, sometimes States within large countries, sometimes parts of huge States like California. Thus, like distribution businesses, their scale is fundamentally outside the control of their managers; it is determined exogenously by politicians. Consequently an international cross-sectional chart of the unit costs of actual transmission systems could be an interesting cross-section through the world's LRAC/LRMC transmission cost curves.

Unfortunately in practice clear evidence is hard to find. In his 1995 book[52] Pollitt reports a wide range of unit costs over a very wide range of sizes, but does not attribute the variations to specific sources such as governance, efficiency or scale economies. Dismukes, Cope and Mesyanzhinov found "strong economies over all relevant ranges of capacity and across all regions of the USA" in their 1998 study[53], but other studies find scale economies that are insignificantly different from one – i.e. broadly flat[54].

Electricity retailing
As Kwoka's US studies show, electricity retailing is often linked up with distribution, and the costs and synergies are hard to untangle. However, where pure retailing figures can be obtained Kwoka found "substantial" economies of scale among European electricity retailers up to 2 million customers, possibly driven by the fixed costs of large IT systems needed to track millions of customers, and economies of scale in 21st century call centres.

Economies of scale in electricity - summary
To sum up, there seem to be strong economies of scale in electricity distribution up to the size of a small town (50,000 people), but beyond a population of 250,000 people served (100,000 customers) scale economies become weak or insignificant. The evidence for transmission economies seems varied. We should

---

[52] Pollitt, M.G. (1995) *Ownership and performance in electric utilities: the international evidence on privatization and efficiency*. Oxford: Oxford Institute for Energy Studies.

[53] Dismukes D, Cope R and Mesyanzhinov D, 1998, "Capacity and economies of scale in electric power transmission" *Utilities Policy* Volume 7 Issue 3 Nov 1998

[54] E.g. Atsushi's 2003 study of Vietnamese transmission and distribution scale economies found at https://www.iaee.org/documents/Mexico/Economies%20of%20scale%20in%20power_IAEE_Presentation%20Atsushi%20Iimi.pdf

not forget though, that most distribution utilities already serve far more people than 250,000 and that the scale of most transmission utilities is determined by political factors, not economic rationality. And of course it is highly ironic that the area with the clearest and strongest economies of scale seems to be electricity retailing – a part of the electricity distribution chain that was not developed until thirty years after Mill wrote Principles of Political Economy[55], the part with no physical grid, and the part where the fixed costs of call centres and IT systems to track millions of customers now dominates!

From gas

We *could* painstakingly review the serious evidence for gas economies of scale by professional economists, which tends to reinforce the electricity findings that there are economies of scale in small networks, serving tens of thousands of people, but they become weaker at larger scales. That would be the standard academic way to proceed, and could well put you to sleep. Instead, though, let us try something more practical, and conduct an analysis of facts which reveal the beliefs and preferences of the experts in the gas business.

The 2005 breakup of the UK's gas industry

Most of the world's electricity grids were usually designed in the first half of the twentieth century on a fairly local scale, with little international trade envisaged or practiced. However, in gas most of the modern world's transmission and distribution grids were created in the second half of the twentieth century, often from the 1980s onwards. As Chapter 2 described, this continues today: gas transmission and distribution grids are still being developed, in Asia, Africa and Latin America, and transmission is very often an innately international business. So the modern world's gas grids are typically designed on a larger scale than electricity grids, envisaging from the outset considerable international trade through LNG or large transmission pipes. So for gas the question of economies of scale is more relevant to policy makers at the large end (more than a quarter of a million connections, say) than at the level of a single town or city, where few doubt that there are significant economies of scale.

The UK's eight gas distribution grids

In western Europe the Netherlands was the first country to discover gas, offshore from Groningen in the North Sea in 1959, and a national gas network was rapidly developed. In the 1960s Britain discovered gas on its side of the North Sea, and a State-owned enterprise, British Gas, was created to develop and exploit this resource, as well as to absorb all the former town gas works (where gas had been created) and their urban distribution grids. British Gas developed and owned some gas fields itself, bought gas wholesale from other field owners, transmitted the gas around a transmission network, and linked up its inherited town gas distribution grids to create regional gas distribution grids across the UK that typically supplied between 2 and 10 million people.

---

[55] The world's first public electricity retailer was a supply of street lighting and electricity for shops to the town of Godalming, UK, in 1881.

By 2005 the owner and operator of Britain's gas distribution grids was a now-privatised company called Transco, which had been stripped of all significant retail or upstream production activities. So Transco was a pure 'natural monopoly', a heavily-regulated, gas transmission and distribution company. The transmission business was run as one operating unit, while the distribution grids were run as eight regional distribution grids, called Local Distribution Zones (LDZs).

The 2004-05 LDZ sale
In 2005 Transco sold off four of its eight UK regional LDZs to three rival utility companies for £5.8 billion. It is true that Transco had been asked to do this by its economic regulator, Ofgem, rather than offering to do this of its own volition, but if Transco had really believed there were strong economies of scale in operating gas distribution grids, they would surely have made a strong public case for this being uneconomic, and not in consumers' long term interest. An economic consultancy, Oxera, did take up part of their case, claiming that the British gas industry might lose some economies of scale and that overall British consumers might lose out[56].

The first thing to say is that whatever economists may have thought, the managers and owners of these rival companies clearly did not believe there are strong economies of scale in managing gas grids – and they, better than anyone else, should know. Secondly, as Pollitt and Steer (2011) noted[57], although there has been no definitive study of gas costs following the de-merger of the British gas zones, one hardly needs this. The plain facts speak for themselves: Pollitt and Steer show gas costs per domestic customer falling around 40% (from around £50 a head to £30 a head) in four years following the break-up of the LDZs, while non-domestic costs fell around 10%. Later in their article Pollitt and Steer attribute much of this to the regulator's ability to 'benchmark' costs better, and incentivise the companies through 'comparative competition' to achieve higher efficiency levels (Chapter 8 explains how regulators can use benchmarking and 'comparative competition' to imitate the effects of competition-in-the-market, improve efficiency, and lower costs).

So economists have to admit that the solid professional judgement of some of the top gas distribution managers to be found in Europe in 2005 – their revealed preference – was that there are no significant economies of scale in gas distribution at a level of more than 2 million people served, and that, on the contrary, it is at least possible *those managers believed there were effectively diseconomies of scale in trying to run collections of gas distribution grids serving regions larger than about 3 million people*[58]. But whatever they believed, the facts since support the managers' and regulators' views that cost gains from improving efficiency through better comparative competition would swamp any

---

[21] Oxera, 2003, British Gas Trading: potential sales of National Grid Transco's Distribution networks: Critical review of the preliminary Regulatory Impact Assessment.

[57] Pollitt, Michael G. & Steer, Steven J., 2012. "Economies of scale and scope in network industries: Lessons for the UK water and sewerage sectors," Utilities Policy, 21(C): 17-31

theoretical scale effects.

From water
In water Abbot and Cohen in 2009[59] undertook a major review of the literature on scale and scope economies in the water industry around the world. Examining 26 papers, 13 had found evidence of some economies of scale, 5 (all studies of England and Wales) found diseconomies of scale, 5 found scale economies being exhausted at different levels, and 5 found either inconclusive evidence or economies and diseconomies existing at the same time in different parts of the water value chain! The significance of England and Wales in this context is that their water companies are far larger than most water utilities around the world, so the results would seem to suggest that the larger English and Welsh companies have exceeded the optimal size, while most of the rest of the world's water utilities exhibit some economies of scale at a very small level but then these get exhausted.

More interesting than these crude results is that the level at which scale economies seemed to be exhausted varies according to geography, suggesting 'natural' *plant economies* of scale play a role: in other words if I have to treat the water or sewage for half a million people it is of course cheaper if I can do it in one big treatment plant, but this depends on whether they all live in one compact city or spread out over 5000 square kilometres. We must compare like with like: we can rely on the engineers to extract all the plant economies they can, but their scope for doing this depends on where people choose to live. Population clustering is not something the engineers, or their utility managers, or their political masters, can do much about. And then, as in gas and electricity, for the cost numbers to tell us anything about economies of scale or scope, we have to assume that each utility is equally incentivised to be efficient by its governance, and further, that it actually achieves the same efficiency in practice.

Evidence of economies of scope
Let's try to do this properly but fast, to stop you falling asleep. In theory firms can extract scope economies by sharing costs between two stages of the value chain or between two similar functions in different utilities. The evidence from the 1970s and 1980s in many economic studies suggested there were significant economies of scope in electricity[60]. This should have led the British government *not* to unbundle the Central Electricity Generating Board (CEGB), the vertically integrated generator and transmission company for England and Wales. In 1991 British Ministers duly ignored this economic evidence and unbundled and

---

[58] Obviously serving a single city like London with around 10 million people has economies of scale, but no expert team argued that there were strong economies of scale in combining all of the, say, western or northern parts of the UK.

[59] Abbott M and Cohen B, 2009, Productivity and Efficiency in the Water Industry, *Utilities Policy* 19, 233-244

[60] Pollitt reviews these in Pollitt M 2008, The arguments For and Against Ownership Unbundling of Energy Transmission Networks, *Energy Policy* 36, 704-713

privatised the CEGB. In 1997 Newbery and Pollitt analysed their unbundling[61], and found that electricity costs rose at first, as new governance arrangements were created, then fell significantly. Overall Newbery and Pollitt estimated the net benefits of unbundling to be a permanent reduction in costs around 5%. Analysing US electric utilities from 1994 to 2006 Triebs *et al* (2010)[62] found similar results: vertical separation produced technical diseconomies (i.e. there were economies of scope) but these were outweighed by increasing efficiency in buying electricity at a lower cost overall. So both these papers concluded that possible economies of scope were swamped by actual efficiency improvements, whether internal or contractual, and it was a good idea for policymakers to have ignored economists' theoretical views.

Arocena, Saal and Coelli (2012)[63], however, find modest (5-8%) scope economies in regulated US electric utilities between generation and distribution, but Meyer (2012)[64], finds large economies of scope (19-26%) between electric networks and retail, and more modest (8-10%) scope losses when distribution-and-retail are unbundled from transmission-and-generation.

In water the evidence for economies of scope is also mixed. Saal *et al*[65] reported that five studies found scope economies between the different services of water and sewerage, but three found diseconomies of scope. Pollitt and Steer (*op. cit*), however, are highly critical of this paper's interpretations of some of the other papers' conclusions. Less controversially, Abbott and Cohen (2009 *op. cit*) report 5 papers showing economies of scope in the water industry, 2 showing diseconomies of scope, and 3 inconclusive or showing economies of scope followed by diseconomies beyond a certain firm size.

Confused? You should be. This is a dog's dinner if ever you saw one. In this book we begin a clearer discussion of this subject by examining long run marginal costs in a forward-looking time-series sense (the only way that makes sense in practice) in Chapter 5. In Chapter 6 we define utility outputs properly, and look at the growth of industry value chains in the modern world to meet consumers'

---

[61] Newbery D and Pollitt M 1997, The restructuring and privatisation of Britain's CEGB: was it worth it?, *Journal of Industrial Economics* 45 (3) 269-303

[62] Triebs T, Pollitt M, and Kwoka J, 2010, The Direct Costs and Benefits of US Electric Utility Divestitures, University of *Cambridge Electric Policy Research Group Working Paper* series EPRG 1024

[63] Arocena P, Saal, D, Coelli T, 2012, Vertical and Horizontal Scope Economies in the Regulated US Power Electric Power Industry, Journal of Industrial Economics Vol 60, Issue 3, pp 434-467.

[64] Meyer R, 2012, Economies of scope in electricity supply and the costs of vertical separation for different unbundling scenarios, *Journal of Regulatory Economics* August 2012, Vol 42 Issue 1, p95-114

[65] Saal D, Arocena P, Maziotis A, and Triebes T, 2011 A Critical Literature Review on Integration Economies and Economies of Scale in the Water Industry, Draft paper, cited in Pollitt and Steer *op. cit.* page 14

rising incomes and rising expectations. In Chapter 7 we run through some of the commonest efficiency measurement techniques that are useful in practice. In the last general utilities section, Chapter 8 briefly reviews the main contractual and regulatory systems that are actually used in practice to maximise efficiency incentives. In an introductory textbook we do not aspire to review all the main theoretical possibilities, still less review all recent developments in regulatory theory; for this you must choose an advanced text.

Overall evidence on economies of scale and scope in grids
It is hard to avoid the conclusion from examining the classic 'natural monopolies' that beyond certain very small sizes by today's standards grids exhibit neither strong economies of scale or scope, nor strong diseconomies.

Then listen to the words of a seasoned industry expert. In 2011 Michael Pollitt, of the Cambridge Judge Business School, who has studied this area across most utilities in many countries, summarised his views:

> ... *Competition thus brings significant benefits in terms of reducing inefficiency. This suggests that rather than focussing on the theoretically optimal scale and scope of the firm, which may involve reducing competition and may not actually be observable, it is important to consider whether firms are under sufficient competitive pressure to lower costs and improve quality. The long run benefits of competition may more than outweigh the short run costs of deviation from optimal scale and scope, even if those were well defined concepts.*[66]

Note his final seven words; this is the considered opinion of someone who has studied this subject for nearly twenty years and soberly reflected on its relevance to the modern world of utilities.

Overall, it is hard to avoid the conclusion that, contrary to the assumptions of traditional neo-classical economic theory, *beyond a certain small size, which in some industries seems to reflect plant economies or be geographically determined, modern evidence shows no overwhelming economies of scale or scope in most network grid utilities.* Yet casual observation shows they are some of the most complete monopolies.

The telecoms paradox
Lastly, we need to consider a paradox that arises in another network utility, which the neo-classical theory of natural monopolies cannot plausibly explain at all.

If we consider the fixed grids originally of fixed-line telecoms cables, now broadband cables, in cities we observe that these are single grid monopolies in small towns and densely-populated rural areas, while in large towns or cities it is very common to have two or more cable grids installed beneath the pavements.

---

[66] Pollitt and Steer ibid. page 11

Furthermore, when we examine the hearts of large metropolises (cities with ten million people or more) we frequently see that three, four, or even a dozen rival cable networks have been laid under the pavements or roads. Central London, for instance, has a "green sheen" of copper and fibre-optic cables containing dozens of rival commercial cables in large streets near financial, media or telecoms centres, as can be seen in Figure 16.

Figure 16: The 'green sheen': laying new telecoms cables directly on top of old

Source: National Joint Utilities Group, UK, reproduced with permission

If there were strong economies of scale in fixed-line telecoms or cable communication networks we would never see rival grids being laid on top of each other. One player would have laid a massive grid and everyone would rent capacity from them. Using the neo-classical theory of natural monopolies the only possible explanation for finding twelve grids on top of each other would be that the Minimum Efficient Scale of the global cost curve for landline grids just happens to be one twelfth of this city's demand at this point. And if we find 13? Well the MES is $1/13^{th}$ of the city's demand. Hmm: about as plausible as a goldfish in a bowl having voluntarily decided to leap into a cat's mouth. If we find cables being laid on top of existing cables the only plausible explanation must be that current demand conditions were not anticipated by the engineers who first specified the grid. And, given such fundamental design inefficiencies, neo-classical economic theory has absolutely nothing to say.

Generic limitations of static neo-classical economic theories
At this juncture, with major discrepancies between the predictions of the neo-classical theory of network grid monopolies and what we observe or can measure about the real world, it is appropriate to reflect on the internal logic and assumptions of the neo-classical theory of natural monopolies.

First, the internal logic. There is nothing wrong with it; if there were, this would have been spotted and the theory forgotten 150 years ago. So the issue is the theory's assumptions, and their applicability to the modern world.

Industries with strong economies of scale
Let us – all too briefly – forget about network utilities and consider some

industries where there is not the slightest doubt that economies of scale are strong, and then consider those industries' structures.

Consider pharmaceuticals. This industry has undoubted vast research, development, and licensing costs for every single drug that is approved by the Food and Drug Administration in the USA, or its European or Asian counterparts. Given that these fixed costs are of the order of $1900 million per drug[67], that the incremental production, distribution and marketing cost of most drugs is typically a few cents per pill, any approved drug's LRMC must slope significantly downwards at common price and usage rates, even for the most popular on-patent drug on the planet.

Technological progress
Yet the pharmaceutical industry is not heavily monopolised, as neo-classical theory implies. And it is not hard to see why: neo-classical theory makes no allowance for technological progress. Yet the pharmaceutical industry's whole business cycle of research, testing, approval, on-patent, and off-patent or generic drug relies on an *assumption of continual technological progress* which is undeniably true in the modern world. Yet this absolutely cannot be allowed in the neo-classical economic model: if we have technological progress the production possibility frontier advances and we have to redraw all our cost curves either lower down or further to the right. Furthermore, there is no guarantee at all that the shape of a new technology's cost curve will broadly resemble the shape of the old technology's cost curve. Indeed, in pharmaceuticals the problem is far worse than this, as the main technological advances are not cost-reducing enhancements but the creation of new possibilities for consumers that previously did not exist. Neo-classical economic theory has very few tools to handle a continually-rising list of goods in the economy.

So is there another example of an industry with very strong economies of scale but little or no technological progress? What about civilian aircraft production, where currently there are just two major producers on the planet – Boeing and Airbus – and Airbus only emerged because a consortium of determined European governments was prepared to subsidise its original Research & Development costs. There are huge fixed costs of design and development in this industry, and if we combine this with learning curve effects driven by cumulative volume produced, the LRMC must look like Figure 13, surely? But, hold on: while some aircraft do have production lives of more than 40 years, which seems amazingly long for a high-tech product, the whole point of new designs and learning curves is that they assume strong technological progress – or else, why would we need to design a new aircraft? If our old aircraft flew fine, sold well, and did not crash, why would we introduce a new one? Only because technology has advanced to make old aircraft uneconomic, or because governments set tighter

---

[67] Source: Mestre-Ferrandez,J, Sussex J and Towse A, 2012, The R&D cost of a new medicine, published by The Office of Health Economics (in 2011 prices) (see http://www.ohe.org/object/display.cfm?serv=2&id=124#124)

environmental constraints on aircraft makers, believing – quite rightly – that companies will themselves create technological progress to make cleaner and quieter aircraft than currently exist.

Industries without technological progress?

Can we think of a non-utility industry with strong economies of scale but without change in the nature of the product? Well, there are basic bulk chemicals like fixing atmospheric nitrogen into solid fertilisers, or the fruits of agriculture, or of mineral extraction, which may technically be almost the same as they were a hundred years ago; but even these can be strongly affected by technological progress in *the way they are produced, refined and distributed*. And the time scale over which these production processes improve is far shorter than a century. Or, if we consider the service sector, could we pretend that there have not been massive improvements in the quality of service provided by doctors, retailers, accountants, civil servants, or school teachers over the last twenty years?

So, in reality the classic picture of high fixed costs causing a continually decreasing LRMC cannot apply to agriculture, or the primary extractive industries, or almost any manufactured item, or the entire service sector in the modern economy, because continual technological progress, which Mill ignored in his original analysis of 1848, completely undermines the assumption of a fixed technology. Unfortunately the neo-classical economists who followed Mill also chose to ignore this effect – even in industries with very long asset lives like water, gas, electricity and rail.

Growing incomes

The other side of technological progress, indeed its direct logical consequence, is that consumers' incomes will never 'stabilise' in the long term, but will grow *continually*. This means we never will reach a long run plateau of demand, no matter how long we live, because there is no steady state. Even for old-fashioned products such as basic utility services, provided income elasticities are not actually zero[68], there is no long run steady state level of consumption for a city's water, energy, communications, transport or health demands. And, given the very long lives of many grid utilities' assets, this means the grid engineers can never configure the grid optimally for today's demands – they are always constrained by their predecessors' assumptions and creations from several decades ago, or the last century. So almost any real network grid will have considerable X-inefficiency of design configuration, due to divergences

---

[68] Alright, I know. Once we meet global goals to reduce carbon emissions and achieve environmental sustainability income elasticities for energy demand will effectively have fallen to zero or negative, but a) this will be a long time coming, b) this will not be true for most of the world's inhabitants, who are nowhere near the frontier of American or European living standards, and c) why should we hit a plateau of constant demand? Technological progress, rising incomes, and social or political constraints on demand might combine to make demand continually fall, or in general fluctuate randomly, rather than stabilise on a fixed level of demand over several decades, as would be required to meet the neo-classical theory's assumptions.

between the rise in actual demand, and its geographical distribution, and the original plans of their predecessors, decades ago.

Analysing industries with considerable X-inefficiency is not one of neo-classical theory's strong points. Once we start entering the realm where most actual observations comfortably exceed the cost curves, neo-classical theory has little relevance. If we add in technological progress, with new cost curves spontaneously replacing old ones, and assume consumers have continually rising incomes with non-zero income elasticities, neo-classical theory is very little use: its fundamental assumptions are continually being eroded away. In practice these difficulties are further compounded by 'output' being a list of exogenous cost-drivers that starts from tangible observations like load, customers, connections and mains length, but then goes on to include service levels, legal, geographical and historical factors such as the climate, city bye-laws and the hilliness of the area or the quality of its raw water sources – all of which are major exogenous cost-drivers in classic monopolies such as the water industry.

In sum how can neoclassical economists explain the frontispiece photo of bunches of cable wound round itself stuck 10 metres up a pole above the traffic? It's a non-equilibrium position and yet it happens all the time in utilities across the world; the only reason we don't see it all the time is that most utility grids are underground. When it occurs to an overhead cable someone snaps a photo and we can all see
   a) Immediately, the apparent absurdity of it
   b) On closer inspection, the logic of the engineer faced with a problem of demand growing at an uncertain rate, and fixed supplies of cable which are cumbersome to haul up a pole.

The reality of many markets today is that they are not in any kind of static equilibrium, and are at best only in a temporary equilibrium. As in the photo, we've packed up our tools and gone home for the night, and there is an observation – like a market price or quantity – which says "As of tonight we have Xkm of distribution wires in our city", but it's just a temporary resting place and has no grander significance than that. Tomorrow that number will change.

The neo-classical model of a network utility resembles a bicycle, on which some economists are stubbornly trying to place a reluctant elephant. Give up guys. A bike is a neat vehicle for certain loads, but for this job let's start with a completely fresh approach.

Chapter Three

Sunk costs and a general sequential model

In this chapter we refine the notion of sunk costs, and then develop a general time-sequential model of market entry and exit that handles sunk costs.

Sunk costs
We are examining the theory that the most distinguishing feature of natural monopolies is that they have abnormally large sunk costs, so we'd better define sunk costs properly.

Sunk cost concepts & definitions – some refinements
Some people say a sunk cost is any cost that occurred in the past – e.g. Wikipedia (accessed 2017). This definition, equating sunk costs with all past costs, does not distinguish between past repeating costs – fixed or variable – and past one-off costs that cannot be reversed. It isn't helpful from the point of view of economic models, so we drop it.

A traditional definition of a sunk cost is *assets which have little or no alternative use outside this market or particular situation*, as contrasted with general assets, such as vehicles or land, which can be put to use in other markets and so have well-determined resale values. This is a much more useful idea – and starts to capture some of life's essential asymmetries.

At heart, it seems a sunk cost must satisfy three conditions:
1. It is not expected to recur – at least not reliably – i.e. it is a *one-off cost;*
2. It must help *create a lasting asset or presence in a market* – a one-off expenditure on ice cream cannot count – unless you are training to become a professional ice cream taster!
3. It is *specific to a particular technology or situation*, so that if the original rationale for the investment disappears the next best use is to scrap all saleable components.

A different formulation is given in a heavyweight modern economics textbook:
"Besides fixed costs, firms from time to time incur initial costs, e.g. when they decide to enter a new geographical market or when they expand

their product line. These costs are incurred once and, often, cannot be fully recovered when reversing the decision. The part of the costs that cannot be recovered are the sunk costs of the firm."[69]

Note that this definition includes expenditure on things besides lasting or tangible assets, that might be necessary to enter an industry, so the definition has got wider in one sense, but also narrower: it envisages this expenditure in the specific situation of a firm entering a market and then deciding to reverse its decision. This is the approach we will adopt, before we go on to make the calculation of these sunk costs a mathematical formula. But, for the moment, we define *sunk costs as the costs of entering a market that cannot be recovered if the entry decision is reversed.*

As you probably guessed, there is an entire economics of sunk costs[70], which distinguishes exogenous sunk costs from *endogenous sunk costs*. The latter are where firms themselves build up sunk costs, such as Research & Development[71], to create entry (or mobility) barriers within a market which (they hope) will deter entrants from entering their particular market niche, or copying particular aspects of their product that differentiate it from rival products. However, in the utilities we do not need to augment entry barriers – they are already huge – so we are only concerned with *exogenous sunk costs*, so-called because they are exogenously given to us by the technologies of the general business environment.

Examples of sunk costs in practice
We should look at some classic exogenous sunk costs to examine their characteristics more closely, and analyse exactly what it is that 'sinks' their costs.

---

[69] Belleflamme P and Peitz M 2010, Industrial Organization: Markets and Strategies, Cambridge University Press, Cambridge UK 1st edition page 15

[70] One seminal text is John Sutton's 1991 Sunk Costs and Market Structure, Price Competition, Advertising And the Evolution of Concentration Cambridge MIT Press

[71] Much of the sunk cost literature uses marketing as an example of an endogenous sunk cost. While marketing is an essential expense of a successful differentiated product it does not meet the requirement of being a one-off cost; everyone agrees that marketing's benefit erodes quite rapidly and therefore one must expect to spend more on marketing, in exactly the same way as one must expect to spend money on maintenance. So marketing is a fixed recurring cost; product Development, on the other hand, meets all three of the requirements for a sunk cost.

Technology-specificity

Figure 17: A clear sunk cost

This electricity transmission pylon is clearly mostly a sunk cost because it has very few uses except as a tower to support high-voltage AC electricity transmission cables. It is *technology-specific*: when a new way of beaming electrical power around the world emerges this tower will be redundant and will only be sold for a fraction of the (inflation-indexed) sum it cost to erect it. But it is *also site-specific*: if population movements result in no bulk electricity demand near this power tower, even though the technology is still viable, new transmission paths will make it redundant and again it could only be sold for scrap.

What about this communications tower?

Figure 18: How much of this communications tower is a sunk cost?

This tower is far less technology-specific. It is already used by several different communications technologies, and, indeed, may have been erected by a firm specialising in erecting such towers, who then lease parts of it off to individual network media. If one technology is made redundant by some new technology the tower's owners may well be able to find replacement uses for the space freed up. And if all these ground-radio-based technologies became redundant the media owners would face the costs of scrapping their transmitter-receivers, so their sunk costs may be considerable; but the tower's owners could still scrap their steel tower and get a good percentage of its original erection cost. It is also less site-specific, in that the site is reasonably accessible by road and the tower could be dismantled relatively cheaply. All in all, this tower seems far less of a sunk cost than the transmission tower.

What about firms' product development costs? Commercial Research and Development (R&D) is almost entirely Development of specific technologies to achieve specific functions or effects. These costs are clearly sunk if that technology loses out to another technology in the constant battle between technologies. Who now remembers the intricate techniques by which wooden sailing ships fought back against steam ships in the mid-19th century? Or the technologies of wooden water mills of a thousand years ago, or of stick-woven fish traps a thousand years before that? Now that we have high quality solid state sound recording systems, 99% of the development funds that went into state-of-the-art tape recorders in the 1970s must just be written off. More importantly for the future of mankind, recalling that artificial intelligence systems have three components – hardware, software and data content – *nearly all hardware and much software development is a sunk cost*, because they are technology-specific, while the data content (the songs, images, text etc.) can be migrated from one system to another. So don't worry: Arnie's 1982 role as Conan the Barbarian will be preserved for future generations. But current IT firms have vast costs sunk into specific technologies which might not migrate to post-2025 technologies.

Site-specificity
How important is site-specificity? Almost all civil engineering work is site-specific, so is all civil engineering a sunk cost? Well, a unique feature in a unique location, such as an individual nuclear power station, is clearly almost 100% sunk cost, due to its combination of technology-specific and site-specific features, but what about an ordinary house or an apartment block? That is pretty site-specific and is a kind of civil engineering, yet it doesn't fit most people's definition of a sunk cost.

What distinguishes a typical house from a nuclear power station or a bridge is that humans are quite mobile and have to live somewhere, so there is usually a general mass demand for houses in an area, and it covers quite a range of styles of house, so even if the original customers decide to move away others will fill their place, albeit at a lower rent/price if the style of house is deemed to be unfashionable. So houses are not usually regarded as sunk costs.

But what about a house that was once a water treatment works, with reinforced concrete walls half a metre thick, which has now been expensively converted to a luxury unique house in remote countryside? Will its owners recoup all the funds they have invested in this quite singular house? That entirely depends on whether there is a mass market for this kind of house. If a sale were forced on the owners or their children, the extent of the write-down entirely depends on whether new buyers can be found who value the original features the current owners have inserted. So the extent of the sunk cost depends on the general attractiveness of the asset in the main housing market, and of course whether there is a general demand for housing in that area. Mining towns where the mine closes and the whole town is abandoned mean that any money spent on properties in this town is a risky sunk cost, even if the houses are perfectly average.

Sinking the sunk cost

Clearly a gas grid is a sunk cost, so are these gas pipes sunk costs?

Figure 19: A sunk cost?

No. Just checking that you are still awake. These are perfectly normal assets which can be bought, transported and sold in the market for gas pipes just like vans, aircraft or any other capital good. They only become sunk costs once they are sunk – i.e. once installed *in situ*.

Figure 20: Sinking the asset

Photo courtesy of High Desert Pipeline Inc. 2014, reproduced with permission

The yellow gas pipe on the left will soon be a sunk cost – getting it out would cost more than it's used value in the gas pipe market, and once the trench has been filled in with earth the cost of the pipe and its installation will be well and truly sunk. Or consider sewers. Even assuming you could dig one up without breaking it, what would its second hand value be? *All* its cost – raw materials and installation – is a sunk cost.

Actually the same logic applies to many bits of technology in industries where technology moves fast. A technology is invented that does some function (e.g. the carburettor in a car engine) but if a superior technology emerges (fuel injection) which does it better or cheaper, all investments made with the old technology – not just by the producers of it, but also by the consumers of it – are sunk costs, because no rational agent would use that technology now. This is an aspect of the vintage theory of capital which we will use.

The elapsed life of a sunk cost asset

Figure 21 shows a magnificent modern sunk cost:

Figure 21: A modern sunk cost: the Millau viaduct in France

© *Arles / Corbis. Reproduced by permission of Corbis*

It is a sunk cost because it is a civil engineering asset *in situ:* if the demand for its services – carrying vehicles from a very specific point A near Millau in southern France to another specific point B on the other side of the valley – were to cease the asset would be worth a fraction of its construction cost. Or, consider the value of a similar sunk cost built two thousand years earlier in another part of southern France by the Romans – one that also happened to be a utility asset:

Figure 22: A classic utility asset – and sunk cost – constructed two thousand years ago

© Tom Bean / Corbis. Reproduced by permission of Corbis

The Roman bridge at Pont du Gard is a classic piece of utility infrastructure. Forming one of 17 bridges in a 50km long aqueduct supplying 20,000 m3 of water a day to the city of Nimes, it was built in five years around 50CE to carry water across the river Gardon. The top part of the structure carried the water in a conduit that had to be watertight, but hundreds of years of water flowing through this conduit left a huge build-up of limescale, as Figure 23 shows:

Figure 23: The water conduit inside the Pont du Gard

Limestone growths created by 350 years of calcium-rich water running through conduit, and the entire 50km of aqueduct, gradually reduced the quantity and quality of water received in Nimes.

Source: author's photograph

According to the available archaeological and textual evidence the Pont du Gard worked well for 350 years before the limestone deposits shown above built up in the water conduit, and the quantity and quality of water delivered deteriorated. But before it could be totally rebuilt Nimes' water system was "withdrawn from service" in 407CE when the 'business environment' changed dramatically – Germanic tribes crossed the frozen river Rhine in January, swept aside the remnants of the Roman army, and plundered all of civilised Gaul, including Nimes. Because the Roman political system had failed to provide security, this changed political and social business environment brought about the collapse of the Roman empire in the west, and the sacking of Rome itself in 410CE[72]. Urban populations fell away, as lives and livelihoods collapsed. Nimes' demand for water transported over the Pont du Gard simply evaporated. Five hundred years later records show local people had stolen many stones from the bridge to build houses. Eleven hundred years after this, preserved and protected by the French government and UNESCO, it is France's fifth biggest tourist attraction. But tourism was not its planned purposes when designed[73]. So, once its primary function was gone the value of this asset descended into its scrap value as a heap of cut stones.

The financial performance of enduring utility industries
Given enough time, the Millau viaduct may one day be just another historical wonder, like the Pont du Gard, or a disused canal or railway, though more beautiful than most. Each of these infrastructure investments may eventually have achieved a total financial return on its original investment, including the sunk costs, which exceeded investors' original expectations, but much depends on the future business environment and the success of the technology embodied in the main assets constructed. This is largely luck. And the infrastructure utility's Investors, Directors and Managers should take little credit or blame for luck.

But what are a typical infrastructure asset's finances like *during* its useful life? Well, a standard financial ratio comparison of real utilities with a typical retail firm (in Appendix 1) shows that the distinguishing feature of utilities is their outstandingly large assets employed (the huge sunk costs of their grids) compared to their sales value or turnover, so that *functioning 'heavy' utilities have an exceptionally low asset turnover ratio*. In the real firms chosen British water companies had asset turnover ratios one tenth that of the giant US telecoms monopoly AT&T, which in turn has an asset turnover ratio a fifth of a typical business like Walmart[74].

---

[72] See Grant Michael, 1993, *History of Rome* Faber & Faber edition page 324

[73] OK, the Romans often built to impress – either their subjugated peoples, or one another (with rich men's public good works) – and there is evidence that the Pont du Gard impressed people at the time, but its primary purpose was always to deliver water to Nimes.

[74] When assets are long-lived we must be careful to value them consistently; see the final paragraph of the Appendix.

A general sequential model
We now develop a general theory of sequential industry entry and exit. Clear your mind of all neoclassical economic assumptions and models. Literally start by assuming nothing. Now imagine a habitable planet with intelligent life forms organised in largely peaceful societies called countries. A few countries are failed states with effectively no government and no rule of law; in such countries life is "nasty, brutish and short"[75.] The other countries, by contrast, have governments generally succeeding in providing security and making laws, a police force effectively enforcing the laws, and a legal system that can apply both obligatory general laws and voluntary private contracts to everyone. These are the essential social and political pre-requisites for a good market-based economy to flourish. Now assume the inevitable financial consequences of an effective rule of law – government expenditure and taxation. Also assume private consumers (households) consume and producers (firms) produce. Producers and consumers make explicit and implicit private contracts with each other, within the framework of the general laws. Government may choose to be a producer (state-owned enterprises) or not, as the political system decides, but due to its primary duty to provide security and a rule of law, government is always a significant employer and consumer of resources.

Now introduce time: *assume the arrow of time travels forwards only in a sequence of steps, and that although some decisions can be reversed over time, others cannot be*. Also assume financial markets work effectively; there is genuine uncertainty about the future, measured by time discount rates which are set around a central interest rate or government yield curve. Technological progress is considerable and occurs in two main forms: *industry-specific technologies,* which revolutionise particular industries, such as iron ships or nuclear power, and *general purpose technologies* which can be applied across many different sectors, such as the two-edged stone knife (in the Stone Age), iron tools, the wheel, the steam engine, the electric motor, the internet, or the smart phone. To market agents, *technological progress appears to be exogenously determined* – i.e. the dates of such key inventions as the pogo stick or the internal combustion engine, and their effectiveness and subsequent rate of adoption, are determined outside the economic system, by exceptional individuals or processes uncorrelated with any short-to-medium-term economic system. Consequently, production possibilities grow continuously, so that incomes rise permanently at the frontier of the richest societies, while other societies are eventually released from their static friezes, and use faster growth rates to catch up.

In short we have a growth model of the kind the Earth has seen in the last three hundred years, with the underlying efficiency frontier advancing at the rate of technological progress, and stochastic short-term economic cycles driving the actual economic performance of countries. X-inefficiency and sub-optimal decision-making are rife, but the Input Output matrix for each country generally improves

---

[75] Thomas Hobbes 1651, Leviathan Xiii.9 "In such condition [anarchy]...the life of man solitary, poor, nasty, brutish and short."

over time, so average living standards rise, although some firms, households, or whole economies grow faster than the frontier (catch it up), while others dawdle around. A few go backwards. Sometimes recessions happen, and the whole planet goes backwards, but these are usually reversed within a few years.

Firms generally use discounted cashflow investment appraisal techniques. Capital is regarded as like concrete: fluid, until it is poured out. Thereafter each asset is largely "set". So capital is thought of as a fluid, fully fungible financial asset until the moment it is spent and embodied in physical or intellectual capital. An aircraft may be a series of potential possibilities until the moment it is ordered, when the design is frozen and the asset embodies the state of technology prevalent at its freezing. Although an aircraft or phone can have its screens renewed or software upgraded, certain features are fixed for good. Naturally in this world the maintenance /replacement decision for existing capital is decided using the rule of the lowest lifetime Net Present Value (NPV) of capital and operating costs; if this is lower for the old kit it is kept and maintained. But if the new kit's lifetime costs are lower the old kit is ruthlessly scrapped, even if the older piece of hardware may still have a significant productive life.

Axioms of a general sequential theory:
We can summarise the main economic assumptions made so far in the following list of Axioms of a General Sequential model
    1. Social and political conditions are such that government provides an effective rule of law: government may not be 100% efficient but the police and courts basically work;
    2. Time proceeds forwards continuously or in discrete steps (a sequence of days, months, or years);
    3. New technologies emerge from time to time, but a technology is never forgotten
    4. Governments may choose to act as economic agents, or take over the operations of an existing agent
    5. Private agents usually consider only their own welfare (profits or consumption), but governments may incorporate social externalities in their decisions, as well as varying laws, taxes, and public expenditure.

The number of players in a market
Within these broad axioms what determines the number of players in a market or industry? The general rule is very simple: *the number of players in a market is the difference between the number of firms that have entered the market to date and the number that have so far quit.* So, let us add the following specific axioms about market entry and exit decisions:
    6. Market entry and exit are determined by free agents (firms) acting within the socio-economic and legal frameworks established by the government of the day
    7. The number of players in a market is determined sequentially over time by the difference between the cumulative number of entries to and exits from that market

8. Private firms make entry and exit decisions based on their own perceptions of future costs and revenues.

Note that Axioms 6-8 cover entry by a private profit-maximising firm. However, Axiom 4 allows governments to enter a market as a producer if, under axiom 5, they deem the societal externalities of their entry and production to be beneficial to society, or for some other reason. So a government could decide to create some piece of public infrastructure such as a road or a Space Agency, or they could establish a trading enterprise, such as a rural electricity company which creates, distributes and sells electricity to millions of homes – even though this company may be likely to lose money[76]. Naturally, in this world there is no guarantee that any of these government agencies will be efficient or profitable. But the same is true of the private sector – *unless* we have contestability and competition to weed out the least effective.

The business environment of an industry or firm
As we move from discussing a general macro-economy to discussing the conditions of a particular market or 'industry' (all the firms in a market, or series of related markets), we must introduce the concept of the business environment. This summarises not just the state of technology at the time (both general purpose and industry-specific) but also prevailing social, political and macroeconomic conditions, and is a wide concept encompassing both the neoclassical economists' term 'demand conditions' and the general equilibrium concept of an Input Output matrix.

The business environment is the whole exogenous environment in which a firm or industry finds itself at any moment in time. It is to a firm what 'habitat' is to a plant or animal, and just as plants or animals can be rendered extinct by loss of habitat, so firms which arise in one business environment and then fail to adjust to a new one can also wither or die. The business environment includes not only the 'macro-environment' of a country, or the world, at a particular time, but also the micro-environment of that industry, including the specific technologies available, the skill levels of employees available on the market, the past profitability and investment levels of firms in this industry, and the inherited industry structure. As we may want to use this model to predict them, the last three terms might seem to be endogenous variables, but the past inherited, industry structure, profitability and investment levels are lagged endogenous (pre-determined) conditions, and so part of the situation given at any moment in time[77].

---

[76] American readers should hold off any sense of incredulity. This might be inconceivable in the USA but in many parts of the world citizens would approve of such a creation IF they felt the benefits to society of this state-subsidized activity were significant. For example most railroads in the world need state subsidies, and will always need them, it seems. American railroads are profitable because of issues unique to the USA which are explained in Chapter 12.

[77] Frameworks for analysing the business environment can be found in any good business economics or strategy text; e.g. Mulhearne C & Vane H 2016, *Economics for business,* 3rd

So we summarise the exogenous environment in which a firm or industry works, and its consumers, customers, suppliers etc. as "the business environment of the USA in 2015", say. We will not distinguish between August 2016 and September 2016, although clearly if we were discussing 2001 we would have to distinguish *pre-9-11* 2001 from *post-9-11*.

Entry and exit decision rules for the firm

What generally determines whether a player decides to enter a market or not? For the private sector Axiom 8 helps. Let us imagine a typical situation in which a management team believes it can accurately gauge future costs and revenues, and is considering whether to enter a new market. The team draws itself a diagram of cash flow over time to reflect the revenues, cash costs and profit possibilities it sees facing the firm, like Figure 24:

Figure 24: The general expected cash flow of a firm considering entering and exiting a new market

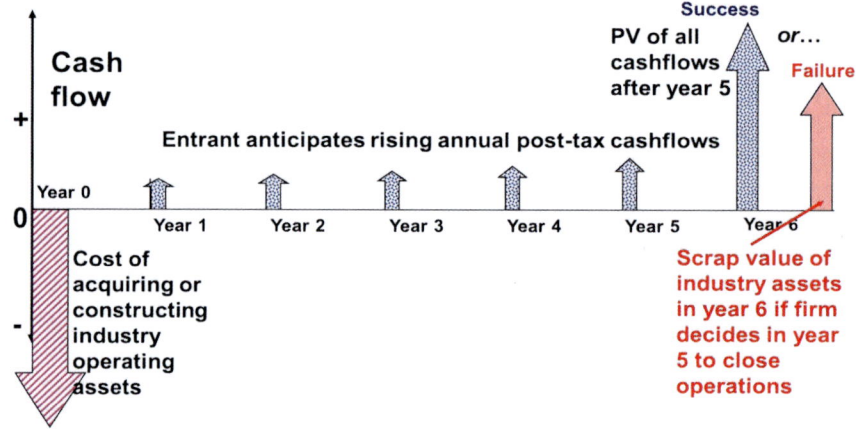

Note that in a cashflow diagram time is shown along the horizontal axis while the vertical axis depicts the net flows of cash into the operation in each year, with cash inflows (positive = cash received in bank) above the horizontal axis and net cash outflows (negative, including risky investments) below the axis. Also, note that all non-cash costs (depreciation, sentimental costs of exiting an industry etc.) are ignored in this calculation.

The management team now considers whether to enter the market, and then whether to exit after, say, six years, or to roll up all profits beyond that into a Year 6 Present Value (PV). Note that 'exit' from a market by this firm (in this situation we mean the investors and top managers), does not necessarily mean that the

---

edition, Palgrave MacMillan, London Chapter 3, or Grant R, 2016, *Contemporary Strategy Analysis*, 9th edition, Wiley, Chapter 3. The author finds STEEPLE (or PESTEL) is generally the best technique to analyse the macro-environment, while for the micro-environment Porter's Five (or Seven) Forces reaches useful predictions far more quickly than the Structure Conduct Performance model beloved of industrial economists of the 1980s.

operation will cease. If this venture is broadly viewed as 'a success' the firm will find buyers who concur that the business seems sustainable, so it can be valued as a PV of continuing future cashflows, which may be similar to the owners' Year 6 PV. A key consequence of this success is that most employees should keep their jobs. However, if the venture is not widely viewed as 'a success' the only option will be to close the operation and sell the assets for scrap[78].

So, in order to enter a market a firm will have to incur some costs of acquiring the resources and capabilities[79] necessary to operate effectively in this industry. Playing in any market requires some resources, and some of these will be unique to this market, in which case they are sunk costs in the traditional sense – assets which have little or no alternative use outside this market or particular situation. But other assets are more widely useful and can readily be sold in second-hand markets for a fair proportion of their acquisition cost – i.e. they are not sunk costs but general resources deployed in this industry (vehicles, land leases, office furniture etc.). So if we came to close the operation (the final arrow in Figure 24) electrical cables, for instance, would be worth just their scrap value as copper wire (which might not be worth the cost of digging it up, so its scrap value would be zero), while the general assets can readily be sold and turned back into cash.

For the sake of clarity it is worth stating that *every real firm entering any market has some sunk costs,* even if it is just the costs and time spent designing its website, or printing initial marketing material like business cards[80]. The issue is never 'Does this market have sunk costs?' but 'How large are the sunk costs to enter this industry or market, relative to other one-off or continuing costs?' In some industries the answer will be 'Negligible' and the investor/managers can

---

[78] This is the function of asset strippers in a modern economy: if a management team fails to create the synergies that keep a firm in business – i.e. allows the firm's total market value to fall below the sum of the market value of its assets – asset strippers buy the whole firm and unsentimentally break it down to its component assets.

[79] For the distinction between resources and capabilities see any modern Business Strategy textbook such as Grant (Chapter 9): "resources are the productive assets owned by the firm; capabilities are what the firm can do."

[80] Marketing costs *to enter* a market contribute to sunk costs as they can rarely be recovered, but economists who regard marketing as a sunk cost have confused the value of a brand at a moment in time (which is a stock concept, and rarely equals the sum of all past marketing expenditure; in the case of business failure the brand's value is usually low) with the continuing repeated fixed cost of marketing (a flow) necessary to maintain the brand value at a given level. In the simplest case of me deciding to enter the plumbing business if my business cards give my contact details and say "Mark Hull Plumber", and subsequently my business does not prosper and I quit the market, I cannot sell these business cards to another plumber, nor can I use them to enter the electrical market. And if my label 'plumber' is too general ("Mark Hull Handyman") the cards lose their usefulness when a potential customer is looking for a plumber: "I wonder if this guy does plumbing...nah he's not a specialist, don't use him.": my sales device has lost its point and was not just a sunk cost but a wasted cost from Day 1.

pass on to other issues, but in this book we consider the case of markets with significant sunk costs.

After entry the firm anticipates making cash profits which will augment its bank balance. The team now contemplates whether to continue in the market indefinitely or to exit after a reasonable period – say, seven years in Figure 25 below:

Figure 25: The sunk costs of entering a market

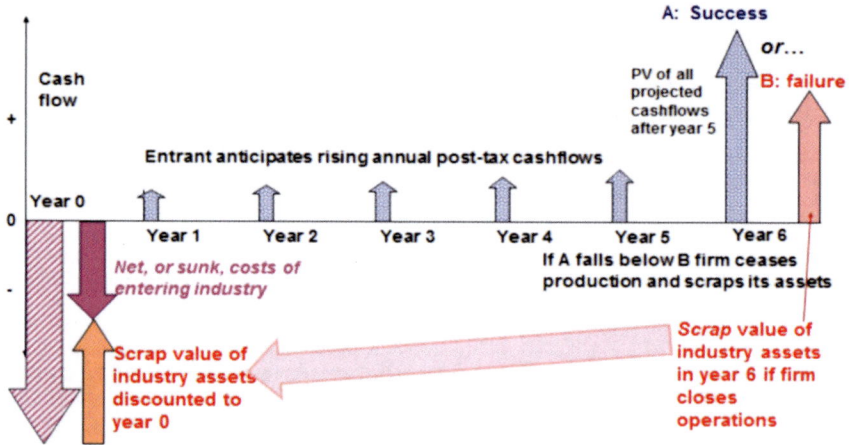

If the firm decides to quit the market the investors and top managers could either close down the entire operation or they could sell the business to another firm as a going concern. If profits turn out to be disappointing and the firm decides to close the business in year 6, the operation's worth would be the scrap value of the sunk costs and the value of its general, or non-sunk, assets, net of the cash costs of winding up the business, laying off staff, etc. Alternatively, the sale price of the firm as a continuing operation in year 6 would simply be the Present Value of all future cash flows; a rational buyer would pay nothing for the sunk assets, as they are only useful in this market, so the acquisition price would simply reflect the discounted value of all expected cash flows at the buyer's discount rate. Consequently, the *capital at risk* when a firm decides to enter a market is *the difference between the gross cost of entry and the discounted future scrap value of the assets, which we now properly define as* **the sunk costs of entering the market**[81].

To summarise the general case: when a firm enters a market it *hopes* that arrow A (the business's value as a going concern) will exceed arrow B (the scrap value), but obviously it does not know what will actually happen. If it enters and its hopes are wrong – the business does not do very well, and no-one will bid for

---

[81] Following Belleflamme P and Peitz M 2010, *Industrial Organization: Markets and Strategies*, Cambridge University Press, Cambridge UK 1st edition page 15.

the firm as a going concern – arrow A falls below B and the best option is to close the firm and scrap the assets. Given that B is the minimum residual value of the firm, the long term capital at risk when a firm enters an industry – its sunk cost – is the net costs of entering less its discounted scrap value. This leads to a very simple entry decision rule:

> ***Does the Net Present Value of all future cash profits exceed the sunk costs – the net entry costs? If yes, enter the market, if no, don't.***

This financial decision is illustrated in Figure 26:

Figure 26: The general entry decision for any firm considering entering a market

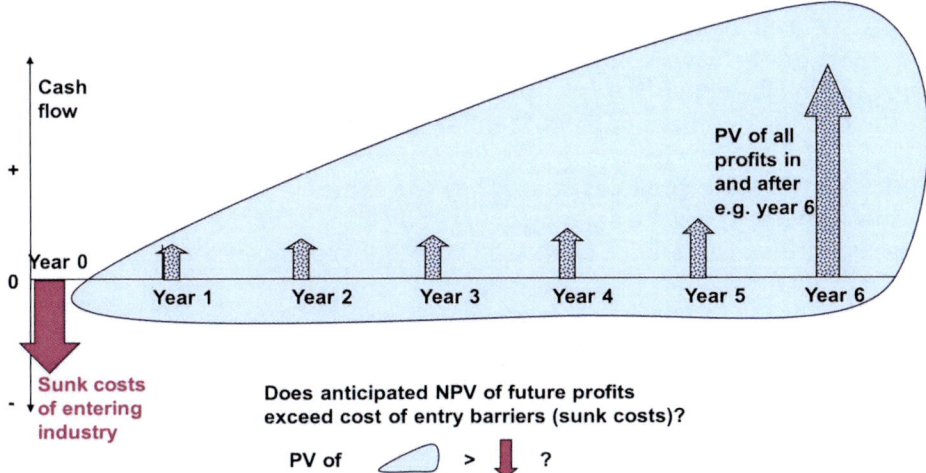

So Figure 26 is a graphic representation of the general market entry condition: *Does the NPV of future profits* (the blue blob) *exceed the sunk costs of entering the industry* (the pink down arrow in this Year)?

Note *there is absolutely no objectivity in entry decisions*: even if we broadly perceive the future as the same, my evaluation may differ from yours. So nineteen management-and-investor teams may decide the projected revenues do not sufficiently exceed the sunk costs to enter, and do not enter. But a twentieth investor-and-management team may disagree. Provided they can persuade enough investors to come up with the funds they enter. But once they enter they have committed their firm, and this becomes an objective, irreversible fact. It is this irreversibility that makes sunk costs unique in a sequence model: *sunk costs are an asymmetry in time* and only a time-sequential model can capture that asymmetry.

Formal statement of the general industry entry and exit conditions
To be clear let us state the general entry and exit conditions formally
The general entry decision:
1. Firm *i* enters market *j* if *i* believes that the risk-adjusted expected Present

1. Value of anticipated cash flows from entering j, discounted at an appropriate risk rate, and net of anticipated sunk costs of entry, is positive

The general exit decision:
2. Having entered a market, firm i exits market j if i believes that the NPV of its anticipated exit path will exceed the NPV of anticipated cash flows from continuing operations in j

Note that the NPV of the exit path in condition 2 could come either from closing operations, or from another firm making a higher offer than the current firm believes likely if it continues operations.

The case of network utilities
In the case of the network utilities we make an additional assumption:
3. **Because network grids usually have few alternative uses, constructing the physical grid for a network utility is a large sunk cost**

This creates far higher barriers to entry than are found in most markets, thus restricting the number of potential entrants for network utilities.

Entry barriers and sunk costs: are they the same?
A sneaky thought may be entering your head: "Is that it? Entry barriers are simply the sunk costs of entering a market. So I can stop reading all those articles about barriers to entry?"

Sadly, no. By all means feel free *not* to read the article about 32 kinds of entry barriers referred to in this book's Introduction, but in no sense is the above argument a complete discussion of entry barriers, just as it is not a complete discussion of all the factors a firm bears in mind when entering a market. Most true entry barriers are hard to quantify or 'financialise'. In fact, business strategists argue that all *the best barriers to entry, or barriers to mobility within an industry, are non-financial*[82] because one of the primary strategic goals of a firm is to make its strategy "non-copiable" by other firms, and any resource or capability that can simply be purchased can, of course, be bought and copied by a rival with sufficient financial resources. So, most of a firm's discussion about whether or not to enter a market should focus on issues of the fit of the proposed business with other aspects of the firm's innate resources or existing business capabilities (economies of scale or scope, other corporate or business synergies, achievement of business visions, cultural, strategic and process fit, etc.). Most of these issues are broad judgements, quite unsuited to precise financial calculation. As the *only* factors being considered in the analysis above are those that can be directly financially calculated, we are therefore saying that *after* all the truly essential strategic issues have been considered, and *a decision to enter looks likely, the above decision rule represents an additional financial constraint which must also be met*. It is a necessary but not sufficient condition

---

[82] For example the entire Resource Based View school of corporate strategy. One does not need to accept all the Resource Based View's arguments to agree with this part of their conclusions.

for a rational firm to enter a market.

The economics of small sunk expenditures
The usefulness of time being irreversible, and sunk costs affecting decision-making is widely underplayed in conventional economic theory. On a small scale, and without assuming all the features of sunk costs, consider the economics of retailing goods which are perishable, or age, or become unfashionable over time. For instance, imagine you are a small retailer who has bought 1000 pairs of socks which you hoped would be fashionable and sell well. Unfortunately, after several weeks, you find you have sold only 50 pairs and now really need the space on your shelves for another item which you are certain will sell better than these socks. Obviously, this sock purchase decision was not one of your best, but your supplier will not buy them back at any positive price, and the second-hand or wholesale market for these items looks completely dead. In short the best alternative to selling them looks to be to dispose of them; this will have a positive cost, which is like selling them at a negative price. Given this, and the urgent need to clear space on your shelves, what is the optimal retail selling price for your socks?

An analysis of fixed and variable costs, adding mark-ups to purchase prices to cover labour, rent etc. does not help us. The original purchase price is also irrelevant to the decision we must now make, because the supplier will not take them back. Whether we make an accounting profit or loss on these socks is equally irrelevant. The only thing that matters now is to set a sequence of prices over time that maximises all future revenues from these un-darned socks. And that is something that most economic tools do not help us with: only a good feel for the market can establish the optimal price path. The bald economic truth is that your socks are a sunk expenditure, and any revenue that you can get at all is better than disposing of them at a negative price. Which is why we sometimes see amazing bargains in the shops: it is not a question of the retailer mis-calculating his marginal costs, or forgetting about his fixed overheads, but of the retailer having recognised a past cost for what it is and re-calculating his options and opportunity costs. Perishable food retailers face exactly this decision every day when faced with unsold stock that is reaching its sell-by date. Their response is dynamic pricing: lowering the price of the unsold food by the hour until it all goes, while trying to scoop as much revenue as possible from customers. We might call this 'scooping the future revenue path'; it is the dynamic equivalent of price discrimination in static markets. As remote booking has become both easier and contractually binding, both the static and dynamic versions of price discrimination are used by airlines, hotels, theatres and other firms to maximise revenues in industries with fixed capacity, low variable costs, and variable demand.

The economics of large sunk costs
We now look more closely at the general sequence of decisions, activities, and cash flows that occurs when a firm decides to sink some large sunk costs.

Lumpy investments

A *lumpy investment* is large one that cannot be divided – one where the first outputs from creating an asset emerge only once the whole asset is finished. Consider the cash flow of an archetypal lumpy investment such as a transmission link – a bridge, tunnel, or a non-stop link between two cities for instance. An example might be Eurotunnel, the fixed link between England and France. Figure 27 shows a stylised version of such a lumpy project's annual cash flows:

Figure 27: The stylised annual cash flow of a large lumpy investment

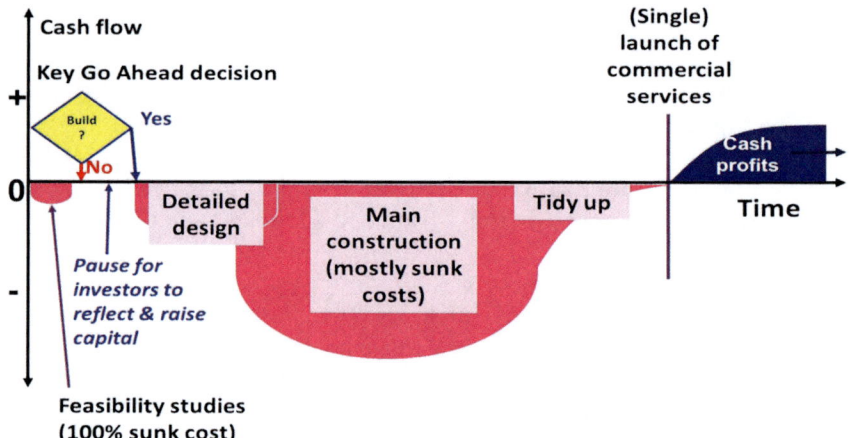

In the case of Eurotunnel the (last set of) feasibility studies began in 1984[83], governmental approval was signed in 1986, raising the capital was done at the same time as detailed design started, serious physical construction began roughly two years after approval was given, and lasted for four years, the tidy-up installations took another two years, and tunnel services were launched in 1994, eight years after the key Go Ahead decision. As with most transport links, revenues have continued to grow in the subsequent two decades with economic growth and deepening of intra-European trade.

Sequential discrete investments

A more general infrastructure investment, though, may have some large lumps, but there are several of them and they can be logically separated, so that *a sequence of expected profitability decisions can be made*, rather than just one key Go-or-No-Go decision at the beginning. In other words, the most profitable parts of the investment can be developed first and if these succeed then the firm

---

[83] Source for these facts is the Groupe Eurotunnel website available at http://www.eurotunnelgroup.com/uk/the-channel-tunnel/history/ . As the site makes clear, feasibility studies for some sort of tunnel began in 1802, the first serious schemes involving tunnel boring machines began in 1880, and in 1960 the design of the tunnels that was actually used was first presented to the British and French publics – 26 years before that design won the concession competition held by both governments. Alternative designs featured a bridge, and a combination of bridges, islands and tunnels.

can make a sequence of subsidiary investments. A typical infrastructure asset such as a railway or a water or energy distribution grid has these characteristics, as shown in Figure 28:

Figure 28: The stylised decision sequence & annual cash flow of a general infrastructure asset

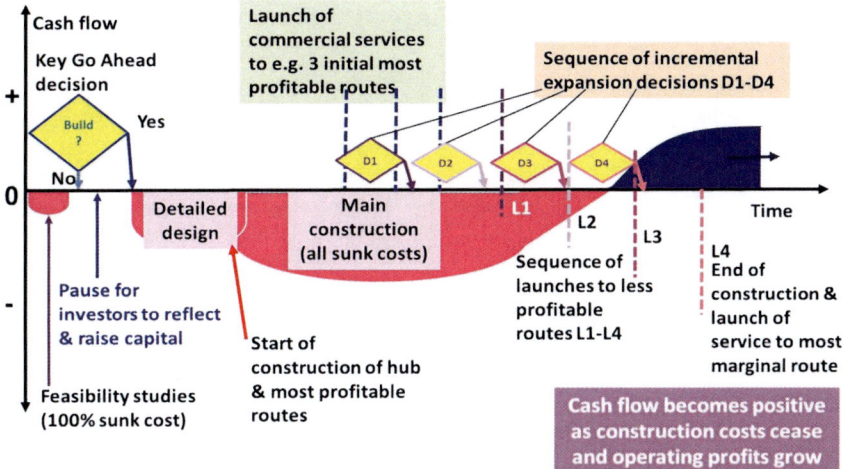

Figure 27 and Figure 28 bring out an important difference in the innate risks of each venture: one-lump assets with only one purpose and a single launch, involve far more risk than assets which are piecemeal, and can be stopped if demand is not as high as hoped – or promised. The de-risking in Figure 28 occurs because

1. The irreversible investment decision is broken down into a series of discrete decisions
2. Before some of the later investment decisions are made time has elapsed after the launch of the first set of services during which the investors and managers can *compare the actual costs and early revenues with those projected* at the time of the key decision, to see if there is a bias in their assumptions, and to check their understanding of the true business environment.

And, of course, the marginal condition is that a utility should stop when it believes that the sunk costs of developing the next route or street will equal or exceed the likely PV of future cash flows from it[84].

---

[84] An example of this was the French government's development of the TGV high speed train system across France in the 1970s and 80s: the initial designs and building of the prototype trains and power systems were the hub sunk cost, along with the Paris-Lyon line which was built and launched in 1983. The French government then took a sequence of individual route decisions, each with huge sunk costs of dedicated line construction (e.g. the western lines in 1990, the northern lines in 1993/97 etc.) The rolling stock was not a sunk cost, as it could be transferred to run on most European railways, though at the time it could only run at top speeds in France. Further lines were developed to the east, and further south, as demand has risen tenfold since 1983, and more lines are still being added.

The different perceptions of investors and managers

We say 'should stop' above because it is possible for the decision-making process to go awry, due to *differences between the investors' perceptions* of future revenues and costs, *and the firm's Directors'* and managers' views. Be aware, though, that there is a general and fundamental asymmetry in this relationship: the infrastructure managers have sunk their careers into a specific technology, while the investors believe they are free to switch funds between their investments and sell out if necessary, so they are only committed to the extent of their current portfolio. Many asset-intensive industries have these characteristics of multiple sequential launches and potential disagreements between investors and managers. Railways were usually developed with a sequence of main 'transmission' lines being developed between distant large cities, and then 'branch' feeder lines were developed to boost demand at either end, or along the route. Fixed telecoms lines were similar, whether undersea cables, onshore 'local loop' copper wires, or fibre optics.

Railways as an example

The history of railway development shows many examples of investors and managers disagreeing about the future profitability of investments[85]. A classic illustration might be the strategic decision to close a loss-making branch line: due to the fundamental asymmetry between investors and managers, the investors may wish to shut the branch line and the managers do not, because of the managers' collective commitment to this specific set of sunk costs, and their view that closing a branch will start to undermine the economic viability of the main trunk line, and thus of the managers' entire careers. There are many examples from around the world; in the USA the early evolution of 'sunshine regulation' of monopolies under Charles Francis Adams described in Chapter 12 of this book was partly designed to protect investors from unscrupulous railroad management teams up to tricks like this either in line development or continuing operations. And in his comparison of the internet bubble of 2000 with the railway bubble in Britain of the 1840s-70s Robert Miller notes the "extraordinary skulduggery" by which the Directors of the London and South West Railway managed to double-track a trunk line from Exeter to Southampton, when a clear majority of the shareholders had explicitly voted against this development[86]. The two boxes below give some examples of what happened in early railways and

---

[85] The author was one of thousands of founding shareholders in Eurotunnel in the 1980s. It has not so far been the financial success that he or most investors hoped it would be. Around 2004 the author asked a professional transport economist with extensive experience of Eurotunnel why the actual revenues were so much lower than those originally projected before the Key Go Ahead decision. The transport economist said "Mark, you have the causality round the wrong way: the revenue projections were whatever they had to be to justify the project." Remember this when looking at all investment revenue projections: always ask yourself 'Who made these projections, and Why?'

[86] Miller R, 2003, *railway.com*, Research Monograph 57 by the Institute of Economic Affairs, London, page 78. Today's travellers on these lines may be rather grateful for the Directors' skulduggery, calling it farsighted.

trace the career of a celebrated but commercially 'failed' serial entrepreneur of marginal British railways.

> **SUNK COSTS IN THE RAILWAYS**
>
> Few industries exhibit the interplay of sunk costs, time, evolving technologies and changing business environments better than railways, especially now that we have more than a hundred years of hindsight with which to understand the business environment of the time. This history also has interesting lessons on the relationship between investors and the utility's managers.
>
> The investors were not just wealthy speculators: a poor curate's daughter, such as the author Charlotte Bronte, invested significant parts of her meagre savings in what she thought were safe, profitable railway investments that would make herself, and the country, richer. Naturally, some railways failed to make an operating profit, let alone repay the original investment, and even some that did found ways to avoid paying dividends to shareholders. Even when the economics were clear, as with Brunel's 1835 Great Western Railway – the first high speed railway in the world, linking London to Bristol – after the investors had paid in all the share capital, one of the first acts of the Board of Directors was to vote themselves each an annual salary of £5000 a year – an enormous sum when a Yorkshire curate like Charlotte Bronte's father was paid a few hundred pounds a year to support his family. In America the ways in which minority stockholders, or just ordinary stockholders, were ripped off by the railroad Directors and big railroad magnates became legion. So famous were the tricks, options, and fine print used to defraud railway investors around the world that in Lewis Carroll's 1876 absurdist comic poem 'The Hunting of the Snark' the evil beast is threatened with the most cunning trap then known to man – a railway share (or stock).
>
> The part of railway history which best illustrates the commercial boundary between success and failure is 'light' railways, where by definition costs need to be cut to the bone to make the enterprise economic. In the UK a certain Colonel Stephens was a pioneer of many of these.

Looking at the two boxes, and with the benefit of more than a century of hindsight, we can see that a huge amount of the ultimate profitability of railways *ex post* depended on exogenous circumstances that were well outside the ability of the railway managers to influence or even predict – the general macro-environment referred to earlier. Just as many canals had been very profitable in the 18th and early 19th centuries in Britain and the USA, so railways were initially very profitable in the mid-19th century, when they replaced canals for freight transport and coaches-and-horses for passenger travel. But by 1890 the first modern automobiles had been invented, and by 1913 Henry Ford had invented mass-production of cars, driving the costs of motor transport down to levels that the upper middle classes could afford. By 1950 in Europe this would remove the core segment of profitable First and Second Class passengers on whom rural passenger railways relied for the bulk of their profits.

COLONEL HF STEPHENS: VILLAIN OR VICTIM?

"A Colonel Stephens railway" is code among some British railway experts for a light rural railway built by enthusiasts which never made a profit in its life, and, frankly, never had a chance of being profitable. The implication is that Colonel Stephens and his railway Director pals duped gullible investors into buying shares in their pet railway projects – he was associated with 35 railway projects – when none of them had a chance of repaying their sunk costs with an adequate rate of return. What distinguishes these from an outright 'Ponzi' scheme – where investors pay into an entirely fictitious scheme, and the investments are simply drained by the fund managers – is that at least the railways were actually built.

But is this fair on Colonel Holman Fred Stephens? A civil engineer who qualified in 1894, he was involved with trains for forty years, and most of his railways were not commercially successful. An analysis of all 35 of the railways he was involved with in his lifetime shows

- 18 projected railways reached the Order stage of a Parliamentary Bill but were never built; so investors did not lose large sums – mainly the feasibility study costs;
- On 4 unprofitable railways Stephens was merely hired as a junior or consultant engineer – his career started as a junior engineer on two light rural railways (Cranbrook and Sheppey); he had a brief role as a consultant in the Isle of Wight Central Railway, and he was hired to convert the Burry Port railway from freight to passengers – he was unsuccessful, but it was making heavy losses when he arrived;
- 5 railways were already built but making losses; he took them over and cut costs, but could not return them to profit – they were all somebody else's sunk costs, demand was well below operating costs when he arrived, and they were in a terminal state (we can now see with full hindsight);
- 4 railways he built were profitable – two were projects where he cut the previously-projected costs and built quick, light passenger tramways (Rye and Camber, and the West Sussex) both of which remained profitable until cars became popular in the 1920s ; a third was the East Kent coalfields railway, where the Tilmanstone colliery line remained open and profitable for 70 years, and the North Devon and Cornwall was a clay freight tramway on which demand rose sufficiently to make it profitable as a light freight railway for 20-30 years (Stephens managed the conversion);
- 4 railways he helped to build never made a profit: two were freight, where the mineral extracting customers were not profitable – Edge Hill, where the iron ore reserve was never commercial (the railway was never officially opened and shut after 4 years), and Ashover where he shrank the gauge to 2 feet to lower costs, but the demand for stone plummeted; two were railways where the passenger demand melted away in the early 20th century as rail lost custom to trams (the Plymouth and Devonport) or to cars and buses (the Kent and East Sussex). Could a railway engineer have done anything about these four cases – other than not build the railway, and make himself redundant?

Villain? Or just an honest railway engineer, born at the wrong time?

Objectively examining Colonel Stephens' lifetime contribution to marginal end-of-line rail extensions, his passenger services suffered from the above general socio-economic trends, while his freight railways were totally reliant on the specific fortunes of the local minerals they carried. The coal on his line at Tilmanstone was profitable for 70 years, so the railway that served it can be deemed profitable for 70 years, while the iron ore at Edge Hill was never economic, so the line was shut before it was officially opened! With a hundred years hindsight, perhaps his only error was to dedicate his life to the wrong technology – rail – when a luckier young engineer in 1890 would have chosen automobiles. But someone else would have been hired to push rail's luck against the competing technologies of trams and automobiles. In the face of such vast forces what can a single human do?

Appendix 2: A financial ratio comparison of enduring utilities with other businesses

The fundamental measure of success in a continuing industry is its *profitability*, which is an agreed measure of profits divided by an agreed measure of assets invested or employed:

$$\text{Firm profitability} = \text{Profits/Assets}$$

$$= \text{Profits/Sales} \times \text{Sales/Assets}$$

$$= \text{'Profit Margin'} \times \text{'Asset Turnover'}$$

This ratio analysis says that there are two fundamental ways to improve the profitability of a firm: raise the profit margin on an average sale, or raise the throughput of sales per unit of capital employed – the turnover of your assets. Or both.

Both profit margins and asset turnovers vary enormously across an industry, and even more so between industries. The former reflects the success of different strategies within the industry, while the latter tells us about the different natures of the industries, and in particular their asset-intensity. So let's examine some typical figures for a couple of utilities and a typical business such as retailing.

Table 2: Key financial ratios comparison of sunk cost utilities with typical businesses

Concept	E&W Water	AT&T	Walmart
	2009 £bn	2013 $bn	2013 $bn
Turnover (= Sales Revenue)	9.7	129	469
Operating Income or Profit (OI)	3.2*	30.5	28
Assets Employed	251**	272	203
Operating Profit Margin (= OI/Turnover)	33%	24%	5.9%
Asset Turnover ratio (Annual Turnover / Assets)	0.04	0.47	2.3
Turnover Asset Ratio (Assets/Annual Turnover)	26 years	2.1 years	0.4 years
Profitability (OI / Assets)	1.3%	11.2%	13.7%

Source: Ofwat consolidated financial accounts of the water industry in England and Wales 2009, Investopedia Asset Turnover ratio, Walmart and AT&T websites accessed 2014.
* NB Current Cost Operating Profit   ** At replacement cost

Table 2 compares the financial performance of the water and wastewater industry in England and Wales, as collated by its economic regulator Ofwat for the latest year available (2009), with the latest annual figures for another large regulated utility, American Telephone and Telegraph (AT&T), and the world's largest retailer Walmart.

We see that AT&T and Walmart have a profitability around 11-14%, which seems a good enough performance compared to alternative investments, such as bank savings or the equity and debt performance of most firms. Also, bearing in mind the innate risks of each business, it seems fair that Walmart, a firm in a very competitive sector, should earn a higher return than AT&T, which contains a lot of regulated businesses, where it is hard to make a loss.

However, both firms achieved their 11-14% return in different ways: Walmart did it by earning a modest 6% margin on everything it sold but selling the equivalent of its entire assets 2.3 times a year. AT&T did it by making a handsome 24% margin on everything it sold but only managed to sell the equivalent of half its assets (0.47) in a year. In the table I have calculated the inverse of the Asset Turnover ratio which shows that Walmart turns over its assets in 0.4 of a year (about once every five months) while AT&T takes 2.1 years to do this. However, the English and Welsh Water industry is an order of magnitude more capital-intensive than this: its margin is 33% but at 26 years its turnover asset ratio is 13 times AT&T's and sixty times Walmart's, resulting in a profitability of only 1.3%. This is not sufficient to draw forth dedicated funds, and is the result of a deliberate decision taken by a former regulator to lower prices; however the clever thing is that all investments since 1990 have earned, and will earn, a different rate of profit, which is high enough to draw forth investors' funds. The regulatory techniques for doing this are explained at the end of Chapter 8.

It is only fair to add that we are not quite comparing like with like here: AT&T and Walmart's assets are valued using conventional summations of the historic cost of each asset, which is standard in business. But the England and Wales water industry's assets are all valued at their Current Cost – that is as if they all had to be replaced this year. For a commercial company like Walmart there should not be much difference between Historic Cost and Current Cost valuations, as most of their assets will be recently purchased (e.g. their inventory), but for a water or telecoms company some of the civil engineering assets will be more than a hundred years old, which is why the British water regulator uses Current Cost valuations. A fuller justification is given near the end of Chapter 8, but the gist is that Current (or replacement) Cost valuations should ideally be used in every industry, and we have them for the water industry, but the best substitute for Walmart is Historic Cost valued assets, so the comparison is mostly valid. And, bringing in AT&T, the comparison shows not only that the water industry is extremely capital-intensive, and especially sunk-cost-intensive, but that in general utilities are capital-intensive – i.e. they have very low asset turnover ratios. This is a result that we draw on in our general conclusions.

Chapter Four

Applying the general sequence model to markets with significant sunk costs

In this chapter we apply the general sequence model of market entry and exit to markets where sunk costs are significant to explain (predict) the natural monopolies, and then look at the wider applications of this model.

The general sequence model of entries with significant sunk costs

We now use Chapter 3's general sequence model to see how the precise sequence of entry and construction decisions works out for markets where entry requires building highly dedicated infrastructure, which are very substantial exogenous sunk-costs. We bear in mind human experiences over the last two thousand years of building infrastructure, and the last three hundred years with the succession of specific technologies called canals, railways, water, sewerage, gas, electricity and telecoms.

Zero entrants

We start from zero, and the introduction of a new business environment, including perhaps a new technology T_1 that provides new services to customers. Groups of management teams and investors ponder the new possibilities, and the predicted sunk costs of building the necessary infrastructure, its expected running costs, and the revenues likely to be generated from the area served. *Where population is very sparse or very poor* all investors will agree that the PV of likely anticipated revenues will not exceed the sunk costs of building the grid, so *no-one enters the market*.

- Sewer services in remote areas like Mid-Wales or northern Scotland are examples of this: because of the sparsity of people and houses, the sunk cost of building a sewer grid exceeds the PV of operating profits any firm could earn from it, so no firm enters the sewerage market here, and houses have septic tanks rather than mains drains.
- This is also why *favelas* or shanty towns have few utility services: there's no shortage of people, but they don't have any money, and with dire poverty there is a strong chance desperate residents will either steal any salvageable installed assets such as wires, taps or pipes, or, failing this, they may just steal

the service provided – e.g. water and electricity theft are common in the poorest parts of the world's poor cities. In these areas responsible utilities only develop services with local political and social backing – e.g. the local community is often directly required to donate labour (at weekends or in the evenings) to help install the infrastructure, so that local residents have a personal stake in the service continuing to operate and take direct action against those found trying to steal essential components[87].

We now consider the general case, where firms are unequal, and some are quicker than others to get their acts together and sink costs, so that *market entry is sequential*. We consider the possibilities of *simultaneous entry* later, as a special case[88].

First mover entry – monopoly
If one management team is quicker than others to organise sufficient backing from investors, and sinks the costs, we have a monopoly – at least for a while. And of course monopoly includes markets which, with hindsight, were wrongly entered, either because investors were foolish, or duped, or because the business environment turned out not to favour the specific technology embodied in the infrastructure's sunk costs – and few people could have predicted this. Thus, with a hundred years hindsight, we can see that the "Kent and East Sussex Railway" that was built in 1900 by Colonel Stephens and friends was always going to be a marginal economic proposition[89] – a light railway carrying little freight in a sparsely populated rural area – and once technology turned towards the internal combustion engine it was always going to be one of those industries that economically limps along, barely paying its operating costs and contributing little towards its sunk costs. Of course many markets *end up* doing this – e.g. many canals and railways around the world – but most of them made a significant contribution for a time towards their sunk costs. Whether that contribution was in line with original investors' expectations is an academic point that need not detain us: there is no point in crying over milk spilt centuries ago.

So we have the case of monopolies that exist but, with hindsight, shouldn't and monopolies that have outlived their original rationale. Many other monopolies exist and *ex post* are still profitable, and always were profitable – energy, water

---

[87] This sounds harsh but life in the favelas is already harsh, and provision of utility services is one of the things that makes life less harsh. Of course theft from the utility is still common, but at least the assets aren't ripped up and sold for scrap. This process requiring the consumer to commit to the technology by sinking some costs as well as the producer sinking costs is discussed more generally in a few pages.

[88] Bresnahan T and Reiss P 1990, Entry in Monopoly markets, *Review of Economic Studies* 57 531-553 was the first article in game theory to make this distinction. However, they model the first mover's prior establishment of an active customer base as a fixed cost advantage over the second mover, which ignores customer switching costs.

[89] For a brief history see http://en.wikipedia.org/wiki/Kent_and_East_Sussex_Railway ; it was mooted many times in the fifty years before it was actually built, but most investors, quite rightly it seems with hindsight, got cold feet.

and telecoms utilities, for instance. Figure 28 in Chapter 3 is the general version of our cashflow diagram of a firm facing large sunk costs; in it a firm develops a main asset followed by subsidiary routes until it reaches its marginal route. Figure 29 shows this as a diagram of a sequence of decisions for first entry into an industry with heavy sunk costs:

Figure 29: The sequence of entry decisions for the first mover in a utility market

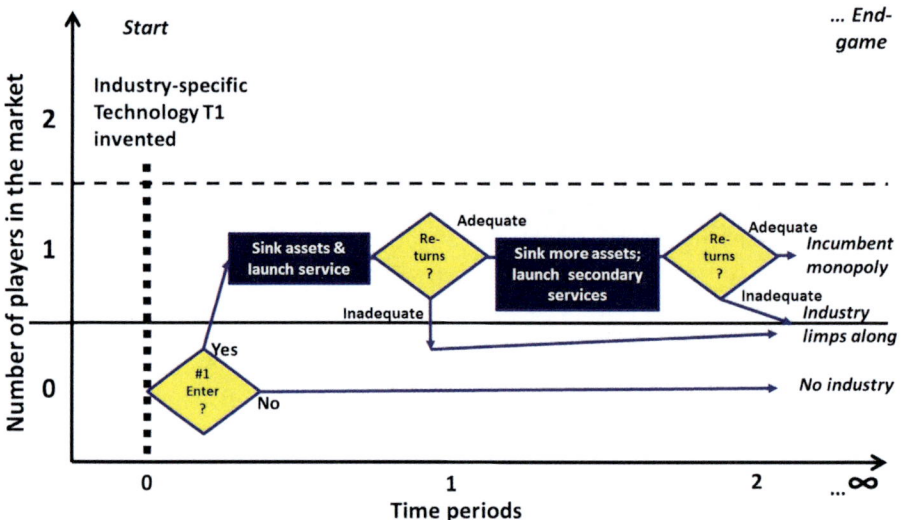

The first decision is the key Go Ahead Decision – do we enter or not? If we enter we must spend the investors' money, commit to our technologies and to their specific sites, and then launch the service, and get the first *ex post* feedback on actual service relative to substitutes and expectations, and our first objective revenues and profits. This delayed decision, at t+1 in Figure 29, is a significant moment for the business, and one that is often ignored. If returns are inadequate now is the time for investors to stop management's plans for riskier secondary investments, though as we saw earlier with the London and South West Railway's double-tracked route to Exeter, managements sometimes succeed in ignoring (or defrauding) investors' explicit decisions.

On the other hand, if actual returns are adequate and prospects for the secondary investments look credibly good, investors may wish to continue investing, or sell out to others with the appetite to do so. However, in the light of a changed business environment since the Go Ahead decision, it may now be apparent to astute investors that the original plans need changing. Long-favoured technologies may be losing out to rival or completely new technologies, or we, or others, may have learned facts which mean that practical implementation of our new technology T1 may need to be tweaked significantly; or certain long-treasured sites may no longer be optimal. If so, now is the time to stop sinking money into the wrong permanent solutions, have those rows with management, insist on the changes, and, if necessary, fire Directors and management teams – or, if you find yourself in a minority of investors, sell your investment, since other investors clearly value the reinvest-with-minimal-change prospects more highly than you.

As shown in Figure 28 this cycle of sinking new costs, launching new services, evaluating new actual revenues, costs and customer feedback, and re-evaluating future options continues in theory until the marginal route is reached. For simplicity this is not shown in Figure 29; instead, we skip to the end game. As time 't' tends to infinity the end game (so far) can be one of three possibilities:

1. Zero entrants   = no industry
2. 1 'limping' entrant   = 1 inadequately profitable incumbent monopolist
3. 1 healthy entrant   = 1 profitable incumbent monopolist – possibly in need of regulation.

In modern economies the exact *ex post* profitability of a firm may be kept hidden, but capital markets still form views about enterprises of interest to them, even if no financial information is made available. *Investors* read signals such as the apparent popularity of a service from any source they can, including anecdotal evidence, and *can generally detect if reinvestment is occurring*. These signs will be taken as signals of the profitability so far, so that in general it is hard to hide the overall *ex post* profitability of the enterprise. If the incumbent appears to be limping along investors will be scarce; only if the incumbent appears to be thriving will new investors usually consider backing a second entrant – unless that entrant has a radically new proposition to offer.

Sequential entry of a second player
There are two ways of obtaining a duopoly: either it results as the end-game from a series of mergers, or it results from just two players entering an industry. We consider end-games later. If the duopoly occurs from entry, either both players enter more-or-less *simultaneously*, or one entry follows another – *sequentially*. Let us use the simple definition that 'simultaneous entry' means the first entrant – Player One – had not launched its core service before Player Two took its key Go Ahead decision – i.e. at some point both players were racing to complete their assets before either had launched. The simultaneous and sequential ways of entering the industry are both shown in Figure 30's decision diagram:

Figure 30: Entry of player Number Two can be simultaneous or sequential

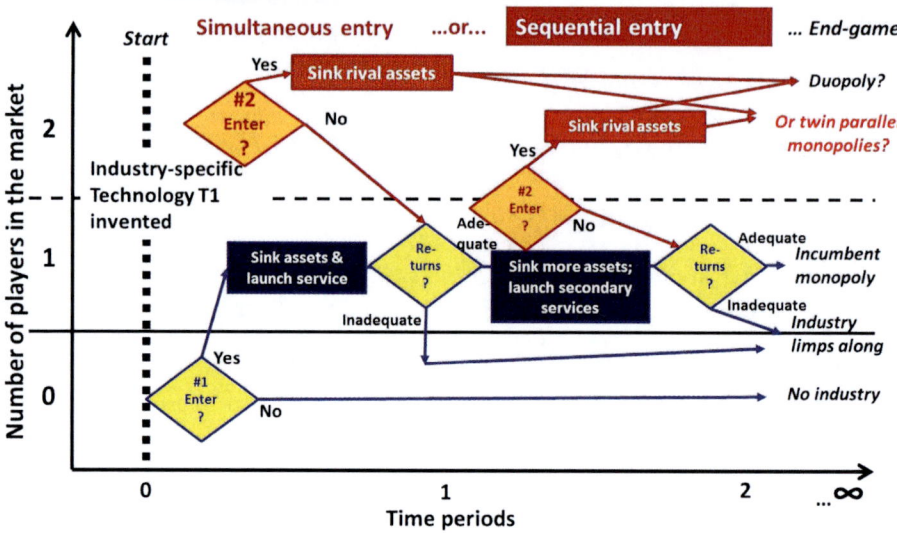

We now consider the two entry options, starting with sequential entry. For a sequential second entry to occur the general starting position is that we have an *incumbent* monopolist who has sunk its costs, launched a service, is making a healthy profit, and is considering a sequence of secondary investments. Repeating Figure 26 from Chapter 3, Figure 31 shows how Firm One originally viewed matters at its Go Ahead decision:

Figure 31: The First Mover's perspective at its key Go Ahead decision

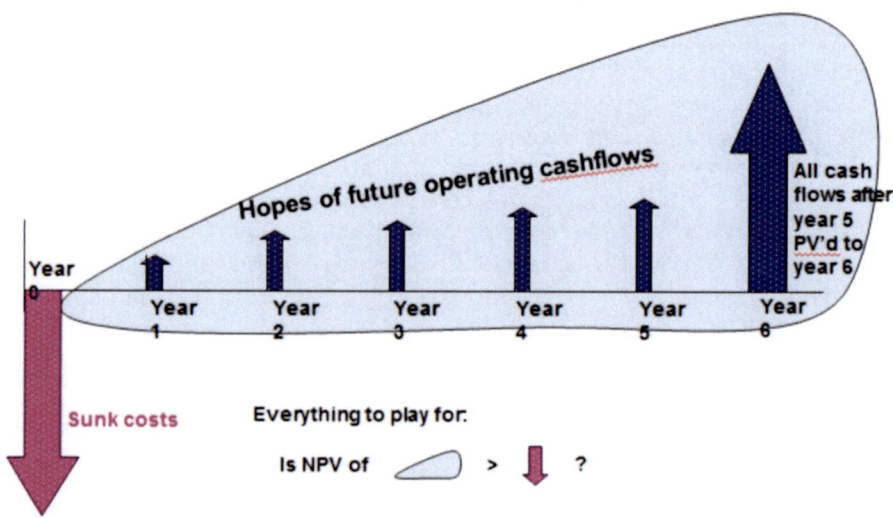

And now Mover One's capital-at-risk is an objective fact, a sunk cost, which it has written into its balance sheet, and it has the beginnings of some operating cashflows, as shown in Figure 32:

Figure 32: Mover One's perspective one year after launching

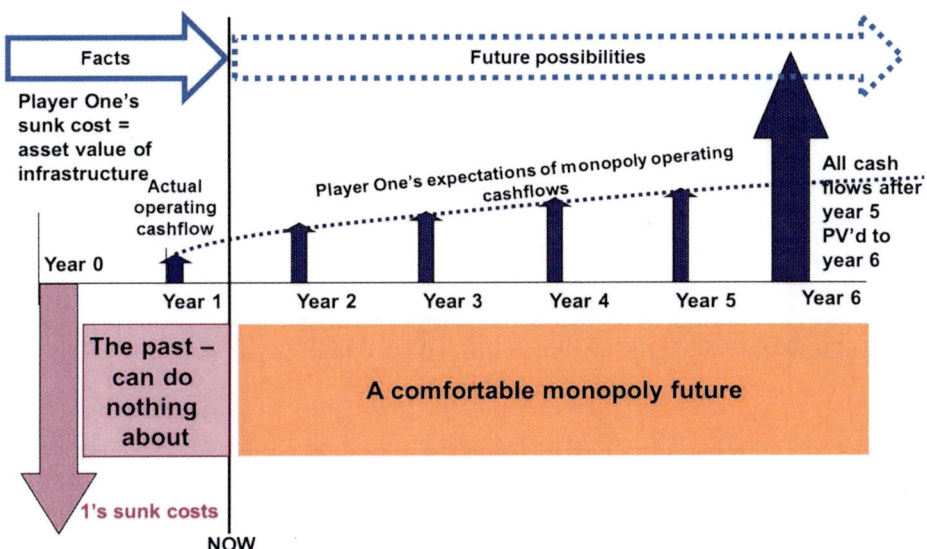

But then, to its horror, it discovers that Mover Two is determined to enter the market and is committed to completing its assets and launching a rival service:

Figure 33: Mover One's perspective after it discovers Mover Two's impending entry

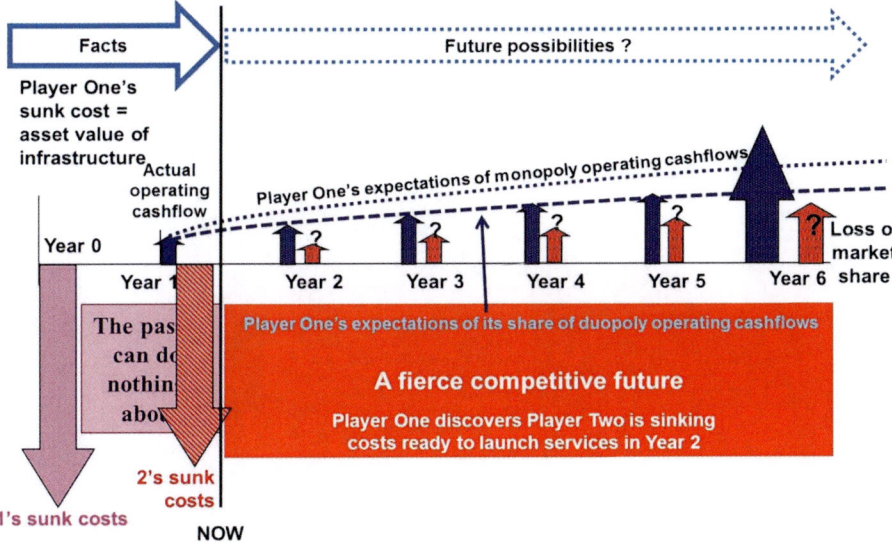

Will Mover One react? You bet: *under all circumstances Mover One will react*. Its best option is to try to persuade Mover Two to abandon its entry, through legal manoeuvres, signalling tactics, entry deterring prices, or even offering to merge. However, if deterrence tactics fail it has no choice but to face up to its reduced prospects and start calculating just how to fight off this challenge, and how much market share it is likely to lose to the entrant.

Dynamic market entry concepts

Before we analyse Mover One's reaction choices in detail we must introduce some core concepts used by firms trying to win customers in dynamic markets. The first is the distinction between *reachable customers* – who can in principle receive your service – and *unreachable customers*, who cannot. For utilities this distinction is typically because of geographical areas – reachable customers live in an area which your infrastructure serves – but it can also apply to customers' incomes, lifestyles or social preferences. For example, there is no point trying to sell electric fridges to households without electricity, or basins with taps to households without piped water, or persuading old people who don't own smartphones to use a taxi app like Uber. For firms selling fridges, basins, or Uber these customers are 'unreachable', and your sales can never attain 100% of the potential market until those customers have been reached by the relevant network.

Networks, of course, don't appear instantly. They take time to build, and, as we have concluded in Figure 28, a rational grid utility chooses to build its grid first in what it expects to be the most profitable segments of the market. Figure 34 shows the evolution of the simplest case: a grid monopoly extends the reach of its infrastructure, and subsequently grows its customer base:

Figure 34: The growth of a monopoly utility's infrastructure and customer base

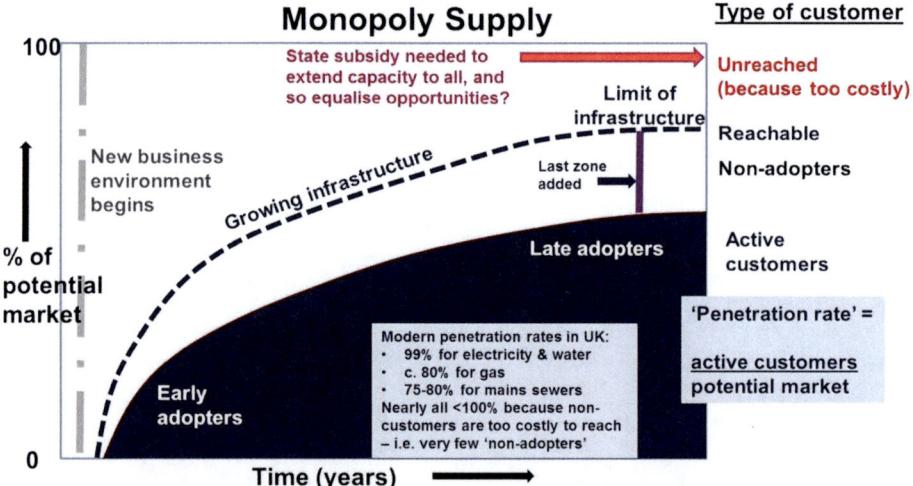

So, after the dawn of the new business environment permitting the innovative service, Mover One marshals the investment funds and management team to start building its grid, rolls it out in the most profitable zones, and starts selling the service to new customers. The first to join are called *early adopters*. As the infrastructure is rolled out the ratio of the next zone's PV of future revenues to sunk costs declines, until at the marginal zone the firm stops growing its infrastructure. Once the infrastructure has been fixed, and the last of the late adopters has signed up, the firm's base of active customers is complete. Those who are not active customers are either *non-adopters*, who don't want this service even when readily available, or the unreached, for whom reaching would require the supplier to receive some kind of government subsidy. The ratio of active customers at any moment to the total potential market is called the *penetration rate*[90]. In modern rich and peaceful countries penetration rates for electricity and piped water are almost 99%, but typically 80% or less for gas (gas cannot match all of electricity's functions) and main sewers (septic tanks and soakaways are cheaper for small remote communities).

The second distinction is between a series of *local monopolies* and *oligopolies*. Do not imagine that if two utilities supply a town we must have a duopoly: a duopoly only occurs if customers are served by two suppliers, *and can switch between*. Consider first the case of a country with seven large cities served by seven utilities which are not connected – the case of most water and all wastewater utilities around the world, as shown on the left in Figure 35:

Figure 35: The extent of competition: cities within a country

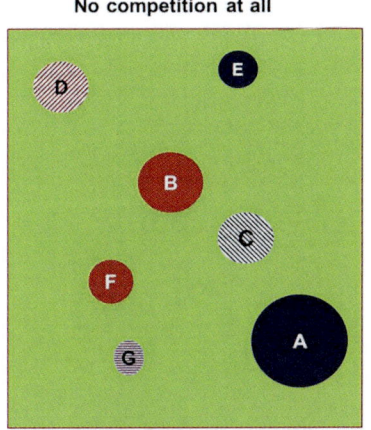
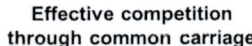
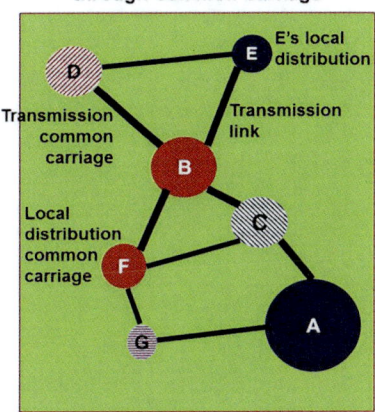

On the left there is no competition between the seven utilities, although if there is an economic regulator of them all, she or he can set up a kind of imitation of competition called *comparative competition*, which is discussed in the latter part of Chapter 8 – the chapter on regulation. However, if the utilities are connected to each other we have a situation like that on the right. It is now possible to have full competition *if*

1. Connection between each city is easy and provided on identical terms for every 'customer'; the 'customers' for the transmission product in this case are the utilities who distribute the product or service to the final consumers

---

[90] Strictly speaking the penetration rate is the ratio of *connected customers* to the total potential market, and in reality connected customers includes active customers and those who have recently moved or died; the latter tend to be less 'active' than live customers, though, presumably, new householders will eventually be active at these premises.

in each city; this condition is called *common carriage* in the transmission system; and if

2. The distribution utilities in each city are required to provide easy access to their customers on identical terms for every utility's customers; this condition is called local *distribution common carriage*; and if

3. Each utility is allowed to acquire end-consumer customers in all other cities; recalling the stages in Chapter One's value chain, if utility A is allowed to provide the retail function in city B, and *vice versa*, then within city B its local utility, B, provides the distribution function – or 'local loop' as it is known in telecoms circles – but the consumer in city B may have signed up utility A to provide the end-services – the retail function. This distinction enables full competition for the retail function between any of the seven utilities in any of the seven cities, although the transmission and distribution functions[91] will still be conducted by monopolies, who will generally need regulating to ensure they don't exploit their positions.

However, a similar range of possible market structures can also logically occur in the distribution function *within* a city. For physically-connected grids within a city it is only possible for a householder to have utility competition in distribution if two or more utilities put their pipe or cable down your street. For reasons that we will shortly divine this is rare in energy and water supply, but more common in the telecoms world. Figure 36 shows some theoretical possibilities:

Figure 36: Possible patterns of competition between distribution zones in a city

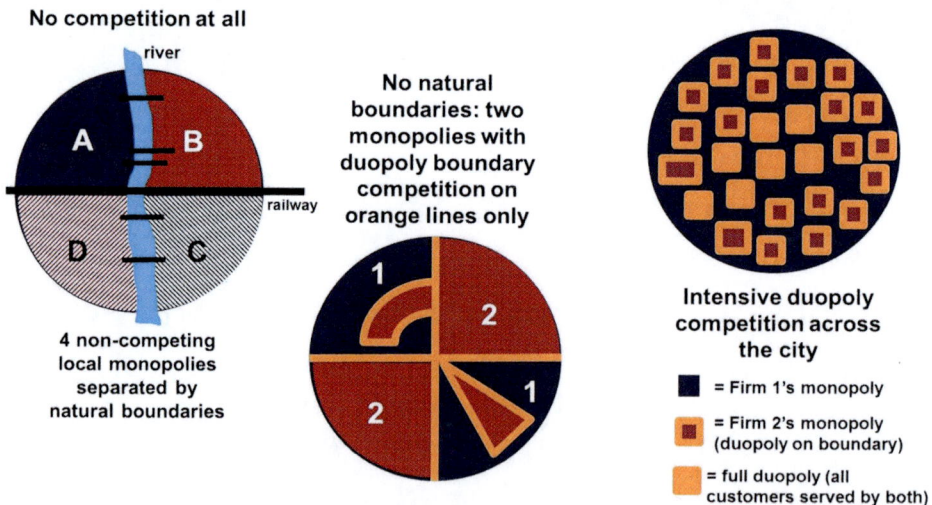

On the left we have the city version of the left diagram in Figure 35, in which four utilities supply customers across the city, but because of wide natural boundaries such as rivers, parks, railways, or trunk roads, all four utilities are cleanly separated by exogenous boundaries; so no customers are situated on

---

[91] See Figure 3 in Chapter One and the following text if you're not familiar with the different utility value chain stages.

streets served by two or more utilities, so no customers have any choice between competing utilities, and every utility has a complete local monopoly.

In the city in the middle diagram there are no wide natural barriers at all. A slow-moving Firm 1 started to supply the city's north west and south east quadrants, but a nimble Second Mover entered the city, made rapid gains in the opposite quadrants, and even beat Firm 1 to some of 'its own' customers in the north west and south east quadrants. Sluggish Firm 1 has been 'outreached' for a large part of this city's customers by a Second Mover who is quick and aggressive at building infrastructure. *Once the race to build infrastructure has finished, however, there is actual competition for customers between the utilities only at the boundaries of their areas*, which are highlighted in orange. All the other customers – the majority of the city – are served by just one of the two monopolies, and so have no choice. Genuine distribution competition is limited to the orange-lined areas, and most customers face their local monopoly.

On the right we have the logically possible case of rampant boundary competition between two determined suppliers. Firm 1 started to supply the whole city, but aggressive Firm 2 entered and rapidly installed capacity in many blocks that Firm 1 had not yet reached, with competition along each boundary. And for some blocks in the city both firms decided to duplicate the other's capacity throughout the block. This city has dense, intensive duopoly competition. This logical possibility is short of all-out duopoly across the whole city, which, in fact, we do see quite frequently in cities over a million people in the fibre-optic cables business.

We conclude from this analysis that two or more different players in a game does not automatically mean we have duopoly or oligopoly. For distribution grid utilities choosing where to build infrastructure, local monopoly is the default arrangement, unless the Second Mover has very strong incentives to duplicate the grid. At its simplest, *why play Second Mover in someone else's game, and be guaranteed competition forever, when you could be First Mover in your own game, and possibly retain that comfy monopoly?* You would only do it if the First market looks much, much richer than the Second[92] and you are supremely confident of your long term ability to beat the First Mover. In addition, for reasons of design simplicity, and lower building and operational costs, utilities will tend to follow the obvious strategy of trying to *dominate contiguous segments* of the total market. So, over time, as shown in Figure 37 two utilities entering the same market will generally try to seek out local geographical monopolies, rather than duopolies:

---

[92] It is just conceivable that if you think the First Mover in Game One is totally incompetent and about to go bankrupt, the market is significantly better, and you have a strong reputation in the market, ...but these are heroic assumptions.

Figure 37: The general evolution of two utilities entering a geographically-segmented market

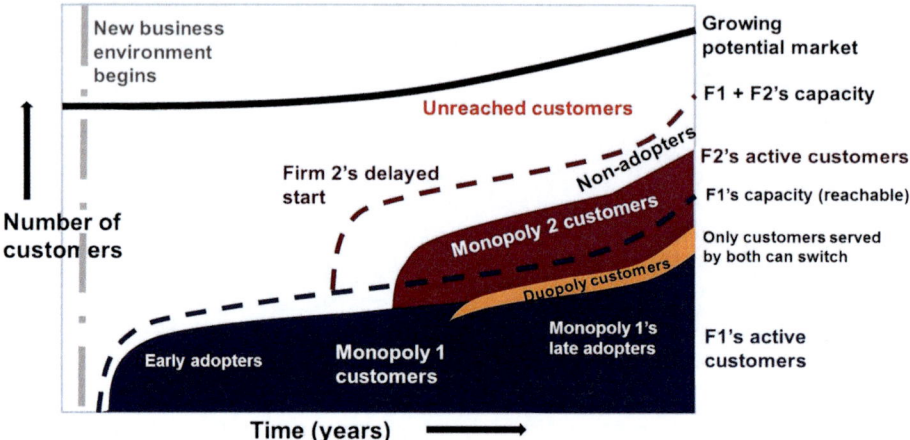

Figure 37 shows the general case of one firm entering before another. If entry happens to be simultaneous Firm 2's infrastructure and customers all slide to the left, to sit directly on top of Firm One's, but little else changes.

Systems modelling of one and two player games through time
We now have some key tools to examine the evolution of dynamic markets. To understand Mover One's range of reactions to Two's entry we must look inside the firm at the main variables of interest to investors, customers and management. The best tool for this is a business systems or 'business dynamics' model which formalises and quantifies a firm's resources and capabilities[93].

Systems model of a monopolist
Figure 38 is a simplified business systems model[94] of the key operations of an incumbent monopolist utility at an early stage in its evolution, such as we saw in Figure 34, when it is still growing its infrastructure and trying to gain new customers:

---

[93] For an explanation of the Resource Based View of a firm see any modern strategy textbook, e.g. Grant Chapter 5.

[94] If you wish to understand business dynamics models more thoroughly texts such as Sterman John D, 2000 Business Dynamics, McGraw Hill, or Morecroft John, 2007, Strategic Modelling and Business Dynamics, Wiley, or the e-book by Warren K, 2012, Strategy Dynamics Essentials available at http://sdl.re/essentials are three standard sources.

Figure 38: A business dynamics model of a developing monopoly utility's resources and capabilities

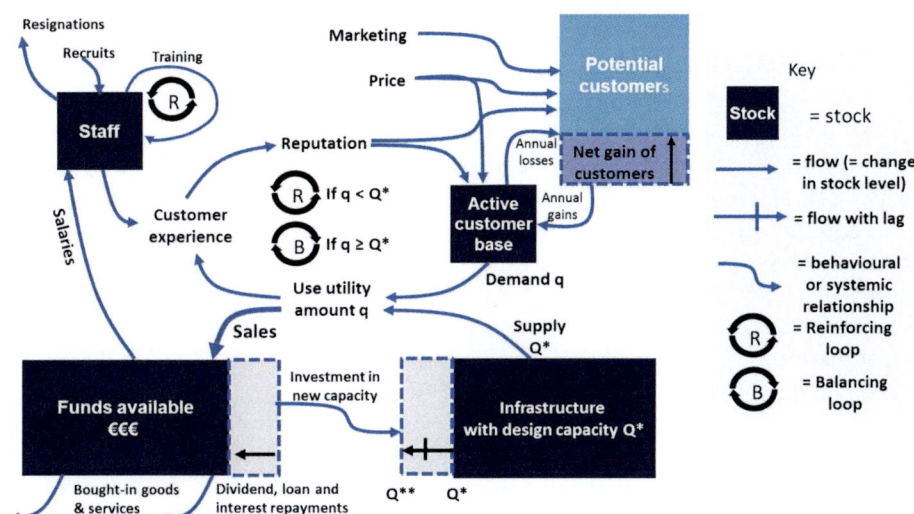

Figure 38 is a general model that would apply to canals, railways, water, sewerage, gas, or electricity, but to give it greater resonance today let us simultaneously imagine – you can do it, you have many capabilities – a specific example of a modern utility providing fibre optic cables to parts of a city which currently has none. The business environment is that demand for broadband is rising strongly, there is a generally acknowledged shortage of broadband capacity in this city, and, once installed, fibre optic broadband (T_1) provides cheaper and faster broadband speeds than previous technologies.

This utility's key *resources* are shown in Figure 38 as blue rectangles. In the bottom left corner its financial funds available include its paid-up share capital and maximum borrowing. This is the stock which is being gradually reduced (the big red negative cashflow lump in Figure 28) to pay for enhancements to the infrastructure – the key physical resource in the bottom right. However, it takes time to build infrastructure, so there is a lag before the capacity of the firm is actually enhanced from the current rating Q*, to say Q**.

On the sales side, the stock of potential customers who have not yet used the service is shown in the top right corner, while the stock of active customers who are connected is shown in the centre. Growing the base of active customers is the utility's highest priority at this stage. In general, if this service requires a permanent connection (energy, water, sewerage, or, in our example, broadband cable) the active customers are those who are reachable (i.e. there is a main down their street), and have been connected, for which there may or may not be an 'access charge' – a non-refundable sunk cost allowing the customer to use the service[95]. If the utility is a transport service these customers may be less committed. Note though, that for passenger transport, buying a season ticket or moving house, or, for rail or canal freight, building sidings or quaysides, all *require the customer to show* some commitment and to *sink sizeable costs* of their own. So, utilities which provide a frequently-repeated service (e.g. commuter trains, rather than infrequent trips) not only require the producers to sink massive costs to provide the infrastructure, but may also ask the consumers to sink significant costs too.

Just to emphasise the model's links to the Resource Based View's theoretical concepts, the incumbent's main *resources* are, as just described, its funds available, its stock of active customers, the physical assets in its infrastructure, and its staff (who can be improved by training). This utility has two main *capabilities*: to buy or build infrastructure enhancements efficiently, or at least effectively, and to use its physical infrastructure to deliver its service to its active customer base; this *core capability* (it is a monopoly) has a quantity dimension (it is limited to a (comfortable) capacity of Q^*) and various quality aspects – reliability, speed, seats available, service levels etc.

Customers' previous experiences of the service provided, combined with the utility's marketing and pricing decisions determine actual demand, q, while the quality of the crucial variable customer experience is determined by the level of q relative to installed capacity Q^*. In short, the system is usually demand-constrained. If demand is less than Q^* the customer experience should be good, reputation and word-of-mouth are good, and demand will tend to rise, in a reinforcing loop. But if q exceeds Q^* there may be congestion, or for other reasons – unreliable technology, unsatisfactory staffing, etc. – the system becomes supply-constrained, actual customer experience falls below that expected, the utility's reputation declines, reducing demand, so bringing supply and demand into better balance and the experience becomes more satisfactory. In other words, provided Technology T1 fundamentally works overall this system should be a balancing loop.

A full systems model of the First Mover's monopoly situation is available online to readers of this book[96]. It is highly recommended that you have a go at playing the incumbent monopolist and see if you can achieve targets such as not exceeding a borrowing capacity of £5bn or returning to a positive cash balance (zero gearing) inside fifteen years. It is even better if you can play this game, and the subsequent steps, in groups. Figure 11 shows a screenshot from a typical game, which has clear elements of the building up of infrastructure and customer base shown conceptually in Figure 34, and the linkages between key resources and variables that is shown in simplified form in Figure 38:

---

[95] This charge may be the only charge levied, or it may be an access charge like a standing charge, on top of which a variable charge is levied, depending on how much the service is used.

[96] It is free and available at http://sdl.re/MHmonopoly1

Figure 39: Screen shot from a systems model of Mover 1's profitable monopoly game

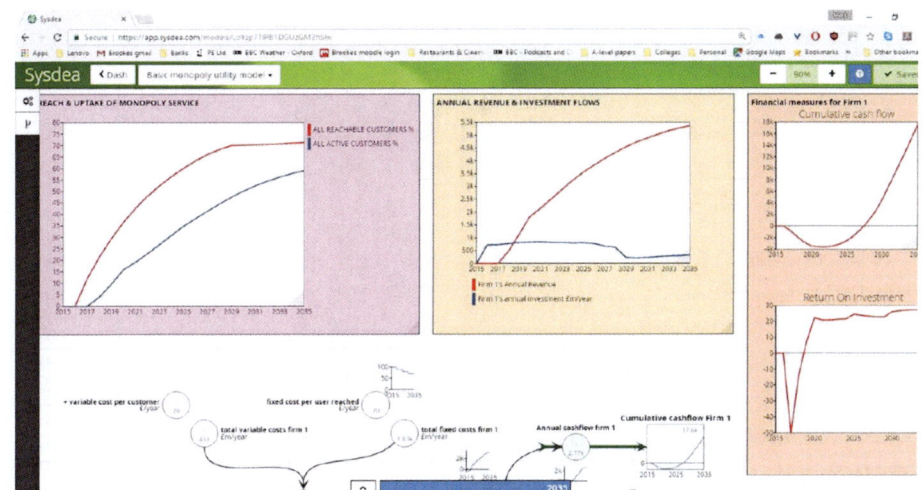

Source: http://sdl.re/MHmonopoly1 a Sysdea systems model that any reader of this book can access

As we can see, after 15 years the First Mover's infrastructure reaches 70% of the market, and around 60% of the potential market are active customers, which is very similar to Figure 34. After six years our monopolist starts to earn a Return On Investment over 20%pa, but at one stage their net borrowings are almost £4bn, and they take ten years to return to a positive cash balance. For simplicity the cash balance assumes no interest charges and no dividends paid out; these are realistic complications that are easily added to systems models, but would inhibit exposition of the fundamentals of building and operating a profitable monopoly utility.

2nd Mover's entrance

Now, let's set loose a second player – Mover Two – and break up this comfortable, cosy monopoly.

In line with Figure 28 and Figure 29 Mover One (the *incumbent*) is seeking to expand its installed infrastructure up to the marginal route, but this eats into a lot of the funds available and is a slow process. Finally, if the consumer has non-trivial sunk costs to incur before using the service (search time, domestic disruption, moving home, or, in the case of energy and water distribution grids, a non-trivial *connection or disconnection charge*) most domestic consumers will not consider simultaneous multiple suppliers of a continuing utility service – i.e. (domestic) consumers will choose to have only one supplier of each utility at a time. This situation contrasts with consumers' weekly supplies from food shops, restaurants or gasoline retailers, where their sunk costs (an example of *switching costs*) are zero. Thus consumers' sunk costs of accessing the utility, and any other switching costs, strongly reinforce their natural inertia – their reluctance to switch their entire individual demand from an established utility supplier to a later arrival.

So, the monopolist has a significant capability and set of resources for any entrant to challenge. But, typically, not all these resources or capabilities will work wonderfully: as viewed by Mover Two, some of Mover One's assets may be in the wrong place, its embodiment of T_1 in sunk assets may be imperfect and only alterable at very large incremental cost, its staff may be the wrong kind of people (e.g. 'techies' rather than 'people people'), its service record patchy after a poor a start, etc. And there are Firm Two's own special advantages – its competitive edge – which makes it different and likely to succeed in the eyes of its managers and investors.

So, the situation in Figure 30 after One has launched is interesting and must have been one that Firm Two envisaged as soon as it realised that Firm One was likely to launch its service first. What did it plan to do? Logically, Mover Two must have envisaged a competitive situation in which the dynamic model would in general look like Figure 40:

Figure 40: Simplified dynamic model of two competing utilities where Firm One launched first

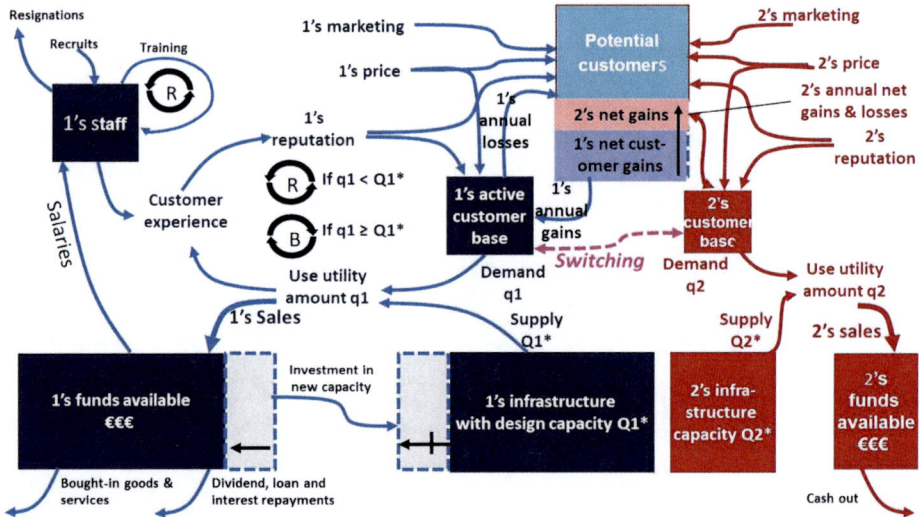

(For clarity the parts of Mover Two's game on the right which mirror Mover One have been omitted)

A fine old rivalry, where Mover One initially has the largest market share, and Two has to earn revenue by gaining customers either from the pool of potential customers or by persuading One's customers to switch to Mover Two. As the second entrant, Two has a big job ahead of it, and must have had some different ideas to Mover One to convince its investors to continue investing. These are its competitive strategies, and we will examine these shortly, but first let us consider the possibility that Mover Two has arrived too late – terminally late.

"Scooping the market"
In general Mover One will try to execute a tactic that we can call *scooping the market* in which it may be able to completely prevent any rational second utility

from entering. How so? First Mover One must develop a product with high enough quality or service levels to satisfy nearly all of the potential market (easier said than done with difficult new technologies). Next, Mover One must develop its local route infrastructure *sufficiently densely* (the sequential decisions in Figure 28) *to capture all the customers in its served geographical area.* Finally, it must market its service so effectively that no late or new potential customers are left unserved. What Mover One will then have done is to *drain the stock of potentially profitable customers in Figure 40*, so that **the only route for Mover Two to gain any customers** and revenue is by tempting existing Mover 1 customers **to switch**.

Figure 41 shows this situation. Mover One has scooped the market and Mover Two – bankrolled, perhaps, by a madman whose giant ego is matched only by his enormous bank balance – has nevertheless pressed ahead building its assets and launching its service. Mover One has had time to drain the entire stock of potential customers, so the only way for Mover Two to gain any customers at all is by enticing some of Firm One's active customer base to switch to Two's active customer base:

Figure 41: Mover Two's business model if Mover One has scooped the market

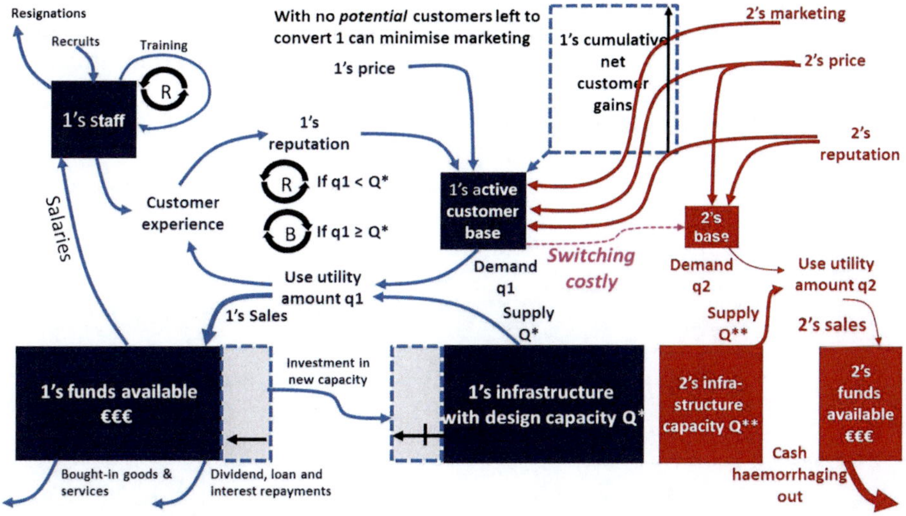

In this desperate situation Mover Two's marketing campaign must be focused on differentiating itself in some way from Mover One or offering a huge price advantage. If there is any significant inertia, or switching costs, or price insensitivity, Mover Two will gain only a few customers at best. Meanwhile cash is haemorrhaging from Mover Two's business due to
1. Very little revenue coming in
2. Continuing heavy infrastructure investment costs
3. Any fixed costs of running the new service
4. The variable costs of servicing Mover Two's customer base
5. The costs of a very expensive marketing campaign, including free trial

periods, discounted access costs, and highly-targeted marketing to persuade just a few customers to switch.

Figure 41 shows the real reason why electricity, gas, water, wastewater, cable broadband and transport utilities are normally monopolies: somehow – often through government policies or an act of licencing – a Mover One was allowed to develop its service first, and then, even if legally allowed to, no sane competitor would contemplate taking it on. If Firm One has laid gas pipes down 19th Street, signed up most houses in the street as customers, and left potential connections for all the others, why would any entrant lay another gas pipe down 19th Street? As we sensed in Figure 36 if Mover One looks like it is going to succeed in scooping the market *it will usually make more sense for Mover Two to try an unserved street and obtain a monopoly of its own*, than to challenge a sitting incumbent. Failing this, if forced to compete, *Mover Two must find some very strong point of differentiation*. But we know from Chapter 1 *this is impossible in commodity products like electricity, gas, water, wastewater, or broadband, and very difficult in transport*[97]. So, if Mover One has scooped a utility market no rational player will enter as Mover Two.

Full systems modelling games of twin entrants
Figures 38-40 are not just pretty, complicated diagrams; they are simplified versions of real system games that have been built to test the theories outlined here. Figure 42 is a screen shot showing the charts from one of these models in which we have Mover One scooping the market and Mover Two trying to enter the market without losing too large a fortune:

Figure 42: Screen shot of a systems model where Mover One has scooped the market

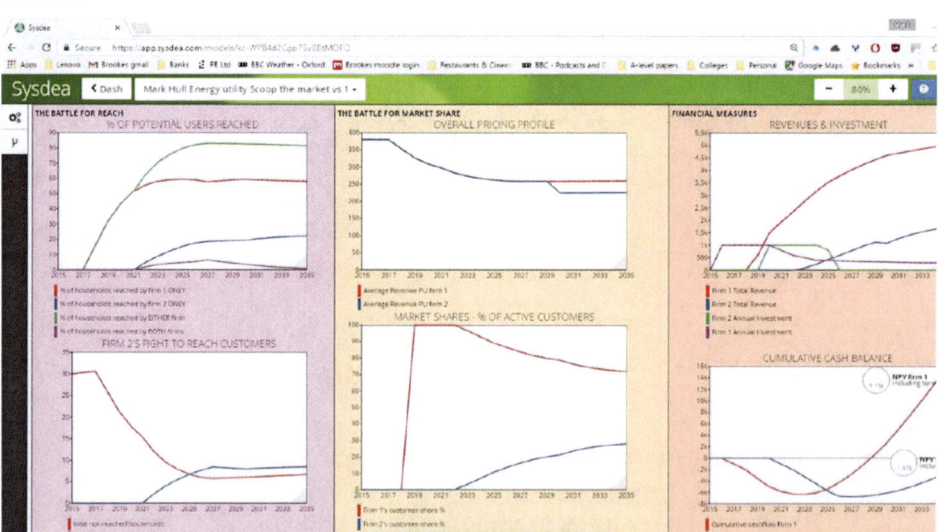

Source: http://sdl.re/MHscooping1 a Sysdea systems model that any reader of this book can access

We see that the stock of potential customers who have not been reached by Mover One has shrunk not to zero, but to around 20%. These are the "unreached" from Figure 34, who are unreached because they are believed to be 'uneconomic' by either entrant: a combination of too costly (too remote) to reach and low revenues when you get there. So, the main commercially viable customers available to Mover Two in this model are those who are already active customers of Mover One, or the most valuable available when Firm Two makes its entry – but still less attractive than the rest of Firm One's customers – or those reachable from One's infrastructure who have not so far taken up One's offer. The NPV of Mover Two's venture is negative because it must acquire 'poor' customers at high cost, and runs very cash-negative with little prospect of returning to a positive cash balance within 20 years of launching its service. This alone would be enough to deter most real investors, but we must also bear in mind that *the simulation has not begun to model Mover One responding to Mover Two's entry*. For example, the top middle chart shows that this simulation assumes Firm Two matches One's prices until Two decides to cut price to gain more customers, but Firm One has not yet reacted. When Firm One reacts, as we know it will, this, with the reaction to the reaction, and so on, can be modelled in advance by both players in one of these dynamic systems models. But the inevitable outcome must be that any successful competitive response by Firm One to Two's entry must eat into Firm Two's profits and cash still further, rendering the NPV of Two's proposed venture still more negative[98].

Proper systems models such as these are used by Finance Ministries and NGOs to predict under what kinds of conditions subsidies may be required from governments, and to predict the likely market structures that will emerge given the fundamentals of each utility and experience elsewhere. You too can use this model to test your understanding of the two-player entry game. It is best done as a class exercise organised by your tutor, since a group of you can conduct more systematic tests – and have more fun – but if you are a solitary student the general duopoly model is available from Strategy Dynamics' website at http://sdl.re/MHduopoly1 .

Simultaneous entry of a second player
Let us now return to the general case shown in Figure 40, of near-simultaneous entry by two firms. In fact the analysis from Figure 37, and the systems modelling of geographically-separable non-lumpy infrastructure, show there is no great difference between simultaneous and subsequent entry, provided Mover Two enters before Mover One has scooped the market of all profitable customers. So, Firm One has entered as a monopoly, acquiring what it regards as the best customers first, fairly closely followed by Firm Two. What is Firm Two's best strategy? The modelling and Figure 37 show there are two stages for both players:

---

[97] Until the business environment changes dramatically: we consider this later.

[98] Of course it will harm Firm One as well, but Firm One is by now in a far stronger financial position.

1. The *battle for reach* is the non-repeated competition to build the best infrastructure; it is non-repeated because the rivals build sunk cost infrastructure which they cannot undo. For both players it has two components:

    I. First, 'reach in' (create infrastructure) to maximise your own monopoly customers from the set of currently unreached customers. You should generally do this first because to challenge you the other player must commit to the sunk cost of reaching your customers, and if he does not commit you will have a monopoly forever

    II. Second, reach the potentially more profitable customers from your duopoly rival's reached customers by duplicating his infrastructure; it is the second best choice because no matter how attractive these customers are the incumbent will react, and even if all goes to plan you will be assured of competition forever (barring mergers)

2. The *battle for market share* in a duopoly utility market is the permanent competitive game to win and retain customers who have real choice because they are reached by both utilities.

In the battle for market share, once Firm Two has reached a potentially profitable Mover One duopoly customer, how can Two win, when Mover One started earlier, has a longer track record, more brand recognition, a larger active customer base, and possibly a good reputation?

Price cutting tactics

Some people's first thought will be to offer a price cut. However, *cutting price alone can never be a true strategy*, because it can be done in an instant by the chief executive, and, if necessary, reversed the next day for new contracts. It is therefore a *tactic*; it can form part of a strategy only if backed by long term product or cost development plans, which we will discuss in the mid-game section.

We can say, though, that a big price cut automatically kills the main point of entering a market – to earn profits – unless Two is absolutely certain that it has a Technology T_2 with a long run marginal cost well below the incumbent's T_1 LRMC. But if Two is in this position it doesn't have to cut prices: it could just show One its actual costs and wait to see how One responds, given that with hindsight it is now clear to all that One originally backed the wrong technology and cannot undo its sunk costs. Firm One might just give up, or offer to merge in return for Two's applied knowledge of T_2. Or it might wait for technology T_3 to turn up, with even lower LRMCs, and jump onto that bandwagon.

If Player Two does not have a T2 with a startlingly lower LRMC, can it ever use lower prices to persuade enough customers to switch? Well, the first thing to say is that if Player Two in Figure 12 is to make any existing customers switch it must comprehensively absorb all of an existing consumer's switching costs. In other words, if the technology invites connection or disconnection charges Mover Two must absorb these, and more, to cover all the consumer's search and experimentation costs. In effect Two must offer an absolutely free Trial Period (plus, probably, a cash incentive) so that a Firm One consumer can try out Firm Two's solution and be assured that at the end of it, if they still prefer Firm One, they can switch back and be no worse off. To make such an offer credible to all potential consumers is a considerable marketing challenge for a firm which is not yet in this market; in practice Mover Two must possess a highly trusted brand name from a relevant similar market, or be a government agency.

So Player One has a clear First Mover Advantage with its own customers here: it does not have to pay the switching costs while Mover Two must, if it is to persuade any customers at all to switch. These costs will then have to be absorbed from Player Two's continuing profits, which is why T_2's LRMC must be well below T_1's LRMC for Two even to consider using price as a significant competitive advantage against an incumbent.

Regarding the continuing usage charges (i.e. the non-access variable or draw-down charges) *if Two enters with a low price Mover One has no options: since it is already committed the incumbent must respond on price and cut its price to any level above its SRMC*. It will not be earning a full return but at least it will be covering its continuing costs, and can try to last the competitive storm longer than Mover Two. The only time it would not do this would be if it had overspent on sunk costs, funds available were low, and a price cut would force it to miss interest or capital re-payments, sending Firm One bankrupt.

Even if successful, Mover Two must get less than 100% of the market while incurring the remainder of 100% of its sunk costs. So if price cutting is Mover Two's strategy, Mover One must respond by threatening to cut prices severely, and the only credible counter-response one can imagine Mover Two making that would actually be a threat to the incumbent would be to reveal that it is backed by an extremely wealthy investor dedicated to their success – effectively that it has an infinite pool of funding available. This is the old strategy known as "My-owner-may be-mad-but-he-is-astonishingly-rich".

Non-price strategies
We referred earlier to Player Two having some "different ideas" for it to compete with Player One. These might be
a) Production ideas, about
   1. how to use Technology T1 better (or on a bigger scale), or
   2. using a completely different set of new Technologies (T2,...), or
b) Demand ideas about how to offer a new or better service to customers, either
   1. geographically or
   2. through differentiation of its product.

To take these in order, if Player Two uses the same technology T1 as Player One but somehow 'better', we see that in general it is most *un*likely that Two will have the same cost choices as One: Two will be using Technology T1, but a different part of the Technology's cost function – e.g. a different scale, or more, or less, capital-intensive[99] – or they will use T1 and the same part of the cost function, but will use it more efficiently, and so be on a lower cost curve[100]. And in b) to achieve geographical or product differentiation Player Two must use either a different technology, a different cost function – e.g. their sunk R&D costs and their fixed marketing costs may be higher – or the geography is different: but that will directly affect any revenues and costs that vary geographically.

So, the *only* circumstance in which the incumbent and entrant will be fighting it out with the same costs is if there is only one technology that really works, there are no significant Learning Curve effects, there was no pioneering learning from Mover One's entry that benefits Mover Two, the product cannot be differentiated, and does not vary by geography. In all other cases the incumbent and entrant will be 'fighting with different weapons', not least because the business environment has changed since both Movers made their Go Ahead decisions[101]. Thus a scenario that riddles the academic literature, of two network utilities competing with identical costs, is one of the least plausible cases imaginable.

Example of a new technology: canals and railways
When it comes to Mover Two using a different technology, T_2, and to technologies fighting it out, the history of transport gives us many relevant examples. Two hundred years ago the best way to carry heavy freight was on a boat on a river, lake or sea. The boat could support the large weight, and water has low viscosity, so once some motion could be applied to the boat through wind, rowing or being towed by a horse on the river bank, the load was moved along very easily if the water surface remains flat (it's not so easy pushing a load up a river or in choppy seas). Despite the risks at sea of boats sinking, or piracy, per tonne. kilometre water transport was far cheaper than land transport by carts, mules, or on the backs of sweating humans. Where peace prevailed considerable sums were spent on infrastructure improvements, building quaysides, deepening rivers to make them 'navigable' further inland, and so on.

Canal technology means building level thin artificial lakes for boat transport, and had been known for millennia in China, and other parts of Eurasia. In the eighteenth century, as the Industrial Revolution got under way in northern Europe and thirteen States of North America, manufacturing began to concentrate production in key inland locations. To bring in raw materials or ship out bulk finished goods, canals that extended the navigability of existing rivers or sea ports inland appeared attractive to aristocratic investors and ingenious

---

[99] Recall that after it has launched the incumbent cannot easily change its capital stock, while the entrant can.

[100] The incumbent will have made Learning Curve gains with its use of T1, but the entrant can learn from any overt mistakes the incumbent made (or other pioneers of T1) and so avoid some expensive pioneering write-offs. These facts alone mean the business environment has changed significantly since the incumbent's Go Ahead decision.

[101] Before it was uncertain if two players would enter the industry simultaneously; now it is a certainty.

manufacturers. So canals were developed in northern Europe and north America to foster and deepen the Industrial Revolution. At its apogee costs to customers from the 1825 opening of the 12 metre-wide 584 km-long Erie Canal to New York fell to just 8% of the costs of the previous technology: horses and carts[102] *Each canal was a local monopoly* and investors understood this, believing they had bought a share in a permanent local monopoly.

But around 1835 canal investors had a nasty shock: they had reckoned without Technology T_2, which was early steam railways. So just as investments like the Erie Canal were being finished and starting to earn decent monopoly profits (at most the entire difference between the alternative more expensive land transport system and the operating costs of the canal) along came railways able to haul hundreds of tonnes of freight in one go, at even lower operating costs. Railways sprouted up, making most canals in the world redundant, until in the twentieth century railways were themselves replaced by road vehicles for much freight and passenger transport.

Different geographies = regional monopolies

However, the arrival of blatantly superior technologies does not happen very often. If no new technology arrives from heaven to help Mover Two, it must find some way to make its product or service different. One difference is geography. As Figure 35 and Figure 36 have shown the default self-interested market structure for a distribution or collection grid is a local monopoly, so if a utility Second Mover finds itself in the Second Mover position in Figure 30, its best option is to race around the city trying to get as many and as profitable local monopolies as possible. At the infrastructure-building stage competition is a fierce race for local monopolies rather than duopolistic competition for customers inside each other's territories. This result holds true for all markets of commodity (homogenous) products.

In most sequential entries this happens in an even clearer way: entrants race to gain monopolies over entire cities, rather than splitting them, vying for the biggest cities first, or, for transport links, vying for the biggest city-pairs. This was seen repeatedly in the history of the early canals and railways. In early British and American railways hundreds of local geographical monopolies were originally started, and those that survived commercially were subsequently allowed to merge into bigger regional monopolies; there was no competition except along the boundaries[103]. And we saw the same logic in the nineteen nineties and noughties with the installation of fibre optic cable networks: the

---

[102] Probably the maximum cost saving, this may have taken years to emerge. Source: Encyclopedia.com entry for Lake Erie "the Erie Canal cut the cost of sending goods from Buffalo to New York City to less than $8 a ton from a precanal cost of $100 a ton" available at http://www.encyclopedia.com/doc/1G2-2536600962.html, accessed August 2016

[103] E.g. in the UK there was competition on the two routes to Exeter, Birmingham and Scotland, because these destinations lay on the boundaries of regional monopolies. By 1923 there was no other competition-in-the-market..

cable companies would race to sign up as the monopoly cable suppliers for whole cities, but would rarely split a city, in effect preferring to win a monopoly over a whole city of 100,000 than a monopoly of half a city of 200,000. Only when all the large and medium city monopolies had gone did they resort to competing down the same street in large cities. We shall analyse the case of broadband cables in giant city centres shortly.

We also see geographical differentiation in a completely different industry: *mining*. Here the output is a commodity sold in a global market with just one price, so the product cannot be differentiated, and the First Mover has a huge competitive advantage in being able to choose the best veins first down which to sink its infrastructure. But unless Player One can obtain a licensed monopoly for the whole mineral reserve, it can rarely commandeer all the resources necessary to mine the whole deposit simultaneously, so it cannot stop Second Movers from sinking their mines and starting parallel mineral production. Do these mines compete locally? No: if we assume some sunk costs – mines of some depth – then significant entry barriers keep down the number of entrants, and for reasons of safety and asset security, the small number of Second Wave entrants tends to spread out over different areas, in effect establishing local geographical production monopolies.

Differentiation

If Player Two tries to make One's existing customers switch it must offer existing customers a significant advantage over One's offering. Besides geography, the main type of competitive advantage is product (sometimes called horizontal) differentiation. The problem for utilities is that in Chapter 1 we learned that, with the exception of travel journeys over 30 minutes, the utilities are all commodity products. So, forget that for most utilities, but it is what is done in other industries with predictable technologies and heavy sunk costs, such as software, automobiles, or aircraft.

We will not here outline the many ways in which companies can sustainably differentiate their good or service, as we only have two competitors at this stage and with two players the degree of differentiation does not have to be great[104]. The subject is covered in all good business strategy textbooks[105] and we will return to consider it more thoroughly as the number of players increases. The main points to note are that some products ('commodity' products) simply cannot be differentiated, while if the product can be differentiated, for this to be sustainable it must be *non-copiable*, which is hard to achieve. If you simply give your product an attractive feature or function which is highly valued by customers, then the first thing rivals will do is to copy it, and they won't rest until

---

[104] E.g. in a small town if there are only two restaurants and many trapped hungry customers the owners only need to put up different coloured drapes and tablecloths for there to be a significant point of differentiation. But this won't be sufficient in Tokyo or San Francisco, where there are ten thousand restaurants.

[105] For example see Grant *op. cit* Chapter 7.

they have achieved it – in their own way. And, of course, their way may be better than yours, if you are honest, so this aspect of rivalry never ends. But if you have a certain style or image which they struggle to match, for whatever reason, then you may have a sustainable differentiation advantage.

Two player entries: conclusions
To summarise, if two players enter an industry with large sunk costs
1. *First Mover Advantage will be strong if*
   a. the ratio of sunk costs to revenues (and hence to other costs) is high – but not so high as to deter the First Mover
   b. the product cannot be differentiated
   c. customer switching costs are non-trivial
   d. individual consumers do not split their suppliers – they generally choose to be entirely supplied by one firm or another, and
   e. no superior Technology T_2 has yet appeared.
2. *First Mover Advantage will be overwhelming*, allowing Player One to 'scoop the market' and to enjoy a permanent monopoly, if the above conditions are met and Player One succeeds in
   a. assessing the market right (geographically, socially, service levels etc.),
   b. applying a winning technology successfully (a big element of luck), and
   c. designing capacity to handle 100% of the likely future market comfortably.

In other words, if the advantages in 1 above apply (as they do for energy, water, fixed-line telecoms and most transport utilities) and Player One plays its cards right, it should be able to scoop the market and permanently deter all competitors from entering until conditions change. Conversely Player Two may successfully enter an industry requiring significant sunk costs if one of the following applies:
1. Player One makes mistakes in the above,
2. Player Two has a rival technology T_2 that gives it a significantly lower LRMC than Player One's, and it uses part of this cost advantage to absorb all the switching costs for an existing customer of Player One – and it has a sufficiently trustworthy brand name to make this offer credible to the entire potential market
3. Player Two can gain a geographical monopoly in an area Player One has not yet developed (i.e. Player Two achieves First Mover Advantage in some markets – twin monopolies)
4. Player Two can successfully differentiate its product from Player One's (duopoly).

If any of these four conditions apply the game from hereon can either be a two-player game of the kind found in conventional game theory analysis, or it may be sufficiently enticing to attract a third entrant.

Middle-games and end-games
Once two players have entered a game with high sunk costs, or more than two players are committed to entering it simultaneously, we can say that an industry

is established and we are analysing what we now define as the middle game. And it is worth adding that this is very much the kind of scenario that can be captured and modelled in business dynamic games, where Firm A may have been the First Mover but entered with a technology and cost structure that, with hindsight, turned out to be sub-optimal, Firm B entered with what we subsequently know to be the right technology, but not in the best locations, and Firm C entered with the least cost technology, the best locations, dynamic competitive advantages, and the most money, but had to gain most of its customers by switching them away from the existing players. A fun game to model, and most realistic, not just for utilities but across all industries, including high tech industries where customer switching costs are significant. Not surprisingly, business dynamic modellers find many of their best commercial customers in these industry sectors.

A third entrant

Figure 43 summarises the decision sequence if a third firm decides to enter the market:

Figure 43: Enter Player Three: the decision sequence

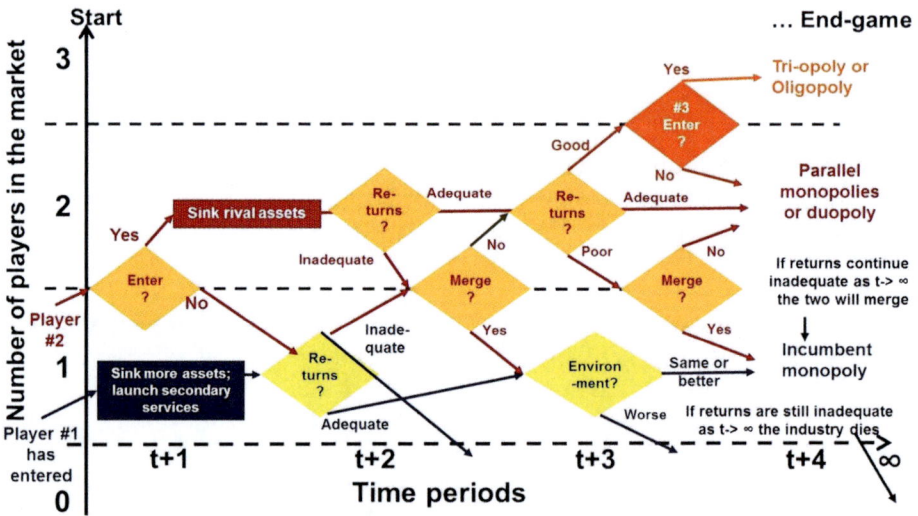

Why should a third player incur large sunk costs to enter a market in which two firms are already slugging it out? Mover Three must believe that
1. The market is large, profitable, and will grow still more
2. It (Mover Three) has some innate strengths over the incumbents that will lead it to be able to create sustainable competitive advantage.

What could these innate strengths be? Well, any of the four conditions listed in the previous conclusion for Mover Two to enter against Mover One, if we replace 'Mover Two' by 'Mover Three' and 'Mover One' by 'Movers One and Two'.

By far the most important condition, though, is that there is a large, potentially profitable market here, which has seen rapid growth to date. The widely-adopted product life cycle theory predicts an S-shaped curve up to a new plateau, but before it happens no-one knows how high the ultimate plateau will be: if this fast-growing *market has currently reached level A*, the *future plateau market, which we can call X*, might be 2A, 20A or 200A. Furthermore, the distribution of expectations is unlikely to be normal; Figure 44 shows some of the possibilities:

Figure 44: Possible distributions of investors' estimates of the ultimate size of a fast-growing market

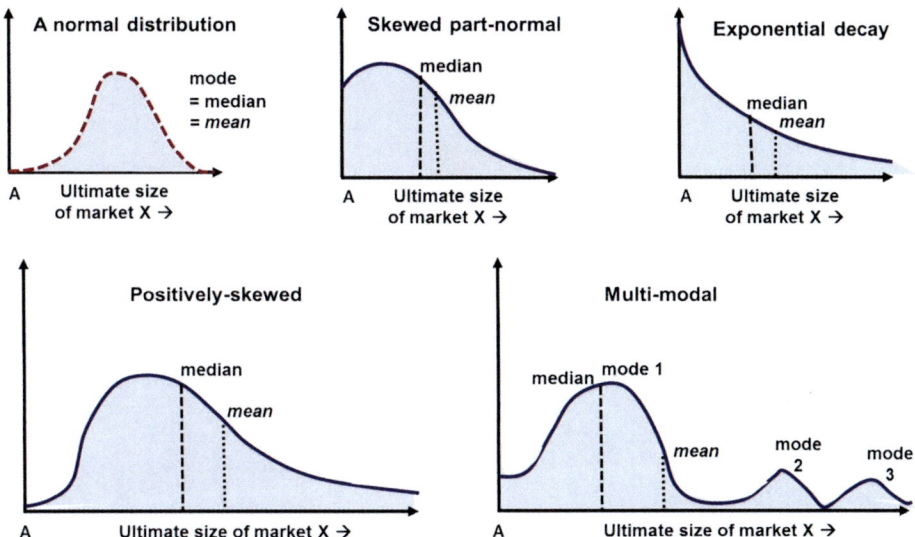

A normal distribution about a central point is unlikely because it assumes that on average we correctly guess an "unknown unknown" future. A more likely outcome is that the distribution of expectations will be positively skewed – at the extreme multi-modal. By definition *Third Mover investors must be long term investors with high X expectations* (on the right) who conclude that although the sunk costs are vast and they are the Third Mover, the market will be so huge that the turnover / sunk cost ratio will be attractive even if they only win a modest share of the market.

Adjustment paths and investment bubbles

Following the successful launch of a new technology with ultimate sales of X, Figure 45 below depicts the paths over time of three separate concepts
1. The adoption by customers of the new Technology 1
2. Actual sales of the new product or service
3. Stock or capital markets' expectations of these sales.

In fact, at the start no-one knows that Technology 1 will work as intended at all, and so the possibility that X will ultimately be zero cannot be dismissed by sceptical investors for some time. We then see that as customers progressively adopt the new technology actual sales take off in the familiar S-shaped curve, but capital markets must try to predict the ultimate X in order to value the company selling Technology 1; so they whoosh off, overshoot, get corrected, undershoot and get corrected a couple of times more, before eventually homing in on the True X. Given that they have to anticipate X on very little information this is an entirely rational path.

We may define an investment bubble as the launch of a new product or service which ultimately achieves sales of zero or very low in relation to early expectations. We then note that *it only needs a few such high X investors who genuinely believe this to create a speculative bubble*.

Figure 45: The time-adjustment paths of 1) technology adoption, 2) capital markets, and 3) sales of a new product

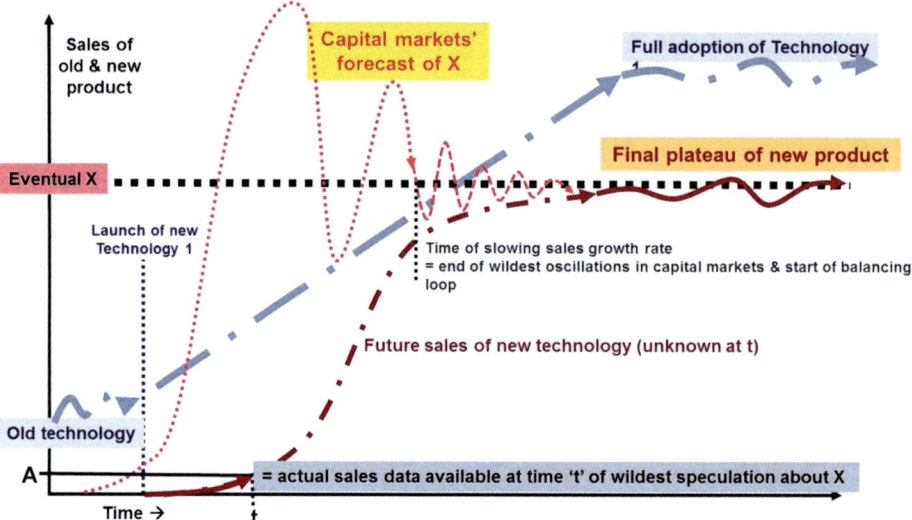

To explain a speculative bubble let us posit two broad classes of investor: a few long term risk-embracing 'fundamentalists' who intend to hold their investments until the market approaches a significant X, and a significant herd of short term 'speculators' who 'close out' their positions (i.e. they liquidate their gains into cash to reduce their exposure) more frequently. The short-term speculators have no long term view of the market at all, but they 'smell' that some (not all) long term investors have very high expectations of X. Cynical speculators (not all short-term traders) then spread a rumour that these high X investors are the 'smart' money – i.e. they are better guessers of the future than most of us. To the extent that this is believed they create an asset price spiral which exaggerates what is already the 'normal' overshoot shown in Figure 45. For a while this rocket ride up makes money for everyone – if you sell out in time – but most consistently it makes money for those who get in early, close out their positions frequently, and gradually reduce their exposure. Subsequently, stock markets wildly guess the actual demand growth with an oscillation that only really dampens once the growth rate of actual sales starts to decline, as shown in Figure 45. Ultimately, although some markets grow fast for more than ten years, of course nothing grows forever, sales growth rates slow, and the stock market settles around the new equilibrium for X. A twin-investor model such as this readily explains the dynamics of investment bubbles, such as tulip mania in the Netherlands of 1637, Britain's railway mania in the 1840s, and the IT bubble of 2000.

So, *by definition, every firm entering as Player Three must be backed by some investors who belong to the optimistic side of the long-term investor community*, and are prepared for some serious risks. They must also have self-confidence in their differences, seeing them as strengths. These investors must feel confident that their firm either has a very powerfully differentiated product (difficult with a utility), or that it can rapidly deploy a Technology that is superior to the other two players' Technologies, in reliability, service quality, and costs. In addition to matching all of Player One and Player Two's services, Player Three must have confidence in their own *dynamic* capabilities – *they must believe themselves capable of* creating the infrastructure and *launching the service faster* than the first two, if they are not to come a very poor third in this race. Previous success in a market that is thought to be similar will buoy such capability confidence.

If Player Three meets all these conditions it enters the race, and the cycle continues, of sinking the assets, launching the service, reviewing the *ex post* returns and the changed business environment, and considering another round of investment. The reason that Figure 43 labels the end-game of a tri-opoly as 'oligopoly' is that the dynamic possibilities of a game with three players are far more numerous, and far less stable than a two-player game. This makes the modelling far harder, which is why so much modern game theory considers just two players. In general there are few unique solutions with three or more players, largely because modelling the feedback reactions becomes too complicated. A simple illustration of how a tri-opoly differs from a duopoly, and is therefore the start of oligopoly, is the modern extension of the oldest version of a two-player linear positioning strategy game, originally devised by Harold Hotelling in 1929[106] ; this is explained in Appendix One to this chapter.

Simultaneous entry of three or more players
Simultaneous entry with sunk costs of several players can be viewed as a special case of sequential entry in which certain timescales collapse, so that there is no knowledge of *ex post* costs, revenues, technologies or markets at the time when decisions have to be made. There is more guesswork, more potential for mistaken entry, and from the point of view of an individual participant the whole venture has the characteristics of a lumpy investment.

However, recall from Chapter 3 that there is absolutely no objectivity in entrants' appraisals of future revenue streams because the future is not known, and is particularly uncertain where new technologies are being commercially applied. Today's students might like to know that in the era before smartphones all the world's major cellphone manufacturers developed successive generations of cellphone, each one providing more specific functions, such as text, email,

---

[106] Hotelling H, 1929, Stability in Competition, *Economic Journal*, 39 (153): 41–57

cameras etc. In the first decade of this century the world's rich cellphone manufacturers each sank hundreds of millions, sometimes billions, of dollars into R&D desperately searching for "The Killer Application" that would give their phone the magic feature desired by the world, and so assure them of the largest slice of the global market. In the end, as history relates, Apple won the competition by designing the world's first smartphone that not only had music, a camera, web browsing and email, as well as the phone/text functions, but also used open-ended software to allow the user to add an infinite variety of personalised Apps to their phone. Apart from their neat design, high quality graphics and great touchscreen innovations, it was the killer software solution that slayed all competition: the traditional phone companies took years to recover, and when they did the entire industry had adopted Apple's idea of open-ended personalised 'Apps'.

In our context the point of the smartphone story is to illustrate how even in a well-established industry with simultaneous entry, differences about the course of future technologies are vast, and there is absolutely no objectivity *ex ante*. It is only with hindsight that we can see what the winning combination of technologies was: the luxury of the historian, but not of the participant. So in an industry which no-one has entered, or perhaps only a very few firms have entered in a different country or business environment, simultaneous entry will include
- More firms making mistakes, because there is no *ex post* information
- A wider mix of firms, since firms such as Player Three who truly believe the future market will be one or two orders of magnitude larger than their more cautious rivals, will be entering alongside their more cautious rivals.

So how does simultaneous entry alter the game shown in Figure 43? In fact we don't need to draw an even more complicated version of this game. The crucial difference is something revealed earlier in the key difference between Figure 40 and Figure 41: the worst possible situation for any player is to arrive after another player has scooped the market, leaving no pool of potential unattached customers, and few active customers. In that scenario Player Two has to win every customer from its rival's installed and active customer base, overcoming customer switching costs, fear of the unknown and simple inertia, all of which requires enormous marketing effort and cost *in addition to* the vast sunk costs of creating the performing asset. So to avoid this, with simultaneous entry of three or more players, the highest priority for every player is to build enough assets as fast as possible to deliver some kind of functioning service to customers, and then, as is commonly agreed in the strategic literature[107], to grow your active customer base as fast as possible – i.e. grow your market share as fast as possible – while growing your reputation and supply capabilities. This frantic phase is likely to be cash-negative and victory may well go to the player with the

---

[107] See the lifecycle section of any business strategy textbook, where sales or market share is shown as the Critical Success Factor in the growth phase of a product or industry – e.g. Grant 8th edition page 217.

apparently most-popular service, the highest sales, and the widest capabilities (*ex post* objectively), who also succeeds in signalling that their investors have the deepest pockets.

As life cycle theory predicts, after growth slows and the market matures, the frantic investment in customers and assets slows, and the business can return to being cash-positive. The least successful firms – or those with the weakest balance sheets – may be forced to seek mergers with the most successful – or players with genuinely complementary capabilities. So, to save operational and maintenance costs, a regional distribution network such as an energy or water grid serving part of a town might seek to merge with another grid serving the same area. But if the network is a transport service in part of a city or region, and the general demand is for integrated transport across the whole city (not just to the city centre) then it will be important for a partial transport firm to offer a city-wide transport service, and so to form long-term alliances, or ultimately merge with, similar transport firms covering different parts of the city.

General conclusions on sequential or simultaneous entry conditions
For a player in a significant sunk costs game, whether entry is sequential or simultaneous, the conclusions are remarkably general and simple: install your performing assets as fast as possible, launch the service early, build up as large an active customer base as you can, and try to drain the pool of potential customers who have yet to try anyone's service to zero. This phase may well be cash-negative for some years. Then give as good a customer service as you can, exceeding anything you promised, and manage customer expectations properly, so that disappointed customers are few. Try to create a monopoly! If you have not actually achieved a monopoly in the frantic growth phase, try to merge or create effective alliances quickly so that you offer customers what they want at an entry-deterring cost, and before politicians get round to regulating the industry. If you succeed any entrant will have very substantial entry barriers to surmount, not just of the sunk costs of creating performing assets, but also of creating an active customer base by stealing your customers away from you. So even if an entrant comes along with a completely new Technology, at a much lower short run marginal cost, as an incumbent, if your customers are broadly happy – particularly if the service is a commodity – winning your customers away from you will prove to be an expensive, lengthy and time-consuming challenge.

And of course, if you are completely successful in creating an effective monopoly you will sooner or later find yourself facing a regulator. Analysis of the middle game can then start to examine a two-person game involving the firm as monopolist versus the regulator, who acts not only on behalf of the consumers, but also on behalf of investors, who by now may have little effective control over the monopolist's management. We start to examine this game in Chapter 8.

Competitive strategies for middle-games
In the middle game, if a firm has live competitors who produce the same or similar products, it needs a strategy for how to beat them, so that it can survive

and thrive. This area of business strategy has been well studied in the last few decades, so let's adopt the most widely-accepted model for a stable business environment, Porter's generic business strategies, which synthesizes two ways of increasing profits with two long term goals for the firm:

Figure 46: Porter's mid-game competitive strategies in a stable business environment

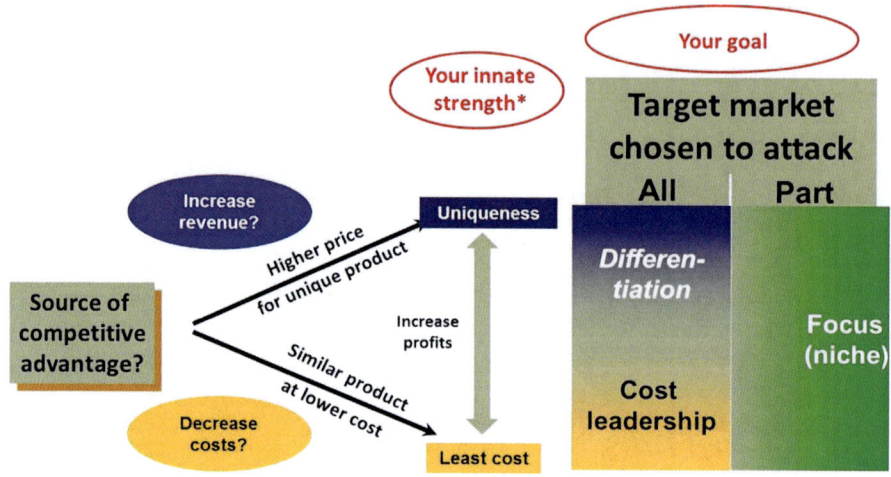

Based on Porter M, 1980, Competitive Strategy, Free Press   * As perceived by the customer

Perhaps Porter's greatest insight was to see that in a stable business environment a firm should execute[108] only one strategy at a time. To be sure, a differentiator can trim its costs, or a cost leader can take routine steps to raise its product quality, but if a differentiator cuts its costs too far customers and employees become confused about what its point of difference over the competition really is. If BMW really cuts its costs to be equal to Ford's why buy a BMW? And cost leadership is an all-out dedication: it's no good basing your entire business strategy on cost *leadership*, if in fact you are second or third by some way to the cost leader, who is always making more profit than you. To those who practice cost leadership successfully there are no half measures. So Porter's view was that if a large firm tries to change its strategy it will often fail (it will get "stuck in the middle") because the lag between strategic decisions and their implementation confuses employees and other stakeholders. Changing strategies in a large organisation will always be seen as internally inconsistent and self-defeating until the moment the new strategy works.

A transformed business environment

To summarise so far, in industries with high sunk costs, if sequential entry is viable there is considerable First Mover Advantage to Player One provided it

---

[108] Economists habitually underestimate the importance of execution of a strategy, as opposed to the analysis and design stages. In fact, where the business environment is stable most of the world's leading companies have strategies that are simple in concept: *the difficult part is executing them* better than their rivals.

plays its cards right. Given a lucky selection of fundamental technology, good applications of this, good geographical locations for its sunk assets and markets, and a sensible designed capacity for the infrastructure, it is possible for Player One to 'scoop the market', leaving just scraps, at most, for subsequent entrants. But what if the business environment completely transforms itself? This might be a sudden move from peace to war, the advent of global warming, the discovery that aliens have been living in Philadelphia for fifty years, or it might be the invention of a completely new technology. The latter happened in telecoms with the growth of computers, the internet, and a booming need to transfer large amounts of digital data along wires.

Recall that telecoms networks configured in the first half of the 20th century assumed a typical house would make about 10 phone calls a day. So this was the thinking that went into designing the 'local loop' telephone wires around most cities in the mid-20th century. By the 1960s the original analogue signals had been converted to digital electronic signals, and data was being transferred along the old copper telephone wires, which were progressively upgraded around the world. By the 1970s fax machines were becoming common in offices, so digital data transfer demand rose thousands of times above the levels originally foreseen in, say, 1920. As computers got cheaper more organisations wanted their own private data networks to link offices, banks and factories around the world, and increasingly rented this service from incumbent monopoly telecoms companies, who, to their delight, found digital data transfer demand rocketing up. The invention of the internet protocol in 1979, and particularly in 1981 the hypertext transfer protocol secure (https), meant any organisation could send and receive encrypted private data securely over any public telephone line. By the 1990s, with the (open) world wide web booming, and private intranet links mushrooming, enabling people to conduct online business securely, the demand for data transfers was growing another thousand - or million - fold.

The upshot was that by the 1990s data was being transferred around and between cities on old copper wires which were continually having to be upgraded. The projections for 21st century demand were for data transfer rates millions or billions of times higher than demand had been when the original First Mover telephone lines were installed back in the 1920s.

How does this change the game? Well, completely. The First Mover may have scooped the market in 1920, but faced with these prospects in the 1990s new companies were entering the landline telecoms market and laying their cables directly on top of the incumbent's. Yes, they had to incur 100% of the sunk costs, but the prospective demand in their new Figure 24 evaluation so far exceeded the installed capacity levels that the decision made good economic sense. The growth of demand had made the incumbent's installed capacity totally inadequate.

The consequence was that in the centres of large cities we now have an oligopoly of actual competition-in-the-market, with many telecoms fixed-line grids right on top of each other, competing head-to-head, as Figure 47 shows:

Figure 47: Utility competition-in-the-market: a 'green sheen' of new telecoms cables laid right on top of old ones

Photo: reproduced by courtesy of National Joint Utilities Group

However, in smaller cities we have tri-opolies or duopolies, because the PV of anticipated demand is not that large in comparison to the sunk costs of laying a new cable grid. And in small towns and villages we still have just the single monopoly, where consumers must wait until the incumbent monopolist, or its economic regulator, decides in its own sweet time to favour customers with an expansion of network capacity.

End-games

One of the weaknesses of current game theory is that most models assume a finite number of rounds of the game, when everyday business life has no such Final Day of Judgement. It seems to us that time continues indefinitely in reality, barring routine apocalypses, so the closest approximation to our perception of reality is to refer to the end-game as being when 't' tends to infinity, as we have, for instance, in Figure 43. The overall situation is summarised in Figure 48 which is a version of a diagram well known to economics teachers the world over who try to explain classic market structures to bewildered students[109]:

Figure 48: The standard end game market structures, and how they are reached

Initial conditions		End-game	End game product is	
Ratio of sunk costs to turnover	Ease of entry (ceteris paribus)	Number of firms in the industry	Commodity	Differentiated
Negligible	Easy	Many	Perfect Competition	Imperfect or Monopolistic Competition
Significant	Hard	Few	Commodity Oligopoly	Differentiated Oligopoly
Very high	Very hard	Two	Duopoly (we match each other's essential features)	
Extremely High	1st mover only	One	Monopoly (no one to differentiate against)	
Impossible	Never made sense	Zero	(No industry)	

Of course, we must emphasise that these end-game positions assume that technology and the rest of the business environment do not change – i.e. the business environment has come to some kind of temporary equilibrium or stasis. ... Hmm... when did that last happen? Some time in the Triassic? OK, but it shows the asymptotes to which we are converging up until the moment the environment does change.

The model applied to non-grid utilities
We have discussed how the sequence model applies very well to classic grid utilities such as electricity, gas, water, sewerage, railways and canals. But the general model makes no reference to grids or networks, only to sunk costs of entry. Thus an industry without a physical grid could still face considerable sunk costs relative to the anticipated market and thus have very few entrants. So if we briefly review 'non-grid utilities' the only question under this theory is how large are all of their sunk costs in relation to anticipated revenues and operating profits.

Posts
Posts can be divided into letters, counters and parcels
    a) letters includes sorting offices, post boxes for receiving letters and postal 'walks';
    b) counters includes a network of retail outlets – local post offices and sub-post-offices – that constitutes a distribution service for products like stamps and postal services, mixed in with private commercial retail businesses;
    c) parcels is a collection-and-distribution network.

The largest financial sunk costs occur in a), for the grid of mailing or posting boxes that needs to be installed on every other street corner in urban areas or in every hamlet of five houses in rural areas. However, the sunk capital costs are small relative to the annual running costs of collecting letters from these, or continuing letter delivery costs, which are largely variable. The bigger source of monopoly power is the network of local sorting offices and delivery walks, which is a classic case of first mover advantage: once a firm has established a national brand it is very expensive for a second mover to duplicate that network completely, yet if the second mover does not, it must pay its rival to complete services it cannot fulfil. However, this does have one big advantage for the second mover: they can 'cherry pick' only profitable routes and leave the incumbent to serve the unprofitable routes. This situation is briefly covered in Chapter 8.

Looking at the difference between letters (competition-in-the-market rare) and parcels (competition-in-the-market quite common) we can liken both postal value chains to typical utility value chains: the bulk-delivery stage between major cities is like transmission, while the 'local loop' is like a distribution network.

---

[109] For example see Krugman P and Wells R Economics 2013, Worth / Macmillan, New York, 3rd International Edition page 374

However, unlike utilities, there is likely to be more competition in the transmission business than in distribution because variable costs form a much larger part of total costs in the bulk business than in the local. Another difference is that many of the assets used in both businesses are not sunk – trucks, vans, aircraft and land all have well-defined second hand values, leading to high fixed costs in the short run, but not to high sunk costs. In this respect posts fits the neoclassical model of monopolies quite well, so the degree of monopolisation may be determined by the steepness of long run economies of scale.

Telecommunications
Obviously *fixed line wires are classic grid utilities*, though they are of course communication grids and so subject to communication grid laws such as Metcalfe's Law[110] rather than to the dendritic patterns of local distribution or collection grids. The copper wires of early twentieth century networks mean these old assets also happen to have a high scrap value, should technologies render fixed landlines redundant, which reduces the sunk costs. The low scrap value of the twenty first century fibre optic cables increases sunk costs, but 'no-dig technologies' that allow remote-controlled machines to tunnel through land without disturbing the surface can reduce sunk costs. It is an ongoing technological battle.

Mobile networks usually require no landlines, but they do need a grid of radio masts to ensure local coverage. Can these masts be used for other purposes? Yes, masts are often shared within telecoms, and of course they can be leased, which largely eliminates the operator's sunk costs. Even for the mast owners most mobile masts are not very large, so their payback period may be quite short, particularly given their multiple uses in telecoms. But there are more sunk costs than just physical costs. For example, non-transferable government licence or franchise fees are sunk costs. The policy recommendation should therefore be either to make licences partly transferable, so that a bidder who has badly over-estimated the value of a franchise can get some of their money back, or for the government to risk-share some of the variable unknown future profits. The latter should not be considered for the routine franchise of a well-established technology, but only if the unknowns are really unknown applications of an untested technology. So, in practice the sunk costs, and hence the innate monopoly characteristics of this half-grid, could be reduced.

Buses
Nearly all bus services are capable of being franchised, and many around the world are either franchised or are totally private sector initiatives. Thus we have competition-for-the-market and, less frequently, actual competition-in-the-market when rival bus companies compete for passengers along the same

---

[110] Metcalfe's Law hypothesises that the value to a consumer of a communications network increases with the square of the number of consumers connected, so the value of a social network with 20 people connected is 4 times the value of the same network with only 10 people on it (a ratio of 400 to 100).

routes[111]. The obvious physical sunk costs akin to a grid are bus stops and the occasional bus depot. Although bus stops are becoming more intelligent (telling customers where buses go and when they will arrive) they are not a major sunk cost. The principle of bearing responsibility for one's actions says that if there is a possibility of a bus service being permanently cancelled the body that initiated the service and then subsequently cancels it should bear the sunk costs. So if a branch of government initiates a bus service they should pay for the sunk costs of stops and depots, and for subsequent maintenance costs, while franchisees in frequent franchise auctions (strong competition-for-the-market) should be selected on the basis of best value for money.

One other main sunk cost is the time and money governments and bus company managements spend bidding for franchises; minimising this over the long run would lead to long franchise periods. But to maximise the consumer benefits from competition-for-the-market, public bodies should aim to have reasonably frequent auctions (i.e. short franchises), so a social optimum would involve an auction process that is as short, effective, and efficient as possible around franchise periods that are quite short. If certain assets play a key role – e.g. city centre locations for bus depots – these may have to be owned by the awarding authority for the auction to be truly competitive. Again this issue is discussed in Chapter 8.

So, if demand will support it (e.g. in large cities), bus duopolies and tri-opolies can co-exist without public subsidy, and companies can enter and exit the industry relatively freely. But if population density is low, public subsidies will be needed to attract even a monopoly supplier.

Radio & TV networks
Physical sunk costs (transmitter stations, booster masts etc.) are negligible in TV and radio networks, either because they are relatively small to begin with, or because they have already been incurred across most parts of the world and will not have to be repeated. (We also assess the general problem of valuing sunk costs that work and should not need to be repeated in Chapter 8).

But there are larger costs of running a network of correspondents: a news organisation needs global coverage – geographically or sectorally – regardless of the 'news' value they bring in (their output or load). "Our correspondent" in Tehran may have a really busy month and file many stories while our correspondent in Omsk may have to wait a long time before a newsworthy story appears. Editors manage this problem by widening the briefs of correspondents in quiet sectors and narrowing the brief of the busy Washington DC correspondents. The fact remains, however, that the raw economics of these businesses are that they are

---

[111] In practice we may have both, as rival bus companies compete-in-the-market for the thickest parts of a transport route near the centre of a large town, but as the branches thin out they tend to have local monopolies at the ends of the routes, competing-for-the-market whenever they bid for these licences from the local council.

often highly competitive while being networks of high fixed costs – not high sunk costs. The only true sunk cost is the development of a network of leads that may one day create a newsworthy story, but these are largely investments of time, and are financially trivial, so they appear in accounts on the Profit and Loss account, not on the Balance Sheet – i.e. as a current cost, not a capitalised cost. So from a strategic point of view, sunk costs are trivial – except for the journalist who incurs them and is then moved to another post before they have filed a really good story – and once again illustrate the principle that high fixed costs do not necessarily create monopolies, but high sunk costs do.

Wider applications of the general sequence model

By definition a sequence model introduces time into an economic theory; this is only useful if time adds something. In this case time coincides with the state of technology, and has the property that it cannot be reversed, which affects two types of economic decision:
- sunk costs – industry- or location-specific assets with no alternative use; once built they exist for good
- capital asset purchases, which embody the state of technology at the time the decision was made, and often cannot be reversed.

The general sequence model can be applied to any industry, regardless of:
- cost-structure, investment lumpiness, whether there is technological progress or not, length of asset lives, or number of pre-existing players
- whether an investment is to be made by private agents or governments, who may additionally consider externalities
- whether the investment is *de novo* or to retain an existing operation.

The theory is particularly fruitful when applied to network utilities supplying commodity services such as energy or water distribution or collection:
- The requirement to construct, maintain and operate a physical grid is a large exogenous sunk cost which constitutes a sizeable entry barrier
- The theory predicts that a region will be served either by no network utility suppliers (if population density is low), or by one (the monopolist), but by two or more if demand rises well above the first mover's network configuration (e.g. buses in big cities, or city centre telecoms). This accords well with empirical observations across the world.

In sum the usefulness of the sequence theory of industry entrances and exits is that it can apply to any industry, regardless of its rate of technological progress, efficiency, capital-intensity, the lumpiness of investments, number of current competitors or any other constraint. Additionally, it corresponds closely to what most well-run firms try to calculate in one way or another before entering an industry. A simple example shows how powerful this theory can be: waste collection is either of fluids or of solids. The commonest fluid on Planet Earth is water and in modern urban societies humans have devised entire networks that supply clean water to us; we use most of this water for cleaning, and then return it in dedicated sewers built expressly for this purpose. These water and wastewater grids are huge sunk costs and the theory predicts convincingly that, if provided at all, they will always be innate natural monopolies. However, solid waste collection is done through a system of bins and carts; there are no large sunk costs here, and consequently few issues of natural monopolies. Job done: the theory makes generally correct predictions.

The limitations of the sequence model are that in many markets the barriers to entry and exit are low, so that after a decade or two thousands of firms have entered and left an industry. Unfortunately, sequence theory does not predict how successful or powerful individual firms will become after entering the market[112]. To explain this the conventional mid-game and end-game theories of oligopoly, monopolistic or imperfect competition, and perfect competition are still useful, particularly if students are taught the dynamics of how these models handle small shocks. Figure 48 explains how these situations arise, but of course does not explain how firms operate in each type of game.

Appendix 2 to this Chapter is for academic readers. It explains the intellectual derivation of the sequence model and compares the three theories of natural monopolies: the Neoclassicals' high fixed costs theory, Baumol et al's 1982 Contestability Theory, and this sequence theory.

---

[112] There is also a practical difficulty in using the sequence model, as any economist who has ever tried to use this method in practice will attest: due to firms splitting, merging, changing their names, and joint ventures, it can be very confusing to try to calculate the number of players in an industry without detailed sectoral knowledge of the firms involved.

Appendix 1: Hotelling's linear positioning model

Harold Hotelling was a mathematician at Stanford, Colombia and North Carolina Universities who taught Milton Friedman statistics and persuaded Kenneth Arrow to apply mathematical tools to general economic theory. In 1929 he had a paper published in the Economic Journal which considered the problem of positioning a store on a street in a small town[113]. This model was one of the earliest applications of game theory modelling to economic situations, and has been modified in the following example to be placing an ice cream vendor on a beach, before being extended[114].

An ice cream seller on the beach – monopoly

Imagine a hot summer's day by the sea. People are going to a beach which is flat and straight but bounded at either end by an unusual combination of midges in a forest (the wind keeps them off the beach) at one end and crocodiles at the other (who don't move much because they are well-fed and sleepy). Behind the beach is a featureless straight road. Gradually the beach fills up uniformly across its area with local sunbathers. The beach area is strictly controlled by the local Council and run on behalf of the sunbathers. Recently the Council has voted to allow one – and only one – ice cream vendor onto the road behind the beach, on condition they sell one flavour of ice cream from a mobile van which is parked on the road. The ice cream seller may not sell ice creams by wandering onto the beach, nor may they offer a second flavour, and anyone who sells ice cream from a boat in the sea will be torpedoed by vigilantes who patrol the coast in submarines.

In effect Hotelling is asking where along the road should the Council place the ice cream vendor so as to maximise social welfare, which in this instance means minimising the walking distance to the ice cream van for the average sunbather?

Figure 49: A hot beach with a uniform distribution of consumers along it

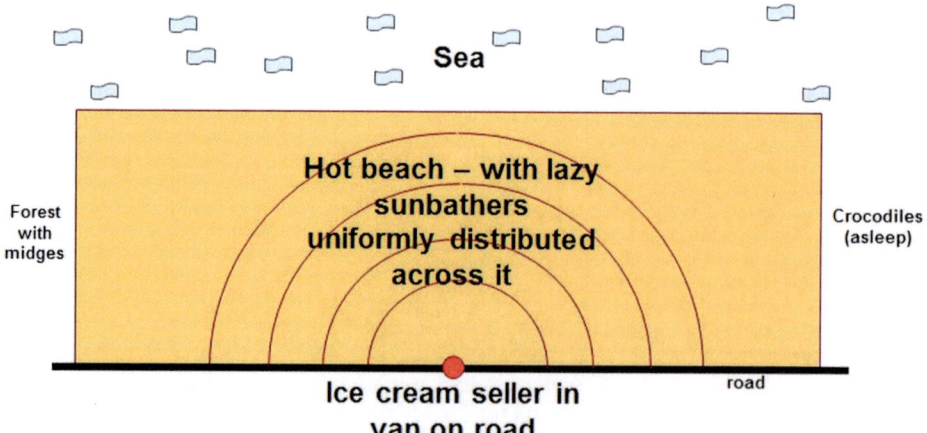

Yes, you can prove mathematically (Hotelling did) that the location in the middle minimises the average (or total) walking distance for sunbathers, and thus is the social optimum.

But what if you were the ice cream vendor, and you could go anywhere along the road to maximise your sales? Where would you position yourself? Yes, you'd pick the same spot – because it is in your self-interest to minimise the total walking distance for sunbathers.

Two ice cream sellers – duopoly
Now consider a complication. The Council changes its mind, has another vote, and agrees to allow two – and only two – ice cream vendors onto the road, but the other restrictions still hold (can't go onto the beach, or in the sea, and both must sell the same type and flavour of ice cream). Where on the road should the two ice cream vendors be placed? Yes, you can prove that they should be placed a quarter along the way in from the boundaries. This is the social optimum for two vendors:

Figure 50: Where will two ice cream sellers position themselves?

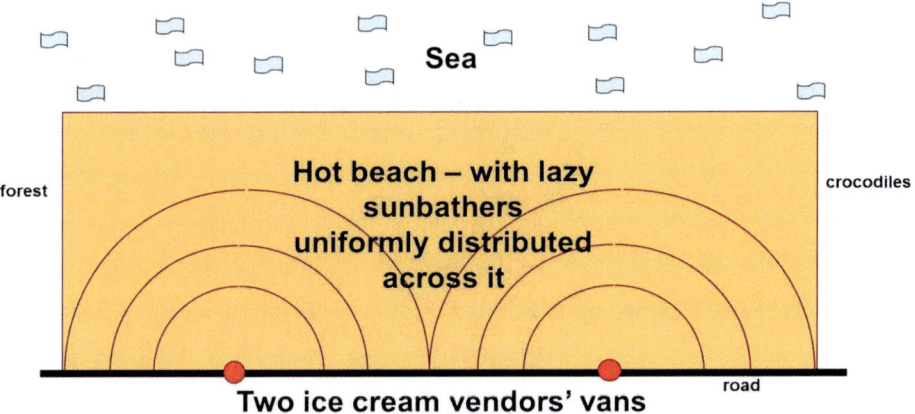

But suppose a Council official places them in these positions at the start of the day and then goes back to her office, not to return for that day. Further, suppose the ice cream sellers know this fact, it being a small town, and all. If you were one of the vendors, would you move, and if so where?

Yes, there's an incentive to move in towards the centre: if you are the left hand vendor you can move to the right and move the customer boundary to the right, stealing customers from the other vendor. You may lose a few lazier customers from the furthest reaches on the forest and the sea, but not as many as you will pick up from the middle of the beach. And, of course, there's an identical

---

[113] Hotelling H, 1929, Stability in Competition, *Economic Journal*, 39 (153): 41–57

[114] The analysis here follows Kay J, 1993, *Foundations of Corporate Success*, OUP Oxford, hardback p243

incentive for the right hand seller to mirror your actions and move in towards the centre from the right. Where will it end? Yes, with the two of you next door to each other in the middle. But this is the monopoly position! Technically, Hotelling has shown that, *given the assumptions of this model, the Nash equilibrium (the position where no player can improve their position given the other players' strategies) for a duopoly is identical to a monopoly.* Despite introducing a second vendor and a plainly superior potential service to customers, unless the social optimum position is policed by the Council it is unstable and will degenerate into the monopoly position. So, adding another player and introducing competition has not improved matters.

Wait a minute...instead of competing, couldn't the two ice cream vendors simply agree to stay in their given social optimum positions? If they did, wouldn't that be stable? Yes it would be stable so long as they both keep to the agreement – indeed, it's superior for precisely the reasons that make it the social optimum: their half shares of the global market in Figure 50 are larger than the half shares from splitting the market in the middle (because they provide better services to the people near both ends of the road, and so sell more ice cream in total). Which gets us to the heart of the issue, theoretically and commercially: in the absence of an effective policeman, *do you trust the other vendor?* If yes, and you can make a transparent agreement, then the ¼ – ¾ position is a stable Nash equilibrium and superior to the ½ – ½ position, but if the vendor with whom you have competed for years retires and her unreliable young sister takes over, trust is broken and you end up drifting to the competitive equilibrium.

A third ice cream seller – tri-opoly
So let's go one step further than Hotelling did and introduce a third player. Obviously the social optimum can be proved to be as in Figure 51:

Figure 51: What is the Nash equilibrium with three sellers?

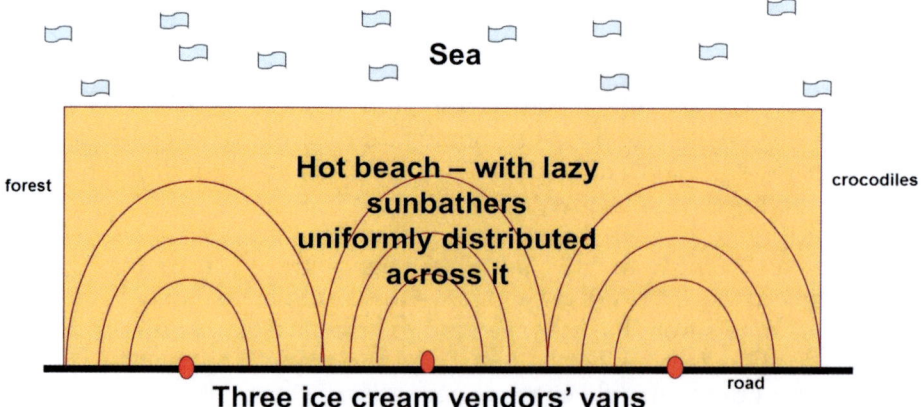

Now, what happens once the town clerk goes back to her office at 9 am? Well there's no incentive for the middle player to change anything, but for the reasons that applied in Figure 50, the two outer players are incentivised to move in to the centre, so that again we end up with two or more players oversupplying the customers in the middle. But is this three in-the-middle a Nash equilibrium? No – if the other two players stay as they are it would be worthwhile for any of the three players to move out from the middle and occupy one of the two outer positions in Figure 51. Why? Well, with all three in the middle the sales of each of them are one third of the total market that the monopolist had in Figure 49, but their sales in Figure 51 are larger because they are getting a third of a *larger total market*, and it is larger because collectively they are giving a better service to everyone outside the middle third of the beach. So where does this game end?

In fact this is a trick question: as specified, this game has no stable equilibrium for three or more players. Life is interesting here, and you always have to keep an eye on the other players, any one of whom can alter their position (strategy) which might require a compensating response from you. Welcome to oligopoly, which, under a Hotelling bounded linear positioning model, begins at three players!

The more technical readers will want to check the algebra of the above models, as a lot could hang on the aggregate laziness function of the customers, which in turn depends on
- The distribution of customers along the beach – Hotelling assumed it was uniform, but it could be anything, such as normal about the centre, or bi-modal at the extremes
- The individual pain (or cost) of getting up and walking to the vendor as a function of distance (the pain function) – Hotelling assumed it was a linear function of distance, but quadratic functions give different answers.

We won't cover that here, but interested readers should go to the original article, and then to modern general treatments such as that in Belleflamme and Peitz[115], which concludes that there are two general forces at work: a *competition effect* driving firms apart, and a *market size effect* bringing them together, and the precise specification of these functions can lead to very different outcomes.

Specific conclusions from the Hotelling model
Looking back on the three models we see that as we increase the number of players from two to three

- The likelihood of breaking trust increases, implying that an agreement between a larger number of producers is harder to sustain than with a smaller number – implying it is harder to make large cartels work than smaller ones
- However, if the game moves away from the social optimum and we have an odd number of players, and can identify the middle player, they might make a good whistle blower to call in a policeman (if one exists);

---

[115] Belleflamme P and Peitz M, 2010, *Industrial Organization: Markets and Strategies*, Cambridge University Press, Cambridge UK, Section 5.2 page 113

- Incentives to differentiate your product from the herd – if it is possible – grow far stronger as the number of players rises[116]. If there are only two restaurants in town you don't need to spend much effort differentiating yourself from the other, but if your market is a vast city, successful differentiation is crucial to surviving and thriving.

General conclusions from the linear positioning model
This model has been used as the simplest possible model of differentiation and what marketeers call 'product positioning' within an industry. Product positioning is an attempt to make explicit the mental maps that consumers use to differentiate products within an industry, and is generally viewed in several dimensions reflecting customers' perceptions of the qualities of different products in an industry. Normally the point of doing this is to plot two key dimensions at right angles on a flat screen or piece of paper and draw a 'product space map' or 'product dimension map' so as to discuss unambiguously the combinations of various qualities that consumers want, and then to link these to different market segments. Chapter 8 shows a general product space map for the business of designing supplier contracts and concessions in the utilities, while Chapter 12 applies this map to railways. Hotelling's linear positioning model can be seen as a bounded one-dimensional product space map – the simplest possible example.

The wider significance of Hotelling's model is that *for its reasonably neutral assumptions* it unambiguously shows that the competitive Nash equilibrium for a
1.   Monopoly is socially optimal and stable
2.   Duopoly is not the social optimum, but the same as monopoly – i.e. the Nash equilibrium is sub-optimal
3.   Tri-opoly does not exist

...unless there are effective policing agencies to enforce a social optimum, or the players reach cooperative solutions between themselves: these are implicit or explicit agreements, either through trust, or easy monitoring-and-recontracting, which, of course, can be seen as cartels.

---

[116] You'd think it was not hard to differentiate ice creams, but as a child in Britain in the early 1960s the author can remember a time when there were only three flavours of ice cream to eat at home. This, of course, was due to there being a duopoly of national ice cream sellers, which in turn was due to the large fixed costs of developing national brand names, and the huge sunk costs of supplying thousands of retailers with ice cream freezers, who otherwise would not have stocked ice cream. As usual, we end with sunk cost theory.

Appendix 2: The intellectual derivation of the sequence model

JS Mill's theory of natural monopolies
In 1848 the Classical economist John Stewart Mill noted the occurrence of Natural Monopolies[117]; he did not really try to explain them, but noted their prevalence among early gas and water utilities[118]. It was left to the subsequent Neoclassical economists to develop the theory of economies of scale outlined in Chapters 1 and 2. This theory argues that networks have high fixed costs and low variable costs, so the LRMC slopes continuously downwards, and the Minimum Efficient Scale is just one producer.

Baumol's contestability and the fixed cost/sunk cost thought-experiment
Following a series of academic articles Baumol, Panzar and Willig combined in 1982 to invent a new theory of natural monopolies based on sunk costs and the theory of contestability. Chapter 1 of their 1982 classic work *'Contestable Markets and The Theory of Industry Structure'*, states

> *"The key requirement of contestability in markets in which the set of techniques dictates that the size of incumbent firms be large relative to market demand is that the entry process be entirely, or almost entirely, reversible without cost. With reversible entry – that is, with costless exit – unsustainable prices will afford incentives for rational entrepreneurs to enter in fact. Such entrants need not fear changes in prices...for if and when such reactions do occur ... that firm need only exit."*
> Baumol W, Panzar J and Willig R, 1982, Contestable Markets and The Theory of Industry Structure, hardback edition, Harcourt Brace Jovanovitch, New York, page 6.

We see here the emergence of the modern definition of sunk costs as the costs which are lost forever once a firm decides to enter a market. The core difference between Baumol *et al* and the Neoclassicals boils down to this: is it really the *fixedness* of the costs of a grid or its *'sunkness'* that creates the monopoly? To illustrate this Baumol *et al* (p7) consider a thought-experiment: imagine a hypothetical pair of cities on which passenger air travel demand is just sufficient for one airline to survive – a natural monopoly. This airline must employ aircraft ("capital on wings") in its operations (whether leased or owned), which means it has high fixed costs but low sunk costs: exactly the opposite economic characteristics of a network grid. More general examples include plant leasing companies[119] which intensively use mobile (un-sunk) capital, such as construction equipment, cranes, or ships; or we can consider the stock in a retail shop. What these example all

---

[117] JS Mill, 1848, Principles of Political Economy, Book 2, Chapter 15 outlines Mill's theory. Book 5 Chapter 11describes it more fully, though without really explaining it, or resorting to use of the calculus.

[118] There were no electricity utilities and very few sewer utilities in 1848.

[119] I am indebted to Dan Elliott, now of Frontier Economics, for introducing me in 1994 to this generalised thought-experiment.

share is that their main assets are highly mobile, and saleable, with thick second-hand markets.

> *"This example suggests the role of sunk costs in determining whether or not a market is contestable [is key]. Clearly, when entry requires the sinking of substantial costs, it will not be reversible because, by definition, the sunk costs are not recoverable. However, if efficient operation requires no sunk outlays, then entry can, by and large, be presumed to be reversible, and the market can be presumed to be contestable."* Baumol et al ibid page 7.

Because all real entry decisions face some sunk costs, *zero* sunk costs is too extreme a definition of a contestable market to be of any practical use. It rules out industries like the small plumber example in the chapter where sunk costs are negligible, not zero, yet the industry, whether stylised as perfect competition or monopolistic (imperfect) competition, is evidently contestable. Of course, Baumol *et al* were academics, but their concept of costless entry usefully pre-figured the real 'Hit-and-run entry strategies' of firms in industries with very low sunk costs, such as pharmaceutical drugs which have gone off-patent. Here, a firm with flexible manufacturing capabilities to make generic pills enters the market for drugs which have sold well and just gone off-patent. On the day the patent expires (known in advance to all) the price of the drug is well above production costs but from this date the technology is freely available to all, so a nimble competitor with no marketing ambitions can produce a new generic drug quickly, publicise it cheaply to the most price-sensitive hospitals, doctors and patients, and make super-normal profits until the price falls towards production costs. Once super-normal profits evaporate the hit-and-run drug maker exits the industry, leaving it to permanent players in the industry – players with sustainable mid-game strategies – to build up production scale, or a brand name, or both.

Unfortunately, Baumol *et al* do not follow up this excellent general sequential analysis and insight, so that the remaining 470 pages of their book assume almost entirely neoclassical fixed technologies and predictable continuing cost curves. They think that the mathematical concept of subadditivity will help them. In case you had momentarily forgotten, in mathematics

A function is defined to be subadditive if $f(x+y)$ is less than $f(x) + f(y)$

- e.g. the square root function is subadditive; you can work out the above proposition for the case of $x = 9$ and $y = 16$, then for $x=25$ and $y=36$.

Trained as neoclassical economists, they instinctively apply subadditivity to neoclassical cost functions, and so define a natural monopoly as an industry where "over the entire relevant range of outputs, the firms' cost function is subadditive."[120] They then show that while economies of scale and scope are

---

[120] Definition 2A2 Natural Monopoly, Baumol *et al* page 17

sufficient to give a subadditive cost function, the converse is not true: a subadditive cost function does not necessarily imply economies of scale and scope[121]. So, in neoclassical theory it may be possible for an industry to be a natural monopoly, without exhibiting economies of scale or scope, though of course it must have a subadditive cost function – by definition!

So, subadditivity is absolutely the vital concept to grasp for the practising utility economist? Hmm; do modern utility economists focus their analyses on the subadditivity of a utility's continuing costs? Or do they accept things are as they are, look at a utility's sunk costs, past and future, and its forward-looking incremental cash costs? Baumol and Co. threw the baby out with the bathwater when they moved on beyond their general sequential analysis on page seven, which, sadly, is why the very useful concept of contestable and non-contestable industries has largely died out of the academic literature in the subsequent decades.

However, let us be crystal clear: *if* the neo-classical conditions of huge long run fixed costs with low long run variable costs apply, the LRMC (and so the LRAC) *will* continually decrease. And the cost function will be subadditive, satisfying Baumol *et al's* conditions. Furthermore, *if* conditions stabilise, and we have static demand with no technological progress, we would expect to see a monopoly eventually emerge – in the absence of public action to regulate or prevent this. The weakness of the neoclassical model is not its internal logic but *its neo-classical assumptions*. Baumol et al started from better assumptions, that sunk costs are key to making entry decisions irreversible, but in their detailed modelling completely ignored the vital insights that sunk costs are an asymmetry in time, and time can be modelled to parallel technology, as an irreversible arrow. Their modelling of customer reactions was also largely limited to static demand curves. In their defence, we should add that back in 1982 dynamic modelling of complex economic systems was limited largely to macroeconomics, and had not been generally extended to microeconomics.

The sequence model of sunk costs
The model outlined here, with irreversible technological progress and sunk costs, can be seen as a version of a standard leader-follower model in which one player enters an industry and a second entrant reacts through quantity-adjustment (Cournot, 1838), a new price (Bertrand, 1883), or by anticipating the other player's reaction function (Stackelberg, 1934). Stackelberg also explicitly discussed first mover advantage (how player 2 might leapfrog Player 1 to appropriate first mover advantage), and usefully considered price war as a 'chicken' strategy which deliberately creates temporary disequilibrium. Of course, this only makes sense if the game is repeated and the lessons learned, which, in turn, assumes continuity of investors and managements.

Extending standard game theory into repeated and sequential games

---

[121] Faulhaber's converse proposition (1975); see Baumol *et al op. cit.* pages 18-21.

undoubtedly increased the relevance of theory to the natural monopolies. But modern "sequential game theory" has evolved with the simplifying assumption that there are two players taking turns, so life is always like a game of tennis (A's turn, then B's turn, A's turn, etc.). By contrast, in reality, third and fourth players may join if they envisage enticing prospects, and a tactic that big firms routinely use to beat small firms is to launch several initiatives at once, following them up in the next time period (when it could be B's turn) with more plays, just as the little firm is reacting, so that A retains the initiative. Due to limited management resources, small firms may not have the capabilities to respond quickly, move after move, in multiple dimensions. On the other hand, small firms can beat big firms through hit-and-run strategies or other commercial guerrilla warfare tactics, where the big firm may not even know it is under attack, let alone what the rival 'customer value propositions' will be. All these real strategies reduce the usefulness of conventional sequential game analysis: only a handful of markets are actually duopolies, and to seize and retain the initiative it may be quite normal for a really dynamic player to take three turns in succession.

In sum, none of these approaches satisfactorily handles the case of calculated risk-takers investing chunks of fungible cash into sunk technology- and location-specific infrastructure that may create a public service utility. In such a game, technology, market demand, and other aspects of the business environment may change during construction of the infrastructure, or soon afterwards, and new entrants may fight with new (or vastly improved) technologies, or find some other way to appeal to customers that Mover One cannot imitate. Very few of these models treat sunk costs as an asymmetry in time, and almost none consider the case of a Second Mover with high sunk costs wondering whether they have the capabilities to enter an industry behind a First Mover who has invested, played most of his cards right, and been lucky to guess markets and technologies correctly so far – i.e. scooped the market.

To capture this effect, we need a model with time and technology as irreversible arrows (a vintage theory of capital) and a sequence of potential players considering entering a series of markets either as parallel monopolists in a series of linked markets, or rival contestants in a single homogenous market. As analysts, economists must also learn to stop racing to the end game: in cosmology, a ripple in the early universe can have galactic consequences later on. So, here, we must carefully consider the initial conditions and the evolution of the mid-game[122].

Following a career as a government economist in the 1970s and 80s, then

---

[122] Not all economists race to the end game: John Sutton's 'Market structure: Theory and evidence', Chapter 35 in Armstrong M and Porter B (editors) 2007, *Handbook of Industrial Organization Volume 3*, Elsevier BV, contains a definitive exposition of the Bounds approach to determining the number of players in a high-sunk-cost industry with, and without, product differentiation. The problem with this from a utility point of view, or from the point of view of many 21st century industries, is that technology is assumed not to change between the first entrant and subsequent ones.

four years managerial experience in very contestable industries, and thirteen years professional utility experience in the nineties and noughties, in 2007 the author came to reflect on his natural monopoly experiences, before teaching an undergraduate module on industrial policy at Oxford Brookes University Economics Department. There were no good textbooks on utility economics, so the author wrote the First edition of this textbook (Basic Network Utility Economics), published in 2013. Chapter 4 of that first edition outlined the general sequence model and highlighted the key conditions under which a first mover could scoop the market, and when it would make sense for subsequent firms to enter. The author then realised that the critical stage when sane Subsequent Movers give up, leaving the First Mover as a monopolist, lacked a formal exposition. This led him to adopt the systems modelling set out in this second edition's Chapter 4, and to make the distinction between the battle for reach (infrastructure) and the battle for market share (active customers) shown in this chapter. The model described here, though, is still quite general, and has not exhaustively tested the critical limits of what is needed to scoop the market against the full range of combinations of producer and consumer sunk costs or switching costs.

Chapter Five

Calculating long run marginal costs of a network utility

The sequence model allows technological progress and permanently growing incomes to co-exist with inefficiency and government intervention. It then usefully determines the number of players in an industry where entry barriers – sunk costs – are significant. This seems a more reasonable approximation to reality than the assumptions needed to make static neo-classical models work. Let us now use this framework to calculate the dynamic equivalent of long run marginal costs in a world of inefficiency and technological progress (Long Run Incremental Costs) for the best known natural monopoly of all: water. The technique, however, is general, and can be applied to any firm or industry.

LRMC in a growing economy: Long Run Incremental Costs

In 1968 Ralph Turvey[123] proposed a practical new way to calculate forward-looking Long Run Marginal Costs for the electricity industry – an industry with considerable technological progress and where demand was then projected to rise continually. Policy makers wanted to develop a rule that would link electricity prices to the expected long run marginal cost of supplying electricity. Turvey's solution, now known as Long Run Incremental Costs, was a practical way of discounting expected future investment and running costs in a dynamic industry. His method is perfectly general and rapidly came to be adopted by professional economists as the standard approach to calculating Long Run Marginal Costs in a time-series sense for a firm or an industry.

How to calculate LRIC for a firm or industry

To calculate a Long Run Incremental Cost (LRIC) we take three broad steps:
1. Calculate the lifetime forward-looking cash costs (capital and operating costs) for each new supply option using the best current technology, and discount each to a Net Present Cost;

---

[123] Turvey R, 1968, Optimal Pricing and Investment in Electricity Supply, Allen & Unwin, London and MIT Press, Cambridge, Chapter 4. Page 44 outlines the method of discounting the investment and running costs needed to supply an incremental unit of demand each year for ever, thus equating LRMC in the time series sense with LRIC.

2   Compare these lifetime Net Present Costs and rank them in sequence, so that we develop the cheapest first, then the next cheapest etc. – to create a least-cost, or *optimal investment path* for the firm or industry;

3.   At any moment in time the Long Run Cost of an incremental perennial unit of supply (the LRIC) for the firm or industry is the latest cost of the optimal investment path discounted to today.

To understand Turvey's marginal cost logic heuristically, imagine an industry currently supplying 100 units a year. However, demand is expected to rise in the future, so the firm or industry has developed an optimal investment plan – a least-cost path of planned investments to meet future demand out to the year 2100[124]. Now suppose a new customer arrives demanding one more unit a year from this year forever. The LRIC is the cost of bringing forward the entire optimal investment path for the industry by one hundredth of a year – or 3.65 days – which is the burden this customer, with their new order, has placed on demand, and thus on the investment programme. Therefore we should charge them for their one permanent extra unit of supply the Long Run Incremental Cost – the cost of bringing forward the investment programme by 3.65 days.

While the LRIC approach was developed for the electricity industry, and is standard procedure in many industries, the most interesting application of the concept, as Turvey himself acknowledges, is to calculate the marginal cost of environmental resources such as water.

Calculating the Long Run Incremental Cost of a piped water system

The LRIC starts from an assumption that we live in a growing economy, with positive income elasticities for the product in question. So, in this instance, long term water demand is assumed to be growing, due to growing per capita incomes or rising population.

The Long Run Incremental Cost of bulk treated water

To optimise long run supply solutions we first need to calculate the long run incremental costs of storing, abstracting and treating raw water. To do this the engineers first assess all the major long term supply possibilities, costing them for capital and running costs, and then calculate average lifetime running costs by dividing the time-discounted total supply over the lifetime of the scheme by the time-discounted capital and running costs for each solution.

For simplicity, let us suppose that the next new scheme will be needed right away. Figure 52 shows a chart of our schemes, starting with the Chairman of the Board's favourite, Scheme 'C':

---

[124] Naturally the discounted value of almost anything that happens out then or beyond is negligible, while our ability to predict technologies available then is even smaller.

Figure 52: Average lifetime costs for each long term supply solution

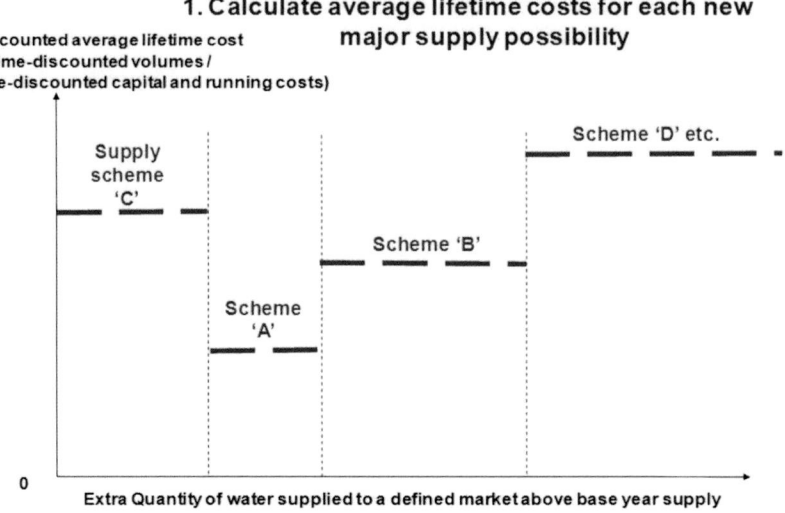

Now we rank these schemes in order, starting with the cheapest first. Figure 53 shows the result: we must start with Scheme A immediately, because the extra supply is needed immediately and A is the cheapest. Once that has been commissioned, installed and all its capacity used (in X years time), we will commission Scheme B. Only then will we start planning Scheme C. Someone is deputed to tell the Chairman the bad news that Scheme C will not start for a long time.

Figure 53: Step 2 – calculate the optimal investment path for a firm by ranking schemes by cost

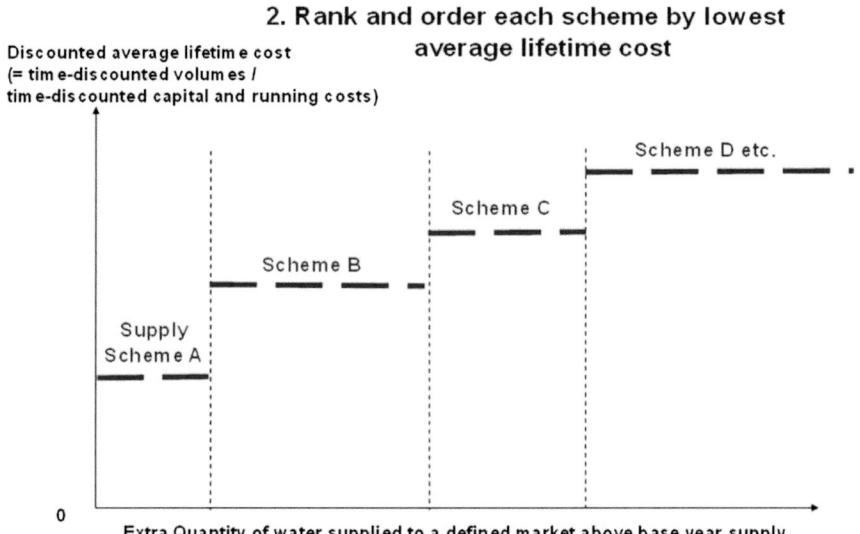

Next we calculate the LRIC for each scheme in succession, as in Figure 34. The Long Run Incremental Cost is the discounted cost of bringing forward the next scheme's capital and running costs by an amount sufficient to meet the increment of supply needed.

Figure 54: Step 3 – the LRIC of abstracting, storing and treating piped water in bulk

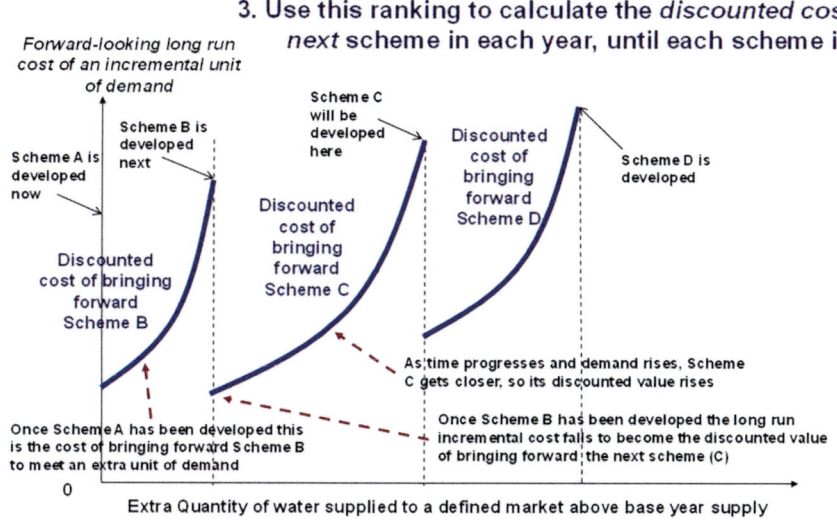

These LRICs inevitably rise as the date for commissioning the next scheme nears: once we have installed Scheme A an increment of demand which brings forward scheme B by three months, or a year, is not expensive if we are bringing forward a large capital cost that will be incurred many years from now by, say, 3-12 months. However, as the date for scheme B nears an increment of long run demand which brings this capital spend forward to next year or this year has a huge cost, so the LRIC rises as we approach the ordering date for the next scheme. However, once Scheme B has been commissioned our LRIC falls again, discontinuously, to a new level reflecting the costs and distant date for Scheme C, the date being determined largely by the capacity of the newly-commissioned scheme, Scheme B.

This weird, discontinuous and rising LRIC surprises some academics and many non-utility economists, but has been double-checked by professional economists, utility engineers and utility regulators. The British water industry regulator Ofwat first issued guidance on calculating LRICs for water and wastewater in 1994, and the latest guidance can be found on its website.

The LRIC for water transmission and distribution grids

Once we have the LRIC for water storage, abstraction, and treatment, we need to calculate the LRIC for the other key parts of the value chain shown in Figure 15. We start with the LRIC for water transmission and distribution grids, which accounts for 30-40% of the total cost of supplying drinking water to a typical household.

One key cost of a modern water grid that JS Mill could not possibly have foreseen in 1848 is the cost of the IT system needed to monitor a grid. These IT systems not only list all the underground assets for accounting purposes, but also maintain registers of the grid's current state, availability, age, condition, performance and many other vital indicators. This has led some commentators to draw the conclusion that the IT system is a large fixed cost, and thus a cause of scale economies. But this is wrong. As well as the hardware, software and set-up costs of an IT system, which are both fixed and sunk once installed, over the lifetime of a grid IT system – two or three decades – the main part of the costs are those of migrating good data from old IT systems to new ones, of checking the data, and then ensuring that all new data entered on the system is both good and up-to-date. Figure 55 shows how IT system costs grow as the grid it is serving grows:

Figure 55: The lifetime costs of a grid's IT system for small, medium and large grids

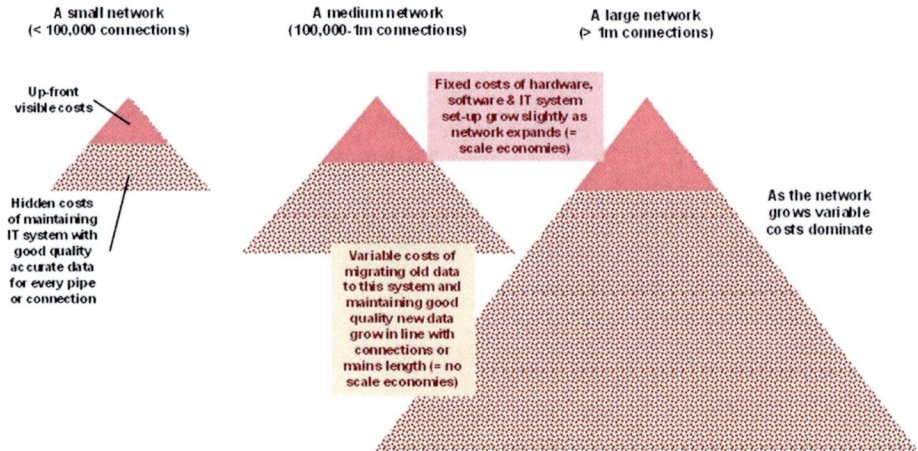

Not many people outside utility industries appreciate how much time and effort goes into maintaining grid IT systems, nor the limitations of these systems[125], and how much of this effort is directly linked to the size of the grid – i.e. is a variable cost in the long run. This, of course, means that the LRIC of an IT system falls, but not to zero, or anything like it. This is shown as the curved line down in Figure 56 – the LRIC's of all the main cost drivers in a water grid:

---

[125] Garbage in, garbage out was never more true than with IT systems about underground assets. Maintaining data quality is really difficult in old systems which have suffered decades of emergency repairs, or war or seismic damage.

Figure 56: The Long Run Incremental Costs of all the main cost drivers in a water grid

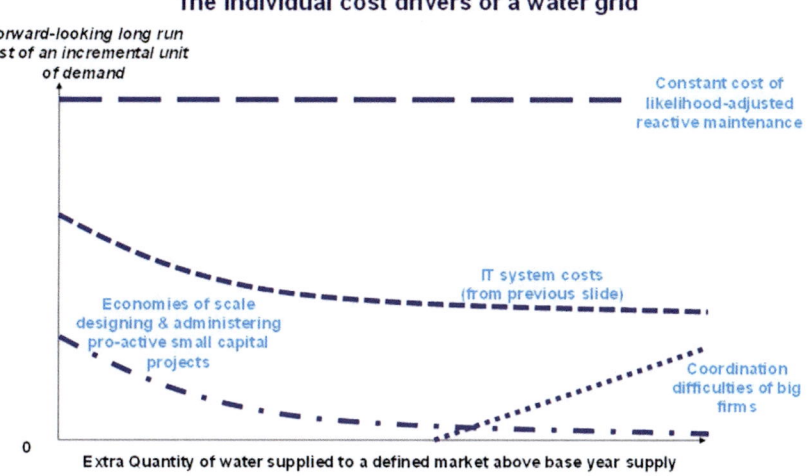

Although IT system costs are an important cost driver in any modern grid, the largest item in the grid's discounted lifetime costs, as Figure 56 shows, must be the actual costs of repairs, or *reactive maintenance*, as the engineers call it, and this will be constant – every extra connection or ten metres of main is an extra asset that can go wrong and there is no reason to suppose that this will decline as the system gets larger. Why should the last connection, or the last ten metres of main, be cheaper to maintain than the first connection or first ten metres? So the bulk of transmission and distribution grid costs should, in theory, be flat.

However a small part of maintenance is planned in advance; this is called *pro-active maintenance* and is the ideal goal of all maintained grids. Indeed large pipelines on offshore oil production platforms, or large pipelines carrying oil and gas above ground, or inside oil refineries and petrochemical works, are generally maintained in this pro-active manner, preventative maintenance being thought to be cheaper than waiting for an accident to happen. But with underground assets useful preventative maintenance is in practice either far too difficult to identify in advance, or simply too expensive. Consequently most utilities – particularly water utilities – wait for accidents to happen and then go and fix them – i.e. *they react*. And when maintenance work is planned there are set-up costs of designing, administering and monitoring the work, so that there are mild economies of scale up to a small size, as shown in Figure 56.

Finally, some observers familiar with small and medium-sized water companies argue there are diseconomies of scale with large networks found in big cities, which lead the LRIC to rise. This is because although theoretically large IT systems can model large grids, migrating and maintaining completely good quality data on these models is difficult, expensive, and rarely achieved in practice at present. Consequently, errors between the theoretical model held on the computer and reality can rapidly creep in, causing considerable inefficiencies in operating large networks. By contrast, the grid networks of smaller cities and towns, with all their main idiosyncracies, can be remembered by a single human brain – that of the town's water engineer, or by two or three senior officers of a medium-sized water company, provided that company has a long and stable management team. These officers are thus able to check the data quality with what they know to be the case in their heads, while their opposite numbers in larger companies do not have this first-hand knowledge because a) the system is too big for one human brain to comprehend it all, and b) they are rarely in post longer than 2-4 years in large companies, and so cannot build up the experience that small company managers can. We thus have plausible reasons for supposing dis-economies of scale, particularly if larger companies suffer from difficulties of co-ordination between departments (you may well have experienced this in your own dealings with utilities) or shortness of time in post by senior managers, which in the author's experience, is far more common in larger utilities than smaller utilities. Figure 36 again shows this possibility.

We are now in a position to combine all the knowledge into a single forward-looking Long Run Incremental Cost curve for a typical water transmission or distribution grid, noting that identical logic applies to the same core parts of the pipe and wire grids for electricity and gas – their core monopoly functions of transmission and distribution. So Figure 57 shows what we believe to be the resulting Long Run Marginal Cost of a water, gas or electricity distribution or transmission grid:

Figure 57: Step 4: the LRIC of a water distribution grid

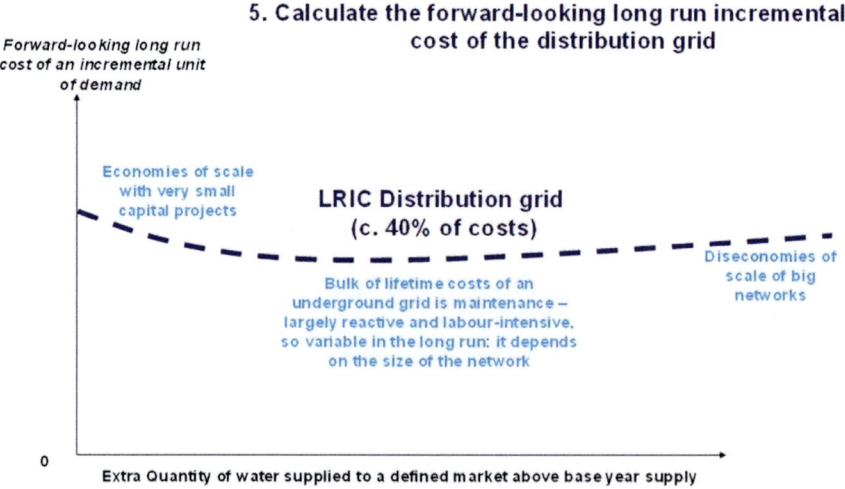

To summarise, neo-classical theory strongly suggests that the static Long Run Marginal Cost of a grid should continually decrease. However, many experienced water industry engineers, managers, regulators, and economists would strongly dispute this: by-and-large the lifetime capital and running costs of a grid that serves 3 million people will be roughly three times the cost of a grid that serves 1 million people. This is chiefly because economies of scale in construction planning are soon exhausted and the continuing costs of an underground grid are mostly reactive maintenance or repairs, which is a labour-intensive series of sporadic call-outs at unpredictable times and diverse geographical locations. Having three times as big a grid to maintain means that on average a company will need thrice as many maintenance staff. So, once we get over economies of scale at a small level – less than around 100,000 connections – the LRIC of a grid should be roughly flat, possibly rising if a grid gets to be horrendously unwieldy, as may have been the case with Transco's eight gas Local Distribution Zones in 2005.

LRIC of water retailing and testing
Retailing water in the 21st century is an activity that has economies of scale because complex IT systems are needed to register and monitor millions of customers, and the suppliers of these systems maintain that they have high fixed costs of installation but their running costs should be low. The author would not disagree with this – adding one extra customer on to a system does not increase costs very much even over the lifetime of the system, and customers usually contact you if their data is incorrect, unlike a buried pipe that is leaking, or a valve that is working but not fully. Isn't it ironic that the one part of the water value chain JS Mill could not have considered in 1848, the retailing of water, is the one part that today fits his model so well?

In addition modern water retailing requires the testing of millions of sample of drinking water a day. This is usually done in specialised laboratories where there are small economies of scale, but once the process has become automated there are few remaining economies of scale.

Figure 58: Step 5: the LRIC of retailing water

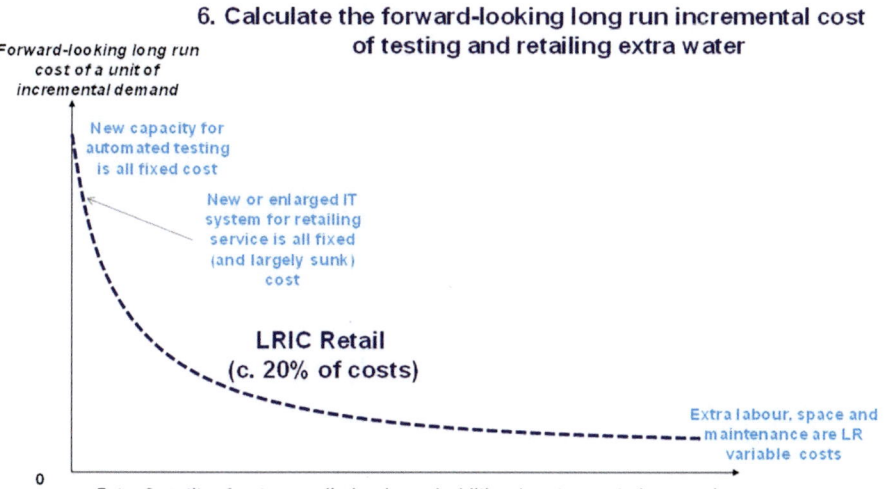

Summary LRIC for drinking water

To create an LRIC for all treated water we combine the LRIC curves of the main component parts shown in Figure 59:

Figure 59: Step 6: add all the LRICs together

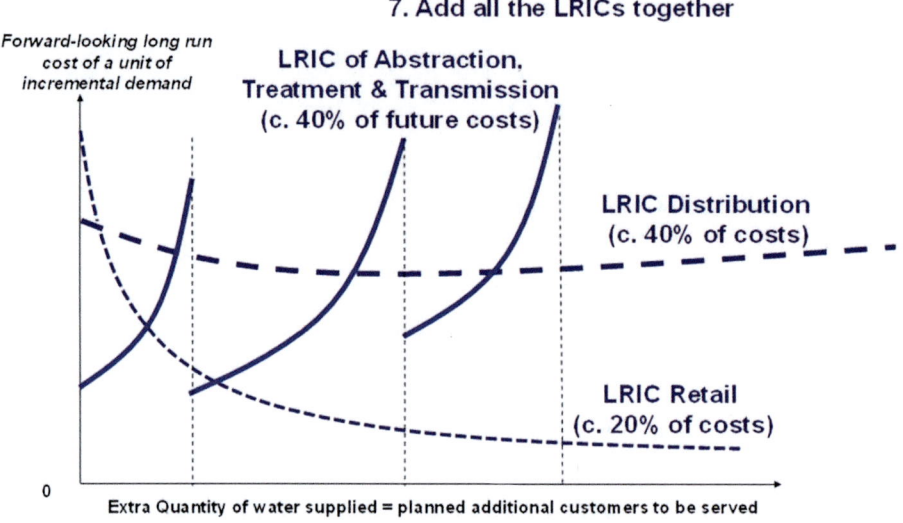

The resulting chart is shown in Figure 60:

Figure 60: Step 7: Summary: the Long Run Incremental Cost of piped water

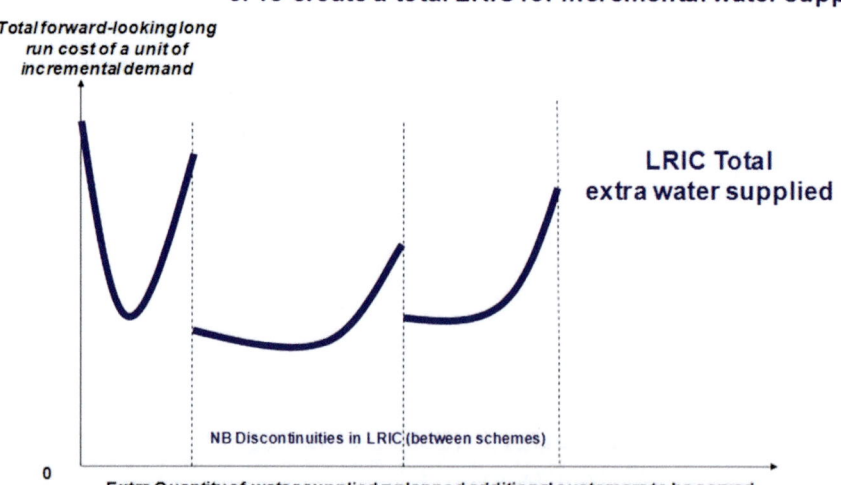

So...our strongest real monopoly, water, actually has *a discontinuous and rising 'LRMC' curve*. Well, Marshall didn't predict that, but can be forgiven as he could not possibly have predicted 21st century utility technologies, or good

20th century economic techniques. Their modern neoclassical followers writing microeconomics textbooks, however, have some explaining to do.

The LRIC depicted in Figure 40 causes terminal consequences for neo-classical economic theories of water grids. Theoretically there is a danger of multiple discontinuous solutions, particularly if demand were to increase and then to fall back. And there is a serious problem if demand falls back, as it is expensive to re-engineer a buried pipe network to be smaller in a city where the population is falling (e.g. Liverpool or Manchester in the UK, Philadelphia or Detroit in the USA).

Fortunately the demand curve for water is nearly vertical (its price elasticity is zero) so if demand is either rising or falling constantly each discontinuity occurs only once, not twice. But this is small comfort to broken-hearted neo-classicists, who will be crying into their beer.

If long term demand is rising, water is such an essential service (demand is so strong and price-inelastic) that a rational unregulated water monopolist would charge an entry-deterring price, rather than risk a second entrant. In England the first economic regulator of the water industry calculated that this would result in prices roughly three times higher than current levels in the late 1990s. Consequently, as a political reality, the author believes water prices always have been, and always will be, regulated to prices well below entry-deterring levels.

Chapter Six

Measuring utility outputs properly, and the evolution of utility value chains

Given how frequently utilities turn out to be monopolies, consumers and taxpayers generally want reassurance that their local utility is using its "monopoly money" efficiently. Consequently, comparing the efficiency of utilities is a major feature of some regulatory systems. We will examine the main ways to measure utilities' efficiency in Chapter 7, but first we need to take a close theoretical look at exactly how economists should measure the output of each stage of a utility's value chain, and then look at how these value chains are evolving in the longer term, as societies become richer and more demanding.

We will concentrate on the classic energy and water utilities, and obviously start by using the main stages of utility production and distribution shown in the value added chain of Figure 8. Those main stages are
- bulk production
- grid transmission and distribution
- retailing.

However, we start with the simple observation made in Chapter 2 that a utility's output is not simply the quantity of energy or water produced, distributed, or sold, but also the service provided with that commodity good. This service element becomes much more important as incomes rise in the 21st century. In addition, many utility outputs are non-obvious – the public has very little awareness of what has to be done to deliver their energy or water, and why it might be a great deal more expensive in one location than another, or why bills have risen so much in the last twenty years. This "work done" is a true output of the industry, even if the public is unaware of it, and must be measured properly if we are to make fair comparisons between similar utilities in different locations. So, a member of the public who just pays their bills and has no interest in utilities can remain ignorant of these factors if they choose, but a good regulator or utility economist should not.

Bulk production
Energy bulk production
On small islands or in remote locations, where transport costs are high, a single energy source which happens to be local will naturally be favoured over expensive competing energy from overseas or from distant neighbours. Thus, due to a geological monopoly, or demand being smaller than the Minimum Efficient Scale, many small islands or cities in remote locations have only one power station, one gas field, or one LNG terminal. This means that the bulk energy production stage in this society is a monopoly, which one would not want to leave unregulated and in private hands, even if the next stage were a public sector monopsony: single seller / single buyer price negotiations are well known to have no particular solution which is stable.

In large societies, however, as Figure 8. shows, bulk production of energy is a contestable industry because the value of the product is high in relation to its transport cost, and so bulk energy is transported considerable distances, and opened up to competition from rival producers. In these cases economists would generally recommend a separation of production from transmission and distribution, to enable the bulk producers to compete in some kind of market for bulk energy.

Water and wastewater bulk treatment
As the wastewater section explained earlier, due to the gravity-fed design of sewage systems, nearly all wastewater treatment works have an innate monopoly of the sewage supplied to them, so efficiency comparisons of sewage treatment plants are an essential task for tax payers, consumers, and regulators concerned about value-for-money. And the same goes for the next stage in sewage treatment, sludge treatment – it is almost always a local monopoly.

Regarding bulk water treatment, in theory a market could be designed to enable water treatment works to compete with one another using the grid's transmission network to bring water from competing sources to a single 'point' of bulk demand. In water a feature such as London's Ring Main – a vast treated water storage reservoir and water main surrounding London – could correspond to major sub-stations in the electricity industry or City Gates in the gas industry, so a market could be established to make water treatment works compete to supply London.

But this has not happened yet, so in reality water regulators find themselves trying to compare the efficiency of wastewater and water treatment utilities or, where regulators have powers to demand the data, comparing the efficiency of individual plants. But what is the output of a water treatment plant? Figure 61 shows some of the problems when comparing the outputs of three different works:

144 | Infrastructure & Utility Economics - Chapter 6

Figure 61: the output of three different water treatment works A, B and C

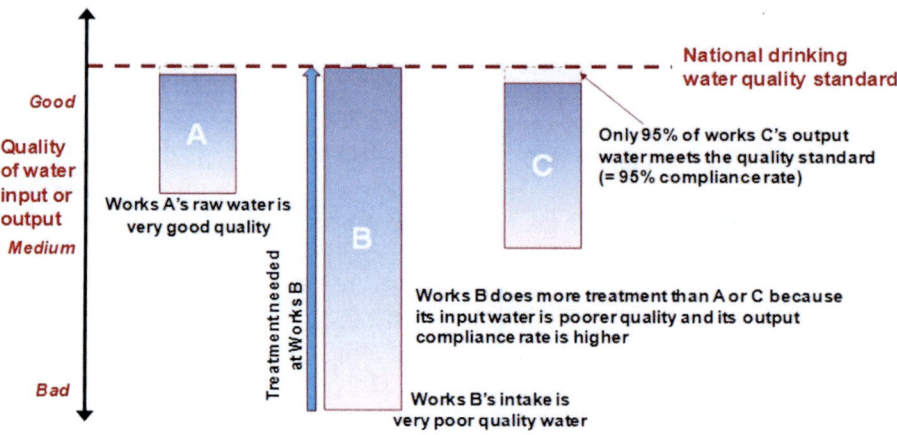

Treatment work done = Quantity of water put into distribution X Treatment needed X Compliance rate

The job of a water treatment works is to turn water of naturally varying quality into a standardised product that meets the quality set by the water quality regulator; we assume this standard is uniform, and does not vary within each State or country. However, the input water quality does vary: some raw water sources are naturally very pure and need minimal treatment, while other water treatment works have to take water from muddy rivers with many physical, chemical or biological impurities that is far more expensive to process. Figure 61 shows three treatment works, A, B and C working with different qualities of input water supplied, Because they have different compliance rates with the quality regulator's standard we have to say that the work done by each plant is the Quantity of water treated x the treatment needed x the compliance rate. If all three had the same cost per unit of water delivered we would have to say that works B is the most efficient because it is doing the most work – it takes the worst quality water in and produces the best quality water out of the three treatment works, so its output per € of costs put in is the best.

We have a mirror image of this problem measuring the output of a sewage (wastewater) treatment works. We can say the quality of sewage is not strained, but is standard; it drops gently from the drains of all houses and across a hundred human houses is quite standard. So the quality of *influent* (the wastewater received) in most sewage treatment works tends to be uniform. But the quality of *effluent* (the water discharged out) is not: each treatment works discharges into a different body of water and the discharge consent standards – the quality of effluent the works is designed to achieve – should reflect the size of the load received (usually measured as the domestic population served, or its equivalent) and the size and quality of the receiving water. So the environmental bodies responsible for setting discharge consent standards tend to set tighter standards for small streams receiving sewage effluent in the steep headwaters of a river, and lower standards for treatment works discharging into big rivers, deep estuaries, or an open ocean with strong offshore currents.

Figure 62 shows how wastewater treatment work can be measured and compared for three different works, A, B, and C:

Figure 62: Comparing the outputs of three different sewage treatment works

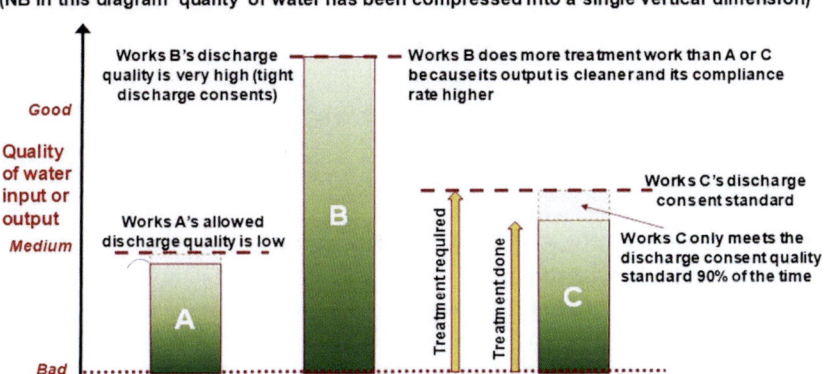

Treatment work done = Quantity of sewage handled X Treatment required X Compliance rate

In this diagram again all the many physical, chemical and biological properties of water quality have been compressed to a single vertical dimension, with good quality shown at the top and bad quality at the bottom. On average over a year all three works receive the same quality influent, but works A has a low discharge consent standard and so does not have to do a lot of work to improve its sewage before discharging it, while B has to do a lot more: it will have more complicated treatment processes to 'polish' the effluent, with more tanks to maintain and more cleaning, more types of sludge to dispose of, and more pumping. It is therefore reasonable to suppose that works B should have higher costs per unit of load received than works A. And although works C has quite a modest target of work required, it is failing to meet this standard 10% of the time, so its work done is the load (quantity, or population served) times the work required by the consent standard times the works' compliance rate of 90%.

Plant economies of scale in the water industry
In practice a reasonable-sized water or wastewater company will have many treatment works that are small or even tiny, serving outlying villages or hamlets, as well as larger works serving towns or cities. Every water engineer knows there are strong *plant* economies of scale for water and wastewater treatment works, caused fundamentally because much of the plant is circular in cross-section: costs tend to increase in proportion to the circumference of the circle, while throughput increases with the area inside the circle so, other things being equal, the unit cost of treating a litre of water, or a human body's waste for a day, is much cheaper for a large town than for a small rural settlement. As

usual these plant economies are most pronounced at the very small level, and tend to flatten out once the population served exceeds a million or so[126]. Water engineers naturally try to exploit these economies of scale whenever possible, but they cannot force people to live together, so in fact this clustering or lack of clustering is a major determinant of a water firm's treatment costs, and so is another factor which is totally beyond the managers' ability to control or even influence. A rural water or wastewater company is going to have higher unit treatment costs than a large city: living in the modern countryside has its costs and someone has to pay them.

NB The fact that there are strong plant economies of scale in treatment does not mean that there are wider economies of scale *at the level of the whole network* (treatment works plus grids plus retail function). The author has heard many investment bankers promote takeovers and mergers[127] suggesting that merging two neighbouring companies will create economies of scale, but the only thing that could cause plant economies of scale to reduce average unit costs across the entire network would be to pipe one town's sewage or water to the other, or to move one town's entire population into the other. Simply merging two water companies is never going to achieve either of these, persuading humans to move houses so as to lower their utility bills does not generally work, and indeed both options assume the larger town has free spare capacity available to handle all the new load. If new capacity has to be built to achieve the saving this will certainly be a more expensive route than treating the water or sewage in their existing separate locations.

Indeed just about the only circumstance in which plant economies can be exploited to reduce costs across a network is *if new capacity has to be built anyway* – i.e. all options involve extra capital costs – *and* the savings from plant economies exceed the extra capital and transport costs of the extra grid. In this case the companies should compare the discounted lifetime capital and running costs of the two options of building extra capacity in the two existing works, with the capital cost of building the grid and one large works, and the extra running costs of the grid and the single larger works.

Thus a proper efficiency comparison of collections of water or wastewater treatment plants between firms should allow for two factors well beyond management's influence:
    1.   the differing qualities of raw input water at water treatment works, or different discharge consent standards at each wastewater works, and
    2.   population clustering permitting *individual plant* economies of scale.

---

[126] For construction reasons, or for reasons of space, there tends to be a maximum size for every kind of cylindrical plant, so that treatment plant for very large cities tend to have repeated cylinders rather than one huge cylinder. Obviously, at this stage in the processing, basic engineering economies of scale have been exhausted.

[127] i.e. clever, highly-motivated, people promoting any deal you can imagine, in order to earn their annual bonus.

Grids

Since a grid is the heart of a network utility monopoly, assessing grid outputs is a key task when assessing the efficiency of a network utility. We recall that the 'output' of a transmission or distribution grid is *not* the quantity of load distributed, but the network's availability and ability to deliver its load to all final outlets at the times and places specified by customers, together with several other dimensions of service quality, and other exogenous cost-drivers which management of the utility cannot control or influence. Among these is the geography of the territory served, local legal constraints or customs, and decisions made by past politicians, regulators or management teams which constrain the network's capabilities today. So the 'scale' variable is not a simple Q for Quantity of output, but an entire 'vector' of potential outputs, each one of which can be a significant cost-driver beyond the ability of the current management team to influence.

To give some examples of exogenous geographical factors well outside the control or influence of a utility management team that can drive up grid costs considerably, consider the general geographical *clustering* of customers' houses in an area, and the number of connections per customer – which affects all utilities – as well as the effects of the *hilliness* of an area on a water company's costs.

Population clustering

Grid utilities do not choose where their customers are: as monopolies they are usually obliged to serve all the customers in a given area, and, over time, it is the customers, or the planning authority, or the town council, or economic or social forces – but certainly not the utility's management – who choose where to place customers' houses. But clustering of customers' houses is a good thing for a network utility because it reduces the average distance between houses, and so reduces the length of main the utility needs to install and then maintain, as Figure 63 shows:

Figure 63: How house clustering reduces mains length and costs

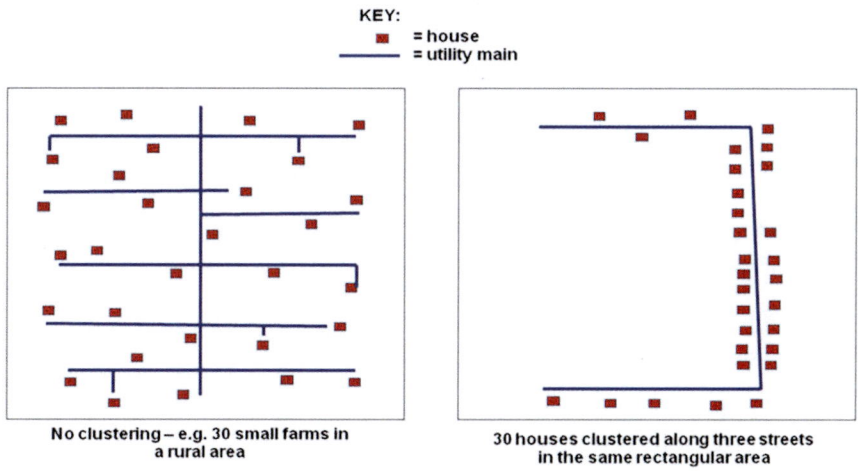

Each rectangle in Figure 63 has 30 houses in the same area but the tightly clustered rectangle on the right has a far shorter length of main than is needed to service the maze of spread out farms in the rectangle on the left. The longer the main needed to serve a given number of customers the higher a utility's costs, *ceteris paribus*, and so utilities with the most house clustering (cities) should generally have lower costs than rural utilities – other things being equal, of course.

Connections per person
The most extreme form of human house clustering is the urban block of apartments. These range from two-storey buildings to tower blocks more than a hundred floors high. As explained in Chapter 1 the utility company is not responsible for the distribution or collection system that is internal to a building, as these are the owners' assets and responsibilities, so the utility company's responsibilities cease at the meter at the property boundary, which counts as one connection, even though it may serve a thousand people.

At the other extreme we have a detached house where a single person lives. This is a very common kind of end-connection for wealthier single people, or an elderly person whose spouse has died. In this case we have an extreme: one connection = one customer = one person served[128]. But in most countries the commonest arrangement is one connection per house, so one connection = one customer = several people. An overall ratio found nowadays by many European and American utilities is that an average household typically has about two and a half people in it – in other words that a typical utility serves two and a half times as many people as it has connections.

The relevance of this is that a utility does not choose the type of home its customers live in – the customers do, given the prevailing housing options and pressures in their area. And each network connection is an asset that ultimately needs maintenance and can go wrong. So if two utilities service the same mains length but one has just city centre apartment blocks while the other serves thousands of individual suburban houses, then, other things being equal the city-centre utility should have lower costs than the rural or suburban utility[129].

The default measures of scale for a utility grid: mains length and number of connections
So fundamental engineering dictates that the two prime characteristics of any utility grid are its prime assets, its prime work-creators, and so its prime indicators

---

[128] In fact the most extreme is a large detached house with several utility connections and just one wealthy resident. This is quite commonly seen in houses with more than one broadband landline.

[129] NB The responsibility – and costs – of pumping heavy tap water up to the top of a tall tower block lies with its owner, not the local water utility. So, you'll be relieved to know, the climax of the film 'The Towering Inferno' celebrates the destruction of private property, not public assets.

of a grid's scale. These are, as just described, its length of mains and the number of connections it has to operate and maintain. For a *transmission* grid we may define 'connections' as the 'stepping-down' points such as sub-stations in electricity, city-gates for gas, or pumping booster stations and pressure-release points for water. For a *distribution* grid the number of connections is, mostly, the number of customer connections. Some economists might argue we should add the number of customers, as well, because the more customers a utility serves the more potential complainers it has, and the more complaints it has to investigate, the higher its costs will be. However, customer numbers and connection numbers are usually very highly correlated, so if one is going to include all three then one should divide number of connections by number of customers to give connections per customer, or its inverse, customers per connection. But if most customers are honest, though occasionally mistaken, then complainers complain ultimately only about real problems with a white noise of mistakes on top, and the real problems are either faults in the mains or faults in the connections. So the author believes that *the true scale measures of a grid are still fundamentally mains length and number of connections*, with a stochastic 'white noise' on top.

Hilliness as a driver of water distribution costs
An additional geographical factor that affects only water grids is height. Height above sea level does not matter for electricity, gas, sewerage, telecoms, posts, or transport, but water is cheap and heavy, so transport costs are a high proportion of its final delivered cost. There is no getting away from fundamental physics that to pump water to the top of a hill requires more energy – and hence more expense – than letting water run down a pipe to a house at the bottom of the hill.

Of course water engineers are not daft and try to obtain water for high communities from as high a source as they can, taking advantage of nature's generosity (the warm atmosphere) in lifting water thousands of metres high when it is evaporated over seas, lakes or woods. But almost all physical geographies require some pumping of water. Figure 64 shows how water is lifted in a largely flat area and describes some of the main concepts used by water engineers.

In Figure 64 raw water is obtained from a borehole in an aquifer and from a river. Both sources of water are low-lying and require pumps to lift the water up to the level of the treatment works. The vertical distance the water is lifted is the amount of potential energy given to the water by the pump, which is called the 'static pumping head'. If a company operates several sources then the *pumping head of its entire treatment network is the average of all the sources' pumping heads weighted by their contribution to total input*.

Figure 64: Lifting water in a flat area

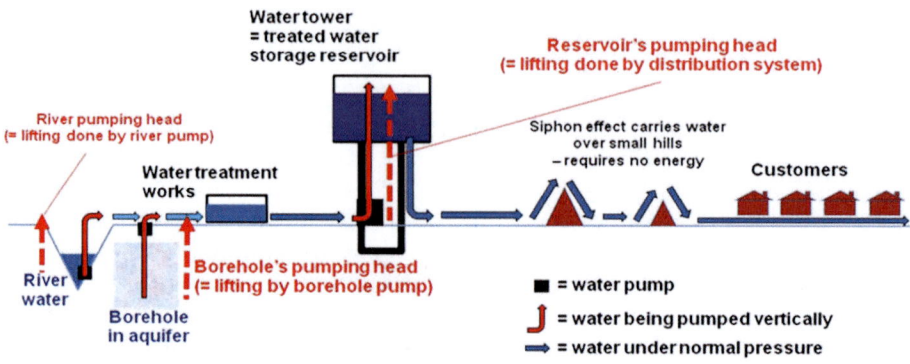

Once treated the water needs to be lifted up for general distribution purposes. Treated water is normally pumped up to a large high storage reservoir – the water towers you have no doubt noticed on many high places. The vertical lift up to the top of the reservoir is called the reservoir's pumping head. Water flows out of the reservoir by gravity and out along miles of distribution pipes to the centres of demand – cities, town and villages. If there are small hills between the main storage reservoir and the customers, provided there is no air leak or break of pressure in the pipe, the siphon effect will carry the water up over small hills and then down again to the customers on the other side.

Now consider distributing water in a hilly area, as shown in Figure 65:

Figure 65: Lifting water in a hilly area

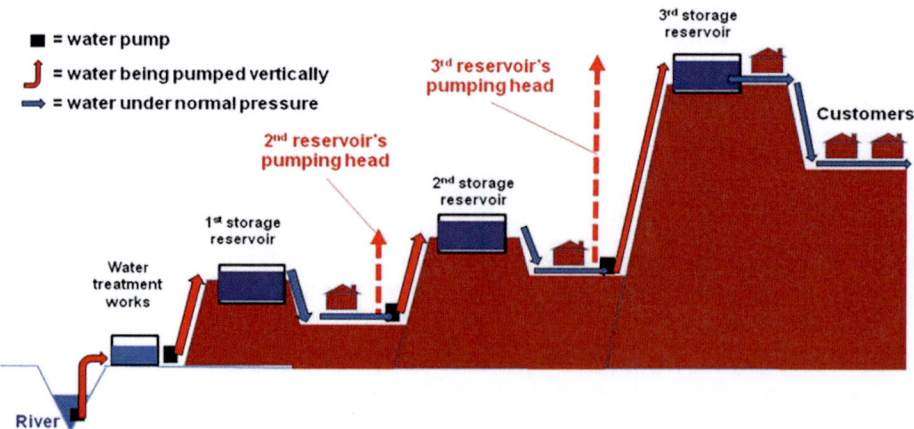

As in a flat area water is lifted by the treatment system from its source to the treatment works, and then it is lifted to the first treated water storage reservoir. This gives it sufficient lift for the first settlement, but it needs to be lifted further for higher towns or villages, and then higher still for the highest reservoir and highest houses on the grid. The distribution grid's total pumping head is the average of all the reservoirs' pumping heads weighted by the distribution input of each reservoir, so it should be clear that the pumping head for a hilly area will be higher than for a largely flat area, and that pumping head is an objective measure of the pumping needed to service a water company's particular piece of geography[130].

To summarise, the outputs of all utility grids can be considered to be the length of mains actively serviced, and the number of live connections supplied, but in the case of water grids we also have to consider the amount of lifting, or pumping head, that their human and physical geography requires them to do. In addition, we also have to remember the quality of the service grids supply, and any other constraints or service conditions imposed on the utilities being compared.

Retail

Fairly obviously the retail part of a utility's functions is a contestable section of the value chain. Chapter 1 lists the main retail functions as

"...customer identification, tariff offering, contract signing, meter reading, billing, debt collection, disconnection, reconnection, and new connections."

These are straightforward tasks revolving around the customer, so the prime indicator of the output of a utility retail business must be the number of customers. As a secondary measure of retail output service levels may vary considerably between countries, states and towns, particularly in rich countries, so any fair comparison between utilities must measure the key service levels accurately. Typical service metrics might include customer satisfaction survey results, customer contact response times (to phone calls, emails, messages), quality of responses to queries, proportion of bills based on actual (not estimated) meter readings, etc. Naturally for these different measures to be used in a rigorous cost comparison the definitions used must be common – e.g. the same customer satisfaction survey, the same definition of quality of response etc.

Growth of utility value chains in the long term

Delivered energy value chains

One can readily appreciate that utility outputs are complex and multi-dimensio-

---

[130] NB This definition of 'static' pumping head excludes dynamic pumping head, which is the energy loss by water friction rubbing against the inside of pipes when travelling long horizontal distances.

nal. As societies become richer the service elements of utility output become more important: a rich Californian household is going to demand a 24-hour service 365 days a year while a household in sub-Saharan Africa may be immensely grateful to receive any electricity, gas or water for more than eight hours a day and a hundred days a year. Yet fundamentally a kilowatt of electricity or a kilocalorie of methane has not changed since they were scientifically defined in the nineteenth century, and once the supplier has achieved 24-hour x 365-day supply most customers do not think much more about their electricity or gas, other than as a cost to be minimised. Of course the social utility of what households can do with the same energy (have better lighting, cook more food, drive further) has undeniably increased but this extra utility is absorbed as additional consumer surplus, and so is not part of the marketed value chain. So delivered energy value chains have not substantially changed in recent decades. If we combine this with a conventional assumption of modest but steady technological progress in each utility industry it is likely that the delivered price of a unit of electricity or gas should fall decade over the decades – assuming constant utility efficiency and a constant real price of primary energy. You may like to check this yourself using locally available energy prices, a GDP or consumer price deflator, and bearing in mind major changes in real primary energy prices since your price series begins.

The long run evolution of water and wastewater value chains

Water and wastewater provision in poor countries

Everyone agrees that safe and adequate water and wastewater provision are essential for human health, and have been deemed since 1976 to be part of the 'Basic Needs' of every human[131]. At the turn of the 21st century the United Nations set eight Millennium Development Goals (MDGs) for the world to achieve by 2015. Goal 7C aimed to halve the proportion of the world without access to safe drinking water (from a base year of 1990), and to halve the practice of "open defecation"[132]. In fact, by 2015 the world had more than met the clean water target (down from 24% of the world without access to safe drinking water to 9%) but had more difficulty with the wastewater target, partly because in 2000 the 1990 base year had been overestimated: we now think the number of people openly defecating fell from 1300 million in 1990 to one billion in 2015, which is a fall from 25% of the world's population to 14%[133]. In 2015 the MDGs were replaced by a more rigorous and internally coherent set of Sustainable Development Goals (SDGs) for 2030, of which SDG 6 aims to "ensure access to water and sanitation for all"[134].

---

[131] The term was first introduced by the International Labour Organisation at their 1976 World Employment Conference.

[132] Open defecation is not using a lavatory, but defecating straight onto the ground or into water. As well as the environmental effects of human faeces, you can imagine the personal hygiene problems if there is no clean running water for washing your hands.

[133] Source UNDESA Water For Life 2005-2015 http://www.un.org/waterforlifedecade/sanitation.shtml accessed July 2016.

United Nations' 2015 SDG 6: ensuring access to water and sanitation for all

The UN target for clean water in 2030 looks achievable, given what has been achieved over the last quarter century and that, at the start, in 2015, there were 'only' 663m people without access to improved water sources. The less good news, however, is that at least (an estimated) 1800m people in the world still drink water with traces – or more than traces – of fecal contamination, which is certainly not acceptable or healthy. The solution to this, though, largely rests on achieving the second part of SDG 6: access to basic sanitation, which includes safe handling and treatment (or at least safe disposal) of 'wastewater'.

In 2015 the UN, WHO and World Bank estimated that "2.4 billion people lack access to basic sanitation services, such as toilets or latrines" and "more than 80 per cent of wastewater resulting from human activities is discharged into rivers or sea without any pollution removal". This means that in 2015 the UN estimated *that a third of the world lacks basic sanitation and over 80% of human sewage on the planet – the sewage from almost six billion people – went untreated*. Indeed, much of it never enters any sewers at all, let alone receives proper sewage treatment: a billion people on our planet still practice open defecation, much of which flows into water sources, while another 1-2 billion use some form of pit latrine (described below). Of course open defecation is what humans have done throughout our history, and what nearly all other animals on the planet do today; at low population densities it does not generally harm the environment, but it is environmentally damaging, noxious and positively unhealthy when practiced by a billion humans on a planet with as little earth as Earth.

In very poor rural areas the best practical alternative is to use pits for human waste, covered by small shelters over the hole, which provide privacy, dignity and some kind of sustainable personal hygiene facilities (ideally clean running water) for the user. These '*latrine pits*' are sustainable, realistic alternatives, and can be far healthier than open defecation, so long as the local community is educated about hygiene, and is encouraged by social and political institutions to install and maintain some kind of running water hygiene facility alongside the latrine. Figure 66 shows the challenge today to achieve the wastewater part of SDG 6 by 2030, and introduces the distinction between 'good' pit latrines – well designed with some kind of running water nearby, so that users can wash their hands afterwards, and well maintained by the local community– and 'poor' pit latrines which fail one or more of the above criteria. In rural areas the key challenge is to persuade communities to build and maintain good pit latrines (or houses with drains leading to safely-draining cesspits). If you want to visualise a poor pit latrine think of the amusing scene in the 2008 film *Slumdog Millionaire* in which the hero as a small boy falls into an unsavoury pool while trying to see his favourite film star – and rest assured that the child actor loved shooting

---

[134] Goal 6 of the UN's 2015 Sustainable Development Goals for 2030: see http://www.un.org/sustainabledevelopment/water-and-sanitation/.

that scene because he was covered from head to toe in chocolate. The reality, of course, is not so pleasant, which is why we must, in the author's opinion, introduce the distinction of poor and good pit latrines, and focus on the crucial criterion of *good maintenance of these latrines*.

Figure 66: The world's wastewater challenges for 2030

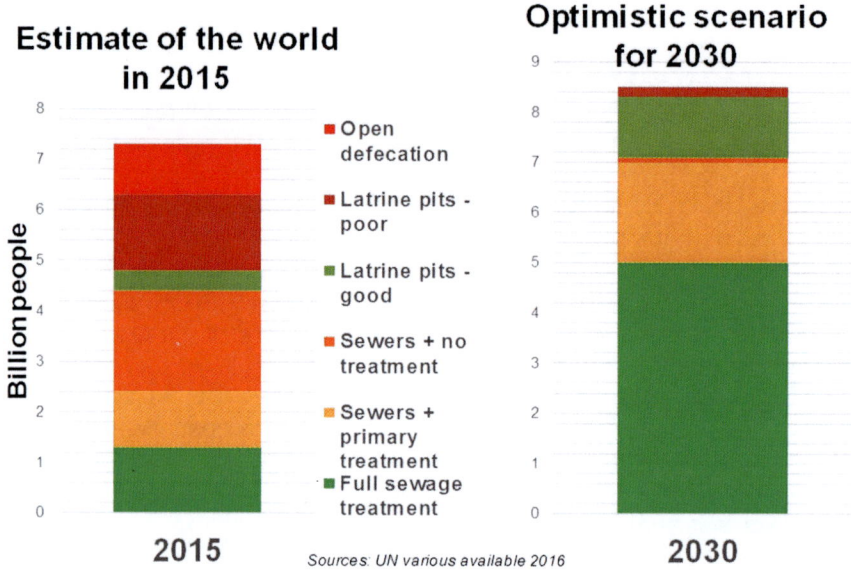

Today only around 1.3 billion humans currently have their sewage treated, and most of these people live in urban areas in rich countries. The world's urban population is expected to rise from four billion people in 2015 to around five billion people by 2030[135] with 28 mega-cities having populations larger than ten million, and with many of those people having incomes less than, say, $3000 a year. The resources required to treat the sewage from another four billion bottoms will be vast[136], but the environmental strain on the world's rivers and oceans of not treating all that sewage are larger still. The first task of course is to capture all the sewage in closed non-leaking, un-blocked, sewer pipes, and this may well be the most difficult task in practice, as digging thousands of small sewers under favelas or shanty houses will not be popular with people who may take direct action against external utilities 'nosying' into their affairs. And keeping all the small sewers unblocked (and free from tree roots) is a huge problem even in peaceful rich countries which do not experience tropical rainstorms. Thereafter someone has to pay for the installation and maintenance of primary sewage treatment (settlement into solids and liquids) and then full secondary treatment to produce a liquid effluent that is cleaner – physically,

---

[135] UNDESA 2014 World Urbanization Prospects https://esa.un.org/unpd/wup/Publications/Files/WUP2014-Highlights.pdf page 7

[136] The calculations behind Figure 66 are the author's estimates based on UN, WHO and World Bank data and estimates available in July 2016

chemically, and biologically – than the receiving water into which it flows. Given that clean drinking water is plain common sense while sewers can be perceived as an environmental nice-to-have, and sewage treatment is purely 'for the birds' (and fish) – in economic terms a positive externality – achieving the wastewater part of SDG6 looks far harder than achieving the clean water part.

Growth of the water and wastewater value chains in richer countries
Reflecting on what it is consumers in richer countries want from their clean and wastewater value chains in the longer run, we come back to the fundamental economics of the product described in Chapter 1. Water is a product that is personally ingested by the bill payer in a household, and by those they love dearly, who may be small and susceptible to trace impurities[137]. Wastewater, by contrast, is a service most householders prefer not to think about at all; it is also almost entirely a social externality, but one that we regard as increasingly mankind's 'responsibility' to provide as stewards of the planet's natural environment. As societies become richer we are therefore prepared to pay for specialist service providers to clean our water or to clean up 'our' environment to ever higher standards.

So, rich societies ask their water and wastewater industries to do more, which means the value chains of European and north American water and wastewater grew strongly in the last decades of the twentieth century. In the twenty first century this process is being repeated in Asia, Latin America and Africa, aided by the global trend for households to move from basic rural sanitation methods to centralised urban sewer systems which permit – and need – sophisticated sewage and sludge treatment. Figure 67 and Figure 68 show this conceptually and offer some predictions for 2030:

The clean water value chain in rich countries
Figure 67: The steadily rising outputs of the global drinking water value chain

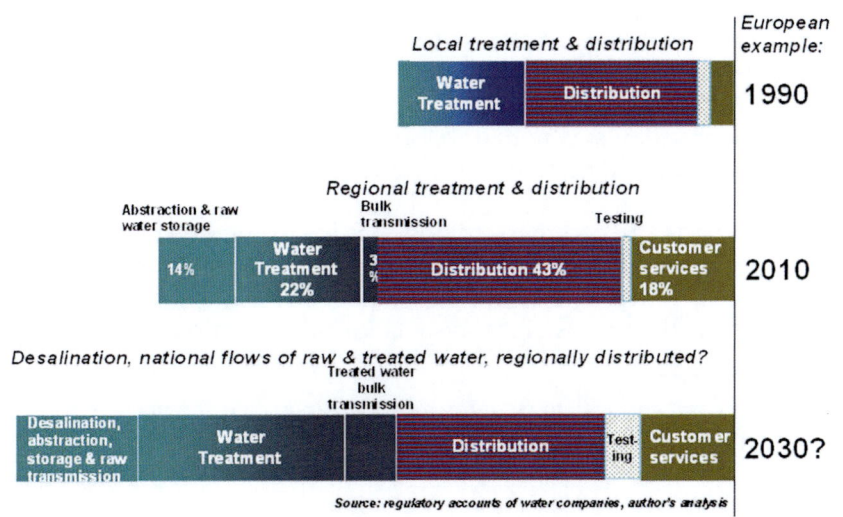

In Figure 67 we see that by 1990 in eastern (Communist) and western Europe, for example, most of the clean water value chain was local village, town, or city water treatment and distribution. Water quality was undeniably variable across countries and the continent and was frequently sub-standard: in one region in England in 1988 half the drinking water had too many traces of agricultural chemicals to pass European standards, and this sort of experience was common across many west European countries. Quite rationally, tap water quality was widely not trusted by the public and bottled water was actually more highly trusted than tap water, despite its generally lower quality standards. Travellers frequently had minor stomach upsets which were attributed to the different standards of tap water, and one of the first questions new arrivals asked experienced business people in a country was "Is the drinking water in city X OK?" Frequently it was not, so experienced business travellers never drank tap water, did not eat salads (washed in tap water) and brushed their teeth using bottled water. There was rudimentary testing of water quality but because standards were set and monitored locally, often influenced by the water supplier themselves, the water companies did not waste a lot of effort conducting tests they knew in advance they would fail, and the public consequently gave test results little credence.

By 2010 Communism was long gone, most countries west of Russia had joined the European Union, and the EU had put real money into standardising and improving water quality across the continent. Considerable resources had gone not just into policing the quality of actual drinking water, but more importantly to improving the treatment processes so they got rid of trace chemicals. Tests were standardised and much more rigorous. Politicians from areas that failed the tests were pressured to spend money raising the quality of drinking water – with generous funding from the EU available. Consequently by 2010 the actual water delivered at the tap approached the theoretical EU standards across western Europe[138] and the same was true in most cities in Eastern Europe, with improvements slowly coming into small towns and rural areas. In addition in some regions transmission grids had evolved to move drinking water between towns and cities in the same area – this being technically feasible once water has a standardised quality. As the value chain has grown – for a better quality product – water bills have risen and companies spend more on billing systems that explain to customers why their bills have gone up, and why their charges are just so – i.e. why one household's bill differs from its neighbours' bills.

Looking ahead one can see these trends continuing, with testing, transmission and water treatment continuing to grow as people expect a uniform product in quantity and quality available across the continent, and indeed across most cities on the planet. In addition, as global populations rise towards 9 or 10 billion, the

---

[137] Large water companies tell me that the most demanding customers in terms of water quality are tropical fish – and their more vocal human owners.

[138] Failure in any one of the 57 European Union standards means that sample fails. Typical compliance (success) rates are now well in excess of 99%.

pressure on global freshwater resources will rise, and so water engineers will have to use poorer qualities of raw water, which in turn means that more resources must be spent turning recycled effluent (which is cleaner than most streams) or even seawater into drinking water. Thus the upstream stages of abstraction, storage, desalination and bulk water treatment should grow quite strongly across the planet, as depicted in Figure 67.

The wastewater value chain in rich countries
Figure 68 shows the same long run evolution, but for the global wastewater value chain. Again Europe is the working exemplar. In many of western Europe's small villages by 1990 wastewater services consisted largely of sewerage (the pipes, with little or no treatment), while larger inland towns generally had some basic sewage treatment. However many coastal towns had little or no sewage treatment – sewage was just piped out to sea a kilometre or so, in theory away from beaches and harbours, but in practice the tides or winds often veer from their planned courses.... Seas that look marvellous to swim in, like the Mediterranean, could look and smell disgusting up close, and underwater the variety of species was shrinking rapidly. Upstream many rivers received treated sewage of various grades, but all too often key villages and small towns had no effective wastewater treatment, while the runoff from agricultural land in field drains and ditches contained animal sewage from intensive pig, chicken, or cattle farming, or phosphates and nitrates from man-made fertilisers that promoted growth of algae and bacteria in the rivers they ran into. In short rivers were all too often sewers, lakes were fetid, and the Mediterranean was starting to hum. In Eastern Europe the situation was even worse with many large cities having no effective sewage treatment, and smaller towns and villages having no sewage treatment.

Figure 68: The steadily rising outputs of the urban wastewater value chain

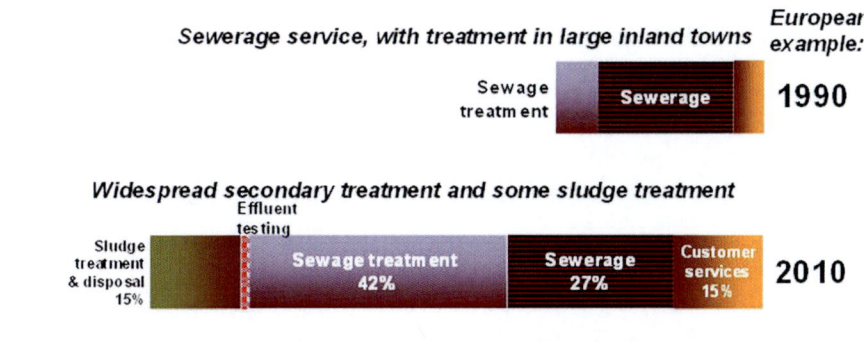

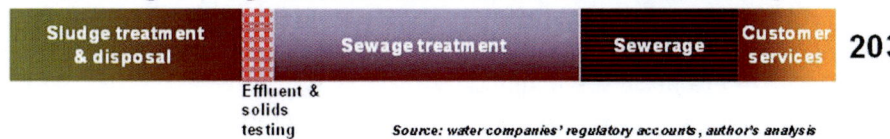

Source: water companies' regulatory accounts, author's analysis

By 2010 the European Union had introduced comprehensive legislation[139], systematic monitoring and, most importantly, funding to clean up all Europe's rivers, lakes, ground waters and seas by 2015. Nearly all cities and large towns in western Europe, including those on the coast, had comprehensive sewage treatment, and all the cities and towns in eastern Europe either already had this in place or had practical plans to achieve it before 2015, with the exception of Albania (Europe's poorest country) and parts of the former Yugoslavia. Measured river quality across the continent was starting to improve and comprehensive plans to improve the North and Baltic Seas had been agreed and funded within the Union. But there was still a massive way to go: although rivers and cities on the land of Europe are becoming cleaner, a 2008 EU study found that manmade solid waste, industrial emissions and sewage accounted for 80% of pollution in the Mediterranean Sea, and that half the large cities around the Mediterranean still have no sewage treatment[140].

Consequently the EU set up a Horizon 2020 programme to de-pollute the entire Mediterranean Sea by 2020, backed and funded by the EU and the European Investment Bank, which can make low-cost loans to African and Asian cities and countries.

In its actions Europe has followed America's pioneering legislation – and implementation – of the 1972 Clean Water Act, which required all point sources of pollution to obtain a licence to discharge water of any kind into a significant body of natural water. In particular the biggest polluters, municipal sewage treatment plants, were required to provide a degree of scientifically-estimated 'secondary treatment', which generally includes settlement of the sewage (primary treatment) followed by proper biological digestion of the liquid that flows out of the first tank. This put an end to cities simply putting all their sewage through a settlement tank and then claiming "Don't worry: our lakes and streams are fine! All this city's sewage is treated." Thirty years later the result was that 53% of America's rivers, 35% of its lakes and 70% of its bays and estuaries were deemed 'good' for all their designated uses (swimming, fishing etc.)[141], while all coastal waters were deemed of fair quality and to have improved slightly since the 1990s[142]. However, America's aquatic environmental priorities have now shifted away from 'point source' pollution, as the following 2010 EPA quote explains:

---

[139] The European Water Framework Directive of 2000 encompassed and exceeded all previous EU legislation to achieve a good quality of water across the continent's surface and ground waters by 2015. All 16 of the 1995-2005 new entrants to the Union (mainly from Easter Europe) were given considerable financial assistance from the late 1990s to help them achieve this in time for 2015.

[140] Source: EU's Horizon 2020 programme, http://ec.europa.eu/environment/enlarg/med/horizon_2020_en.htm accessed August 2010.

[141] Source: EPA 2004 Report to Congress.

[142] Source: EPA National Coastal Condition Report III, published 2008.

> *"Over the last 30 years, stressors have shifted, as demonstrated by EPA's National Aquatic Resource Surveys. These recent surveys found that nutrient pollution, excess sedimentation, and degradation of shoreline vegetation affect upwards of 50 percent of our lakes and streams. .... Sources of these stressors vary regionally, but the main national sources of water degradation are: agriculture, stormwater runoff, habitat, hydrology and landscape modifications, municipal wastewater, and air deposition"*[143].

Stewardship of the planet is like being a parent: the job never ends.

Looking ahead to 2030 Figure 68 predicts that the coverage and depth of sewage treatment, and especially sludge treatment, will continue to grow, as well as more rigorous testing of effluent and sludge, including all its trace elements. It is ironic that much of the extra 'value' in the wastewater value chain – though most people would never describe sewage or sewage sludge as 'value added' – comes from processing sewage sludge into healthier and more environmentally-friendly forms of treated sludge, before recycling or burning it. Conscious that if this sludge is to be recycled it must be wholly acceptable, effort is now turning to removing trace metals and chemicals from sewage sludge, so that they are not recycled through soil into our plant foods and then accumulate in the bodies of mammals such as humans or the mammals we eat.

Environmental success stories
The true 'value added' from the complete removal of toxins from the sludge / soil / plant cycle and the sewage / effluent / natural water cycle is that our 'natural' surface and ground waters are returning to the healthiest state they have been in for hundreds of years. London, for example, was founded two thousand years ago in a reasonably healthy location, but the effluent load from the human population rose so much that by 1750, and for two hundred years after, the river was toxic to fish, animals, and humans alike. Fifty years after comprehensive[144] sewage and sludge treatment was started in earnest all along the River Thames, predators at the top of the natural food chain such as salmon and otters, which had not been seen for centuries, have returned to most of their traditional haunts.

The task ahead
But London and the river Thames are small successes compared to the main task ahead. In 1984 the author was fortunate enough to finish working in the USA and spend several months travelling around the world with his girlfriend snorkelling in warm tropical seas before returning to Europe. Best of all was Tahiti. Flying in it looks every bit the tropical idyll: green jungle-festooned volcanoes tower over

---

[143] *"Coming together for clean water: EPA's strategy for achieving clean water"* EPA page 1, August 2010.

[144] It must be comprehensive: untreated sewage from even a few houses can taint an entire river basin and stop the return of the top predators in the food chain.

shallow turquoise lagoons, ringed by honey-coloured atolls dotted with palm trees, which are surrounded by a rim of white breakers, indicating the coral reef that keeps out the big waves and sharks of the vast Pacific ocean.

But it is beneath the water's surface that the Society Islands, as Tahiti is properly known, sublimely surpass other tropical islands' seas. The Society Islands have by far the greatest biodiversity I have ever seen, especially on the more remote islands – and there are hundreds of them. Spend thirty minutes with a mask and snorkel 'face down' on the lagoon side, or on the ocean side of these atolls, and it is possible to see far more species of fish than you can count. What happens is that unless you happen to be a marine biologist swimming around with an underwater-writing log book, after about thirty minutes snorkelling, and noting thirty species or so in your head, you forget which species you have counted, and which are new, and become confused. The same goes for varieties of coral. After half an hour cruising around at a location you take a break, walk along the atoll beach for ten minutes and re-enter the water to find dozens of new species of fish and coral that you did not see on your earlier swim, as well as at least a dozen or two varieties you have already seen. The same experience was repeated on several different islands. Of course there were many wonderful fish and corals off islands in Papua New Guinea, on (then-remote) beaches in Thailand, along the southern Indian coast, and on beautiful Sri Lankan beaches, as we travelled around the tropics, but for sheer underwater visual diversity the Society seas were in my opinion unmatched[145]. And I could think of no reason for this other than the total remoteness of the Society Island archipelago. It is smack in the middle of the Pacific Ocean, thousands of miles from the nearest large cities or industrial works of any kind. The warm tropical seas of this natural environment have been largely undisturbed for around 400 million years[146], so that biological diversity has been given an unparalleled stable environment in which to proliferate, and the result is the amazing spectacle you can see through a $10 mask today.

Capturing all the sewage

Treating all an area's sewage is relatively straightforward for sewage engineers – yes, there is such a profession – provided the sewerage system captures all the sewage. It sounds trite to say that a sewage works cannot treat sewage it never receives, but in fact a large part of the art of cleaning up an area's sewage is the art of capturing all the sewage in that area. This may appear to be a straight-

---

[145] I have since swum in the Red Sea, off Mauritius, Malaysia and Brazil, but the only place that has come close to Tahiti for species diversity is Australia's Great Barrier Reef.

[146] Excepting, of course, Earth's Permian, Triassic, and Cretaceous Disasters, which, in their days, devastated 96%, 50%, and 75% respectively of all marine species on the planet. However, while hundreds of thousands of old species were rendered extinct in just a few million years each time, new species seem to have evolved to fill the environmental niches very rapidly – no more than thirty million years. Given that the last Disaster was 65 million years ago this gives bags of time to evolve thousands of fish and coral species in each micro-environment.

forward job of consulting a sewer map and installing sewage treatment works near the lowest point, but we should learn from the experiences of wastewater companies like England's North West Water. By 1990 they had some of the worst polluted seas around the British Isles, inheriting sewage treatment works for major cities like Liverpool and Manchester from its predecessor organisation, but having no sewage treatment and just sea outfall pipes for many large towns and villages along its coast. Just 30% of North West's beaches complied with European standards[147]. So North West designed a vast sewage improvement capital programme costing more than a billion pounds over the next ten years to install state-of-the-art sewage treatment in every resort along the 430 kilometres of coast for which they are responsible. They obtained approval for this from all their regulators, spent the money, and installed the treatment works. Then they awaited the results of European Bathing Water tests to show that North West England now had nice clean 'Blue Flag' beaches. Unfortunately the biological tests of seawater showed no such thing. Sewage was leaking into the sea from other sources that the sewerage grid had failed to capture. North West engineers realised the sewer maps they had inherited from local government engineers were inaccurate and so had to survey the entire coastline again, before designing sewers that would capture the sewage from every last isolated house or hamlet on the coast, or on rivers near the coast, and divert that sewage into the nearest sewage system.

With 20/20 hindsight we can now see that North West Water was always going to have to build both the extra sewage treatment works and the new 'interceptor' sewers, regardless of the accuracy of the maps they inherited, but if, with the wave of some magic wand, they had known the true situation earlier, they could have designed the overall capital programme more efficiently, and achieved Blue Flag status on the most popular bathing beaches more quickly.

So what are the learning points for cost-effective sewage capture? Firstly, as with all underground asset networks, any map is compiled only on a best-estimates basis – i.e. using the best information available to the map-maker – but some crucial information may have been withheld, through ignorance, laziness, or particularly if the person volunteering the information (a home-owner or property developer, say) has an incentive not to disclose the information – for instance, incurring higher charges if they report a development. This means sewer maps[148] are the most inaccurate maps of all underground utilities, as the other grids are at least typically developed in one broad era of history. Secondly, housing development is a process that goes on over dozens of decades and is frequently 'piecemeal' – a single house can be developed on the coast, or on an estuary, and the person responsible for updating the sewer map could easily

---

[147] Data sources: Ofwat annual reports, North West Water annual reports, UK Climate Impacts Programme.

[148] The sewers of mediaeval Paris clogged easily, rendering them useless, and were shown only on very bad maps. The sewer authorities used to roll giant stone cannon balls down them to dislodge blockages, but even these often got stuck.

forget to add a single house to their map, particularly if the house is not connected to a sewer and discharges straight into the sea or estuary. Yet, unlike every other utility grid, it is precisely the houses that are NOT connected to the system that will ultimately be the problem. And if, five years later, the developer builds another house next door for his brother, using the same 'sewage system', we start to have a collection of houses not shown on the map all discharging raw sewage into rivers or the sea.

The third factor is history and the irreversibility of time. If planned before being built, sewerage is fairly cheap to install, and straightforward to treat, but if the settlement came before sewerage was invented 'retro-fitting' sewerage down every street would be incredibly expensive. There is not just the normal cost of digging up the road and making the connections, but also the fact that, unlike electricity, gas or water, sewers are very sensitive to gradients: the sewer will not drain properly if it is too shallow, while if it is too steep solids separate from liquids. So a sewer's depth below the house in a road is critical, not just so that the sewage from that house will drain away properly but also so that at the end of the road the sewer will flow properly into the larger sewers that lead ultimately to the treatment works. The consequence is that it is almost impossible to conceive of 're-sewering' a town that already has sewers: the costs would be astronomic. Figure 69 below gives a simplified idea of what the sewer system for an old town looks like if sewage treatment has just grown, and never been planned:

Figure 69: A simplified pattern of the sewers in an old town straddling a river

Sewers nearly always run under streets, which in old towns can wander around apparently at random. Underground the small sewers converge into bigger ones, but the maze of sewer pipes that actually emerges into a river or the sea can be big or small, old or new – a truly random mess. The city illustrated above happens to straddle a large river, but one can easily see how a coastal resort would simply resemble half of this pattern, with hundreds or thousands of sewers draining straight into the sea, or an estuary, or a river. It is impossible to consider relaying all the town's sewers.

This was the problem facing Eugene Belgrand in Paris in 1855, and Joseph Bazalgette in London in 1856. The cunning solution these titans of the sewage world adopted had first been attempted (in modern times[149]) along the right bank of the Seine in Paris in the 1660s and 150 years later under Napoleon[150]: it was to create an *interceptor sewer*, a large sewer which intercepts all the little old sewers just before they drain into the river, and carries their sewage down to a central point of treatment. The key idea is shown in Figure 70:

Figure 70: Designing interceptor sewers along a riverbank

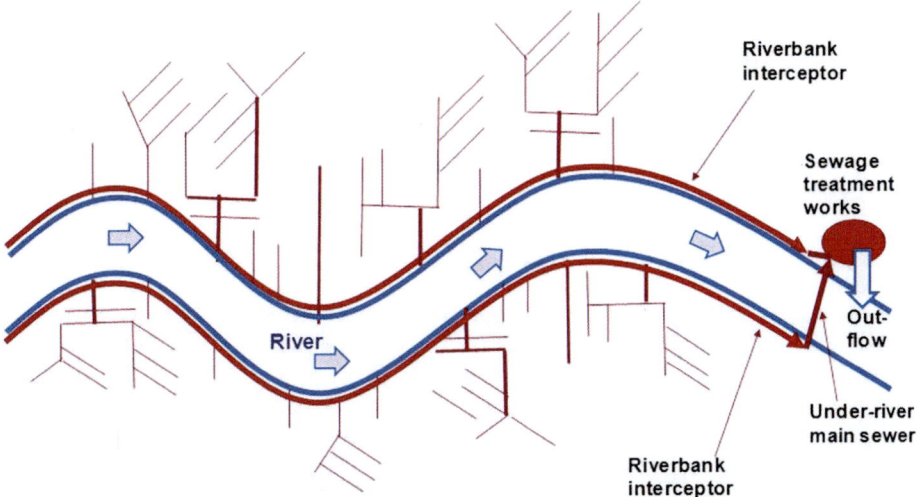

For historical accuracy I should add that the 19th century Paris and London interceptors did not lead to sewage treatment at the end; instead the outflow was merely dumped downstream in the Seine, or in the Thames estuary, where tidal currents took it out to sea. The London plan also required several vast slow-moving steam-powered sewage pumping stations. The key point, though, is that once the interceptor sewers had been built it was easy to add on a treatment works, while without them a sewage treatment works would be quite useless.

Indeed so clever is the idea of interceptor sewers that there is a tendency today among sewer engineers to call all large arterial sewers 'interceptors', even if they are designed from day one to be large receiving sewers. Achievement of Sustainable Development Goal 6's sanitation targets will require many of the

---

[149] Obviously the Romans were the first serious European sewer builders. Many of their sewers can still be seen today under cities such as Rome, Paris, Istanbul, London and York, or the forts along Hadrian's Wall.

[150] Source: guide to "Les egouts de Paris".

world's large but poor cities to develop interceptor sewers all around their cities, and then feed these into modern sewage treatment works to achieve the green results we hope for in Figure 66. Thus the wastewater value chain in Figure 68 for whole countries by 2030 will not only have a lot more sewage treatment in it, but will also have a lot more sewerage expenditure in it, and given that most inhabitants of slums or *favellas* cannot afford this sort of expenditure, it will be richer folk who will be paying for this public good.

Stewardship of the planet – and its costs
Since the author's trip to Tahiti it has been his belief that the greatest consequence of the 1960s 'Space Race', and America's triumph in reaching the moon, has been the photographs of our planet taken from the moon, or from spacecraft orbiting the moon, like Figure 71.

No more was it possible for educated people to assume the Earth's resources were infinite, though increasing in scarcity and therefore price, as implicitly assumed in conventional neoclassical economic models. After two thousand years searching, mankind had finally found the Garden of Eden – all around us. We could now deeply understand the message in Genesis that knowledge brings power, and power creates responsibility in beings that are morally aware.

Figure 71: Power creates responsibility in beings that are morally aware

Earthrise from the moon, taken by Apollo 8 on 29 December 1968 and reproduced by permission of NASA

These photographs show us one of mankind's urgent roles – stewards of the planet – and, as I was later to learn, the humble, completely automated, totally silent, occasionally smelly, town sewage treatment works has a very significant part to play in that self-imposed role. We may pollute individual fields or rivers and fix them quite quickly, as London has cleaned up the River Thames in fifty years, but if major pollution spreads to our seas we could seriously reduce the biodiversity of something as vast as the Pacific Ocean, so that even the technological possibilities available to our grandchildren would be stretched for centuries to remedy that damage.

I hope you agree it is a good thing that wastewater value chains around the world should continue to grow, and that planet Earth should strive to attain the Millennium sanitation goals, not just to improve human health, but also for environmental reasons. But, as economists, you also know that someone has to pay for all this sewerage and sewage treatment, and as they are public goods this will probably require either taxpayers or some element of cross-subsidisation between sewage "customers". You know very well who will pay: you will and I will. We have no choice. Once you've eaten the fruit of knowledge there's no going back. But if you find yourself chewing this textbook you've taken the old adage "Read, learn and inwardly digest" a step too far. Time to get out, eat, drink, and be sociable, because you need to return to do some serious work in Chapters 7 and 8.

Chapter Seven

Measuring the efficiency of utilities

The core concepts of productivity and efficiency

At its heart the economic concept of productivity compares inputs, or resources, with outputs. In microeconomics outputs are what an organisation is trying to achieve, and we have just spent Chapter 6 describing utility outputs, and how they are growing in the industry value chain. So the core concept of productivity is a simple ratio:

$$\text{Productivity} = \frac{\text{Output}}{\text{Input}}$$

In microeconomics we say one firm is more productive than another if it produces more output per unit of input. *Efficiency is* the related notion of *how a firm is doing compared to others or compared to what is possible.* Of course, what is possible is constantly changing: technological progress advances each year, relative prices change each year, firms reconfigure parts of their long term capital stock, hopefully with capital of a recent vintage, and try to improve their efficiency, while rivals do the same or better. To a large degree the terms productivity and efficiency are used interchangeably[151], which is strictly wrong, but since the Production Possibility Frontier is constantly changing and the social aims (the governance and strategic goals) of utilities vary widely we shall see that both terms *productivity and efficiency are innately relative concepts*, tied to particular *comparators* (companies used for comparisons) and *to a particular time*. But just because they are relative concepts does not mean we cannot quantify our comparisons.

---

[151] A point made in the excellent text *"An introduction to efficiency and productivity analysis"* by Coelli T, Prasada Rao D, O'Donnell C and Battese G 2005, (2nd edition), Springer, New York, page 3. This book is highly recommended for all students intending to pursue this subject more seriously, far exceeding in clarity, heuristic exposition and coverage all comparators the author has seen. Professionals will want to digest Coelli, Estache, Perelman and Trujillo's 2003 *"A primer on efficiency measurement for utilities and transport regulators"* World Bank Institute, Washington DC.

Measuring inputs: first, the pragmatic approach

So, at heart we need to compare outputs with inputs. Chapter 6 has just reviewed utility outputs in some detail, and we know they are complex (multi-dimensional) and in the case of the water industry, growing, as our environmental awareness grows. But what are our inputs? Traditionally the economists' answer used to be Factors of Production: capital, labour, land, and possibly energy or entrepreneurial spirit. However, economic theory clearly says that all factors of production are substitutable to some extent, and more importantly, we live in a world where most of these factors carry monetary values: capital, labour and land all have their prices, so cannot we just add these monetary costs up and say the total cost is X?

And you'll be delighted to learn that, with the exception of certain parts of public sector economics where it is hard to price some inputs, the answer essentially is "Yes, that is precisely the best route."[152] Of course there may be practical difficulties involving inflation-adjusting to common-year prices if making comparisons over different years, adjustments for shadow prices or costs if some prices are suspect, adjustments for exchange rates, Purchasing Power Parities and the like, if we are making international comparisons, but *these are second order-refinements*. The first order priority is to measure inputs as the total financial cost, and fortunately this can be related to something not only that customers very well understand – their bills – but also professional managers understand well: various definitions of the costs of their company.

It may seem strange that we need to say anything as obvious as the above, but in fifteen years professional experience the author has seen several papers in which serious academic or professional economists chose one or two factors of production as one of their measurements of inputs. It seems hard to credit, but serious papers have been produced comparing utilities using something as obviously fallacious as output per labour input as one of the main measures of inputs[153]. Not only is this obviously wrong from the point of view of economic theory, but utility managers just laugh at this nonsense, which does the economics profession no good at all. The reason that practical managers laugh at this is that they know the naive economist doing this study has calculated total labour inputs using some measure based on the number of employees a firm or industry records as being employed there. But a firm can easily sub-contract its functions to a contractor, whose employees are not counted in the firm's labour force, and hence not counted in the economist's labour inputs. This is particularly common where a utility's employees' main roles are functions such as maintenance or repair (e.g. network grids), and where patterns of contracting and sub-contracting vary dramatically, e.g. after restructuring or privatisation of

---

[152] As a micro-economic text, rather than a macroeconomic text, we can ignore the difficulties of the Sraffian critique of aggregating heterogeneous capital stock where the rate of profit itself determines relative capital prices. Let's keep it simple: market prices are fine unless you have very strong reasons to object to them.

[153] You might expect a good textbook to name the offenders, but that would be cruel.

a utility. This is why total cost is a far better measure of inputs: if the money is spent on labour it will be recorded as a cost whether the person is employed by the utility or not. So if we want an efficiency estimate that is at least correct as a first order of magnitude then we must include all inputs in the denominator (the bottom part) of our efficiency ratio.

Just to reinforce the importance of including all costs, including capital costs, in utilities you will be aware that many of the staff of a utility are engineers – gas engineers in the gas industry, electrical engineers in the power industry etc. Most engineers spend part of their careers working on capital projects which are enhancements to the existing network, not part of the system's ongoing running costs – its Operations and Maintenance ('O&M') or Income and Expenditure ('Profit and Loss') costs. Several engineers have said to me "I worked in my company for ten or fifteen years before my salary began to appear on the company's costs as a Profit and Loss item".

So the first argument for including all costs is that to ignore them is to ignore a major part of the costs. The second argument is that all factors of production are substitutes – what one firm chooses to do with a labour input another firm may choose to do with units of capital, energy or land. Should customers, regulators or academic economists interfere with this? No: it is the utility management team's job to evaluate the factor-substitution possibilities, to decide what in their opinion is the least cost solution, and to implement this decision efficiently. So an economic study comparing labour inputs has fundamentally misunderstood the situation, and is useless to a utility economist, although it may have its own academic purposes (usually, to advance an academic's career through showing off some new partial technique).

Naturally, the same argument applies to all other partial cost approaches: some regulators focus on operational or running costs, ignoring capitalised costs for a variety of reasons. A common excuse is "the data is not available". This is weak, pathetically weak. It is like a lazy or corrupt policeman who says he cannot find the evidence to charge a suspect with a serious crime, when the evidence appears to be lying around, and he simply cannot be bothered to go out and find it. It is a regulator's job to set fair prices and the regulated companies must give them whatever data they require to do that job. The regulator should not force companies to waste resources on exercises producing trivial data, but *this is crucial data* for the evaluation of companies' efficiency, and thus has a top priority. It may take persistent effort over several years to assemble this data on consistent definitions for many companies but regulators and *regulatees* (regulated companies) have that time and should use it well. If, for legal or other reasons, a regulator does not have responsibility for enough regulatees to conduct a good *comparative efficiency assessment* they should hand over the business of evaluating regulatees' efficiency to a party who can obtain this data for sufficient companies to make a good comparative evaluation. If necessary this may mean obliging their regulatees to provide the data needed on the definitions required by that third party. Regulators can, and often do, achieve very satisfactory results from this kind of collaboration.

Another objection to using certain versions of capital costs is that one would not want to use costs that include depreciation costs – because accountants or utility Finance Directors control these and can arbitrarily assume different lives for similar assets. True. My preference is to ignore depreciation and focus only on cash costs, which might require averaging over a couple of years if there have been very lumpy maintenance expenditures in some years. But if you wish to use depreciation and regulate an industry with long-life assets, such as the heavy utilities, you must face up to this, and devise accounting policies such as Infrastructure Renewals Accounting that overcome these objections and arrive at total costs that include capitalised costs as well as operating costs. You may need to calculate replacement costs for all capital stock so that you have a way of comparing companies' different capital from different price eras (this is crucial when assets last a century and price levels change by a factor of a hundred). Difficult and time-consuming though these cost concepts may be to prepare for both the regulators and the regulatees, it is better to spend the industry's time and effort obtaining good quality data from all, than to place serious weight on conclusions drawn from partial cost analysis, which will inevitably be a house built on foundations of sand.

So, as economists, we have a remarkably simple theory: the ideal *utility management's objective ought to be to make the utility deliver all the outputs society requires of that utility at the lowest cost.* And to measure utility efficiency, we should *use a multi-dimensional output divided by a single figure of total cost*, drawn up using the same accounting definitions for each company under comparison, which does not have to equal each company being regulated.

The theoretical approach: allocative efficiency or productive efficiency?

Having clarified pragmatically where we want to end up, let's now review the theoretical kind of efficiency we are considering: are we measuring allocative efficiency or technical (productive) efficiency, or both? Begin with Figure 72 which summarises the relevant part of Microeconomics 101 using a single output twin input model (the reasons for doing this are explained shortly). So we have a set of firms (utilities) in an industry employing two inputs. Let's imagine that input 1 is labour, or more generally, operating costs, so the horizontal axis shows output per unit of input 1 – e.g. output per man.hour – increasing to the right. In this diagram the further away from the origin O the better. Let's assume that input 2 is capital, measured in thousands of euros of capital stock (of a particular vintage), and this increases along the vertical axis – again the further away from O the better. Finally, we recall that the boundary of the production set – the limit of what is possible given today's technology – is called the Production Possibility Frontier (PPF): it indicates all points of productive efficiency, and to avoid corner solutions we shall assume that it is concave to the origin.

Figure 72: The two types of economic inefficiency in a single-output twin input model

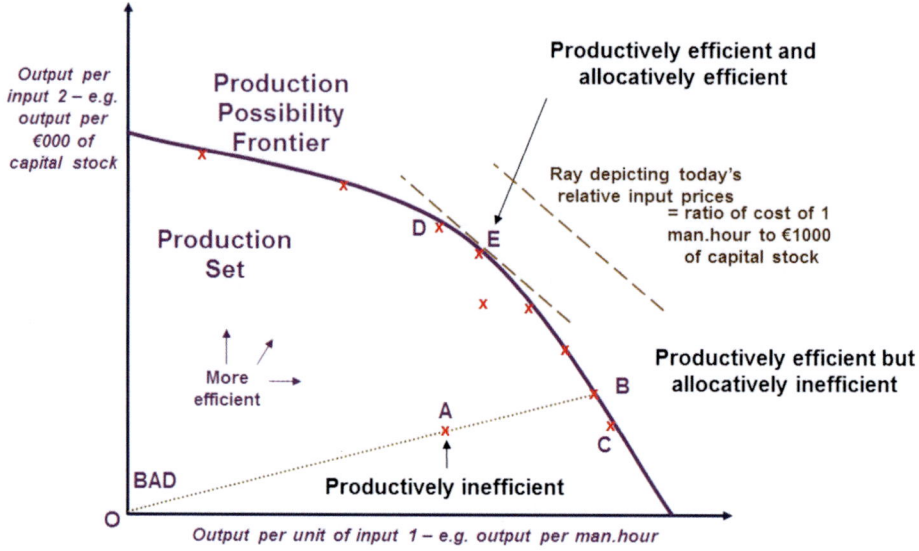

Productive or technical efficiency

Figure 72 shows the efficiency of ten firms in the industry, each marked with an X. Firm A is well inside the production set, not close to the Production Possibility Frontier and is obviously inefficient. Firm C can produce the same amount of output per capital unit as firm A, but more output per unit of labour, while Firm D can match A's labour efficiency but vastly exceed its capital efficiency. Firm B uses capital and labour inputs in the same ratio as Firm A but manages to produce more output altogether, and is the most efficient firm using this input mix, so it is on the PPF. B is productively efficient, as are all the firms on the Production Possibility Frontier.

So, given that we have pragmatically concluded that networks have multiple outputs and a single input – total money costs – why are we considering a single output twin input model? The point is that unlike the managements of all other commercial firms, the managers of geographical grids have no choice over the outputs they must supply – these are totally exogenously determined – so the managers' only production choice is what combination of inputs they should use to minimise the costs of serving the externally-determined set of outputs. Since these two-dimensional charts of PPFs can only handle three variables, and we want to illustrate a point about the choices available to utility managements, for the purpose of this discussion we must have two inputs, and will have to collapse all outputs into a single dimension. Figure 72, therefore, illustrates the archetypal choice facing a utility management team when considering whether to go for a capital-intensive low-running-cost solution or a capital-parsimonious high-running-cost scheme.

So A is a typically inefficient firm, while B, C and D are productively efficient utilities, close to, or on the PPF – firms which could be used as reference points for Firm A. And, indeed, the simplest of these ratios – the ratio of OA to OB – is exactly the measure which is used in 'DEA', which is one of the techniques we will shortly discuss; so if A were 70% along the ray between the origin O and the point B then DEA would say A was 70% efficient compared to its known comparator, B, on the Frontier.

Allocative efficiency
Besides rays emanating from the origin, such as OB, we can also have straight lines on this chart that slope the other way – from the top left to the bottom right. The slope of these lines shows a trade-off between one input and another, and since money can be used to purchase either input the slope of these lines can represent the relative prices of these two inputs per unit of cash. In other words these trade-off lines can indicate budget constraints. The tangent of our budget constraint lines with the PPF gives our point of allocative efficiency – firm E in Figure 72 – which is both productively and allocatively efficient.

To show this consider the budget of efficient firm B. We could draw a line with the general slope of our budget constraint through B up to the left, where it happens to hit firm F on the PPF, as shown in Figure 73:

Figure 73: Firms D and E are more allocatively efficient (cheaper) than firms B and F

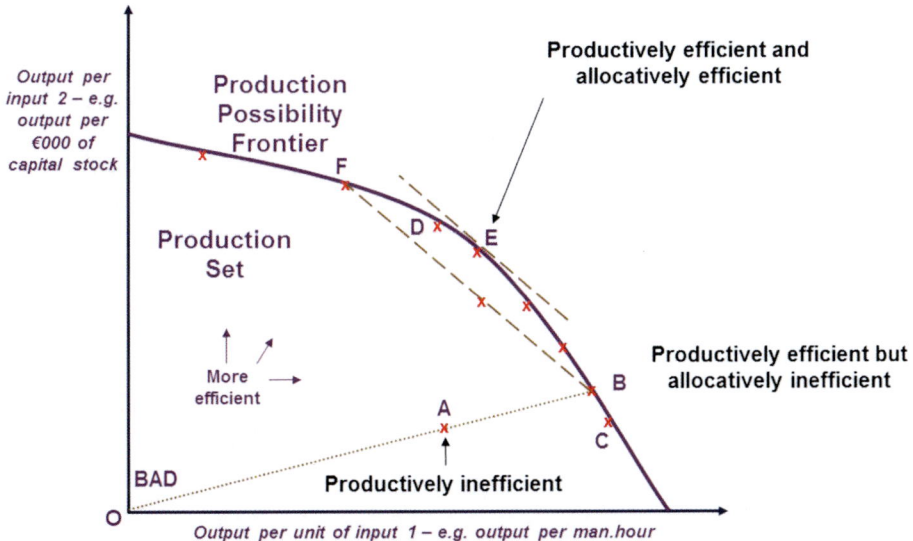

EB and F have the same budget as each other, as will all the points on that line, but firms D and E and all firms along the PPF chord FDEB will be able to produce more than B and F from the same budgets[154], so they are allocatively more efficient, and E is the most efficient – best value – of all, given those relative prices.

Productive or technical inefficiency and X-inefficiency: same idea, new words

By the 1960s the grip of neoclassical assumptions on western economists was so strong that the first professional American economist to suggest that productive or technical inefficiency might be a significant phenomenon in reality had to invent a new name for it. Mainstream economists were so divorced from reality, and so in thrall to neoclassical assumptions, that they could not imagine substantial productive or technical inefficiency without at the same time invoking monopoly theory, or at the very least monopolistic competition. So in 1966, when Harvey Liebenstein[155] looked explicitly at some industries around the world that were thought to be competitive, such as textiles, printing and pottery, he reproduced serious evidence showing that many real firms were likely to be at least 30% away from any relevant efficiency frontier, while pointing out that his academic colleagues were devoting serious time to estimating allocative inefficiencies from welfare losses that were fractions of one per cent of GDP.

For his point to be taken seriously by academic economists, and for it to be published in the American Economic Review, Liebenstein then had to coin a new term for the old concept of productive or technical efficiency. He called it 'X-efficiency'[156], and concluded that

> "in a great many instances the amount to be gained by increasing allocative efficiency is trivial while the amount to be gained by increasing X-efficiency is frequently significant."

Liebenstein gently chided our profession with quotes from another distinguished economist, Mundell, that unless some of his colleagues changed their analytical approaches "some one inevitably will draw the conclusion that economics has ceased to be important"[157]. In 1890 Marshall had defined economics as "a study of mankind in the ordinary business of life"[158] but seventy six years later what should have been a commonplace observation about the practical world of economics had to be re-invented as a breath-taking new idea for the economics profession to take it seriously. How low had the economics profession sunk!

---

[154] In this diagram, because of the definition of the axes (with costs on the denominator) lower budgets are to the top right.

[155] Harvey Leibenstein, "Allocative Efficiency and X-Efficiency," *The American Economic Review*, 56 (1966), pp. 392-415. It is incredible that professional economists should have wilfully ignored technical inefficiency for half a century, and is a point of shame for the economics profession, since the rest of society thought we knew something about this.

[156] "Our primary concern is with ...an initially undefined type of efficiency that we shall refer to as 'X-efficiency'" Leibenstein page 392.

[157] Liebenstein page 394 footnote 1; perhaps Mundell should have said relevant rather than important.

[158] Marshall A, 1890, Principles of Economics

Allocative or productive efficiency?
So what should we be examining: allocative efficiency or productive/technical/X-efficiency? Or, fifty years later, and particularly for utilities, does Liebenstein's conclusion still hold good?

I think most practical economists would say that as a matter of casual observation most of us believe that the average business operation is nowhere near its true Production Possibility Frontier, and that the PPF is only really glimpsed in wartime or when firms face panic measures or a crisis. And, almost by definition, those situations exhibit rather strange parts of the PPF, usually constrained by past sub-optimal capital decisions (with hindsight), and very probably by sub-optimal management – or the firm would not be in that situation in the first place. Later in this chapter we will discuss different theoretical concepts of the PPF, but if we stick with the simple notion of a static, clearly-defined PPF, it is very likely that Liebenstein's result still holds good. Of course competitive conditions in each industry matter, largely driven by the height of entry barriers, and we will examine possible distributions of inefficiency within the production set of various types of industry later in this chapter, but anyone who has ever run a real business, or even worked with them, nowadays tends to believe that allocative inefficiency is a nice theoretical concept to consider but productive inefficiency is very likely to be an order of magnitude (i.e. at least ten times) more important.

Furthermore, all engineers or managers recognise the concept of productive inefficiency, though many struggle with the notion of allocative inefficiency. If explained to them they tend to say 'I don't know what planet you economists are coming from, but productive or technical inefficiency is what we all mean by 'inefficiency'". So if an economist is to be much use in practice, productive inefficiency is what we should focus on.

A couple more theoretical arguments support this conclusion. First, note that in the diagrams the softly-touching tangent of the budget constraint with the PPF gives the beautifully unique point of allocative efficiency, E. But this is a trick of the paper, a consequence of our assumptions. If we had assumed three inputs, or two outputs, we would have a line of contact points – which gives us an infinite set of allocatively efficient solutions. And if we had three outputs and two inputs we'd have a two-dimensional 'facet' of allocatively efficient solutions etc. So there is nothing intrinsically wonderful about a point of allocative efficiency – it is not some kind of Holy Grail, just a set of efficient points within the entire set of productively efficient points, one of an infinite but arbitrary set of points on a big horizon. There is an analogy with watching the moon's reflection on a calm sea. It's very beautiful, but there is no special significance to that particular point in the sea: it was an arbitrary spot, depending on where the observer and the moon were that evening.

Sorry to break that little romantic moment. Now consider that, relative input prices can change, and frequently do – e.g. real wages tend to rise each year by a predictable amount, while the cost of capital varies randomly about a constant long term trend – *so what was the resource constraint in some past year will not generally reflect current resource constraints, or this year's relative input prices.* This is the big difference between sequential economies and their static counterparts: in the sequence model decisions were made in the past, the capital of that vintage was 'poured out', probably sub-optimally (knowing humans as we do), and we now have to live with those past decisions until the capital wears out or has to be replaced using a forward-looking decision. So, like all general equilibrium solutions, *allocative efficiency points are a set of points that were transiently optimal:* they seem to be a set of touching points on what was once the horizon, but we have now sailed on and our horizon has been redefined.

Should this matter in utility economics? Well, with the exception of the hardware and software of IT systems, yes, most assets are very long-lived, so the relative price of capital to operating costs such as energy or labour may have changed very significantly since the decision to commission a particular asset was made.

And yet our pragmatic conclusion is that we should add up all inputs at current relative prices to create a single cash-based cost concept which is our single input, and then see which of the utilities in our industry can achieve all its multiple outputs in that sector for the least cost. By using current relative input prices we are comparing all the firms with a set of current allocatively efficient hypothetical firms. So we do use both concepts. Just recall that changes in relative input prices between two years can make last year's allocatively sub-optimal firm this year's optimal firm. And one of the main reasons for adding all inputs together to make inter-firm comparisons is that the allocation of funds into particular resources, such as operating costs and capital costs, is a managerial decision that regulators and politicians should not interfere with. It is management's job to manage, and micro-management of the industry by politicians or the regulator should be strongly resisted.

Unit cost comparisons

Now let's turn to something refreshingly simple. The most basic efficiency measure is the good old unit cost figure beloved by management accountants and practical managers the world over. A unit cost is the inverse of our definition of efficiency: it is an input (a cost) divided by a unit of output, not an output divided by an input. An example might be an electricity unit cost of, say, 4 cents per kilowatt. Obviously, a generator with costs of 3 cents a kilowatt is more efficient than one with costs of 4 cents a kilowatt.

Bulk energy generation

So, handily, in the two most contestable parts of the value chain – bulk energy generation and utility retailing – we can calculate simple unit costs and use them. Bulk energy production is measured as a single scalar output (units of physical energy) by all companies in the same sector and this is divided by a total cost figure, including an agreed measure of capital costs, to achieve the unit cost figure for each production unit. These are then compared across different plants, firms, and industries as the standard measure of generation efficiency. In some countries a central administrator or a market mechanism uses these measures to 'shut in' (close down) production from marginal plants. The unit cost of the first plant shut in (not producing), or the unit cost of the plant one below (that was just allowed to produce) is then regarded as the short run marginal cost of the industry at that particular moment. So, in these parts of the value chain we have a close relationship between basic accounting measures and the components of neoclassical economic theory. And obviously, to calculate SRMC we need short-term accounting definitions of costs (variable or incremental costs), while to calculate LRMC we need longer term cost definitions.

Utility retailing
In utility retailing, everything revolves around the customer, and since utility outputs are commodities we could simply compare retail costs per customer[159] In fact this metric is commonly used by utility retailers and regulators, provided that (because some types of customer are more expensive to serve than others) customers have been grouped into agreed market segments – domestics, commercials, industrials etc. – using standard definitions of each segment..

Unit cost approach – the limitations
So, we can use straightforward unit cost comparisons for bulk energy production and utility retailing. But the output of a grid is not units of energy or water, it is the service of providing availability to the customer through kilometres of mains, thousands of connections, and all the other demographic, legal, geographical, historical and political factors beyond management's control. Because the outputs of transmission and distribution grids, and all water treatment and wastewater treatment plants, can only be described in several dimensions, any efficiency measures must also have those dimensions. At best simple unit costs for a grid or a water treatment plant will give a partial impression; at worst that impression could be seriously wrong.

Regression measures of efficiency – including multiple outputs

Water and wastewater treatment – a simple regression
The output of a water treatment works has been summarised in Chapter 6 as

Treatment work done = water quantity X treatment needed X compliance rate

so let us assume that this data has been calculated for every treatment works operated by a water company, and the company's total output is the average of all its treatment plants' figures weighted by each plant's contribution to the company's total distribution input. (For wastewater treatment exactly the same

---

[159] Variations in service levels are not often the retailer's fault and so can usually be ignored.

concepts and processes apply). Let us further suppose that we have this output data and input or cost data for 10 water companies, whose efficiency we want to compare as shown in Table 3:

Table 3: Example of water treatment outputs and inputs for 10 companies

Company	OUTPUTS Treatment work (litres x 10^9 a year)	INPUTS Annual costs (€m)	EFFICIENCY Work/cost (litres / €)
A	6	125	48
B	60	750	80
C	35	500	70
D	20	225	89
E	30	325	92
F	40	500	80
G	20	300	67
H	30	500	60
I	15	450	33
J	8	250	30
Average Company	26	393	67

Just staring at the figures above it seems clear that company E, producing 92 litres of treated water work done per €, is the most efficient water producing company, followed closely by company D.

A scatter plot of these ten companies helps us to visualise their efficiency positions, which is drawn in Figure 74:

Figure 74: scatter plot of ten water treatment companies' efficiencies

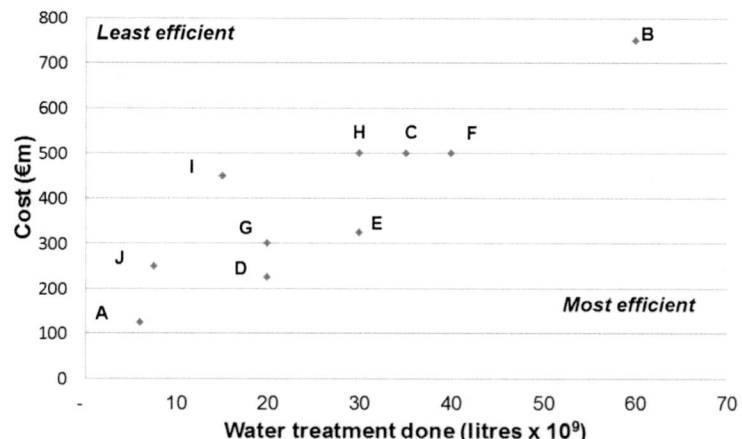

If we just look in the middle at companies F, C H and E, then E and H produce an output of 30 but E does it at lower cost than H so E seem to be more efficient. And comparing H and F, they both have costs of 500 but F produces more than H, so F should be more efficient than H. In general the best place for a company to be is with the lowest costs, down in the bottom right hand corner.

But we can go further. To test a hypothesis most economists' minds naturally turn to econometrics. Could we run a regression between the points in Figure 75 to see if there is a general link, and if so, how strong is the average correlation between total costs and water treatment work done? Let's try:

Figure 75: Simple regression of water treatment costs on treatment work for ten companies

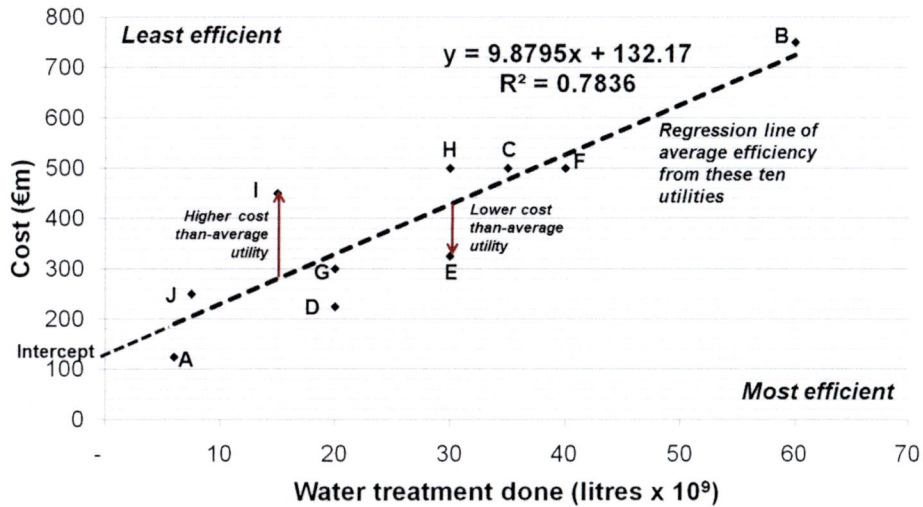

So we have a regression, and there appears to be a significant correlation, which we could sort of see by eye from Figure 74. The R^2 of 0.78 means the regression line is 'explaining' 78% of the variation, which is pretty good for a cross sectional regression, and translating the 'x's and 'y's into the concepts we know the equation is saying

Cost of water treated (in €m) = 132 + 9.9 x water treatment done (in billions of litres)

for the average water company out of these ten. In fact our smallest company, A, has lower costs than the intercept term, €132m, and it has an output bigger than zero, but this is because A is more efficient than the average company of these ten, *and the regression line only attempts to describe the average company*, not more efficient companies such as A or E.

Corrected Ordinary Least Squares
Could we use this regression approach to attempt to define the most efficient

companies, and then measure actual companies' inefficiency? The most obvious approach is to shift the regression line down until it approaches the most efficient utilities we can actually observe. We can do this most simply, as in Figure 76, by reducing the intercept but keeping the slope the same until we arrive at a line that just includes our most efficient company or companies (D and E in this case). This line is called the Corrected Ordinary Least Squares line, or COLS, and we are using it because we assume that our best guess (based on just ten data points) of where we think the production frontier lies is that it is somewhere below the dashed OLS regression line, that it should roughly include points A, D and E (as we know they are possible), and the slope of the frontier should reflect all the evidence we have from the other seven comparators – which is reflected in the regression line.

Figure 76: Using a regression line to guesstimate the COLS efficiency frontier

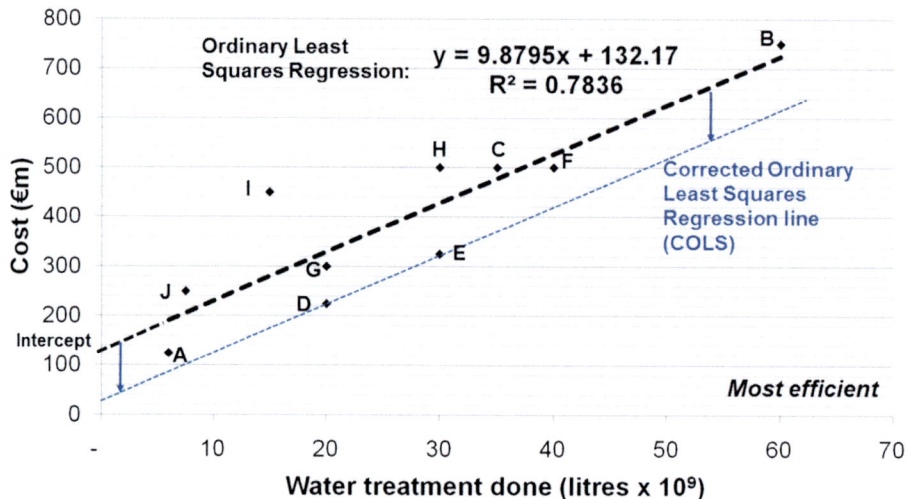

In practice most regulators take a cautious view when estimating the frontier, bearing in mind the statistical 'noise' in companies' annual cost figures and the other significant assumptions made in this methodology[160], so most rein back their estimate of the frontier to some arbitrary definition between the original OLS average line and the absolute COLS line. Nevertheless the principle of COLS is used by regulators in their efficiency modelling of utilities[161], so we are now using a professional method.

So we now have a couple of tools to analyse grid efficiency – scatter diagrams

---

[160] For instance the assumption that the frontier is a straight line is, of course, our own direct assumption caused by employing OLS which imposes a linear trend. This is an assumption we make purely for our own ease. The frontier, of course, may not be linear, but then we would have to use a non-linear estimation method, or a non-parametric method.

[161] For example British water regulator Ofwat has used versions of COLS in much of its water efficiency modelling since 1994.

and regressions – and the good news is that regressions at least can be extended to handle all the output dimensions we need. Provided we have data, and we have checked and groomed it to remove dubious stuff, we can build spreadsheet databases like Table 3 to create as many efficiency variables as we have good data for, and then run multiple regressions to check whether our companies have more than one significant cost-driver that is well outside the utility's ability to influence using a variety of potential measures of exogenous cost-drivers. For example, in water and wastewater treatment it would be highly desirable to make an allowance for *plant economies* of scale, which are clearly natural economies of scale dictated by the local water environment, by having a second output measure of average treatment plant scale, or a variant of this idea. The disadvantage with multiple regressions, of course, is that we cannot easily illustrate them in charts like Figure 75 and Figure 76 because that would need 3- or more-dimensional diagrams.

Twin outputs – for a grid

The output of a grid is complex. Let us start by reducing grid outputs to the bare minimum: length of mains broadly describes the total physical scale of the grid in kilometres, while the number of connections broadly summarises the other main assets that can fail (bends, valves and connections) and the customer servicing work that is required. When comparing two or more grids we can divide each utility's mains length and number of connections by that company's combined operating and capitalised costs to get two efficiency measures, as shown by the hypothetical example in Table 4:

Table 4: Example of grid outputs, costs and efficiency measures for 10 utilities

Company	Mains length	Connections	Cost	Mains Efficiency	Connections efficiency
(units)	km	(000s)	€m	(km of mains/€m)	(Connections / €m)
A	8,000	700	125	64	5,600
B	30,000	3,500	750	40	4,667
C	20,000	2,500	500	40	5,000
D	12,000	1,500	225	53	6,667
E	25,000	1,100	325	77	3,385
F	20,000	3,000	500	40	6,000
G	16,000	1,000	300	53	3,333
H	25,000	2,000	500	50	4,000
I	25,000	2,000	450	56	4,444
J	10,000	1,750	250	40	7,000
Average	19,100	1,905	393	49	4,854

Our twin efficiency measures are outputs divided by inputs – the inverse of a unit cost – and show that company E seems to be the most efficient at delivering kilometres of operating and fully- serviceable mains, while company J seems to be the most cost-effective in providing connections per million euros of cost. But at the same time company E seems one of the worst in connections efficiency, while J is poor at mains efficiency. E and J are both best and worst? How can we make sense of this? Is there in fact one company that really is the most efficient all round?

Again, a scatter plot of mains efficiency against connections efficiency helps illuminate our problem:

Figure 77: Scatter plot of mains efficiency against connections efficiency for the 10 utilities

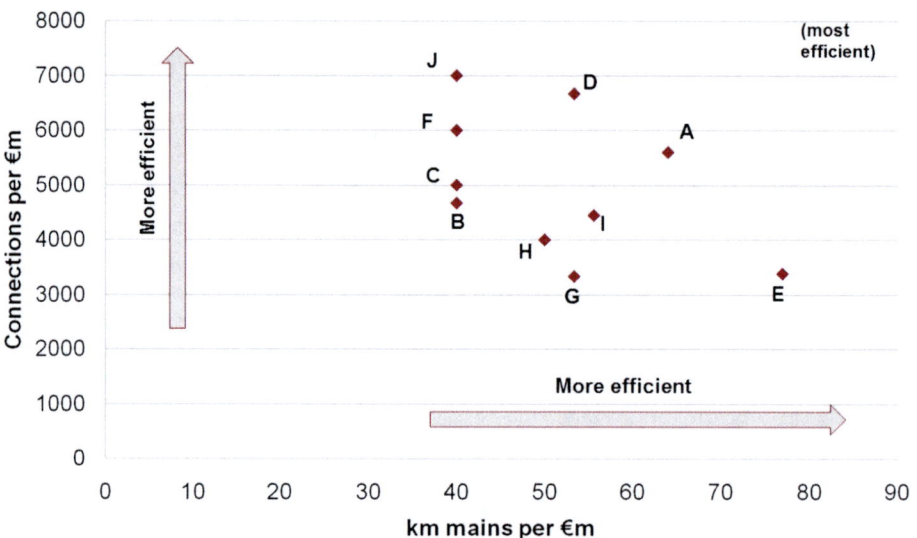

The axes of Figure 77 are drawn so that efficiency increases away from the origin (the bottom left hand corner), and the highest efficiency would be a position near the top right hand corner. From the diagram it is clear that E must be more efficient than G, while J must be more efficient than B, but from their combined scores utilities A or D look like having better claims to being the most efficient overall. So, again, a simple scatter plot diagram has told us a lot more than Table 4 does.

Cross-sectional econometrics
Can we run a regression through Figure 77? Sure. Figure 78 shows the result of running a regression simply in Powerpoint graphic software:

Figure 78: Using a simple regression to compare the efficiency of 10 utility grids

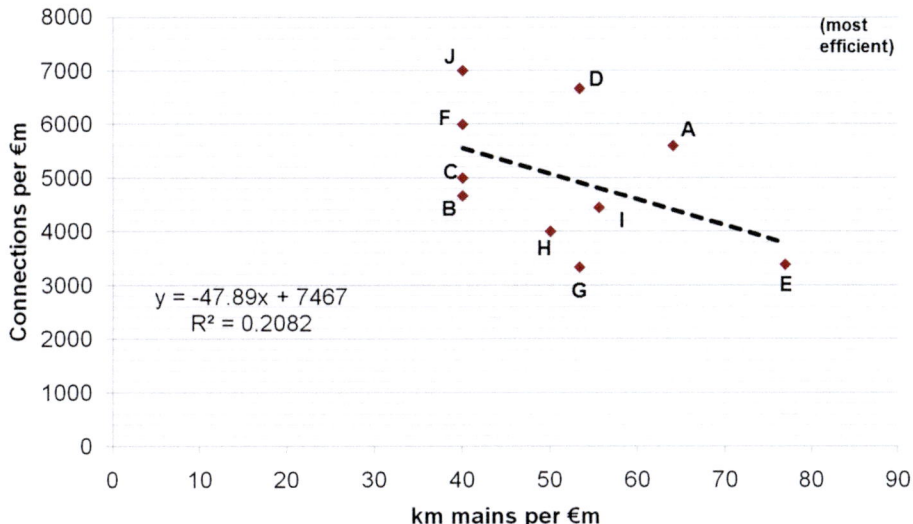

Obviously the regression does not appear to be a particularly good one, as the R^2 is only 21%, but this is not a time-series regression, so an R^2 of only 21% is not terrible. The statistics are picking up a tendency that is fairly apparent to the naked eye from Figure 56, so we are on to something, and it makes theoretical sense. Removing the 'x's and 'y's, and simplifying a little, the regression equation in Figure 78 says

connections efficiency = 7467- (48 x mains efficiency)

in other words connections efficiency is negatively correlated with mains efficiency – companies tend to be quite good at either one or the other. Obviously company A appears to be pretty good at both, but on each single measure alone it is surpassed by company E or J, as we noted earlier.

Using regression techniques to measure inefficiency

Efficiency is a relative concept, placed in time and space, and the most efficient firms that we have evidence of are firms A and D. In the absence of evidence to the contrary we might assume that one of them could be 100% efficient, and thus actually producing on the production possibility frontier – though of course this may change next year or the year after. But can we quantify just how inefficient the less efficient firms are – at least relative to the most efficient firm?

One approach is to use the regression line itself. This regression line is an indication of the central tendency of our data, so, by the very nature of the statistical equation which produces it, the line must go through the middle of our data set, both in terms of going through the mid-point of the ten (the average firm) and in terms of the slope (the average trade-off between mains efficiency and connections efficiency).

Figure 79: Estimating a production frontier using a regression

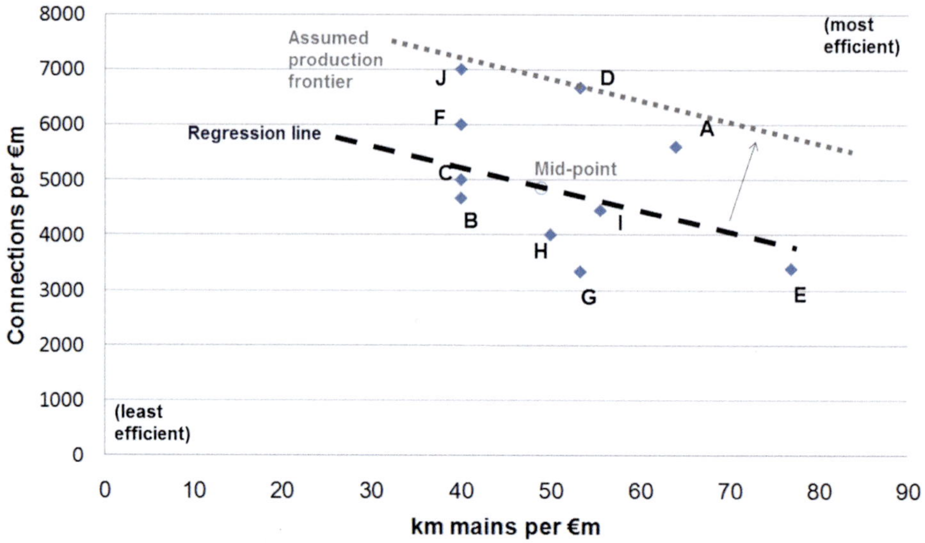

Just as with COLS, if we use this average trade-off line as an indication of the shape and slope of the production boundary then we could slide it out to the right and up until it hits our most efficient firm. In this case the most efficient firm turns out to be firm D, given the slope of the regression line. We now assume that our best guess (based on just ten data points) of where we think the production boundary lies (it is clearly at or beyond firms A and D) is somewhere about where the dotted adjusted regression line is in Figure 79, since we know D is possible and the slope of the line reflects all the evidence we have from the other nine comparators. We can now measure each utility's efficiency relative to the frontier.

Data Envelopment Analysis (DEA)

However, what should we do if the scatter plot of our utilities' efficiency turns out like Figure 80?

Figure 80: The regression slope has the wrong sign

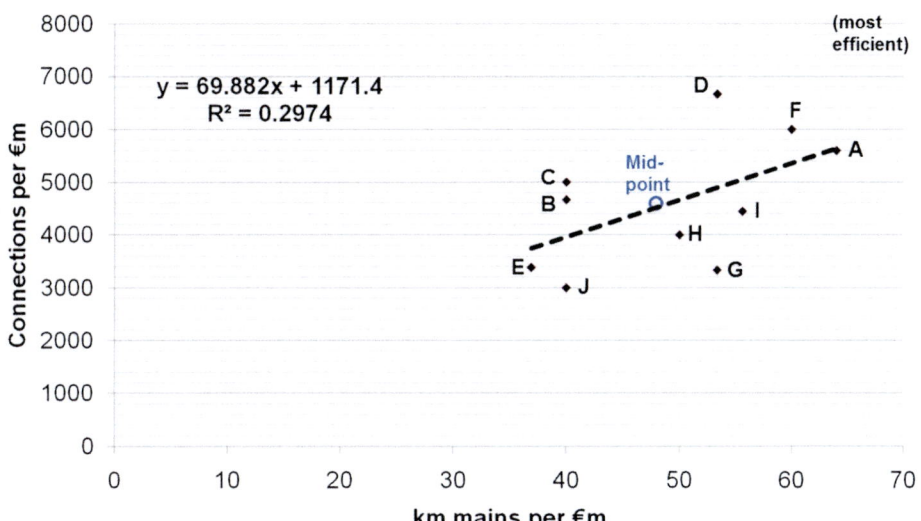

In fact just three data points have been changed between Figure 79 and Figure 80: one component each of the outputs of points E, F and J has altered. However, these three changes to our data[162] have completely changed the slope of our regression line, and in a seriously bad way, despite the improved R^2. Professionally, these regressions are described as "counter-intuitive", which is a polite way of saying either our theory is wrong or the observed world is mad. Since we do not generally believe the world is mad, clearly we have some work to do with our theory.

Why is this regression slope so bad? Well, the negative slope of Figure 79 implies that there is some kind of trade-off between mains efficiency and connections efficiency, which we know theoretically ought to be true. If you run the leanest, meanest utility in the region and then, suddenly in one year, there is a major housing development in your patch, so that what was 20 km of your rural mains with almost no connections now has an additional 10km of mains and another 10,000 extra connections for you to service, there is no way your costs can *decrease*. Over time, in an average year, your costs can only *increase*. So we know with 100% certainty that additional mains and connections must each increase a utility's costs. Yet the regression in Figure 80 says:

Connections efficiency = 1171 + 69.9 x mains efficiency

---

[162] You may like to think of this from a hypothetical regulator's point of view as having received data from ten companies, running a quick regression to test your model, then, because you have suspicions about some of the data, querying all companies' understanding of the data definitions, and then receiving the revised (true) data shown here, which gives a regression with the 'wrong' slope.

in other words if you can improve mains efficiency you can also improve connections efficiency. Well, yes that's true *if you are inefficient*: reduce your costs and you will simultaneously improve both efficiencies. But if you are already the leanest, meanest utility in the land you cannot. In other words the frontier cannot be shaped upwards: if you are on the frontier then there must be some trade-off between those who are mains-efficient and those who are connections-efficient.

So what's gone wrong? A trick of the data, or a rubbish regression? No, the R^2 is a respectable 29%, and in fact the t-statistic on the 'x' coefficient is a healthy 2.5, which we can retain with 95% confidence. From a purely statistical point of view there is no reason to reject this regression – it's just the economic theory behind it that's rubbish. However, if we look closely at the scatter diagram we can see three data points which do appear to be both efficient and on an apparent downward-sloping frontier: points D, F and A. *Their* relationship is not rubbish.

So why hasn't the statistical package picked up the trade-off effect between these three points and reflected it in the regression slope? Well, the answer is it has, but the negative correlation between these three efficient utilities has been outweighed by the generally positive correlation between the other seven points.

"But they're inefficient!" you may want to exclaim "– they shouldn't dictate the shape of our production frontier." Yes; you're quite right! But no-one told the statistical package that, so it includes every observation and treats each equally. In fact, having drawn the scatter plot, we could have excluded all the inefficient observations manually, and done a regression of just the three efficient points, but we would get a pretty thin regression (with one degree of freedom).

So the resolution of our "counter-intuitive" regression is that a regression process necessarily treats every observation equally – efficient and inefficient alike – and the "true" negative trade-off relationship between the three most efficient utilities was drowned out by an accidental positive relationship between the seven inefficient utilities.

We need some new tools of analysis. Data Envelopment Analysis, or Data Envelope Analysis for short (DEA), adopts a completely different approach to the econometric approach. It starts from a very firm theoretical foundation which says that if you are measuring something like efficiency you had better have some pretty clear theoretical ideas about how an efficient organisation behaves, and how it differs from an inefficient organisation. In other words it *assumes you know* what the outputs and inputs of an organisation or society are, and *what an efficient organisation looks like*. This might seem a pretty reasonable assumption, but we will need to come back and re-examine this, because agreeing what is beyond management's control it is not always dead easy.

The idea was invented by MJ Farrell in a classic paper in 1957[163,] who applied it immediately to agricultural inputs and outputs. The basic concept applied to our example is shown in Figure 81:

Figure 81: DEA: the basic idea

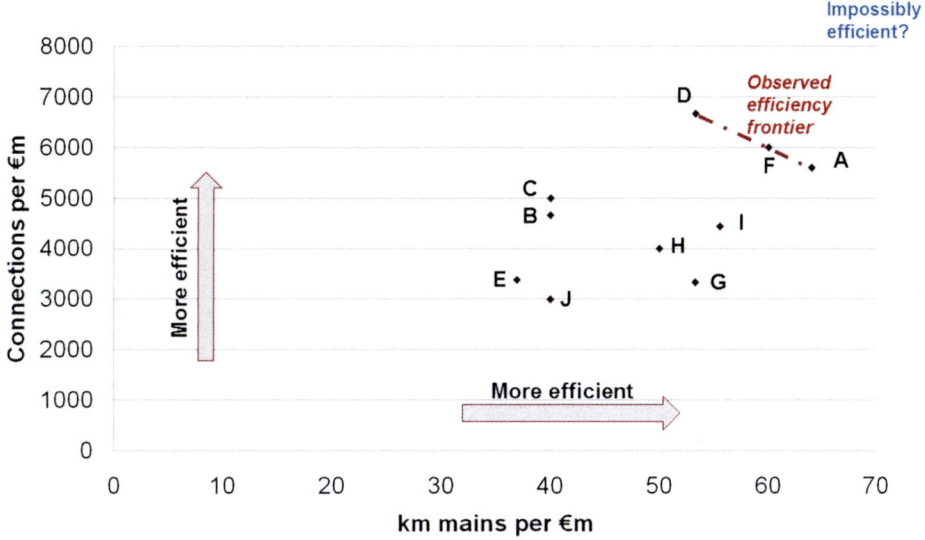

Because we know efficiency increases to the right and upwards, companies D, F and A are the most efficient. If a company could be further above or to the right of them it would be even more efficient than these three, but we do not have any such companies in our sample, so we do not know if this is possible. That area has to be marked *'Impossibly efficient?'* just as old maps used to mark unknown lands as *Terra incognita*. Then, if we draw a straight line between D and A (and in our example that line happens to go through F) it seems a reasonable assumption (and is no more than an assumption) that all the points along this line are also possible: that is, if utilities can attain the positions of D or A it seems reasonable to assume other utilities could also attain positions between them that are straight line combinations of them. Utility F is in fact just such a linear combination of D and A. All points along this line would then also be as efficient as D and A. So, based on our little sample of ten utilities, we seem to have an observed efficiency frontier, and to back this up we have three points on or near it.

So, following the idea of Figure 79 should we extend this frontier indefinitely – instead of just interpolating between D and A, should we also extrapolate beyond it? Now that would be really risky. We have no evidence to do this, and if we carried it on indefinitely until we hit the axes themselves there are a bunch of theoretical reasons for thinking this would be wrong. The main theoretical reasons are that we generally believe production possibility sets tend to be

---

[163] Farrell MJ (1957) "The Measurement of Productive Efficiency", Journal of Royal Statistical Society Series A 120, 253-290.

convex – in other words they cluster together, creating an oval or blob of possibilities around the origin, rather than allowing us to whizz off towards infinity, as very acute lines would.

To be safe, therefore, we should not go beyond what our sample has shown to be possible. We know D is possible, but have no evidence that a utility can be more 'mains-efficient' than A (no points further to the right), and no evidence that any utility can be more 'connections-efficient' than D. Our (observed) production possibility frontier can therefore include the dashed line in Figure 60 but cannot go further than that, and so must stop at D's connections efficiency and A's mains-efficiency, as in Figure 82:

Figure 82: Measuring efficiency using the DEA frontier

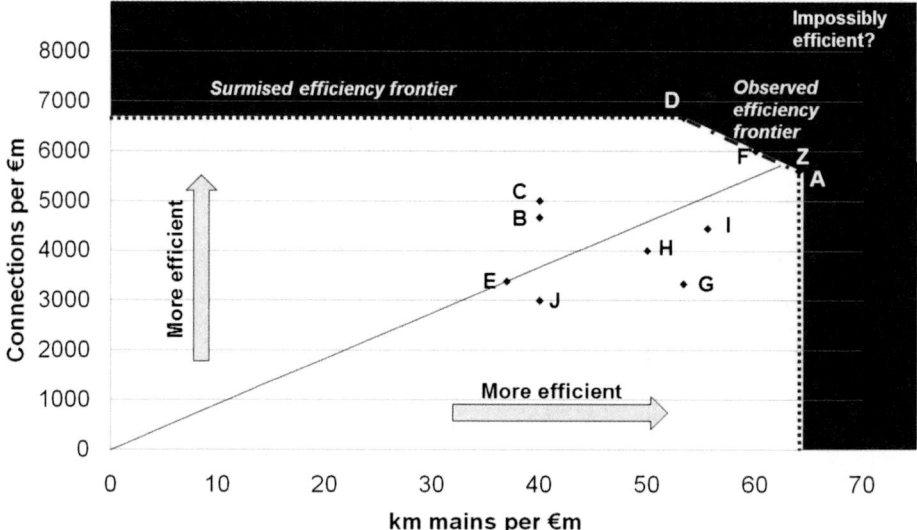

Our production possibility frontier now consists of three parts: an observed frontier and two 'surmised' or assumed frontiers. But at least it is convex and does not stray outside what we know is possible. Can we use it to measure the efficiency of the companies we believe to be less efficient? Farrell said yes. Let's take a typical company like E which is not fully efficient. *If E could reduce its costs by 10% the number of mains and connections it has would not change but both its mains-efficiency and its connections-efficiency would increase by 10%.* In this diagram E's apparent position would move out along a ray from the origin O, past the point E and out 10% towards the frontier. Could they not continue this, reducing costs until they hit the observed frontier at a point, let's call it Z, somewhere between D and A? We believe Z is possible because companies D and A have achieved similar but slightly more outlandish versions of this.

So we think company E could cut its inputs until it achieves point Z but is currently at point E. If the distance OE were 6 units and the distance OZ were 10 units this would mean we believe that E is currently achieving only 60% of what it is capable. Its efficiency would therefore be 60%.

This is the principle of DEA efficiency measurement, and once Farrell had outlined the idea it needed to be operationalised. This was eventually done in 1978 in the form of a seminal paper and a computer program by Charnes, Cooper and Rhodes[164], before being evolved into sets of standard software that you can now buy online, or obtain from your faculty's resources.

A quick question before you rush to the library facilities to get the DEA kit to rate your football team or your economics professors: how should we measure the efficiency of a company like G, which, if we continued on the ray OG would hit the vertical 'surmised' (or assumed) frontier? Is that fair, or should we measure G's efficiency relative to an extension of the observed efficiency frontier DA, which would be much further out into space. The answer is we remain conservative and say that the vertical surmised efficiency frontier is the only frontier we have any evidence for, so that is the base line of 100% efficiency. This means all points with more 'extreme' mains- or connections-efficiency than D or A may get off slightly lightly. Yes, there is nothing we can do about that except widen our data set. Which leads us to the concept of trying to create a global efficiency frontier.

Expanding the sample efficiency frontier

DEA gives us a great tool to measure firms' X-inefficiency but we would really like a lot more observations to be sure that our sample's observed production possibility frontier is anywhere near the true maximum possible. And not only do we want confirmation that utilities D and A really are efficient (we want more observations around D and A), we particularly want more utilities on the efficiency frontier that are more outlandish than D or A's mains and connections combinations. Then we would have less of the frontier as a surmised frontier, and more of an observed frontier:

Figure 83: Expanding the DEA frontier

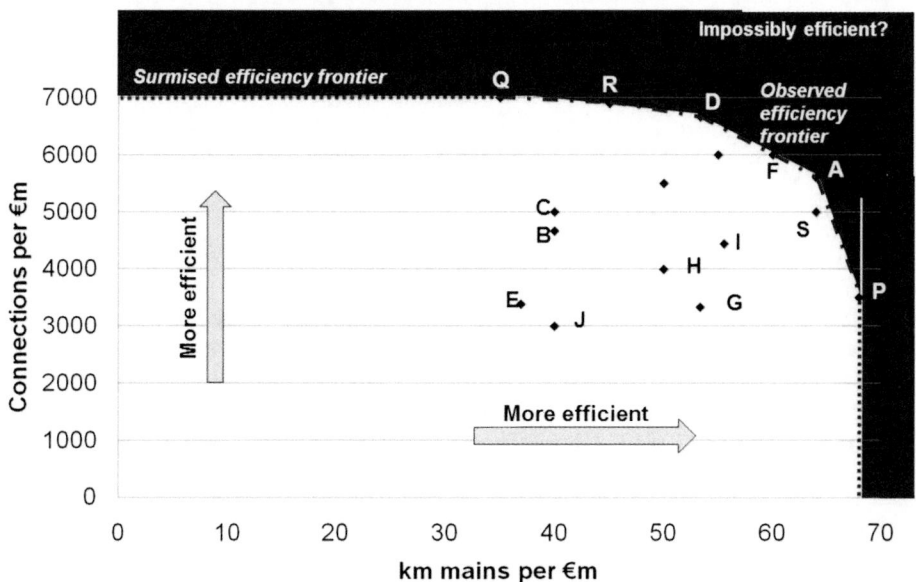

In Figure 83 only 4 new observations have been found – P, Q, R and S – but they are all very useful. P extends the mains efficiency frontier slightly, while S confirms that A is not an anomaly (a data mistake), and R and Q extend the connections-efficiency frontier and confirm that D is not a mistake. Points P, A, D, R, Q now define the observed efficiency frontier, which has become a lot more convex, and its observed range (the curved portion) now covers the triangle of data possibilities for all data in our sample. This means the efficiency of every utility in our sample can be assessed against an observed frontier (a linear combination of two of P, A, D, R and Q) rather than against a surmised efficiency frontier.

Figure 84: Expanding the production possibility frontier

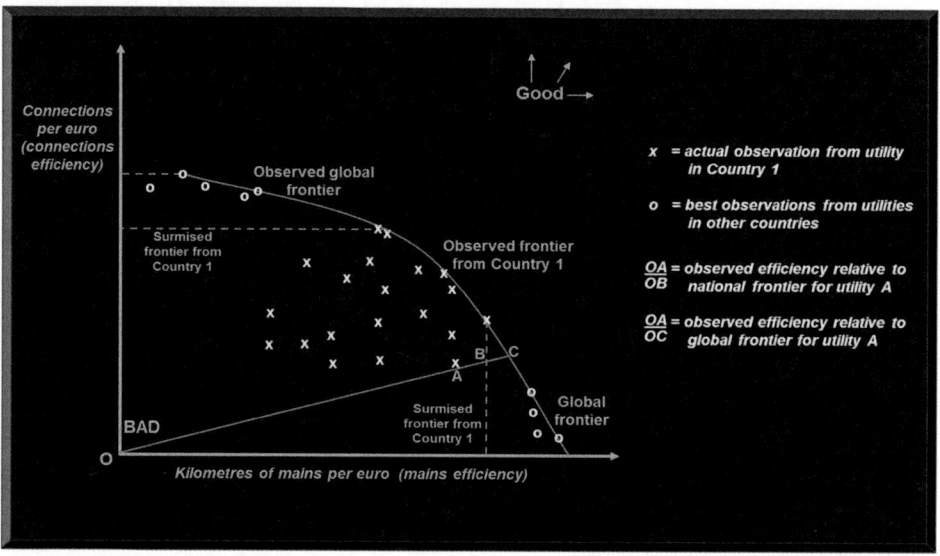

If we continue to expand our data set we should eventually get a much smoother convex production hull, as seen in textbook diagrams, and in Figure 84. This diagram also shows the benefits of international collaboration between regulators using the same data concepts and definitions. A regulator from Country 1 or State 1 may have a good bunch of data from their territory, marked in Figure 84 with X's, but another country may have a far lower population density than any of country 1's regions, and so the bulk of their observations – both efficient and inefficient, marked with O's – will be down at the bottom of the chart, say below the ray OAC. This is good because any efficient utilities here that exceed mains efficiency B will define the frontier away from the assumed vertical frontier out to a more truly global frontier. And collaboration with a third country or State which has more cities and dense towns might lead to more data points at the top of the chart, expanding the frontier above the assumed horizontal frontier. Gradually our frontier can become an indication of global best practice.

---

[164] Charnes A, Cooper W, and Rhodes E (1978) "Measuring the efficiency of decision-making units" European Journal of Operational Research, Vol. 2, p429-444.

Different definitions of the productivity frontier

At first sight the productivity frontier seems a straightforward concept: it is the combination of points of maximum observed productivity at any moment in time. But we know that the data set we have is only a partial view: somewhere in the world there could be similar utilities which are efficient but use combinations of inputs and outputs that the firms we observe do not have - in other words they define other parts of the frontier. From this we can infer that if we had perfect information about every utility on the planet we could define the global frontier of observed productivity for each year. This seems straightforward, and is shown graphically in Figure 85.

However, we know that no firm staffed by real humans is as efficient as it could possibly be; if technology froze and the external environment (customers, regulators etc.) stopped changing their wishes, firms could probably improve on their current positions a little. There must be some waste or X-inefficiency even in the most efficient actual firm, which could in theory be eliminated. So every actual observed frontier must lie within a production set that depicts the theoretical possibilities of the current state of technology. We could call this the Zero Waste Frontier, shown in Figure 85 as the dashed line slightly outside the observed global frontier.

Figure 85: Three theoretical definitions of the productivity frontier

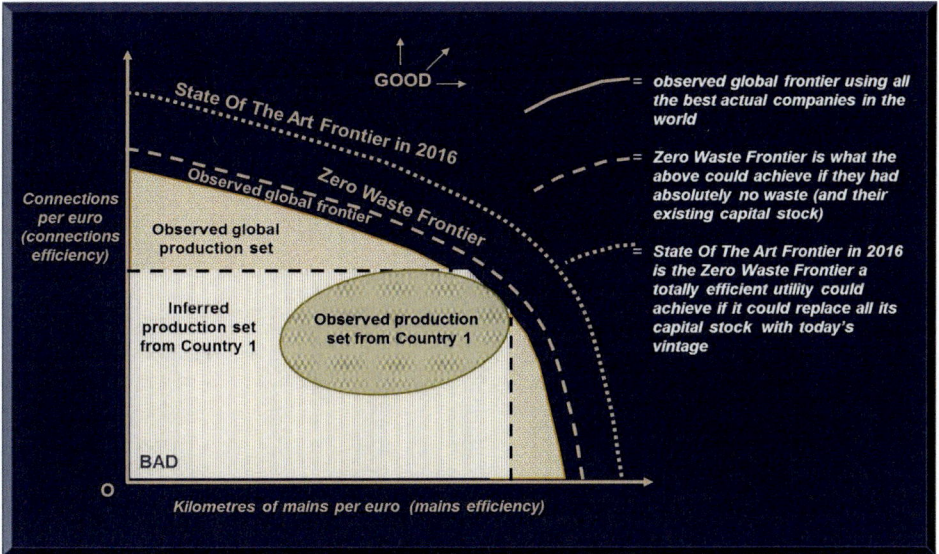

However, even the Zero Waste Frontier is not the absolute limit of efficiency that could be achieved today. With technology frozen at today's level, we can imagine the best companies in the world replacing all their capital equipment with the very latest capital stock and we would see what they could produce. Such a boundary ought to be even better than their current one, so we could call it the State Of The Art Frontier (SOTAF) for this year. It is the most that any firm could produce using all combinations of the best technology available to us this year. In a world of improving technology SOTAF is what Marshall's Long Run Marginal Cost was to neoclassical economics: the boundary for a capital stock optimised for current conditions with current technology.

In reality firms work with the capital stock they have and cannot replace their entire capital stock every year – particularly utilities whose assets sometimes have very long lives. After all, *even if* a firm had complete freedom over its capital budget, there is a replacement rule which says a firm should replace a piece of capital only when the discounted lifetime cost of the new kit, including its purchase cost, is lower than the discounted lifetime cost of the old kit's higher maintenance costs. So, if capital improvements are not sufficiently large for new kit to pass the replacement rule – possibly because the firm bought a new piece of kit just three years ago – even firms with complete capital freedom would not find it economic to replace all their capital with the latest year's new vintage.

In the world of heavy utilities, if we then add the realistic constraints that technological progress in operating, maintaining and servicing pipes and wires is pretty modest, the assets are very long-lived, and much of the world's utility capital spending is severely constrained by politicians or regulators, we have to concede that the most we could ever observe is a global frontier of efficiency reflecting each company's actual capital stock, which is a complete ragbag of past vintages of capital inherited from previous managements, and of past capital/running cost expenditure allocations.

This lead us to the paradox that a firm that commissioned a major piece of capital equipment last year, but uses it inefficiently, has the potential to be a lot more productive than a firm with old capital which uses it very efficiently. It might seem unfair to penalise utilities' managements because they have been starved of capital for decades, but this is the inexorable logic of comparing costs properly: in a truly competitive world high costs, whatever their origins, are regarded as excuses and given short shrift.

Thus, as Figure 85 shows, an observed global efficiency frontier for the year 2016 necessarily implies two further frontiers beyond it: the Zero Waste Frontier slightly beyond the observed frontier, and the State Of The Art Frontier which is well beyond all we observe, and would be the production possibilities if the best companies in each sector of the frontier could replace all their capital with this year's vintage. We might think of these as like the solar system's Kuiper belt and Oort cloud: theoretical bands of rocks and particles that ought to exist, way out there, beyond the observed solar system. Until recently the Kuiper belt was a purely theoretical construct, but we have now viewed Pluto and other dwarf planets up close, and know they are the biggest lumps of it. The Oort cloud, on the other hand, is a thousand times further away, and remains almost entirely invisible to us – at present it is just a theoretical conjecture about the place where comets and other 'periodic' bodies spend most of their lives before zooming in around the sun and becoming visible to us (and approachable by our space craft). But we know comets don't just suddenly come into existence and then cease to exist – they have to live somewhere. And we also know that if even the most efficient firm in an industry could replace all its capital equipment with the latest kit it would be much more productive than it currently is. So there has to be a second hypothetical boundary beyond the Zero Waste Frontier which is the most we can envisage any firm producing per unit of input, using today's technology. The difference with heavy utilities is that the distance between the ZWF and the SOTAF may be much larger than in other industries because of slow technological progress and the long asset lives, and may be heavily influenced by previous capital spending allowed by past politicians and regulators.

Patterns of industry inefficiency: potential distributions inside the production set

We first considered using Data Envelopment Analysis because a regression of firms' actual performance gave us a 'counter-intuitive' (theoretically wrong) result. That was because the seven inefficient firms in the industry outweighed the three efficient firms and happened to be grouped badly from the point of view of economic theory. This seems like a general weakness of all econometric approaches: if we do not weed out the inefficient firms in advance, chance clusters of inefficient firms may lead us to erroneous conclusions about the structure of an industry's efficient possibilities. We do not want the chance structure of inefficient firms well inside the production possibility set to lead us to false conclusions about the shape of the industry's efficient firms – its Production Possibility Frontier. Yet until we do an efficiency analysis we do not know who is efficient and who is not, so who should we weed out?

This reasoning is precisely why many efficiency economists prefer the DEA approach. Define your efficiency concepts clearly, identify those firms on the frontier, and then use the frontier to measure the efficiency of the inefficient. It's a strong starting point for a good debate, but let's hold off awhile evaluating different techniques, until we have looked at some other issues. However, *the shape of the inefficient* is something that deserves closer study now.

Economists rarely consider potential distributions of inefficiency, largely because mainstream attention is focused on contestable industries where competition should eliminate firms who lag far behind the frontier. Why should economists care about possible patterns of inefficiency? Either these firms will recover their competitiveness and bounce back close to the frontier, or competition will sink them, they will become bankrupt, and cease to exist. Either way less-than-optimal performance is just a transitional path with nothing surprising depending on it.

Well, that may be true in a competitive industry, but the general entry and exit conditions of Chapter 3 say intense competition is very unlikely for a utility. So, to do a worthwhile utility efficiency analysis we must consider possible patterns of inefficiency within the production set. This is particularly true when we come to examine the technique of Stochastic Frontier Analysis, but also important when comparing the DEA and econometric approaches. However, before we get there, let us dare to imagine what possible patterns of inefficiency within an industry might look like. Figure 86 shows some plausible possibilities:

Figure 86: Possible distributions of inefficiency in some selected industries

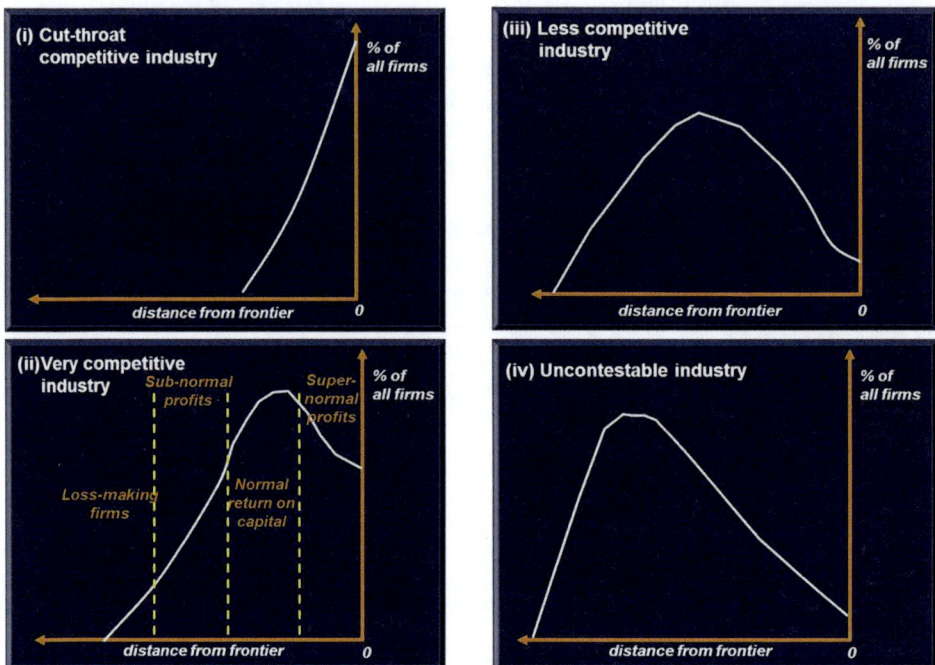

The horizontal axis of these diagrams is worth discussing because it is reversed from conventional axis-definition. So the frontier is at the right of the axis, and the distance from the frontier (inefficiency) increases the more to the left a firm is. Or, if starting from the left, picture it as a slice through the production set of any of the diagrams from Figure 77 to Figure 85 starting from the origin, which is 0% efficient, and heading out to the frontier on the right which is 100% efficient. The y-axis (the height) shows the number, or proportion, of firms to be found at this distance from the frontier, and inefficiency decreases as you approach the frontier.

In (i) above because the industry is assumed to be ruthlessly competitive, any firm that does not keep up with the frontier quickly ceases to exist. The assumptions obviously preclude large entry and exit barriers, and it seems that just staying with the pack at the frontier is the name of the strategic game. Restaurants in a big city, or the music, or fashion industries might be examples of such a market structure.

In (ii) it seems possible that a very competitive industry would have many firms around the frontier, earning a super-normal rate of profit, more firms just a few paces off the frontier, earning normal profits, and then there would be a rapidly diminishing tail of firms making sub-normal profits or losses who had better modernise and improve their efficiency or become history. Our previous discussion of the Zero Waste Frontier and the SOTAF seems apt here: in both i) and ii) it must be possible for firms to be at or very close to the SOTAF, which in turn implies either very little capital is used in these industries (the examples cited in i) above), or capital is very cheap, so the replacement decision is not expensive, or technological progress is so fast in this industry that the gains from replacing old vintage equipment with the latest stuff are massive (e.g. the Information and Communications Technology industries) so everyone furiously replaces all their capital stock every two or three years, because it is part of the cost of staying in business in this industry.

In iii) above we have a more conventional, less competitive, industry, with possibly more barriers to entry, and a fairly symmetric distribution of inefficiency – and profit, presumably – around a mean that is some distance from the frontier. Our ZWF and SOTAF concepts seem relevant here.

Finally, in iv), we have an un-contestable industry with very high entry barriers, such as a grid utility. The interesting question is whether the distribution of inefficiency should be skewed to the right, as in i) and ii), symmetrically as in iii), or to the left as I have shown in iv). I believe the general answer depends on the real efficiency incentives and capital freedom permitted by the regulatory regime, and that in most of the world's utilities these incentives are not strong, so a rational utility management team would head for the quiet, comfortable life, and the distribution would be negatively skewed to the left – i.e. the distribution's mode is away from the frontier.

In short, because a monopoly faces competition only from its nearest substitutes, and for utility products these are distant, unless one invokes stiff regulatory incentives – or strong peer pressure, or social stewardship as powerful incentives – there is no general reason to suppose the *average* utility will be close to the observed frontier, and no reason to suppose the observed frontier will be close to the ZWF or the SOTAF in a slow-moving, capital-intensive, long-asset-life utility. Rather, there seem to be strong reasons for supposing that the proportion of firms close to the frontier will be less than those well inside the observed production envelope.

Theories, facts and Bayes
We have found methods to assess grids' twin outputs of mains length and connections, and two methods, econometric OLS regressions and DEA, to assess efficiency at an instant in time. Furthermore, both methods can easily be extended into more than two dimensions, our only problem being that it is difficult to draw diagrams of this on two-dimensional paper. Yet in several cases the scatter diagrams have been rather useful in telling us what is really going on.

Rationalism, empiricism and Kant's synthesis
There is, though, a big issue at stake here, submerged but now surfacing, which affects our choice of ways of estimating utility efficiency. It is about the different

philosophical approaches we can adopt to obtain better measures of efficiency.

First, though, I should add that many students find philosophy very boring, and if you are one of those feel free to skim a few pages to the heading about Bayesian approaches, because you need to understand Bayesian concepts in order to make informed statistical choices. The bit before is designed to give those who like philosophy some background to the issues which affect us in the little world of efficiency measurement, as well as explaining why the distinction between positive and normative economics is both theoretically wrong and practically useless.

Rationalism

In late mediaeval Europe for a couple of centuries there were two broad schools of philosophical thought: the rationalists and the empiricists. The rationalists were found mostly on the mainland of Europe and included philosophers, mathematicians and scientists such as Rene Descartes, who wanted to show that all rigorous intellectual disciplines could be derived from cold logical theoretical reasoning. Descartes' famous discussion concluding "*Cogito ergo sum*" ('I think therefore I am') was his attempt to prove to a very persistent doubter that although one could doubt many things in the world, such as the existence of God, or Hell, or even a table in front of us[165], he, Rene Descartes, must exist because he could think. The rationalists' ideal was really the world of mathematics and pure logic, where there are pure proofs – proofs such as the internal angles of a triangle adding up to 180^0 –which they held, once proven can never be disproven.

Empiricism – and Leonardo da Vinci

In a sense the empiricists started from the opposite position – all knowledge begins with the senses: observable or empirical facts are the key, not theories. Of course they did not ignore theories. Indeed one of their earliest leading lights, Leonardo da Vinci, said

> "He who loves practice without theory is like the sailor who boards ship without a rudder and compass and never knows where he may cast."

But he also went on to say

> "If you find from your own experience that something is a fact and it contradicts what some authority has written down, then you must abandon

---

[165] 'How can you *prove* that this table exists?' was the doubter's persistent question. Just because it appears to be there, and you see it or feel it, does not prove the table exists; after all, things appear to exist in a dream but we know with 100% certainty those images are not real. Are we in fact all existing in some giant dream – for example God's dream? And if so, do we have free will, or does God really know what we will do in the future, but allow us the illusion of free will? If you like this sort of debate you will probably enjoy a University course in philosophy and metaphysics.

the authority and base your reasoning on your own findings."[166]

So theories are fine but closely-observed facts are superior. And few people could observe something and draw it as well as Leonardo. Having been granted permission to dissect and draw corpses (a rare privilege in those days) and having a quick and curious mind, as well as a heaven-sent ability to draw, Leonardo knew what the inside of a human body looked like, and drew it in wonderful detail. So we have dozens of his notebooks full of drawings as accurate as he could make them of bodies, muscles, spines, pelvises, brain cavities etc. which were a revelation for medical students at the time, who could not get ready access to cadavers for dissection. Instead, medical lectures in those days were held in a theatre with the lecturer, who himself would never touch a body, standing a long way from the cadaver, ordering a surgeon where to cut and telling students what they should see based, on a 1300 year-old textbook by Galen. Galen, we now know had based his theories not on dissections of humans, which were prohibited under Roman law, but on animal dissections, so his anatomy book was wrong from the moment he wrote it. Leonardo's art-training had taught him to draw from meticulous observation. The lecturers insisted that Galen's text must be true, no matter what contrary evidence appeared in front of the students' eyes when the corpse was dissected. Leonardo's reaction was to continue to draw exactly what he saw, men, women, babies in the womb, fruit, trees, streams etc., as well as things that might be, like helicopters and submarines. He was determined to link theories about 'what should be there' to closely observed facts, but if in doubt he trusted what he saw. Leonardo had little time for academic lecturers who might have grand theories, but had never personally dissected a human body or so much as drawn a cut apple accurately.

Later philosophers, scientists and political theorists shared Leonardo's scepticism about pure 'theory' and built a philosophy which said that while mathematics and logic are useful, only direct observation of reality can give you the key facts which logic needs to drive a rational argument forward. For instance, you can argue for ever about whether a black swan can exist[167], but once you agree it is possible for it to exist the only way you can settle the issue of whether it actually exists is to go and find one. This requires first-hand observation (in an experiment that can be repeated by others) so that it can be taken to be a well-established fact. This, of course, put them on a head-on collision with the Christian church, which knew that God could not be observed directly, only indirectly. This may have been why many of the strongest empiricists were found in Protestant countries like Britain, the Netherlands and Germany: the position of the church in Roman Catholic countries was strong enough to make scientists as distinguished as Galileo publicly recant their deeply-held beliefs.

---

[166] Source: Quotation from Leonardo cited in Tarshis J. 1969. Father of modern anatomy: Andreas Vesalius. New York: Dial,103

[167] At this time none had ever been seen, but it was thought they might possibly exist.

Kant's synthesis

Of course neither of these extreme intellectual positions was completely right, and many serious thinkers tried to provide a persuasive intellectual synthesis that squared their liking of mathematical and logical proofs, their growing knowledge about the universe, and their religious beliefs. It was not easy, but the great German philosopher Immanuel Kant came to some worthwhile conclusions which are still useful today. Essentially Kant said[168] that a statement about the world can be either *analytical*, derived from pure logic and maths (an *a priori statement like 2+2 = 4*), or not analytical, which he called *synthetic*. He then divided synthetic statements into those that are factually true or not (which he called *synthetic a posteriori*) such as whether a black swan does actually exist on planet Earth or not, and 'the other sort' – *synthetic a priori*.

As it happens Kant's *synthetic a priori* statements are some of the most interesting statements you can make. All injunctions ("Don't open the door in a jet flying at 30,000 feet!") are *synthetic a priori* statements, as are exhortations("Love thy neighbour as thyself") or moral statements ("Murder is wrong"). So is a simple little sentence like "I love you": it may sound factual, an a posteriori statement of the world as it is, but if course it is often a wish, and it may be conditional ("... provided you love me") or it may even be a deliberate lie. Yet most people would say these are some of the most meaningful statements a human can make (when you mean them!) which is why we write songs and poetry about them. Also much academic knowledge or theorising comes into this category. For example it is hard to devise a simple experiment that simply and conclusively confirms or refutes a grand scientific theory like evolution or general relativity, precisely because they are so general: a sceptic might say these concepts have become so big, that, like the concept of God, they are irrefutable (or un-falsifiable, to use the language of scientific methodology) because they can be subtly re-defined if they appear to fail one very specific test[169].

When considering *synthetic a priori* statements be very careful with your words,

---

[168] Kant I *'Prolegomena to any future metaphysics'* 1783

[169] Of course science is much cleverer and more agnostic than this: we do not actually believe that any of these models are "the truth"; we simply use them quite shamelessly and only if they are useful. We do not believe that light is particles or light is a wave: we know light is just light, and may not be like anything we can understand at the human level. But using particle models of balls colliding into each other, or water waves, can help us understand some of its properties. Similarly, if we build a bridge the engineers will use Newtonian physics even though they know this theory is not absolutely true, and is in fact contained within Einstein's relativity physics. We do not use the more general theory of relativity because in practice we do not need to use it. But if engineers had to plan the trajectory of a spacecraft to the Centaurus stars, four light years away, they would have to use the extra explanatory power of Einstein's relativity theory to get there accurately. In short, ultimately we don't believe scientific theories are true, we believe they are useful. This is my starting point for economics: I don't believe economic theories alone are wholly true (how could they be in the Social Sciences?), but they must be useful – i.e. get me to a logical conclusion I could not reach by common sense.

and distinguish concepts precisely. The statement "Murder is illegal" is an *a posteriori* statement: it can be checked by checking the laws of the country you are in. But "Murder is wrong" is a moral statement, just like "Mankind should be stewards of planet Earth". It is the 'should' that makes it a *synthetic a priori* statement: such statements are not self-evidently true, like 2+2 = 4, or some mathematical lemma, nor can they be shown to be true by observing the world.

Positive and normative economics
Kant's distinctions are relevant to economics because some influential twentieth century economists, including Milton Friedman and Paul Samuelson (both of whom I greatly respect), got hold of some of these ideas, but also confused them, by adopting some ideas from an early twentieth century school of philosophy called the Logical Positivists. This brief (now largely discredited) school included some first rate philosophers such as Wittgenstein, and others now forgotten. These young men hated the part of philosophy we are discussing, metaphysics, and rejected Kant's *synthetic a priori* completely, boldly declaring that all meaningful statements were either analytical *a priori* or synthetic *a posteriori*. Well, as we have seen, their ideas were never going to catch on with the public, which loves its love songs, nor with serious scientists. Eventually they were largely ignored even by other philosophers. The founder of scientific methodology, Karl Popper, wrote his seminal "The Logic of Scientific Discovery"[170] in reaction to their work, in so doing inventing the modern concept of *falsifiability* of scientific hypotheses, which is probably the most lasting contribution the Logical Positivists made to intellectual progress. The most famous English-speaking logical positivist was the Oxford philosopher AJ Ayer, who concluded his views on it many years later with the wonderfully pithy

> "I suppose the most important [defect]...was that nearly all of it was false."[171]

Unfortunately two great but then-young American economists tried to apply Logical Positivist distinctions to economics. Paul Samuelson, followed by Milton Friedman[172], reasoned that all economics could be divided into positive ('what is') and normative ('what should be') economics, it being strongly implied that positive economics was rigorous and scientific while normative economics was vague, wish-driven statements about value-judgements that could, and should, be handed over to non-economists.

---

[170] Originally 1934 *Logik der Forschung*, translated by Popper in 1959 as "The Logic of Scientific Discovery".

[171] Hanfling, Oswald (2003). *"Logical Positivism"*. Routledge History of Philosophy. Routledge. pp. 193f

[172] Samuelson's *Foundations of Economic Analysis* (1947). Friedman's thoughts were summarised in his 1953 *Essays in Positive Economic."The methodology of positive economics"*. The first wave of critics soon emerged, arguing economics could never be value-free – e.g. Myrdal G, 1954 *The Political Element in the Development of Economic Theory*, trans. Paul Streeten (Cambridge, MA: Harvard University Press).

For example in consumer theory a utility curve shows points of indifference, or equal satiation. In positive economics it leads to the idea of a Pareto improvement, whereby the gainers from a social move benefit more than the losers, so that in theory the gainers could compensate the losers and still be better off. So Pareto improvements are a good idea, a powerful piece of positive economics, because they are rigorous and logically true; the fact that compensation of the losers by the gainers was rarely done in practice because the losers were often the least powerful in society was held to be 'not an economic problem' but one for politicians, sociologists or whoever. Or, when I was an undergraduate, a typical general equilibrium text might begin "Let us assume that politicians have clearly specified the social welfare function...", which de-coded means "Assume politicians have made all the those really difficult value-judgements and trade-off decisions about who should gain and lose from each possible policy action we may take." Yet we know these limitations – these value judgments – are the very reasons why many good economic ideas (such as land redistribution or reform of property laws) are not put into practice: economists make a theoretical case for it based on positive economics and Pareto improvements, and politicians say "You guys just don't live in the real world! I couldn't contemplate that for a moment" (because of some obvious-to-them value judgements).

So applied economists advising real decision makers have long rejected the distinction between positive and normative economics as being useless in practice. Actually the real world is full of interesting, vital, value judgements and sometimes these value judgements are made by politicians or even an entire electorate, but sometimes it is economists who are required to make some critical value judgements. Example? When, after a recession, the Governor of your country's Central Bank says "I believe the economy is growing again." This is not positive economics: it is a value judgement, or a statement of hope, based on logical thinking and some positive economic models. And the reason the man or woman got their job as Head of the Central Bank is precisely because they were thought to be good at making value judgements[173] like this. As a micro-economist the value judgements you will make will be on a smaller scale, but they will to some extent determine your conclusions. Fine. Don't be afraid to make value judgements; just be open and honest that you are making some and do not pretend that you have made no value judgements. Unless you wish to be a theoretical mathematician nothing worthwhile involves no value judgements.

Bayesian approaches

Which brings us to the Reverend Thomas Bayes, an 18th century churchman interested in games of chance – though purely for intellectual reasons, of course. Bayes researched a popular lottery of his day and reached some solid mathematical conclusions which were published after his death by his friend

---

[173] Let us hope this was the reason they got the job, and not because they were the President's brother.

[174] Bayes, Thomas; Price, Mr. (1763). "An Essay towards solving a Problem in the Doctrine of Chances.". *Philosophical Transactions of the Royal Society of London* 53: 370–418

Richard Price[174]. His most famous conclusion is now called Bayes theorem and it concerns 'conditional probability', which is the probability of one thing *given that* we already know another thing – like a fact, or a theory. Mathematically we can write this as (or, let us define our notation as)

P(A || B) means the probability of A given B

so P(A || B) means the probability of A being true, given that we have observed fact B.

The simplest version of Bayes theorem is

$$P(A || B) = P(B || A) \frac{P(A)}{P(B)}$$

where P(A) and P(B) are the absolute or 'prior probabilities' of A and B being true – given no other information at all. Naturally, being a mathematical equation, Bayes theorem assumes we can observe or calculate some of these probabilities, P(B || A), P(A), and so on, and that is what Thomas Bayes had spent years doing, until he had proved this theorem mathematically. Eleven years later this work was independently repeated and extended by the great French mathematician Pierre-Simon Laplace, in 1774[175], though being a better mathematician, Laplace proved it more generally and applied it to several different areas of science besides games of chance.

Now let's apply Bayes theorem to econometrics. We may have a theory, or Hypothesis, H, that expensive utilities are inefficient, and we may have some evidence or data, D, on utility costs which we hope will act as some kind of a test of our theory. We have observed actual costs, D, so we *could* take this as given – as a fact. But in truth it is not the last word, or definitive proof of anything: there may be a stochastic process (pure chance) determining what we actually observed, so that if we had repeated the 'experiment' we might have got different cost data – for instance if the weather had been different that year, or there had not been a recession in the construction industry etc. So D itself may have a probability distribution, and the actual D that we observe was just one of many similar ones we could have seen; indeed, if we knew something about those stochastic processes we might be able to describe the probability distribution P(D) and work out what the probability was that we would observe the actual D that we did observe. In other words we might be able to work out the prior probability P(D) in advance using a completely different model or system from the main one we wish to test – for instance a weather model, which has no economic components at all, or a macroeconomic model in which our sector is a negligible bit.

---

[175] Pierre-Simon Laplace (1774/1986), "*Memoir on the Probability of the Causes of Events*", Statistical Science 1(3):364–378

We now repeat Bayes theorem replacing A and B with H and D

$$P(H \| D) = P(D \| H) \frac{P(H)}{P(D)}$$

which is just a piece of algebra replacement.

However, translating algebra into efficiency concepts, what this now says is that the probability of our Hypothesis H being true, given that we have observed fact D, is the probability of D being true if H is true times the ratio of the prior probabilities of H and D being absolutely true – given nothing at all. The 'reverse' probability, $P(D \| H)$, to the thing we are interested in, $P(H \| D)$, is called the *likelihood function*; it is the likelihood of us observing fact D *if (or given)* that our Hypothesis H is in fact true.

What does this likelihood function $P(D \| H)$ mean? Well, one interpretation is that it's the point of the differences from the regression line that we calculated earlier, isn't it? That regression line says that if our hypothesis is true (i.e. given H) then we expect the costs (D) of the inefficient to be higher than average (the regression line). Or, using DEA, efficient firms will define the production frontier and inefficient firms will be inside the production set on a ray between the origin, them and the frontier. So inefficient firms will have higher costs per unit of outputs delivered than the efficient hypothetical firm Z will have on the frontier. If they could shrink their costs they would move out along the ray towards firm Z.

Bayesian handling of useless data
One way to check you understand the application of Bayes theorem is to consider the usefulness of data that is rubbish. I mean pure rubbish – just absolute nonsense. Supposing we have some hypothesis, H, given that D, the date clock, says 6 July. But in fact the date clock is stuck at 6 July and always says that. What now is the probability, P(D), that we will observe D = 6 July? Well it must be 100%; it can't say anything else. Is this data, D, telling us anything useful? Absolutely not. Now let's plug P(D) = 100% = 1 into Bayes theorem:

$$P(H \| D) = P(D \| H) \frac{P(H)}{P(D)}$$

but P(D) = 1

$$P(H \| D) = P(D \| H).P(H)$$

but *P(H || D)=P(H)*: the probability that our Hypothesis is true given Data D is simply the prior probability of our Hypothesis, P(H) – because the data is worthless

$$P(H) = P(D \| H).P(H)$$
$$P(D \| H) = 1$$

of course it is – because

$$P(D) = 1$$

So we have come to the totally trite conclusion that was our original assumption. Great! But now do the process in reverse and we start to understand why Bayes theorem is so useful when designing scientific experiments: what we really want in any scientific experiment is the opposite of a stopped clock: fascinating data that could only have occurred if our hypothesis were right. *Ideally we want P(D) to be as low as possible* (we want some very unlikely data to turn up), *and we want the likelihood function P(D given H) to be as high as possible* ("...the probability that we will observe Data D if our Hypothesis H is true, is very high").

A classic example of a wonderfully-designed experiment that used this logic to confirm a major theory was Eddington's 1919 demonstration of relativity, which effectively showed that a ray of light could be bent by a very large mass. This experiment measured the exact position of a star known to be just behind the Sun during a solar eclipse, a brief period when our Moon comes between the Sun and the Earth, and blocks out the Sun's brilliance. Eddington travelled to Principe, an island off West Africa, where the eclipse was total, and took photographs of the eclipsed Sun through a telescope. His photographs showed that the predicted star could still be seen when it was behind the Sun – i.e. over the Sun's horizon. The only alternative explanations to the theory of relativity (Newton's Laws) were either that the star moved its position a few light years while it was behind the Sun, and then mysteriously moved back again afterwards, or that, somehow, the Earth wobbled off its normal, almost circular, orbit during the eclipse, before wandering back to its well-worn path round the Sun soon after the eclipse ended. Both are incredibly unlikely! So the probability of the data observed, P(D), was very low. What do we think was really happening? Because the Sun is so massive the light from the star was bending round the Sun so that we could see over the Sun's horizon and behind it. So a ray of light could be bent by a huge mass such as the Sun, contradicting Newton's laws, and confirming part of Einstein's hypothesis of relativity.

Applying Bayesian methods in economics
So we have gained the Bayesian insight, which may have taken Thomas Bayes years to formulate (this is pure speculation), and probably took a genius like Laplace a few hours. What Bayes' insight adds to modern statistical work is to say that if you have strong views or theoretical beliefs about your hypothesis, why not try to calculate the 'prior probability' of your Hypothesis, your P(H), directly, as a number (like 70%) or a probability distribution (such as 'Normal

with a mean of 70% and a standard deviation of 5%')? From the point of view of Bayes theorem as a piece of pure maths, it does not matter if your prior probability is even subjective – a complete value judgement. After all, if there had been alternative explanations for Eddington's observations two thousand years ago these would have involved Gods moving stars about in the sky and other explanations that we now regard as totally fantastic. So the P(D) of Eddington's experiment was only very low because we have subjectively ruled out explanations that our ancestors believed were totally credible. And in the world of economics, since the demise of positive economics we accept that all practical work requires some value judgements, so who better to make those value judgements than you, so long as you are open, realistic, and honest about what you have assumed? After all, if you go over the top and just *assume* your theory is true (P(H) = 1) your conclusions will be as weak as water[176]. So you have an incentive to be fair and realistic, and if someone else wishes to repeat your experiment with different priors they can. The next step is then to quantify your Data prior probabilities, P(D), of experimental error, false positives and the like as objectively as possible, using models or techniques that are independent of your main experiment. And finally you need to work out the likelihood function P(D || H) - the probability of your Data occurring given that your Hypothesis is true, which of course you want to be as high as possible – "...the probability that we will observe Data D if our Hypothesis H is true is very likely."

Bayes and the parametric vs non-parametric debate
Figure 80 showed how a random set of seven inefficient comparators outweighed good data from three efficient firms to give us a regression with a misleading slope – in fact a coefficient that we know (with 100% certainty) was wrong. We used that result to justify using the DEA approach, in which we *a priori* define being efficient as having lower costs per unit of multi-dimensional output, and concluded that among efficient firms there must be a trade-off between mains-efficiency (dimension 1) and connections-efficiency (dimension 2 in Figure 80). A Bayesian would say that DEA is the assumption that our "prior" or theory is 100% correct (P(H) = 1) and the data will show whatever it shows.

The problem with DEA is 'What if we are slightly unsure about our theory?' What if we have quite reasonable doubts about whether something is a cost-driver that is beyond management's control or ability to influence? For instance a utility's management team might claim that past capital expenditure was something they had no control over, and so they have heavy operating costs, and high total costs, in comparison with other companies at present because of decades of under-investment in new capital stock by previous management teams. Hmm. Well, theoretically they may have a point: clearly none of the current management team could be responsible for the consequences of past capital decisions taken before they were born, or before they became qualified

---

[176] According to some religious authorities, 'Scripture', being God's Word written down, cannot be argued with, and so has (P(H) = 1): you either believe it or you are a non-believer.

water engineers, or, in fact, before they joined the company. But were they responsible for capital decisions taken just three years ago, when the same people were Board Directors but under a different CEO. Hmm. Not sure about that... where should responsibility stop?

The DEA approach says we reach some theoretical definition – a precise list of factors which can be quantified and will be allowed as exogenous cost-drivers – and then feed these into our DEA model as network outputs. The DEA model is then so constructed that if we define there to be 6 allowed exogenous cost-drivers (6 outputs), at least 6 utilities will be declared to be 100% efficient by our model, and all the others will be compared to a linear interpolation of that 6-dimensional space and given an efficiency rating less than 100%. A practical weakness is that in a small data set – e.g. the ten in Figure 80 – more than half the data set will be delighted to know they are 100% efficient. Indeed, in Figure 83 we have only two dimensions of output but six firms defining a smooth convex hull, so with just two outputs we have six firms that are 100% efficient[177]. A regulator, trying to incentivise general efficiency, might be less pleased with the result than the six firms. This is the general weakness of using DEA: for a reasonable number of exogenous cost drivers – say 6 – unless the regulator is lucky, and the same firms keep on coming top, there is a fair chance you will end up with 20 or 30 100% efficient firms, and will need a very large data set – two or three hundred utilities – to derive useful incentive implications.

DEA is an example of a *non-parametric* approach – it gives us no statistical guidance at all on whether something should be included as an exogenous cost-driver or not. But if we have doubts about our theory, from where else should we obtain guidance? The pure Bayesian says use other models entirely to derive your priors P(H) and P(D) independently. By contrast, the parametric approach that is often attempted in practice, and is justified by being called a standard 'Hendry' econometric testing-down approach[178], treats the data as right and whatever theory is correct will emerge from the data. So a data set is collected, groomed to remove obvious anomalies or dubious datum points, a set of reduced form possible explanatory factors (exogenous cost-drivers) is derived, and then the testing down begins, with explanatory factors being thrown out if their t-statistics are not 95% significant. The author and former colleagues have certainly seen this approach used by regulators, arriving at sets of exogenous cost-drivers that contain many sensible factors but some other factors that are at best dubious and at worst 'counter-intuitive'[179]. It is a purely inductive and empirical approach, the exact opposite of DEA, largely ignoring theory, and assuming the data must be 100% correct.

---

[177] In multiple output analyses a factor that helps to reduce the number of firms deemed 100% efficient is that one low-cost firm may define the frontier in several outputs, or dimensions.

[178] This is most unfair to Hendry himself, who always stressed the importance of being crystal clear about one's alternative theoretical models before attempting even the most basic regressions.

Cross-sectional comparisons – a suggested approach
So which to use? Parametric testing-down or non-parametric DEA? Or do we have to be Bayesians and assign either arbitrary priors to our data and our hypotheses, or develop completely independent parallel models to justify our data and hypothesis priors? Bayesians would say that if we aren't at least 50% sure of our basic theory – e.g. that productivity is output divided by inputs, and efficiency is having higher productivity than others – the whole exercise is a waste of time.

Well, if we are determined to be really rigorous we must use the last approach and justify some data and hypothesis priors from genuinely independent data and independent theories or models ('The Literature'). We can be very sure that productivity is output divided by inputs; the hard part is turning conflicting models and data from different parts of the world into precise numbers, like 70% for theory A and 30% for conflicting theory B. Or deciding when a management team or set of owners become responsible for a company's inherited circumstances. However, if we recall Eddington's test of relativity, the best approaches construct an experiment so well that any plausible alternative hypotheses would be exceedingly unlikely to explain the data – i.e. the absolute probability of the data P(D) being observed must be close to zero, while the likelihood function (P(Data) given the Hypothesis) must be close to one.

Use significance levels below 95% when testing down
When deciding whether to accept or reject a hypothesis most econometrics text books use 95% confidence limits because the first scientists to apply the statistician RA Fisher's 1925[180] results thought that this was a reasonable level of confidence to have in an important scientific theory. But the practical econometrician in our exercise is looking to see if Factor X, which can be quantified, could be a significant exogenous cost-driver beyond the influence of a utility's management. The difference with general theoretical circumstances is that they are more worried about wrongly accepting a false hypothesis (a so-called 'Type II error'), while we are more concerned with wrongly rejecting a true hypothesis (a Type I error).

This is not semantics. When comparing utilities' efficiency if there is a chance that factor X could be a significant cost-driver we should give it every reasonable opportunity to shine through: the factor X that we have objective, quantifiable measurements of may be a rather poor proxy for the true but unobservable, or unquantifiable, factor Y, and there could well be a very good theoretical linkage between Y and utility costs that is beyond management's control. Ideally we

---

[179] The technical term for bonkers. Again, let us spare their blushes; we do not need to rake over old coals. However the author has examined four generations of water models used by Ofwat since 1994 and several generations of models used by Ofgem and its predecessor regulators, as well as models used by other regulators around the world.

[180] Fisher RA Statistical Methods for Research Workers, Edinburgh: Oliver and Boyd, 1925, p.43.

would model the linkage between X and Y as a sub-system within our general system of equations, but because Y is unobservable or unquantifiable we cannot, and so have to accept X as a sub-optimal, but at least quantifiable, proxy for Y.

In practical terms this means ultimately that if we are really sure of our X and Y sub-theory then any significance greater than 50% should be enough for a regulator; 50% might be a bit bold, if you are a junior regulator in your first job, but draw comfort in your own value judgements (your priors) from the following facts:

1. "Only 80% significance" means that the statistics are telling us that it is 80% likely that X is an exogenous cost-driver, beyond management's control, and 20% likely that it is not – that we have a random coincidence of numbers. *In other words it is four times as likely that X is an exogenous cost-driver than it is not.* Why would you bet on the 20%? Yet several regulators have employed econometricians who did. And a significance of "only 67%" still means it is twice as likely that X is an explanatory factor, and so on, right down to 50%.
2. The significance of explanatory variables can fall at one stage in testing down and then later rise as other explanatory variables are dropped.

Stochastic Frontiers Analysis

A generic problem with all our Ordinary Least Squares regressions so far has been that the thing we are most interested in – a utility's efficiency – is a residual, an error term between what we expect from theory and what we observe in practice. This methodology of residuals is well known in the history of science, but it has always been acknowledged as being obviously weak. Where possible we will always prefer a more direct approach. By contrast the non-parametric approach of DEA measures efficiency explicitly, but runs the risk of including some explanatory factors which should not be included because they got there by chance – by a stochastic process.

If we consider the error term in an OLS efficiency regression then theoretically we are saying it includes both a random white noise error term – let's all it 'v' – and a term for utility efficiency – let's call it 'u'. What if we could separate these two out? Then we would have an explicit measure of the thing we are interested in – utility efficiency, allowing for its operating environment.

This is precisely the thinking that led to the invention of Stochastic Frontiers Analysis (SFA). In 1977 two papers appeared within a month of each other in major economic journals advocating and justifying SFA[181]. The two papers had

---

[181] Meeusen W and Van Den Broeck J, (1977), Efficiency estimation from Cobb-Douglas Production functions with composed error, International Economic Review, Vol 18, 2 June 1977 and Aigner D, Lovell C, Schmidt P (1977) 'Formulation and estimation of stochastic frontier production function models', Journal of Econometrics 6 1977 21-37. Of course both papers had been written in the couple of years preceding this.

been written independently but essentially came to the same conclusions about devising a new measure of estimating production frontiers and individual firms' distance from them.

So our underlying equation describing what drives costs in our industry is, in matrix form,

$$y = f(X\beta + \varepsilon)$$

Where X is a matrix of values of exogenous cost drivers for each firm in the industry, beta is a vector of coefficients to be estimated by statistical processes, and the error term ε

$$\varepsilon = v + u$$

Where v = *noise* – stochastic numbers with a mean of zero and a normal distribution and u = *utility efficiency* – a one-sided distribution, which can vary but never exceed the stochastic frontier. This is the thing we are seeking – our Holy Grail.

So we have de-composed the error term into two bits, a normal error term with a mean of zero and a normal distribution, and a one-sided efficiency term 'u'. But what specification should our error term have? What should an efficiency term look like in theory? Both sets of original pioneers, Aigner *et al*, and Meeusen and Van den Broeck were concerned with a general application to all industries, rather than to utilities, and so took the conventional view that competition would force most firms to be efficient. Consequently they tried distributions that were skewed towards the frontier, rather than away from the frontier, as shown in Figure 87:

Figure 87: Distributions of inefficiency typically assumed in Stochastic Frontiers

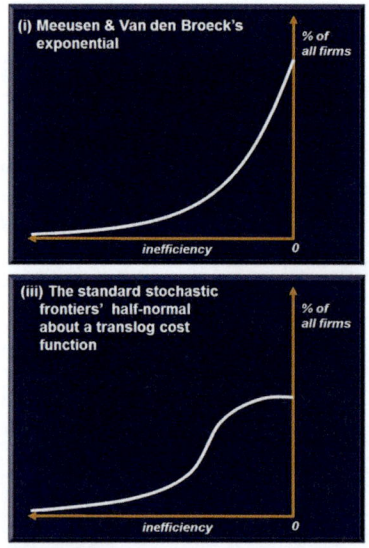
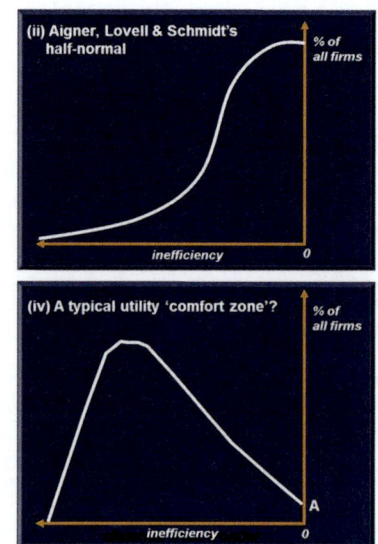

Over the subsequent years stochastic frontiers has become a popular way of estimating frontiers in business economics because of its good theoretical properties, but as ever, it has some limitations:

1. Having to be estimated using maximum likelihood estimators, we cannot prove the estimates are unbiased, whereas if we could use Least Squares we know they are unbiased;
2. For practical purposes this is not usually a major handicap because in practice SF estimates often turn out to be statistically indistinguishable from OLS estimates;
3. This is rather handy (we have confidence the estimates are unbiased) but, on reflection, shows that the novel idea of splitting the error term into two prior distributions is not in practice doing much work.

So, overall, a disappointing result. Why is this? Is it the prior assumption about the specification of the efficiency term? Both Meeusen and Van den Broeck and Aigner, Lovell and Schmidt tried a variety of assumed distributions of inefficiency, including exponential and half-normal. In the intervening years it has become traditional to assume a half-normal distribution about a translog cost function.

Problems with using stochastic frontiers in utilities

However the problem with all of these models is that they assume the distribution of inefficiency becomes *thicker towards the edge of the production set* – in other words their default assumption is that firms tend to be efficient, indeed firms tend to be frontier-efficient, and only exceptional laggards are seriously inefficient. What if the distribution of inefficiency is the other way round? What if only exceptional firms are very efficient, while most are a little bit lazy, or quite a lot lazy, and just follow the pack? Particularly in a non-contestable industry such as network utilities the normal default hypotheses seem to be round the wrong way. Figure 87 from pure theory, could well be the case for a non-contestable industry like a network grid.

So while Figure 87 (iv) shows what we suspect to be true for utilities, Figure 87 diagrams (i)- (iii) show distributions that have actually been tried by stochastic frontiers practitioners. All three of them fundamentally slope the wrong way: they are 'positively' skewed towards the frontier when (iv) shows that what we think we want is a negative skew towards the lazy (but safer!) middle.

Non-traditional assumptions of inefficiency distributions in utilities

Before proceeding any further, it is worth saying now that if we were arch-empiricists and really had no prior theoretical view about the distribution of inefficiency within a production set we should logically assume the simplest distribution of all: a uniform distribution – a flat line – all the way from the centre of the production set to the frontier. That would certainly be easy to test, but does not seem ever to have been tried.

Real world inefficiencies

Surely that's going too far, you might ask? Surely no real utility would occur near the centre of the production set, being allowed to produce almost nothing and still consume resources? Do not be so sure. In many parts of the world this would be unthinkable, but a huge amount depends on the strategic goals and governance arrangements of the utility – what it has been set up to do, how it will operate, and who is monitoring it – as well as its business environment and corporate culture. These real internal values and beliefs of an organisation and the environment in which it operates have a huge influence on an organisation's actual delivery of outputs. If the President of a country believes that the main purpose of a particular utility is to provide his troublesome nephew with a job that keeps this nephew out of the political arena and allows him to make some serious money (besides his salary) from bribery on company contracts, then we have a utility that is rotten from the top. If this situation is allowed to continue the rotten-ness will spread and our 'long run equilibrium' will be a utility that does the bare minimum for the President and his nephew to stay in position, including, for example, providing no service at all outside the capital city. Do not for one moment imagine there are no utilities like this on planet Earth in the twenty first century.

More significantly, the differences in business environment, corporate governance, strategic goals and corporate cultures can lead many utilities not to focus on efficiency and outputs as their highest priority. In many countries a job in a state-owned utility is highly prized as one of the few sources of cash income in a desperately under-employed economy, so not only do employees try very hard to get family relatives and friends appointed to other positions in the utility, but also in countries with a serious AIDS problem the list of employees on "long term sick leave" can be massive. In a country with no social security network managers are understandably reluctant to strike terminally ill colleagues off the employee roll, but the consequence is that in some countries significant proportions of utilities' payrolled staff do no work at all and never will.

Potential inefficiency distribution assumptions for stochastic frontiers

So for utilities let us not be neoclassical, and assume that the pattern of inefficiency must slope up to the frontier. We should at least test for a uniform distribution, and there is a strong possibility that even in well-run countries with close monitoring of utilities, the pattern of inefficiency for the non-contestable utilities could slope down from a band of acceptably-inefficient firms to a few efficiency fanatics at the frontier, as shown in Figure 87 (iv).

For the classic case of a utility producing two outputs from one input (total costs) Figure 88 depicts how an industry's efficiency scatter plot would look if it followed the standard half-normal distribution assumed by most SFA practitioners:

Figure 88: Possible patterns of inefficiency: the standard half-normal distribution

By contrast Figure 89 shows how a completely uniform distribution of inefficiency would look:

Figure 89: A uniform distribution of inefficiency within the production set

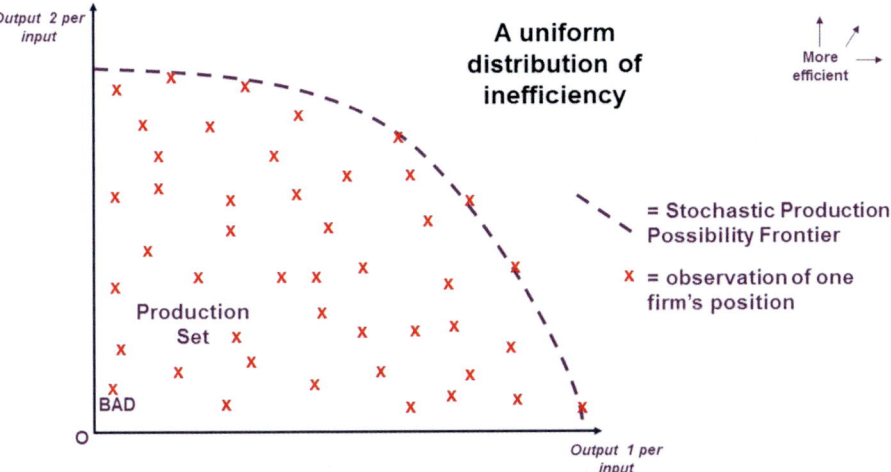

To test for this using stochastic frontiers is far simpler than the standard case: the technical efficiency term u = a constant. One might ask why this assumption is not the default standard assumption – the null hypothesis – in all efficiency studies examining non-contestable utilities?

As a third option Figure 90 shows how the hypothesised distribution of utility inefficiency from Figure 87 (iv) would look when mapped out in two dimensions:

Figure 90: The 'comfort zone' distribution of utility inefficiency

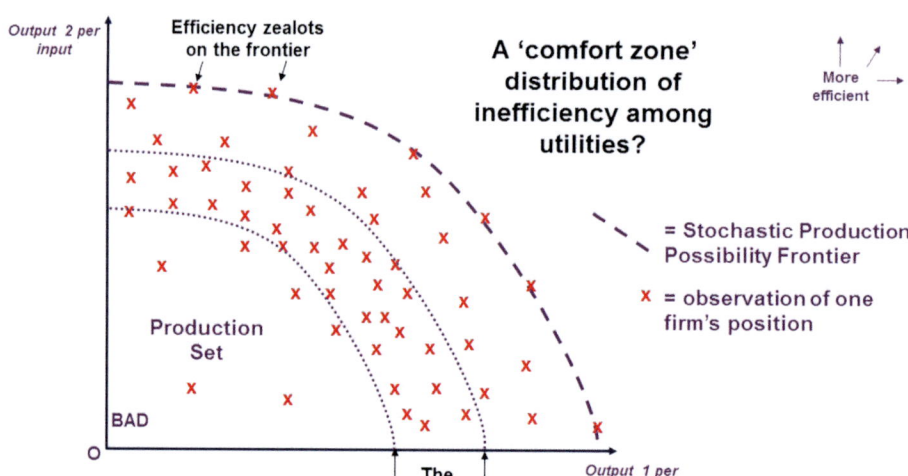

This distribution is a mixture of the previous two distributions, but with firms concentrated not near the frontier, but in a band in the middle, in what we might call the 'comfort zone', while only a few efficiency zealots define the frontier, and a few real stinkers define the centre of the production set. But how could we test for this distribution using stochastic frontiers?

Reversing the assumed error distribution from an upwards slope to a downward slope (using this definition of the horizontal axis) is no statistical problem, but we have to reach a decision on what the intercept A at the frontier of Figure 87 (iv) is going to be. It cannot just tail off asymptotically, as conventional stochastic frontier assumptions do at the other end, or we will never observe it at all! Yet stochastic frontiers theory calls for a bounded, one-sided, error term to represent inefficiency. So we must arbitrarily curtail the tail, and decide the height of that tail at the intercept. Effectively we are *a priori* assuming the proportion of the industry that will actually achieve the frontier. We could try different heights to see which works best, but in fact we know with 100% certainty that an A greater than zero exists: there must be at least one company in our data set that defines, or is close to, the frontier of observed best practice for that data set. So this gives us a simple rule that the minimum value A can have is $A_1 = 1/n$ where n is the number of firms in our sample, and we could try $A_2 = 2/n$ etc. if we want to assume that a genuine 'frontier' must have at least two firms on it, or $A_3 = 3/n$ if we want our frontier to be a little bit stochastic, etc.. Beyond that it rather depends on how large our sample is and how well spread over the convex hull the efficient firms happen to be; in other words we may have to see in practice, from scatter plots and the like, what works best. We will then have linked our theoretical definitions and concepts of 'stochastic production frontier' to assumed distributions of efficiency in a satisfyingly Bayesian manner.

In the deep interior of the production set, beyond the modal zone of comfortably inefficient firms, the pattern of the tail-off at the opposite (inefficient) end of the distribution is depicted in Figure 87 (iv) as asymptotically declining. Do we have any theoretical justification for this? A little bit: even the most corrupt President wants some services provided for the citizens, or the citizens may revolt and demand the removal of the extremely corrupt utility President, so there will be some pressures for every utility in the world to produce some outputs. So the pattern of inefficiency at the centre of even the worst global utilities should tail off towards the centre of the production set.

Total Factor Productivity (TFP)

At the start of this chapter we said that productivity is innately a relative concept, and that it improves over time. We now therefore turn to measuring efficiency over time. The most widely used measure of productivity improvements over time is Total Factor Productivity (TFP), sometimes known by purists as MultiFactor Productivity (MFP)[182]. At its heart *TFP measures the growth of outputs between two periods in time and compares it with the growth in inputs*. If outputs have grown more than inputs we have productivity growth, while if the reverse, we have become more inefficient. Usually TFP is positive, and so we have some productivity growth which can be attributed to two broad causes: technological progress or an increase in technical (or productive) efficiency.

Just to clarify, the relevant equation defining a 'Hicks-Moorsteen' Total Factor Productivity index, or HM TFP[183], is

$$\text{HM TFP Index} = \frac{\text{Growth in Output}}{\text{Growth in Input}} = \frac{\text{Proportionate change in Output quantity index}}{\text{Proportionate change in Input quantity index}}$$

There are some truly excellent aspects to TFP:

- *It makes no theoretical assumptions at all* about firms being in equilibrium, efficient, incentivised, motivated by profit, owned by private enterprise or the state, or whatever; in other words it can be used anywhere at any time;
- Provided you can create adequate quantity indices *it can be generalised beyond a firm to an industry, and beyond an industry to an entire economy*.

Yes, this is actually how we measure technological progress of the world's economies[184]: Gross Domestic Product is a single measure of an economy's

---

[182] According to *Coelli et al* (p 64) the difference is philosophical: MFP purists say that it is impossible to list all the possible inputs of a firm, and particularly for something as complex as an industry or an economy, so any realistic index can only be called an MFP, not a *Total* Factor Productivity index.

[183] Diewert in 1992 attributed this independently to Hicks and Moorsteen in 1961.

[184] The technique was first devised by Robert Solow in the second of his seminal 1957 papers on growth theory: Solow R 1957 *Technical change and the aggregate production function* Review of Economics and Statistics, Vol. 39, No. 3 (Aug., 1957), pp. 312-320

outputs, so we compare an economy's GDP growth at the top of our equation with growth in all the inputs of the economy, such as population (or estimated labour hours per year), growth in the estimated capital stock, land area cultivated etc. in the bottom. The residual – called *the growth residual*, because, of course, the sum of all the input growths never exactly equals the growth in output – is the economy's TFP productivity measure, an inseparable amalgam of technology and technical efficiency improvements (or changes if things have got worse).

So, all in all, TFP is a pretty general tool. The difficulties in macroeconomics are the well-known limitations of GDP as a measure of true economic output, and the practical one of getting comprehensive data to create those aggregate input quantity indices. In microeconomics things ought to be simpler.

We recall from first year economics and the fundamentals of creating an index, that we need a way of converting a vector of characteristics into a single number using something like a weight or a relative price function. So, to create a Cost of Living index from three goods, energy, food, and rent, we would take the price index for each and weight it by the share (or quantities) of energy, food or rent in total household expenditure. The change in the cost of living is then the change in our overall index of the three components weighted appropriately. But to create the total index we must adopt a rule about whether we are going to keep the quantity expenditure weights as they were in our base year (a Base-weighted index), or choose those of the end year, or a Current-weighted index (the weights change each year), or chain together a series of base-weighted indices, as is often done in practice.

To create a TFP measure we need to create quantity indices, and so must make exactly the same choices about the relative *prices* of each input: should the prices that we use to calculate total output be Base-weighted, Current weighted, or a Chain of base-year weights?

For inputs, as argued before we would generally just use one, money, which equals total cash costs, which, as has been pointed out, uses current relative prices in each year (a Current-weighted index). And of course we must remove inflation from the cost measures. But what about outputs? If we try to measure a single utility's outputs, how would we value an extra customer or connection against an extra km of main? Unlike contestable industries, utility outputs are not sold separately with their own prices, so we have no relative prices from which to create the value of a unit of output in one dimension against a unit of output in another.

Unfortunately this problem is insuperable. So TFP, or HMTFP to be accurate, cannot be used to measure productivity growth of individual network utilities in a single-input multiple-output model unless some arbitrary decision is made to drop all output measures except one, and then simply compare changes in this one output variable with changes in deflated costs. Effectively we are examining changes in (the inverse of) the simple old unit cost model, gaily dismissed 40 pages ago as woefully inadequate. However, one has to say that when compiling sectoral TFP measures for an entire industry this is pretty well what is assumed (e.g. the water industry is typically measured by changes in water delivered per € of cost, the gas industry by gas delivered per € etc), so network quality or service enhancements – *the actual network functions* – *are usually completely ignored* in favour of traditional 'load' measures of output, with the additional comment that such *industry TFP measures necessarily apply to the average of the whole industry.*

Malmquist measures

So, traditional HMTFP measures are no use in trying to measure network productivity properly. They also suffer from the disadvantage that they cannot separate technological progress from technical efficiency. We need a new kind of productivity measure that can handle multiple outputs without trying to collapse them all down into one output using a relative price function, because we don't have that vector of relative prices and never will.

In 1994 Fare, Grosskopf, Norris and Zhang[185] devised a version of a 'Malmquist' productivity index which analysed the residual from Total Factor Productivity gains into two components: shifts in technology and efficiency increases. They then applied this in a macroeconomic context to look at the growth residuals of 17 industrialised countries between 1979 and 1988 and concluded that America, as the richest country in both years had grown entirely due to improving technology, while the fastest growing country, Japan, owed half of its rising productivity growth to catching up the frontier (efficiency gains).

This application of DEA-based ideas into the evolving subject of Malmquist indices is a brilliant fusion of cross-sectional DEA or regression techniques (which do not need prices to weight together different outputs into an aggregate output) with the conventional time series approach of index numbers. Appendix 1 to this chapter describes how Malmquist indices were developed over the course of the twentieth century, but our main concern here is to use them to measure different utilities' network efficiency.

Malmquist measures – when the industry average does not move

Figure 91 shows a simple case of a Malmquist measure using a twin-output single-input model of firms in an industry ten years apart:

---

[185] Fare R, Grosskopf S, Norris M, and Zhang Z "Productivity growth, technical progress and efficiency change in industrialised countries" *American Economic Review* 1994 84, No.1

Figure 91: A Malmquist measure of utility grids' efficiencies and frontier shifts – the simple case

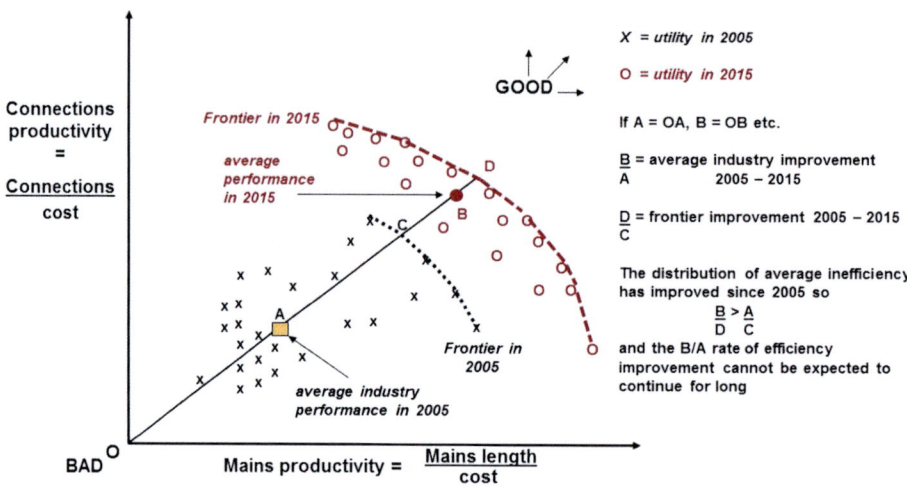

The horizontal axis of Figure 91 is the familiar dimension of all network utilities, their mains length productivity (mains length divided by cost), while the vertical axis reflects another essential dimension – connection productivity. Recall that for most distribution networks (but not transmission grids) the number of connections and the number of customers served are closely linked, in both a cross-sectional and time series sense, so an alternative vertical measure might be number of customers divided by cost. Using data from the year 2005 the individual firms' productivity is shown with an X and a section of the global frontier is observed, shown as a dotted line. Most firms were some way from the frontier in 2005. Separately, but on the same chart, another DEA analysis has been performed using data for the same industry ten years later, with each firm now shown as a O. In 2015 most firms were closer to the frontier, the dashed line, and, in this case, the observed frontier defines a wider range of production possibilities than it did in 2005.

In this section let 'A' be shorthand for the length OA, D be the distance OD etc. The movement between the frontiers over ten years can be defined as the ratio D/C, though of course it could vary as the frontier may not grow uniformly in each dimension. The line CD, though, has the advantage that it goes through the average points, A and B, for the whole industry in both years. So if the regulator were to sum up their entire industry's productivity gains over the ten years this would be the distance ratio B/A, and this could be broken down into two components, an average efficiency catch-up by firms in the industry of (B/D)/(A/C) – e.g. say, from 50% in 2005 to 80% in 2015, so a 60% gain in technical efficiency – and the frontier shift of D/C – say another 20% – giving a total productivity gain for the industry over ten years of 92% (= (1.6 x 1.2)-1).

Malmquist indices thus have the great advantage that not only can they be used to define how industries and their frontiers have moved in the past, but also they can be used directly to set cost-reduction targets in the future. Given the example above, when setting target efficiency rates for the next ten years, it would be wrong for the regulator to think that average productivity can continue to increase at 92% per ten years (6.7% a year). While the frontier may continue to progress at 20% per ten years (a strong prior assumption in Bayesian terms), if the industry is already averaging 80% technically efficient, catch-up efficiency cannot possibly exceed 25% without going beyond the frontier. We may also choose to apply a prior probability that at least some firms will be inefficient, giving a catch-up factor less than 25% - say 20%. Thus a challenging but fair target might be 44% over the ten years (= (1.2 x 1.2) -1).

The key learning insight is that the combination of multiplying the technical efficiency catch-up measure by the technology frontier shift measure should equal the total actual productivity gain over the two periods.

Total productivity gain = technical efficiency catchup x technology frontier shift

So if we use the algebra of Figure 91

$$\frac{A}{B} = \frac{\frac{B}{D}}{\frac{A}{C}} \times \frac{D}{C}$$

– which of course must be true (when you cancel out the Ds and Cs the RHS = LHS) – and then replace with the numbers suggested

$$1.92 = \frac{0.8}{0.5} \times 1.2 = 1.6 \times 1.2$$

Malmquist measures – the general case
The data in Figure 70, though, has allowed us to make the rather convenient assumption that the line joining A and B is a ray that goes through the origin – in other words that the average ratio of mains length productivity to connections productivity has not changed in ten years. In general this will not be true, either for the average, or for any given firm in the two years being considered, particularly if there is a long time between the two observation. For instance, as people become richer and population densities across the planet rise, the connection density (connections per km of mains) should rise and so B may generally drift upwards, above the OA ray[186].

---

[186] Obviously this would be offset by any trend for utilities to extend their networks into increasingly remote rural areas.

Figure 92: Illustrates the general Malmquist case for a utility network with two outputs

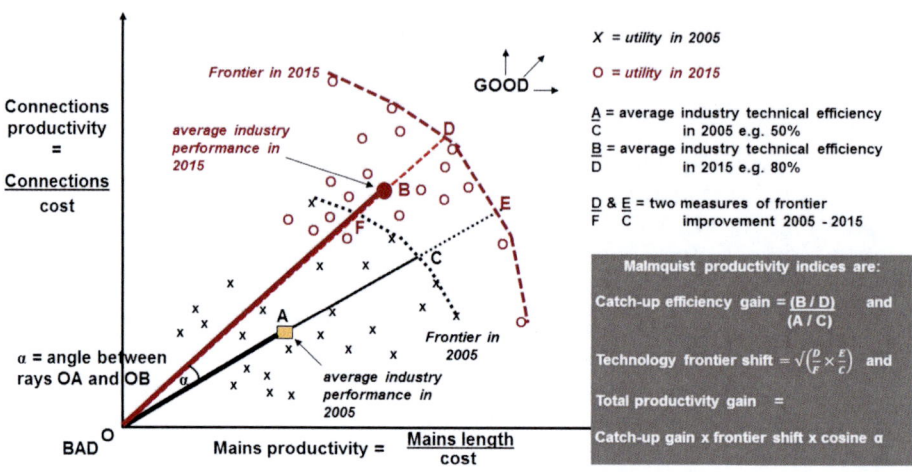

The base concepts from Figure 91 still apply, so B/D is the average efficiency in 2015 and A/C is the average efficiency in 2005. Again let's assume that technical efficiency has increased from 50% in 2005 to 80% in 2015 so there has been a 60% catch-up increase. What has changed in Figure 92 is that we have two rates of frontier shift, E/C and D/F, which might be, say, respectively a 26% gain and a 40% gain. We simply take a geometric mean of these, which for two variables means multiplying them together and taking the square root (i.e. 1.26 x 1.4 = 1.76; square root of this is 1.33 or a 33% gain).

So, using the algebra in Figure 92 we specify the Malmquist measures, but must make an allowance for the shift towards more connections efficiency, which means multiplying by the cosine of α, the angle between the rays OA and OB.

Total productivity gain = technical efficiency catchup x technology frontier shift x cosine α

$$\frac{B}{A} = \frac{B/D}{A/C} \times \sqrt{\left(\frac{D}{F} \times \frac{E}{C}\right)} \times \cos\alpha$$

Just so that we are clear let's give our hypothetical points in this case some real measurements consistent with Figure 92:

	A	B	C	D	E	F
Distance from the origin O	50	104	100	130	126	93

In Figure 92 the angle α is about 12½°, so its cosine is 0.976.

So to check let's plug these values into the formula above

$$\frac{104}{50} = \frac{104/130}{50/100} \times \sqrt{\left(\frac{130}{93} \times \frac{126}{100}\right)} \times 0.976$$

so the total efficiency gain

$$= \frac{0.8}{0.5} \times \sqrt{(1.4 \times 1.26)} \times 0.976 = 1.6 \times 1.33 \times 0.976 = 2.128 \times 0.976 = 2.08$$

$$= \frac{104}{50}$$

Note that there is no requirement for the two frontiers to move evenly away from the origin, so in general (as in this case)

$$C \neq F \text{ and } D \neq E$$

Possible Malmquist frontiers when technology is forgotten

More extreme shifts in the shape of the PPF are of course possible – at least theoretically, and in practice if a large time were to pass between the two observations. Consider an extreme case where the technologies developed in practice have taken very different paths over an entire century, so the angle between two firms, or the industry's centre of gravity is 60^0, for instance (so its cosine is 0.5), and the PPFs have evolved like Figure 93:

Figure 93: Twin output PPFs after a century

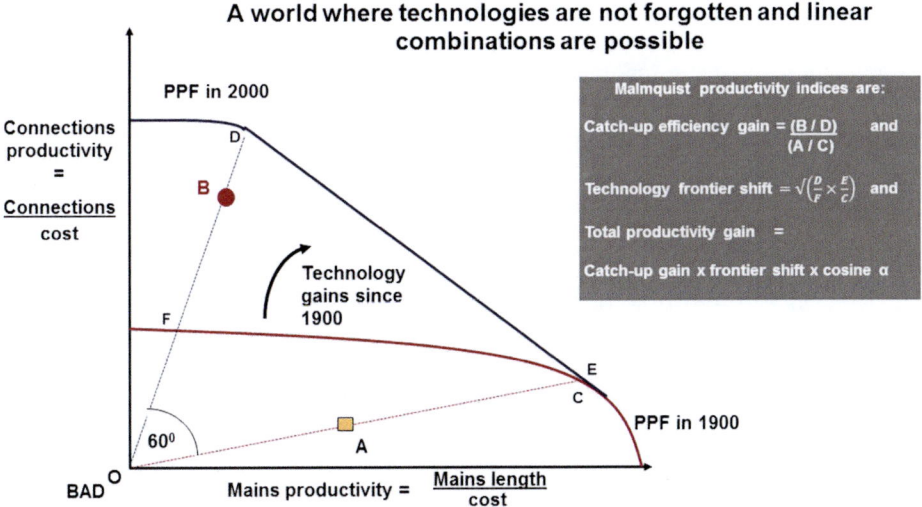

Figure 93 assumes, as we have been doing consistently since Chapter 3 (axiom 3), that a technology is never forgotten. But what if it were? Or, imagine that we have two radically different technologies on planet Earth at the same time but the practitioners either don't know of each other's existence, or, if they do, cannot practice the other technology effectively because they lack the capabilities and resources (skills or raw materials in conventional microeconomic terms). The two Production Possibility Frontiers might look like Figure 94:

Figure 94: A world where technologies are forgotten

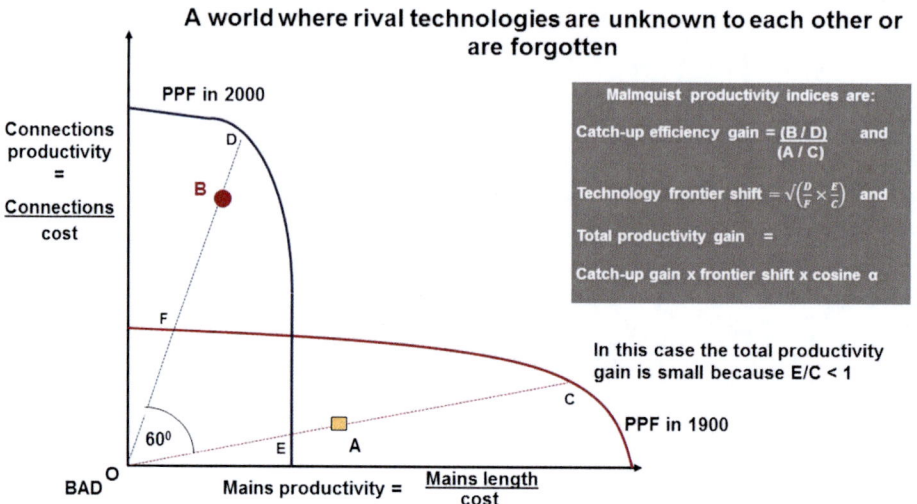

In this world our Malmquist total productivity indices are lower because E/C < 1, unlike Figure 92 and Figure 93. This shows the true cost of forgetting knowledge.

Stochastic Malmquist frontiers
The frontiers in the charts above are shown as DEA frontiers for simplicity, but the same technique could of course be applied using stochastic frontiers. However, the distribution of inefficiency also changes over the ten years, so the correct specification of the inefficiency term in the 2015 stochastic frontier (a traditional positively skewed one might be appropriate, given the new efficiencies) could well differ from that specified for 2005. One suggestion would be to do a DEA measurement first and look at the scatter plot – i.e. look at DEA versions of Figure 92 for each pair of output productivity indices and then test alternative distributions of inefficiency, with some priors about how efficiency ought to have changed under the regulatory regime – was it the regime that incentivised these efficiencies effectively or not?

Malmquist indices allowing for economies of scale or scope?
The above Malmquist model assumes that there can only be two causes of productivity growth over time: catch-up with the efficiency frontier and technological progress of the frontier (frontier shift). In general, it is also possible that the technology frontier has increasing returns to scale (decreasing LRACs) at some point, or that there may be joint production economies – i.e. there could be economies of scale or economies of scope. In 1999 Grifell-Tatje and Lovell[187] proposed a more general Malmquist index to include scale efficiencies,

---

[187] Grifell-Tatje E and Lovell C (1999) "A generalised Malmquist Productivity Index" *Sociedad Espanola de Estadistica e Investigacion Operativa*, 7, 81-101
[188] Balk BM (2001) "Scale efficiency and productivity change" *Journal of Productivity Analysis* 15, 159-183

while Balk in 2001[188] included all four sources of growth in the most general Malmquist productivity index yet produced; Balk's index and discussion of all productivity indices to date is excellently summarised in Coelli *et al* (pages 74-81); a detailed review of that is best left to professionals. What we can consider is whether we wish even to consider allowing economies of scale or scope in analysis of network utilities' efficiency – which, of course, was the question we asked in Chapter 2.

Our first answer would seem to be 'Yes, of course. Why not?' But then we consider what we are trying to do. Typically, we are trying to assess utilities' efficiency, and their productivity gains in order to rate management and investors' contribution to that. But management and investors cannot control or even influence the scale or scope of their utility[189]: the utility does what it does, has the scope that is given it, covers the geographical area prescribed on a map, and provides the services it is required to do on the scale demanded by its customers and its political masters. Management and investors cannot change the scope or scale of a utility: only its political masters – or possibly its regulator – can do that. So it depends what one is trying to do. If you are a regulator trying to determine a fair efficiency target for a utility for the next few years it would be unfair to allow economies of scale or scope as potential sources of productivity growth, but if you are undertaking a major survey to see whether the scope or scale of firms in an industry should be altered by politicians variable returns to scale and more comprehensive Malmquist indices should be allowed.

Panel data

Whichever technique is used, DEA or stochastic frontiers, it is inevitable that the more convex the production set the more utilities will be rated as 100% efficient, and so the more firms will be set an efficiency incentive based only on the rate of frontier progress. Some regulators do not like this, particularly if they believe data from 'the outside world' would show their regulatees are not very efficient, but they cannot readily obtain this data in a form fit for their use. Other regulators are simply short of good comparators in their industry – e.g. there is usually only one electricity transmission network per country, and these can vary widely in scope and scale.

For these and other reasons it has sometimes been argued that regulators should "use panel data" to supplement their shortage of cross-sectional observations by extending cross-sectional data through time – e.g. add in data from your, say, 12 comparators this year to data from the previous year, and to the year before that, so that you will have 36 observations from which to create a frontier and thus your efficiency measurements. Reasons for doing this would include

---

[189] By scope we may consider other parts of the utility value chain – e.g. there may be synergies between distribution and retail, or sewerage and sewage treatment, or water and sewage treatment, that a utility with a single function cannot extract.

1. It is more data, and more data cannot harm, it can only help
2. It gives you more degrees of freedom
3. It is inherently more stochastic: if nothing has changed except exogenous factors like the weather then three observations of a utility are more likely to give you a stochastic probability distribution around the 'true' value rather than the single-shot cross-sectional approach which could be unduly influenced by abnormal weather / economic conditions etc.

You should spot in a trice some of the problems with this approach. Now discuss the merits and de-merits with other students and your tutor. The author's views are given in Appendix 2 to this chapter.

The importance of good quality data
In practice obtaining data on a consistent basis across companies and over time is the most difficult task here, as it is throughout the utility value chain. Individual utilities can try to do this voluntarily through 'efficiency clubs' all subscribing to the same data definitions, pooling data, and paying a trusted consultant or trade association to analyse the data and produce efficiency rankings, which can be public (available to all subscribing members) or anonymous (the company knows that it is Company F but does not know other companies' letters). The author has put together and run several efficiency clubs and would say that even when the analyst does not know in advance which tools the data will show to be most useful, generally about 90% of the effort goes into obtaining raw data from companies and then ensuring that it is consistent, while only 10% of the effort goes in analysing the data and presenting the conclusions.

However, if a regulator gathers data for efficiency comparison purposes they can enforce consistent data definitions within the firms over which they have jurisdiction, and can try to persuade other utilities to adopt the same definitions so as to widen the set of comparators. The British water regulator Ofwat has jurisdiction over water utilities in England and Wales but has at times extended their data pool to include utilities in Scotland, Northern Ireland, the Netherlands and Australia. Similarly British energy regulator Ofgem uses international data to compare the efficiency of the national gas and electricity transmission systems and Oftel does the same for landline telecoms.

Well done! You've reached the end of a really long and difficult chapter. I hope you've still got as much hair as when you started it. We're nearly there now: Chapter 8 is the last general one, but I don't think it is quite as difficult as Chapter 7. And it has the great merit of being shorter. Take a breather, give yourself a chocolate biscuit, and come back ready to conquer 'Competition, concessions and regulation – the main options in practice'.

Appendix 1: The intellectual development of Malmquist indices

Progress on this was made slowly and sometimes obliquely. Following Laspeyre and Paasche's pioneering 19th century work defining Base-weighted and Current-weighted Indices, the seminal work bringing together all previous work on Price or Quantity Index numbers and developing rigorous comparisons was done by Irving *Fisher* in 1922. Noting that a current-weighted price index tends to understate inflation because consumers react to those goods becoming the more expensive by buying less of them, while a base-weighted index overstates inflation for the opposite reason, Fisher proposed an *Ideal* index[190] which was the geometric mean of a base-weighted and a current-weighted index.

In 1926 a Bank of France economist, Francois Divisia, faced up to the tricky problem of how to create an ideal aggregate money supply index from different components of money. He could just add up the components, as was standard practice in most countries, but that assumed that 100 Francs of cash is as likely to be used in the next transaction as 100 Francs of illiquid financial instruments such as a long-dated bond – which it plainly isn't. To arrive at an ideal liquidity-weighted index of the total quantity of 'money' in circulation Divisia[191] proposed a new Index to aggregate weights of different kinds of money supply components into total money supply, the *Divisia* Index, which were continuous liquidity-weighted average quantity and price indices. The only trouble was that Divisia's maths was too good for his own good[192], as his indices require time to be *continuous*. Well, you and I may perceive time as continuous (one moment flowing into the next, with occasional interludes when you wake up, embarrassed and dribbling, in the middle of an economics lecture), but for practical economic purposes, quantities and prices are measured in *discrete* time (a year's worth of output or input etc.), so a Divisia index is not actually a workable proposition, more an intellectual dream.

In 1936 a Bank of Finland economist called Tornqvist proposed a practical Divisia index formula for discrete time; he cut the Gordian knot by taking the weights at the beginning and end of the time period being considered, or for two adjacent periods, and simply averaged them using a geometric mean. Thus was born the principle of a *Tornqvist* index for prices[193]. In 1953 another Scandinavian economist, Sten Malmquist, created the mirror-image Tornqvist *quantity* index, now called a *Malmquist*[194] index, to measure consumers' improving utility levels over time from higher consumption of several goods, and in 1961 Moorsteen[195]

---

[190] Fisher, I. (1922), *The Making of Index Numbers*. Boston: Houghton-Mifflin.

[191] Divisia, F. 1926. "L'indice monétaire et la théorie de la monnaie." *Revue d'écon. polit.*, LX, No. 1: 49-81.

[192] Do you have this problem? Such a bind, isn't it?

[193] Tornqvist, L, (1936), 'The Bank of Finland's consumption price index,' *Bank of Finland Monthly Bulletin*, no, 10, pp, 1-8,

[194] Malmquist S: "Index Numbers and Indifference Surfaces," *Trabajos de Estatistica*, 4(1953), 209-242.

[195] Moorsteen, R. H.: "On Measuring Productive Potential and Relative Efficiency," *Quarterly Journal of Economics*, 75(1961), 451-467.

independently did the same for producer theory. Finally, in a seminal 1982 paper catchily referred to as CCD 1982b[196], Caves, Christensen and Diewert proved some desirable properties (such as transitivity) for 'Malmquist indexes', provided all firms were efficient and produced on a translog production function. This gave the Malmquist index deserved fame and legitimacy (though Moorsteen seems to have got short shrift).

But the fundamental problem stopping the use of these Malmquist indexes in measuring network outputs was that the component outputs had to be priced. Finally, in 1989, Fare, Grosskopf, Norris and Zhang[197] applied Malmquist indices at the macroeconomic level to break down Solow's GDP 'growth residual' into technology shift and efficiency improvement. From our point of view, though, their greater contribution was to apply Malmquist indexes using Farrell's DEA concepts and definitions of distance from the frontier, since these measures handle inputs and outputs in multiple dimensions without requiring prices to aggregate them. Fare et al used this approach to compare growth in non-comparable inputs of capital and labour with growth in a single output – GDP. Thus the modern Malmquist index was created as a multiple-input single-output measure for traditional macroeconomists[198], a single-input[199] multiple-output model for utility economists, and a multiple-input multiple-output measure for general economic use.

Quarterly Journal of Economics, 75(1961), 451-467.

[196] Caves DW, Christensen LR and Diewert WE "The Economic Theory of Index Numbers and the Measurement of Input, Output, and Productivity." Econometrica, November 1982, 50(6), pp. 1393-1414.

[197] Fare R, Grosskopf S, Norris M, and Zhang Z "Productivity growth, technical progress and efficiency change in industrialised countries" *American Economic Review* 1994 84, No.1

[198] i.e. assuming all indices of happiness and wellbeing are compressed into conventionally-measured GDP.

[199] Assuming prices are 'correct' and we have no problems with input externalities, shadow prices, exchange rates etc

Appendix 2: panel data inadequacies

The most obvious remark is that if we have several years' worth of data stretching over, say, five years, then we can use this panel data to create Malmquist indices of catch-up and frontier shift. So the Malmquist approach we have been using has already extracted nearly all of the useful information out of this data provided we are careful and have data for enough years for the two frontiers to emerge distinctly. However if we only have a few firms − say less than 15-20 − the cross-sectional data may give us too few degrees of freedom for an econometric approach to work and using the DEA approach we could easily end up with the majority of them defining the observed frontier if we start to allow ourselves three or four outputs.

Regarding the idea of just mixing up say three consecutive years' worth of data for 12 firms to get 36 observations academic readers may be horrified that anyone could suggest such a bad idea, but the author has heard it seriously suggested − by lawyers trying to persuade the UK's Competition Commission predecessor that a merger between two water utilities should be allowed. The Competition Commission's predecessor did not entertain the idea for long.

The first thing that is wrong with simply mixing cross-sectional and time-series data is that it violates the assumptions about the observations being independent. In a cross-sectional regression or DEA the observations are assumed to be independent but when we introduce a second year of observations the second set is not independent: the links between where a firm is this year and where it will be next year are far stronger than any links it has with its comparators. So you have not really got more degrees of freedom, just repeated observations of the same fundamental point. Thus the first two advantages listed three pages ago are nullified but the third one is reinforced, namely that repeated observations of the same point can give us a probability distribution about a point rather than single snapshot of where it happened to be at one random instant.

However, for this third argument to be true we would need every firm not to vary at all between our first year and our last year, so that we can see the effects of changes in random exogenous variables like the weather and the economic environment on each firm's costs and output measures. Across an entire industry the likelihood that no firm will have any significant changes going on over three years is negligible. Not only will there be major cost-saving or capital enhancement schemes proceeding in several firms but there will also be changes in senior management, IT systems and many other 'soft' systems, processes or cultural values that mean that a company in 2014 is not the same company it was in 2012. In that case we have a series of still photos of a firm changing in front of our eyes, not repeated snapshots of the same unmoving firm, complicated by random changes in exogenous variables. The entire argument is specious.

Finally we cannot ignore technological progress over time as the panel data enthusiasts are. If we were doing this in an industry like telecoms the frontier is moving at something like 8% a year, so the frontier would have moved 25% in three years. In such an industry no firm can afford to freeze itself for two or three years or it will be commercially dead. But even in slower moving heavy utilities like energy, water and rail, frontier progress is of the order of 1% a year at least, so frontier movements can combine with inflation adjustments, relative price movements and weather effects to give quite significant exogenous shocks between the first year and the last. This point is reinforced by the erratic pattern of individual firms within an industry: we say that an industry frontier shifts smoothly but the reality is that individual firms install the latest technology and suddenly leap forward 10% or 20% to define the frontier for a year or two. Then another firm installs the new latest technology and it redefines the frontier, while the first firm keeps its 'new' system for many years. It is like watching a herd of grazing buffalo move across a plain: the herd seems to move slowly and steadily but individual animals move some distance, stop for some time to graze, and then walk on a significant distance. The movement of individual animals is more jerky than the movement of the herd. This reinforces the earlier remark that in reality no industry is likely to stay 'constant' for three years, and even if a regulator were to make an exception for one firm, and say "OK, firm B, we will keep your observations in for the first two years but omit your third year because you installed some new kit" every firm in the industry could claim something similar.

In short there really is no substitute for independent cross-sectional observations. Regulators must collaborate to obtain the best globally-applicable data or fade into inefficiency and irrelevance.

Chapter Eight

Competition, concessions and regulation: the main options in practice

General competition policies to rebalance consumers' interests
In countries that bother with such niceties[200] a high market share will attract the attention of competition authorities or regulators charged with looking at matters from the point of view of the whole of society, a point of view which must explicitly consider consumers' interests as well as producer's interests.

In the USA the arm of government that generally investigates this is the Justice Department, while within Europe at a global or continental level it is the European Commission. These bodies have significant powers to tame some of the mightiest companies on the planet. For instance around 2000 the Justice Department and the European Commission simultaneously examined the way Microsoft obtained and used its dominant market positions. These examinations took up many years of Microsoft's top management time, resulted in Microsoft paying huge fines, caused them to make their software more accessible to other software suppliers, and may have led to changes in the top management of the richest company on earth at the time[201].

So global corporations face some powerful competition bodies who can control access to markets of 800 million of the world's richest consumers, and try to ensure that monopoly power is checked in certain ways. More typically, though, monopoly power exists at national or local levels, and so the problem falls on the

---

[200] In 2001 the author was working in Brazil when the largest beer producer, with a reported 65% market share, was allowed to take over its next largest rival, with a reported 20% market share. Clearly this Brazilian government did not worry too much about potential abuses of market power by large companies, even for something as close to consumers' hearts as beer. South Africa is another hot country where the market share of the largest beer producer is well above 80%, so economists' concerns with potential abuses of market power are by no means universal.

[201] During these lengthy investigations Bill Gates stepped down as CEO, which could have been for business or personal reasons. Whatever the reasons, he has since donated dozens of billions of dollars to benefit a billion of the world's poorest citizens and persuaded other rich folk to do the same.

shoulders of national governments. Provided a government views the interests of society as being fairly close to those of consumers[202], they will create competition authorities to investigate and if necessary break up firms that create or act collectively as though they are a monopoly. The main reasons governments do not equate consumers' and society's interests are
- For national security – e.g. the US Department of Defense does not buy equipment from foreign suppliers if US suppliers make equally good products
- For social infrastructure: many countries nationalise and subsidise certain monopolies which actively develop the country or promote national or social cohesion– e.g. railways, electricity, gas, water, bus companies
- For national pride – e.g. the French government has traditionally viewed its national interests as not necessarily being aligned with French consumers. Relevant examples include the persistence of Electricite de France (EdF) and Gaz de France as large national vertically integrated energy suppliers within a European energy scene where separation of functions has commonly brought significant advantages to European consumers[203].

But the default assumption is that *in general, governments tend to equate society's interests with consumers' interests*. So they establish laws and competition authorities to act on behalf of consumers by reining in monopolists' powers and super-normal profits.

Competition policy in the USA

In the USA the Antitrust Division of the Justice Department is responsible for competition policy, using laws, some of which were created 120 years ago to break up oil or rail 'trusts' (monopolies), or a financial regulator such as the Securities and Exchange Commission, or State prosecutors.

Trusts and anti-trust law

What is, or was, a 'trust'? It was a secret, but not then illegal, agreement pioneered by John D Rockefeller and his partners in 1882[204]. After seven years in the booming American oil refining industry Rockefeller founded Standard Oil in 1870. It rapidly became one of the world's first "integrated oil majors", a major

---

[202] This is a big "if"; see footnote 198.

[203] Technically, to comply with EU rules, EdF and GdF have been internally separated, but they are both ultimately owned by the French state, and the effectiveness of the separation can be judged by the scarcity of solar power panels in sunny southern France. Only if one views EdF as an integrated power company, including its role as a generator with many nuclear power stations, can one understand EdF's incentives not to promote distributed solar connections as strongly as they are in many other countries, and thus to capitalise fully on southern France's naturally sunny position.

[204] When asked in 1910 if he had thought of the company that Standard Oil would become Rockefeller said "No Sir. I wish I had the brains to think of it. It was Henry M Flagler." Source Edwin Lefevre, in "Flagler and Florida" from *Everybody's Magazine*, XXII (February, 1910) p. 183.

producer and shipper of crude oil (through pipelines, ships, railways, canals and by horse), by far the largest oil refiner in the world at the time, and a major oil wholesaler and retailer. The crude oil production stage was – and still is – fragmented; the 2007 movie 'There Will Be Blood' is violent and dramatically disappointing, but is the best visualisation the author has seen of the cut-throat nineteenth century oil production business, vividly depicting the origins of standard industry terms like 'oil well', 'barrel', 'well-head', or 'blow-out'.

The next stage in the value chain, refining, was more, well, refined, requiring conventional chemical engineering and business skills, and more capital; it was therefore more concentrated. Standard Oil realised they could effectively appropriate most of the (super-normal) profits in the entire American oil value chain[205] by monopolising the refining stage so that they became monopsonist buyers of crude oil nationally and monopoly sellers of kerosene for lighting and cooking. They were acting on a Federal scale, yet regulated by State laws which were rapidly becoming inadequate for businessmen who benefited from the national railroad network, reliable water transport and the invention of the telegraph to transmit prices and orders. Standard Oil could easily move goods between or around States, or from the Gulf of Mexico to the Atlantic or the Pacific. If their actions had been known to the American people Congress might have moved rapidly to pass laws prohibiting this, but the 1882 agreement establishing the Standard Oil Trust (a holding company owning 41 oil operating companies) enabled Rockefeller and his 36 partners to merge their refining assets, to allow 9 of the 37 stockholders to hold their stocks "in trust" for them all, and to keep this agreement secret. Though it was no secret at the time that Standard Oil had a stranglehold on American oil refining, and national monopolies were not illegal, it has since been estimated that they then refined around 90% of America's oil[206].

Although kept officially secret, word about 'trusts' had leaked out sufficiently for politicians to want to be seen to be acting. In 1890 Congress passed the Sherman Antitrust Act which said

> *"Section 1. Every contract, combination in the form of trust or otherwise, or conspiracy, in restraint of trade or commerce among the several States, or with foreign nations, is declared to be illegal. Every person who shall make any contract or engage in any combination or conspiracy hereby declared to be illegal shall be deemed guilty of a felony, and, on conviction thereof, shall be punished by fine....*

---

[205] This is an economic analysis of what they were doing: Rockefeller and company merely thought they were making oodles of money in the oil industry. However, they were well aware of what they were doing strategically to the industry. Note also that consumers benefited from strongly falling oil prices during this period, in part made possible by Standard Oil's exploitation of many kinds of economies of scale.

[206] Segall, Grant (2001). John D. Rockefeller: Anointed With Oil. Oxford University Press p48-49 and p67.

> Section 2. Every person who shall monopolize, or attempt to monopolize, or combine or conspire with any other person or persons, to monopolize any part of the trade or commerce among the several States, or with foreign nations, shall be deemed guilty of a felony,...."

In what was left of the 19th century the Sherman Act was used against unions, who were seen as labour cartels, but slowly its power was turned against business monopolies and cartels. It took a determined investigation by journalist Ida M Tarbell, whose father had been driven out of business by Rockefeller's ruthless but legal tactics, to track what was really happening in the oil industry. She published her findings in 19 instalments of a popular magazine and then in her 1904 book *The History of the Standard Oil Company*. This pushed the politicians to start prosecuting Standard Oil in 1906 using the Sherman Act. When this prosecution, which was inevitably fought all the way to the Supreme Court, finally resulted in a conviction in 1911, Standard Oil of New Jersey was obliged to break itself up into 34 companies. In the century since it is interesting to see that many of these companies have re-agglomerated. Standard Oil of New Jersey, for instance, which was abbreviated to 'SO', then to 'Esso', and then to 'Exxon', is still the world's biggest oil company, having merged with Mobil (Standard Oil of New York) along the way, while SO California became Socal and then Chevron, Standard Oil of Ohio (Sohio) and Indiana (Amoco) became part of BP, Continental Oil became part of ConocoPhilips etc.

The Sherman Act was reinforced by the Clayton Act of 1914 which added the following activities as anti-competitive behaviour:
- price discrimination between different purchasers, if such discrimination tends to create a monopoly
- exclusive dealing agreements
- tying arrangements
- mergers and acquisitions that substantially reduce market competition.

Today national or international competition policy in the US is the responsibility of the Antitrust Division of the Justice Department, while local issues are investigated and prosecuted at State level.

Competition policy in Europe

At the time of writing 28 of Europe's 40-odd countries belong to the European Union (EU), which has more than 500 million people. Countries *not* in the EU include Switzerland, Norway and some parts of the Balkans and eastern Europe. Any country joining the European Union must sign two founding treaties: the Treaty on European Union (which says it will join the Union), and the Treaty on the Functioning of the European Union (TFEU) – which states how the Union works. The main TFEU contains 358 Articles (EU laws) which countries must adopt and then pass into national laws in their own country. One important Article, 26, says that the Union *"...shall adopt measures with the aim of establishing or ensuring the functioning of the internal market"* and defines the Union's **internal market** as *"an area without internal frontiers in which the free movement of goods, persons, services and capital is ensured"*. One of the main means of achieving the internal market is competition policy, which is set out in Articles 101-106 of the TFEU.

Article 101
Article 101 says
> "1. The following shall be prohibited as incompatible with the internal market: all agreements between undertakings, decisions by associations of undertakings and concerted practices which may affect trade between Member States and which have as their object or effect the prevention, restriction or distortion of competition within the internal market, and in particular those which:
> (a) directly or indirectly fix purchase or selling prices or any other trading conditions;
> (b) limit or control production, markets, technical development, or investment;
> (c) share markets or sources of supply; "
> [... two other examples of prohibited behaviour are listed]
> 2. Any agreements or decisions prohibited pursuant to this Article shall be automatically void.
> 3. The provisions of paragraph 1 may, however, be declared inapplicable in the case of:... [firms which promote] "technical or economic progress, while allowing consumers a fair share of the resulting benefit"...[it imposes several further conditions].

Note that an 'undertaking' is a firm. So Article 101 is a law designed to promote unfettered competition, banning explicit or implicit price agreements, and, at its heart, stopping firms collaborating in a *cartel – a formal or informal organisation whose behaviour aims to act as if all the players were a single monopolist.* Paragraph 2 means that a firm cannot be prosecuted if it breaks an industry agreement, since the industry agreement is itself illegal, while paragraph 3 allows the Commission some grounds to make exceptions.

Article 102
Article 102 says
> "Any abuse by one or more undertakings of a dominant position within the internal market or in a substantial part of it shall be prohibited as incompatible with the internal market in so far as it may affect trade between Member States.
> Such abuse may, in particular, consist in:
> (a) directly or indirectly imposing unfair purchase or selling prices or other unfair trading conditions;
> (b) limiting production, markets or technical development to the prejudice of consumers; ..."
> ... [Two other examples of abuse are listed.]

Immediately we see that the fundamental anti-monopoly concept is *abuse of a dominant position*, which is a loose economic concept, designed to give the

European Commission's Competition Directorate flexibility: flexibility to see if consumers really are suffering, and flexibility to do something pragmatic to remedy competition, and improve consumers' overall welfare.

Article 103 empowers the Commission to propose detailed rules ('Directives') that will achieve the main Articles in practice, while **Article 105** empowers the Commission to enforce the Articles and Directives – to be, in effect, both 'investigating policeman' and Judge and Jury. **Article 104** sets out transition arrangements for new member countries, while **Article 106** clarifies principles for state-owned monopoly services.

As a result of these Articles the Commission has given itself investigative powers such as summoning witnesses, or requiring companies to provide files or records, as well as punitive powers such as fining companies or blocking mergers.

As this is not a book on competition economics we will not here discuss the formal and informal rules by which the Commission decides to investigate particular firms or industries. Suffice to say that one of the lowest market shares of a company investigated for its dominant position was just under 40% in the BA/Virgin case of 2004. Another example concerns Microsoft: at the turn of the century, and with near-monopolies of PC operating systems and office software, Microsoft was investigated by the Commission for several years before and after 2000. The Competition Directorate has the power to fine a company up to 10% of its *global* turnover, which is sufficient to wipe out some companies' profits for a whole year. In Microsoft's case they were fined €899m in 2008[207]: not crippling for a company with a turnover exceeding $50bn, but it took up many man.years of senior executives' time, and forced Microsoft to publish more of its technical codes augmenting access for other software suppliers – albeit rather late.

Summary of EU competition policy
So EU competition policy applies across all members of the European Union and is based on of the two founding Treaties of the Union. Note that no Article refers to perfect or imperfect competition, comparisons between monopoly positions, welfare losses etc. Instead they aim to protect European consumers from potential abuses by cartels – groups of firms in an industry trying to enforceagreements that might damage consumers' interests (Article 101) – or by individually powerful firms who are described in Article 102 as having a 'dominant' position in the European internal market.

Note that where the relevant market is deemed to be of national or sub-national scale, firms come under the jurisdiction of national laws which must reflect Articles 101 and 102 in their own competition legislation. So, for instance, the UK passed the 1998 Competition Act, in which Chapter 1 repeats what is now Article 101 but applies specifically to firms registered in the UK, and states that all agreements or contracts which prevent, restrict, or distort competition are

---

[207] Article 23 of the European Commission Decision of 27 February 2008.

illegal, unless specifically exempted. Chapter 2 repeated the forerunner of Article 102 and says any conduct (a very general phrase) which constitutes abuse of a dominant position is prohibited within the UK. The 2002 Enterprise Act states that the Director General of Fair Trading is responsible for enforcing competition policy in the UK, while it is the *Bundeskartellamt* in Germany, in France the *Autorité de la concurrence*, and in Italy the *Autorità Garante della Concorrenza e del Mercato*.

Overall goals for injecting competition into utility monopolies

Chapter 4 concluded that where network utilities with significant sunk costs exist it is very likely they will be monopolies, unless the first mover was unable to 'scoop the market' or there has been dramatic technological progress since the network was configured. These results are general, and likely to hold regardless of the ownership, governance, or strategic goals of the utility.

Given that we have known for thousands of year that 'monopolies are bad' the issue for policy makers is how to inject as much of the normal 'competitive spirit' into an industry which has innately strong monopoly elements. *Most economists would argue that genuine competition-in-the-market is strongly preferable to regulation*, so, if *sensible, an industry should be vertically re-structured to enable genuine competition to flourish in the contestable segments.*

Restructuring an industry to promote as much competition as possible

So, most economists would argue that getting the overall structure of the utility's industry right is the most fundamental requirement. How should we achieve this? As ever, Figure 8 from Chapter 1 is our initial guide. So, omitting the bread and milk examples, let's repeat it but with some modifications to aid a general discussion:

Figure 95: General value chains for heavy utilities

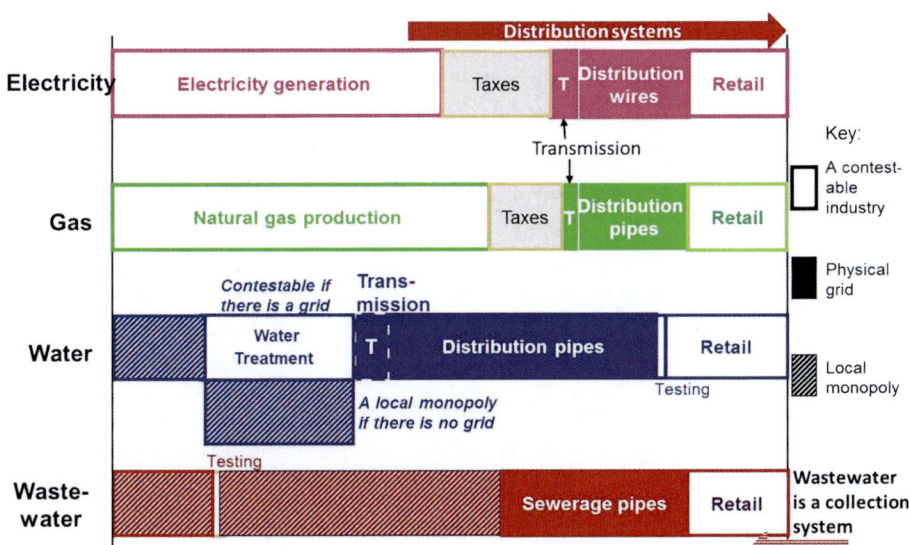

The innate monopolies are the core wires and pipe businesses that distribute – or in wastewater's case collect – energy or water. Thus the transmission and distribution networks will never[208] support genuine competition in the market so long as there are vast sunk costs of entry and no game-changing shifts in technology, such as occurred in telecoms in the 1990s. We should add to this virtually the whole wastewater value chain because of the innate local monopolies of sewage treatment (for sewage treatment to exist at all the collection network of sewers must drain down to a single point which is the influent point for the sewage treatment works) and sludge treatment (sewage sludge is only produced where sewage is treated, so both are local monopolies).

The big difference between Figure 95 and Figure 8 is in clean water. The innate monopoly of water is just like the case of gas, except the value of the pipe business in water is relatively greater (because water has a lower value per cubic metre than gas), but water treatment has two possibilities: in the water world if water comes from surface sources, local geography is very likely to constrain the feasible sources of water to just one source – a big river or lake – which, combined with strong engineering economies of scale, usually means that surface water treatment is best exploited using just one plant, and thus a local monopoly. However, if a regional water grid exists enabling several different water sources to compete to supply overall demand in the area, competition between water treatment works is at least feasible, and so water treatment is in principle contestable – as actually happens in energy grids. So Figure 95 shows clean water as having two possibilities depending on whether there is a regional water grid or not. It has to be said that in most places around the planet there is no such grid, and that one is likely to find water grids only where consumers are rich *and* water is either very scarce (e.g. Israel) or population density is very high (e.g. England and Wales, or the Netherlands) or water comes from a network of boreholes into an aquifer. Thus the reason that Figure 8 shows clean water as contestable is that it was based on the dense network of water grids in England and Wales which were strongly reinforced after that industry was privatised in 1989. So, Figure 95 should be viewed as the general diagram explaining the contestability of the classic heavy utilities while Figure 8 is the diagram for utilities in England and Wales.

In all the above cases the core utility is a monopoly which could be private, and regulated, or kept in public ownership with some set of (preferably explicit) strategic goals, governance, and monitoring arrangements. Bulk energy production (electricity generation and gas fields) and the retail functions are in principle contestable, and so *could be fully competitive if there are several such sources, competition is legally allowed, and if competition is actively supported by government.*

---

[208] It is surprising how many theoretical regulatory papers the author has read containing phrases like "...until competitive conditions prevail the best system of regulation is ...". Those authors have not accepted that there never will be competition so long as there are overwhelming first-mover advantages and huge sunk costs.

This last condition (active support for competition) is contentious; my view is that this is a necessary condition but some experienced regulators express the view that active government support for entry and competition may not always be necessary. From both the theoretical considerations about long-lasting first mover advantage in Chapter 4, and practical experience, I remain sceptical, believing that incumbent monopolists have an enormous capacity to abuse their dominant positions, and thus if entry is desirable it will generally need to be actively encouraged. Rather than using the tired analogy of a playing field that may be level or not, a better metaphor might be a well-tended garden of competition. Gardens don't happen naturally: gardeners must do a lot of deliberate planting, encouragement and weeding. In practice what matters is that at the time any utility industry is restructured major value judgements must be made about the relative capabilities and strengths of the incumbent and any potential entrants, the importance of any consumer surplus likely to arise from entry, and the likely effects of 'cherry-picking' entry on any non-economic consumer segments currently served by the incumbent, including any Universal Service Obligations it may have. This is a major subject in intermediate utility economics and is not pursued further here (in this textbook on basic utility economics). In the end-game mature state of oligopoly or perfect competition, we can all agree that competition may simply require passive monitoring by the regulators, but this is not a quick process. In the case of British wholesale energy markets, as we shall see in Chapters 9 and 10, it took ten to fifteen years to break up state-owned monopolies sufficiently for observers to say that there was genuinely strong price competition among electricity generators or gas producers most of the time.

Monopoly concessions or outsourcing
As competition-in-the-market is impossible for the innate monopoly parts of the value chain, could we not at least attempt the second best solution, competition for-the-market? The general answer is yes, but this is a specialist subject in its own right; in this section a general textbook cannot provide more than the briefest overview of some vast commercial possibilities – and problems.

The main concession possibilities
Concessions are a kind of outsourcing contract and there is an array of possible outsourcing contracts ranging from a simple functional contract through to very complicated possibilities. Figure 96 shows this in the form of a standard marketing product space map:

Figure 96: A product dimension map of utility outsourcing and concession

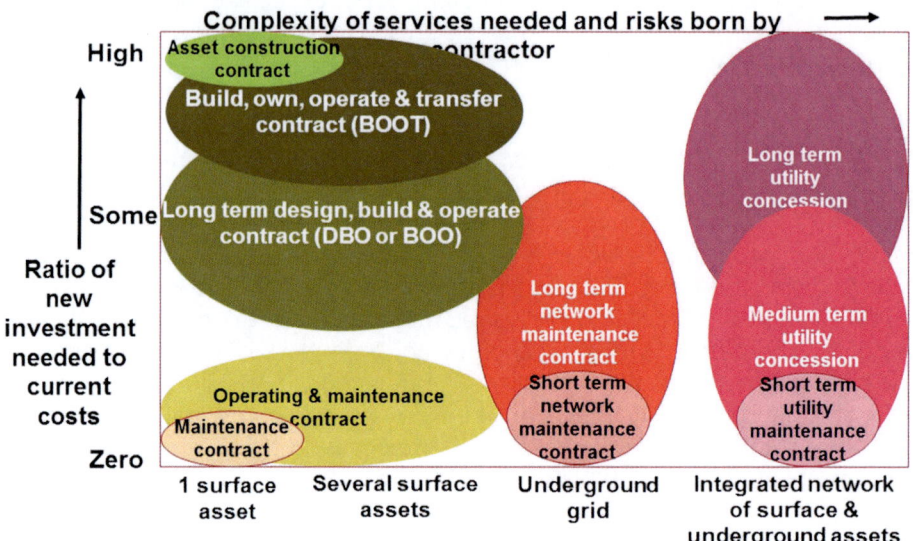

The horizontal axis shows the complexity of the service provided, or in economic terms the number of outputs needed to specify the contract fully (i.e. the range of risks born by the contractor), while the vertical axis measures the ratio of funds needed for investment compared to ongoing operating and maintenance costs. So in the bottom left corner a community could hire a private contractor to perform one function in a single surface asset, such as cleaning out the tanks in an existing sewage treatment works. Or they could ask a contractor to maintain and operate an entire sewage treatment works for a year or two, or several power stations around the city etc. Or, in the top left corner, a community could hire a contractor to build a new power station or a water treatment works to a detailed design specification, and then once built, hand it over to the city – the kind of standard fixed-price construction contract that cities place every day.

Moving to the right matters get more complicated. Sometimes capital equipment is tricky to operate and so it is only formally accepted ("commissioned") once it has been proven to work reliably. If there are teething troubles the city might want the constructor to overcome these before handing it over, and to train its permanent staff in how to run the new kit. In this case a Build, Own, Operate and Transfer (BOOT) contract is the best solution.

However construction contracts require a detailed specification, or design, which is expensive for the city to draw up. Moreover contractors and cities have found over the years that separating the design (by the city) from the building and operation by the contractor can be very inefficient, so a more efficient solution may be to *outline* what you want – say, a gas-fired 800MW power station – rather than draw up a detailed design, and let the builder do the detailed design and construction, maximising synergies in the design and construction phase. Once built the contractor must then prove to the city that it works efficiently and reliably, and train the city's staff, so this requires a period of operation. This arrangement, where the contractor maximises design and construction synergies but also absorbs all the design, construction and commissioning risks, is called a Design Build and Operate (DBO) contract, and as you might imagine DBO contractors have figures showing that the savings from a DBO contract over a standard construction or BOOT contract can be massive. Whether this will be true or not is an important value judgement by the city, but in the author's experience the scale of capital efficiency savings can dwarf operational efficiency savings.

A slight variant on a DBO contract is the Build, Own and Operate (BOO) contract, in which the contractor retains ownership of the asset and sells its output to the city for an agreed price over the operating life of the asset, rather than being paid a fixed sum once the asset is commissioned. The main difference is cash flow: in a DBO the contractor has a negative cash position for a few years at most, while in a BOO the contractor will only get their construction costs back over the lifetime of the BOO contract, which might be as long as twenty years or more, so they will need to arrange long term finance, possibly raising a bond on the asset – and possibly asking the city or its political friends to 'underwrite' (guarantee to buy) part of the bond issue.

Moving further to the right a network grid is a far more difficult set of assets to describe or specify the outputs of, and so maintenance contracts for underground grids will be either short term, specific and open-ended from the contractor's point of view – 'We will charge you €X per call out' [but not regulate the number of callouts] – or fixed price but longer term, with thick contracts that take ages to negotiate. As in all commercial contracts an arbitrator will be specified to sort out cases which were not fully covered in the lawyers' thick document, but as the duration of the contract lengthens the likelihood that the arbitrator will actually be called in increases.

And at the far right of Figure 96 we have contracts to run and maintain an entire section of an integrated utility. Again, short term contracts – to keep things ticking over in an emergency – are likely to be open-priced (a lengthy list of of tariffs per service done) so that the buyer (the city) retains all the financial risks via the number of jobs done, which is entirely demand-driven.

Finally, above these contracts, we come to genuine concessions. Here the public sector buyer wants to transfer significant operational risks to a private contractor, and to squeeze out super-normal profits from the contractor by having frequent auctions. Auctions of retail outlets in busy shopping malls are common, so why not try them here?

Common utility concession problems
The biggest single difference is that in a few hours in a shopping mall any bidder for shop premises can see exactly the state of the assets they will be using and so can quickly establish their starting position. By contrast, any bidder for an

entire city's electricity, gas, water or sewage network will have to spend months examining as many assets as it can, and then will still have very little idea about the true state of all the underground assets. So bidding for a utility concession is a very costly process (transaction costs are high) and bidders are only likely to do due diligence and incur these costs if they have a very high probability of winning the auction. Indeed they will want to be one of only a handful of bidders at the auction – two or three at the most – and if they get the slightest hint that they might be losing the race to land the concession, the best option for them is to cut their expensive bidding losses immediately and withdraw from the bid. Consequently it is not uncommon to see the number of bidders for a concession start out at ten or more, then for there to be coalitions among bidders, to reduce their competitors and increase individual chances of winning (though of a smaller share of the total), and then in the final stages for all but one or two to withdraw. Some auction!

So, if the rules of the bidding game allow this, one way to reduce the relative costs of the bidding process is to join coalitions of bidders and fight for a share of the city against fewer bidders. If you lose the bid at least you have reduced your bidding costs, while if you win you can take your time to examine the true state of the assets, and the commitments you have made under the licence, before trading shares in a proven concession with your partners using much better information about the concession. Another way is to lengthen the period of the concession. This is common, but it has two big effects. First, obviously, the auction frequency declines. But this is the chief advantage to consumers of this kind of competition over regulating a private monopoly. Second, the role of the arbitrator is likely to grow. In fact for a twenty year concession the role of the arbitrator becomes indistinguishable from that of a regulator of a private monopoly with a twenty year operating lease. It seems as though all roads lead to regulation.

Recall some fundamentals of economics: we need an absolute minimum of three players for a market to exist (one buyer and two sellers, or two buyers and one seller), the parties must be genuinely independent, the more parties we have the less likely it is that collusive behaviour will emerge, and that the managements (not necessarily the firms) should have absolutely no guarantee of support from governments should they make poor decisions. So we need at least two or three credible bidders for the concession, who are independent, and arrangements must be made to ensure that if external politicians, regulators, or the concessionaire's managers make such poor decisions that the company becomes technically bankrupt, overall services will continue.

For concession decisions we need to make additional assumptions about the initial state of affairs at the start of the sequence, the transparency and accuracy of data about that state, and the ability of the owner/buyers to assess the state of their assets. If you thought specifying all the outputs of a network in Chapter 7 was difficult, specifying all the outputs for a concession contract is far more complicated – let alone (from the city's point of view) trying to monitor them *independently of the concessionaire*.

Our core problem is that we think we want to hire an efficient agent to perform some functions which we believe are tightly specified. Our problems start when the agent realises that matters on the ground, or under it, are different from our original specification. It is a bit like putting your car in for servicing: if all you want is two tyres changed, then that can be specified and done for a fee agreed in advance. But if, in the process of doing this, the garage sees other things that render your car illegal, dangerous, or unsafe should they not consult you so that you have the opportunity to fix these at the same time? Yes, obviously. So garages call you up during the day with the "...bad news that we have unfortunately discovered ..."And then it becomes a game of trust: how much do you trust them that what they recommend genuinely is the least-cost solution going forward? Going on from this, if you book your car in for something less well-specified, such as an annual service, the garage will only ever give you a minimum figure: "We will do X, Y and Z, which will cost €€€€s but of course if we find anything else we'll call you [and the price will go higher]."

This example captures the essential difficulties of specifying and monitoring concession contracts. *Specifying*, and pricing in advance, all possible eventualities in a contract rapidly becomes impossible beyond a year or two, particularly if the concessionaire's responsibilities include several plants and some underground assets (which are generally impossible to verify before or after the contract), while *monitoring* the concessionaire's delivery of the outputs becomes a full-time job for a rapidly growing army of inspectors. Add to this the vagaries of future civic desires (no Council can bind its successors not to change their minds, nor to respond to changes in national legislation, nor to want extra services), incomplete knowledge of assets at the outset (imagine you were the prospective concessionaire trying to inspect all the gas pipes under a city in the hectic weeks before submitting your bid), differing cultural or engineering values, and the possibility of minor corruption (the inspectors become apologists for the concessionaire) or worse, full blown corruption, and we have some formidable barriers to a smooth regular concession auction. It just doesn't work like the concession of a shop in a retail mall where everything is transparent and contracting costs are low compared to the value of the concession, so you can have auctions every couple of years.

The final major difficulty with long term utility concessions concerns the state of assets when they are returned to the long term owner – the public sector. In the last five or ten years of the concession there is a real risk of the concessionaire skimping on maintenance, or failing to replace assets that are likely to fail with new assets. The city can specify in the concession contract exactly how much the concessionaire must spend on maintenance prior to handing the assets back but if it does so the contract has become input-based for the last X years rather than output- or performance-based, and so the city has lost all incentive effects to minimise maintenance costs.

Concession and outsourcing conclusions

Do not conclude from the above that outsourcing parts or the whole of a utility value chain is doomed to failure. Many cities around the world have large parts of their core utility services provided through a variety of outsourcing or concession arrangements, including water services in many towns in France. But the costs of submitting a utility bid can be a significant proportion of the costs of the concession over its lifetime, unless you go for a very long concession, in which case the essential benefits of a concession (frequent auctions to compete away supernormal profits) evaporate away. The experts in it say that a large amount depends on trust which has to be built up both ways over many years. This again precludes frequent auctions, which are deliberate trust-breaks. Economists view high trust situations as a network of implicit contracts, which can of course be ruptured by external parties' actions or the arrival of new players in the game. In the author's experience most long term concessions end up mimicking the situation where the regulator regulates private sector operators, which we are just about to discuss. So, in the special case of complicated utility networks it is simply not true that competition-for-the-market is self-evidently second best and other forms of promoting competitive behaviour are demonstrably third best. Overall, we conclude that this is a specialist area with many practical difficulties and some clever ways round those difficulties, which experts will explain to you – for a handsome fee – but it is not an area for beginners.

Policy conclusions on promoting competition in utilities

We can now come to some preliminary general policy conclusions for economists and policymakers about promoting competition in utilities:

1. Analyse the industry value chain in your area and *assess which parts are susceptible to genuine competition* in the market; they must a) be in principle contestable – refer to Figure 95 above – and b) have several credible independent players ready to make a contestable market competitive;

2. *Break off the potentially contestable businesses* provided they really would be both competitive and financially viable on their own in your circumstances, and use general competition powers to support genuine competition in these new markets; the government may well need to 'level the playing field' for the first twenty years by giving competitive advantages to small entrants fighting for market share against a big incumbent;

3. *For the remainder consider a variety of concession options* and take expert advice;

4. If a concession seems not to yield what a community wants, or only with great difficulty, and you can obtain effective and independent regulators for a relatively modest cost, *consider privatising the remaining monopoly parts and regulating them*;

5. If there are strong cultural or social aversions to regulating private monopolies, or the cost of obtaining effective and independent regulators is likely to be high, or large parts of the utility value chain will need public subsidies for the foreseeable future, *retain the remaining parts in public ownership*, set explicit strategic goals, corporate governance rules and acceptable values for the organisation, and establish a well-resourced body to monitor the utility.

These are some interim rough-and-ready conclusions. We will make sector-specific recommendations in the light of some major global experiences in Chapters 9-12, and draw general conclusions in Chapter 13. As you would expect, the World Bank has far more detailed policy conclusions for professionals.

The basic idea of regulating a monopoly
We now consider the possibilities once a political decision has been taken to allow a utility to operate as a regulated private monopoly.

Regulation methods
The fundamental goal of all economic regulation is for the *regulator to set a maximum price* for the regulated company – or *'regulatee'* – that makes a 'fair' allowance for both the costs and profits necessary to attract the capital required for the utility to continue to operate.

Figure 97 shows a typical utility incurring running (or operational) costs, maintenance costs, and some maintenance costs which are 'capitalised' – i.e. costs which are not treated as costs to the Income and Expenditure account but as additions to the balance sheet's list of physical assets for the utility[209]. Note that different utilities have very different ratios of operating to maintenance costs: the running costs of a fossil-fuelled power station (chiefly fuel) are very high in relation to its maintenance costs, while a sewer network has almost no running costs at all (gravity is free) so all "operating costs" are maintenance costs.

Figure 97: Regulating a monopoly: the basic idea

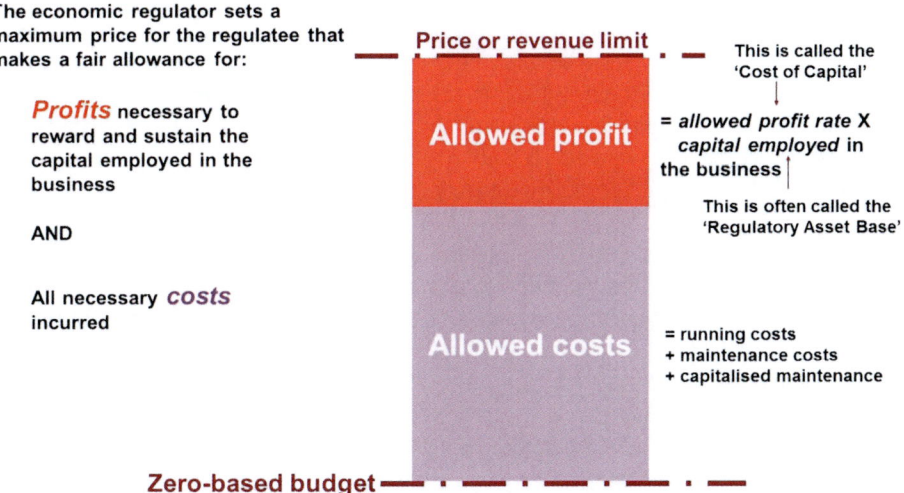

---

[209] Typically accountants will want to 'depreciate' these assets assuming some theoretical asset life, and the depreciation will be charged to the Income and Expenditure account.

In addition the utility must make sufficient profit to attract enough investment funds for it to continue to operate. The amount of money invested to date in the business is called the capital employed in the business, while all new future funds are called investments. In a sequential model the distant past does not matter too much because 'the past is a foreign country: they do things differently there'[210], and anyway nothing we do now can change it. But the recent past is another matter: it may well affect how external investors view the future, which very much does matter.

If investors view the future as like the recent past then they will want a good return on their investment, adjusted for the relative risks of investing in a utility compared to other investment opportunities. In fact under most regulatory regimes there are very few investments as safe as a utility, so this is normally one of the lowest risk investments an investor can make. Nevertheless an investor will demand some return on their money for them to offer it as equity or debt. The profit rate is the amount of profits the utility earns divided by the capital employed in the business. The lower the price that the regulator allows a utility the lower will be its profits, and so a key question for most regulators is what is the lowest profit rate they can allow that will still induce sufficient investments for the utility to continue to do its job (to continue to provide all its outputs)?

Besides raising prices, another way to increase profits would be for the utility's management to reduce costs and so increase efficiency. But in fact this is hard work; it requires real effort and is personally very risky for an individual manager: reducing the size of your own empire is not something most humans willingly choose, making close colleagues with whom one has worked for years redundant is not a pleasure, and the prospect of losing your own job means that most managers and employees will be natural opponents of any radical plan to cut costs. Plus, actually redesigning new structures and processes for a slimmer organisation with lower costs, itself takes time which most engineers would prefer to spend maintaining and optimising their network. Quite reasonably, they argue that if they had wanted to become blood-letting cost-cutters they would have joined a Management Consultancy or the Human Resources Department.

As someone who has run a manufacturing company and had to cut costs significantly, I can say that cutting costs by firing good people is emotionally by far the hardest job I have ever had to do. Professional cost-cutters concur that this is some of the hardest managerial work around: the lead partner of the cost-cutting section of the utilities practice in a large consultancy says "As a CEO, if you seriously want to cut costs and are not focused on it 110% of your time, you will fail. You have to live it and breathe it. This is not a job for the faint-hearted." [211]

---

[210] LP Hartley 1953, "The Go Between"; opening sentence.
[211] Graham Butler, partner at IBM Business Consulting Services, Utilities practice London 2005-09. One could respond that of course he would say this, having a cost-cutting product to sell, but he means it, having started his cost-cutting career in a utility and having helped dozens of utilities since to cut costs. Like butchery or surgery, it's a nasty

Principal Agent theory
So, just as turkeys don't vote for Christmas, utility managers don't want to cut costs beyond the easy or obvious, and any realistic regulatory model must separate managerial incentives from investor incentives at the outset, while acknowledging political or other pressures on any regulator as being real. Since 1980 a great deal of regulatory economics has been done under the formal assumptions of 'Principal Agent' theory, which it is not out purpose to summarise here. We note simply that the core assumption of Principal Agent theory is that managers are 'agents' of the Principals (the owners), hired to represent the owners' interests (maximising profits), and they sometimes wrongly become diverted from this objective by their own personal interests. Much of this analysis concerns ways of minimising bad deviations from profit maximisation.

General criticisms of Principal Agent theory
It is worth standing back at this point and noting that only an economist, and a certain kind of economist, would view matters like this. Any other social scientist – business strategists, organisational behaviourists, sociologists etc. – would start by saying that we have different groups of individuals coming together to achieve some common aims through the social institution of a limited company, but some of their aims will necessarily diverge, and it is the manner in which they handle these conflicts – or minimise them, to use the sort of word economists prefer – that is worth generalising. One could analyse the internal workings of a company using an informal stakeholder model, or the increasingly sophisticated models of business strategy measuring the building of internal resources and capabilities, or create metagame models of a firm with owners, managers, other employees, and other stakeholders all having roles in the game, but with these players in the game sometimes disagreeing on the rules of the game, leading to occasional periods of mutual harming. Any one of these models would be a more holistic approach than Principal Agent theory.

Specific criticisms of Principal Agent theory
While Principal Agent theory could, in principle, be modelled through game theory, its greatest weakness is that it tends to assume the Principals are multi-talented people who know best what they want to achieve, and how best to spend their money. Managers, on the other hand, are viewed as mere ciphers, people who, in a sense, get in the way of the owner maximising their profit.

In fact, of course, people do not always know what they want, or how best to achieve it. In an ice cream shop I may know best what flavour of ice cream I want. But students of engineering at most universities in the world do not get much choice in their first year syllabus because their teachers say "We know what you want to know and when you need to know it – better than you do". Or, in the world of politics, taxation-minimisers claim "I know better than the government how to spend my money". Do they? If they want defence from hostile foreigners,

---

business, but if you have to undergo it you would rather it were done by someone who has done it before.

do they really know better than the Joint Chiefs whether to spend money on an aircraft carrier, or a weapons system, or essential logistical back-up? If they want an efficient public service do they really know better than top public servants whether to spend money on this kind of IT system or that kind of IT system? When you look at it closely this claim is often hollow: I know how best to spend my money in the ice cream shop because I am well-informed about ice cream flavours and have the tummy to prove it. It is not true when decisions become very complex or I am out of my experience.

In the business world it is patently not true that the shareholders of a firm are multi-talented masters of the universe while a firm's managers are mere ciphers, or agents. In an age of mass computerised share-trading many shares are "owned" by very short-term players with no long- term interest in the company at all. And although long-term shareholders such as myself, can easily buy shares in IBM, to imagine that I could run IBM better than its top management is ridiculous. Good management is actually a scarce resource, it directly creates firm capabilities, some of these will hopefully be sources of sustainable competitive advantage to the firm, and thus of (super-normal) profits. Thus most managers actually view profits as having been created by them – not by the owners. One top manager once said to me "All the shareholders provide is a certain type of long term risk capital"[212]. And so we move to more rounded theories of the firm as a vehicle in which different groups collaborate to add value to a joint enterprise, and then stake claims on the total. John Kay concluded in Foundations of Corporate Success[213] that profit is the residual added value left after all other explicit claims have been taken. Alfred Marshall famously argued that in the long run this residual super-normal profit would shrink to zero because the creators of all economic rents would rapidly appropriate them. But Marshallian analysis does not solve the problem of multiple claimants on the same bit of profit, which can lead to disputes between claimants that could kill the goose that lays the golden egg; nor does it admit that super-normal profits might endure for decades in some successful firms, even when operating in competitive markets.

The second specific criticism of Principal Agent theory is that it assumes that going after something directly is the best way to achieve it. This might seem a truism, and a good piece of counsel generally, and one that in economics we generally accept, but for some really important long term goals this can actually be bad advice. For centuries it has been commonplace to advise teenagers that they won't find love or happiness by explicitly seeking it, but they might find their heart's desire while doing other worthwhile activities. Taking this wisdom up to the level of a whole economy John Kay's book "Obliquity"[214] convincingly explains why seeking oblique solutions to society's deepest desires is often the most satisfying long term solution. It is a good read, and an excellent cure for Principal-Agent-itis.

---

[212] Michael Allan, former President, Du Pont Japan Ltd, in a private conversation.
[213] Kay J, 1993, "Foundations of Corporate Success" Oxford University Press, Oxford, hardback version, page 216
[214] Kay JA, 2011, "Obliquity" Profile Books, London.

A use for Principal Agent theory

Having said this, the one area of corporate life where Principal Agent theory seems a really good model of what actually goes on is the world of Mergers and Acquisitions (M&A). Here the Principals are the investors, while the Agents are the Boards and CEOs of merging companies, and their advisors – investment bankers, accountants and lawyers – who are all heavily incentivised to 'Do a deal, no matter what business strategy or logic dictates'. The evidence strongly suggests many mergers have no long term rationale, and are not in the acquiring firm's long-term shareholders' interests, but it is this latter group who must ultimately pay for all the advisers' fees and deal-making[215]. Yet M&A deals continue to dominate many a wealthy investment banker's annual bonus package, while diverting CEO and board room time away from running the firm's core businesses.

Incentivisation under more holistic management theories

Having established that managers might actually be talented individuals who have the capacity to create profits where none existed previously, we examine how real incentives for owners and managers can be created in a wider, more useful, framework than Principal Agent theory. Sometimes it can be viewed as a 'game' but we must be careful with this word in utility regulation, as it carries different meanings for different readers. By 'gaming', utility professionals tend to mean that someone is lying about their position or intentions[216], while academics tend to see only agents maximising self-interest. The managers, investors, regulators, and customers who have been lied to do not take such a dispassionate view of 'gaming' as an academic can.

Figure 98, based on Figure 97, shows the general situation facing any regulator who wants to reduce costs in their industry:

---

[215] Johnson, Scholes and Whittington, 2008, 8th edition page 359, summarising much serious research, says "As many as 70 per cent of acquisitions end up with lower returns to shareholders of both organisations". Grant, 2010, 7th edition page 450, notes that although the acquired firm's shareholders nearly always do well – because acquirers typically pay a 25% takeover premium – "For acquiring firms studies show that the returns are either negative or insignificant from zero." The quality of the kinds of studies referred to is generally shown by how they estimate the counter-factual: what would have happened if the merger had not gone ahead.

[216] See, for example, the concluding quote about the California electricity de-regulation experience in Chapter 9.

Figure 98: To grow profits in a utility regulators and investors have to incentivise managers

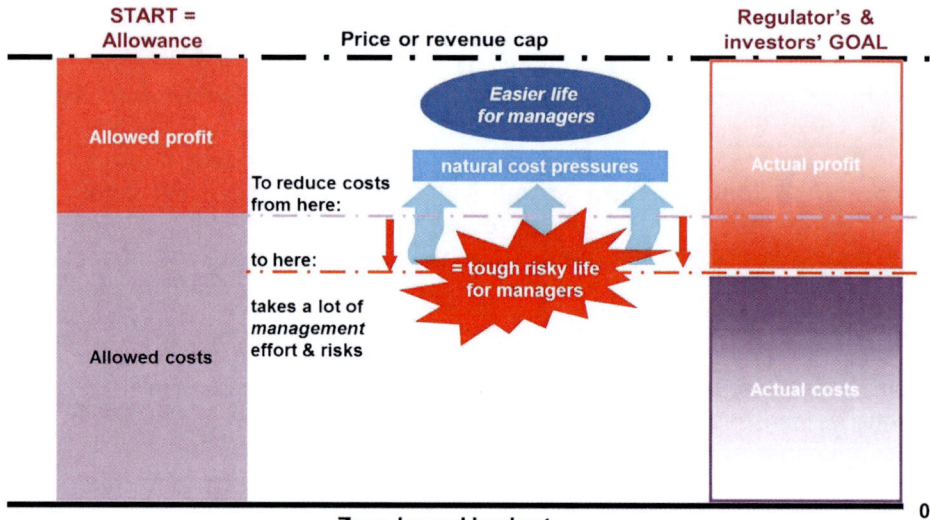

The regulator may set the situation on the left, but in the long term wishes to achieve the outcome on the right, by getting managers to lower costs and increase profits. This, of course, is the perennial goal of investors. But these intentions will always be opposed by two innate processes: natural pressures for costs to increase – inflation, new technologies, better relations with all suppliers – and natural human indolence – our preference for the comfortable life. So if anything is to happen in reality *the regulator and investors must persuade or incentivise the utility's managers to make it happen*, as well as 'doing their day job' – running the business operationally and planning for the future. As we have said cutting costs involves a lot of discomfort and personal risks for managers, as shown in Figure 98. The regulator's cunning plan, of course, is to allow extra profits for a while before ultimately lowering prices and passing the efficiency gains on to consumers. Thus any regulator seeking to increase the efficiency of their regulatees is implicitly playing a multi-time period game or 'dance sequence' of moves involving himself, investors and managers[217].

Running cost incentives

If a regulator simply allows greater profits this rewards shareholders, who can influence the Board of Directors, and so middle management, but it is an indirect route requiring an efficient market for managerial control. More generally we can conclude that regulators should try to find better ways to motivate both the investors (shareholders and debt-holders) *and* the managers – i.e. *both company incentives and managerial incentives matter.*

---

[217] Note, though, that for many regulators' improving efficiency is not their prime goal: for a discussion of overall regulatory goals, and where cost reduction fits in see Chapter 13's very brief Conclusions.

In practice utility managers often see themselves as 'stewards of a network' they did not build but are temporarily in charge of. Unlike, say, investment bankers, utility engineers are not fundamentally 'money-driven' people. Of course they have mortgages and other bills to pay, and are not going to refuse any extra money offered, but the idea of earning a lot more money is not what gets them out of bed in the mornings, or makes them tick as human beings. In fact one of the best rewards for them, and for society at large, might actually be the freedom to spend some capital (in particular) as they think fit to optimise the system of which they are stewards. So extra profits could actually help them, but the company will have to earn extra profits before any of it can be given to managers for their 'pet projects'. So, effective managerial incentives *could* be made to depend on company financial incentives, even if direct financial incentives would not.

Capital incentives
We now turn to the other part of the revenue allowance: allowed profit. The fundamental algebra is

Allowed profit = Allowed Cost of Capital (CoC) x Allowed Capital Employed

The allowed capital employed is often called the *Regulatory Asset Base* or RAB for short.

Given that no regulator wants to go down in history as the regulator who bankrupted the industry they are regulating, regulators will tend to err (if they are human) on the side of allowing a higher general cost of capital than is strictly necessary to finance the industry. Straightaway this gives a very slight bias to capital decisions. If the allowed CoC is even slightly higher than necessary to finance the industry there is now an incentive for the regulatee's managers to *'gold plate' their asset base – i.e. to spend more on capital assets than is economically efficient*. Recall that the asset base of a network utility – the sunk costs – is frequently massive, so even a 0.1% error on the allowed CoC in the regulatee's favour will translate into € millions of extra profits, especially for the capital-intensive utilities of railways, water, sewerage, gas, and electricity distribution.

Turning to the capital base, from the regulatee's point of view, unlike a firm in a competitive market, once an investment has been allowed into the Regulatory Asset Base it will earn this allowed profit *forever!* This applies regardless of whether the regulator has overestimated the CoC, got it right, or even slightly undershot it. Investors will get that return forever, and no management team in a competitive firm can boast that. So regulatees have every incentive to bid for more capital spending than they strictly need so that the regulator will allow them higher investment and they earn higher gross profits forever. Regulators, on the other hand, need to appear as 'hard but fair'. Because each capital base decision is unique to each utility and time, there is less personal risk to the regulator of being widely criticised, so they can afford to be tougher on capital spending than on the CoC: the regulatee will gripe, for sure, but their position in the game obliges them to. So the actual core disputes under nearly all forms of regulation centre around allowed specific investments, rather than the necessarily more theoretical discussions about the general allowed profit rate (the Cost of Capital) for the industry.

"Gold plating" the asset base has therefore long been known to be one of the traditional dangers of all forms of regulation, and has much practical and theoretical evidence to support it[218].

Revenue control or price controls?
Before examining the main forms of regulation we must deal with a technical difference that disturbs purists. Should the regulator be setting a price control or a revenue control? Well, given that the regulator is seeking to restrain a firm's monopoly tendencies the goal is to limit the firm's revenues. But the way that a monopolist sells their services, and thus can possibly exploit its monopoly position, is usually by raising its price above long run marginal cost. If a regulator intervenes to limit prices they should restrict the firm's revenues, and so as a first order approximation the two are roughly the same. Obviously, though, a regulator cannot restrict prices where the service is not sold by units of quantity. For instance, if water is sold unmetered 'per connection, per year', as it is in many British households[219], then the water company does not sell water by the cubic metre and so the regulator must set some kind of revenue limit, or at least a revenue per customer limit.

In the more usual case where the service is sold per unit (e.g. 'The tariff for your local gas monopoly is €X per unit'), actual revenues always differ from planned or allowed revenues because the total *quantity sold by the utility always differs from what was assumed*. Therefore in practice regulatory regimes must contain a set of complicated rules covering how these differences should be adjusted during or after the period to which they refer. But this is mind-numbing stuff, not worth frying your brain for. The principle is obvious: the regulator should take back excess revenue the firm should not have got, or give it back as soon as possible if they are short[220].

In practice revenue and price caps usually differ very little. In both, a price or

---

[218] Averch H and Johnson L, 1962, 'Behaviour of the firm under regulatory constraint' *American Economic Review* 52: 1053-69 is the classic theoretical article. For a practical illustration just walk in to the headquarters of your local monopolised utility and look around you.

[219] At the time of writing approximately 40% of British households pay for water according to the size of property they have, in a series of property bands that are used to set property taxes. Large customers and all new houses pay for water on a unit basis. If unmetered water charging sounds barmy recall that it is one of the cheapest ways to retail water, that Britain is fairly wet, water is not scarce in half the island, and so water's shadow price here would be very low anyway.

[220] Note the word "should". This is not to say that this is actually done in practice.

revenue per customer is announced in advance and cannot easily be changed after it has been set, while the quantity assumptions will inevitably be wrong and have to be cleared up after the event. So, in what follows we will use the two terms revenue cap and price cap almost interchangeably.

Rate of Return (or Cost of Service) regulation

Figure 99: American utilities at a glance

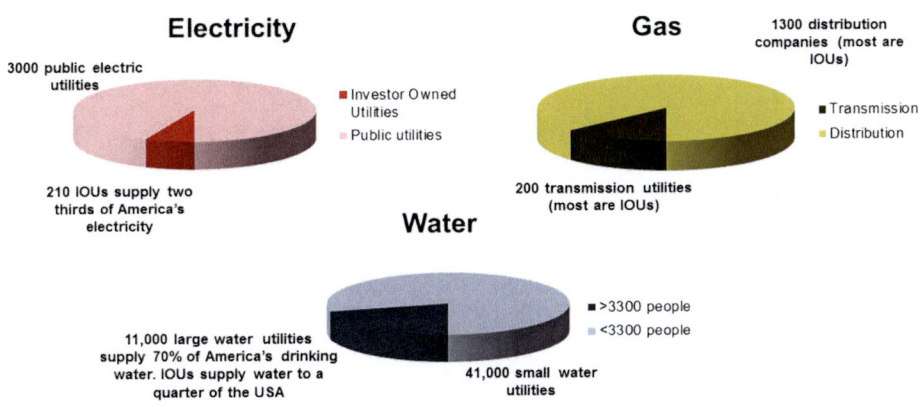

Sources: Energy Information Administration Energy explained website, 2007 Power Industry Overview, Environment Protection Agency Factoids, and National Association of Water Companies, all accessed August 2011

Because of its general aversion to mixing government with business, and therefore to public ownership of trading enterprises, America developed more privatised utilities than any other country in the twentieth century, and so led the way in developing ways to regulate private monopolies. Figure 99 summarises what has recently been published about them by the Energy Information Administration and the Environment Protection Agency. So, we see that although there are three thousand publicly-owned electricity utilities, most of America's electricity is distributed by the 210 regulated private monopolies, called Investor Owned Utilities (IOUs), and that America's gas is transmitted and distributed by 1500 gas utilities, most of which are IOUs. In water there are an astonishing 51,000 utilities, but 70% of America's drinking water is supplied by the largest 11,000 utilities; unfortunately the EPA does not say how many of these are privately owned, but the National Association of Water Companies estimates that private water utilities supply water to 73m Americans[221] – almost a quarter of the USA.

Chapter 12 of this book contains a section on American railroads, which describes the emergence from 1870 of economic regulation of privately-owned utilities in the USA. Eventually the most popular form of regulation became the Rate of Return or 'Cost of Service' approach, in which the regulator set an allowed Cost

---

[221] NAWC website Private Water Solutions accessed August 2011

of Capital – the Rate of Return – for the sector and firms were allowed to earn that profit rate, or a bit more if they could beat it. Profit rates were discussed between regulators and the Investor Owned Utilities, often in very legal language, and based on the outcome of this profit rate decision, new prices were set until such time as they were changed again. It is worth emphasising that prices were, and are, set in nominal terms, and once set they are not generally revised until the utility asks for a rise again, which might, once, have been more than ten years, before the emergence of widespread inflation. The rise of inflation since the 1970s means rate settings have become more frequent than they were a hundred years ago. We do not here describe the detailed rate setting processes adopted, or the methodologies used to derive the Cost of Capital, as these subjects vary by State and regulator.

Cost of Service model – and the over-bidding game
Given an allowed return on capital one main question concerns the amount of investment that will be allowed to augment the Regulatory Asset Base: how does a regulator decide what an appropriate level of investment is for each company? The other main question is how should the regulator determine a fair allowed cost base for each company's running costs? In general these are determined by the regulator following representations by each utility. But the regulatees have a clear incentive to overbid both bids, which the regulator must allow for, so by how much should the regulator knock back the bids? There is general agreement that there is an *information asymmetry* here: that the regulatees know better than the regulator what they need, and what they can 'make do' with as a minimum – which is bound to invite a good regulator to make comparisons between their regulatees and other similar utilities. In sum we note there are few incentives to be efficient in this model, but very strong incentives to make a good rate case.

In 1993 Laffont and Tirole provided a general theoretical model of this situation which students of regulatory economics are often taught, but as its practical influence seems to be limited this book will skip that exposition. The conclusion of a Laffont-Tirole model is generally that a regulatee will minimise costs provided it is able to keep the profits caused by its information asymmetry, but if it is not allowed to keep these profits for long, cost-minimisation incentives are weaker[222]. ...Hmm ...smart regulators had sort of guessed that some years before. We will shortly return to the issue of how long gains made by the management should be kept by the firm.

An alternative, very practical approach, is to use a technique beloved of Finance Ministry officials the world over. These operators know a thing or two about knocking expenditure bids back, and it was summarised to me once as: *'Keep going until you can see the panic in their eyes'.* But this sort of double-bluff poker game does not seem the best way to optimise essential utility expenditure

---

[222] Crew M and Parker D, 2006, International handbook on regulation, Edward Elgar Cheltenham page 9

plans. It is 'a bit extreme' and, more importantly, is not conducive to a *repeated game* where expectations of similar treatment at the next review could lead to lower regulatory risks and so a lower cost of capital. In practice US regulation is very heavily 'fact-based' (on past facts) and practical. Regulators tend to look at actual costs in a (past) 'test' year, subject the test year's costs and performance to various tests of appropriateness, and, if satisfied, then build past costs into forward-looking allowed prices or 'rates'. The general weakness is that the past (base) year might include vast amounts of X-inefficiency in its costs – i.e. *unlike Figure 98 the budget is not zero-based*.

The Gain Sharing model
A refinement to the basic Cost of Service model used in many American utilities is the Gain Sharing model in which regulatee company profits earned above the allowed Cost of Capital are formally "shared" with consumers in a *stakeholder* model. Following what is now conventional business governance practice, but was pioneering in its day, 'stakeholders' are defined as consumers, plus investors, plus managers and others, often including government, 'the environment' etc. The underlying principle seems a good one: if the utility as a whole can exceed the cost and investment efficiency targets set by the regulator these gains will be shared between all the stakeholders. So, for instance, if profits are higher than envisaged the government will benefit from higher tax takes, or 'the environment' might benefit from a power utility exceeding its air pollution reduction targets, or a water utility taking less water from a river than it initially said it would need.

In practice the ratio of gains to be kept by each stakeholder is usually heavily skewed (70% or more) towards society in the form of consumers, which usually means that utility management will not contemplate radical cost-cutting. If we summarise results using the rate of profit earned and compare what actually happens with what was planned (an allowed Cost of Capital) then effectively, three things can possibly happen under the gain sharing model, as Figure 100 shows:

Figure 100: Management incentives under traditional US Gain Sharing regulation:

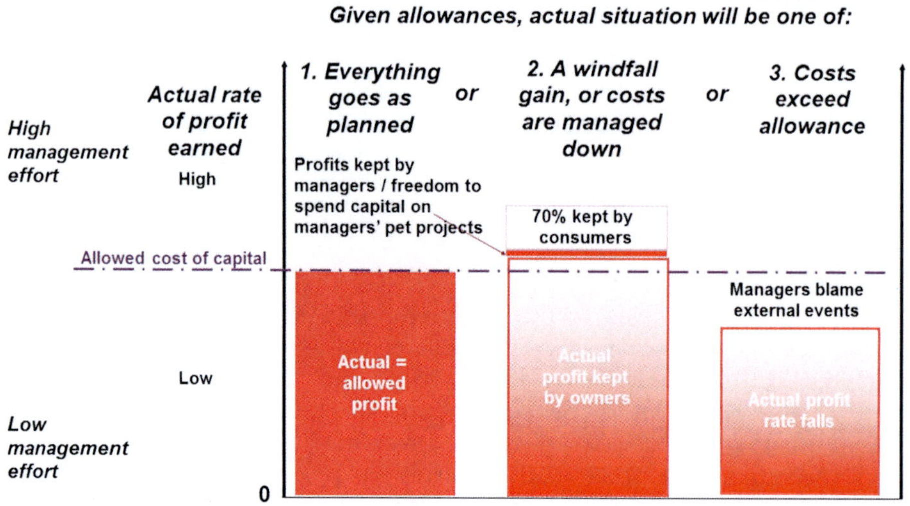

Given allowances, actual situation will be one of:

	1. Everything goes as planned	2. A windfall gain, or costs are managed down	3. Costs exceed allowance

High management effort — Actual rate of profit earned: High
Profits kept by managers / freedom to spend capital on managers' pet projects
70% kept by consumers
Allowed cost of capital
Managers blame external events
Low management effort — Low
Actual = allowed profit
Actual profit kept by owners
Actual profit rate falls

The first possibility is that it is just about conceivable that 'the plan was perfect'. Fine, but trivial. Enough said.

Secondly it is possible that there was either a windfall gain to the utility (benevolent weather, lower suppliers' prices than expected etc.) or management successfully reduced costs, causing lower-than-planned costs and higher-than-planned profits. In this case management takes the credit, consumers take 70% of the gains, and investors take most of the rest of the profit. There may be something left over for the environment, and a tiny amount for managers to spend on their pet updating or optimising projects.

In the third case external events or cost overruns cause higher-than-planned costs and lower-than-planned profits. In this case something unexpected must have happened in the external environment (there's always something unexpected) that managers can blame for the increase in their costs, which they may try to recoup through an extra rate-setting exercise.

So, in sum, there is
    1. Very little 'upside' incentive for a regulatee manager to reduce costs under any scenario;
    2. In the third situation, where costs have risen,
        a) Few regulator want to be criticised for unfairly ignoring firms' pleas for assistance following some exogenous event that plausibly could have raised firms' costs, so, provided they are sure the event occurred, and increased costs, most regulators will make *some* allowance for this effect
        b) Management has more real information than the regulator and passes on only information which supports its case, omitting any 'windfall' factors which could have acted the other way

c) Under gain-sharing eventually prices will track behind cost increases, so shareholders may suffer for a while with lower-than-planned profits, but there is little management incentive to reduce costs

d) So most management effort goes into convincing their regulator that this cost increase was real, external, and large, instead of finding ways to reduce costs.

e) In passing we note this is another example of an *information assymmetry* favouring the regulatee.

The most extreme form of regulatory information inequality is called 'regulatory capture' where instead of controlling the industry's prices and profits, the regulator is controlled by the regulatees, and is fed only information that suits their purposes[223]. A regulator who wants to avoid capture must find ways to redress this information imbalance.

General incentives under Rate of Return regulation (in practice)
Under Rate of Return regulation the general incentives for network utility managers might be expected to be:

1. Grow your capital base as much as possible: put every effort into getting more investments included in the Regulatory Asset Base – i.e. *gold plate the asset base*
2. Because cost reduction incentives are so weak, *put your effort into making cost-increase excuses, not cost-reduction exercises*.

However, because generations of US regulators had been educated knowing these dangers, US regulation has become very pragmatic, a tradition of "working things out' as you go along", to quote Crew and Parker[224]. The fundamental framework of rate-based regulation does have long term consequences, though. This framework is that once rates are set they will not be changed by the regulator unless the company starts making (what the regulator regards as) excessive profits, and by mirror image, the company will not apply for a rate-setting review unless its profitability is (what it regards as) far too low. And because regulatees under a gain-sharing regime can always apply for a Cost Of Service rate review from which they must be allowed future costs equal to past costs, incentives for X-inefficiency reduction can be very weak.

In practice this has led to some strange 'counter-intuitive' developments. One set of foreign observers with an intimate knowledge of several US power utilities

---

[223] The classic case in modern times would be regulation of the financial sector by the Federal Reserve in the decades up to 2010: not only had the Chairman and the previous Chairman made their careers as advocates of 'light touch' bank Regulation, the only other potentially powerful regulator – President Bush's Secretary of the Treasury – had made his career in one of the main banks exploiting light touch regulation to the full, and being so successful that he ended up as CEO of his bank.

[224] Ibid page 9

described them privately as being seriously under-invested on the capital side, but with "obscene" labour remuneration at the top of the management tree[225]. Thus operating costs, and particularly investment, had been excessively trimmed year after year by senior managers who had pocketed some proportion of the savings, while the infrastructure itself was, in the opinion of external experts, rotting away. Clearly this could not have continued forever, but it is an endemic problem when regulating utilities (probably the best examples can be seen in Chapter 12 on railway regulation), and illustrates the general difficulties for any regulator in monitoring all a utility's outputs (as described in Chapter 6).

Yardstick regulation

Shleifer's vision

In a theoretical article that was eventually published in 1985, MIT economist Andrei Shleifer[226] noted that standard cost-reduction incentives were extremely weak for America's privately owned regulated monopolies under their existing "cost-of-service" form of regulation, and that this would logically produce high inefficiency. Briefly reviewing other possible remedies, Shleifer argued

> "What the regulator needs is some relatively simple benchmark, other than the firm's present or past performance, against which to evaluate the firm's potential. With such a benchmark, he can decide what the firm's costs ought to be, and set the price accordingly."

Shleifer dismissed benchmarking against state-owned utilities as "too different from private firms" and "not necessarily efficient". Instead he proposed comparing private utilities' costs with other private monopolies' costs and called the scheme "yardstick competition". His core idea is shown in Figure 101:

Figure 101: Shleifer's benchmarking yardstick: the core idea

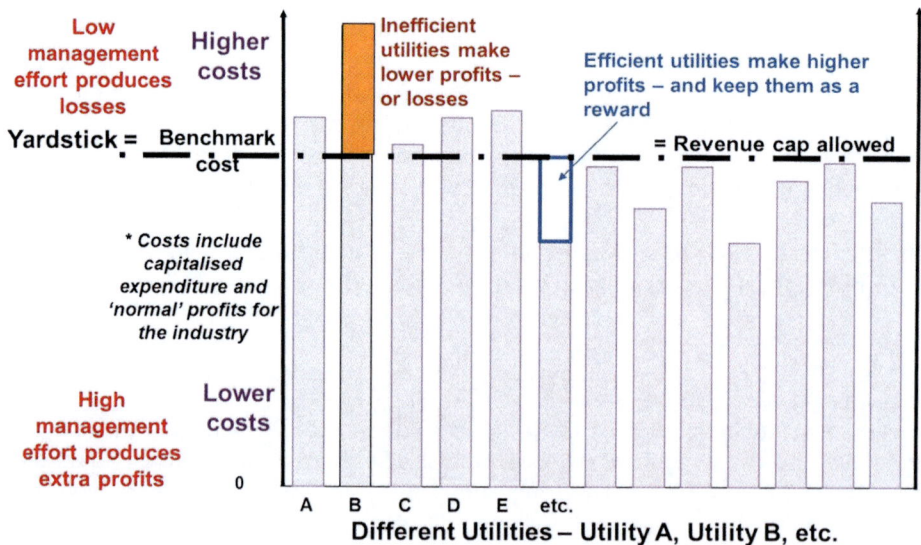

The horizontal axis of Shleifer's yardstick compares a number of utility companies, while the vertical axis shows their *total costs, including an allowance for a normal rate of profit for the industry*. It is, therefore, *a comparison of companies' actual revenues with what he proposed to allow*. Very simply, Shleifer proposed setting every company's revenue equal to total normal costs, and deriving 'normal costs' from a comparison, or benchmarking exercise, using what he called a *yardstick*. In his first example Shleifer assumes all firms have identical costs, and so his yardstick is a simple average, as shown in Figure 101. He then relaxes the assumption about firms being identical and shows that provided the differences between firms are "observable" the regulator could set an environment-adjusted revenue cap that is socially optimal. What Shleifer calls 'observable' differences in costs we can more accurately call quantifiable[227] differences – i.e. we can use numbers (in different dimensions) to describe the differences between firms. Or, in business terms, we can describe this as quantifying the exogenous cost-drivers that are beyond management's control, which, of course, is just what we have spent Chapter 7 analysing.

So, either by simple averaging, or by doing a more sophisticated benchmarking of the firm's operating environment, the regulator arrives at a fair yardstick estimate of each firm's efficient costs based on factors that the firm's managers cannot influence. This yardstick includes an allowance for a normal rate of profit given the risks of that industry[228]. The regulator then sets this level as the firm's allowed revenue base for the next period. As *firms are given advance notice of this level they have time to react to it, and so can plan and execute cost reduction strategies in time to benefit from the yardstick*, rather than simply being beaten by it[229]. Firms that succeed in reducing costs will be allowed to keep extra profits, subject to the clear implication that their new lower benchmark will form part of the basis for estimating (someone's) costs for the next round of price setting. In practice this means that shareholders and management would keep the extra profits for one period before handing them over to consumers as consumer surplus.

---

[225] The author must respect the confidentiality of this source, but note that the managers making the comments about 'obscene' remuneration levels were themselves earning salaries approaching or exceeding seven figures.

[226] Shleifer, A, 1985, A theory of yardstick competition, The Rand Journal of Economics 16, 319-327

[227] We can observe and agree that a couple are in love, and that this is significant, but we cannot usefully quantify it.

[228] Yes, there is a small circularity: the regulator is himself or herself one of those risks, called regulatory risk. Fairly or not, regulators assume this is small. In practical terms political risk (the risk of politicians changing laws) is far bigger than regulatory risk because regulators are aware of, and try to minimise, regulatory risk, while politicians will do whatever they think needs to be done while they have power.

[229] Shleifer called his model sequential, but in the core analysis promptly collapses all time periods into one, which is like inventing a dance routine with just one step. However, in the conclusion he clearly considers a sequence of steps, a repeated game, and the possibilities of collusion.

However, firms that do not cut costs will be beaten by the yardstick: they will pay the penalty in terms of earning sub-normal profits, or even produce losses[230]. The Owners or Investors are then incentivised to change this management team for one that can cut costs, and managers are incentivised to cut costs in order to keep their jobs. In this manner regulated utilities' investors and managers are being persuaded to operate like companies in a fully competitive industry.

Collusion

In his conclusion, in order to consider the possibilities of collusion between regulatees, Shleifer explicitly considers the sequence that forms the game of repeated yardstick regulation: the cost-estimation and regulatory decision making period, then the price control and cost-cutting period, then the subsequent round of efficient-cost-estimation and decision-making etc. He concludes the risk of collusion should be low if

1. The regulator can punish firms for collusive behaviour
2. The number of firms regulated is large

The second conclusion is hardly new – it has been known in practice for centuries, and has been proven in formal game theory for decades – but it usefully reinforces the general point made earlier that regulators must either have direct responsibility for a large number of regulatees or have access to a set of data from a wide set of similar utilities. The first conclusion says regulators should carry a big yardstick – backed by heavy legal powers if needed, such as the right to terminate a company's licence to operate or to force companies to supply certain kinds of data.

Summary of Shleifer

So the heart of Shleifer's vision was to focus attention on how regulators should spend significant resources fairly estimating what an efficient monopoly's costs should be, starting from what we would now call '*a zero-based budget*' *rather than from a budget based on past years' actual costs* – which of course includes past and current inefficiencies. For our purposes Shleifer is in effect saying 'Let's focus regulatory and management attention on what efficient costs should be.'

America's reluctance to implement Shleifer

Given that Shleifer was directly addressing American regulators and monopolies with theoretical rigour about a vital practical issue, it may be surprising that his work had little immediate impact in the USA. But one must view these institutions – both the regulators and the regulatees – in their historical and political context. With the exception of railroads and telecoms, most American utilities have local roots, and so their regulators are usually local, often based in individual cities, or at the most having State-wide jurisdiction[231]. They have been

---

[230] Given that the gross operating profit margin for a utility with large sunk costs can amount to 40% of turnover it would take managerial ineptitude on a truly stupendous scale to make routine losses while running most heavy utilities.

established under State laws and so can only be changed by Acts of each State's legislature. So if a State has a hundred local utilities and there are 50 States...you can do the math.

In additions, for historical reasons explained in Chapter 12, lawyers have traditionally played a big part in administering US regulation in practice – far more so than in any other country. This may once upon a time have been because they were the only professional people in a small town capable of reading a complicated contract and interpreting it objectively, or because lawyers are highly regarded in American business, but for whatever reason many of the people charged with applying regulation in practice have legal backgrounds. So what, you may ask? An important difference is that Anglo-Saxon lawyers have a very high regard for 'Precedence' – previous decisions on a subject by a high authority. Economists, on the other hand, are by nature more sceptical, tending to wonder, first if the earlier authority actually got the decision right, and second if circumstances have changed: to paraphrase a remark attributed to John Maynard Keynes, we might summarise economists' views as "When circumstances change, we reserve the right to change our minds."[232] To lawyers, of course, this is proof that economists are inconsistent, unreliable people, while economists tend to regard regulatory lawyers as a bit conservative. Plus, as lawyers, they don't regard inefficiency as the greatest crime in the world (they're right: it isn't), and with regular price settings from now to eternity, they have no incentive to change the law – merely an incentive to interpret it differently each time.

Could this system be changed? Only by political action. But translate this into the reality of American politics, where making changes to laws needs politicians to see a real benefit from legislative action, and you can imagine most politicians' reactions: "Just because some economist has written a theoretical paper saying we should change the way we regulate our utilities, you think I should use my limited political capital to change a hundred old laws. Is the old system working that badly? The lights are still on and there's water in the taps. Can you guarantee my constituents immediate big price cuts if I get this through? No? Well, frankly, I've got bigger fish to fry..."

The emergence of price cap regulation

Chapter 7's review of efficiency measurement noted that American economists in the 1960s were so in thrall to neoclassical assumptions that technical inefficiency was simply not an issue: most American economists just assumed it away. Harvey Leibenstein's article on the likely scale of X-inefficiency[233] referred

---

[231] Obviously this is a generalisation ignoring bodies such as the Federal Energy Regulatory Commission (FERC) which sets some electricity transmission tariffs etc.

[232] What he actually said, according to Alfred L. Malabre in Lost Prophets: An Insider's History of the Modern Economists (1994) p. 220, was "When the facts change I change my mind. What do you do, Sir?"

[233] Leibenstein H, 1966, "Allocative Efficiency and X-efficiency" American Economic Review 56, 392-415

to in Chapter 7 was read, but it had little lasting effect on the psyche of most American economists. Consequently they were not overly worried by the inefficiency critique of Cost of Service regulation, and were not inclined to push their politicians to reform US regulation methods. So it was abroad, in Chile and Mrs Thatcher's Britain of the 1980s, that Shleifer's ideas were first implemented, with stunning speed, directness and success.

Revenue cap regulation on the UK
Unusually for a European, in the UK Mrs Thatcher viewed state-owned enterprises as innately inefficient and an unnecessary drain on the nation's resources; she wanted to reduce the state to its core governmental functions. In 1982 she started examining ways to privatise profitable, state-owned businesses such as the state-owned airline, British Airways (BA), and the national phone company, British Telecommunications (BT). BA was fundamentally in a contestable and increasingly competitive business, so it could be simply sold off, and told to survive and thrive in the global airline industry. This happened in 1985.

BT, however, with its near-monopoly of land lines, at a time when few people had mobile phones, was a trickier intellectual problem. The company clearly faced exciting technological possibilities that were thought to be constrained by the 'dead hand' of a bureaucratic state utility, but its core landline business might need regulating. Draft legislation was put to Parliament to allow the creation of a competitor, Mercury, and to require the government and regulator to promote competition in the telecoms industry. Finally, in late 1982, economist Stephen Littlechild was commissioned to review the options for regulating BT's monopoly profits after it was privatised, against a general expectation that these would dwindle quite quickly, as new competitive markets developed.

Littlechild's 1983 price cap
British policymakers and economists, including Littlechild, were well aware of US-style Rate of Return regulation, with its Cost of Service and Gain Sharing variants, but were generally sceptical of the whole idea of regulation, because of its drawbacks of inefficiency and gold-plating, which were the very opposite of the attributes Mrs Thatcher wanted from privatisation.

So no policymaker in Britain wanted Rate of Return regulation. The hard part was finding a workable alternative. The first alternative Littlechild considered was having no explicit regulation of BT at all, and simply allowing competitive market forces to emerge. The second option, promoted by the professional British government economists, recommended a version of what we have called gain-sharing, in which 52-75% of any excess BT profits would be returned to customers. A third option was suggested by Mrs Thatcher's Personal Economic Adviser, Professor Alan Walters: keen to privatise state-owned monopolies, but also to minimise the kind of welfare losses discussed in Chapter 1 of this book resulting from too low a quantity and too high a price, Walters advocated a scheme designed to expand BT's outputs by having a progressive scale of tax rates being imposed on BT (on top of normal tax rates) formally linked so that the tax rates fell as the quantity of BT's outputs grew. In addition Littlechild considered a form of regulation by profit ceilings in which BT's profits would be capped if their profit rate exceeded a rate that was about twice their estimated cost of capital.

Littlechild had a really difficult task to do, few quantitative tools to help him, and very little time, but he was given freedom to consider alternatives. As he later admitted[234], in the week before the report was due, a fifth option came to him: what about a temporary price or revenue cap? It would be a demanding price cap – hopefully promising customers that their bills would not rise with inflation – so that would make it politically appealing, but what made it economically appealing was that the price cap would incentivise BT to minimise costs and capital expenditure, and be innovative, and the more they did so the more profits they could earn for their new shareholders.

Consequently Littlechild summarised his views in a Table of ranked preferences in his report, which, with a few changes to adopt the language we are using, is shown in Table 5:

Table 5: Stephen Littlechild's 1983 ranking of the options for regulating British Telecommunications

Ranking: 1 = best, 5 = worst	Form of regulation of BT				
CRITERION	No explicit constraints	Gain-sharing	Output Tax	Profit Ceiling	Price Cap (RPI-X)
Protection against monopoly	5	3	2	4	1
Efficiency & innovation	1=	4=	4=	3	1=
Burden of regulation	1	5	4	3	2
Promotion of competition	1	5	4	2=	2=
Sale proceeds & prospects for BT	1=	4	5	3	1=

Source: Based on Littlechild S (1983) 'Regulation of British Telecommunications' profitability' HMSO London, pages 1-2 and 37-39; Littlechild's 'MRR' has been called Gain-sharing, 'ORPL' an Output tax, and 'Local Tariff Ceiling' is Price Cap.

Littlechild concluded that the scheme with no explicit financial controls had the best overall properties except for its complete lack of protection against monopoly power, which was so serious that it could not be recommended. The other schemes had undesirable effects and might be hard to implement in practice, with the exception of the price cap, which says, in effect to a regulatee 'This is the maximum price: now make as much profit from it as you can'. This

---

[234] See p4 of Jon Stern's 2003 paper *What the Littlechild report actually said* London Business School Working Paper 55 available on http://www.london.edu/facultyandresearch/research/docs/1_LittlechildJSFINMay03.pdf

had strong efficiency and innovation incentives, good profit prospects, and therefore sales proceeds, and good protection for the customer via the price cap guarantee. After all a price cap is only a *maximum* price: if competitors enter with lower prices the incumbent (ex-monopolist) can always cut their prices, so customers win either way. As the telecoms market was expected to become increasingly competitive a price cap had the core advantage of mimicking market competition that Shleifer notes; so in 1983 Littlechild was ahead of, and anticipating, the revenue-cap part of Shleifer's 1985 paper.

Indexing for inflation: the RPI – X formula

An endemic weakness of the Rate of Return / Cost of Service system of regulation is that it sets prices in nominal terms forever. In times of inflation (Britain had suffered from double-digit inflation in the 1970s and 80s) this meant that real prices were soon eroded away by inflation, leading utilities rapidly into losses. In America, where rate settings had once been quite rare events in a utility's life, inflation, though lower than in the UK, was still significant, forcing utilities to apply for rate settings every few years. So it was essential for any workable British scheme to have some kind of inflation-indexing formula built into the general revenue cap to avoid price re-settings every year or two. But Littlechild also wanted to insert efficiency incentives into the indexing formula to demonstrate that the privatised monopoly was delivering real gains to the British public.

Consequently he seized on an earlier formulation for setting revenues, when something called a 'Buzby Bond' had been debated[235], to modify its formula into a general revenue cap formula for indexing individual or collective revenues for inflation, but with an efficiency incentive, 'X':

Revenue cap next year = revenue cap this year x (1+ RPI – X)
where RPI = the Retail Prices Index (the inflation index then used in Britain)
and X   = an arbitrary number designed to bring benefits to customers, and promote innovation & efficiency

Littlechild noted that although the Buzby Bond debate had assumed an X of 2% in its formula[236], the Department of Industry had already used the same formula to set BT's revenues for that year, but with an effective X of 5%. Furthermore, in the latest year BT had almost hit its X of 5%. So his revenue cap would offer politicians the hope of significant real price cuts, as well as simulating competition prior to the introduction of real market competition[237].

Believing that competition would soon make regulation redundant, Littlechild proposed RPI-X as a temporary rule for indexing BT's real prices down for the first five years from current levels without requiring annual rate determinations. Then

---

[235] Littlechild *ibid* page 34 13.5
[236] Littlechild *ibid* page 35 13.11
[237] Littlechild *ibid* page 34 13.4. In 13.12 he says it would be a gamble for BT to offer *nominal* price freezes (or cuts).

"In any event, an automatic reference to the MMC [the overall body then regulating profits in the UK], after, say, five years, seems appropriate[238]"

He said nothing about the methods the MMC might use to determine BT's regulated revenues from then on.

With the benefit of hindsight we can interpret the factors that allow variable X to be sustained year after year: it is the unique combination of catch-up efficiency by individual firms' managements and general technological progress across an industry, with which we are so familiar from Chapter 7. And the general rate of frontier technological progress in telecoms was about to get very high in the late twentieth century. However Littlechild says this interpretation formed no part of his thinking in 1983, or subsequently, when regulator of the electricity industry[239]. For him X was simply a firm-specific dividend which could, and should, be yielded to consumers.

The government liked Littlechild's practical reasoning, accepted his conclusions, and privatised British Telecommunications in 1984/5 by selling its shares in two tranches of a 'Public Offering' and establishing a brand new regulator, Oftel, to set prices and monitor BT. This proved a popular move, reducing state intervention in the national economy and getting the public sector out of making pure business decisions. BT was free to make whatever commercial decisions it thought best, creating new mobile phone companies, buying foreign phone companies or suppliers, and installing high speed fibre optic landlines to respond to the massively growing demand for data flows, while the government raised billions of revenue from the flotation to lower taxes or reduce Britain's national debt (in fact it did both).

So Mrs Thatcher and her cabinet decided to follow this by privatising all the profitable utilities they could, as well as airports, ports, bridges, roads etc., as summarised in Table 6[240].

Table 6: The main British utility privatisations of the 1980s and 1990s

Company privatised	Industry	Year
British Telecommunication	Telecoms	1984
British Gas	Gas exploration, production, transmission & distribution	1986
British Airport Authority	Airports	1987
British Airways	Airlines	1987
10 water authorities	Water & sewarage	1989

---

[238] Littlechild *ibid* page 35 13.14
[239] Private correspondence with the author in 2014.
[240] For clarity, many dozens of smaller privatisations are not shown.

Table 6: The main British utility privatisations of the 1980s and 1990s - continued

Company privatised	Industry	Year
12 electricity distribution companies	Electricity distribution & retail	1990
2 generators and National Grid	Electricity generation & transmission	1991
Rail Track, 12 TOCs and 3 Roscos	Railway track, operating & train leasing companies	1994-97
British Energy	Nuclear electricity generation	1996

Source: Various official publications by the British Government and British Parliament.

In fact, so great was her determination to privatise state-owned entities that, as we shall see in Chapters 9 and 10, some basic economic precautions about competition were completely overruled by other considerations. The privatisation program rolled on, and the vast state enterprise British Gas was hurriedly floated off as a vast private monopsony and monopoly in 1986.

Littlechild's 1986 report on the water industry

In 1986 Mrs Thatcher instructed her Environment Secretary to consider various options for privatising the water industry. Water had three major differences from most of the other sectors being considered for privatisation by the British government:

a) As Figure 95 shows, or Figure 8 in Chapter 1 shows (for Britain), water, and especially wastewater, are the least contestable of all the heavy utilities, with at least three fifths of the water value chain and four fifths of the wastewater value chain being non-contestable natural monopolies;

b) Water is water, and as Chapter 1 explains, because people pour it down their children's throats, or consume it personally, and because it is so closely tied to the natural environment, people feel differently about water compared to electricity or gas; opinion polls at the time showed that while there were majorities in favour of privatising state-owned energy companies, privatisation of water was opposed by around 70% of the UK's population;

c) Although potentially very profitable, water promised to be 'cash-negative' for ten years or more; this meant it would suck in more money for operations and investment than it would pay out to investors in dividends and interest payments. This is highly unusual for almost any industry, but improving drinking water, and particularly sewage treatment, would need *several billion £s to be invested every year for the foreseeable future* to comply with upcoming European legislation. Once explained to her, Mrs Thatcher was appalled at the prospect of this vast investment programme being funded by the British taxpayer; she wanted Britain's dynamic new financial sector to fund it privately. Indeed her fears on this proved well-founded: it is a matter of fact that to clean up decades of under-investment, and to prepare for 21st century standards, *the British water sector was significantly cash-negative every year for 25 years after privatisation.*

These constraints meant that the prospects for competition in the industry were extremely remote, and that privatisation of the water industry would require serious public health, environmental, and economic regulation by permanent, heavy duty, regulators. Stephen Littlechild was again commissioned to review the best form of economic regulation, only this time he knew regulation would be a permanently repeated game, and he, like everyone, was not keen on Rate of Return regulation.

Since the publication of his 1983 BT report, the RPI-X formula had been widely cited and admired in the UK as a practical formula for what might be called inflation-indexing-but-not-quite the revenue of privatised quasi-monopolies. A complication of the water industry was that water was not metered for most British homes, so the cap would mostly be a revenue cap rather than a price cap[241], but as we have already discussed this is not usually a big problem. And Andre Shleifer's paper on yardstick regulation had been published in the Rand Journal in 1985, showing that some form of comparison between companies could help set revenue caps when the regulator was asked to set an overall level of charges that would be fair to everyone – consumers, investors, managers, and other stakeholders.

The way was clear for Littlechild to recommend that some form of revenue-cap regulation be permanently used in the water industry. Given that all the water companies had existing tariffs and standing charges, he concluded that when tariffs came to be fundamentally reset the general RPI-X formula could be applied to their previously-determined revenues, but with unique Xs for every company. Although these overall Xs would be a matter of judgement by the regulator, this judgement would reflect many factors:

"In deciding how far to revise X ... the economic regulator needs to examine the company's production methods and investment programme. He must ascertain the scope for cost and price reductions through increased productivity and efficiency and the need for capital expenditure. He needs to predict the consequences of X on what the company will do, how it will do it, how consumers will be affected and how others will react.... So permanent regulation is more complex than temporary regulation." [Littlechild S, 1986, para 10.20]

In other words the regulator's X judgement should reflect his or her assessment (or perception) of the scope for cost and profit reductions, the firm's forward-looking unique investment needs, its consequent projected financial viability over the period for which the revenue cap applied, its particular consumers' needs, and the knock-on effects of any major changes in all this for other stakeholders such as local government or the natural environment. As you can imagine, this is much easier said than done!

Once the initial X had been set to bring revenues back to the target vicinity for

---

[241] For unmetered homes water and wastewater were charged proportionate to the property's value assessed for local property taxes.

that company, Littlechild said that the regulator could apply different company-specific Xs for each subsequent year. The effect would be to set a sequence of annual revenue caps for the whole of the review period as shown in Figure 102:

Figure 102: The change in a utility's revenue cap = RPI - X

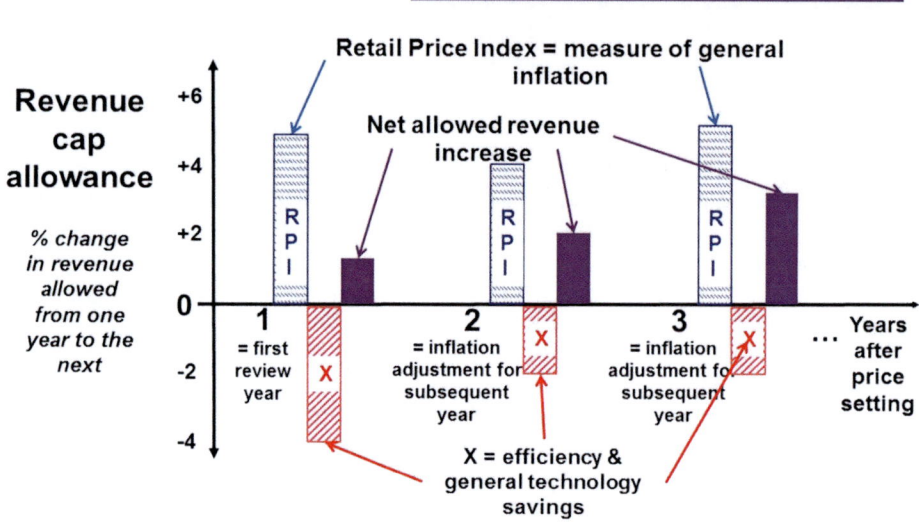

Naturally if inflation turns out to be less than the X-efficiency savings the formula will lead to nominal price falls, as Littlechild had discussed in his 1983 paper.

Explicit modelling of all Littlechild's factors

However, if X is to include *all* the factors Littlechild listed in para 10.20 of his 1986 paper, and not just efficiency savings, 'X' must reflect required investments and required increases in operating costs, the firm's financial viability, and other stakeholder requirements. In the succeeding decade, as these concerns were applied in practice to the water industry, and those cost-drivers started to bite seriously, the first water regulator made this breakdown more explicit in his revenue settings. He explicitly agreed that environmental or health concerns would dramatically increase some water utility's capital expenditure and operating costs for 'Quality' reasons; or customers might demand 'Service' level improvements, such as a lower risk of being flooded out of their homes by sewage in sudden storms. If allowed, these investments would drive up a firm's borrowings, its interest payments, and its operating costs. So firms were required to list all their plans for the next twenty years in giant spreadsheets submitted to the regulator's office, where desired capital expenditure ('capex') and operating cost ('opex') increases had to be listed under these allowed headings. The regulator then made efficiency adjustments to these bids (he disallowed certain investments, or reduced them) before putting the whole bag of inputs into a financial model of each firm and projecting its financial position forward ten to twenty years. He then imposed industry-wide (frontier) and firm-specific (individual catch-up) efficiency savings, as outlined in Chapter 7 on both projected capex and opex.

Finally, if a firm's financial position was still untenable, its allowed revenues were increased until its projected financial position for the entire time horizon was bankable. A stylised version of this explicit modelling of Littlechild's '10.20 statement' is shown in Figure 103:

Figure 103: A stylised version of the RPI-X revenue cap used in the water industry in England and Wales after privatisation

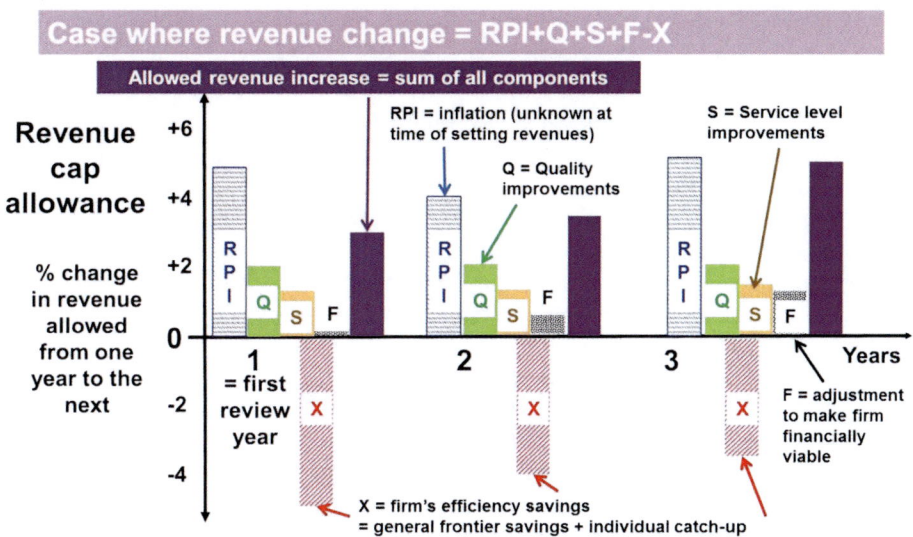

Figure 103 shows that the English and Welsh water regulator would set revenue caps for each water utility using a combination of explicit allowances for Quality, Q, and Service level, S, improvements, each requiring capital expenditure and possibly opex increases, less a combined general frontier efficiency factor and a company-specific efficiency factor. The sum of this created a revenue profile which might then be augmented to ensure financial sustainability for the firm over the revenue-setting period, though the precise details of the limiting financial ratios were not revealed – i.e. this part of the calculation (if it was a calculation and not a 'gut feeling') was kept implicit. Similar approaches, though less explicit, may have been used by other regulators, but all agreed that in the end the revenue- or price-cap set was a judgemental package which had to be "viewed as a whole" by investors, consumers, managers, regulators (in water this meant economic, health and environmental regulators), government (in all its branches), and any other stakeholders.

An Appeals process
Clearly a lot depended on the regulator being fair to a wide array of stakeholders considering a wide range of revenue-determining factors. Littlechild added one further safeguard of fairness into the process: if the utility's managers or investors thought they had been treated too harshly they could appeal against the regulator's decision (or Determination, to use the language eventually adopted) and ask the country's highest competition body at the time, the Monopolies and Mergers Commission (MMC) to review, and, if necessary, override the regulator's decision. In this process the regulatee and the regulator would be treated

equally by the MMC. This recommendation, along with the rest of Littlechild's report, was adopted by the government, and the appeals process was actually used by several utilities after subsequent price reviews. However, while some firms were awarded higher revenues by the MMC under appeal, one or two regulatees ended up with *lower* revenues than they had originally been given by the regulator – and had no choice but to accept this ruling: appeal was no one-way bet.

Implementation of revenue cap regulation in the UK
As each privatisation was considered, the government adopted Littlechild's general price-cap, or revenue-cap, regulatory framework. New regulators for energy, water, transport and media were created, and Littlechild himself was appointed regulator of the newly privatised electricity industry in England and Wales in 1989, while the Government's Deputy Chief Economic Adviser, Ian Byatt, was appointed economic regulator of the privatised water industry in England and Wales. So the most lasting effects of Littlechild's regulatory recommendations were felt not in telecoms but in industries such as energy, water and rail, where demand did not grow significantly more than envisaged when the networks had been commissioned.

And even in telecoms, where BT had been the first firm to be regulated using an RPI-X revenue cap, as recommended, a price review was held after five years which continued to apply an RPI-X revenue cap to BT's regulated sales. The expected boom in new telecoms services (mobiles, rival landlines, and broadband IT networks) did occur over the next twenty years, but the decline in the relative importance of traditional regulated revenues was not as rapid as had been expected. Consequently the relative importance of BT's regulated business did not decline as rapidly as Littlechild had expected in 1983, so even in telecoms revenue-cap regulation remained important for 22 years. Eventually, though, as described in Chapter 4, telecoms data transfer demand rose a thousand-fold, then a million-fold, and then a billion-fold over the levels that had been assumed when land lines were first laid in the 1920s, and many new players entered the mobile and landline industries, creating a situation of massive growth, but also genuine competition-in-the-market for BT, in which the standard regulatory game played quite a minor role.

Pure price-cap or pure rate of return, and *ex ante* or *ex post* price setting
Thus Littlechild had proposed that a price- or revenue-capping regulator would have to look at all the components listed in our opening diagram on regulation in Figure 97. This has led some economists to say that *at the limit* (if you reset prices every year, say) Price Cap regulation and Rate of Return regulation end up being the same, since you end up doing the same process in both approaches[242].

---

[242] E.g. Littlechild and Michael Beesley wrote a paper on this for the Bell Journal in 1989, conceding that RPI-X and rate of return would eventually converge for repeated regulation.

But there are crucial differences:
1. price cap regulation specifically does *not* do this every year; instead, *as Shleifer maintained, it is a sequential model of regulation deliberately sending price signals several years in advance*, informing investors, managers, employees, suppliers and customers of these future relative prices, inviting them to form medium-term profit, employment, or consumer surplus expectations, and thus to calculate their own actions several years ahead; recall that no other sector of the economy has this guarantee of future relative prices; thus the period for which prices are set in advance matters crucially: if prices are set for only a year or two we do not have a realistic time for managers to cut the cost base effectively and permanently, and earn rewards from their uncomfortable actions, so the method cannot be considered a price cap;
2. Rate of return regulation starts with the presumption that the firm is efficient; yardstick price caps start with the assumption that all firms are unequal, and only a few will be efficient; yes, at the frontier RPI-X could be applied to annual price adjustments under rate of return, but that's the whole point of the yardstick: in an industry of local network monopolies there are managerial incentives for most firms *not* to be near the frontier;
3. there must *not be any attempt at adjustment after the event to allow loss-making firms to make up losses incurred, or to claw profits back from firms that have earned super-normal profits*. This is sometimes called an *ex ante* system, in contrast to an *ex post* system, and is a vitally important condition of price cap regulation.

Yardsticking in practice
So, by 1990 Shleifer had defined three of a yardsticking revenue-capping regulator's main jobs:
1. From a zero base estimate a fair benchmark full-cost price for an efficient firm in your industry, including an allowance for profits that will ensure sufficient funds from investors;
2. Estimate a fair rate of technological progress for the industry frontier in each year beyond;
3. Apply these conditions to set revenue caps for future years for all firms in your jurisdiction

and on both tasks 1 and 2 there seemed to be some practical routes forward to arrive at real numbers. Littlechild, meanwhile, had noted the excellent general incentives of an existing British mechanism for inflation-indexing a state-owned enterprise's revenue cap with explicit, though arbitrary, efficiency incentives, and had promoted its use as a permanent tool for regulating monopolies. The British Government had listened and adopted Littlechild's revenue-cap recommendations when privatising energy, water, telecoms and other state-owned quasi-monopolies, each subject to a similar form of revenue-cap regulation. In the subsequent decade Shleiffer's theory and Littlechild's practice would be brought together more closely, as the section around Figure 103 above indicates.

But that still leaves many important technical questions unanswered. Three of the biggest are:

1. For how long should the period of price controls be set? Three years? Five years? Ten years? and, related to this:
    a) For how long should companies be allowed to keep efficiencies that they create?
    b) If being benchmarked to some global frontier of best practice, or something approaching the SOTA described in Chapter 7, which requires optimisation of capital (and hence an optimal configuration of the network), how long a period should companies fairly be allowed to catch up with the 'efficiency frontier'?
2. How exactly do you set a cost of capital that will be fair for the future?
3. How do we treat the value of past sunk costs, and should this be different from how we treat present and future capital expenditure?

We examine these three questions in turn.

The regulatory period & the optimal time for keeping efficiencies

While the length of the period for which prices are set, and the optimal time for keeping efficiencies can be formally analysed, this can only be within a set of well-defined assumptions, nowadays likely to be a repeated game. It is not our purpose here to describe such models, or even to summarise the literature; that is the job of your regulatory tutor. Instead *we examine what happened in practice* in the pioneering period when revenue-cap regulation was first implemented, and consider any general lessons from this.

Using a process of trial and error over the period 1985-2005 British regulators settled on a normal regulatory price-setting period of five years. This seems to have emerged as an almost entirely pragmatic value judgement, despite receiving many theoretical papers on the subject (some of them written by my then-employers). The practice may have started with Littlechild's original recommendation that the RPI-X should last for "..., say, five years" in his 1983 paper. During the 1980s privatisations the regulatory periods were usually not defined in the founding legislation or licences, leaving this up to regulators or companies to decide. In water, for instance, prices were originally set at privatisation for ten years, but there was a provision for the regulator or companies to call for an 'Interim Review' of revenues any time after five years. Not surprisingly, from the regulators' point of view[243], each regulator decided to take advantage of this, so five-yearly Reviews and price terms became common practice, although little was enshrined in licences or legislation until the 21st century. In water Interim Reviews then became something that either a regulatee or the regulator could

---

[243] The regulator's term of office was only five years: it would take an oustandingly brass-necked regulator to look at an industry and say 'Naah: I think my predecessor got everything perfect. There's no need to have a price review during my five years in office. Now, pay me a significant salary for just monitoring the industry.'

call for, if an objectively-defined Relevant Change of Circumstances occurred[244] that fundamentally undermined the assumptions of the main five-yearly Price Determination.

So five years emerged pragmatically as the duration for each term of prices. Why five years? You might wonder if it had anything to do with behavioural considerations on cutting costs significantly and permanently. If so it should be linked to the typical terms in office of a utility's CEO, as these are the humans who will have to drive through all serious cost-cutting. As a matter of fact few CEOs are in office for more than five years, even in the staid world of utilities, so most will be doing well to see through one cost-cutting round and a couple of other major achievements in their period in office. Another factor concerns the organisational practicalities: the author can vouch from personal experience of three major utility cost-cuttings that it can take two years to draw up a major cost-cutting programme and implement it thoroughly, and another two years to let morale in the organisation recover. So, from the organisational behavioural point of view, to make efficiency incentives work in practice in a utility, as Shleifer imagined them to in his article, price-setting periods might need to be around five years. The author has been assured by a former British regulator that this sort of argument was not regarded as a relevant consideration at the time, but one might ask why not?

And why not have a gain-keeping period longer than five years? If they can call for an Interim Review at any time, as in water, investors would certainly prefer longer periods, as they get to keep gains longer[245]. And, given that price reviews require a lot of information gathering and senior management time in regulatory discussions, the true costs of each price review for both regulators and regulatees are considerable. So the transaction cost of a Periodic Review is significant, suggesting that the longer the regulatory period the better, provided either party can call for an Interim Review if problems get too serious. Issues of the regulator's term in office are also relevant, but the regulator's term should, of course, be determined by the length of regulatory period, rather than the other way round.

This author believes that business practicalities (rightly) dominate. The trouble with very long price control durations is that recent real events are being judged against an allowance or plan which looks 'longer in the tooth' as each year passes, and gradually becomes totally archaic. This may seem an unsophisticated answer to a question that theoreticians love to analyse, but the truth is that in most businesses reality starts to deviate from plans after a year or two, and after three years there is usually quite a significant gap between the assumed or planned starting position for this year and the actual starting base for this year – the 'inherited adjustments to base' we might call them. In economic terms these inherited adjustments to base are such things as the quantity discrepancies

---

[244] An event that altered predicted revenue by more than 5 per cent.
[245] The Laffont-Tirole argument.

already discussed (actual against planned), changes in relative prices in the economy – real fuel prices, capital availability, supplier costs etc. – and general changes in the economy such as new tax rates, new technologies, new environmental or social constraints, or fresh demands by consumers.

So, after three years, 'inherited adjustments to base' have become significant and are getting larger by the month. They are starting to dominate the implementation of a regulatory plan which seemed realistic when assembled, but is looking increasingly antiquated. People have changed jobs on both the regulator and regulatee sides, and internal defenders of the ageing plan are becoming scarce. However, if we know that a new Regulatory control period is only two years away, we can focus on that, and stop worrying about the inadequacies of the old plan. Four years on and we are only one year away from the new period, so that is the focus of all our regulatory effort; it just is not worth asking for an 'Interim Review' for one year, when that would take 3-6 months and the whole situation is being reviewed anyway. Both regulator and regulatee know that they could, if desired, include an item of "Backlog adjustments to base" from this Period as a designated issue in the next Periodic Review, thus saving the need for a full Interim Review.

Thus five years seems an eminently practical compromise between our desire for social efficiency – preferring longer terms – and the realities of business life and a global economy that changes daily. Perhaps ten years might have been optimal in the nineteenth century, when the rate of technological progress was less than 1% a year, and people had seven year apprenticeships and twelve-year training periods, but, in the twenty first century, five years is about as long as anyone can realistic plan ahead in business[246].

The period for keeping efficiencies
The duration of the regulatory period links to the question of how long investors should keep the gains from efficiency, though they do not *have* to be the same. In principle we could have a regulatory period of five years and allow efficiency gains to be kept for three years, or for ten years. But then we would have to devise a general way of guaranteeing that gains from one Period will be transferred to the next, so that one regulator binds their successor, to a certain extent. In fact, the same question arises even if both periods are the same but the efficiency gains are not made in the first year of the Regulatory period. Thus, if both periods are five years but a new management team takes over a regulated utility in the third year of a regulatory period, determined to cut costs substantially in the fourth year of the Period, so that the full-year extra profits are experienced in the fifth year of the Period, the incentive effects of yardstick regulation would be greatly reduced if all subsequent gains were wiped out at the start of the new regulatory price control period.

---

[246] However, Ofgem recently moved to an 8-year period, but again with the option of a 4 year review: this may be a consequence of record low interest rates, or it may be just a desire to lower the Cost of Capital to reflect the very low political risks of renationalisation in the UK.

To avoid this, British regulators decided to maintain full efficiency incentives, which meant tying their successors' hands, by guaranteeing that all cost savings, both of operating (P&L) costs and investment, or capitalised expenditure, would always be kept for a full five years from the date that actual expenditures fell below those assumed by the regulator. On the operating costs side this is straightforward, but to maximise capital efficiency while minimising gold plating incentives for capitalised expenditure, for five years after a utility has achieved a capital efficiency (spending less on capital additions than allowed but still achieving all the new outputs) the regulatee's gross profits are based on the larger Regulatory Asset Base originally assumed by the regulator. Then, after the five years the RAB is reduced to the actual capital expenditure incurred. Thus regulatees' investors always keep efficiency gains for five years, whether they are running costs ("O&M costs", as they are known in US utilities) or capital costs.

The Cost of Capital

Obviously this book is not going to tell you the answer to the Cost of Capital. It is a specialist subject, and reams of stuff has been written on this, all of it clever and some of it good. If your text does not include the Dividend Yield and Capital Asset Pricing Models, Miller-Modigliani, adjustments for tax, and several alternative theories, find a text that does.

A note of caution. Be wary of theories that rely a lot on equity betas to determine the Cost of Capital for a regulated utility: in essence these betas generally are correlation coefficients between a firm's share price and the total stock market index (the Dow Jones, Nasdaq, FTSE 100, Hang Seng etc.). Equity betas make sense for most firms in an economy, the theory being that the firm's profit prospects are in part tied to the whole economy's prospects, and the stock market index is a good leading indicator of the economy. But this is not true for a pure regulated monopoly utility, such as a gas or electricity transmission or distribution utility, or a water company[247]: in the medium term a well-regulated utility's profit prospects are determined by only two factors: political or regulatory risks, and the utility's management. Neither of these is in any sense correlated with the state of the 'economy' so the R^2 on the regression that derived the beta is far more important than the beta itself; the R^2 *should be* close to zero and the beta *should be* meaningless[248]. In practice most utility R^2s and betas are little

---

[247] Just to repeat once again, the output of a utility distribution *network* is *availability*, not load (units of energy or water), and the demand for network availability is constant, not cyclical. And for water and wastewater 'generation', there is no theoretical reason why demand for this load should be cyclical. In post-industrial economies, where manufacturing is a far smaller part of the economy than services, water and wastewater demand in offices mirrors domestic demand: you still have to flush the lavatory whether you are employed or unemployed.

[248] Short term (daily or weekly-measured) utility betas do exhibit higher R^2s and low positive values of beta less than one, which the author can only ascribe to misunderstanding by some players in the market of the true nature of regulated utilities, or by more sophisticated traders using utility stocks as some kind of temporary store of value before re-investing in their next play.

different from zero, when measured over several years, which is what matters for regulators when setting the Cost of Capital. This should also be the germane consideration for most long-term investors, who should want some proportion of a well-diversified pension portfolio invested in utility shares because of the low risk of the utility's profit stream collapsing to zero – which cannot be said for most other investments in the corporate sector[249].

Valuing past sunk costs and Infrastructure Renewals Accounting

This is a serious issue, and one, so far, to which far less theoretical attention has been paid than to the Cost of Capital. The core question is how to value past capital expenditure, some of it spent more than a century ago. In practice, as we have said, with the exception of American Investor Owned Utilities, most utilities in the world have been owned by some arm of government, and so we are usually talking about capital expenditure authorised by past public authorities, and funded by taxpayers, ratepayers, or bond holders. As outlined earlier, the inescapable consequence of time-as-an-irreversible-arrow is that we cannot change the past, and so the regulator could, if they have the legal authority to do this, draw clear financial lines through the past and say, for instance, "I am going to treat money spent before 1868 in one way, money spent between 1868 and 1989 in another way, and all money spent since 1989 in a third way." So long as the regulator is clear that all expenditure in the recent past, currently, and in the future will be treated in a way that will not change, then investors have a reasonable regulatory assurance of how their funds will be treated from now on.

This freedom was cleverly exploited by the first regulators of both the electricity and water industries in the UK. In water, Ian (afterwards Sir Ian) Byatt had inherited a set of water utilities with Historic Cost accounting values of the assets on their books going back more than 150 years. This meant, as an example, that the value listed on its Balance Sheet of utility A's total physical assets could include a water treatment works commissioned in 1989 at a cost of £10 million, while neighbouring utility B's identical water treatment works, commissioned in 1926, was valued at its 1926 historic cost of, say, just £10,000. Of course there had been massive cumulative inflation between 1926 and 1989, which accounted for most of the thousand-fold difference in the valuation of the same asset. Clearly Historic Cost accounts cannot possibly treat past capital expenditure values fairly where asset lives are long. Indeed, going right back to Chapter 4 and the fundamentals of valuing a sunk cost, we might call this the Pont du Gard problem, or, since the Pont du Gard is no longer used for its original purpose, more accurately, the Istanbul cisterns problem: should the value of the underground cisterns (large tanks holding water) built by the Romans and still used today in the Istanbul water network be their historical cost when commissioned by the Romans in the second century (X million sesterces)? What exchange rate should we use

---

[249] Finance theorists will not be happy with such a simplistic dismissal of CAPM, but the onus is on them to prove that equity betas measured over 5-10 years (the relevant period) really are significant – and are actually used by regulators to determine the Cost of Capital, rather than being ex post rationalisations of numbers they first thought of.

between Roman sesterces and modern Turkish lira, and can it possibly have any useful meaning? In general, the problem is how to value a sunk cost that is well and truly sunk, and most unlikely to be repeated?

Clearly the accountants' normal Historic Cost principle for valuing past capital expenditure cannot be used for valuing assets with useful lives lasting several decades. Fortunately Ian Byatt had 'form' on this subject[250], and he induced the adoption of Infrastructure Renewals Accounting in the British water industry, which is one utility accounting method now considered potentially useful by the World Bank. This method of accounting is a specialist subject, beyond the scope of this book. The relevant point, though, is that under this accounting method assets can be valued at their 'Replacement Cost', which is what it would cost in today's money to replace the asset if, for instance, it needed to be replaced after an earthquake or a terrorist attack. So we have a method which can be used to value the Istanbul cisterns or the Pont du Gard, but it assumes we would rebuild them using modern technology, rather than stones, slaves and Roman hand-saws.

The practical (political) problem for Mr Byatt was that if he used the Replacement Cost of the English and Welsh water industry's assets in 1989 as his starting Regulatory Asset Base[251] this would have led to water prices being roughly three times higher than they currently were. Politically, this was a non-starter. So, having checked with the government (the inheritors of all past public sector investment), Ian Byatt decided to re-value all capital expenditure prior to privatisation into a new sum that he would define as the 'Initial RAB'[252] – a sum that was arbitrarily and heavily written down from its replacement cost. So, going forward a company's RAB would consist of two parts: its (past) written-down regulator-determined Initial RAB and its continually-growing new RAB of cumulative capital expenditure on network enhancements valued at full cost. The whole RAB was then indexed for inflation and would earn the full Cost of Capital, so investors were guaranteed that *every future £ spent* would earn the full CoC.

But how to arrive at a written-down Initial RAB? Mr Byatt noticed that by coincidence the stock market value of the companies averaged over the first 100 days after flotation would do just fine as his Initial RAB, allowing water prices

---

[250] He had previously chaired a British government report examining accounting methods for treating long-life infrastructure investments: Byatt, I.C.R 1986, Accounting for Economic Costs and Changing Prices, a report to HM Treasury, HMSO, 1986.

[251] Neither Mr Byatt nor other British regulators formally adopted the term Regulatory Asset Base, preferring phrases such as Regulatory Capital Value, but RAB has entered the literature and is widely understood, so it is used here.

[252] Mr Byatt faced opposition to this revaluation from some smaller Water Only Companies who had previously been privately owned dividend-controlled companies, under regimes that had been abolished by the 1989 Water Industry Act. They claimed that they had been assured that all their past private investments would earn full replacement cost returns, but these claims were not upheld.

to stay at roughly the same levels, and giving the appearance of being an objective number reflecting the stock markets' acceptance of this RAB as a fair initial valuation. He went ahead and did this, and the matter passed largely unremarked by the stock markets.

But it is only when considering coolly the logic of his proposal that one notices the apparent circularity, shown in Figure 104:

Figure 104: Circular Logic

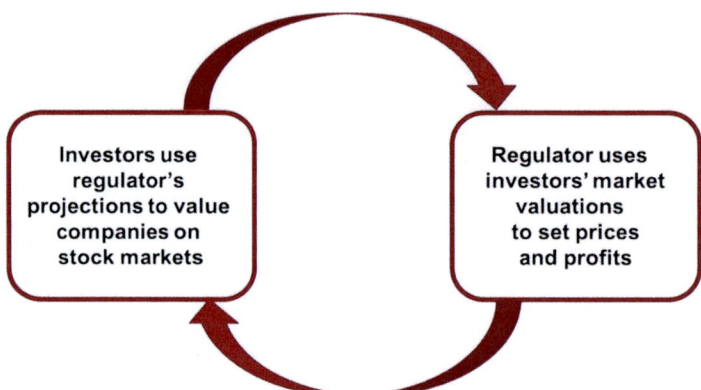

Was Byatt using circular logic? He accepted stock market valuations of companies to set their RABs which were then used to set new stock market valuations. Indeed, what were the investors trying to guess when they valued the companies, if not how much profit future regulators would allow? If investors had known what he was going to do they would have valued the companies far higher, of course.

But this ignores the advantages of time-as-an-irreversible-arrow. What really went on occurred over quite some elapsed time, and resembles a spiral not a circle, as Figure 105 shows:

Figure 105: Setting regulatory asset values over time: the Byatt causal spiral

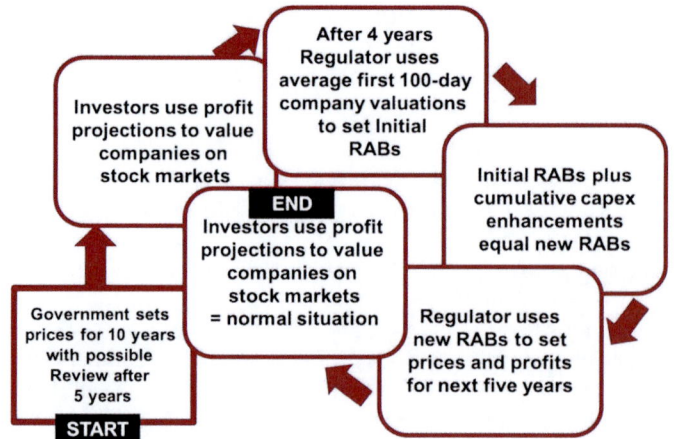

Because time had elapsed between the initial stock market valuation and his use of it as a retrospective evaluation of the Initial RAB, Mr Byatt prevented the circularity of Figure 104, and thus the possibility of investors determining their own future profits.

A neat trick, you may think, but a shame it can't be repeated, because this book has explained the trick, the cat is now out of the bag, and if any new regulator tries this, investors will immediately overvalue the shares on flotation, guaranteeing themselves spectacularly high profits for ever.

But in fact Byatt and Littlechild's trick *can* be repeated. Governments and regulators simply have to collapse stages one and three of Figure 105 by defining the Initial RAB on privatisation as whatever number they wish, and markets will have no choice but to build this into their projections of future profits[253]. Governments could, if they wish, for instance, choose to write down all past capital assets to zero, ensuring low utility prices for many years to come[254]. In so doing, they will, of course, have set the most wonderful example of entry deterring pricing, and reinforced those regulated utilities' monopoly positions virtually forever, unless technologies change beyond recognition.

With economists of the calibre of Stephen Littlechild and Ian Byatt showing how regulators at the top of their game made revenue- or price-cap regulation work in practice, we conclude this chapter reviewing how to check the monopoly power of innate network monopolies. There may be other models of monopoly regulation besides Rate of Return or Cost of Service, Gain Sharing and Revenue Cap but they have yet to be widely demonstrated to work well in practice. In the remaining chapters of this book we examine the experiences of some countries around the world that tried to restructure, privatise and regulate network utilities, and see what has happened a quarter century after Andrei Shleifer first proposed introducing 'comparative' competition or yardsticks as a way to set revenue caps for monopolies.

---

[253] This arbitrariness – and circularity – of initial RAB was one reason why the state government of Victoria specified the RABs of its electricity distribution companies in founding licences or legislation when privatising them in the 1990s.

[254] Steven Littlechild informs me that this was done to Guernsey's electricity system some years ago.

Chapter Nine

Electricity restructuring and privatisation lessons

Introduction – general papers

Over the last quarter of a century more than 150 countries are estimated to have engaged in significant reforms of their electricity systems[255]. No two countries are the same, and even within one country (e.g. the USA or India) conditions can be very different, depending on national and local politics, history, geography and personalities. So this chapter examines some of the most striking successes and failures of global electricity industry restructuring and privatisation: the progressive evolution of electricity markets in Scandinavia, Chile and Argentina's radical structural reforms, the Thatcher-ite revolution in Great Britain, and the contrasting experiences of Texas and California. We conclude by trying to summarise the views of a few experts who in turn have attempted to draw lessons from the hundreds of professionals in this area who have devoted years of their lives to this subject.

The Scandinavian electricity market
Nord Pool

Norway is the large country in northern Europe where the warm moist Gulf Stream meets mountainous western Scandinavia. Consequently Norway has a lot of rain and snow at high altitude, and with only 5 million people in this large territory, hydroelectricity generates 98% of its electricity. Government policies to promote the use of electricity, by attracting electricity-intensive industries, have been successful, so that per capita electricity consumption is three times the European average, yet the country still manages to sell 8-10% of its annual electricity production as exports.

Sweden, the country sharing the main Scandinavian peninsular, has some hydroelectricity but many more people, so Sweden is innately energy-poor relative to Norway, which, in addition to its hydroelectric potential, also discovered both oil and gas offshore in the 1980s. Low-lying Denmark to the

---

[255] Glachant J-M & Perez Y 2011, 'The liberalization of electricity markets' page 165 in *The International Handbook of Network Industries* ed Finger and Kunneke, 2011, Edward Elgar.

south of Norway, and Finland to the east of Sweden, were still more un-blessed by nature with energy, so that Finland, Sweden and Denmark would always tend to be energy importers, compared to Norway's innate energy exporter. It only seemed natural, therefore, for these four politically distinct but culturally-close countries to want to trade electricity between them.

It started back in the 1970s, when most of Norway's 80 hydroelectric power stations were publicly-owned. In 1971 the Norwegian government allowed a cooperative energy "pool" (the Samkjoringen) to be established, which coordinated spot electricity trades between the country's generators, so that they could meet aggregate Norwegian demand at lowest opportunity cost to themselves. Given that it is easier to move electricity around a grid than water between two mountain lakes, the generators with the greatest reserves of water were allowed to produce electricity and sell it to those with the least water. "The pool acted rather like a spot market in stored water" Newbery deftly summarises[256].

By 1992 Chile and the UK had restructured and privatised their electricity industries (see later in this Chapter). With this overseas experience, and twenty years domestic experience of the pioneering Samkjoringen electricity market, the Norwegian Parliament took the market a stage further by explicitly introducing "... competition as a tool for ensuring a more efficient and reliable energy supply."[257] Following an Energy Act the Government in 1992 split the vertically integrated electricity company into a generator called Statkraft and a bulk transmission company called Statnett, which became the Norwegian Transmission System Operator (TSO). Statnett's responsibilities included monitoring and operating the transmission grid and its cross-border links to Sweden and Denmark, and allowing Third Party Access (TPA) to any other parties who might wish to trade electricity across their grid. Revised tariffs for connecting electricity between any pair of connections were issued in May 1992, and were available to any trader whether Norwegian or not. The wholesale electricity pool was renamed the Statnett Marked, but none of the companies involved was privatised.

The effect of this, according to Newbery, was to integrate the Norwegian electricity market so that trades were corralled through this market and generators were forced to focus on efficiency and maintaining adequate cost-effective capacity. 20% of generating capacity was owned by Norsk Hydro, a private company, but the other 80% was owned by around 30 vertically-integrated local public municipalities, each of whom was in effect putting their supply-demand imbalances through the Statnett Marked. The price of electricity on this market was thus beginning to say something significant about the opportunity costs of water and electricity across Norway.

---

[256] Newbery D 1999, op .cit. page 246
[257] Nord Pool ASA 2004, The Nordic Power Market: electricity power exchange across national borders' an introductory training level document page 7, available at http://www.fer.unizg.hr/_download/repository/Nord%20Pool%20-%20The%20Nordic%20Power%20Market.pdf

Figure 106: The evolution of Nord Pool in the 1990s

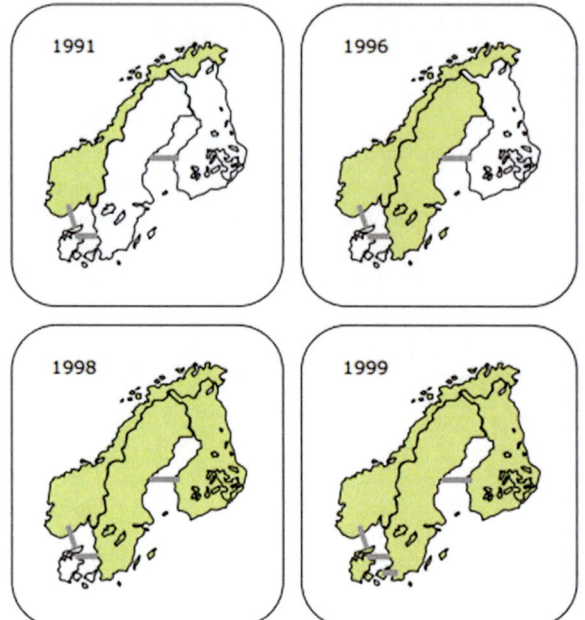

Source: 'The Nordic Power Market' Nord Pool ASA page 8

At the same time the Swedes matched developments by creating Svenska Kraftnet in 1992 as their Transmission System Operator, with broadly the same TSO responsibilities as Statnett. By 1996 the two systems and tariff terms matched up well, so that by 1996 the two systems could run in parallel as the Deregulated Nordic Power Market, or 'Nord Pool' as it came to be known. Figure 106, based on the company's own training documents, shows the geographical evolution of Nord Pool.

Following an internal merger of its transmission companies Finland was able to join from 1998, and in 1999 two Danish transmission companies became the fourth and fifth members of Nord Pool. To complete the separation of electricity trading from transmission wires a Helsinki-based electricity exchange El-Ex had been founded in 1996 which published prices for local Finnish electricity trades. In 2002 Nord Pool Spot AS was created to run the marketplace operations and to monitor and publish wholesale prices. It also took on a new responsibility, to act as a central 'counterparty' to every trade so that the market evolved from being a series of bilateral agreements between generators, suppliers and large customers, to being a centralised market where every contract was with the market-maker, and the market-maker had the responsibility of balancing the system both physically and financially.

The significance of the Nordic electricity market today
Trading in electricity derivatives (products or services which depend on the price of electricity or complement electricity trades) had begun in the 1990s. This continued apace, and in 2005 Nord Pool started trading EU carbon emission

allowances. As the EU market for carbon emissions is continental, and Scandinavia has a lot of renewable electricity, the Nordic market brings together a lot of northern European supply and demand. In 2007 Nord Pool was acquired by the American stock exchange NASDAQ, and in 2010 changed its name to NASDAQ OMX.

Other countries would follow this progressive evolution of electricity trades into a formal market and then change the form of the market as conditions evolved. The global significance of Nord Pool is that it was one of world's earliest multilateral electricity markets, and it shows that one does not *have* to privatise, nor create uniform legal models, to inject significant market signals into the electricity systems of a diverse set of political states. Recall that Denmark, Finland and Sweden fully participate in EU energy, environmental and competition policies which strongly affect all electric utilities in the EU; Finland even uses the euro as its currency. However, Norway is not in the European Union at all.

Nordic exchange, PJM and similar models of centralised trading
There are parallels between the Nordic power exchange and arrangements such as the American PJM system. PJM, originally standing for Pennsylvania, (New) Jersey and Maryland, is the Regional Transmission Organization that manages the high voltage transmission system to 60 million people across a belt of the eastern USA from New Jersey down to North Carolina, and west to Illinois. In these models a large number of independent electric utilities, who are usually vertically integrated to varying degrees, and may be publicly- or privately-owned, agree to
 1. cede certain operational powers to an independent System Operator who manages the physical characteristics of the electrical system (frequency, voltage and stability), as well as achieving an overall energy balance in the system "in real time" (meaning every second of every day);
 2. create a market operator whose function is to manage markets in electricity trades which financially and physically balance in the short and medium term future. Long term balance, in which we mean building new power stations, is of course a more tricky issue, both commercially (because of the sunk cost risks involved) and politically, so the market operator's responsibilities usually stop a defined number of months out from the present.

Of course the two roles can be combined in one organisation and they feed off each other: without a system operator market trades cannot be physically delivered, and without market-based prices for derivative services, such as synchronising frequencies[258], the system operator would have to impose arbitrary charges for synchronisation which some parties would regard as unfair.

---

[258] Using alternating current all the power plants' generation cycles have to be synchronised with the system so that all the 'peaks and troughs of each wave' coincide; whenever a plant starts up it has to attune to the system and any deviations from the system standard have to be corrected, usually by the plant itself, but in time to a signal sent by the system operator.

Of course this is not the only arrangement for electricity trading, and many countries which do not have such a centralised market and grid operator would say that they manage to trade electricity on a voluntary and bilateral basis quite happily, as and when the need arises. The author recalls attending a European electricity conference in the early 1980s in which the overall conclusion of 40 or 50 European electricity utilities present was a very clear view that electricity trading was strongly beneficial to European citizens, and that the best way to promote it was to keep the politicians well out of it. They, of course, had reckoned without the long term effects of certain South American generals and a British Prime Minister called Margaret Thatcher.

Chile and Argentina

The history of electricity industry restructuring and privatisation begins earlier in Chile than in Europe, but as ever significant microeconomic developments must be viewed within the political context of the time.

In April 1982, in order to divert attention away from domestic difficulties of rampant inflation and strikes, the generals running Argentina at the time decided to invade 'the Malvinas', or as the British call them, 'the Falkland Islands'. These are a group of windy islands in the Southern Atlantic Ocean, with just 1813 people then on them, five hundred kilometres to the east of Argentina, to which Argentina has long laid claim. The long term consequences of this decision were fateful for both the generals and Britain.

The immediate consequence was that the British Prime Minister, Mrs Thatcher, sent a military Task Force which evicted the conscript Argentinian army, and returned the islands to British rule. The medium term consequences were that the Argentinian military *junta* was overthrown and Argentina re-emerged as a democracy. An intriguing possibility is that the main long term consequence of the Falklands Conflict may have been that after 1982 the idea of generals running countries was largely discredited not just in Argentina, but across the whole of South America. Less disputed is the fact that Mrs Thatcher won the next British General Election, if not the next two, on the back of her Falklands victory with massive majorities, and these majorities not only kept Mrs Thatcher in power for eleven years but also gave her the confidence and Parliamentary muscle to ignore critics and listen to her inner convictions. She felt empowered to embark on some radical economic experiments affecting all British utilities, which we describe in the next section.

Chile

In 1973 a military junta headed by General Pinochet had seized power from the democratically elected socialist President Allende of Chile. The generals brought in a number of young economists to help run the country economically, who were known as The Chicago Boys, because many of them had been educated at Chicago University in the USA. The Chicago Boys tended to have strong free-market sympathies, yet they were running a country where many core institutions, including all the utilities, had been nationalised and state-controlled for decades.

A fundamental feature of Chile's electrical system is that it is composed of four unconnected parts, each separated from the others by hundreds of kilometres, so when we discuss regional monopolies readers should bear in mind that locally these can be absolute monopolies (what is the substitute for electricity in cold southern Chile?). In addition 60% of Chile's electricity was then generated from hydroelectricity, and there was sufficient storage capacity to buffer electricity from one day to the next, so unlike Nordic countries, Chile did not desperately need the hour-by-hour electricity prices required by some countries. However, the young economists wanted market prices to send signals that would improve the energy-using efficiency of utilities, send the right signals to investors about the need for new generation, transmission and distribution capacity, and send the right price signals for conservation and usage to energy consumers.

In 1978 the Chicago Boys, backed by the generals, decreed a Law to create a National Energy Commission (CNE) and pushed forward policies to unbundle the electricity industry and make all utilities behave in a more commercial fashion. The two state-owned electricity utilities, ENDESA and Chilectra, were vertically separated into generation and distribution-and-retail companies in 1982, and the generation and distribution parts were further unbundled geographically.

But incumbent utilities don't give up without a fight; ENDESA was allowed to keep the role of Transmission System Operator, as well as being a major generator, while the distribution-and-supply companies were of course local geographical monopolies. Furthermore if a large industrial customer wanted to switch suppliers to a non-incumbent retailer the incumbents were not required to separate the tariffs into a generation and a transmission/distribution component, so large customers could not readily compare prices. Some industrial customers also reported that generators were unwilling to supply them directly, in case they offended their biggest customer – the incumbent distributor. So there was little increase in competition for large customers and none at all for the average domestic customer. In the largest system, accounting for three quarters of Chile's electricity, ENDESA's role as transmission system guardian also enabled it potentially to restrict access to rivals in a way that would ensure it was not disadvantaged as a generator. In fact there was no guarantee of open access for generators to the transmission system until 2004, nor any obligation on the transmission companies to build extra transmission capacity ahead of generation. In other words the field of generation competition was far from level. CNE acted as regulator of competition in generation, and as price setter for transmission and final supply prices.

By the time of the Falklands Conflict between Britain and Argentina in 1982, Chile's electricity utilities could be privatised under a stable regulatory regime, and foreign investors were allowed to buy control of generators and distribution monopolies. Privatisation progressed, so that by 1991 there were 11 generators, 21 distribution companies and two vertically integrated companies[259]. So restructuring and privatisation had occurred in Chile by 1991, but the success of these reforms was limited[260]. First, bearing in mind the physical isolation of the four systems, and that ownership of generation companies has been allowed to cluster into three main families of generators, the structure of generation cannot be very competitive. Secondly because the system operator in the largest market caps prices at $150/MWh "the spot market does not yield prices that are high enough when generating capacity is fully utilised to balance supply and demand", so private investment in generation is too low. In the past the government has intervened to procure generation rather than let it spontaneously occur – as it should in competition-in-the-market.

So, despite its early start on the rest of the world, with serious deficiencies in the structure of generation and wholesale electricity markets, possibly one-sided access to the transmission system for many years, and huge bargaining power by incumbent retailers, the Chilean system falls well short of a comprehensively restructured free-market electricity industry.

Argentina
Following the disgrace of the generals, elections were held in 1983 and Raoul Alfonsin was elected President. His government was followed in 1989 by President Menem, who embarked on radical reforms of the energy sector. In 1992 the whole electricity industry was broken up vertically and horizontally. Firstly it was forbidden for a player in one function to have any involvement in another vertical function of the industry. Second, generation was broken up so that no generator had more than 10% of capacity. Third, transmission and distribution were recognised as natural monopolies and privatised, but regulated, leaving one transmission company (Transener), three federal distribution companies, and 20 regional distribution companies. By 1993 there were 40 generators, nearly all private, and 70 firms trading in the wholesale electricity market[261].

In theory the fourth strand was to create a regulator, ENRE, with powers to award licences, determine tariffs, and resolve disputes. Although ENRE had considerable legal powers, in reality the fear was that it would be dominated by the host of private companies, so it was given as little to do as possible. So, for instance, any decision to invest in more transmission capacity had to be proposed and approved by users of the network (beneficiaries), not decided by the regulator in response to requests from beneficiaries of the line.

Generally Argentina's system is thought to have worked quite well, given the country's overall situation, with a comprehensive restructuring right from the beginning, but retail competition has been disappointing or non-existent.

---

[259] Newbery 1999, page 120.
[260] This analysis follows Joskow 2006.
[261] Perez-Arriaga I, 1994, The Organisation and Operation of the electricity supply industry in Argentina', Energy Economic Engineering Ltd,, London, cited in Newbery 1999 page 251

The UK after 1990: continual reform eventually produces competition

By the 1980s the UK's electricity industry was similar to most west European countries. After two world wars, local utilities which started out in a variety of forms of public and private ownership before 1920 had been merged and nationalised into very large state-owned corporations. There were clear geographical divisions: in England and Wales the value chain had been split in two: electricity distribution and retailing were provided through 12 regional state-owned monopolies. Generation and transmission were the responsibility of the Central Electricity Generating Board, which owned and operated 74 power stations with a combined capacity of 58 GW[262]. These were mostly large coal-fired stations, but included a dozen nuclear-powered plant (8 quite modern), a few oil-fired plant, and a pumped-storage scheme in a mountain in Wales to provide immediate surge power for system-balancing. Figure 107 shows how the industry was organized under state ownership:

Figure 107: The UK electricity industry in 1989, prior to privatisation

State ownership of the main companies in England and Wales:
Central Electricity Generating Board — 12 regional distribution companies
Electricity generation | Transmission wires | Distribution wires | Retail or 'Supply'

In Scotland the two electricity suppliers were regional vertically-integrated public corporations:
North of Scotland Hydroelectric Board – hydroelectric and fossil-fuelled plant
South of Scotland Electricity Board – mainly coal-fired generating plant

While in Northern Ireland there was just one public corporation:
Northern Ireland Electricity Service – coal & oil-fired generating plant

Scotland was linked by high voltage transmission wires to England and Wales, and England was linked to continental Europe (France) with an undersea cable. Northern Ireland was linked to the Republic of Ireland, and eventually to Scotland by an undersea cable

Northern Ireland was physically isolated from the rest of the UK, so its electricity service was a classic stand-alone vertically integrated electricity utility. It had some links to the Republic of Ireland, to the south[263] but these often did not work.

Scotland was also distinct, but there were two Boards with a combined capacity of 10GW, one serving the vast bulk of Scotland's population in the south, and one serving the geographically large but sparsely-populated highland and islands of northern Scotland. The two were linked, and southern Scotland was

---

[262] For many of these facts I am indebted to David Newbery's Electricity Liberalisation in Britain, 2004, Cambridge MIT, Cambridge Working Paper in Economics 0469.

[263] There was an interconnector but it was periodically blown up as part of Northern Ireland's 'Troubles'.

linked to England by several main transmission lines. Due to its two modern coal-fired and two nuclear power stations, and due to its low population and de-industrialisation in the 1980s, Scotland tended to be a net exporter of electricity to England. England, in turn was linked to France and the rest of the European grid through an undersea cable with a capacity similar to a large modern power station. The French government had responded to the two oil crises of the seventies by commissioning around a hundred nuclear power stations for Electricite de France (EdF), which started to come into service in the early eighties; by 1990 France, like Scotland, was a net exporter of electricity to England, and to other neighbours.

Wholesale electricity markets - the Pool and its successors
Looking at the whole electricity value chain, the British Department of Energy decided that the best way to privatise the industry, while introducing competition-in-the-market for electricity, was to create a wholesale electricity market into which all the generators would bid to supply, and from which all retailers would bid their demands. They called this market 'the Pool', and it was designed as a 'Day Ahead' market, splitting every day into 48 half-hour slots and trading all slots each day ahead[264]. Wholesale markets require a firm to operate them (the New York Stock Exchange, the London Metal Exchange etc.), and Pool trading rules had to be developed, and to evolve, since this was a pioneering wholesale electricity market. This took some time, and the launch of the Pool in 1990 was considered to be something of a national security risk. In the end it went smoothly and the lights have stayed on ever since.

One of the aims of the Pool's economist creators was to make prices reflect the Short Run Marginal Cost of generation plus an uplift for dealing with transmission constraints, other losses, and a capacity mechanism addition. Consequently one of the fundamental Pool pricing principles was that the price that each electricity buyer paid for each half-hour slot of electricity was the bid price of the last marginal unit, which the economists hoped would be strongly linked to the marginal unit's SRMC. So every buyer had to pay the market-clearing price, and every supplier who bid a lower price than the market clearing price was asked to supply the quantity they offered, but got the market-clearing price.

Wholesale electricity trading is a specialist subject in its own right, and one in which professionals have made careers as advisors or designers[265], but in general the broad conclusion is that there have been several generations of organised wholesale market, as the time and geographical scope of the market has

---

[264] Initially only one day ahead; the future trading time was lengthened in succeeding years.[No, I think the Pool always set the price one day ahead. Contracts for differences were traded bilaterally and could be for any period ahead]

[265] For a detailed history of the evolution of British wholesale electricity markets see the CRI's Industry Brief Simmonds G, 2002, Regulation of the UK electricity Industry 2002 edition, CRI Bath, available at http://www.bath.ac.uk/management/cri/pubpdf/Industry_Briefs/Electricity_Gillian_Simmonds.pdf or Newbery's 2004 Cambridge Working Paper Newbery CWPE 0469

widened and new categories of players have entered. In brief the four main stages were:
1. The original 'Pool' for England and Wales was launched in 1990
2. Pool arrangements were revised several times, but one of the biggest underlying changes may have been in 1998 when competition for domestic customers was permitted, so retailers had to buy as economically as possible or risk losing millions of household customers. In addition Contracts For Differences in electricity bid began to be traded as financial instruments between generators, buyers, and increasingly hedgers and speculators, which added a raft of financial players into this bidding game.
3. In 2001 NETA changed three main aspects: 1) bidding in the system changed from one in which the National Grid Company (NGC) told the generators which plant to run, to one in which the generators told NGC which plant they would run; 2) most trades (about 95%) became bilateral, between the buyer and seller, rather than involving the Pool or a central Exchange; and 3) financial trading of electricity became even easier, through a set of four related bilateral years-ahead forward and spot markets which effectively allowed 'futures' trading, so that purely financial players – who wanted to bid with real money but did not want physical supply or delivery at all – were actively welcomed, rather than just tolerated.
4. BETA (in 2006) widened the transmission and trading market to bring in Scotland.

Forward and futures electricity market trading
In a basic textbook like this step 3 requires a little explanation: in a **forward** market buyers and sellers (firms) generally contract with each other to deliver goods at a future date for a price that is agreed today. So you and I may contract today to buy-and-sell some electricity in two months' time, and this contract is legally binding: neither of us can get out of it without agreeing to another contract, possibly involving other people. If we are both happy with this forward deal then you and I have both settled our future worries about prices changing, and can both get on with our ordinary business, for me, for instance, of generating electricity efficiently and for you retailing it cheaply to domestic customers. In financial parlance this is called 'constructing a hedge'.

In a **futures** contract we similarly agree to trade goods for some future time at a price agreed today, but *it is generally expected that there will be no physical delivery*. Before that date arrives each of us must undertake a second action: we must 'zero our physical position' – ensure we don't actually have to deliver or receive the goods – by making the exact reverse physical contract to our earlier one at the best prices we can now obtain – or tell the market administrator that we will be actually supplying or taking delivery of the physical good. So if you had bought 1 GWh of electricity for delivery on 17th February from 10-10.30 am (because that is what you need to run your business as an electricity supplier) you must now sell that quantity of electricity at that time and place, in a second futures contract, and then buy the physical quantity you need on the ordinary 'spot' market at the spot price. The only difference is the price will have changed between the date of the two contracts, so you will have made a financial profit or a loss on your futures contracts. The clever thing, though, is that this futures profit or loss exactly offsets the change in the price of electricity on the spot market, so by taking out a futures contract you have insured yourself against future changes in electricity prices. This is really the advantage of a futures market: it has 'financialised' your position while the oppositely-balanced physical trades leave every participant doing whatever their firm does – producing bulk electricity (me, as a generator), retailing it (you, as a supplier), or nothing (the hedgers or speculators).

Because futures contracts are so standardised and permit zero physical positions the entry barriers in this market are low, so it can be profitable to construct futures trades even when spreads are small. Consequently purely financial players – hedgers[266] and speculators – can participate, adding liquidity and much greater trading volumes to the market[267], which in turn reduces the transaction costs of trading.

With hindsight this 15-year path to the current British wholesale electricity markets could have been shortened a bit, but in general countries looking to create wholesale electricity markets must expect to go through several evolutionary stages unique to their circumstances and time. No-one should repeat the British stumbles, but you generally have to walk before you can run.

Generation and transmission

Figure 108 summarises the changes in the electricity sector since 1989:

Figure 108: summary of the evolution of the privatised electricity industry in England and Wales

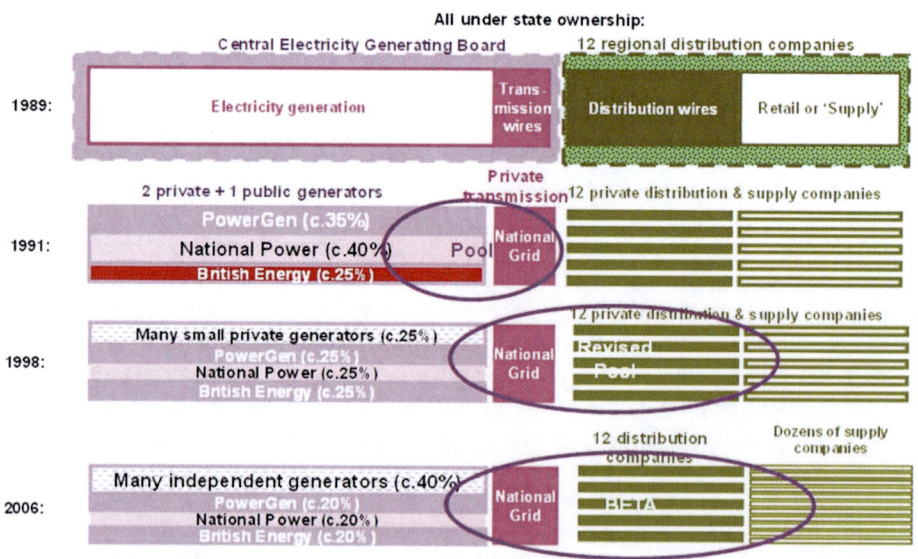

Data sources: various including Competition Commission/MMC 1996 Report on merger between National Power and Southern Electric

Under state ownership there was one vertically integrated public corporation generating and transmitting electricity in England and Wales: the Central Electricity Generating Board (CEGB). In 1991 the CEGB was split into four parts:
1. The national high voltage transmission network was separated off; initially shares in the **National Grid Company** (NGC) were given to the distribution companies (the Regional Electricity Companies, or RECs), but eventually these were sold off in a public flotation. Note that the *National Grid does not own electricity but simply 'wheels' it from the power station to the take-off substations* where it is needed, levying a charge on the electricity owner for this service; as a private monopoly this charge is regulated, originally by OFFER and now by Ofgem.
2. The 1991 privatisation created two wholesale sellers of electricity who generated power from fossil fuels (mostly coal, some gas and oil); each had more than 20 large stations:
    - one had 52% of the CEGB's generating capacity (**National Power**)
    - the other inherited 34% of the CEGB's capacity (**PowerGen**)
3. The remaining 8 GW of nuclear power stations were collected into a new company called Nuclear Electric:
    - this was kept under state-ownership because it was thought investors would not like the risks of owning and running nuclear reactors; however, once the Pool had been running successfully for several years and the government judged that investors were prepared to contemplate owning nuclear reactors the newer power stations were transferred to a company called **British Energy**, which was privatised in 1996.

National Power, PowerGen and National Grid were privatised in 1991 and the first two started trading immediately in the Pool as private companies.

---

[266] Who might be 'a hedger' but not want physical delivery? A firm like a supermarket chain or a rail network operator, that buys (or sells) a lot of electricity, the price of which is very closely linked to the wholesale price of electricity but is not actually wholesale electricity. A supermarket doesn't actually want 1 GWh of electricity at one time (the wholesale electricity market) but its aggregate position across a thousand stores may amount to this much electricity, so they could hedge all or part of their future position today using futures markets. Of course there are many other ways to solve their problems besides a futures hedge, each with its own risks and costs.

[267] Most finance textbooks describe and distinguish the two kinds of market. Don't worry if initially you confuse the two because a) the author did not understand the difference for many years, and b) it isn't necessary for most network utility economics – though obviously if you have a test tomorrow, or are charged with assessing or introducing market trading into your utilities you had better get to grips with this stuff now. Some other fundamental differences between futures and forward contracts are that futures contracts are centrally registered with an administrator (the 'Exchange') and are subject to margin calls; and in many (but not all) futures markets everyone's counter-party is the Exchange itself. NETA was one of those exceptions, as it was a set of decentralised optional bilateral markets where generation was self-despatched and prices received were 'pay-as-bid'. The Pool, by contrast, was a compulsory centrally despatched market where everyone (buyer or seller) traded with the Pool authority and everyone received the same Pool price.

> Given your knowledge of competition theory now ask yourself the following questions:
>
> a) Given Pool rules, and that nuclear power has very low short run marginal costs (unlike a fossil-fuelled power station, which must buy primary fuel for each unit of electricity generated, a nuclear power station costs little more to run than to leave it on stand-by), what pricing and quantity strategy maximises Nuclear Electric's profits?
>
> b) Given this predictable pricing strategy (which Nuclear Electric and British Energy did follow), what kind of market structure is this called and what pricing consequences do you expect – e.g. from the ice-cream-seller-on-the-beach version of Hotelling's model?
>
> c) Given this logical analysis, why did the government create only two fossil-fuel generators out of the CEGB's generation stations in 1991? Why did it not create, say, five companies?
>
> d) Given their starting points, why did National Power and PowerGen allow their combined share of the market to decline from around 75% in 1991 to around 40% fifteen years later?
>
> Discuss this with your fellow students. The Appendix to this chapter gives the author's answers.

Investment risks
Over this period many British, European, Asian and US firms including Dynegy and Enron (see California) entered the generating game in Britain by buying individual power stations sold by National Power or PowerGen, or by buying entire British generators, or building new gas-fired power stations. Some left after only three or four years having lost hundreds of millions of $s or €s, but others stayed and entry continues to this day. This is a risky business, even for 'professional' generators.

Degree of competition achieved
Because of the availability of cheap primary fuels in the UK, and the varying environmental constraints imposed by successive British governments, and because electricity is a secondary fuel whose wholesale cost depends on world prices of oil, coal and gas (Figure 9 in Chapter 1), it is difficult to create a unique *counter-factual* of what would have happened to British electricity prices if the industry had not been restructured and privatised. It is therefore hard to say whether British consumers have benefited from privatisation through lower *prices*. In 1997 Newbery and Pollitt[268] concluded that generation *costs* were permanently 6% lower than the counterfactual of continued public sector ownership which, discounted at the public sector's 6% discount rate amounted to a 100% return on the £10 billion sales value of the generators and NGC. The

---

[268] Newbery DM and Pollitt MC (1997) 'The Restructuring and Privatisation of the CEGB: was it worth it?' Journal of Industrial Economics XLV (3) 269-303

distribution of these £10bn of benefits, though, should be of great interest to policymakers, as Newbery and Pollitt found that in the British case *all the benefits of privatisation went to investors: none accrued to consumers.* And in a general, anecdotal, sense most industry experts expect something like this: almost all experts would agree that a competitive market has led to better decision making in terms of new capacity, plant operation and volume of reserve margin.

In 2000 the two UK electricity industry regulators, Littlechild of Great Britain and Horton of Northern Ireland, repeated this study taking account of cost reductions and regulatory price reductions after 1997. Their counter-factual assumed that a state-owned electricity sector would have had to increase prices to cover a larger investment programme than the private sector actually achieved, and so some benefits had accrued to customers. Overall their study found that *generation costs were roughly 12% below what they would have been if the electricity industry had continued in State ownership,* that the benefits totalled £20bn – twice what Newbery & Pollitt had found – and that *half the benefits had accrued to investors and half to consumers.*

Drivers of lower electricity costs
In the 1990s a quantity of North Sea gas with low opportunity uses in Europe became available and the Department of Energy decide to allow UK power stations to burn it as a primary fuel. Thus the government and the regulator, Stephen Littlechild, informally backed a policy to reduce generation costs – and the market power of the duopolists. The combination of cheap gas prices, low construction costs, and high electricity prices at the start of the decade made the scale of profits available from gas generation irresistible for entrants (and incumbents), resulting in a 'Dash For Gas'. From 1993 an additional 20 GW (32% of system capacity) was added within 8 years, much of it by new entrants, which directly undermined the duopolist's prices in the Pool. Consequently wholesale electricity prices fell during the 1990s. But circumstances and government policies change; in the twenty first century global energy and world oil demand rose, so gas prices generally rose steeply up to 2008, meaning wholesale electricity prices rose, negating the earlier falls. After 2008, as world LNG trade and North American gas fracking rose, most world gas prices fell away again, resuming the downward fuel pressure on UK electricity generation costs, but government policies now switched to backing renewable fuels, which were more expensive.

Electricity distribution and supply
By 1989 the distribution of electricity in England and Wales was organised into 12 publicly-owned area distribution 'Boards', with names like South Eastern Electricity Board (SEEBoard), London Electricity Board, etc. These regional monopolies undertook both the 'distribution' (see Chapter 1 for a description of these activities) and 'supply' functions (the electricity industry's name for the retail function), but from the outset the government and regulator aimed to separate the contestable retail businesses from the innate distribution monopolies in a carefully planned manner. The 1989 privatisation programme envisaged the opening of the retail market to competition in three stages:

1. Competition for about 5,000 very large customers above 1MW – from 1 April 1990
2. Competition for about 45,000 large customers above 100kW – from 1 April 1994
3. Competition for all 22 million customers – from September 1998.

In order to maximise sale receipts and maintain security of supply in the first phase of privatisation the 12 regional monopolies were privatised in 1990 as joint distribution and supply companies. Only in the succeeding decade were the *supply* businesses progressively prised away[269] from each distribution business:

1. In 1990 the 12 RECs were privatised as geographical joint distribution and retail monopolies regulated by OFFER (headed by Stephen Littlechild); they were free to buy electricity from whomever they wished in long and medium-term wholesale contracts;
2. The 5,000 very large customers (such as major airports and giant factories) in 1990 were freed to by-pass the RECs, using long- and medium-term contracts, or they could use their existing REC's special tariffs for very large users; the 1991 launch of the Pool meant that both the RECs and the very large users could buy Day Ahead (spot) electricity in the Pool to top up any short term needs;
3. The additional freedom for the 45,000 large industrial buyers to choose their supplier from April 1994 meant that tens of thousands of large customers could switch retailers. Being very price-sensitive customers, many did switch suppliers to new industrial specialists in electricity retailing. The effect on the overall market was initially limited: a few dozen specialist companies entered the Pool as relatively small volume buyers which fragmented the buying side more; however, with the rise of more small generators the sellers' duopoly was starting to break down, so the cumulative effect was to create a real market with many buyers and sellers of a commodity product;
4. The final freedom for all 22 million households to choose their electricity supplier came into force over a six month period from September 1998. The spirit of competition grew slowly, with 10-12% a year of customers switching, though many switched only to one of the other large RECs or the generator duopolists who had decided to become retailers as well as generators. Totally new entrants to the industry said that it was hard to fight incumbents with 100% market shares who had such advantages of enormous market buying power, retail economies of scale (in billing operations, call centres, and IT systems), brand recognition by almost 100% of customers, and local knowledge. It is worth noting, of course that these formidable entry barriers were small obstacles to the existing players in the energy game: to the RECs who expanded out of their home area, or to the two generators, National Power and Powergen, or to the rogue monopolist with an even stronger

---

[269] Technically each REC had always had two licences at privatisation – a distributor's licence and a supply licence for roughly the same area – and they were just progressively separated in the 1990s. The widespread perception was that the supply businesses were levered away from very reluctant RECs

national energy reputation, British Gas, so it is not surprising that the retail electricity game stayed very much within the energy industry.

5. In 2000 the Utilities Act forced the privatised distributors to separate their supply businesses from their distribution businesses, both legally and commercially. The dozen former Electricity Boards' Public Electricity Supply duties were abolished and they were obliged to create different business names for each business, separating their offices, depots, IT systems etc. They had to ensure that customer IT records were separated between the distribution business – which must have the name and address of every property in the geographical area to do its function – and the supply business, which did not need this if its market share was to fall below 100%.

6. A decade after the Utilities Act 2000 was passed we might say the era of full-on retail competition in British electricity markets had arrived. However, while there is serious competition in each area of the country *it is oligopolistic competition in each region:* the biggest six retailers have 99% of the national retail market which has provoked considerable social and ultimately political opposition.

Some people doubt that competition has been worth it. A 2001 study by NERA[270] showed that the direct costs of introducing full retail competition in the UK (£131m a year) roughly equalled the direct benefits of lower bills (£123m a year) but ignored the value of time (at least an hour) spent searching for new suppliers. Furthermore the benefits went to the 11million switchers while the costs were born by all 26 million households, so at conservative estimates of the value of time NERA estimated the 15 million non-switching households were losing around £6 a year each to introduce competition from which they did not benefit[271].

Is choice between the same six suppliers across the country in every region better than the lack of consumer choice offered twenty years ago: no choice of local supplier but having a dozen legal monopolists across the country? Most economists would value the option to choose your supplier positively, and most consumers would agree. *Having the freedom to choose suppliers changes the balance of negotiating power enormously*, and this is something the NERA study did not value. Consumers often refer to removing the 'arrogance' of monopolists– the tacit presumption that they are doing the consumer a favour by deigning to supply you, and then following this with "...and of course you will do things our way" when it comes to things that ought to be mutually agreed. Such matters include suitable times to read meters[272], or the choice of very restricted tariffs

---

[270] Gordon MacKerron *Costs and Benefits of 100% Electricity Market Opening*, 2001, NERA Energy Regulation Brief

[271] Critics of NERA's study say it failed to take account of the impact of retail competition in reducing generation costs.

[272] The author recalls a time in the 1980s when his electricity bill was estimated for two years because he worked five days a week. The London Electricity Board refused to organise meter readings for his flat on Saturdays, or in the evenings, saying this was not

restricted tariffs for customers in unusual categories, or excessive 'administrative charges' for small items which some regulator has forgotten to ramp down.

Today, while the small business sector has scores of specialist electricity retailers, the domestic sector (households) may appear to have competition from dozens of major household name retailers such as British Gas, Virgin and Tesco, some of which can be seen as fronts for the Big Six electricity retailers. Competition has at times been fierce, with the regulator investigating some competitors' sales methods for persuading people to switch suppliers 'on the doorstep'. However, due to the commodity nature of electricity as a consumer good[273], the boring-ness of the product, the thin margins, the importance of brand recognition – especially when buying online – most consumers (other than the retired) cannot be bothered to investigate alternative tariffs before enduring the hassle of switching suppliers. In the modern world if your friends catch you spending time investigating alternative electricity suppliers they will grab you by the ears and say "Up, you hermit! You've got to get out more".

Distribution
The natural monopoly *distribution* businesses have remained as 12 separate companies, heavily price-cap-regulated by an economic regulator (currently Ofgem), although some consolidation of ownership has occurred. As with transmission, the distributors do not buy electricity in the wholesale market – they simply wheel it through and charge customers for connecting or disconnecting from the local grid. Their sole function is to 'keep the lights on' – even if you haven't paid your bill (it is the retailers' responsibility to get money out of you!).

Summary evaluations of benefits of competition
There is little doubt that introducing competition in the contestable sectors of the UK electricity industries combined with heavy regulation of both the contestable and non-contestable parts has

1. Lowered costs of generation by at least 6% below what they would have been under public sector ownership; this is a straight welfare gain;
2. Lowered potential demands on public sector investment
3. But also permanently eliminated dividends from a generally very profitable part of the public sector; though this sum should be reduced by tax payments from private companies;
4. Achieved substantial private sector investment in generation, transmission, distribution and supply (retail); but not all of this investment was efficient: Edison Mission managed to lose $1.15 billion in two years buying and selling power stations in 1999;

---

their policy, nor would they give meter reading appointment times for periods of less than half a day. The author replied that it was not his policy to take half a day's holiday to stay in his flat for a two minute meter reading, so both sides continued using the company's estimated meter readings. Eventually the London Electricity Board gave in, and sent round a meter reader on a Saturday.

[273] OK, green electricity commands a small price premium in most countries.

5. (after 15 years) ended the 'arrogance of retail monopolies' and given all consumers a real choice of suppliers.

Major British mistakes made along the way that could have been avoided include
1. Not splitting the generators early on into at least, say, five different firms

..er that's about it. There were other mistakes, such as privatising British Energy and then bailing it out seven years later, or possibly replacing the Pool with NETA, at a cost of £700m, when Newbery argues that it was the governance arrangements of the Pool that should have been changed[274], but these were implementation failures and so *minor*, not major, mistakes – for instance updating the Pool once more, rather than replacing it with NETA, would not have been costless.

Texas and California: contrasting approaches, different results

Progressive reform in Texas

In a State with a strong sense of self-belief and entrepreneurial spirit, electricity generators were always likely to spring up in Texas. Being also blessed by nature with a lot of oil and natural gas, in the twentieth century Texas was almost bound to be an electricity exporter. The crucial link was to develop a reliable transmission grid within the State, and then to connect it with neighbouring States. When the Second World War broke out several utilities banded together to create the Texas Interconnected System (TIS) to facilitate the reliable exporting of surplus electricity to bordering States who were in temporary deficit due to war production. After the War, due to population growth, and with the rise of air conditioning and electricity-using appliances such as fridges, domestic electricity demand grew strongly within Texas. The TIS continued to strengthen transmission within the State to increase the grid's reliability, and maintain exports. In 1970 The Electricity Reliability Council Of Texas (ERCOT) was formed with two employees; gradually it grew to absorb all TIS's useful functions[275].

ERCOT: the USA's first ISO
Systematic reforms of the entire electricity industry in Texas began in 1995, when the State legislature amended the Public Utilities Act to permit competition in generation to be fought out through a wholesale market. However, unlike some States, Texas did not rush to initiate competition in generation immediately. Rather, the State's Public Utility Commission began by steadily expanding ERCOT's role as transmission grid coordinator. In 1996 ERCOT officially became the USA's *first Independent System Operator, a non-profit organisation with an explicit remit to allow equal access to the transmission grid for any generator or buyer.*

---

[274] Many people disagree with Newbery; Littlechild argues there was no political constituency for changing governance alone, and it would not have been effective.
[275] See ERCOT's history at http://www.ercot.com/about/profile/history/ accessed August 2013

Building on its 1995 legislation, in 1999 the Texas Legislature voted to vertically separate the State's electric utilities into generation, transmission, distribution and supply, and explicitly reinforced ERCOT's roles as

1. Planning and operating a reliable transmission grid within Texas
2. Providing wholesale market settlements
3. Permitting open access for any shipper to wheel their electricity across parts of Texas
4. Developing sufficient codes and processes to permit retail switching and competition.

Not all of this could be done immediately, and being a cooperative, rather than a competitive, non-profit organisation ERCOT did a lot of consulting before gradually meeting all of these objectives. Part of the difficulty, of course, was that incumbents did not want to be split up, so the vertical separation took a long time and resulted in some uneven distributions of generation power. One must recall that in the early years, at a time when a lot of gas-fired generation was being constructed, Enron (headquartered in Houston) and similar 'asset-light traders' were still powerful players with collectively huge investments in gas and electricity assets across this State and many others, playing determined and complicated games across the USA.

For the benefit of younger readers it is worth emphasising that Enron was not always a corrupt organisation. Enron started out like hundreds of others as a mid-Western gas trading company owning some pipelines. While most of the blame for its subsequent failure must lie where the US Courts apportioned it – on the three most senior individuals – the author (like thousands of others) first became aware of Enron, and then doubtful about it, in the late 90s, because of its promise always to increase quarterly earnings. Nothing grows forever – just look at the actual history of any real company. But Enron insisted they would always grow exponentially, and they took aggressive retribution against firms or individuals doubting their claims. In the author's view, the fundamental cause of Enron's downfall was its Chairman's refusal to admit that quarterly earnings growth must ultimately suffer some reversals. After growing phenomenally from 1985, continual quarterly earnings growth became ever-harder to maintain in the late 90s, and so large-scale fraud and corruption set in, as the key operators just below the Chairman, knowing what they had had to do to achieve the last quarter's earnings growth, realised what he did not: that this record could not be maintained indefinitely. Corruption became endemic because they knew the end was nigh.

The point of this minor digression is to note that although Enron was headquartered in Texas, it was not always a corrupt firm, and most of what they did was normal or acute (but legal) energy trading. They introduced techniques from financial trading that are now standard tools in energy and carbon trading, and mastered the concept of asset-light energy trading (see later under California). They were emulated by other companies, and were undoubtedly a powerful force to be reckoned with in the progressive evolution of Texan electricity markets.

Opening of the Texas retail market
The biggest change affecting consumers in Texas was the opening, seven years after being first envisaged, of the Texas retail electricity market. As of 1 January 2002 6½ m individuals and corporations served by investor-owned utilities in most cities were free to choose or switch their power suppliers, and public cooperatives were invited to join the process. Many consumers did switch suppliers, with TXU reporting that 69% of large commercial and industrial customers in Texas had switched suppliers in 3 years, and 20% of domestic households[276]. By 2007 ERCOT reported that 46% of domestic customers had switched supplier[277] after 5 years of retail competition, making it, on this measure, the most competitive electricity market in the USA.

The 2010 Texas nodal market
In 2001 ERCOT consolidated its ten regional control areas into one and had developed sufficient protocols to centralise power scheduling and procurement of ancillary services. Partly because of the size of Texas – a grid with 550 generation units linked by 65,000 km of transmission wire – it seemed impossible to decide on a central pricing point for the system, which kept delaying development of the wholesale market. In 2003 ERCOT was instructed to create *a 'nodal' market*. This is one in which prices are set not for one notional point, or set of equal-price-points in the system, but for many.

In 1st December 2010 the Texas nodal market finally went live, with ERCOT dispatching generation for all the units by issuing marginal prices for more than 8000 nodes. It has functioned continuously since, public and private sector investment in the State has continued, service levels remain good, and Texan customers have continued to enjoy freedom to choose their electricity supplier.

California: the starting position
In 1994 California's electricity generation, transmission, distribution and retail functions were split between three vertically integrated incumbents: Pacific Gas and Electric (PG&E), Southern California Edison (Edison), and San Diego Gas and Electric (SDGE). Infrastructure was generally well developed but demand was rising, particularly in southern California, while supply for the State's 32m people[278] came from around the State, but with northern California, and Oregon and Washington to the north exporting hydroelectricity to the south. The primary fuels were the full range of coal, oil, nuclear, solar, hydro and gas, but new capacity was turning strongly to gas, partly because north America's gas

---

[276] Source TXU reported in Sioshansi op cit. page 73.
[277] Source ERCOT history website.
[278] http://www.census.gov/population/projections/state/9525rank/caprsrel.txt was the official Bureau of Census figure at the time; California's population rose to 36 million by 2000, a rise of 14% over the ten years.

transmission grid was well developed and new sources of gas were being developed, but mainly because gas was viewed as a clean primary fuel with low harmful emissions.

During the 1990s some infrastructure constraints developed. New plant generating capacity within the State was delayed, and although existing capacity was uprated, and generation utilisation rates rose significantly, a main transmission link between the northern and southern grids ('*Path 15*'), with a transmission capacity of about 8% of the State's generating capacity started to be used heavily. For the rising population of southern California dependence on this single path was far higher than 8%.

In sum by 2000 the Supply Demand balance for electricity in California was tight and getting tighter. Gas was usually the most expensive primary fuel, so it tended to be the marginal fuel that set electricity prices. Midway through 2000, in response to a fall-off in drilling activities in the two previous years, natural gas wellhead prices started to rise.

California's restructuring & reforms
In 1996 State Governor Pete Wilson started formally to deregulate the industry. To avoid the mistakes of the early English market, 40% of the incumbents' generating capacity was forcibly sold off to mainly out-of-State generators, many of whom were the new breed of 'asset-light' utilities such as Enron, AES, Reliant and Dynegy, who bought minimal real assets but traded all forms of energy in as many markets as possible. While incumbent regulatees tended to use more long term contracts and regulated prices, the asset-light utilities disliked regulation and did a large amount of short-term energy trading, believing themselves to have a competitive advantage over incumbents with their superior energy trading skills. Enron Chairman Kenneth Lay was reported to have told the Chair of the California Power Authority:

> "In the final analysis, it doesn't matter what you crazy people in California do, because I got smart guys who can always figure out how to make money."[279]

This statement was reported as testimony to a later enquiry, and gives the flavour of Enron's general approach to all business suppliers, rivals and customers. While Enron was the most extreme, the other asset-light energy traders also thought like this: arrogantly. The Bible says "Pride goes before destruction, a haughty spirit before a fall"[280] and today we commonly use the term *hubris* to describe overbearing arrogance, especially before a fall.

---

[279] Testimony by S David Freeman to the Subcommittee on Consumer Affairs, Foreign Commerce and Tourism of the Senate Committee on Commerce, Science and Transportation on April 11, 2002 of a phone conversation between himself and Kenneth Lay in 2000.
[280] Proverbs 16:18.

Gas-fired electricity generation was the first port of call for the new entrants: natural gas could be bought in a combination of long, medium and short-term deals with classic financial instruments (forwards, futures, options and other derivatives) to minimise risks if prices moved adversely. The gas was then handed over to conventional power station managers who generated electricity according to a plan notionally provided by the administrator of the California Power Exchange (PX, the day-ahead market in wholesale electricity), though in fact ultimately devised by their own traders. The electricity output was then sold on wholesale markets using the same principles to close off a firm's position so that combined electricity and gas trading profits for an entire year could in theory be "locked in" and written into the Profit and Loss account in a few weeks of intensive trading. The profits from a few days energy trading could easily swamp any profits made from weeks of electricity generation – the normal source of profit for a power generator.

Globally, Enron took this principle to its logical conclusion by locking in profits from multi-year deals – sometimes up to ten years ahead! – and writing those future profit into that year's profits, unhindered by US accounting rules at the time, or by their auditors, Arthur Andersen.

While the Transmission grid (operated by the California Independent System Operator (ISO)) and Distribution functions would obviously have to remain highly regulated functions, the main change in the Retail function was to separate it from Distribution in the incumbents, and to open it up to new entrants and general competition, allowing the designers of the new framework to claim the *possibility* of a very competitive market. So the same asset-light energy traders who ran electricity generation could also supply electricity to domestic customers, or, more likely, to larger commercial customers. However, given that the incumbents were local monopolies starting with 100% shares of the mass domestic market (households), and with very well-established trading records, it was always very likely that the three incumbents would retain most of their domestic markets, at least for the first decade or so[281], so that nearly all the entrants' actual customers were likely to be large commercial customers. Domestic customers took too long, were too expensive to win, and the retail margin per customer was too small. Furthermore, the legislation had already guaranteed all domestic customers a 10% price cut without doing anything; "Why would anybody switch to a competing supplier under these circumstances?" Sioshansi asks rhetorically[282].

The final reform was to create a series of wholesale electricity markets based around the California Power Exchange (PX), and market administrators, and the necessarily complex sets of rules for electronic trading were established, tested

---

[281] In England energy incumbents still had 99% of the domestic market ten years after their legal monopolies were abolished.

[282] Sioshansi F 2006, Electricity Market Reform: What has the experience taught us thus far?' in Utilities Policy 14 63-72.

and sent live in April 1998. Furthermore, to force all the players to use these markets, long term contracts were outlawed, so that all wholesale power generated had to be sold and bought through one of the two PX markets.

The 2000 – 2001 California meltdown
In the second half of 2000 gas wellhead prices started to rise[283] and this led to some clear signs of abnormal trading conditions in electricity markets, as daily PX prices started to exceed 1999 price averages by factors of up to thirty. In southernmost California SDGE was able to pass on some of these much higher costs to its furious customers, but the other two incumbents faced retail prices that were capped by regulators at levels well below wholesale levels. Having been forced to sell generating plant that produced electricity at around 3 cents a kilowatt hour, they were now having to buy it all on wholesale markets at anything from 11 to 50 cents per kwh while selling it retail for a regulatorily-capped 6.5 cents per kwh[284]. Of course their generating arms made large profits but these were 40% smaller than their retail needs. Enron and the energy traders were declaring record energy trading profits while California's incumbent retailers headed for bankruptcy.

Blackouts first hit the San Francisco area during the summer peak of June 2000, and SDGE filed a complaint in August that markets were being manipulated. In December the grid operator, ISO, declared California's first ever Stage 3 emergency, meaning generation reserves were below 3%, and the State only avoided blackouts by switching off two huge water pumps. In the New Year, on January 17th and again on the 18th, the State suffered rolling blackouts. Governor Gray Davis declared a State of Emergency and bought power on the wholesale electricity markets at very high prices on behalf of the increasingly bankrupt incumbent electricity retailers.

In the next few days the Federal Energy Regulatory Commission (FERC) ended the requirement for retailers to buy all their electricity needs through the PX, and abolished the wholesale rate schedule, so effectively ending the PX in January 2001[285]. On February 1st 2001 the Governor authorised the Department of Water Resources (DWR) to make long term energy contracts on behalf of the incumbents, and DWR set up contracts lasting up to 18 years. Later that year PG&E filed for bankruptcy, while Edison worked hard on a plan with the State to avoid that fate. Both companies' previously grade A bonds were reduced to junk ratings.

California trading and gaming
Today's readers may not appreciate how the heady spirits of the Millennial era

---

[283] Energy Information Administration Annual Energy Outlook 2002 page 33.
[284] Speech by Fred Keeley, Speaker of the California State Assembly, March 2001, available at http://www.commonwealthclub.org/archive/01/01-03keeley-speech.html and accessed 19 July 2010.
[285] EIA, page 32.

affected global corporate attitudes. As a consultant at the time, the author worked briefly for several of the companies mentioned, though not for Enron[286], and not directly on electricity in California. What was common around global utility markets at the time, though, was a confident belief by these traders that short-term financial trading was superior to longer term contracts, and that nearly all forms of market pricing, no matter how short term, were superior to longer term decisions or rulings by regulators or politicians.

The principles of asset-light trading
Most experienced economists generally presume that financial markets are efficient (i.e. they process new information rapidly) and unbiased over time, so that persistent liars will be found out[287]. So it ought not to be possible for a single player to distort a thickly-traded financial market, unless they have some other asset they can lever at the same time, such as media access (helps share-tipping), or a hard-to-obtain licence, or real physical or commercial assets that can influence real supply or demand. To a pure financial trader the main advantage of tying up risk capital[288] owning non-trading assets such as customers, power plant, or transmission lines would be to lever them so as – to use a phrase that was popular a hundred years ago – to 'corner the market': i.e. to distort the market for a while so that one can make a profit.

Applied to the situation in California several experienced traders entered the market and bought assets that might have a disproportionate influence on prices. So, many entrants bought one of the larger power plants sold by the incumbents. When wholesale electricity prices looked like spiking upwards it would be possible for the trader owners of this power plant to tell the engineers to undertake maintenance, communicate this urgent maintenance 'need' to the market (though not the true reason why), drive prices even higher, and then stop maintenance, and switch on power to sell at the highest possible rates.

Clearly 'Path 15' was another highly desirable asset. However, this was an integral part of the incumbents' Regulatory Asset Bases, and so not directly for sale. But *capacity* on Path 15 (i.e. the right to use the line) could be bought and sold on the new markets, so Enron and others bought significant rights here. A letter in 2000 from an ex-Enron energy trader to State Senator Barbara Boxer alleged

---

[286] Although knowing nothing of Enron's abuse of accounting principles or the moral fibre of its senior personnel, it was clear at the time to the author that Enron's strategy for expanding into global water could never work, as the elapsed time needed to develop international water concessions far exceeded the corporate planning horizons of most US corporations, and particularly impatient companies like Enron.

[287] The Efficient Markets Hypothesis takes this commonplace observation further, but in its strong form is more contentious, especially when combined with the Rational Expectations Hypothesis.

[288] Obviously the first step any seasoned trader takes to reduce the risk-capital (equity) tied up in owning an asset is to financially leverage the asset, by borrowing against it.

"There is a single connection between northern and southern California's power grids. I heard that Enron traders purposely overbooked that line, then caused others to need it. Next, by California's free-market rules, Enron was allowed to price-gouge at will."[289]

A later investigation showed that Enron devised half a dozen schemes to systematically harvest congestion charges from the grid operator (ISO) while generating or transmitting no electricity whatever[290]. And, of course, perfectly legal gaming could simply buy Path 15 capacity when it was cheap, sell it when it was dear, drive up wholesale prices in southern California, and create an entirely legal speculative profit for the trader at the expense of millions of southern Californians.

In addition gas-fired generators could on occasions influence some of the officially quoted gas price indices, which were sometimes based on very few actual physical trades, so that integrated energy traders could make huge profits at the gas trading stage that more than offset losses in the electricity generation or trading functions. A subsequent investigation by the FERC concluded:

"- Markets for natural gas and electricity in California are inextricably linked, and dysfunctions in each fed off one another. Spot gas prices drove electricity prices, and manipulation of price indices apparently drove, at least in part, dysfunctions in the natural gas market. The [full FERC] report makes recommendations for steps the Commission can take to assure price indices accurately reflect market prices.
- Staff concludes that large-volume, rapidfire trading by a single company at Topock, a California border trading hub that was incorrectly thought to be liquid, substantially increased natural gas prices throughout California."[291]

Finally, Enron engaged in some games that were simply commercial frauds. These had names such as Deathstar, Congo Red, and the Forney Perpetual Loop, and were variations of a basic commercial scam known to American bankers as 'check kiting' whereby a principal sets up a dizzying array of counterbalancing trades between parties that seem to be independent but are in fact controlled by the principal, and then suddenly negates all the internal trades, scooping up outsiders' funds and running away[292]. In this case Enron collected 'congestion fees' from the grid operator (ISO) before cancelling the energy trades, and not returning the congestion fees because Enron could not be traced as the

---

[289] Letter from David Fabian to Senator Boxer, February 13, 2002, p.1, quoted in Congestion Manipulation "DeathStar", McCullough Research (June 5, 2002) at p.4 and retrieved on 19 July 2010.
[290] See McCullough Research at http://www.mresearch.com/pdfs/19.pdf   Executive Summary, accessed July 2010.
[291] http://www.ferc.gov/industries/electric/indus-act/wec/enron/summary-findings.pdf written on 26/3/2003 and retrieved on 19/7/2010.
[292] See McCullough Research at http://www.mresearch.com/pdfs/19.pdf   pages 4-5 accessed July 2010.

principal. Caught out once by the PX with an early version of this scheme in 1999, Enron paid a trifling $25,000 fine, promised it would not reoffend, and then repeated the scam on a bigger scale from 2000 onwards. It was not found out until the State's 2002 investigation.

California: the immediate lessons
Reflecting on the lessons a year later, S David Freeman, an experienced energy executive who was appointed Chairman of the Power Commission in the middle of the crisis, testified to the Senate Committee on Commerce, Science and Transportation that he believed:

> "...[Electricity] is a public good that must be protected from private abuse. If Murphy's Law were written for a market approach to electricity, then the law would state 'any system that can be gamed, will be gamed, and at the worst possible time.' And a market approach for electricity is inherently gameable. Never again can we allow private interests to create artificial or even real shortages and to be in control.
> ...In electric power, we must have openness and companies that are responsible for keeping the lights on. We need to go back to companies that own power plants with clear responsibilities for selling real power under long-term contracts. There is no place for companies like Enron that own the equivalent of an electronic telephone book and game the system to extract an unnecessary middleman's profits. Companies with power plants can compete for contracts to provide the bulk of our power at reasonable prices that reflect costs."[293]

But, quite aside from gaming by Enron and a herd of others, the truth is that there were underlying severe flaws in California's restructuring. After extensive investigation in 2003 the FERC, who had not covered themselves in glory during the crisis itself, substantially agreed:

> "...supply-demand imbalance, flawed market design and inconsistent rules made possible significant market manipulation as delineated in final investigation report. Without underlying market dysfunction, attempts to manipulate the market would not be successful."[294]

Without a tight Demand / Supply balance, transmission constraints, caps on retail prices but not on wholesale prices, and an absolute requirement to make players put all flows through the daily market, it is possible the Californian crisis could have been averted. But there can be no doubt that Enron and their imitators aggravated the situation, and might have made even a perfectly-designed and –implemented set of new markets unworkable. With hindsight we know that such greedy people were bound *to try* to kill the goose that laid such

---

[293] Testimony to the Subcommittee on Consumer Affairs, Foreign Commerce and Tourism of the Senate Committee on Commerce, Science and Transportation on May 15, 2002.
[294] FERC ibid paragraph 1.

handsome golden eggs. The regulation designer's job, of course, is to ensure that excessive 'Greed-is-good' cannot bring about the total systemic failure that was in fact seen in California.

A longer-term comparison of the electricity reforms in California and Texas

Because it was great fun we have spent more time analysing the failures of Californian electricity restructuring than examining the successes of the Texan revolution, begun in the 1990s, but only completed fifteen years later. And you can – if you survive them – learn more from your failures than successes. Some years on it is worth drawing considered comparisons between the steady progressive reforms that went on in Texas and the fireworks that backfired in California, bearing in mind that, due in part to the FERC's inability to pass any Federal-wide legislation[295], major reform of the electricity sector in North America has pretty well stalled over the last decade.

Lessons from California
Some people have said that California's reforms would have gone fine if California had had sufficient generating capacity. Joskow strongly disagrees, pointing out that the crisis happened in mid-winter, while California is a summer-peaking system[296]. Also, he notes that the New England states, New York, New Jersey, and Pennsylvania had all implemented very similar reforms at the same time, experienced exactly the same gas price shocks as California did, and yet they did not melt down.

Another cause of California's problems has also been shown to be an excuse: the drought in the western USA pushing a tightly-constrained system over the limit. Amundsen *et al*[297] reject this, calculating that the Nordic system suffered a far worse drought a few years later and managed to survive without resorting to mandatory rationing, blackouts, financial ruin and price-gouging by generators.

So, do we just conclude that the old North Eastern American systems are reliable, the Scandinavians are robust, but the Californians are 'too flaky'? No, there are satisfyingly reliable analyses that even allowing for players breaking the law and deliberately trying to game and break the system, with better policies the meltdown could have been avoided.

The serious faults in the California reforms of 1996-2001 must be reckoned to be:
    1. Capping retail prices while requiring retailers to buy from a free wholesale market was suicidal
    2. Medium and long term contracts should not be discouraged – if traders want these regulators should let them have them

---

[295] Glachant and Perez page 164.
[296] Joskow 2006, in Sioshansi and Pfaffenberger, page 12.
[297] Amundsen E, von de Fehr N and Bergman L, 2006, The Nordic market Chapter in Sioshansi & Pfaffenberger op. cit cited in Sioshansi 2006 page 70.

3. In the absence of a sizeable volume of long term contracts, the regulators should have foreseen the potential systemic risks involved and ensured that both the generators and the retailers had sufficiently hedged their forward positions to avoid unsustainable financial positions
4. Regulators must have sufficient legal powers and financial and human resources to be vigilant, and if necessary rapidly suspend or terminate the licences of any traders they suspect of any kind of malpractice or manipulation; lengthy legal investigations followed by a $25,000 fine and a promise not to reoffend were a joke
5. California's Independent System Operator was neither sufficiently Independent nor much of an Operator: allowing players to book and then not use capacity on lines that were well known to be system bottlenecks (Path 15) was madness. Part of the problem is that these things are more obvious in retrospect than they were at the time.

Even the clear-up was a mess. Littlechild noted that "The California Legislature required the Department of Water Resources to purchase electricity in behalf of customers, which it did via large quantities of very long-term contracts at what turned out to be excessive prices"[298]. Sioshansi estimates the total costs of California's "botched up market" at $70 billion[299]. For this kind of money America could have bought a couple of aircraft carrier groups and invaded half a dozen small countries.

California's problems have certainly not been solved for good, merely shelved for a few years, at great expense to Californian ratepayers. Issues of inter-state coordination and efficiency across the south and the north have just been put in the deep freeze. Building new generation or transmission capacity is a big sunk cost, yet private investors will not do this unless they have some guarantees that they will at least be legally allowed to sell their product (one of the worries of nuclear power companies, who face the riskiest sunk costs of all) and that they will not face subsidised competitors. So a national solution seems impossible yet the problem has escaped well beyond the control of individual States; it reminds the author of the situation prior to passing the 1890 Sherman Anti-Trust Act.

Some international conclusions about electricity industry reform
In a 2006 article[300] Paul Joskow reviewed the vast literature and global experiences of restructuring and privatising the electricity supply industry (ESI) and summarised these in ten "textbook" components which make for successful reform of the ESI. Joskow's summary has been further summarised in the Box in Table 7.

---

[298] Littlechild S 2006 Foreword in Sioshansi and Pfaffenberger op. cit page xx.
[299] Sioshansi 2006 page 73.
[300] Joskow P 2006 Introduction to Electricity Sector Liberalization: Lessons learned from cross-country studies in Sioshansi F and Pfaffenberger W (eds), Electricity Market Reform: An International Perspective, Elsevier, Amsterdam.

Table 7: Joskow's Top Ten Textbook Tips for successful electricity sector reform

Tip	Action	Why?	Watch out for...
1	**Privatise** utilities	Focuses managers on performing	State pursuing own political agenda
2	Vertically **separate contestable from monopoly functions & insist on equal access** to all monopoly parts	Competition where possible, regulation where necessary	Cross-subsidising of competitive activities from monopoly
3	**Create** several truly **independent generators**	Produces real competition-in-the-market; is helped if there is excess capacity	If necessary intervene to break up collusion and promote competition
4	**Create an Independent System Operator** to manage the grid, schedule generation, and balance quantity & physical parameters of electrical system in real time	Keeps the lights on	State moves to protect state-owned assets or enterprises; ISO does not need to own the assets, merely manage them
5	**Create** wholesale electricity **markets** in real time	Allows process of market discovery to work and produce meaningful prices	The markets will change over time; so should systems, regulators & players
6	Apply regulatory rules & support network institutions to **promote efficient access to the transmission grid**	Allows buyers & sellers to compete and exchange wholesale electricity fairly	Allocating scarce transmission capacity fairly; efficient siting and interconnection of new generators
7	Unbundle retail tariffs to **separate supply from distribution and transmission charges**	Allows consumers to choose between fairly competing suppliers	Incumbents raising artificial entry barriers or exploiting former assets such as customer lists unfairly

Tip	Action	Why?	Watch out for...
8	Where retail competition will not be allowed **make monopolists buy some power in wholesale markets**	Uses market-based signals to show true cost of this wholesale electricity	If distributors self-generate value this electricity at market-related prices
9	**Create an independent regulator** with good information about costs, service levels and comparative performance of regulated monopolists	Stable independent regulation promotes confidence, private investment, and managerial focus on performance	Political interference with regulators; regulators must have sufficient legal powers, resources (esp. skilled staff), and time to make fair comparisons
10	**Reform the reforms!** Create temporary transition mechanisms that will serve a series of short-term goals – and then replace them	No plan is perfect; learn, then modify as you go	Agents using transition mechanisms to block change rather than promote it

Sources: (Joskow 2006, modified and simplified by Littlechild (2006)[1], Sioshansi (2006)[1] Glachant and Perez (2009)[1], and this author (2013))

We will not go over all the tips, but for Tip 1 one might ask if privatisation is absolutely necessary? Economists usually shy away from making strong political statements, yet this seems an unusually direct piece of political advice. The point that Joskow and the other authors are trying to make when they endorse this, though, is primarily not political but practical. Following our fourth and fifth axioms from Chapter 3, a government and its electorate can still choose to establish and run state-owned utilities, giving them a variety of social objectives (e.g. maximising availability of the service, for instance, for reasons of externalities), and if this is the people's view of what they want from a utility then state-ownership may well be the best vehicle to achieve it. Furthermore there is no inexorable law that says that public utilities *must* be grossly inefficient or hugely distorting – efficiency benchmarking exercises typically show a wide dispersion of efficiency with no clear distinctions between publicly-owned and privately-owned utilities. However, IF the politicians have decided that they really want to improve the efficiency of their electrical utilities, then Joskow and others are saying that in their experience the best way to stop the State from letting any other social objectives get in the way of efficiency improvements is to privatise the utilities and let the managers focus on improving their organisation's performance and efficiency.

Regarding Tip 4 there is no requirement for the ISO to be privatised, or to own the transmission assets: it merely needs to have free rein to control the system as it thinks fit, and to have the legal powers and resources to do so. Examples where it does not own the assets include ERCOT, the ISO which manages 85% of the electricity in Texas[301], and PJM in the eastern USA.

Finally regarding Tip 10 (reform the reforms) we should contrast the experiences of those States which Littlechild rates as successes (in his 2006 review of Joskow's paper) with those he regards as failures. Scandinavia, Argentina, the UK, Texas, and Victoria (in Australia – not discussed here, but examined by Joskow and Littlechild) all started comprehensive reform programmes and then *pursued that goal for more than a decade until they had achieved competition in the contestable markets* (quite often oligopolistic, but given economies of scale this is what one's going to get, especially in retail) *and strict regulation (or at least strong local accountability) of the innate monopolies.* In democratically elected countries this means successive governments must steadily but unwaveringly continue reforms begun by their predecessors – a view we shall see reinforced in the other utilities. No matter how brilliant your plan, or how strong your resolve, you can't expect to change a utility industry in a year. Of course, if you are serious, you had better start with some fundamental changes at the beginning, but, as the case of Argentina shows, you must keep on reforming the industry to achieve the full potential available.

All of these reinforce Tip 9 – create a powerful independent regulator responsible not just for setting regulated prices, but also for promoting and ensuring competition. As Littlechild says, competition is a process of discovery, and a process that has to be actively managed. Part of this means continually checking that the industry's regulator is independent and strong. In the UK, for instance, lobby groups and opposition politicians[302] have argued that after an initially strong and independent start in the twentieth century, the electricity regulator has now been captured by the Big Six retailer/generators.

---

[301] Source: ERCOT website http://www.ercot.com/about/index accessed August 2013.

[302] For instance in 2013 the then-Labour Party Leader Ed Miliband announced the next Labour Government would break up the Big Six retailers, freeze prices, and replace the energy regulator Ofgem with a new regulator that was 'fairer' to consumers. He did not win the 2015 General Election, but his successor, Jeremy Corbyn, has called for equally radical, or even more drastic, reforms.

Appendix: answers to questions about the UK's privatisation

a) Bidding at almost zero prices ensures that all of Nuclear Electric's available capacity will be called into production, but Pool rules mean that the electricity generated will receive the price of the marginal producer plus uplift. So Nuclear Electricity has a very simple profit-maximising strategy: bid very low prices for all available capacity.

b) Given that neither of the two fossil-fuelled players can match Nuclear Electricity's SRMCs, the fossil players must cede all of this market share to Nuclear Electricity. Nuclear Electricity is therefore effectively not in the pricing game, so we are left with prices to be decided between the two fossil-fuelled players. Newbery reports that the two fossil-fuelled generators set the pool price 90% of the time, while Nuclear Electric, Scotland and France "hardly ever set the pool price"[303]. This is a duopoly and Hotelling's model says they should collude on price, and that this solution will be stable. Their behaviour suggests that National Power and PowerGen could have done this 90% of the time.

c) The Energy Minister and the government's economists did not want only two fossil-fuelled generators to be created, but, as we sometimes see (e.g. when wars start accidentally) the situation got out of control and became victim to its own timing. In order to hit the timescale for privatising the electricity industry it became necessary to sell shares in two large generators rather than in several smaller generators.[304] [305]

d) National Power and PowerGen did not 'allow' their market share to decline; it was imposed on them by regulators and the Monopolies and Mergers Commission requiring them to progressively sell off power stations with the explicit purpose of reducing their market share.

---

[303] Newbery op cit page 5

[304] The official story, which is affirmed by several participants, is that National Power (then called 'Big G') was originally to have had 40% of the total capacity and all the nuclear power stations (why did the bankers suggest such a crazy original plan? Because the Prime Minister wanted nuclear privatised, and this was the only way they could see of doing this). But then it became clear – presumably from some kind of opinion polling – that including nuclear power stations with twenty years productive life in them would not achieve a realistic valuation of their future NPVs, and indeed could actually reduce Big G's market valuation. By then it was too late to split up Big G into several smaller companies, and so the actual privatisation of generation consisted of gathering all the fossil fuel plant into two firms and selling it all off in two lumps, Big G (with no nuclear plant) and Little G – a perfect duopoly.

[305] It is possible that in Cabinet discussion of the privatisation a 'national interest' argument may also have played a minor role, in that two large private firms would be more significant players in the global International Power Producers (IPP) market than, say, five smaller companies.

Chapter Ten

Gas restructuring and privatisation

Introduction
Recall from Chapter 1 that most gas companies in the world were formed later than electricity companies and tend to be larger, both geographically and financially. The value chain has nearly always included strong private sector elements, as gas fields were often geologically indistinguishable from oil fields and so are naturally linked to the strongly private sector world oil industry, unless politicians have made determined moves to nationalise gas production in their country. Even if the upstream gas industry is state-owned the private sector is often invited to come in and improve operational efficiency or augment the exploration effectiveness of the nationalised corporation. Downstream the gas transmission networks have developed as fast as needed, the pace dictated by the availability of upstream gas and the spread of distribution networks across cities. Of all state-owned utilities gas is probably the most frequently profitable utility across the world prior to any restructurings and privatisations.

The sources of natural gas
To understand the emergence of successive waves of gas energy it helps to understand five main types of natural gas that we currently believe occur in the earth's crust. Let's begin with some elementary oil and gas geology.

Oil and gas represent the penultimate stage of decomposition of the bodies of plants and animals living on the earth's surface long ago. They have not fully decomposed (the ultimate stage) into carbon dioxide, water amd a few other minerals because their bodies were surrounded by water, mud or sand soon after death, and the surrounding liquid ooze gradually hardened as the entire area sank into the earth's crust and became sedimentary rock overlain by newer sedimentary rocks. Most of these fossil fluid organic remnants were squeezed out onto the earth's surface in the succeeding millions of years and evaporated or decayed in daylight, but in a few places the geology was such that the fluids were trapped in pockets deep underground. The geological features that are necessary to trap and preserve these fluids are
   1. One of the succeeding layers of rock above the fossil fluids must have

been impermeable to oil and gas (a ceiling to stop the fluids rising up to the earth's surface)
2. Preferably there should be also be a floor beneath the fluids to stop the fluids being squeezed down

The American government's Energy Information Administration website has some good general sources of information for students of the gas industry. One excellent schematic, copied in Figure 86, shows five kinds of gas occurring naturally – although there are a few other sources not generally found in the USA, such as gas hydrates (natural gas trapped in ice crystals in permafrost, or on the ocean floor):

Figure 109: The five types of natural gas

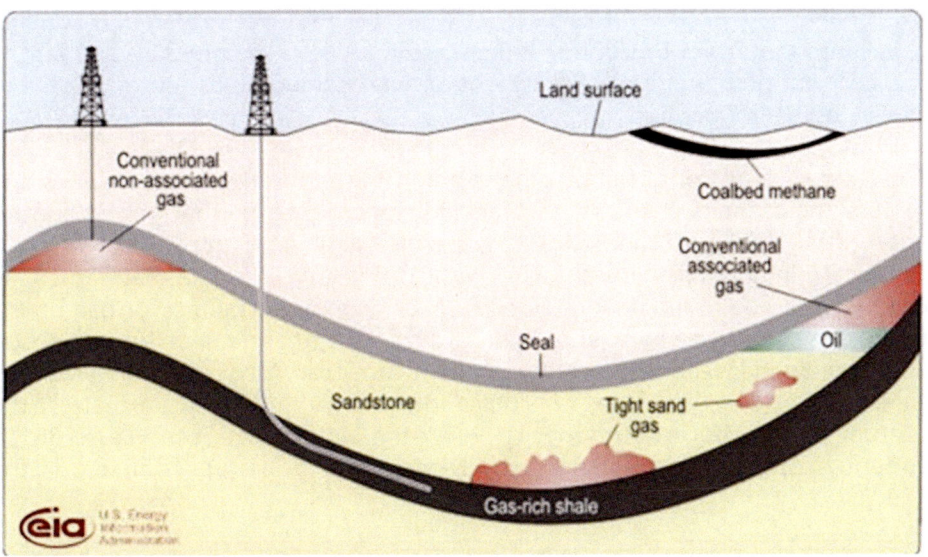

Source EIA website, reproduced with permission[306]

In rough order in which they have generally been found, the five types of gas found naturally in America are:
1. Coalbed methane – methane in coalmines
2. Associated gas – 'wet' gas that was originally produced as a by-product of an oil well
3. Non-associated gas – a pure 'dry' gas field
4. Tight sand gas – gas that is held in compression in the beds below oil fields
5. Gas-rich shale – 'shale gas' that is accessed by fracturing ('fracking') the shale rock below an oil or gas field.

In mediaeval times, miners had long known that coalmines sometimes produced

---

[306] From the EIA's website http://www.eia.gov/kids/energy.cfm?page=natural_gas_home-basics accessed August 2012.

huge quantities of lethal gases, and originally just tried to open up shafts so that this killer gas could be vented out to the atmosphere. Once methane had been recognised as a reliable energy source, and gas grids had been developed (in the twentieth century), it was possible to attempt to cap this gas and sell it off to the gas grid owners. Gas was next generally found in the nineteenth century associated with oil, as the result of natural decomposition processes creating a continuum of alkanes[307] and longer hydrocarbon chains, all the way up to heavy oils. The heavier gases and associated liquids (natural gas liquids) were easier to trap, transport, and sell, while methane was often regarded as a nuisance and flared off, until a nearby gas grid had been developed. By the 1920s methane was finally recognised to be an excellent fossil fluid and was actively sought for the first time in capitalist north America and in the communist Soviet Union. An ideal (non-associated) gas source for humans was a dome (or 'anticline') capped by a sealing layer of rock: this was just what the 'rock doc' ordered. By drilling a well into the top of this dome, humans could relieve the pressure and let the gas flow out quite naturally, the weight of overbearing rock squeezing gas out like water in a fountain.

The last two types of gas source have only emerged in the last fifty years and require the technique known as 'fracking' to produce natural gas at current gas prices. Tight gas sands are "low permeability sandstone reservoirs that produce primarily dry natural gas. A tight gas reservoir is one that cannot be produced at economic flow rates or recover economic volumes of gas unless the well is stimulated by a large hydraulic fracture treatment and/or produced using horizontal wellbores" according to the American Association of Petroleum Geologists[308]. Gas-rich shale is a similar sort of thing but found in shale at the bottom of a hydrocarbon deposit (below the sandstone – see Figure 86.) It currently constitutes a quarter of all US gas production – up from zero in the 1990s.

The North American gas industry
History of the North American gas industry
Although native Americans had found crude oil seeping out and used it to waterproof boats, the history of the modern American petroleum industry began in 1821 when a certain William Hart dug a well 27 feet into coal shales in Fredonia NY, and then bored another 43 feet into the shale to find a source of natural gas[309]. He capped the borehole before piping the methane to the town using hollow wooden logs sealed with tar. The gas was used for lighting in many buildings in Fredonia, as Hart's gas borehole and pipes rapidly attracted rivals. Fredonia became a tourist attraction, and the Fredonia Gas Light Company, formed in 1858, became America's first public gas company.

---

[307] Recall school chemistry? Methane is the lightest (CH_4) followed by ethane (C_2H_6), propane, butane, pentane etc.?.
[308] From the American Association of Petroleum Geologists' Energy Minerals Division website, accessed August 2012, at http://emd.aapg.org/technical_areas/tightGas.cfm
[309] The difference between a well and a bore hole is that you can fall down a well, but a bore hole is too small.

The world oil industry is usually said to have begun in Pennsylvania in 1859 with Edwin Drake's first successful well dug specifically to find crude oil[310]. This thick black liquid was refined and supplied for cooking, heating, lighting and lubrication purposes, until by 1920 the invention of the internal combustion engine, its use in trucks, cars, ships and aircraft, and the mass-production of cars, had started to transform the demand for fuels into the world we know today. Gas was normally seen as the plain younger sister – the unwanted gooseberry even – to oil's global success until the 1920s when oil producers started to develop large fields of non-associated natural gas which they had stumbled upon while prospecting for oil.

Geography of the North American gas industry
At present there are around 5000 individual gas fields, half a million km of large transmission pipes, and over 400 underground storage sites in the USA alone[311]. Figure 110 from the EIA shows that the main modern sources of conventional gas in the lower 48 States of the USA are
1. The Western Gulf / Gulf Cenozoic area in Louisiana around the Mississippi delta, offshore in the Gulf of Mexico, and in southern Texas
2. The Fort Worth and West Texas Permian basin
3. The Anadarko / Arkoma basin of northern Texas and Oklahoma
4. Four basins in Wyoming (making Wyoming the third largest producer after Texas and Louisiana)
5. The Appalachian basin – declining production until the advent of fracking
6. Three more Rocky Mountain basins in Colorado, Utah and New Mexico
7. The Williston basin in North Dakota, which continues into Saskatchewan and Montana

In addition to these there is substantial gas production in Alberta and British Colombia in Canada, and smaller production in Mexico.

---

[310] Edwin Drake's great achievement in finding oil was his invention of a steel casing (a hollow steel tube) to prevent his borehole collapsing in on itself when he went to the great depth of 16 feet; the casing allowed him to continue drilling until he struck oil at 69 feet. Within a day of his finding oil this way his method was copied by rivals.
[311] Data generally come from various EIA publications or websites.

310 | Infrastructure & Utility Economics - Chapter 10

Figure 110: The main sources of 'wet' and 'dry' natural gas in mainland USA

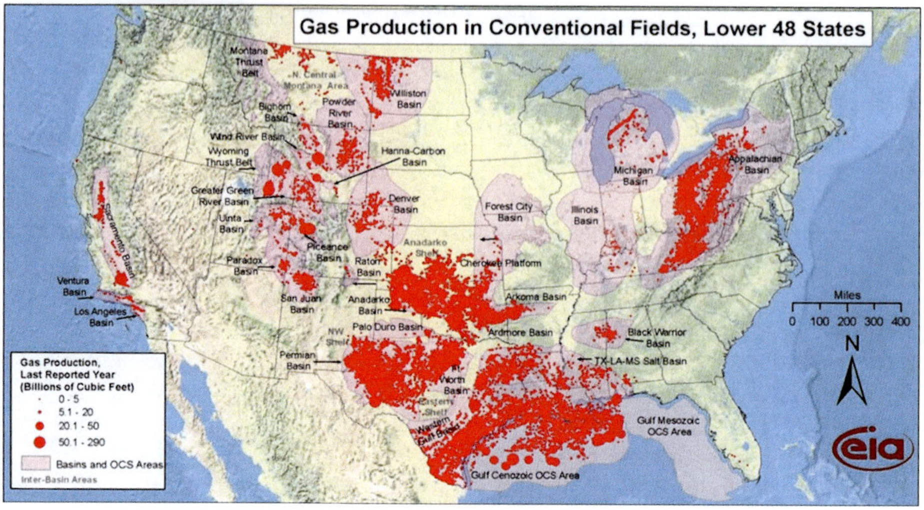

Source: EIA website at http://www.eia.gov/oil_gas/rpd/conventional_gas.jpg reproduced with permission

The other quality that comes across clearly from Figure 110 is how diversified production is: there really are thousands of fields and no great natural concentrations at all. The same is true in Canada: the world's third largest gas producer, after the USA and Russia, also has thousands of gas fields but no 'giant' or 'supergiant' fields. Given that it is a commodity product, if ownership could be kept as as fragmented as the fields, and if it were not for the sunk cost of building the pipelines to move the stuff, natural gas would be a textbook example of perfect competition!

Growth of the North American gas grid
In the late 19th and early 20th centuries gas was found on a small scale across many parts of continental North America and local pipelines were built to send it to local towns and cities. As more gas continued to be found in the 1940s and 50s transmission grids grew to connect the South in the USA with northern States, and gas from the Rockies to the centres of population further east. Almost half of the entire US gas transmission grid was built in the 1950s and 60s, and the same is true in Canada, where the TransCanada and West Coast pipelines were completed in 1957.

Both the USA and Canada have significant storage that can be drawn down in emergencies, and the Canadian grid is entirely integrated with the US system. Canada exports around a quarter of its production to the USA, and continues to find significant quantities of conventional and shale gas in Alberta and British Colombia, but production and exports have fallen in recent years due to the significant rise in domestic US production from tight sand gas, shale gas and coalbed methane which has enabled the USA to overtake Russia as the world's largest gas producer. Figure 111 shows how Canadian production has fallen since 2005 while US production has risen:

Figure 111: North American gas production since 1970 (Bcf pa)

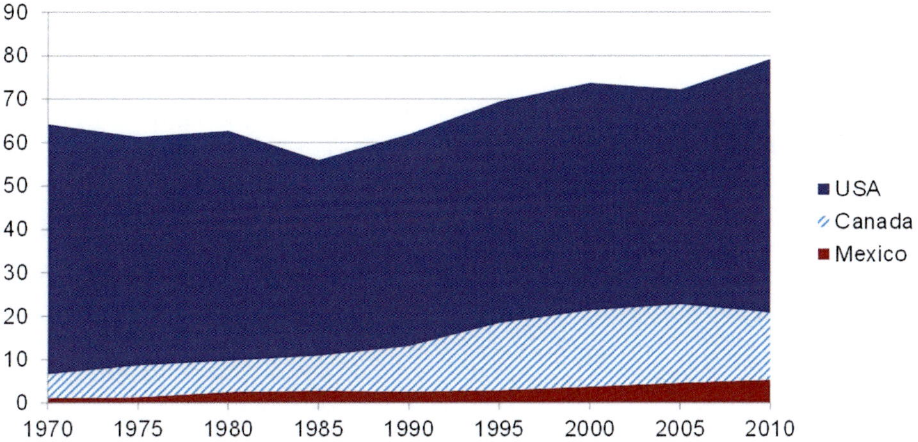

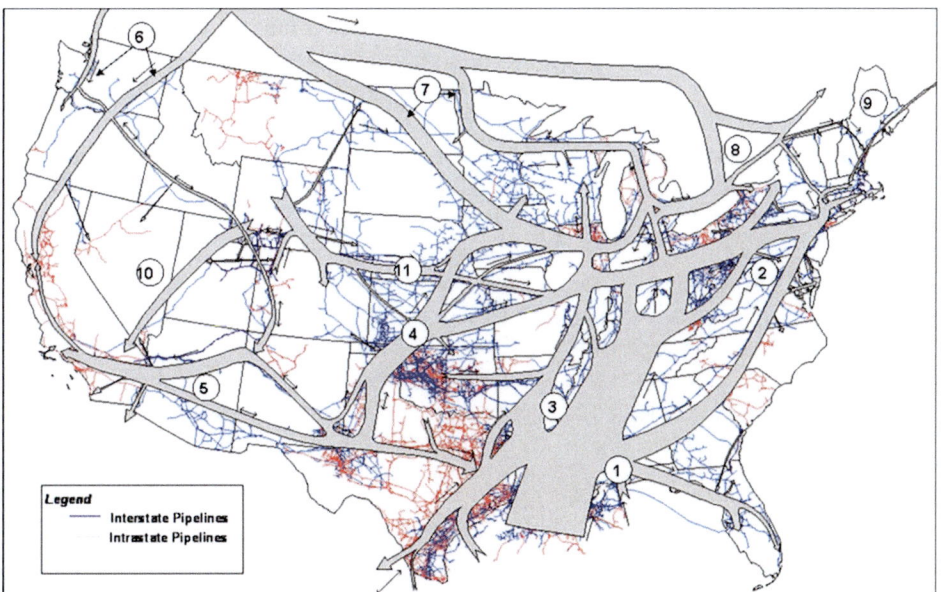

Source: BP Statistical Review of World Energy 2012 Gas Production since 1970 in bcf per year

Figure 112 shows the main gas movement routes within the USA, including imports from Canada and exports to Mexico:

Figure 112: The main gas transport routes of North America

Source: Energy Information Administration website[312]

---

[312] EIA's website main gas transportation corridors, accessed August 2012 http://www.eia.gov/pub/oil_gas/natural_gas/analysis_publications/ngpipeline/transcorr_map.html

So we see that the main movements of gas in the USA are towards the midwest (e.g. Ohio) from the Gulf, from Canada, and from Oklahoma, with submovements west to California, and up and down the eastern seaboard from the Gulf.

Fundamental competition issues of North American gas markets
Recalling the gas industry value chain we fundamentally observe in North America
- *Fragmented production* from thousands of fields in two supplying countries
- A *dense transmission network* which should be able to transport gas from almost anywhere to anywhere in the lower 48 States (or Canada), including several rival routes for most common city-pair combinations
- Over *70 million retail customers*[313] spread across the continent

Given the strong private sector origins of the industry, therefore, the only competition issues might in principle relate only to
1. Regulation of the innate local monopolies of *distribution* grids in each city or region, or
2. Any *concentrations of ownership* among producers, transmission grids or buyers.

Deregulation of the retail gas monopolies
However, in practice the local monopoly distributors of gas referred to in 1 above also usually became the monopoly *retailers* of natural gas in most American and Canadian cities, who were typically regulated by State economic regulators. In the 1960s and 70s various national politicians tried to deregulate parts of the regulated transport network, including Presidents Nixon, Ford, and Carter, and to extend this to the energy networks. After the first OPEC oil price hike of 1973 President Carter signed an Emergency Natural Gas Act in 1977 at Federal level to regulate and de-regulate parts of the gas industry, which led 21 States ultimately to introduce Natural Gas Choice Programs.

Natural Gas Choice Programs
These Programs allow domestic and small commercial customers the freedom to choose their natural gas supplier (retailer), thus restricting the monopolists to their core function of the distribution monopoly. Figure 113 shows the state of these programs nationally in 2009:

---

[313] Canada has 6 million gas customers (source Canadian Gas Association), and the USA has 65m (source EIA).

Figure 113: States with Natural Gas Choice Programs in 2009

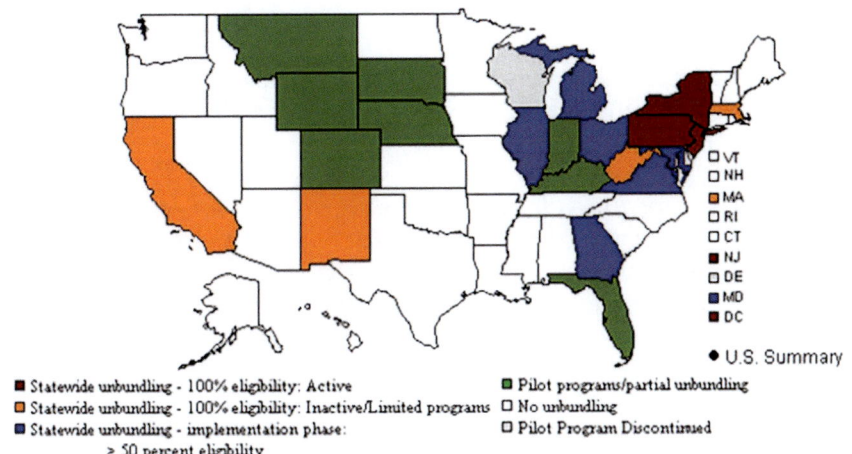

Source EIA website August 2012 http://www.eia.gov/energyexplained/index.cfm?page=natural_gas_customer_choice

However, Figure 113 does not look especially healthy: although in theory 54% of the USA's 65m gas consumers have a choice, most of the 21 States' Programs are inactive (e.g. California), stuck in implementation (e.g. Illinois), or have been abandoned or are still at the Pilot Stage (e.g. Florida). Still being implemented, or at the pilot stage, a third of a century after being Federally encouraged suggests we might see significant gas retail choice nationwide by the 22nd century. Alternatively, we might not! An external observer might conclude that the process has run into some determined local or State opposition – or even lobbying and vested interests.

Not everywhere is resisting retail competition. Natural Gas Choice Programs allow independent retailers to emerge who will buy gas wholesale, ship it to the customer's city, wheel it through the distributor's pipes and sell it on to the final consumer. *Provided sufficient retailers emerge* competition-in-the-market should ensue and consumers will actually have a choice, while the monopolist is restricted to its core local monopoly functions. Of course that proviso is a significant condition: independent retailers cannot be obliged to enter the market, and have to choose to enter it, weighing up the costs of general marketing and persuading individual customers to switch against the likely gross profit margins they will make from those customers. And, being gas – a derived demand and a commodity product – we know most customers are likely to switch on price grounds, unless an enterprising retailer can devise ingenious new tariffs or fascinating additional services which incumbent monopolists cannot, or will not, imitate.

So even where retail gas competition is legally allowed there may be none in practice. Overall, though, the EIA reports that by 2009 around 15% of the 35m eligible customers had switched from their incumbent distributors to independent retailers ('marketers'). Note though, that residents in just three States – Ohio, Georgia and New York – accounted for three quarters of all the switching customers[314].

Other concentrations of market power in American gas markets

Let us return to the other possible causes of market power in the North American gas industry and consider them in turn.

Producer power –measured by a Herfindahl-Hirschman Index
Given that there are five thousand gas fields, and none of them on a global scale is giant, the only way for there to be a concentration of market power is if field ownership is concentrated in a few hands. Current production figures by producer are shown in Table 8. These show no great concentration of field ownership: the market leader, Exxon, had 12% of the market in 2011, and the four largest have around a third of the total market. One could draw another concentration ratio at the largest 12 producers with two thirds of the market, but where does one stop? This 'exponential decay' distribution is typical of most industries, and so a general measure of market concentration was proposed by Hirschman in 1945 and Herfindahl in 1950 which is the sum of the squares of market shares. Their reasoning for squaring market shares was that very large market shares have a much bigger potential for influence in a market than medium market shares – i.e. one firm with a 30% share has far more power than three firms with 10% each. A Herfindahl-Hirschman Index (HHI) using the modern working definition – where we square the market shares as percentages – is also shown in Table 1. This modern HHI measure can range from 0 (perfect competition) to 10,000 (=100 x 100) for an absolute monopoly, or 5000 for an equal duopoly (= 2,500 + 2,500), and several competition authorities use a rule that an HHI measure above 1000 or 1500 indicates a concentration of market power sufficient to trigger a competition investigation.

Table 1: Calculating a Herfindahl-Hirschman Index (HHI) of US gas producers for 2011

Rank	US 2011 Gas Production by Producer	Daily Volume (mcf a day)	Market Share (%)	100 x Market Share	Square of this	Cumulative Square
1	Exxon Mobil	3917	12.0%	12	143	143
2	Chesapeake Energy	2751	8.4%	8.4	70	213
3	Anadarko	2334	7.1%	7.1	51	264
4	Devon Energy	2027	6.2%	6.2	38	302
5	Encana	1879	5.7%	5.7	33	335
6	BP	1843	5.6%	5.6	32	367

---

[314] EIA website ibid, accessed August 2012.

Infrastructure & Utility Economics - Chapter 10 | 315

Rank	US 2011 Gas Production by Producer	Daily Volume (mcf a day)	Market Share (%)	100 x Market Share	Square of this	Cumulative Square
7	ConocoPhillips	1617	4.9%	4.9	24	391
8	Southwestern Energy Co.	1368	4.2%	4.2	17	409
9	Chevron	1279	3.9%	3.9	15	424
10	WPX Energy Inc.	1133	3.5%	3.5	12	436
11	EOG Resources	1113	3.4%	3.4	12	447
12	Royal Dutch Shelll plc	967	3.0%	3	9	456
13	Apache	865	2.6%	2.6	7	463
14	Petrohawk Energy Corp	853	2.6%	2.6	7	470
15	Occidental	782	2.4%	2.4	6	476
16	Ultra Petroleum	649	2.0%	2	4	479
17	QEP Resources	648	2.0%	2	4	483
18	El Paso Energy	632	1.9%	1.9	4	487
19	EQT Resources	497	1.5%	1.5	2	489
20	Cabot Oil & Gas	490	1.5%	1.5	2	492
21	Exco Resources	488	1.5%	1.5	2	494
22	Newfield Exploration	480	1.5%	1.5	2	496
23	Range Resources	398	1.2%	1.2	1	497
24	Noble Energy Inc.	388	1.2%	1.2	1	499
25	Pioneer Naturak	344	1.0%	1	1	500
26	Cimarex Energy	329	1.0%	1	1	501
27	Marathon	326	1.0%	1	1	502
28	Plains Exploration & Production	306	0.9%	0.9	1	503
29	SM Energy Company	275	0.8%	0.8	1	504
30	Quicksilver Resources	263	0.8%	0.8	1	504
31	Forest Oil	242	0.7%	0.7	1	505
32	Energen Resources Corporation	196	0.6%	0.6	0	505
33	SandRidge Energy	190	0.6%	0.6	0	506
34	Linn Energy	175	0.5%	0.5	0	506
35	W&T Offshore, Inc.	147	0.4%	0.4	0	506

Rank	US 2011 Gas Production by Producer	Daily Volume (mcf a day)	Market Share (%)	100 x Market Share	Square of this	Cumulative Square
36	MDU Resources	125	0.4%	0.4	0	506
37	McMoRan Exploration	123	0.4%	0.4	0	506
38	Unit Corporation	121	0.4%	0.4	0	506
39	Stone Energy	108	0.3%	0.3	0	507
40	Hess Corporation	100	0.3%	0.3	0	507
40 = Approximately "Whole Market"		32,768	100%	100	507	= HHI

Source: Natural Gas Supply Association based on published company records; includes Alaska

Note that for simplicity I have assumed that the entire market is just the largest 40 American producers. In fact it is *likely there are thousands of producers*: although one firm can own several hundred large fields, it is quite common for firms or individuals to own only a share of a field, so the smallest thousand fields might be owned by five thousand owners, each with a small share of a small field. Be thankful I have simplified; real economics is messy.

So the Herfindahl-Hirschman Index of US Natural gas producers is around 500[315]. In 1982 the Justice Department adopted the HHI as its default measure of industry concentration; its current (2010) horizontal merger guidelines state that a market with an HHI up to 1500 is 'unconcentrated', a market of 1500-2500 is 'moderately concentrated', and one above 2500 is 'highly concentrated'[316]. The US gas producers market is therefore unconcentrated and would not warrant investigation in the USA, or other countries using similar measures, such as Mexico or the UK. A cartel would be highly illegal, and of course there is no such suggestion, but, just operationally it would be hard to see how, say, the top ten or twenty gas producers could organise a successful implicit or secret cartel, given the thousands of other producers, significant imports from Canada, and shippers' capacity to import significant LNG from around the world. In addition spot, future and forward wholesale markets exist, are thickly traded, and keenly analysed by traders and regulators alike.

Transmission market power
What about a concentration of market power among the owners of transmission pipes? In Canada the National Energy Board (NEB) has had responsibility for monitoring all aspects of Canadian energy since 1959. 70% of Canadian gas

---

[315] Adding another 1000 small producers each with 0.0001% shares is not going to raise the HHI any more; adding in producers 31 to 40 only raised the HHI from 504 to 507. Furthermore adding in the joint production of 1000 small producers increases the size of the total market, so reducing the market shares (and thus the HHI) of the top 40.
[316] Available at http://www.justice.gov/atr/public/guidelines/hmg-2010.html

comes from Alberta, including the vast majority of exports, and Albertan gas was linked into the US system in the 1950s, before it was linked to Ontario. The seven major long distance Canadian pipelines are, naturally, local monopolies, and so are regulated by the NEB using variants of Rate-of-Return models; the NEB's latest reports show these pipelines earning Returns On Equity of 7½ - 11¼% in 2009[317].

In the USA the Federal Energy Regulatory Commission (FERC), or its predecessor the Federal Power Commission, has had responsibility for regulating interstate gas pipelines and wholesale gas sales since the 1938 Natural Gas Act. A 1954 Supreme Court decision gave FERC responsibility for setting wellhead gas prices, but these were removed in 1983 under President Reagan, as one of his major deregulation initiatives. FERC undertook to promote more competition in energy markets at that time, and produces many regular analyses of oil and gas markets.

The FERC regulates interstate gas pipelines using a standard Cost of Service model[318] where

Allowed Cost-of-Service Revenue = Allowed Return (= Rate Base X Overall Rate of Return)
    Plus   Operation & Maintenance Expenses
                 Admin & General Expenses
                 Depreciation
                 Non-Income Taxes
                 Income Taxes
    Less   Revenue Credits.

The allowed overall rate of return is usually set as the actual weighted average of the firm's debt and equity, with an allowed cost of debt for a 'Baa' rated bond, while the allowed cost of equity "is derived from a range of equity returns developed using a Discounted Cash Flow (DCF) analysis of a proxy group of publicly held natural gas companies". As examples the manual mentions a cost of debt of 8¼% and a 14% Return on Equity as allowable for a new pipeline company, which combined with a 70% (debt) gearing gives an overall allowed rate of return of 9.975% after tax. It is beyond the scope of an introductory text to assess the actual profits earned by interstate gas pipelines, although the FERC admits that to achieve a robust network it has had to allow "good" returns on gas transmission pipes[319]. However, it is clear that any generous profits earned are not due to excessive *market* power by the regulatees but either to successful

---

[317] NEB Canadian Pipeline Transportation System – Transportation Assessment 2009, Table 4.2.
[318] FERC Cost-of-Service Manual 1999 available at www.ferc.gov/industries/gas/gen-info/cost-of-service-manual.doc
[319] Commissioner Moeller's Australian presentation November 2010, slide 25, available at www.ret.gov.au/Documents/app/_documents/moeller-usa.ppt

regulatory case-making, or the easy cost-pass-through characteristics and possibly generous allowed profits innate in Cost-of-service regulation.

Local monopolies and thin markets
Chapter 9's explanation of California's failed electricity restructuring mentioned an unsavoury episode in which firms traded gas at a key border location where in fact gas was thinly traded; with a few large trades one significant player was able to move a key local market. Is this kind of exploitation of a local monopoly or a thin market possible more generally? It might not affect national figures, but could conceivably allow a few companies to squirrel away some tidy local monopoly profits.

Yes, this is always possible, and there is no defence against it except a vigorous and vigilant police force: adequately empowered, funded and staffed regulators or competition authorities.

North American gas market conclusions
So in general we conclude that the US gas industry is unlikely to suffer from abuse of market power at the producer stage, and that the transmission and distribution stages of the value chain are generally Cost-of-Service regulated, so any weaknesses there lie with the form and process of regulation, but there could be significant market power from local distribution grids carried over into the retail chain for as many as 47 of the 50 States.

The UK: exploding a vertically integrated monopoly after privatisation

In the UK because this was the second of the Thatcher government's utility privatisations (after telecommunications) with 20/20 hindsight almost everyone would now agree that the British Government made major mistakes and learned valuable lessons from its flotation of the state-owned monopoly British Gas. Recall that in this era Chile and the UK were pioneering the restructuring and privatisation of utilities (starting in 1985) and there had been little time to learn lessons. The USA's model of fragmented privatised utilities checked by Rate of Return regulation was not thought to be a good model for the rest of the world, even by such admirers of Ronald Reagan as Margaret Thatcher and General Pinochet. The British privatisation was therefore rushed and there was no attempt prior to privatisation to restructure the vertically integrated monopoly of British Gas, in part due to the government's desire to maximise sales receipts, and partly due to tactical brinkmanship by the forceful CEO of the utility.

Background
In the 1960s natural gas had been discovered quite close to the British coastline in the North Sea and over the next thirty years oil and gas fields were developed by many private companies. In 1973 the British state-owned gas industry was restructured into the British Gas Corporation (BG), in order to develop a national transmission system to spread the gas around the country and to expand the distribution of gas from town gas networks into surrounding rural areas[320]. As

oil and gas continued to be found in the '70s and '80s, private sector oil and gas firms were awarded long exploration and production licences with high rates of marginal taxation offset by allowances for capital expenditure to develop the fields; British Gas joined some of these venture as an offshore gas explorer and producer. Oil was usually regarded as more valuable because it could be sold freely on world oil markets while gas could only realistically be sold to British Gas: to get to alternative continental European markets would have required a major pipeline down the middle of the North Sea which was too expensive for the owner of a single gas field to contemplate. In fact this was completed, but a decade later, by a Norwegian / German partnership in 1995[321].

So a typical private sector gas producer in the British sector of the North Sea could effectively sell their gas only to British Gas and would need to make a long term contract to justify the large sunk costs of developing the field in the first place. It was therefore obvious that a wholesale gas market similar to that developed for British electricity could not realistically be promoted when privatising BG. As the only buyer (a *monopsonist*) British Gas (BG) could drive prices down depending on their need for this gas. They showed no inclination to export surplus gas to any other markets in continental Europe, nor to allow gas producers to use BG's transmission pipes to wheel gas through to south east England, where short undersea pipelines could have been constructed to gas networks in Belgium and northern France. Having a state-sanctioned monopoly of the transmission and distribution pipes in the UK, British Gas had 'cornered the market' for gas around this island in north western Europe.

The top half of Figure 114 shows how the UK's gas industry was structured in 1985:

Figure 114: Privatisation of British Gas

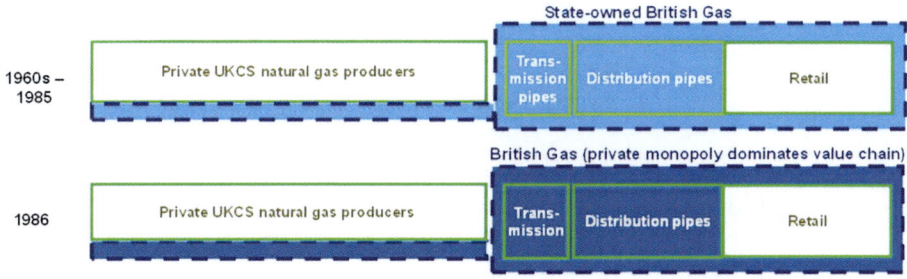

Given this double monopsony-and-monopoly it was not surprising that British Gas should dominate the gas value chain in the 1980s, nor that its profits were a significant source of revenue for the government, equivalent to a percentage

---

[320] The penetration of gas into British households subsequently rose from 70% to 83% by 1999 (source: http://www.eci.ox.ac.uk/research/energy/downloads/countrypictures/cp_uk.pdf)

[321] Europipe 1 commissioned in 1995 was followed by Europipe 2 in 1999.

point or two off income tax[322]. Being the Conservative Government's second major privatisation, Mrs Thatcher told Energy Secretary Peter Walker to privatise BG quickly. The investment bankers advising the government said privatisation of BG as a single profitable monopoly was the quickest way to float the company and would maximise sales receipts. Economists and oil and gas companies warned Walker of the competition consequences of privatising such a mammoth company with multiple monopolies, but BG's CEO, Dennis Rooke, threatened to resign if Walker split up the company, which would have put the flotation back by half a year at least. So Walker privatised BG as a vertically integrated national transmission, distribution and supply monopoly with significant upstream interests, as shown in Figure 114, and BG was able to continue dominating the UK gas value chain for many years.

How to abuse your market position / play to your strategic strengths
After privatisation other players in the gas industry immediately complained about BG's practices and a Monopolies and Mergers Commission (MMC, which later became the Competition Commission) investigation was ordered by the Director General of Fair Trading (DGFT) in 1987. Thus began a lengthy series of investigations by the DGFT and MMC which continued for the next ten years, as the initially limited powers of Ofgas were progressively increased and the monopoly power of BG was slowly whittled away by Ministers and the general competition authorities. To give a flavour of these investigations the very first inquiry (MMC 1988) concluded that BG
1. refused to publish open prices to industrial customers,
2. practised extensive price discrimination between its non-tariff (industrial) customers, (its selling prices were inversely related to the ease with which a customer could switch fuels),
3. refused to supply 'interruptible' gas to some customers (interruptible gas is much cheaper than normal gas and is supplied only to those large industrial customers who have their own storage or can choose when to burn gas in large quantities) and
4. refused to make the terms for access to its pipe network commonly available.

In short BG's practices in this era seemed the very definition of 'abuse of a dominant position' (see European Union Article 102 in Chapter 8)[323].

Breaking-up British Gas 1994-1998
British Gas was a huge corporation, one of the largest on the London Stock Exchange, with a predominantly male engineering culture. Regulation was a novel concept in Europe. After eight years of this 'rogue elephant' private corporation trampling over gas consumers and other gas players, in 1994 a little-known Treasury economist, Claire Spottiswoode, was appointed economic

---

[322] i.e. without the profits from British Gas the Treasury would have had to set income tax rates 1-2% higher.
[323] Does this remind you of John D Rockefeller a hundred years earlier?

regulator of the gas industry. Not always consistent, highly interventionist (happy to micro-manage the regulatee), and liable to send flowers to colleagues, Spottiswoode was not everyone's idea of a gas regulator, but this was no routine regulatory situation. She and a few staff worked out of a small unprepossessing office in London, and were largely ignored by the giant macho corporation of BG, which preferred to negotiate directly with government Ministers and top officials about key issues such as energy policy, tax breaks and access to its pipelines.

Legal separation of the gas businesses
Backed by the government, new legal powers, and findings by the DGFT and MMC, Claire Spottiswoode started to get a grip on British Gas – and then to carve it up. British Gas, which had fought a determined rearguard action, continued to prevaricate, to the growing annoyance of Ministers and the regulator, causing Ofgas to become close micro-managers of BG. BG itself became annoyed by 'regulators who know nothing' of gas engineering getting involved in the minutiae of the Network Code that was then being developed between BG, Ofgas and the private gas shippers. This Code was critical to separating the pipe transmission and distribution businesses from the retail and production ends of the value chain, by allowing all "shippers" equal access in principle to the monopoly pipes businesses. The regulator, on the other hand could not allow BG to dictate this Code to its own advantage, which was the natural inclination of most of the BG staff deputised to negotiate with the shippers to create this new beast: if the pipe monopolies were ever to be separated from the production and retail businesses it was critical to allow all shippers equal access in principle to the monopoly pipe businesses, and the Network Code defined those access rules. And in these negotiations delay was a strong tactic used by BG to block any move it did not want: the longer it took to reach agreement the more months BG had to exploit its double monopoly and stop the Code coming into force.

Eventually the hard job was done, the Government passed the 1995 Gas Act, in which licences in the industry were awarded by the regulator (no longer the government), and it would become illegal for a gas transporter (a pipeline operator) to hold a gas shipper's or retailer's licence, and a workable first version of the Network Code was launched in March 1996. Because of the new Gas Act BG was forced in February 1997 to divide itself into
    1.   A national retail company using the well-known brand name British Gas, owned by a new company called Centrica (shareholders in BG were given shares in Centrica)
    2.   A transmission and distribution monopoly called Transco, owned by BG plc, which renamed itself Lattice Group in 2000[324]
    3.   Upstream gas production and storage fields that were split between Centrica and BG.

---

[324] Presumably the cheapest name available in the Corporate Name bank.

Two developments complemented this legal break up of British Gas plc. From 1994 to 1998 a wholesale market for gas involving shippers on the UK Continental Shelf (UKCS) and large gas users gradually emerged. Active among the large gas consumers were new gas-fired power station operators taking advantage of gas being allowed to be burned in power stations (the 'Dash For Gas'), the decline of inefficient old coal-fired power stations in the Revised Pool wholesale electricity market, and more gas coming on stream from the North Sea. A surge of gas production combined with slippages in the construction of these efficient gas-powered stations created a bubble of gas which was released onto the embryonic spot and futures markets, causing spot prices to decline from 18p/therm to 10p/therm in 1995 and to stay around 12p for the next three years. This fundamentally changed the nature of the UK gas market[325]: for the first time a wholesale gas market between producers and bulk consumers had developed serious volumes of business in the UK, and it was not going to go away.

The other development was that in April 1996, one month after the Network Code was launched, retail competition in the 'franchise market' (domestic consumers) was inaugurated as a trial in the South West Distribution zone, rapidly followed in the other seven distribution zones. By December 1998 retail competition for households across the UK had been attempted, and was succeeding. Centrica's market share had fallen from 100% to a plateau around 75%, with entrants being able to win customers over by offering substantially lower prices than 'British Gas', based not on any efficiency gains[326] but on the significantly lower spot and short term prices they were able to obtain in the wholesale gas market[327]. The situation was now as shown in the top part of Figure 115:

Figure 115: Restructuring of the privatised UK gas industry 1995-2007

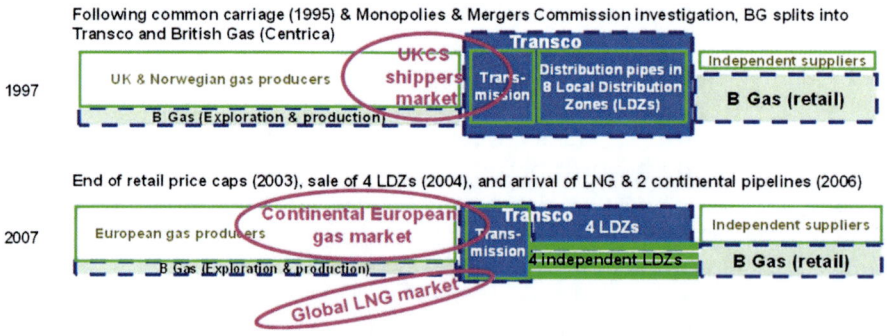

---

[325] Newbery David M *Privatization, Restructuring and Regulation of Network Utilities 2001*, The MIT Press, Cambridge Massachusetts, page 372.
[326] The entrants had to establish energy trading companies, acquire billing systems and lists of potential customers, advertise themselves, and actually persuade customers to 'sign on the dotted line' and switch away from British Gas, all for a normal retail margin around £20-30 a customer a year. The author recalls energy players and consultants at the time estimating it cost around £50 to win one new energy customer.
[327] Newbery p 375

Levelling the playing field

With the back of the beast broken one might have thought abuse of a dominant position was dying. But BG was still in an incredibly strong position: through Transco BG controlled the entire national transmission and distribution system, and the entire national storage system consisting of the Rough gas field, the Hornsea salt cavity, and five LNG sites, which were used to store gas in the summer and release it for the winter peak. Matching this, through its retail arm Centrica, BG owned a major gas field (Morecambe Bay) with large 'swing capacity' (production could be varied to shadow demand), had 75% of the national gas market, a national brand name known by 100% of British energy consumers[328], the freedom to attack the entire national electricity market – following deregulation of the electricity industrial, commercial and domestic markets (see Chapter 9) – and some old long term contracts supplying it with cheap gas (as well as more expensive modern long term contracts). This was far from a 'level playing field': it was still strongly tilted towards the incumbent.

Post 1998 reforms to promote upstream competition

The private sector shippers, the government, the regulator, and the MMC therefore combined to continue to reduce BG's and Centrica's market dominance in ways:

1. As already mentioned, two Europipe gas pipelines going down the middle of the North Sea in 1995 and 1998 offered potential UK Continental Shelf (British) gas producers the possibility of a route to continental European buyers, providing a potential link between the two main European gas systems so that prices might not diverge too grossly;
2. To open up the storage market the regulator and MMC told BG to auction capacity in its Rough and Hornsea storage facilities, subject to no single bidder buying more than 20% of capacity; these auctions were held in 1999, releasing 83% and 100% of the storage capacity respectively[329]. Stripped of their tactical value in the gas market, BG/Lattice sold off its Rough and Hornsea assets over the next two years.
3. Originally designed to export UKCS gas, a 235km undersea 'Interconnector' between Bacton in England and Zeebrugge in Belgium was opened in 1998, directly linking UK gas flows and prices to mainland European export prices; from 2005, as UKCS production declined, compressors were installed to allow reverse flows, so that after 2007 the Interconnector could export up to 20bcm and import up to 25 bcm a year (23% of annual consumption) into the UK[330]; this gas could be Dutch, Russian or even Norwegian;

---

[328] The rival electricity retailers competing in the gas market (such as Manweb and London Electricity) were well known in their own areas but much less well known outside their original geographical electricity monopolies, while in the electricity market everyone had heard of British Gas.

[329] Ofgem 2000 cited in Hawdon D and Stevens N 'Regulatory Reform of the UK Gas Market: The Case of the Storage Auction', *Fiscal Studies* 2001 vol 22 No. 2 p 230'

[330] Source: The Interconnector's website at http://www.interconnector.com/index.html

4. A second direct pipe (the BBL from Anna Paulowna in the Netherlands to Bacton) was commissioned in 2006, allowing 15bcm more continental European gas to be imported into the UK (14% of consumption); again this gas could be Dutch, Russian or Norwegian;
5. In 2007 a 1,166km undersea pipeline from the large Ormen Lange gas field connected Norwegian gas fields directly to the UK; more interestingly its intersection in the middle of the North Sea at the Sleipner platform also connected these fields to the southbound Europipes, thus potentially allowing Norwegian producers to switch destinations depending on medium term prices in the UK and continental European markets;
6. Three terminals importing Liquefied Natural Gas (LNG) into the UK were developed this century; the first on the Isle of Grain opened in 2005 and can now handle 12% of UK consumption, while the second two in Milford Haven in Wales are capable of handling 25% of the UK's consumption; the long term contract sources of this gas are Algeria and Qatar; note that LNG terminals also provide storage, and even a competitive alternative to the transmission network, as they are in the south, where the bulk of demand is.

Chapter 1 noted that even ahead of any appraisal of the prospects for shale gas, Europe is well placed to import pipeline gas from three continents (Europe, Africa and Asia), and it is clear from the above that the North Sea has several grids crossing it, so that producers can now move gas to buyers across north west Europe, including the UK and Ireland. Correspondingly wholesale gas prices across north west Europe should be much closer, and price differences may be larger across time (spot vs medium or long term) than across internal political divisions. In addition Europe has significant LNG re-gasification terminals. Given that LNG has been a 'buyers market'[331] for many years, and supplies can come from a dozen countries around the world, western Europe is one of the main global markets setting prices for gas, and British players, as both producers and consumers, are at the heart of that market. Consequently the upstream position of the UK gas market changed completely between 1997 and 2007: as shown in the bottom half of Figure 2, there is now strong competition to supply all north western Europe, including the UK, with wholesale bulk gas at prices that could be said to be as close to current world spot levels as practical.

Downstream competition and regulation within the UK since 1998
Given the demise of British Gas and that the UK has increasingly purchased gas at free-market world levels, the challenge for regulators has been to manage competition within the retail sector and to regulate the monopoly pipeline businesses.

---

[331] A market where desired supply substantially exceeds desired demand, so that buyers generally hold the upper hand.
[332] An industry name for British Gas, EDF Energy, E.ON, RWE npower, ScottishPower, and Scottish and Southern Energy.

Retail competition

Compared to 1998 when Centrica, through its brand name British Gas, had 100% of the gas market and no electricity customers, by 2010 'The Big Six'[332] energy companies had 99% of domestic consumers. Centrica's market share of gas-only customers has of course fallen, but only from 100% to 75%, while the Big 5 electricity retailers still average a 73% market share of electricity-only customers in their former monopoly areas[333]. So, since domestic competition has been allowed (and competition is generally acknowledged to have been fairly intense) the end result after 12 years of intense competition is that three quarters of customers have not changed from (or changed and then gone back to) their original incumbent monopolist retailers. Of course millions of customers have switched suppliers, 16½ m customers have switched to an out-of-area electricity retailer, and nearly 17 m customers have decided to get both fuels from the same supplier, none of which was possible before domestic markets were opened to competition. So one cannot say the results have been negligible.

Ofgem currently believes, though, that half the UK's domestic customers are "disengaged" (not responding to any new tariffs or marketing innovations) or "permanently disengaged" (never have switched, never will), while another quarter are "passive" (have switched in the past, but not switched in the last year, and probably will not switch again)[334]. One reason for this is the plethora of tariffs facing UK energy customers: this has gone from around a dozen in 1998 (for any individual householder) to 200 in 2007 to 400 in 2011[335]. Even for active customers (the remaining quarter) this is a ferocious task to keep up with, and most people just ignore it. Ofgem has decided that too much choice is a bad thing when it comes to 400 energy tariffs, and is taking action to require retailers to simplify their tariff numbers and structures.

Regulation

The memorably-named Lattice Group was bought by National Grid in 2001 and Transco's assets kept separate. On the distribution side, Chapter 2 has already referred to Transco's 2004 sale of 4 of its 8 Local Distribution Zones to independent gas transporters, indicating that the professionals who manage these operations do not see significant economies of scale in operating gas distribution networks at a level of 1m or more customers. The regulator – Ofgem by this stage – was keen to develop yardstick regulation using independent comparators, and believed that having different owners and operators for these otherwise unchanged LDZs would improve the dynamics of comparative competition.

Regulation of the high pressure National Transmission System (NTS) has followed the same broad yardstick framework described in Chapter 8. Comparative competition of the NTS has been developed by reviewing all the energy

---

[333] Ofgem 2011 Retail Market Review Figure 2.5 page 31
[334] Ofgem ibid page 29
[335] Ofgem ibid Fig 2.1 page 22

transmission grids (the NTS in gas, the two electricity transmission grids in Scotland, and the national electricity grid in England and Wales) at the same time. The allowed after-tax rate of return on all transmission grids was set at 4.4% plus inflation in 2006, compared with 4.8% plus inflation for the distribution grids. This is far lower this than the 10% return allowed by the FERC on p 317.

Other gas examples – Japan

Although Russia has enormous gas reserves, is the world's biggest gas exporter, and has 50m gas consumers, we will not examine the industry here because it was distorted by massive corruption in the 1990s, which is unlikely to be illuminating to economics students. You don't need an economics textbook to tell you that corruption is massively inefficient. When two of the prime suspects sued each other in the London Courts a few years ago the average economics student should sympathise with the average Russian citizen, who just sees a huge loss of economic rent that could have been used for the welfare of all Russians. Instead, we shall look at a country that is the opposite of Russia – Japan, the world's largest importer of natural gas.

The test of any scientific theory is 'Does it lead to useful counter-intuitive predictions[336]?' By now you have sufficient knowledge of utility theory to be given just a few bare facts, and for you to make your own predictions about what the Japanese gas industry should be like.

Japan Quiz (for non-Japanese readers):
The sole facts I will tell you are that Japan is an advanced industrial economy with a little coal and some nuclear power, but no oil or natural gas production to speak of; there are no gas fields with exportable production within 4000km of the main Japanese islands[337].

Using the facts above predict the answers to the following questions:

Supply:
1. What transport mechanism will be used to move gas from gas fields to Japan?
2. From where (roughly) would you expect Japan to source its gas?
3. Per thermal unit, do you predict gas will be cheaper than other fuels in Japan?
4. Given the transport mechanism, will the supply hubs for gas within Japan be concentrated in one or two places, or will they be spread out?

---

[336] Predictions you could not make just using common sense. Common sense is essential in business and economics, but beware: common sense tells you the earth is flat and the sun goes round the earth. This is why we learn theories.
[337] Unless a commercial gas field is found under Sakhalin, as has occasionally been suggested.

Demand:
1. Japan has 130m wealthy people; will they be able to afford imported gas?
2. Tokyo has more than 8m people, Yokohama, Osaka, Nagoya and Sapporo have populations of 2-4m, and another 8 cities on the three main islands have populations exceeding 1m. Much of the internal terrain is mountainous. Do you expect to find
    a. one integrated gas grid across all three main Japanese islands, or
    b. one large grid on each island, or
    c. lots of separate grids surrounding each major city?
3. Given this would you expect to find only a few gas distribution companies or many?
4. (More difficult) Given what you know of Japan's general political and business policies, would you expect Japanese gas companies to be publicly or privately owned?

The answers are given in the Appendix to this chapter.

Appendix: Answers to the Japanese gas company quiz
The following are the author's suggested answers to the quiz questions (they may not be right)

1.   Liquefaction is the obvious way to transport natural gas to Japan. A 4000km pipeline from the gas fields of Siberia would either have to cross China (which both Russia and Japan might regard as a strategic weakness) or be built across remote and mountainous parts of eastern Siberia before crossing the sea to Honshu. A 4000km undersea pipeline from Indonesian gas fields would be even more expensive. These sunk costs are simply too big.

2.   Liquefied Natural Gas could come from any LNG liquefaction plant in the world; currently the world's largest exporters are Qatar, Malaysia, Indonesia, Australia, and Nigeria, and Japan imports from all five of these plus Russia, Brunei and ten other countries.

3.   Given liquefaction, transport and regasification costs, one would expect gas to be more expensive per thermal unit than coal or oil.

4.   Costing only several hundred million dollars each (not several billion), one would expect regasification plants at many locations on the coast near large cities. In fact more than 30 LNG plant had been commissioned around Japan's coasts by 2012.

5.   Yes Japanese customers will want gas and be able to afford it – up to 50m of them[338].

6.   With dozens of supply points and internally mountainous terrain spread over three islands we do not expect one integrated grid across Japan or even one large grid across each island. Given the prevalence of earthquakes, the possibility of catastrophic underground pipeline breaks means extra safety features may be costly.

7.   Consequently we expect to see many gas utilities across Japan, each with their own supply hub and grid based around one or two large cities, or sections of a giant city like Tokyo. We would also expect to see some electricity utilities installing LNG regasification plant so as to use gas as a primary fuel, and possibly piping surplus a short distance to any large industrial customers.

8.   Japan generally favours private ownership of assets, although the Ministry of International Trade and Industry can play a major role organising and merging firms in the private sector. The electricity industry was originally publicly owned, but privatised after the War in 1951, and now has nine regional companies. As is normal around the water world, the Japanese water industry is publicly-owned but very fragmented with more than 1000 utilities mostly owned by small municipalities. The gas industry started in 1645 (yes 1645, not 1945) and has grown strongly since the OPEC oil embargo of 1973. By 1995 there were 243 gas utilities in Japan of which 172 were private and the rest municipally-owned[339]. According to Taki of the

---

[338] Almost a third of Japanese households are single persons.

[339] Taki H 1996, 'The Japanese gas industry' page 7 accessed August 2012 at http://academiccommons.columbia.edu/item/ac:98933

Tokyo Gas Company, each has its own separate monopoly area of supply, with few interconnecting pipelines.

Well done for completing the quiz. You've earned a drink – Kanpai!

Chapter Eleven

Water privatisations, concessions and trading

Water industry theory

Water was one of the few examples of a natural monopoly that JS Mill had for his 1848 textbook, but the reality is it does not fit his assumptions and theory. Chapter 5 concluded that the time series version of the long run marginal cost curve with rising incomes and evolving technologies – Turvey's Long Run Incremental Cost curve – is generally shaped as in Figure 116:

Figure 116: The long run marginal cost of drinking water – again (for derivation see Chapter 5)

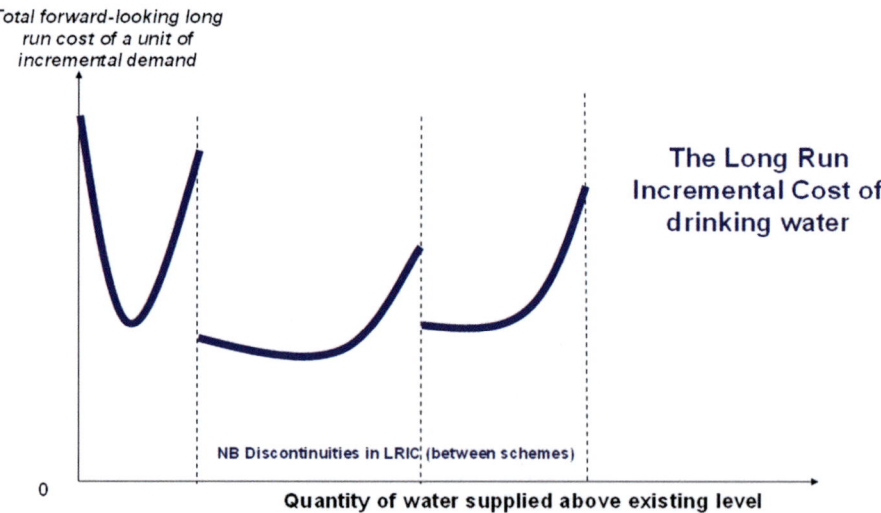

This is not what neoclassical theory assumes. The real reason water is a strong monopoly is its sunk costs; these must be analysed in a model that explicitly considers time – as in Figure 117:

Figure 117: The sunk costs of water

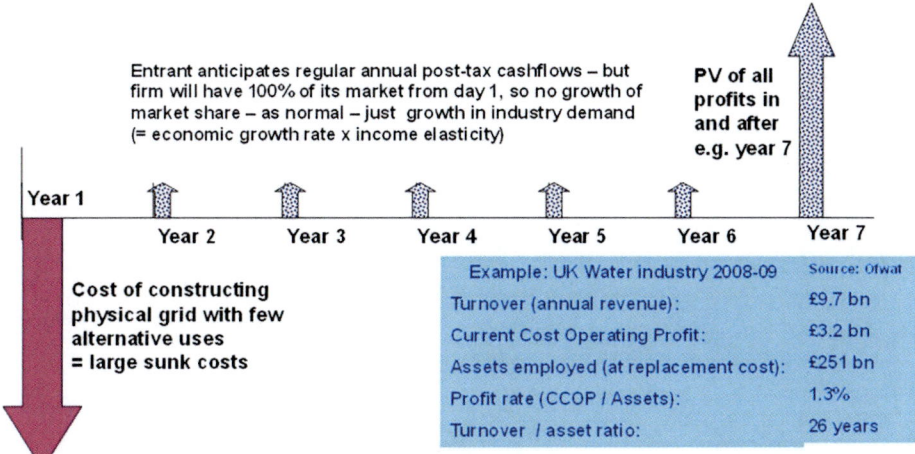

Figure 117 shows that modern water companies in England and Wales earn just over 1% operating profit on the replacement value of their assets, meaning that it would take them almost 80 years to earn the sunk costs of their networks if they had to rebuild these from scratch. The last section of Chapter 8 showed that this is because in England and Wales the regulatory value of their sunk assets before privatisation was massively written down below full replacement cost so that water prices would not promptly triple. There is nothing unusual here about the English and Welsh water industry: *as a generalisation world water prices are significantly below the price that would be needed by private firms to justify investments if entrants or incumbents used replacement cost accounting.* In practice, of course, most water utilities around the world are publicly owned and so rarely have balance sheets adding up past sunk costs, but even if they do their balance sheets play no role in determining current water charges or future investment. So this is not a factor in the public sector. And in the private sector firms do keep balance sheets but only a very few use replacement cost accounting. All private firms use historic cost accounting, where past expenditures are added up in money of the day; this means that modern inflation vastly undervalues assets that were built a century ago. So, because of inflation and long asset lives the return on normal (historic cost) accounts in the water industry looks far higher than the return on assets if they were valued at replacement cost.

For a private sector firm considering entering the water industry this leaves a significant problem which we identified in Chapters 4 and 5 as the real cause of the monopoly: even if the incumbent firms have not scooped up all the cheapest water resources, and customers will contemplate switching suppliers at the same price, any entrant would have to incur sunk costs at replacement prices to earn a severely subnormal profit (1.3%). The incumbents have set a strongly entry-deterring price. In terms of public policy this is well known and accepted: water and wastewater have significant positive externalities, so they are usually publicly owned and publicly subsidised.

Competition, concessions and regulation: the general prospects

Looking at the water value chain the prospects for introducing competition look bleak, and in wastewater look minuscule, as Figure 95, repeated from Chapter 8, reminds us:

Figure 118: The contestable parts of the modern water industry's value chains

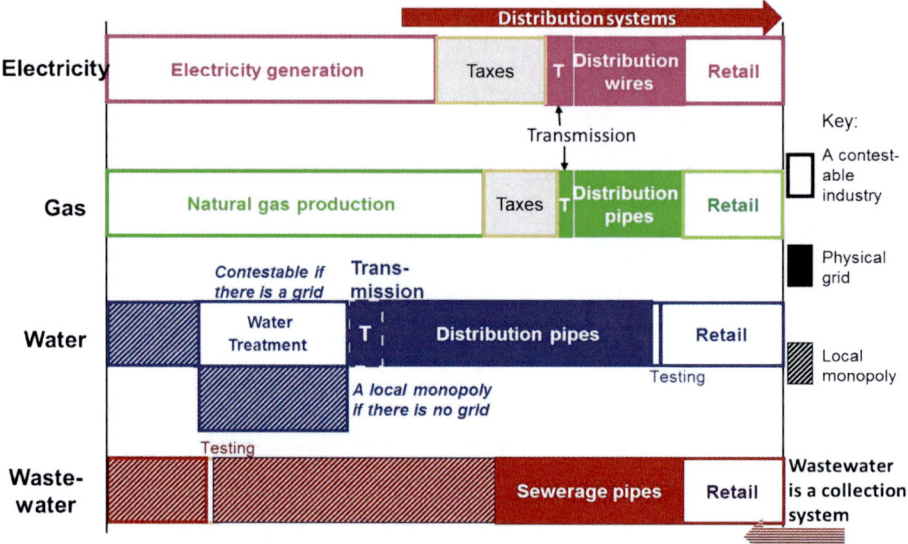

Chapter 8 concluded that if there is a regional or local water grid linking the clean water sources then it would be possible for several water treatment works to compete with each other to supply clean water to a transmission and distribution grid, along the lines of the gas and electricity grids, where one power station or gas field competes with another to deliver energy to wholesale markets. However, this is inconceivable in the wastewater chain because sewage treatment works are almost never connected to each other: bulk sewage is not pumped around our countries[340] looking for the cheapest processing offer – at least not so far this century! In clean water a grid is most likely where there are many small groundwater sources, or the population density and living standards are high, as in the Netherlands or England.

---

[340] As a consultant the author suggested this to Brussels City in the late 1990s, when that large municipality was considering how to treat two thirds of its sewage. Unfortunately the city decided to share the sewage across two large plant rather than considering a scheme whereby three sewage treatment works with long term access agreements, connected interceptor sewers and spare capacity would compete to utilise their excess capacity to process sewage in a spot, forward or short term market. A vintage opportunity was never considered: slight plant economies of scale were preferred to permanent competition-in-the-market. Such a scheme could still be considered for the major new cities planned on China's eastern seaboard, or any other vast city where the Council suddenly decides to treat the sewage of several million people – provided the city has more faith in long term competition than in modest engineering economies of scale.

In conclusion it is hard to see how genuine competition-in-the-market can realistically be introduced; there may be restructurings and vertical separation within the value chain, but privatisation of assets is almost bound to involve heavy regulation of private monopolies. Competition-for-the-market is possible, and is often found in practice for large cities, but the general theory of Chapter 8 leads us to expect short-term contracts where the city retains nearly all the risks, or long term concessions involving a lot of trust, and arbitrators who, if they have not been 'bought' by one side or the other, resemble independent economic regulators.

The UK's experience since 1989: consolidation but no vertical separation

Background

In nearly all countries around the world, including the United States, sewerage and sewage treatment are provided by public utilities. This was true in England and Wales in the 1980s, where many small town and rural sewage networks had been consolidated in a 1973 reorganisation of local government. Drawing on principles first established by the French government in the 1960s, which recognised that the natural ecological unit for administering all matters of inland water quality and quantity should be a river basin, the British government created ten regional Water Authorities organised by groups of rivers. They had names like Thames, Severn Trent[341] and South West. These Authorities were responsible for monitoring the quality and quantity of water in the natural environment, for licensing the quantity of water abstracted by all users, licensing the quality of effluent put back into the natural ecosystems, and operating three quarters of the clean water networks and all of the wastewater operations in England and Wales.

Thus in clean water the ten Water Authorities were responsible for issuing licences to extract water and applying for licences to operate water works, while in wastewater they were responsible for setting and monitoring discharge consent standards in rivers that received sewage effluent, and for operating the sewage treatment works to achieve those standards. On the plus side if there were a problem, or some credit to be had, there was no question where responsibility lay. On the negative side, as often happens in public sector operations, if there were a problem about which most consumers or citizens were ignorant the Water Authorities, as both operator and monitor, could keep quiet about it and few people would know. Indeed they habitually did, and when campaigners and journalists with hard facts to back up their cases complained about matters, the Water Authorities did what public bodies all over the world do, and blamed insufficient public capital expenditure. Indeed it was precisely this prospect – citizens, lobbyists, the media and civil servants pointing out that Britain failed to meet European Union water quality standards, and so would require massive capital expenditure on drinking water and sewage treatment plant – that

---

[341] Two river basins backing onto each other around Britain's second city of Birmingham.

caused Mrs Thatcher to say we must privatise these bodies and get those enormous future liabilities off the State's books. Water privatisation was considered in 1984 but with a strong public campaign against it the proposal was put off until after the 1987 election. When this was won Mrs Thatcher asked her Secretary of State for the Environment, Nicholas Ridley, to examine ways to privatise the ten large Water Authorities urgently. Ridley hired consultants and, scenting deals and money, investment banks offered good people to help think through the nexus of issues.

The 1989 framework for regulating private water monopolies
By nature an inveterate free-market politician, Ridley was a radical who quickly saw that serious issues of public policy were involved. Drawing on his advice, he decided that the public health aspects of drinking water were fundamental and should be dealt with by a specialist body, while the Water Authorities' detailed environmental standard-setting and monitoring functions could continue in another kind of public agency. The operational water and wastewater functions could be separated into private monopolies that would be regulated by an economic regulator. All three regulators would report to his Department. The ten public operators would be privatised with an explicit condition that the economic regulator must allow them sufficient profits to attract the enormous private sector funds that would be needed for the capital expenditure to meet EU standards. The industry would thus have three regulators, as shown in Figure 119. But the economic regulator would be the one who 'held the ring together' financially, if either of the other two wanted to strike out in one direction or another:

Figure 119: Heavy duty regulation: the three regulators of a private water utility

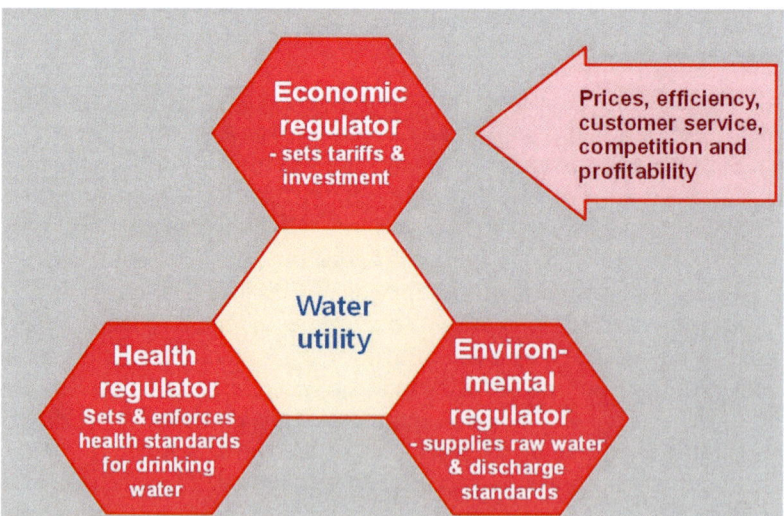

So in England and Wales the following regulators were established:
- An *economic* regulator (eventually de-personalised and) called Ofwat, was set up in 1989;
- A *health* regulator, called the Drinking Water Inspectorate, was set up in

1990. The smallest of the three, it is deliberately kept completely separate from the other two regulators, and granted full whistle-blowing powers if it detects the slightest threat to the public health from tap water, and is empowered to test (or make water companies test) the quality of drinking water at all stages of the process from underground aquifers or muddy bogs to reservoirs, treatment works, pipes, and drinking water in customers' homes;

• An *environmental* regulator was set up, initially called the National Rivers Agency but changed in 1996 to the Environment Agency (EA) so that it had responsibility for monitoring all aspects of the natural environment including water (including the coastal seas), on land, and in the air, and for setting detailed local standards. By far the largest regulator, in terms of budget and people, but having been created essentially out of ten of ten independent Water Authorities, the NRA and the EA had strongly regional origins and so were accused in the first twenty years of having weak national policy coordination[342].

But for a water company in the private sector world, having voluble customers backed by an ever-hungry media, hard-nosed investors, a large workforce, and powerful politicians whom a firm must keep happy, the three regulators are just part of the picture. The managers of some private water utilities would have you believe they are vulnerable entities in comparison to the strong external forces acting on their firm shown in Figure 120:

Figure 120: Overwhelmed? The 6 main forces acting upon a private water utility

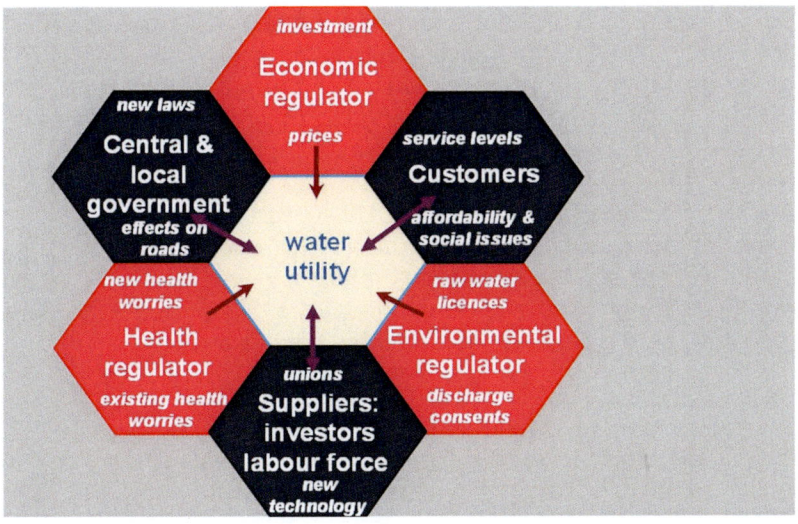

---

[342] TIn the early 2000s one official described British environmental policy to the author as being like an empty elevator shaft: general policies were drafted at European level and placed into what should have been a carefully-controlled elevator going down. But in practice the elevator was often not there, just an empty shaft: the UK Department of the Environment allowed policies to drop through barely considered, as did the EA nationally, so they landed in the basement on the desks of EA officials in local offices who

In addition to the ten former public Water Authorities, originally 29 smaller Water Only Companies (WOCs) were released into the same unified regulatory regime. These companies supplied water but no wastewater services to about a quarter of England, and had always been privately-owned dividend-controlled monopolies under a former separate legal framework. Most of them were the result of hundreds of public and private initiatives from the previous two centuries set up to supply water to villages or towns across the country. These were then merged independently from the public Water Authorities under a dividend-control regime whereby, effectively, reserves and planned maintenance were the residuals in the annual budgeting process[343]. The WOCs had long histories and were proudly independent of the newly privatised Water And Sewerage Companies (WASCs), but were nevertheless subject to the same Water Act and governed by the same three water regulators.

The 1989 privatisation
In July 1989 the government passed a Water Act establishing the new regulators and the private water and wastewater companies; in November 1989 the industry was floated on the London Stock Exchange. The sale was deemed a financial success and the government received £6.5bn from the sale of the ten companies. The three regulators were rapidly established.

Privatisation – the short term results 1989-94
To offset against the £6.5bn sales received by the British Treasury one must also consider that
- in the year before flotation HM Treasury completely 'wrote off' nearly £5bn of the £5 1/2 bn debt owed by the ten WASCs to central and local government (i.e. it turned past loans into gifts);
- To sweeten privatisation still further, in the year before privatisation the Treasury made financial gifts totalling £1.6bn to those companies expected to have the highest burdens of future capital expenditure; this was a straight gift, not a loan, and was designed solely to boost their balance sheets; colloquially it was known as the *'Green Dowry'*;
- The companies were *sold at a discounted price*: their share prices rose by an average of 22% in the week after they were floated[344], which was a wonderful profit for the underwriters of the share issue – far higher than probably could have been obtained by a public auction;

---

effectively formed uncoordinated regional policies. Of course this was an exaggeration. One Minister who did try to get an intellectual grip on matters was David Miliband (Secretary of State for the Environment 2006-07) but he did not have enough time in office to get to grips with water.

[343] Charges to customers and dividends were externally controlled, opex was management's best guess, reactive maintenance was whatever it would be that year, and so proactive maintenance and reserves were the residuals.

[344] Jenkinson T and Meyer C (1994) *The costs of privatisation in the UK and France* in Bishop M, Kay J, and Mayer C (eds) *Privatisation and economic performance*, Oxford University Press, New York page 294

- Although not cash-positive operations, the *water utilities were making significant profits before privatisation*[345]; privatisation forced the public sector to give up all prospect of water utilities in steady state making major profit contributions to the public sector in future, as the publicly-owned energy utilities had been doing;
- Finally the privatised water companies were allowed to inherit low tax-paying positions for the first ten years of their privatised lives.

Because the combined debt write-off and Green Dowry exceeded the flotation receipts obtained from the share sale, and because of the other gifts, private investors were essentially paid a significant sum to take the English and Welsh water industry off the public sector's hands[346]. For a profitable industry, even before the industry started to engage seriously in cutting costs and increasing efficiency, this was a privatisation of profitable businesses that yielded zero net receipts to the public sector – other than freeing it from the obligation to spend billions meeting current environmental and health standards.

Privatisation – the long term results

Service levels – availability
A water service is useless if it doesn't have any water. Normalising to remove individual years of extreme weather, properties suffering unplanned supply disruptions lasting longer than 12 hours have fallen from 0.33% in the first five years after privatisation (incomplete records were kept before privatisation) to 0.21% in the years 2005-2010; recent years have included some of the worst droughts seen in almost 100 years and some of the worst floods seen in 130 years. Properties at risk of low pressure declined from 1.3% in 1990-95 to 0.01% in 2011-12 – a hundred-fold reduction. Across all other measures of performance and service that Ofwat has measured – a good two dozen, ranging from properties at risk of sewer flooding to public correspondence responded to within a defined time – standards of performance have risen significantly for all companies on each measure since privatisation. There is also no doubt that comparative competition – publishing individual companies' performance levels in annual publications – has played a strong role in incentivising companies' managers to improve their performance.

Quality of drinking water & discharge consent standards
As described in chapter 6, although in theory drinking water quality standards across western Europe were uniform in the 1980s, the actual levels achieved were highly variable. The UK was not the worst offender, but for some English

---

[345] Experienced readers will know the difference between profits and cash instantly. Students with no training in company finance must ask their tutors to explain how a firm can make a healthy profit and still be cash-negative.

[346] A 1997 World Bank Report estimated this subsidy at £1.3bn – source Caroline van den Berg Water privatisation in England and Wales, IBRD, page 2 found at http://rru.worldbank.org/documents/publicpolicyjournal/115vdbrg.pdf

Water Authorities 20% or more of the water produced in the 1980s did not meet all the relevant EU standards – especially for nitrates and residual agricultural chemicals which required expensive additions to surface water treatment works. Within ten years 99% of all water distributed met all EU standards, and in recent years this figure has exceeded 99.95%, based on the Drinking Water Inspectorate's regime of millions of routine weekly tests.

On the wastewater side, companies met the environmental discharge consent standards for the effluent from their sewage treatment works in 99% of tests for the first time by 2003-04. More ambitiously, as explained in chapter 6, the amount of sewage captured by interceptor sewers, and the quality of effluent emitted by sewage treatment works, strongly affects the quality of seawater for swimmers on beaches. In 1990 only 78% of bathing waters in England and Wales met EU standards, but the latest figure is now 98.6%[347]; the overwhelming cause of this has been major efforts by coastal wastewater companies such as North West Water, South West Water, Southern Water and Dwr Cymru /Welsh Water, backed by massive capital expenditure programmes.

Prices

Water prices and total charges have risen in nominal and real terms. In the first ten years nominal prices doubled, increasing by 46% in real terms[348], but in 1999 Ian Byatt reset prices significantly lower. After this average charges continued to climb in real terms, exceeding the 2000-2001 peak again by 2008, as shown in Figure 121:

Figure 121: Average water charges in England and Wales since 1989 in 2006-07 constant prices

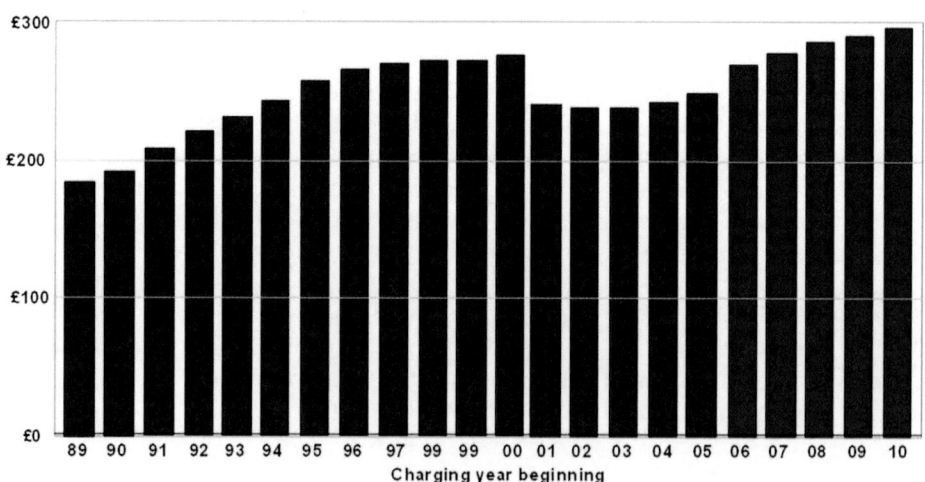

Sources: Ofwat Memo to House of Commons 1998; Presentation by Regina Finn to Agbar Group Barcelona June 2007, Ofwat website accessed August 2011

In the latest Price Determination, average bills will have stayed flat in real terms (allowing for inflation) up to 2014. Undoubtedly, therefore, water prices have risen under privatisation, but as Chapter 6 pointed out, unlike energy products, *nearly all water utilities in Europe, America and Asia have significantly increased the quality of their clean water and waste water outputs*, as well as service levels, and this has certainly been true in the UK. Customers may not have noticed these improvements in service, because normal service goes unnoticed and is hidden but they are real and have had real cost consequences which have to be paid for one way or another. In England and Wales it is the customer who pays for it.

But could the price increases have been lower? Ofwat claims that water and sewerage "bills are more than a third lower than they otherwise would have been, as a result of our challenge to companies to be more efficient"[349]. Naturally the counter-factual (what would have happened if the utilities had not been privatised under this regulatory regime) needs articulation and examination, but Ofwat's claim seems to be based on examination of the cumulative amounts by which Ofwat has knocked back the revenue bids at each successive round of price settings. Naturally this is open to the criticism that some of those claims were artificially raised as part of the regulatory gaming process, and that a suitably hard-nosed Environment Department or Finance Ministry could have achieved the same results. The author doubts that a central government department could have achieved all of this, though: knocking back well-assembled cases requires specialised data, industry knowledge, talent, and powerful yardsticks[350]. Given the track record in England and Wales since 1989 it seems more conjectural to argue that all of this could have been achieved purely within a public sector framework of cash bids and fierce rebuttals than to argue that it might be achieved under yardstick regulation.

Capital expenditure and financials
Ofwat financial reports show that the privatised industry had cumulatively invested around £100bn (in modern prices) since privatisation, and that annual investment equals 40% of the industry's turnover in recent years – about twice the level of investment achieved under public ownership in the 1980s[351]. The industry was cash-negative every year from 1990 to 2015, yet gearing, measured

---

[347] Source: Ofwat *Service and delivery performance of the water companies in England and Wales 2010-2011* page 4.
[348] Source Ofwat *Memorandum of 18 March 1998 in House of Commons Research Paper 98/117*, cited in Lobina E and Hall D UK *Water Privatisation – a briefing*, PSIRU research paper of February 2001.
[349] Ofwat Service Report 2010-2011, page 4.
[350] For instance, following poor performance in a drought in 1995, a very forceful CEO of Yorkshire Water was dispensed with by the then economic regulator. We will never know what pressures Ian Byatt put on the Board of his company to fire him, but having the power to terminate his company's licence to operate for failure to supply can only have strengthened Byatt's position. A Finance Ministry negotiator would not have had this power.
[351] Source Ofwat *Financial performance and expenditure of the water companies in England and Wales 2010-2011* pages 14, 17 and 30, and earlier years' reports; the figures are quoted in 2010-11 prices.

by net debt to Regulatory Capital Value (RAB in Chapter 8's terminology) rose only to 70%. After a quarter of a century of heavy investment to replace poor infrastructure and upgrade water and wastewater networks to the levels expected by modern consumers, there are signs that the investment programme has finally eased off and the UK water industry will now be cash-positive.

At the second five-yearly Price Review in 1999, when Ian Byatt announced price decreases for most firms, London equity analysts furiously berated him, loudly alleging that he would render the industry, or several firms in it, un-fundable. But the firms themselves did not appeal to the Competition Commission for a review of their price limits[352]. When asked if the water firms would be un-fundable the next year the equity analysts said 'Not next year – but very soon'. 2000 came and went. Asked again if water utilities would still be un-fundable they insisted 'Very soon'. 2001 arrived, and with it 9/11 and a major stock market crash; still the water firms were fully funded, issuing ever-longer-dated debt and index-linked bonds. Eventually by 2003 those analysts still in their jobs had to admit the industry was still solvent. Fifteen years later, despite being cash-negative for the entire time, the industry is still fully solvent and issuing 20-year index-linked AAA-rated bonds[353]. The author repeats this story only to show that economic regulators must be tough and ignore all short term warnings of doom from those with a product or a financial forecast to sell.

The experience of regulation since 1989

RPI-X
Littlechild's RPI-X formula was the natural starting point for adjusting revenues between price determinations, but, as just indicated, because of the need for capital expenditure to improve the quality of water or sewage treated, most firms in the industry were expected to be cash negative. RPI-X therefore had to be adjusted upwards at price determinations to allow the firms to be financially viable. It therefore became 'RPI-X +K' where 'K' allowed capital expenditure for quality and service enhancements – an uplift sum that would enhance revenues sufficiently for the firm "to finance its functions", as the 1989 Water Act put it. Ofwat subsequently lobbied for this to be changed to be for "an efficient firm" [to finance its functions]. The price determination software model used to determine its own price limits was released to each firm during the Periodic Review discussions.

Economies of scale
Chapter 3 reviewed the evidence on economies of scale in the water industry, and found little evidence for this once a utility serves more than a hundred

---

[352] Some firms had appealed in the previous Review and ended up with worse price limits than Ofwat had set, so Appeal was always a two-edged sword.
[353] E.g. in 2011 Sutton & East Surrey issued a 20-year £100m index-linked bond rated AAA by all three Agencies paying 95 basis points (0.95%) over the comparable government bond (source: Royal Bank of Scotland press release 2011). NB: not all water companies retain AAA ratings.

thousand people. In brief, Ofwat has found over two decades of yardstick regulation that the smallest companies are frequently some of the most efficient and lowest cost, having adjusted for operating environments.

Mergers

Starting from the position that the more independent comparators it has to judge the frontier the better, Ofwat has resisted merger bids unless there is a strong case that lower costs will *immediately* produce lower prices that can be passed on to consumers. Promises of future efficiency gains that will eventually be passed on to consumers are not enough. Mergers of WASCs have been effectively banned and so, as Figure 122 shows, mergers are either between WOCs (e.g. the five companies in 1989 that form the current South East Water), or the absorption of a WOC by a neighbouring WASC, such as Yorkshire Water's takeover of tiny York Waterworks.

Figure 122: The 17 exits from the water industry in England & Wales 1989-2012

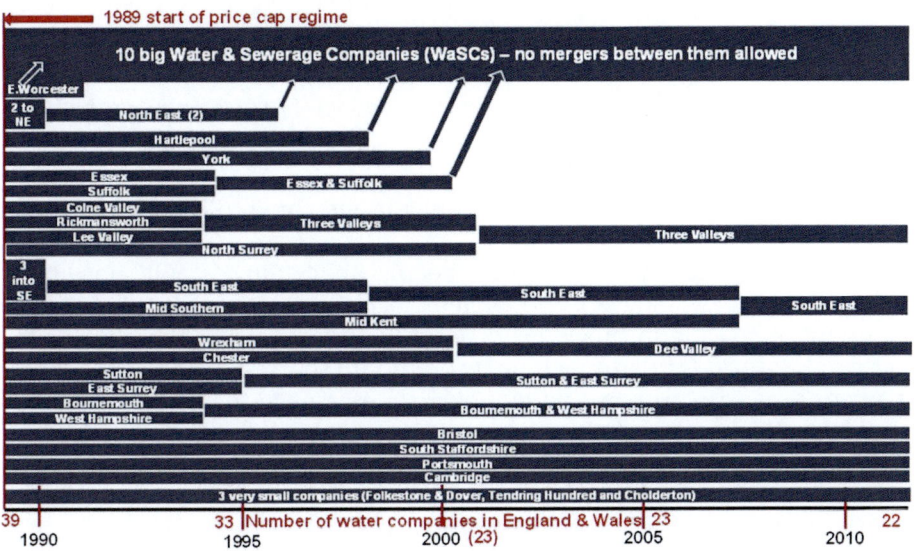

Despite Ofwat's opposition-in-principle the total number of WOCs has been reduced by merger over the quarter century from 29 to 12, currently, though one WOC is tiny (Cholderton serves 2000 people) and some WOCs are owned by WASCs or common holding companies (e.g. Veolia owned companies in three areas) but must report data for each company separately to Ofwat.

Costs and reform of the regulator

In 2006 Ofwat was changed from a single regulator reporting to the Secretary of State for the Environment to a Board structure reporting to, and accountable to, Parliament. Instead of a 'Director General of Water Services' with personal accountability for the industry's prices, profits and performance, Ofwat now has a non-Executive Chairman and a Chief Executive, employs around 220 FTE staff, and costs around £23m to run, equivalent to 0.2% of the industry's turnover.

Introduction of competition?

Introducing competition in water is always tough. Ofwat has tried. The results for wastewater are shown in Figure 123:

Figure 123: the structure of the wastewater (sewage) industry in England and Wales

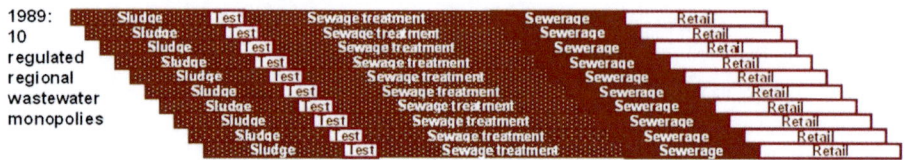

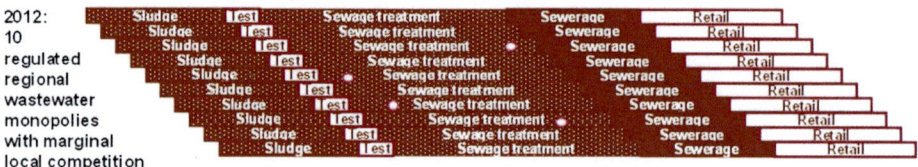

○ = spot competition in large customers

Only in a few isolated cases has the regulator been able to introduce elements of competition. These so-called "inset" appointments are where private entrants provide specialized services more cheaply than the default "incumbent" monopoly supplier. These services are such functions as specialized pre-treatment of sewage in breweries or food factories, so that the effluent from the site corresponds to normal domestic strength sewage and so is not charged at a very expensive tariff by the monopolist. In essence these specialist service providers are arbitraging between the incumbent's tariff differences for different strengths of sewage and an ability to weaken the effluent to normal strength sewage; if they can do it cheaper than the incumbent's tariff quality differential there is clearly an efficiency (and welfare) gain to be split between the customer and the entrant.

On the drinking water side there has been a little more evolution of the industry structure:

Figure 124: evolution of the drinking water industry since privatisation

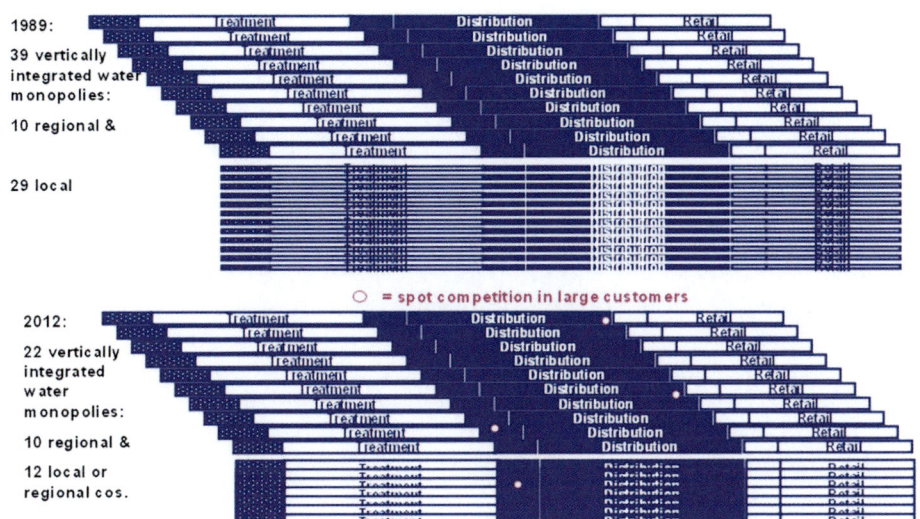

Again small amounts of spot competition ('inset appointments') have been introduced, but despite several licences being awarded for inset appointments very few customers actually receive water from new entrants, and all inset appointments serve large commercial or industrial premises (not households). Developing a Network Code for water has proved every bit as difficult as it was in gas in the 1990s, without any massive economic rents to benefit consumers and upstream producers. Given the entry-deterring upstream prices and small retail margins in water, there were never sufficient incentives for retail competition to benefit domestic households.

Overall conclusions
By and large the English and Welsh water sector is thought to have one of the more stable and dependable incentivised regulatory regimes in the world. Most observers conclude that the industry has worked largely as Nick Ridley wanted. There has not been any significant competition-in-the-market, but that was always going to be difficult to achieve and sustain in water and wastewater. However, regulation using comparative competition has worked surprisingly well, though it does require a large number of independent companies. The Water Only companies have been particularly helpful here; in wastewater ten utilities gives too few degrees of freedom given the range of exogenous cost-drivers, and so the regulator has been forced to go for second-best comparators by demanding sub-company information.

Chile 1988- 2008
Chile is one of the few countries besides 'the Anglo-Saxons' (the USA and UK) to contemplate privatising water and wastewater industry assets – i.e. privatising the ownership. A key factor distinguishing Chilean water reform from similar moves elsewhere in the world is that the process was allowed to take a long time,

being supported by several Presidents in succession. A determined programme of establishing powerful, independent, well-qualified regulators, and a parallel process of improving the service outputs and efficiency of the water and sanitation departments led to the *utilities being socially valued and profitable enterprises before being privatised*. This contrasts with many attempted utility privatisations around the world where governments have simply, and rapidly, tried to 'export some difficult problems' to the private sector.

Chile's story begins in 1977 with the unusual creation – in the water world – of a national water utility, SENDOS, which may have been linked to the country's generally very dry climate and the perceived need occasionally to move water large distances. In contrast to most countries' situations this gave the Chilean water industry a set of national standards. This meant later in the 1980s, when considering water restructuring possibilities, that the national government had the option of creating regional water units that were divisions of an existing coherent body, rather than a ragbag collection of incompatible city and town water departments, as is usually the case around the world when trying to create regional or river basin water utilities.

The modern reform process began in the late 1980s when one of the military governments proposed twin parallel reforms:
- To extend access to clean water and sanitation to 100% of the urban and rural populations
- To raise water and wastewater tariffs so that the water utilities were self-financing.

As in the UK, the Chilean government took a national view of the water industry's problems and decided in 1990 to create a single national water regulator, the *Superintendencia de Servicios Sanitarios* (SISS) to have responsibility for adjudicating on local water and wastewater utilities' capital bids, operating efficiency and tariffs. SISS was given a chief executive, or Superintendent, appointed by the President, a budget around $2m enabling it to hire 80 staff, and a remit to allow water utilities to earn a rate of return equal to base rate plus 3-3½%, though with a nominal rate no lower than 7%[354]. Explicitly adopting Shleifer's benchmarking ideas, the SISS established an imaginary or model water company, and estimated efficient costs which became the benchmark for real water companies' costs. Borrowing a tariff regulation model from the Chilean electricity and telecoms sector, the efficient costs were then used to set the tariffs for real city or regional water companies.

In parallel with setting a competent and well-resourced national regulator in place, the government set about improving the water and sanitation utilities'

---

[354] Foster V, 2005, Ten years of Water Service Reform in Latin America, World Bank Water Supply and Sanitation Sector Board Discussion Paper Series, Paper No.3, January 2005 , page 15, available at http://siteresources.worldbank.org/INTWSS/Resources/WSSServiceReform.pdf

service levels and coverage while still under public ownership. In 1988 13 regional water utilities were created out of SENDOS, largely based on SENDOS's regional directorates, and kept in the public sector. The 'rewards' for utilities which achieved service improvements were publicly-funded capital expenditure and modest tariff increases which led the utilities to be self-funding, and thus largely independent of political support.

By the late 1980s Chile had some of the highest rates of access to clean water and basic sanitation in South America, and the final hurdle was proper sewage treatment. The government's adoption of this as an environmental goal meant that it faced the kind of capital expenditure requirements that were driving Mrs Thatcher to privatise the water utilities in England and Wales. Privatisation of the 13 utilities occurred in three main waves: in 1998 the five largest companies, accounting for three quarters of Chile's connected customers, were semi-privatised when the government sold 51% of its stake in these utilities.

After 2000 the Socialist governments of Presidents Lagos and Bachelet were far less ideologically keen on asset sales, and so the second wave of privatisations in 2001 sold more shares in the same companies to the private sector, but the third wave in 2004 of smaller utilities, with more expensive water in smaller and drier regions, was a series of 30-year operating concessions to service assets that remain owned by the Chilean state. All the utilities and concessions, however, remain regulated by the one national water regulator, SISS.

Water concessions or franchises

Colombia – Cartagena 1994
Some privatised water concessions have worked really well. For instance in 1994 the city of Cartagena in Colombia signed a 26-year operating and maintenance concession with a company called Aguacar, which was 50% owned by the city and part owned by the global Spanish water firm Aguas de Barcelona. With finance part-provided by the World Bank, Aguacar raised the hours of water coverage from 17 to 24 hours a day, and access to piped water from less than 70% in 1995 to 99% in 2005, while increasing sewerage access from 55% to 75%[355]. 60% of the new connections were estimated to be to families in the poorest quintile. Water leakage and theft, which was originally estimated at 40% but was discovered to be 60%, was rapidly reduced to 40%, and the successful collection of fees ratio was increased from less than 50% to 95%, so that by 2005 the concession had become cash-positive.

This is an excellent record for any utility that serves large numbers of very poor people to achieve: one of the many unsung triumphs of the utility world and a considerable improvement in the daily lives of hundreds of thousands of people. It requires a lot of technical and commercial skill to set up commercial

---

[355] UNDP Public Private Partnerships Case Studies For Development, Cartagena, available at http://www.ncppp.org/undp/cartagena.html

agreements like this, and vast reserves of hard work, trust and genuine good will to deliver results like this.

Bolivia – Cochabamba 2000!
Few agreements in the history of utility franchising have a reputation to match Cochabamba. For many people around the world at the time it symbolised all that was wrong with capitalism and globalisation: for them it was the water industry's equivalent to California's electricity debacle – an agreement that, given the combination of poor structural arrangements and forceful companies and personalities, had failure written all over it from Day 1. Some observers were surprised that the Mayor of the City was not left hanging from a lamppost.

Cochabamba is Bolivia's fourth largest city with a population around 600,000 and a metropolitan population around a million. Founded in 1571 in a valley in central Bolivia to provide food for the legendary Inca silver mines of Potosi, in the twenty first century Cochabamba is a thriving city, but has also featured in intelligence reports as a hub for the South American cocaine trade. Allied to strong vested interests and local traditions of corruption, a bloc of ex-coca farmers (from a US-sponsored drug program) settled in Cochabamba, adding to the problems of urban unemployment and an underground economy. Popular sentiment was strongly opposed to water privatisation, but in 1997 the World Bank had required the privatisation of Cochabamba's water utility as a condition of a US$20m loan to the national government[356].

Water was supplied by the city's municipal water department but the service was very poor (often 4 hours a day) and access to water and sanitation was 50% at best. A sole, unsolicited, bid for the Cochabamba concession emerged, and a 40-year contract was signed with this bidder in 1999 which required an immediate 38% tariff increase. Because the concessionaire, backed by Bechtel and local engineering and construction firms, required the building of a large reservoir and dam on the Misicuni river, which was two and a half times as expensive as an alternative water resource, the World Bank severed all links with Cochabamba in 1997. Nevertheless, the World Bank's name was associated with the failed privatisation. Within three months of signing the deal there was an explosion of opposition, riots, the imposition of martial law, and ultimately the deaths of seven protesters[357], before the contract was repealed and the tariff increases rescinded. Today Cochabamba still has severe water problems: only half the population is connected, those that are, get water 3-4 hours a day, the rest pay private water vendors rates that are much higher than the official tariffs, water losses have risen from 43% to 50%, and there is still corruption and nepotism. And the expensive Misicuni project rolls on, as ever promising jam tomorrow but not actually delivering a drop of water.

---

[356] World Bank Operations Evaluation Department Precis No. 222, 2002, Bolivia Water Management: a tale of three cities, http://lnweb90.worldbank.org/oed/oeddoclib.nsf/DocUNIDViewForJavaSearch/EE95EE729B8A87CB85256BAD0066C3A4/$file/Precis_222.pdf

Comparing Carthagena and Cochabamba

Table 9: Comparison of Carthagena and Cochabamba water concessions

Pre-existing conditions	Bid process and contract design	Delivery
CARTHAGENA		
Suspicion of privatisation and foreign water companies	Several bidders reduced to one in final year of negotiations	Experienced water managers hired local agents to involve communities in designing local plans
Adequate water resources	Experienced international water company combined with city council	Required local community to get involved and contribute work before extending network to their area
Bidder took time to learn about Carthagena's conditions	Leakage reduction prioritised to yield resources before extending system	Carefully controlled programme to extend network bit by bit once resources are available
	Good governance and management of concessionaire	
COCHABAMBA		
Severe water resource problems requiring major leakage reduction and new resources	One unsolicited bidder	Failed to involve local communities and get them on board
Tradition of local corruption; powerful drug lords live nearby	Concessionaire contains hated US firm and 4 local engineering firms	Mayor out of touch with his people
Strong anti-globalisation and anti-privatisation feeling by many Bolivians	Committed to $180m Misicuni project to develop new water resources	Young foreign water engineers with little experience of running water concessions
Displaced coca farmers add to unemployment & black economy	Failed to prioritise leakage reduction	Imposed 38% tariff increase before delivering local benefits

---

[357] Bonnardeaux D, 2009, 'The Cochabamba "Water War": an Anti-privatisation Poster Child?' Policy Network website http://www.policynetwork.net/sites/default/files/Cochabamba_March09.pdf

Pre-existing conditions	Bid process and contract design	Delivery
Cheapest water resources ruled out by Mayor and local vested interests	Contract gives monopoly of water resources to concessionaire, including aquifer, which annoys local farmers	Company out of touch with its customers
World Bank had required privatisation of water as condition of loan to national government	Weak governance arrangements	Mayor insists on appointing CEO of concessionaire

Although we can draw many lessons from Table 1 the truth is the first column is sufficient for any external observer to say "Don't get involved" in Cochabamba. And that is exactly what experienced international water companies and the World Bank did from late 1997. Unfortunately for the World Bank its name was tied in popular perception to Cochabamba because of its earlier condition that the city's water utility should be privatised; today, of course, it is a wiser institution.

'Nuff said. Sometimes a simple table of comparisons is the only analytical tool you need.

Argentina – Buenos Aires 1993-2006
Although styled a Water Concession the two most striking things that contrast this concession with the previous two are the scale of the area being served (the Buenos Aires Metropolitan Area has 9 million people, including nearly 2m very poor people)[358] and the fact that the most significant issues concern not clean water but wastewater. The core wastewater challenge was to improve one of the world's dirtiest rivers, the Matanza-Riachuelo, which was little better than an open sewer, and several other tributaries of the Del Plata river. Besides containing enormous quantities of domestic sewage (only 2% of Buenos Aires' total sewage was then treated) the Matanza-Riachuelo river contained vast quantities of organic matter from tanneries and meat processing factories, and heavy metals such as copper, zinc, chrome and lead. To do this the contract sensibly envisaged that in the first ten years sewerage coverage would be raised from 58% to 73% and primary sewage treatment (settlement and removal of solids) from 4% to 73%. In the second ten years – from 2003 to 2013 – it was planned that secondary sewage treatment (proper biological treatment of the

---
[358] World Bank 2001, Buenos Aires Concession case study http://siteresources.worldbank.org/INTPSIA/Resources/490023-1120845825946/sa_buenos.pdf
[359] It had been just 4% in 1993.
[360] Eustache, World Bank Institute presentation 1999, Privatizing and regulating water and sanitation: Argentina's experience, slide 18 on World Bank website accessed July 2012.

liquid effluent) would rise from 14%[359] to 88%, requiring huge investment by the concessionaire[360].

Originally signed in 1992 as a 30-year contract to start from 1993 in fact Suez's concession lasted only 13 years before President Nestor Kirchner revoked it. Despite its size and enormous challenges, the original concession had an exemplary bidding process, some very sensible contract features, and was won and administered by France's Suez SA water company, one of the world's most skilled and experienced water companies. In its first five years, it was widely held up as an example of a well-constructed concession operated under a good contract by seasoned professionals.

However, the original contract also had some major flaws, principally that the concession contract did not adequately cover the city's two million slum inhabitants. Slowly the concessionaire responded to this criticism and desire to change the carefully-negotiated original contract, by introducing locally cost-reflective, but completely unaffordable, charges – such as the US$600-800 bill per slum household to be connected to the network. This was completely unrealistic for slum dwellers and the very opposite of what was socially needed. Eventually a compromise, spreading the costs of new connections over the entire network, was agreed[361], but this took seven years to implement. By such clumsy tactics Suez created social and political difficulties for itself, which one would expect an experienced company to have solved from the start. By 1997 it had fallen short of its original contract performance targets in both capital expenditure and output measures, and by 2000 the concessionaire was falling seriously behind its original coverage targets. A report commissioned by the World Bank criticised the concession for having some serious contract flaws resulting in perverse incentives for the operator, poor information, politicised and weak regulation, and a general lack of transparency in the regulatory process, so that "public confidence in the process has eroded"[362].

For its part the regulator was so weak that it was completely bypassed in the 1997 contract renegotiation that went on between the concessionaire and the pro-privatisation President Carlos Menem. After he was replaced by a President more critical of privatisation the regulator suddenly hauled in Suez for earlier violations of its contract, revealing to all that he was entirely driven by the political process. Overall, Suez maintained that 2 million people had gained access to clean drinking water and 1 million to sanitation during their concession, and that they were refused an important price increase in 2001. The case went to arbitration and ultimately (in 2010) the International Centre for the Settlement of Investment Disputes agreed with Suez.

---

[361] The explicit commercial recognition of the underlying economics, that providing wastewater services is a positive externality.

[362] Alcazar L, Abdala M and Shirley M, 2000, "The Buenos Aires water concession" Volume 1, World Bank Policy Research Paper WPS 2311 resume on http://econ.worldbank.org/external/default/main?pagePK=64165259&theSitePK=469372&piPK=64165421&menuPK=64166093&entityID=000094946_00042605364386 accessed July 2012.

Some general conclusions about water or wastewater regulation and concessions

The Buenos Aires water concession well illustrates the general points outlined in Chapter 1 that wastewater is chiefly a positive externality, and in Chapter 8 that arbitrators of long term concessions ultimately become regulators. It also illustrates the practical difficulty of establishing powerful independent regulators who can carry a big yardstick and get a grip on a utility that faces the entwined difficulties of meeting both its input and output targets. The contrast between the Buenos Aires concession, and the power and independence of regulators in Chile, the USA and the UK, and the generally satisfactory performance of their regulatees, is strong.

Given the economies of scale and scope there is a strong case for establishing three or four global regulators of water and wastewater utilities, by which all concession agreements agree to be bound – after all we wouldn't want to establish an unnecessary monopoly of a single global regulator, would we? As ever, the practical difficulties will be political: it will take very bold politicians to recommend using a regulator from another country. But international institutions like the World Bank and the large global water companies would have a persistent long term interest in using a few really good quality economic regulators.

Water trading

Alternative theoretical concepts

Can water be traded, and should water be traded? These are two different questions. On the first there is an unequivocal answer. Yes: it can be defined, measured out and sold at the wholesale level, just as it is at the retail level.

Should it be traded? Economists' standard advice is that the scarcer a commodity becomes in a monetised economy the more benefits there are to be had from trading it. So, if the quantity of free fresh water in the biosphere is fixed, water is distributed unevenly around the planet, and the number of humans is rising, economists' advice is unusually uniform: water should be traded, and it is likely water trades will increasingly benefit the humans on the planet.

Opponents – possibly most humans on the planet – ask is it right to trade the stuff of life, something so valuable to life as we know it that nothing can survive without it? In most countries, especially hot ones, water has long been valued so highly that it has been seen as a God or an essential spirit. Even in modern scientific terms, although water seems chemically simple, we are still learning more of its properties each year. In sum, for philosophical, spiritual, moral and environmental reasons, many humans value water so highly that they think it wrong to treat water as a commodity like wheat or iron ore. For these reasons social conventions in many countries prohibit the direct trading of bulk water itself between private sector agents, and politicians do not wish to risk unpopularity by introducing new arrangements to encourage direct water trading. Indeed Roman law, on which many European laws are based, held that water is innately a public good, and should not be traded.

Yet despite social unpopularity, economic necessity often has a way of making itself felt. If water cannot itself be traded, are there ways to trade water resource endowments, or water *rights*, so as to achieve improvements in the overall allocation and distribution of of resources? This indirect way of trading water may offend fewer people and yet achieve a very similar result. Let's examine each route in turn.

Direct trading of water
Direct trading of bulk raw water does occur in some richer (and generally cooler) countries. Sometimes this is between different parts of what is essentially the same industry value chain (vertical trading) but it can also be between neighbouring vertically-integrated companies (horizontal trading). In the former case, though, given the monopolies that must exist in water value chains, vertical water trading is unlikely to add genuine new independent price signals unless one could create a relatively free market in wholesale water, as in the energy sectors. Buyers are likely to be local monopsonists, and sellers are likely to be local monopolists. And if one of these is not publicly-owned, a regulator may intervene to set prices well below entry-deterring prices. So in general one would not expect the prices that result from such contracts to fulfil any optimality criteria from general equilibrium theory; optimal prices require arms-length trading between buyers and sellers with several alternative options. Prices may be specified in these water contracts but they mean little.

Chapters 10 and 11 have shown how long it can take to establish stable, relatively free market trading in electricity and gas. Even in the absence of such full scale water markets it is possible that trading between arms-length (independent) rival water utilities might in principle give some useful price signals.

Water contract structures for horizontal trading
If water is to be directly traded the first thing to consider is the structure of the contract. Unlike trading fish, where the fish is there, and all you have to do is to look at it, sniff it and do the deal, or not, trading water requires considerable infrastructure (pipes) to be put in place before a single cubic metre can flow. Aside from the sheer engineering mechanics of the operation (connection points, pipe diameters, who will pump, pumping pressures, volumes, notice periods etc.) the parties must also agree whether the supplier will decide the quantity of water to be traded (a push contract) or the buyer will decide (a pull contract). In general pull contracts are favoured, which is fine for the buyer but leaves the seller with the problem of how much spare capacity to set aside if the buyer suddenly demands their full contractual entitlement[363]. Setting aside

---

[363] Of course the reverse is true in a push contract: the buyer has to figure out what to do with excess volumes of water if the seller should decide to 'open the valves' fully. Good notice periods are essential to reducing costs.

this spare capacity has an opportunity cost which should be reflected in the contract's terms. And no matter whether it is a push or a pull contract, adequate notice periods of the intention to trade a specific volume of water in a specific time period are essential to reducing unnecessary costs.

To avoid contracts falling apart under these conflicting constraints economists generally favour
1. Absolute contract property rights
2. Large financial penalties if either party fails to meet its contractual obligations.

Term 1 is necessary to stop one party defaulting due to so-called *force majeur* circumstances: if the seller can default and claim a drought or some government order stopped them from delivering the specified amounts the contract cannot be relied upon by the buyer and becomes much less valuable. Term 2 backs up Term 1 by ensuring that a seller who has allowed their circumstances to deteriorate to the point where they cannot honour their contracts pays a very high financial penalty which should far exceed the buyer's costs of finding alternative supplies in emergency (i.e. at least the buyer won't lose financially if the seller fails to deliver). Economists claim that all commodity markets have both terms with reason – to avoid moral hazard – and that both terms were essential in developing successful energy trading. These are practical illustrations of Coase's theorem: unregulated trading between private parties can improve overall resource allocations provided property rights are fully defined.

So, if water contract prices are to reflect costs accurately there should be at least two parts to the contract: a price for putting the infrastructure in, and a price for drawing each unit of water down. As soon as we view matters this way, and knowing the general cost structure of the water industry, we see that the vast bulk of the payments will be for putting the infrastructure in place. As the infrastructure price will generally be the larger, but should also fall the longer the period over which initial costs are amortised[364], long term contracts are likely, and this price may need to be reviewed or indexed for inflation. The call-down price for each unit of water actually shipped should reflect short run opportunity costs on both sides, including directly variable costs such as the seller's pumping and chemical costs, and the buyer's short run opportunity costs of meeting demand via alternative supplies at short notice. This price may need to be reviewed periodically for inflation and other changes to the grids. It can, however, be demonstrated that an options contract with specified call-off rights will always be superior to a straightforward call-off contract.

Physical trading of water in practice

Trading between vertically separated entities

---

[364] Recovering the costs of your connecting pipes over 20 years will cost less per year than if you have to do it over 5.

While wastewater services are rarely vertically split, responsibility for services is sometimes divided vertically through the clean water value chain, as we have seen being imposed in the electricity and gas industries. In Australia, for instance, the city of Melbourne's water has long been split into a wholesale water supplier which provides abstraction, storage and treatment, and three 'retailers' who purchase bulk treated water from the wholesaler, distribute, and retail it to their own designated parts of the city. This approach seems to have worked well for a long time, but, as earlier noted, no-one pretends that the prices of water traded are more than an administrative *fiat*.

Horizontal bulk water trading

In the UK most water utilities have "bulk supply agreements" of one kind or another with at least one of their neighbouring water companies, and these have sometimes been significant proportions of a company's total supplies[365]. But most of these contracts date from times before 1989, when at least one of the companies was in the public sector, and the other may have been a dividend-controlled (essentially a cost-plus) company, and the engineers who drew up the contracts "over a pint in the pub" set arbitrarily low tariffs which have then been (at most) indexed for inflation. The prices, therefore, again are rarely thought to reflect the true 'value' of the water, in any kind of economic sense.

A major reason for this is that all raw water abstracted in England and Wales, for each type of licence required, is sold for the same price by the Environment Agency (EA), the government's sovereign owner of all naturally-occurring fresh water. Thus water from a borehole in dry southern England, where water licences are very scarce, costs the same to a water company or any other abstractor as water from an identical borehole in the northern Lake District, where rainfall is three times as heavy and water plentiful. Furthermore the general level of the EA's abstraction tariffs is set on a cost-recovery basis[366], so that EA licence fee revenues equal the costs of administering the abstraction licencing system.

A 2009 review of water industry competition and innovation in England and Wales by Martin Cave recommended that this deficiency be rectified, but it was a very muted request and not completely thought through from the environmental point of view: abstraction charges in southern England are about 0.3p a cubic metre for water that sells for around 80p a cubic metre, but the difference in LRMCs of different water companies in southern England is of the order of 30-50p a cubic metre, so the revealed scarcity value of raw water is roughly a hundred times greater than its selling price (from a publicly-owned monopoly). Logically one could argue that Professor Cave should simultaneously have recommended that all suppliers of raw water into natural water courses (such as

---

[365] E.g. prior to mergers the former Water Only Companies Essex and Suffolk Water and Mid Kent Water used to obtain more than 10% of their Distribution Input from bulk supplies.

[366] Section 42 of the 1995 Environment Act establishing the Environment Agency requires this.

good quality treated effluent from sewage treatment plant that discharges into a river) should *receive* the same level of charge from the EA for providing valuable raw water equal to its quality-adjusted scarcity value. With a cash volumetric value for each cubic metre in the man-made water-and-sewage system roughly a hundred times its current value, price-sensitive water users such as water and wastewater utilities, farmers, fish farmers and golf courses would radically alter their leakage and other operational behaviours markedly, radically improving the efficiency of the British water economy.

So, the environmental scarcity value of raw water does not remotely affect the price of raw water charged in England and Wales. Although a few water economists are aware of this enormous distortion British politicians have yet to be persuaded of the consequences of it. Given the fundamental mispricing of raw water sold by the Environment Agency in southern England, to expect the prices of those small parts of water supplied that are traded between two companies somehow to reflect economic fundamentals, even if the companies are arms-length traders, is quite unrealistic.

Trading water rights – the theoretical debate
The superiority of options trading of physical water reminds us of one conclusion in Chapter 2 that the fundamental output of utility infrastructure is availability. If, fundamentally, buyers are prepared to pay substantial sums for the option to call down water at a pre-specified price why not trade water endowments directly – i.e. trade the right to abstract water from nature directly?

Until the recent Australian successes, rarely in economics had so much been written in theory with so little follow-through in practice, as the subject of the economics of water rights. This section is a very brief introduction to this vast topic. But to deepen your insights into the human drama behind this kind of dry analysis watch the film 'Jean de Florette' or its sequel 'Manon des Sources'; they really bring out what water means to traditional farmers in hot climates.

The fundamental advantage of trading water rights
Because private land can sit above an aquifer, or abut, or contain, inland or coastal surface waters, in any country where water rights follow from land rights and land can be privately owned, it is possible to achieve some degree of trading in water rights by trading land. Except in water-plentiful countries like Ireland, Finland or northern Canada, access to a good water source will always add to land's value, particularly in dry regions. So if water is scarce and land can be traded, effectively water can be traded through land trading.

Direct trading of water rights separates the water properties of a piece of land from the land's other characteristics. This allows the owner of a piece of land to split its characteristics and sell different parts to different owners. So a farmer or a water company might buy the water rights of a piece of land, while a developer might buy the land's good location and pleasant views. In principle, therefore, in a national economy a better overall optimum price vector should result because two markets have replaced one. Accordingly, many countries have decided to permit trading of water rights independently from land trading, and in preference to direct trading of water.

The main advantages
Free-market enthusiasts (many economists) argue that Coase's theorem should be allowed to work: governments should just define property rights adequately and stand back, letting the twin markets of water rights and other uses of land find their own equilibria. Provided there is a fair market with many independent buyers and sellers, free market solutions will improve overall resource allocation. All the government has to do is define property rights fully in law, establish an overall public body to administer the water market[367], enforce the rule of law, try to reduce transaction costs and barriers to exchange, and keep an eye on indicators of competition for any abuse of market power. Each individual agent is incentivised to use water as efficiently as possible by virtue of being able to sell any unused capacity in the market.

The main disadvantages
Critics say that this libertarian view ignores the innate realities of water: to use it – for irrigation, fish farming, recreational or domestic use – almost always requires considerable sunk costs building infrastructure to move it to where it is needed. Of course there are exceptions – farmers can move a herd of thirsty animals into a field and the animals will find the river, or farmers on low-lying land bordering a river in flood can just open an irrigation ditch onto the river, and let it flow in – but such instances are all too rare. Infrastructure sunk costs naturally raise transaction costs, and if they vary between classes of user – e.g. a water utility wants to install an inlet, a pump and 5km of pipe – this class of user is going to want a higher degree of certainty and a longer contract than farmers who simply want to give their cows a drink up to ten times a year.

In addition water supplies vary considerably and unpredictably, even in the 21st century. The overall river basin managers can over- or under-estimate the volume of water available that will not put stress on regional resources, so in practice *decisions made by the central market administrator – or river basin manager – can be the major cause of either inefficiency* (too conservative in releasing water) *or environmental disaster* (letting too much go) in a water trading scheme.

Finally, property rights are not always absolute; sometimes, to be practical, they have to be "conditional and overlapping"[368], depending on supply or other exogenous conditions, so that in fact rights may be expressed as a share in a

---

[367] Strict libertarians would say that if the public wishes to retain water levels above zero for ecological or environmental reasons the public body should buy such water just like any other agent, rather than setting a minimum water level greater than zero. Few politicians would buy that.

[368] Bauer C 1997, Bringing water markets down to earth: the political economy of water rights in Chile 1976-95, World Development Vol 25 No.5, page 640

total amount of water that e.g. an irrigation canal happens to be carrying at that time, rather than as an absolute number of cubic metres per time period[369].

Chilean water trading

In Chile a military government set up the country's 1981 Water Code, in which all raw water was formally ceded to be the property of the state, but the right to abstract water could be assigned to any private party. Once passed on to a private owner the water right could then be divided, added to, sold on, mortgaged or transferred to another party, just like land: it was a freely tradable piece of property. And, just like land, it could, in principle, be taxed by the government (though ultimately the generals shied away from that).

Water rights sales have occurred, and are recorded, but they are low: Bauer, a long-term Chilean researcher, found just 0.4% a year of irrigators selling water rights in Los Andes province (23 a year out of 5,400 irrigators over a 12-year period) and in Los Angeles (13 a year out of 3,300 irrigators), and other researchers have found similar low rates of water rights transfers. By contrast straightforward land sales, including associated water rights, were four times as popular[370]. Thus we can conclude that it is certainly possible to sell water rights in Chile, and it has been done a few thousand times, but land transfers are more common than water rights transfers, and little volume flows through these water rights markets. Bauer reports that transfers are mostly between irrigators; transfers from farmers to other water users have occurred, as cities or mining operations have expanded, but are generally uncommon.

Why are they not more popular? Practicalities, really, Bauer maintains. First, geography: supplies of Andean snowmelt water are unpredictable, and as the structures which divert water into irrigation canals are temporary and rough-and-ready, the volumes of water flowing are unknown and unpredictable; thus the 'water right' being sold is typically a share of an unknown volume of water. Secondly, history: many rights come from prior use claims, but often these were not recorded in the 19th and 20th centuries, and they may conflict with current users claiming to have legal rights awarded by military governments in the 1980s, who gave a presumption of ownership in favour of current water users in 1981. Having three separate Registers of water rights doesn't help too. Then there are the roles of people's expectations and beliefs: a belief that water is sacred, has been hard won from nature, and is essential to living if you are a farmer. And, according to Bauer, a belief that water prices are much higher than they actually are, combined with an expectation that water rights prices will rise from current levels as human populations grow. The effect of these is that most farmers "refuse to sell even a fraction of their water rights"; most actual sales

---

[369] Ibid page 641.

[370] Bauer ibid page 645; he cites Hearne R, 1995, The market allocation of natural resources Transactions of water use rights in Chile, PhD Dissertation University of Minnesota, Minneapolis as confirming that transactions in central and northern Chile were very limited.

are people leaving agriculture, disposing of inheritance or the economically desperate[371].

"Lordy – What a minefield!" you may be tempted to exclaim. But life is messy, and practical economic structures must deal with that. For some light relief let's look at water rights trading in the western USA.

Trading water in the western USA
Irrigation in the Americas has a long history, including, of course, the Incas who derived much of their empire's income from irrigated agriculture. In what is now the western USA irrigation has enhanced crop yields for thousands of years[33], being most recently practised by Pueblo peoples such as the Hohokam, the Zuni, Hopi and the Opata, but not the Navajo, who arrived here after 1400. It was the arrival of European settlers, and Federal English-based laws after 1850, that changed all this.

English-based law generally presumes that any action is legal unless it is specifically outlawed. It also appeals to natural reason (what a reasonable man would decide is right), places emphasis on precedence or first usage, and likes to be as specific as possible. In the context of water rights this tends to mean
 1. A piece of land can be defined, fenced off and owned 'freehold' – forever: this presumes settled farming, and is of course an alien concept to nomadic peoples, who ask rhetorically 'Although a man may own a knife or a hunting bow, how can he own the land, the sky or the waters?'
 2. A person who accesses water from their freehold land (*a riparian right*) is allowed to do so unless someone else can show this is theft of their water – i.e. anything can be freely taken from nature, but you must not steal another human's water
 3. Where demands conflict the first person who can show they had *beneficial use* will have the highest claim (a principal known as *First In Time, First In Use - FITFIU*)
 4. Where water supplies vary seasonally or annually, water rights and contracts become more complicated – conditional, rather than absolute.

From first principles we know that points 1 and 2 means that land bordering a river or lake will have associated rights to access the water there, and in hot territory that means this land will be more valuable than land with no water access rights. When there are only a few settlers this has few consequences, but if the number of farmers rises considerably, insufficient water can be left in the river for downstream communities, or for what we would term environmental or ecological reasons.

An interesting version of this is seen in Indian territories 14,000 km away. In the Deccan, in central India, a giant aquifer underlies the whole plateau and fresh

---

[371] Ibid page 648.

water to supply irrigation ditches can be accessed by any farmer willing to incur the (sunk) infrastructure costs of drilling a well. Consequently nearly every farmer has dug a well and the water table has fallen – as in the western USA, *under standard English law the environment comes last*. However, the Deccan situation has an environmental solution, albeit an unfair one: the water table has fallen so far, and the wells have become so deep and expensive, that in effect wealth rations water – only the wealthiest farmers can afford to re-bore wells deep enough to reach the water table, and so an equilibrium water table may soon be stabilising[373].

No such naturally regulated system works with surface waters in hot deserts: once abstractions exceed flows the river dries up. Immediately we see that anyone downstream with prior rights (point 3) may claim upstream sources are 'stealing their water', and we have the first source of legal disputes. If we add seasonal or annual fluctuations (point 4) to this we have a second source of legal disputes. Next, add in the complications of different jurisdictions of English laws, each being limited to only one State, while the rivers peacefully wind through several man-made legal units called States, and we have jurisdictional issues conflicting with the realities of physical drainage. Now add in the realities of lost certificates, forgeries (don't forget Jean de Florette), and native American unfamiliarity with English legal processes, and we can soon reach a point where modern cities and farmers are suing each other about water rights using laws based on customs and practice in mediaeval (wet) England, while the needs of the natural environment and the needs of people who were here hundreds of years earlier are completely ignored.

Politicians or the highest lawyers in the land had to intervene and create over-arching rules or laws. The first of these was to unbundle FITFIU water rights from ownership of land (riparian rights), which was first demonstrated in a court case in Colorado in 1872 and was adopted in Colorado's Constitution of 1876. Within 20 years most western States had also adopted the 'appropriation doctrine'. These decisions allowed the settlers to begin trading water rights separately from land. Then in 1908 the Supreme Court ruled that Federal (not State) Law applied to issues of native American water rights, and that their land rights automatically included prior riparian rights[374], even if the native people developed beneficial use after American settlers[375].

And so water trading within sets of defined rules began. Two things could be traded:
- Permanent rights could be sold ('sales'); or
- Leases for X amount of water within a right could be sold for a number of years ('leases')

---

[373] The author learned of this situation when working on a World Bank mission in India in the 1990s.
[374] Up to a maximum called the Principal Irrigable Area.
[375] Winters v. United States decision 1908.

Most water rights were to absolute volumes of water in a year, and these did not vary with the overall supply of water in a river, as Chilean rights do. So when supplies dried up environmental uses habitually came last, and each licensee was entitled to use up their full legal right in the FITFIU sequence until the most junior (recent) licensees received none. Gradually some environmental use was recognised as a 'beneficial use' in certain areas. A condition with serious adverse effects in some States was the use-or-lose provision whereby licence holders who did not use their entitlement every year might forfeit their licence, which has obvious perverse effects.

How busy are America's water markets? One study found just under 1100 deals between 1990 and 2003[376], which is less than two a week – for an area half of the USA. Half the deals were leases and, being once-only deals, they naturally constituted 96% of the water traded over the 13 years[377]. The volume of leased water, however, averaged just 2000 GL a year, which is tiny given that Los Angeles alone consumes 636GL a year and drinking water is a far smaller proportion of total water use than irrigation. So there has not been a vast quantity of trading, and the main reasons cited are high transaction costs (building the infrastructure to move the water) and the stochastic nature of supply. Many observers note that farmers seem to value their permanent rights far higher than industrialists. Obviously farmers who are giving up farming for good – e.g. selling land for development – might decide to sell any associated water rights, but it seems few others are willing to do this and take a chance on buying leases in the market.

Australia: successful trading of water rights
Let's now look at a hot dry country where property rights are well established and socially ingrained, generally the water users have some alternative uses for their land or time (so agents perceive defined opportunity costs for water), and the authorities did their homework (i.e. learned the lessons from Chile and the western USA) before making proposals. They then followed these proposals by creating the right new bodies, hiring and empowering talented people, and providing adequate funds to make the whole thing work.

Although there had been informal water trading (as there often is) in South Australia, Australian water rights trading started properly in 1994 when the National Water Commission was first given the legal power to separate water rights from land rights. A series of reforms was considered and initiated, and revised, but to jump to the present, what exists now is trading of two main kinds of licence:

---

[376] Alberta Innovates (a research organisation affiliated to the State of Alberta) 2010, Water trading: the western US experience; a presentation given to the Alberta branch of the Canadian Water Resources Association March 2010 accessed July 2012 at http://www.cwra.org/resource/Proceedings/AB_BranchConference_2010/John%20Thompson.pdf.

[377] Counting the water sales only once; of course you should not do this as their limits apply each year forever.

1. A water entitlement is defined as
 A perpetual or ongoing entitlement to exclusive access to a <u>share</u> of water from a specified consumptive pool as defined in the relevant water plan.

2. A water allocation is defined as
 The <u>specific volume</u> of water allocated to water access entitlements in a given season, defined according to rules established in the relevant water plan.

There are many other kinds of water rights, helpfully summarised on the Australian Government's National Water Market website[378]. These include rights for watering stock, and irrigation or delivery rights (which are tradable within irrigation systems), and one for native water rights. Note also that native water rights a) exist, and b) are not tradable. They are awarded to specific people or communities for ever for personal, domestic and non-commercial purposes. Note too, that in contrast to peoples of the South Western USA, many native Australian peoples had no tradition of using irrigated agriculture as their main livelihood; their impact on overall water tables or river flows is therefore likely to be negligible.

So an *entitlement* licence is a *share* of a specific source of raw water that exists forever – like Chilean licences – while an *allocation* licence is a *specific volume* of water that will be supplied this year, or next, or some other agreed future year – like a pure commodity market agreement. Thus if a farmer or other water user with defined entitlement shares (or with none) sees a dry weather forecast and predicts low total water flows, and so a low entitlement *volume* for herself and her crops or animals, she can increase this by buying a specific volume of water on the allocations market, and the water goes to whoever is prepared to pay the highest. As in all markets, those with the lowest internal valuation of the commodity sell it to those with the highest valuations, so that overall resource allocation is improved.

The latest figures show this set of markets seems to be working well:
1. The total number of individual trades exceeds 30,000 a year[379]
2. The volumes of water traded are substantial: 1204GL a year of entitlements and almost 3500 GL of water allocated in 2010-11[380] were traded in that year; the annual trade in entitlements is around 5% of all entitlements in Australia, while the volume of water allocated and traded last year is roughly twice Melbourne Water's entire storage capacity;
3. The value of water traded exceeded a $3 billion (US$3 billion) in 2009-10;

---

[378] National Water Market "About rights" http://www.nationalwatermarket.gov.au/about/rights.html.

[379] Presentation by James Cameron CEO of National Water Commission to a World Bank conference January 2011.

[380] Australian Water Markets Report 2010-11 Executive Summary provides most of the figures cited in this section.

4. The markets respond to natural supply conditions as one would expect: 2010-11, was the wettest year on record in most of Australia, including in the Murray-Darling basin, which is the drainage heart of the continent. The effect of this welcome rain was that the volume of entitlement trading went down, the volume of allocation trading went up, water entitlement prices fell slightly (10%) while allocation prices for water in the year crashed to just a fifth of the previous year's levels[381], and the total value of water trades halved from A$3 billion to A$1.5 billion

5. Even in a wet year like 2010 the volumes traded rose by 30% (entitlements) and 120% (allocations) since trading was first reported by the National Water Commission, in 2007

6. Considerable volumes of water are traded between States or Territories, and changes in the pattern of trades reflect changes in their relative water endowments.

The cost and timeliness of transactions is actively monitored by the National Water Commission, registration is kept as clear and simple as possible, volumes are metered, information is published rapidly, accounts are actively monitored, enforcement resources are significant, and action is swift. Transparency of allocations and operations are key, which is why a high premium is placed on publishing a lot of general and specific market information rapidly. In addition the Federal Government faced up to a very serious potential problem of previous over-allocation of water rights by funding a government buy-back of entitlements, and freeing up its own agents to enter the markets as they deem best. Reminiscent of a central bank buying back its own government bonds, this is the kind of action governments must be prepared to do if they are to 'make markets work' given a real legacy of past actions, decisions made with information that we later realise to have been wrong, or simply priorities that have changed.

Despite promising auguries so far, whether these markets can really withstand the full range of climatic change that Australia can face, and will face in the next half century, remains to be tested.

Lessons from Chilean, American and Australian water rights trading
For water markets to improve economic efficiency they must lead to a better allocation of resources. However, if you are a farmer and all you know is how to farm crops with irrigated water, you perceive no other opportunity cost for your time and effort – because you cannot imagine other economic livelihoods, or perceive them to be a betrayal of the values your parents, grandparents and ancestors toiled for throughout their working lives. The notion of selling your water rights would be like committing suicide. Any attack on your community's water rights will be viewed as strongly as an attack on your life: it is an attack on your community's very economic existence.

---

[381] Ibid Chair's Foreword page III

Despite low volumes, it can be argued that water trading has worked in Chile since the 1980s, as where water use changes seem appropriate, trades between sectors have occurred in the 'right' directions, and farmers and publicly-owned water utilities have bid up the cost of water rights to sensible levels. This has been helped by the water utilities being allowed to have sensible (sufficiently profitable, but not outrageous) tariffs to start with. But the evidence seems to be that those selling the rights are only those who can see alternative lifestyles for themselves and therefore define a lower opportunity cost for the water than the would-be buyers. It is the shortage of such people that appears to restrict the growth of the Chilean water market.

Another observation is that the sunk costs of creating the infrastructure in Chilean irrigation canals (diverting water from the snowmelt rivers) have effectively been minimised by creating rough barriers called *bocatoma* "made of stone, wood, brush etc."[382] that have to be largely rebuilt every year; changes in these compared to rival bocatoma, as well as changing river flows, alter the actual volume in each canal every year. However, a reason for low trading volumes within each canal network is that physical delivery of extra or less water requires both buyer and seller to alter the size of barriers outside their own properties to divert more or less water into their properties – a considerable transaction cost – and even more works to intervening properties if the two are not close neighbours (a 'prohibitively' high transaction cost).

And the western USA? They might do well to learn from Chile's determination to use national bodies to supervise private sector uses (though not the system of three water licence registers!) and study Australia's well-considered mechanisms, which succeed in moving water rights between States and users.

---

[382] Bauer page 646

Chapter Twelve

Restructuring of rail

Total transport demand and modal demands
Demand for transport falls into two categories: human cargo, or 'passengers', and other cargo, called freight. Human cargo is generally more demanding, so the transport service's characteristics (speed, frequency, punctuality comfort etc.) can lead to strong non-price preferences for one mode of transport over another, and differentiation between different suppliers using the same mode of transport.

Total demand for passenger transport is rising in advanced economies, but slower than GDP, so crude income elasticities[383] of total passenger demand against GDP are usually less than one (0.4-0.7 in the USA over recent decades, around 0.8 in Europe). In emerging countries, where people are still breaking away from traditional ways of life that did not involve a lot of travel, crude income elasticities for passenger travel may exceed one for several decades, leading to double digit growth rates in demand for transport infrastructure to be provided (or funded) generally by governments.

Total demand for freight is strongly affected by the development of a country's industrial base, so it is rising very strongly in countries like India and China, which became the 'workshops of the world' in the early 21st century. In advanced economies the crude income elasticity of freight transport is around 0.7 (USA) to 0.9 (European Union). In total, therefore, for advanced economies growing at trends of 2-3% a year, freight demand is rising at 1½ - 2% a year while passenger demand is growing more slowly, at 1- 1½% a year.

Patterns of intermodal transport demand
Figure 125 shows the commonest modes of transport used by passengers (total demand is measured in billions of passenger.kilometers) in four of the world's largest economies:

---

[383] Geometric growth rate of transport demand divided by geometric growth rate of real GDP; obviously this figure ignores relative price changes and other second order economic interactions.

Figure 125: Modes of transport used by passengers in 4 regions of the world

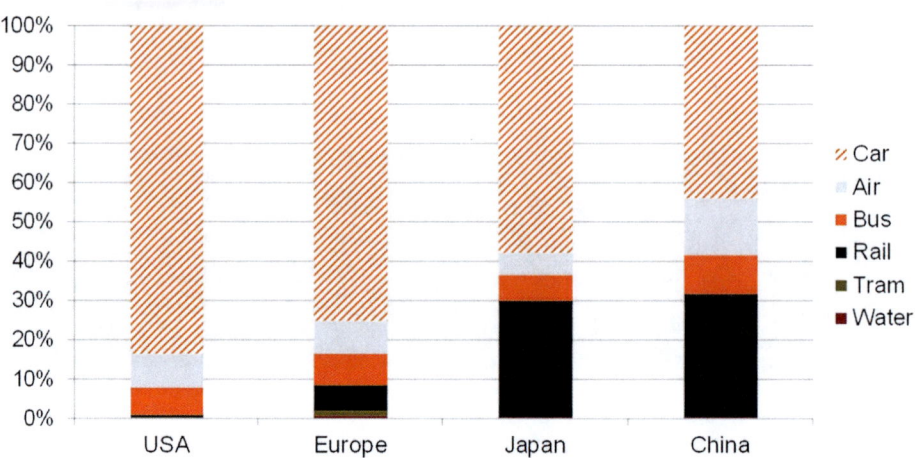

Sources: EU transport statistical pocketbook 2015; all figures 2013 except Japan 2010 and China bus figure from 2010

The dominance of the car is obvious, except in China, although car transport is rising strongly in China and it is by far the world's largest market for new cars at present. While car use is rising strongly in emerging countries like China and India, car's share of the passenger market has been falling for some time in America, Europe, and Japan. Passenger rail is barely used at all in the USA, not much used in Europe (behind buses and air travel), but is the most used in China and the second most used in Japan. In all countries air travel continues to increase its share of the total, undoubtedly because of its speed, but where governments have invested in high speed rail (in Asia and Europe) rail's share is rising. In Europe, for instance, rail's share of the market fell throughout the twentieth century, but since 2000 rail's share of passenger transport has been rising, partly, one suspects, because of road traffic congestion, and partly because of the growth of high speed rail routes (many faster than 300km per hour) which substitute for air travel within the continent[384]. In Italy, Sweden and Germany more than 25% of passenger rail travel is on high speed trains, while in Spain and France this figure exceeds 50%.

---

[384] Although high speed trains are slower than aircraft-in-the-air, they run to and from city centres, and connect easily to local trains and bus routes, rather than having to use airports 20-50 kilometres outside the city centre.

Figure 126: Modes of transport for freight around the world

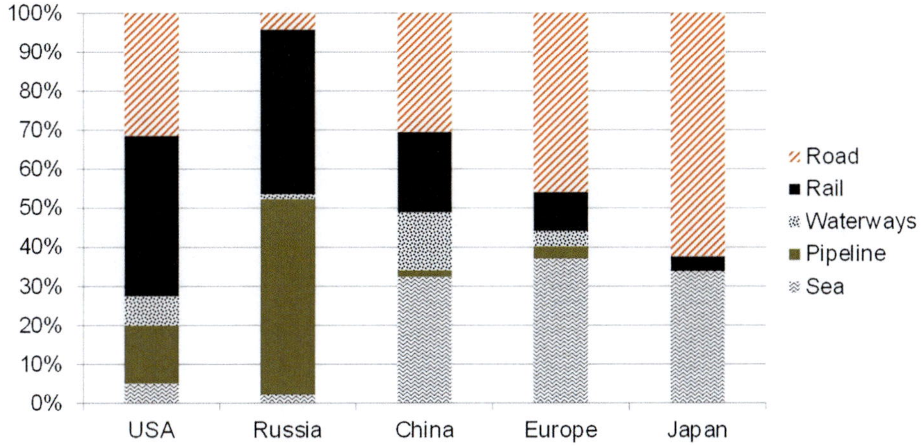

Sources: EU transport statistical pocketbook 2015; all figures 2013 except USA 2012

For freight Figure 126 shows that in the USA, road is the commonest way to move freight, followed by rail, while in Russia oil and gas pipelines move the most stuff, followed again by rail. In the USA rail freight has been rising until recently (the above figures are for Class 1 rail only) while in most other countries rail's share of freight is falling. China, which is the world's largest internal freight market by far, moves more freight by rail than America, and 50% more by road, but moves ten times as much as America on water, by sea or rivers. The islands of Japan and the sea-indented continent of Europe also move a far greater weight of freight by sea than by rail.

Combined, Figure 125 and Figure 126 show the differences between American and Russian railways (huge volumes of freight but not many passengers) and the densely-populated continent of Europe and Japan, surrounded by seas, which move most heavy freight by water, leaving the railways to move passengers around faster than they can drive, and sometimes faster than they can fly. The stark contrast between the two types of rail system is shown in Figure 127 where revenues from passengers and freight are compared for the American and British rail systems:

Figure 127: Sources of modern rail revenues

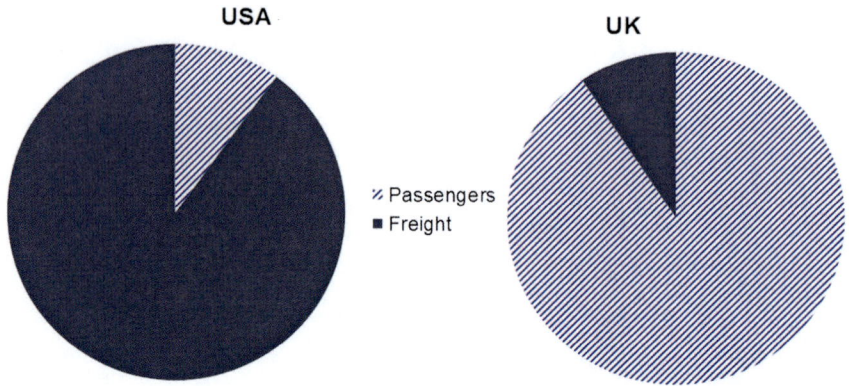

Sources: APTA Public Transportation 2013 Factbook Table 35, Association of American Railroads Railroad Facts p 3, GB National Rail Trends 2012 & estimate based on Rail Value for money study (2009)

(Note that the revenues in Figure 127 are those from customers only, and exclude any subsidies from public funds)

The implications are clear: American railroads are predominantly freight-driven while European railways are passenger-driven.

Fundamental economic characteristics of surface transport

Recall, first of all, that unlike the "commodity products" of water, gas or electricity, public *passenger transport is a differentiable* service (each supplier can make customers sharply aware of the difference in service) if the journey is long enough (generally over 30 minutes). *Freight* transport, on the other hand, is very much a *commodity product*: price rules, so customers nearly always select the lowest priced service.

Second, once set up, all surface transport has low marginal costs for the individual user, and often negative consumption externalities of pollution and congestion, which mean the social marginal cost exceeds the very low private marginal cost. However, maintaining 'the track' on which the road or rail wheels run usually has substantial infrastructure maintenance costs which are largely fixed – they do not vary much with an increase in short term loads. But if an increase in long term load does in fact worsen the track's condition, and demand rises continuously, it may be some time before any effect is detected on the track's condition. A maintenance 'backlog' will then have built up, which comes as an unpleasant surprise to the infrastructure funders, who are often taxpayers.

Third, in most countries it is common for the government to delegate a publicly-owned agency to maintain the infrastructure. This agency is effectively the track manager and steward of the public assets; it may be a government Department for roads or rail within a Transport Ministry, or a public body such as Indian Railways or the Federal Highway Administration in the USA. Within their externally-determined budget the track manager must decide where, when and how to undertake maintenance, and to make minor quality or service improvements or capacity expansions. Decisions about major expansions of capacity or service quality are usually raised to the political level; if they are efficient governments will use social cost benefit analysis to determine these priorities. The overall level of funding is then determined by the priority the government gives to rail or road transport compared with competing demands on public spending. But for the millions of routine minor decisions the governments' problem is how to incentivise the track manager to provide a socially-optimal service within its budget.

Some regulated utility concepts may help here. The track agency can be funded using a simple Pay-As-You-Go (PAYGo) system whereby it is given an annual or multi-year spending limit. But the funder – government – then has little or no idea about the extent to which provision is being made for depreciation and renewals, or for servicing the effective debt on the highway agency's assets. If the agency were given a Regulatory Asset Base along the lines described in Chapter 8 the government could make comparisons between the different publicly-owned track managers, and between them all and commercially-funded transport modes around the world for which data is available. Naturally the caveats in Chapter 8 about writing down or up the inherited RAB to something suitable would be central in setting the inherited asset base, but as time goes by the inherited asset base becomes less relevant. Just so we are clear let us stress that the inherited RAB dictates only the (past) base, but all (future) additions should be approved by a political or regulatory body which has at least considered using social cost benefit analysis.

The problem of optimal incentivisation of the infrastructure managers in transport is exactly the same as it is in other utilities. Whether publicly or privately owned, good management needs clear indicators of infrastructure condition, capacity, availability, serviceability and delivered service levels, and these need to be publicly accounted for, with clear rewards systems for good stewardship of the infrastructure, allowing successful management teams some discretion in spending capital or maintenance funds to enhance the network.

Rail's general characteristics
One of the most important differences between road and rail is that, while roads are generally viewed as intrinsically 'profitable'[385], for the last hundred years rail has been a loss-making service in most countries. In other words, using conventional supply/demand analysis, the rail demand curve is not far enough out to the right for the MC=MR condition to meet at a profitable quantity of output – or, some politicians would say that due to inefficiency in the rail industry, the cost curves are not shrunk far enough to the left for this intersection to be a profitable solution. Actually, politicians don't speak like that ...it's the sort of

---

[385] In the sense that if a country chose to privatise them all, using tolls or road pricing they would easily make a profit.

thing economists interpret politicians to say. Real politicians use phrases like "Read my lips:...No... new... taxes"[386] – before getting elected and being forced to introduce new taxes to solve a budget crisis. Economically speaking, railways can be viewed as providing three main kinds of service:
1. Infrastructure: tracks, stations, bridges, tunnels, cuttings, signals, sidings etc.
2. Rolling stock – the 'trains'
3. Train services – what customers buy: a transport service from A to B; in densely populated countries this is mostly passenger with some freight; the passenger service is the differentiable part of the train "product", though significant differentiation requires the customer to be on board for more than a short time[387].

Bearing in mind the need for public subsidies, Figure 128 depicts the three kinds of service:

Figure 128: The general economic structure of the rail industry

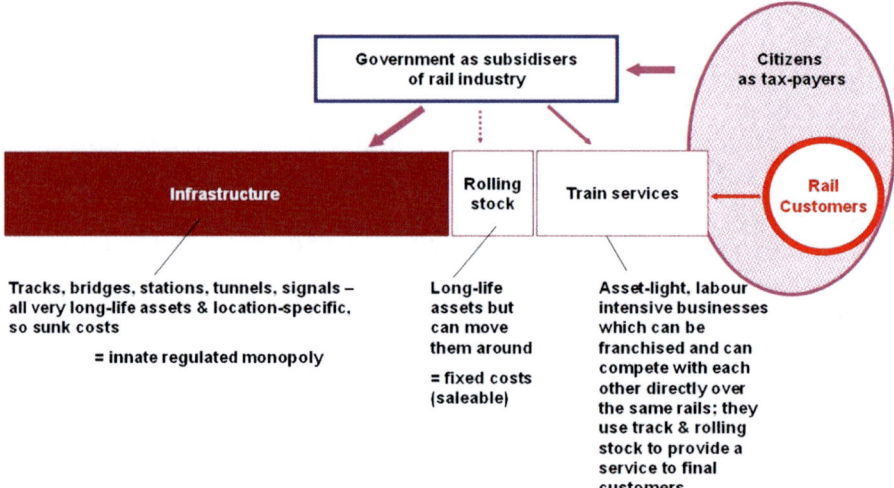

Note the difference between rail users and the non-rail-travelling public – a potential source of major conflict, which is why this distinction is drawn heavily: it can be argued that this is a *hidden resentment* in society, between rail users and those who do not like rail (or possibly any form of public transport). This is because, while few would quarrel with the positive consumption externalities that flow from establishing grids for water, sewage, electricity and gas, some

---

[386] George HW Bush 18 August 1988 to the Republican National Convention, on accepting the Republican Party's nomination. President Bush Senior did not want to introduce new taxes, but was eventually forced to by the checks and balances of the American political system.

[387] So it is hard to differentiate underground or short commuter rail services, except through the well-established measures of frequency of service, reliability and punctuality, which can all be written into the conditions of service that all suppliers must meet. True differentiation of a good or service cannot be written into a contract.

(not all) members of the non-travelling public believe rail should not be subsidised at all.

The proportion of revenues from customers vs non-customers

To compare the contributions of rail customers with subsidies paid by all tax-paying citizens Figure 129 shows the contributions to operating funds from all sources for the American and British rail networks:

Figure 129: Sources of operating funds for two national rail systems

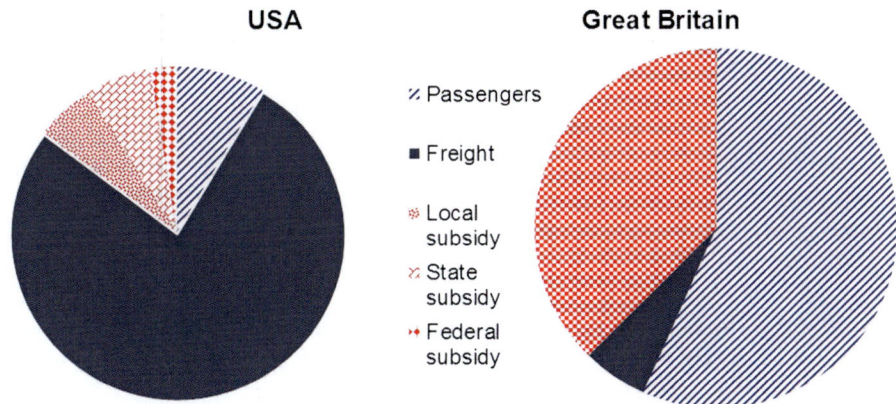

Sources: APTA Public Transportation 2013 Factbook Table 26 & estimates, Association of American Railroads Railroad Facts p 3, GB National Rail Trends portal Government Support

Note that although these figures contain some estimates, differ widely between countries, and change from year to year, public subsidies make an important contribution to most countries' rail funding, but this is far smaller in the USA (less than a quarter of total operating funds) than in the UK (currently a third of all funding). In fact the British system is thought to be one of the least subsidised rail networks in Europe – i.e. British rail passengers pay some of the most cost-related fares in Europe – and the proportion of funds provided by subsidies has decreased recently.

US freight – profitable, competitive & de-regulated

Figure 126 has shown that rail is the commonest way to move freight around the USA, while Figure 127 shows that this freight demand drives the American rail network. Figure 129 shows that US railroads are not heavily subsidised in comparison with many other countries – indeed the freight networks are profitable, while taxpayer subsidies are provided by counties, cities and States to benefit passenger transport, presumably to ease traffic congestion or to get people to and from work in the central business districts of their local city.

Sunshine regulation

Although rail is one of the oldest network industries around, and contains some very strong cultural traditions, the US rail industry has pioneered several forms of regulation of profitable monopolies. After the initial wave of private sector investment had created the first railroads in the 19th century, New England grandee Charles Francis Adams II wrote a book "Chapters of Erie" in which he satirised railroad bosses and exposed how the rail companies were able to create enormous monopoly profits. He was quickly appointed to a body called the Massachusetts Railroad Commission and began to have a significant impact on railroad prices and profits, despite the fact that this Commission had no formal legislative or regulatory powers. "It had really no power, except the power to report, but these reports were strong enough to command respect, and even obedience." (AT Hadley 1885, quoted in Henry, Matheu and Jeunemaitre, 2001[388]). So in 1871 Adams wrote to the Massachusetts Railroad noting that the cost of a locomotive had fallen from $30,000 to $12,000 and asking what effect this would have on their fares. Fearing a public backlash and political action, the railroad sacrificed $500,000 of profits by cutting their rates (Henry *et al*).

In 1984 Professor of Business History Thomas McCraw reviewed Adams' influence and christened the Massachusetts Railroad Commission 'the Sunshine Commission'[389] because of their effective exposure of facts to the light of public knowledge, and the potential for substantial public disapproval. The practice has since been called Sunshine Regulation because it relies on a strong sense of values in a community, and public accountability, without any formal legislative backing. However, Adams' actions were not totally consumer-focused: at a time when there were no regulatory agencies or formal powers to control monopolies, he believed that businesses would benefit from regulation to protect them both from capricious political actions on behalf of customers, and actions by unscrupulous financial traders dealing in railroad stocks and bonds. He thus anticipated some of the main roles of an independent regulator today.

The emergence of Rate of Return Regulation
Following Adams the 1890 Sherman Act established the first 'anti-trust' laws, although these were not used effectively against monopolies for two decades, and had to be strengthened in 1914 by the Clayton Act (see Chapter 8). In the meantime Alexander Graham Bell had invented and patented the telephone. Protected by its patents, the Bell Company, and its long distance division American Telephone and Telegraph (AT&T), grew a considerable monopoly of long distance and local phone lines. By 1885 it was earning a 50% real Return on Investment, but when its patents expired competitors rushed in, its market share fell, and by 1907 returns had fallen to 5%. Bell's financial backers replaced him with Theodore Vail, who reasserted the company's grip on local networks and long distance calls, restoring profitability to 15% by 1912 (Henry *et al* Chapter 1). But Vail was no short-sighted capitalist, and saw that if he pushed profits too high political action would force AT&T to reduce its profits. Following two years of nationalisation in the First World War, when it returned to private ownership Vail proposed a compromise:

---

[388] Henry C, Matheu M, Jeunemaitre A, 2001, Regulation of Network Utilities: the European experience, Oxford University Press, Chapter 1 page 3.
[389] McCraw R, 1984, Prophets of Regulation: Charles Francis Adams, ... Alfred E Kahn, Harvard.

- An external body would set Bell's rates (its prices)
- Bell would have an obligation to provide a universal service to all phone users

His proposal was accepted and became the standard rate of return model for regulating American monopolies. Initially the Bell Company's was regulated directly by the US Congress, but from 1934 the Federal Communication Commission was appointed its regulator.

The Interstate Commerce Commission 1887-1980
In rail an 1887 Act had created the Interstate Commerce Commission (ICC) to regulate railroads. Seven Commissioners were appointed who could have no commercial links to the railroad industry, nor could any of the staff they hired to help them. Thus the ICC became one of the first independent and powerful economic regulators in the world, acquiring 500 staff by 1909. Initially lacking direct powers to enforce railroad prices (rates), its first duties were to eliminate unfair price discrimination between similar customers, but the Hepburn Act of 1906 gave it power to set railroad rates as well as those of bridges, ferries and pipelines. This Act also gave the ICC powers to inspect railroads' financial records and require railroads to provide information in the forms prescribed by the ICC, as well as requiring them to set maximum prices that were "just and reasonable", with the ICC defining what was just and reasonable. A regulatee could appeal against an ICC decision to a federal district court, or beyond directly to the Supreme Court. This Act therefore enshrined the hold of the legal profession over economic regulation in the USA, which continues today.

Following the rise of cars and trucks for local transport, and over-extension of the network, rail demand began to wane on many of the less-used branch lines. A 1920 Transportation Act required the ICC to develop a plan to consolidate the hundreds of regional railroads into more viable commercial units. Harvard Professor William Z Ripley helped the ICC develop this plan, which was unveiled in 1929 and became known as the Ripley Plan. It proposed the merging of all existing railroads into 21 regional monopolies but was contested by the railroads, and eventually abandoned by Congress in 1940.

After World War Two competition from cars and trucks, aided by the new interstate highways, dramatically reduced passenger demand for rail transport to the point where most railroads ceased to provide passenger services at all. After the 1930s there was very little passenger interest in railroads, except for large city commuters. On the freight side there was plenty of competition from water, roads and even air. By the 1970s railroads came to be perceived by the American public and its politicians as strictly commercial ventures: market forces should be allowed to work, and if a lack of demand led to a railroad closing no-one (except vested interests in the industry) would regret its passing. The ICC was seen as an unnecessary part of a rail industry which should sink or swim purely on its commercial merits.

Falling demand for passenger services in America led to the failure of the largest passenger train company Penn Central in 1970, which forced Congress and President Nixon to create and subsidise a new company, Amtrack, to provide intercity passenger transport in the lower 48 States. Nearly all the existing passenger railroads providing intercity services joined Amtrack. Although President Nixon and Congress may have viewed Amtrack as doomed to fail within a few years, in fact demand has doubled since 1970, strongly so in the 21st century, so that subsidies today account for only 20% of its operating costs. Short distance local passenger trains continued to exist and be financially supported by States, counties and cities in their region.

Deregulation of rail 1976-1980
Penn Central's bankruptcy, combined with lobbying from agriculture and industry, started Congress down the road of deregulation. The Railroad Revitalization and Regulatory Reform Act of 1976 (the '4R Act') was the first of a wave of laws deregulating road, air, water and rail transport in the USA. The 4R Act tidied up some arrangements to establish Conrail, the freight successor to Penn Central, gave Amtrack permission and funds to buy vital tracks to complete its services across America, and partially de-regulated rail freight. The latter included allowing the ICC to exempt certain categories of freight from regulation, barring their jurisdiction where one rail company alone could provide the entire services needed by the customer, and allowing prices above long run marginal cost, or customer-agreed prices if the railroad did not have market dominance (when considering all forms of freight transport over the market concerned). The 4R Act also committed Congress to "foster competition among all carriers by railroad and other modes of transportation".

This process of deregulation was completed four years later in the Staggers Rail Act of 1980. Staggers ended the practice of general price increases, banned the practice of railroads intervening collectively to set rates for services they did not themselves provide, and allowed railroads the freedom to set any rate they liked unless the ICC deemed there was no effective competition for rail services. Regulating prices effectively ceased, and the ICC was formally abolished in 1995[390].

Competitive rail freight since 1980
One of the key freedoms given to railroads in 1980 was the right to close lines that did not make a profit, which the ICC had previously required railroads to maintain. In the quarter century after 1980 tracks fell nearly 40%, from 270,000 track miles to 170,000,[391] track density more than doubled from 3.4 to 8.9 million ton.miles per mile of track, so that operating costs per ton.mile fell 67%. Bitzan

---

[390] The ICC Termination Act of 1995 handed the ICC's residual duties to the Surface Transportation Board of the Department of Transportation..
[391] Winston C, 2005, in 'The transformation of the US Rail Industry', in *Railway Reform and Competition* edited by de Rus G and Gomez-Ibanez J Edward Elgar, page 6 of the chapter.

and Keeler estimated total cost savings at $2-3.3 billion a year[392]. A Department of Transportation's Freight Management and Operation's study noted that costs and prices halved between 1980 and 1990, while the industry's lobbying organisation, the Association of American Railroads currently claims that since Staggers real prices have fallen 45% (after inflation), volumes have doubled, accidents have fallen 76%, and the industry has invested over $500 billion in maintenance of the grid, or capacity and service enhancements[393]. After several decades earning returns below its cost of capital, the Surface Transportation Board calculates that the rail freight industry's return on investment exceeded its cost of capital in 2006, and has exceeded it ever since.

US rail conclusions
In sum, few would deny that deregulation of the US freight rail industry has allowed successful "competition in the market" to occur, where "the market" explicitly includes other transportation modes by road, water and air. Customers have been well served with faster service and lower prices, and the industry is now profitable, with both rising demand and a rising share of the US freight market. Passenger rail is small and locally subsidised, but demand is rising this century, which may ultimately eliminate the need for a subsidy on passenger operating costs too.

Sweden's slow progressive reforms

Background
For those unfamiliar with Europe let's examine some fundamental facts about Sweden's rail geography and history. First, Sweden is a physically large country by European standards (1500km, or a thousand miles, from north to south), with a population density only two thirds that of the USA or one sixth that of China. Second, heavy freight is important, carrying steel, paper and forest products, with iron ore carried on one line in the north. Third, if a Republican President Nixon found it difficult to shut down passenger trains in the USA, the idea of shutting main passenger lines in Sweden is politically unthinkable in any era by any government.

Historically the State played a crucial role in designing and building Sweden's railways from 1853 onwards, although private railways were also allowed. By 1985 a state monopoly called Statens Jarnvager (SJ) owned all the track and operated nearly all the trains, but had problems of falling passenger and freight demand, inefficiencies that were obvious to all, and low levels of financial maintenance and investment in the network. Reminiscent of the long sequence of progressive utility reforms in Chile pursued by governments of all political persuasions (see Chapter 11), continual reform of the Swedish railways has been

---

[392] Bitzan J and Keeler T "Productivity growth and some of its determinants in the deregulated US railroad industry" Southern Economic Journal vol. 70, pp 232-253.
[393] Association of American Railroads 2012, *The impact of the Staggers Rail Act of 1980*, available on website at http://www.aar.org/~/media/aar/Background-Papers/The-Impact-of-Staggers.ashx

pursued by a succession of governments from different political parties over a quarter of a century, but all pushing in the same general direction.

The reforms of the 1980s and 90s

In 1986 the government decided to grasp the nettle and put rail transport on the same level as road transport: government would own and maintain the track (the infrastructure) while private companies would operate trains on the tracks, forcing the train operators to act more like commercial companies. Baumstark summarised the central idea:

> "Infrastructure construction, maintenance, financing and the infrastructure pricing system would be based as much on political decisions as they are for roads, while the supply of services would be based on the free initiative of agents."[394]

The government decided to introduce three reforms simultaneously:
1. Significantly renew investment in the network
2. Introduce the possibility of competition along some of the main operator's routes
3. Involve regional governments in the definition and financing of regional transport services

Ideas 2 and 3 were to be pursued by the regional governments opening selected local train routes previously run by SJ to competitive tendering. Since none of these routes was profitable the authorities would have to pay an explicit subsidy, but obviously the winner would be the tenderer asking for the lowest subsidy, given the service and tariff levels specified by the regional government on that route[395]. This process took a year to organise and got underway from 1988. Unprofitable long distance passenger routes were opened up to tenderers four years later, being auctioned by the central government, and SJ won many of these routes. Freight services were opened up to any operator who wished to run a train down the tracks ("*open access*") from 1996, although SJ inherited all existing contracts. SJ was permitted to retain its monopoly of profitable long distance passenger routes that were high speed.

Baumstarck summarised this sequence in a diagram similar to Figure 130:

---

[394] Baumstarck L, 2001, The pioneering Swedish experiment in railway regulation, Chapter 5 in Henry et al op. cit, page 96.

[395] The regional governments were familiar with this process from having used it to procure bus services which could be profitable or not.

Figure 130: Swedish rail reforms in the late 20th century

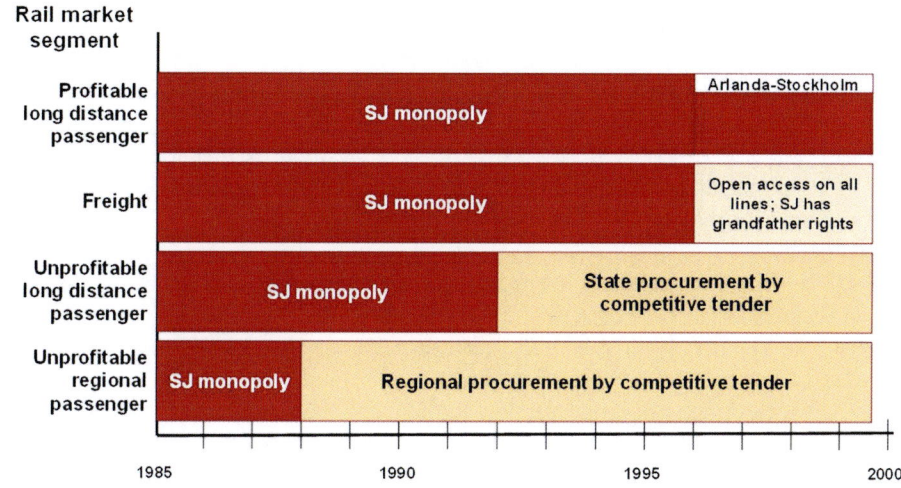

Source: after Baumstark The pioneering Swedish experiment in rail regulation Fig. 5.2 page 98
Source: Baumstarck in Henry et al Chapter 5

The infrastructure of the railway – track, stations, signalling etc. – was transferred to a State body called Banverket, which then benefited from a five-fold increase in investment by the government in the railways during the mid-1990s. This completely reinvigorated the railways and allowed the creation of a high speed rail network and substantial upgrading of track and signalling systems, benefiting not just long distance passenger travel but freight and all other market segments as well. This was Leg One of the government's tripod approach above.

Effects of the twentieth century reforms

The results of these reforms were that the efficiency of the railways undoubtedly increased and costs fell strongly on the routes put out to tender by an estimated 20-25% (Baumstark page 102). While freight volumes stopped falling and stabilised, passenger demand rose dramatically on the high speed trains so that by 2000 a quarter of all passenger.kilometres were high speed (from zero a decade before) and in the next decade both total passenger and high speed demand increased by another 50%[396].

21st century problems and reforms

According to a recent paper by the Stockholm Centre for Transport Studies[397] Sweden's current main passenger rail problems are:

---

[396] EU Transport Statistical Pocketbook 2012 Table 2.38.
[397] Alexandersson G, Hulten S, Nilsson J-E and Pyddoke R, 2012, "The liberalization of railway passenger transport in Sweden – outstanding regulatory challenges" *Centre for Transport Studies* Stockholm available at http://www.transguide.org/SWoPEc/CTS2012-5.pdf.

1. Tender overbidding – this affected the incumbent SJ, which overbid for large unprofitable passenger services in the 1990s, went bankrupt in 2003, and had to be refinanced by the State (given money) to the tune of SK 1.8 billion (about €200m) to make it solvent;
2. Track access fees are too low (covering only 10% of track maintenance costs); the government plans to raise them threefold by 2020, but will keep them below cost-recovery because of rail's positive externalities
3. Track capacity problems have arisen, particularly in rush hours around the three largest cities; this may be a direct consequence of the previous problem
4. The bidding process for track access encourages operators to supply trains that are too short at peak times; despite open access in all sectors (from 2012) the incumbent SJ still has 80% of the market by revenue 25 years after competition was first initiated
5. The decision-making models which in theory decide the availability of access paths to the track (whether the track is free enough to allow a train operator to have a popular route at a particular time) omit some key interdependencies, which means that the model has to be manually overridden; in practice the train planning timetable barely alters from one year to the next.

Sweden's current problems are the inevitable results of the previous century's successes. Demand has risen, competitors to SJ have entered, and the tracks are sometimes congested. Public investment in the railways peaked in 1995 before falling back to levels substantially above pre-reform levels, but this has not enabled system capacity to expand as much as demanded. And there have been good developments: rail has increased its modal share of passenger transport, benefiting road congestion and the environment, 7 independent companies have entered the market to provide competition for the incumbent, SJ, and Sweden's railways are faster, safer and much better linked to the rest of Europe. Along with the other 27 members of the European Union, Sweden's railway policy must be consistent with policy frameworks agreed in Brussels, which generally should benefit the Swedish system, particularly the profitable high-speed trains and freight.

For a book as cheap as this one is you cannot expect to find the answer to all Sweden's current railway dilemmas. If you like this kind of problem, though, think about becoming a transport economist – just don't expect all your advice to be listened to. Remember the fate of the Greek prophet Cassandra.

Many of Sweden's problems are very similar to those found in the UK, which learned some lessons from Sweden when undertaking major industry restructuring in the mid-1990s, but decided to privatise all train operating companies and the track provider as well. Lessons from one country could well carry across to the other.

Britain's restructuring and privatisation

Background
The rail network in the UK is dense, befitting a densely-populated island with high incomes that was one of the first countries in the world to develop a network of long distance railways. Having originally been founded as hundreds of entirely private small railways in the 19th century, several waves of mergers left the network effectively controlled by four regional private monopolies (the 'Big Four') by 1923. To maintain efficiency in the Second World War the railways were not nationalised, but the socialist Labour government of 1945 nationalised the railways from 1948, and they stayed as nationalised British Railways (latterly 'British Rail') for half a century.

Mrs Thatcher's radical Conservative government of 1979 wished to reduce the role of the state and privatise utilities, but recognised a major problem: unlike telecoms, electricity, gas or water, rail was not profitable and so would need some form of continuing subsidy to attract private investment and managers. Rail was therefore left to be the last privatisation and occurred under her Conservative successor, John Major; it was not repealed by subsequent governments.

Figure 131: Number of passenger journeys on British railways since 1921

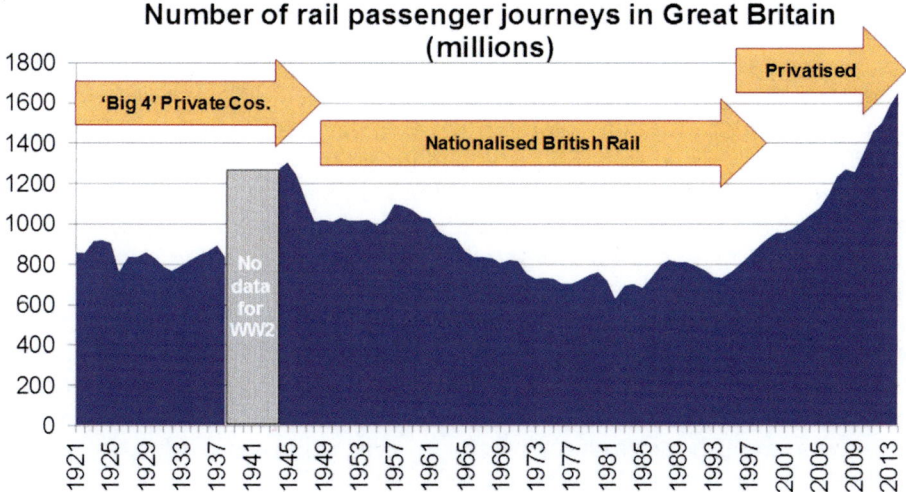

Sources: Office of Rail Regulation website, Department for Transport, NBER

Figure 131 shows the history of demand for passenger rail travel in Great Britain over almost a century, but to imagine the British government's perceptions in the 1980s and 1990s you must cover the right hand end of the chart (after 1993) with a piece of paper: neither politicians nor transport planners knew the future, and nobody predicted the doubling of passenger numbers that has actually occurred since privatisation in 1994-97.

> **Quick Quiz on a century of British rail demand**
> 1. The 'demand' shown in Figure 131 is not the best measure of rail passenger demand. What would be a better measure of demand? Why?
> 2. Why have I not used this better measure in the chart?
> 3. Some people might be tempted to look at Figure 131 and draw direct inferences such as 'Demand rises when an industry is privately-owned and falls under public ownership'. This is far too simplistic and ignores other events in society. What other influences will have had a major effect on rail demand over this time?
> 4. Using some of these factors explain why you think demand rose between the 1920s and the 1940s?
> 5. Why did demand fall between 1947 and 1982 (the nadir of demand)?
> 6. Why do you think demand rose in the late 1980s and then fell back in the early 90s?
> 7. (Most importantly) Why has demand doubled since 1994?
>
> *(Answers in the Appendix to this chapter)*

Maintenance, financial and cultural issues

As already explained, the British system is dominated and driven by passenger demand, not freight, which tends to lose money. In the 1970s a 200 km an hour diesel-powered high speed passenger network had been introduced between most large cities in Britain, which was significantly faster than driving. But these did not make a profit, and even the heavily-used commuter routes carrying millions into London and other large cities each day, lost money, due to the long operating hours requiring double-shifts (6am to 2pm and 2pm to 10pm). And, as in Sweden and most countries around the world, regional passenger services were locally vital to the car-less in society, but lost a lot of money. Closing any of these lines would encounter determined local opposition and might lose the politician who proposed it their seat in Parliament.

Only a very few rail routes made a profit – e.g. the route to Gatwick airport from central London. The hope of the rail industry was that greater automation of trains, signalling, ticketing and information systems would reduce these losses *if* the railways could have significant funds to invest. This was the big 'if' as far as Mrs Thatcher was concerned: she had no intention of investing billions of public funds on an inefficient state monopoly such as British Rail. Culturally the rail industry seemed to her, and other outsiders, like a clique of 'boys-with-trains' and its attitude to customer service was summarised memorably as "We could run a lovely train company if only we didn't have to carry all those passengers". In addition, following years of reduction of public expenditure the industry claimed that a "maintenance backlog" had arisen: the infrastructure was wearing out. Mrs Thatcher distrusted this argument, saw failing rail demand, and tended to regard the whole rail system as a bottomless pit of public expenditure. Her colleagues and successors agreed to some extent, but were determined only to make extra maintenance and investment funds available from the public purse if significant cultural and structural shifts also occurred to shake up the complacent rail industry: it must change its view of the fare-paying public from *passengers to customers* – whose needs would drive everything. If a structure could be devised in which the private sector could be invited to introduce both efficiency and private investment they would sanction extra public investment in the infrastructure.

Privatisation 1994-1997
Learning from successful US freight deregulation, innovative Swedish passenger restructuring, and the privatisation and restructuring of other British utilities, John Major's Conservative government decided on a radical restructuring to maximise privatisation. The central Swedish idea of separating the infrastructure stewardship from train services was adopted, but all parts would be privatised to infuse commercial logic, efficiency and funds throughout the system.

In 1994 the infrastructure – tracks, tunnels, bridges, stations, signalling systems and land – was transferred to a Limited Company called Railtrack which had a new top management team. It was floated on the Stock Exchange in 1996. The train services were to be provided by privately owned Train Operating Companies (TOCs). Looking at a value chain like Figure 128 the government decided to privatise the infrastructure as a regulated monopoly which would receive access fees from Train Operating Companies; Railtrack's access fee revenues would have to be topped up by public sector subsidies. The TOCs would generate and receive fare revenue, lease trains from rolling stock companies (ROSCOs) and pay access fees to Railtrack along with all their other costs. All TOC routes would have to be subsidised initially, but some should become profitable if the commercial managers could succeed in attracting new customers. Each TOC would tender for a multi-year franchise on a group of routes in the same geographical region but competition in the market would be permitted and encouraged, so that a rival TOC might seek approval to create a new route, and, if granted, compete directly against a franchised route. Figure 132 shows how the restructuring began, and progressed, in the first fifteen years after privatisation:

Figure 132: the evolving structure of the British rail industry during and after privatisation

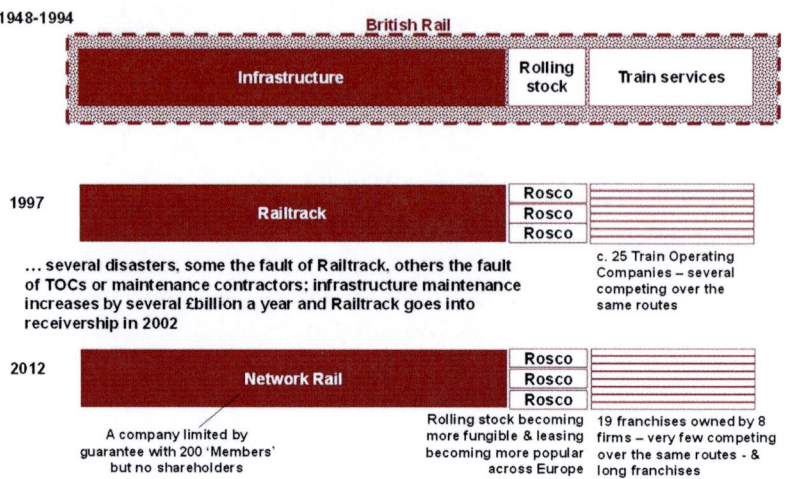

The rolling stock

One of the unique aspects of the 1994-97 British Rail privatisation was the establishment of rolling stock companies (ROSCOs). Why create these? The fundamental idea was to avoid the general end-of-franchise asset valuation problem described in Chapter 8, and thus to reduce the sunk costs of bidding for a franchise. So, given that rolling stock generally has a theoretical life around 25 years, in order to have efficient bidding for a TOC franchise of say 5-8 years, it was thought necessary to have a general buyer and seller of rolling stock who would 'make a fair market' in rolling stock whenever a franchise changed hands. Should this company be a monopoly? No, so three were set up. That at least was the idea, and it might have worked if the network had been in steady state. In practice, other than the high speed trains, much of the rolling stock was actually older than 25 years and urgently needed renewing. So TOCs grudgingly accepted the existing rolling stock as the only equipment immediately available, but they and their customers fundamentally wanted new rolling stock. Unfortunately it would take 3-5 years from ordering to get new rolling stock delivered, which was a long way into a typical seven year franchise.

New rolling stock did not fit into the frequent auctions short-franchise model. Another assumption which proved wrong was that most of the rolling stock could be used across the network: although all the network had been owned and operated for fifty years by one vertically integrated state monopoly, and British Rail had tried to standardise, the differing heights and widths of bridges, tunnels and platforms it had inherited from the different private lines (and different regional power systems) meant that much rolling stock was effectively dedicated to certain lines or regions. *The rolling stock was thus often region- or route-specific, and so a sunk cost*. The operating companies recognised this and simply wanted new equipment for their line; but that would require long franchises to make amortisation of the capital cost-effective.

The issue was most clearly seen on long distance routes such as the west coast route from London to Birmingham, Liverpool or Manchester and Scotland. This was an electrified route that did not reach 200 km an hour because of track restrictions and old rolling stock. Ordering new trains would take 7-10 years to deliver an entire new fleet, which the operator, Virgin Trains, was prepared to commit to, provided its franchise was extended to 15 years. Virgin thus only used the ROSCOs' trains until it could own its rolling stock. The deal was done, and Virgin and Railtrack committed to a simultaneous upgrade of the line and rolling stock. Virgin's trains were delivered from 2002, and the new track upgraded by 2005 at a cost around £10 bn, allowing Virgin to benefit for the last seven years of its franchise. Virgin appeared to lose its franchise in 2012, but appealed that the franchise evaluation system was faulty. The government's evaluation system was independently checked and found to be unfit for purpose, so Virgin retains the franchise at the time of writing. But whatever happens on this line Virgin has created some fairly 'dedicated' assets: although the trains could be used on other routes they are most valuable on this one.

The original rolling stock model did not work well for the first ten years, as running a TOC tended to require ordering one's own rolling stock. This, though, may be ending, now that the fleet has largely been modernised. Unregulated leasing companies owning modern *interoperable* rolling stock seem to be thriving across Europe – with backing from the European Union's rail policies – and so the sunk cost of route-specific rolling stock is gradually being replaced by a standardised trans-continental fixed cost, akin to the profitable American model.

The operating companies' franchises
In 1994 the British Rail routes were operationally grouped into 25 shadow franchises which were tendered and awarded from 1996-1997. Seven commercial companies emerged to hold 18 of the franchises, and a new company, Eurostar, entered offering 300 km per hour services to Paris and Brussels through the recently-opened Channel Tunnel.

Competition on the tracks and competition for the tracks
Following economic fundamentals the original concept was that where possible competition-in-the-market ('on the tracks') should be preferred where possible over competition-for-the-market (franchise auctions), and indeed competition on the tracks was achieved for some years on inter-city routes and regional routes such as the eastern and western regions[398]. It was popular with regular customers who liked having a choice of trains and services, but (unofficially, of course) was less popular with the operators (obviously), and the infrastructure owner – for the same reason as in the Swedish case: the models used to plan routes did not have all the relevant information, so that some knock-on effects of introducing a new route were ignored by the model, which had to be manually over-ridden. So although 'open access' to the track – meaning that any operator

---

[398] EU E.g. in the late 1990s Oxford to London was served by three different TOCs during the day.

could request a single new route in another's franchise area – was introduced in 2002, in practice it could only occur on lightly used routes where, by definition, demand was light.

The consequence was that, possibly due to information asymmetry[399], successive regulators allowed competition on the tracks to wither away in practice over the succeeding 15 years, thus throwing away one of the main potential large benefits of rail separation and privatisation. The consequence was that by 2012 the UK was left with 8 groups of independent firms operating 19 franchises with a median contract period of nine years, and four franchises lasting 15 years or more[400]. The original franchises had lasted typically for seven years[401], but franchise lengths grew for the reasons described. In sum, therefore, the British government has abandoned competition on the tracks, and reduced the competitive part of competition for the tracks to competition once every ten years or so. This is a very long way from being active competition-for-the market, and even further from being the active competition-in-the-market that the UK had in the late 1990s. Defenders of the current system would point to the massive private sector investment drawn in to meet the doubling of demand, quicker train times, improved punctuality, and better safety records.

Infrastructure provision: Railtrack then Network Rail
Railtrack was given most of British Rail's fixed assets – and liabilities – and floated for £1.9bn in 2006, a sum criticised by the National Audit Office three years later as being only a quarter of its then current market value[402]. Of course the replacement value of these massive assets would have been hundreds of times this figure, but all these costs were truly sunk; everyone knew that Railtrack could not survive as a commercial firm without several billion a year of government subsidies, so the company's market value (its *de facto* Regulatory Asset Base) was just a few billion.

A less-noticed aspect of privatisation had been the disposal (with all staff) of nearly all British Rail's maintenance capability, which was transferred to private engineering firms, who promptly received large contracts from Railtrack to maintain entire sections of the network. This outsourcing had been designed to infuse commercial efficiency into the vast maintenance function, but they had forgotten a vital aspect of the contracting theory of the firm: *outsourcing large complicated functions to contractors means the overall service provider (the*

---

[399] i.e. regulators possibly did not have enough operational information to challenge views put forward by TOCs or the track owner that competition on the tracks could not or would not work.

[400] House of Commons Transport Committee Eighth Report 2008-09 Rail fares and franchises, Table 1 page 8

[401] Affuso L and Newbery D, 2001, Investment, reprocurement and franchise contract length in the British railway industry, Department of Applied Economics Cambridge University, page 4.

[402] National Audit Office1999, 'The flotation of Railtrack' at http://www.nao.org.uk/recommendation/report.asp?repId=386

buyer) must create and strengthen its buying expertise, to complete technical inspections and ensure that the contractors have actually achieved what they promised. In the rush to privatise, Railtrack got rid of too many skilled engineers.

Given the history of a maintenance backlog, and rising demands placed on the track, maintenance started to fail and was not noticed by Railtrack. In 1997 seven people were killed and 139 injured in an accident at Southall; in 1999 31 people were killed and 520 injured in an accident at Ladbroke Grove. Suspicions began to rise. Then in 2000 a 185 km an hour accident at Hatfield shocked the nation: although only 4 people were killed and seventy injured, a train left the track and ripped along the sleepers at 115 mph when the rail underneath it collapsed due to inadequate maintenance. Railtrack and its contractor had to admit a major failure in its stewardship at this point, but, worse, Railtrack had to admit it had no idea how many Hatfields were waiting to happen across the network. All high speed trains in the country were speed-limited for up to a year while every piece of track was inspected. Repairing the damage after Hatfield cost Railtrack nearly £750m which made Railtrack lose £550m; it sought extra funds from the government and then, amazingly, paid a substantial dividend to shareholders. This was too much for the Transport Secretary, Stephen Byers, who placed Railtrack into administration – the step before bankruptcy.

Wheels had to keep rolling, though, and Railtrack was replaced by Network Rail, a 'Company Limited by Guarantee'. This means the current owner and steward of the UK's rail infrastructure, Network Rail, is a privately owned commercial company with no shareholders, only 200 "Members", and is not a for-profit company, which explicitly recognises the nature of its reliance on subsidies to continue existing. Figure 133 compares the rail industry's two main sources of income over the last quarter century, revenues from fare-paying passengers and government subsidies, in constant prices:

Figure 133: The two main sources of income for the British rail industry 1986-2013 in constant prices (2013-14 £m)

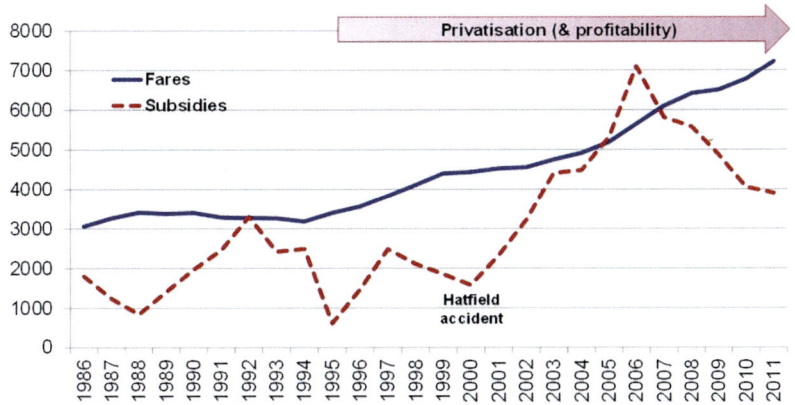

Sources: ORR rail portal passenger fare revenue and Government support to the rail industry excluding freight subsidies, deflated using Financial Year GDP deflator

Clearly before Hatfield the government had been hoping to reduce trend subsidies, although some major capacity upgrades were due in the new century. Hatfield meant the government had no choice but to take the maintenance backlog story seriously and fund it. Figure 133 shows how subsidies rose three-fold in the six years after Hatfield, before falling back to a level about twice as high as the 1990s, in real terms. At the same time British rail fare revenues continue to grow at 7% a year this century after inflation, reflecting the combined effect of rising real prices and strong demand growth, as road congestion worsens and better, more frequent, and faster trains come into operation.

The British railway system now seems to be on a more even keel than previously, with all political parties supporting the current structure and agreeing that investment subsidies must continue, but hoping to wind down operating and maintenance subsidies. The infrastructure provider, Network Rail, is a quasi-autonomous steward of the nation's rail assets, a sort of mutual company that needs government subsidies to survive, but seeks to make a profit within access charges set by a regulator using socio-economic analyses. In 2012 the Coalition government announced a new wave of major rail investment projects, government subsidies, and projected fare rises that aims to reduce subsidies to just a quarter of the total income stream – significantly lower than the levels in either Figure 129 or Figure 133.

Current issues
Not everything is solved though. Some outstanding issues include:
1. Does Network Rail really face appropriate long run cost-reduction incentives?
   - E.g. if senior managers save a lot of money on maintenance or a new capital project can they keep it to spend on their own pet projects, or must they rebuild reserves?
2. Is Network Rail free to borrow on its own – could it issue bonds?
3. Corporate governance: how are Network Rail's Directors appointed? (Who guards the guardians?)
4. The latest rounds of TOC franchises will pay significant sums to the government, but only if the operators hit ambitious passenger growth targets, and then only for the last few years of the franchise. Can incentives be sharpened so that the government and operator share risks, including 'windfall' (exogenous) ups and downs, more fairly?

Conclusions about rail sector reforms
From the point of view of utility economics the experience of rail de-regulation and privatisation in the USA, Sweden and the UK offers classic lessons about sunk costs and franchising that reinforce the general points made in Chapter 8. The problems of regulating the innate monopoly of the fixed infrastructure are less of a problem in rail than in other utilities because rail usually makes a loss. In the US freight business this is not true – after thirty-five years of deregulation and strong demand growth rail businesses are making profits above their costs of capital – because there is no doubt that strong intermodal competition exists,

and where it does not customers have recourse to a residual impartial body to determine a fair tariff. In other countries excessive profits are not the problem; indeed an injection of fare-paying revenue is strongly welcomed.

To illustrate a general framework for mapping rail restructuring solutions we can therefore consider on one axis a spectrum of public control going from a state-owned and state-controlled monopoly (found in many countries in the world,) through a regulated monopoly, to competition for the market (a closely-specified concession contract) to, finally, competition in the market (unregulated firms in open competition with each other). If we make this the vertical axis and put the degree of vertical separation on the horizontal axis, we have a rail sector restructuring options map as in Figure 134:

Figure 134: Strategic options for reforming the rail sector

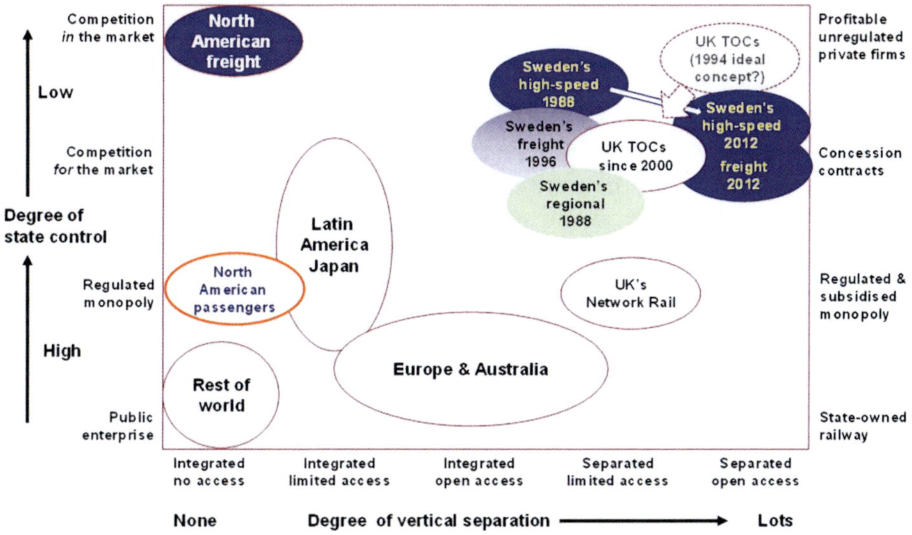

Sources: adapted from Laperrouza's 2011 reworking of Gomez-Ibanez (2004)

Clearly North American freight is the only example of genuine competition in the market. Although Europe, Russia and China might hope to emulate this rail freight position in a few years they will need to ensure two fundamental conditions are in place
- demand is sufficiently dense to make rail freight profitable in the first place, and
- the rail network is sufficiently dense to promote competition between rail suppliers that eliminates gross economic rents *within* the rail network

Two technological developments aid this process: containerisation of loads is undoubtedly reducing transaction and switching costs between rail and other transport modes, helping rail cooperate with road transport to offer a factory-to-factory or factory-to-depot service. This increases inter-operability between rail, road, water and air. The other is radio tagging of trucks and loads to monitor the progress of cargo. Given what the high-speed logistics industry already does online to monitor deliveries it seems ridiculous that there isn't a phone app to do this, but that logic ignores vested interests. Years after inter-governmental agreements and Brussels Directives to promote standardisation across European freight systems, rumours still persist of entire trains going missing for days on end within the European rail network. One would not be surprised to hear of similar problems – with a similar root cause – in Russia or China.

Sweden's pioneering separation of track from operating services explicitly acknowledged that unprofitable lines should be subsidised by the local transport authorities while intercity lines should be subsidised by the national government. Gradually more open access is being allowed to these individual concessions. Britain followed and tried to go further by allowing open access and competition on the tracks between passenger operators from the start, which was popular with customers but was allowed to die off by the Department of Transport in its first decade. Britain's further separation of rolling stock from operational services did not work well initially, due to the inherited stock needing to be replaced, but once trains had been updated (around 2010) and demand growth was confirmed as a long term trend in modern Britain, the separation of rolling stock and the new operating franchises began to look profitable. Both the Swedish and British reforms may have been designed largely nationalistically, but they now look set to be boosted by European initiatives to promote train interoperability (standardisation) on a continental scale.

On reflection standardisation and cashflow are the keys. Cashflow is largely post-tax profit plus depreciation less investment. The private sector is simply not interested in entering a sector unless it can see the possibility of super-normal profits, which requires a reasonable likelihood of normal profits (as in US freight) and some pockets of 'upside' (super-normal profits). One reason North American freight is profitable today is that it was standardised in the early twentieth century, while Europe is still struggling to achieve that. And, as we have seen in other utilities, if we want private sector investment to replace public investment, society must be prepared to allow the private companies to keep super-normal profits for a while.

Since most railways in the world are far from achieving competition-in-the-market we can return to our standard model of concessions from Chapter 8 and ask if this can be modified to suit the modern railway industry (Fig 135):

Figure 135: The standard utility concession model

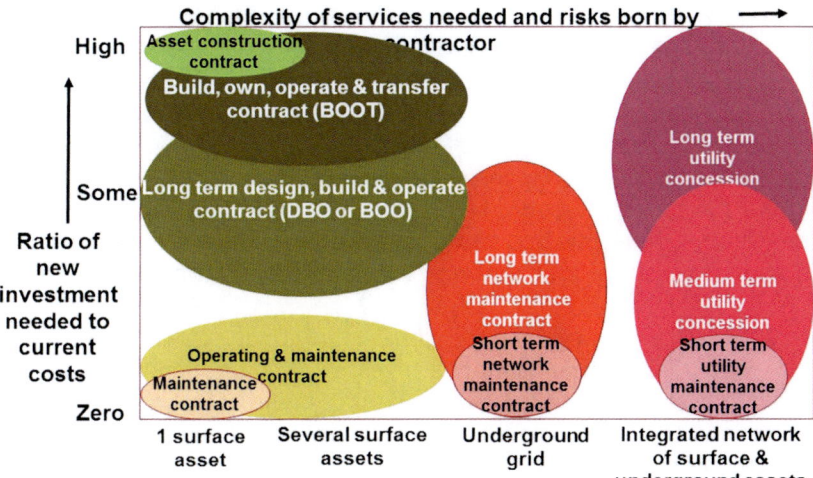

Cashflow is on the vertical axis, decreasing as more investment is needed to keep the service going to the required standard. This reflects the common occurrence of state-owned monopolies being under-funded, with ancient capital equipment and maintenance backlogs; in addition a major wave of new investment may be needed.

On the horizontal axis the standard model has a spectrum of types of concession ranging from very simple standard assets to very complicated and specific networks of assets. We could equate this to the degree of sunkness in a train operating company's concession. So, reversing the direction of both axes in Figure 135 and redrawing the horizontal axis as increasing asset standardisation (i.e. a reducing component of sunk costs), we emerge with Figure 136:

Figure 136: Product space map of train operators' routes

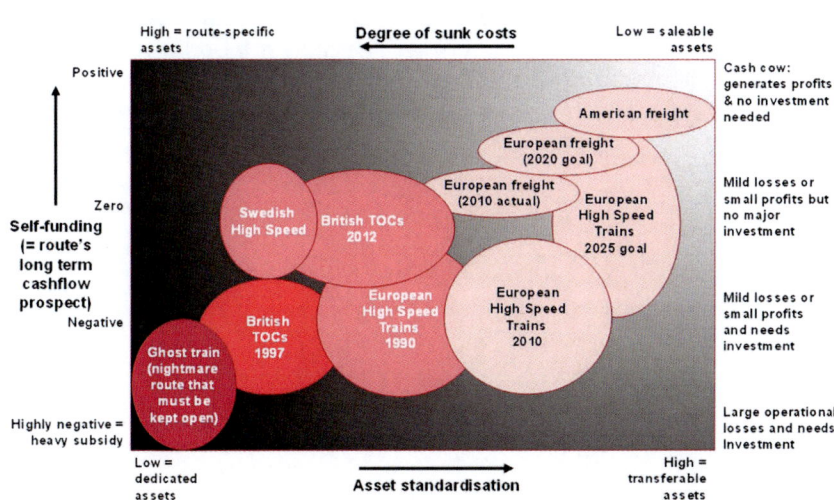

In the top right hand corner North American freight routes have very standardised operating assets – mainly rolling stock (this diagram ignores all track assets) – and generate cash. European freight is considerably less standardised and profitable, but is becoming more standardised across the continent. European high speed trains evolved with different national standards in the 1970s, particularly in France and Germany, but have become more inter-changeable as more new high speed tracks are built to common European standards. For a private company there is far less risk involved in signing a concession than there would have been twenty years ago, if private concessionaires had then been permitted. Competition to run high speed and all passenger concessions is rising, as the growth of train leasing companies across the continent testifies.

At the bottom left hand corner are the 'ghost train' concessions: nightmare routes that make heavy losses, need a lot of investment and where most of the big assets are highly route-specific. Mountain railways with low bridges and tunnels, very tight bends and steep gradients need specialist rolling stock that may not be usable on other lines. Looking back some of the early Swedish and British operating concessions had some similarities, but over the last twenty years their specificities tend to have been reduced, and the investment needs substantially addressed, so that the concessions look more commercially appealing today.

The inter-relationship of new track and rolling stock assets
Positive externalities in rail networks render private investment in major new infrastructure sub-optimal, so major enhancements should be public sector decisions and investments. But provided private investors are left with some prospect of temporary super-normal profits, the public sector can leverage private investment to complement its own investments. So a new track or major upgrade is always a sunk cost and will typically be a public investment, but this can be complemented with private funds if they create non-sunk assets – i.e. if the private assets are mobile and standardised. Hence the strong desire to standardise networks over entire continents, or globally, which could yield material benefits for the European, Russian, Chinese, Japanese, Indian, and Australian governments. Despite this, if an upgrade requires significant route-specific private investment, a long term concession will be inevitable, while the private investor reaps a return for their risky investment, but once the system achieves steady state, shorter concessions extracting more rent, may be feasible.

Appendix to Chapter 12
Answers to the Quick Quiz
1. A better measure of demand would take into account how far people travel as well as how many people travel. Multiplying passenger numbers by the distance they travel in kilometres derives the measure called passenger.kilometres which is probably the best single measure of passenger demand. These figures are of course published annually and quarterly by the modern rail industry.
2. The reason I have not shown passenger.kilometres in Figure 131 is that these figures are not available for early years, while the number of passengers is, and I wanted to summarise a century of rail travel in one simple diagram. In practice, too, the number of passengers varies more from one year to the next than the average distance travelled (a very smooth series), so passenger numbers gives most of the story.
3. You could usefully use PESTEL or other simple tools to help list the major influences likely to affect demand between one decade and another. So
    a. Political   War   WW2 probably massively increased passenger demand; it was certainly much higher in 1946 than in 1938
    b. Economic
        i. Rising incomes leads to rising demand for travel – which does not have to be met by rail alone
        ii. Rising incomes can also lead to wider car ownership as the cost of owning and running a car as a proportion of average income fell; this means greater use of private cars, which are a substitute for rail
    c. Social
        i. Rising car ownership from the 1940s to the 21st century as car travel becomes more fashionable (this can be either a social or an economic factor): Mrs Thatcher is thought to have believed that any man aged 30 or older who did not own a car, and so travelled by public transport, was a failure
        ii. Greater availability of high-speed roads (provided by government) meant that you could drive long distances at high speed and get back in a day
    d. Technological The reliability of cars over long journeys improved considerably between the 1940s and the 1970s, so that by the 1980s driving 200 miles in a day was perfectly reliable
    e. Environmental / Ethical
        i. Congestion is a form of pollution and this started to rise strongly from the 1980s
        ii. Greater pollution from cars became a major social concern in the 21st century
    f. Legal   While trains were free to do 120mph or more, the imposition and enforcement of 70mph speed limits on cars meant that trains became faster than cars for long distance inter-city travel from the 1970s
4. Between the 1920s and 1940s rising incomes led people to travel more on business and for leisure

5. From 1947 to 1982 was the golden era of the motor car. Cars became simultaneously cheaper, faster, more reliable and more fashionable (allowed more personal independence), and the supply of high-speed roads was increased by the government's development of motorways and fast 'A-roads'. Road travel boomed. Rail was left to be used by people commuting into work, children going to school, and by the poor and elderly.

6. The late 80s blip up of demand and subsequent mid-90s dip are probably phenomena of short run macroeconomics: the British economy went through a short-term economic cycle of boom in the late 80s (rising incomes so higher rail demand) and decline in the early 90s (higher unemployment so fewer commuters).

7. The most important factor in the doubling of demand since privatisation is greater congestion on the roads. Due to costs constraints, lack of space, and people objecting to demolishing homes to make way for roads, the government could not build more high-speed roads to meet peak demand. Road congestion rapidly built up in the 1990s, and the rising time taken to get into city centres led people to use rail far more for daily commuting and inter-city travel. It is possible this effect drove some of the rise in demand in the late 1980s as well.

Chapter Thirteen

Some overall conclusions

Economic theory
As the opening quotation from Leonardo da Vinci suggests, where theories do not adequately explain the facts one must replace them, no matter how well-born their pedigree. As the best way to explain why network utilities are commonly monopolies the high fixed costs argument may be commonly taught in economics textbooks, but it is neither necessary nor sufficiently supported in evidence. A sequential model using heavy sunk costs is undoubtedly supported by the facts and explains far more, being able to predict why grids may have any number of players from zero to a dozen or more, but why a monopoly is the most common number of players above zero. It also makes far fewer restrictive assumptions than the neo-classical model, and is general: it can be applied to any industry, but only yields interesting results when sunk costs are significant.

Measuring efficiency
Measuring utility efficiency is not as easy as in other industries because many cost-drivers are determined by geographical and historical circumstances, by past political decisions, or by past specification errors which viewed in the current context may have built in permanent design inefficiencies. Economists have a useful role to play, and a fair set of tools to compare utilities' technical efficiency, which is far more important in practice than allocative efficiency. The best way to model utilities' technical efficiency is to treat all the exogenous circumstances as outputs of the network, all the inputs – operating and capital costs combined – as cash expenditure, and to rate the management's task as minimising costs given the need to supply the exogenously-dictated outputs. OLS Regression and Data Envelope Analysis are explained as good starting approaches, but stochastic frontiers assuming an appropriate prior inefficiency distribution (for a non-contestable industry) should give better cross-sectional comparisons, provided observers justify their distribution assumptions rationally. Starting from first principles, a Bayesian approach to justifying inefficiency distributions is explained and recommended in Chapter 7. Finally, to measure efficiency over time, and to distinguish between catch-up efficiency and frontier progress an economist should use Malmquist indices; again some new measures or approaches are explained using simple diagrams.

Competition, concessions and regulation

Competition-in-the-market can be introduced in utility retailing and in the bulk production stage provided there is a grid to connect the power stations, gas fields or water treatment works. In this century sewage treatment works are not linked by grids so very little competition is likely for the entire wastewater industry. Competition-for-the-market may be the Second Best option in other industries but for network utilities it has such high transaction costs that it rarely leads to efficient solutions unless contracts are very long, in which case the frequency of auctions is negligible – destroying any real idea of 'competition'. Economically it is also hard to distinguish these arrangements from a regulated licensed monopoly; an arbitrator usually has to be appointed whose functions increasingly resemble those of an economic regulator.

The Rate of Return, gain-sharing, and yardstick price cap methods of regulation have been considered. Rate of Return models tend to assume efficiency. Rate of Return and gain-sharing offer very few efficiency incentives in practice to the managers who must actually implement them, particularly if targets are set based on 'last year's budget' rather than a zero budget. Shleifer's yardstick regulation is explained as innately a sequential model assuming utilities have different levels of efficiency, and requiring time to elapse between decision-making periods of the regulator and the regulatee's management; this means it cannot collapse to the Rate of Return model without losing its core properties.

Yardstick price cap regulation has been made to work effectively in Chile, the UK and other countries, and can yield significant increases in service levels and efficiency, though some of this may come from the 'peer-pressure' practices of comparing rival utilities' performance rather than from the intricacies of the price-capping rules and incentives. For yardsticking to work the regulator must carry a big yardstick – have enforcement powers including that of terminating or suspending a company's licence to operate or trade, and sufficient legal powers to force firms to supply data on consistent definitions – and have a large enough number of comparators to make a fair assessment of where the global frontier currently lies in relation to their regulatees. This probably requires collaborating with other regulators around the world.

Professional texts

You now have enough information to know if the next step for you is to say 'Thank God that's over!' or to continue with professional texts. But there are few professional texts covering more than one utility that are practical, general (not tied in to just one country's frameworks), cheap and good. The (short) Appendix to this Chapter lists some professional texts that may help you, but in general these are collaborations by many academic or professional authors and so may not have a unified intellectual framework lying behind them. They are also not cheap!

One notable exception is David Newbery's *Privatization, Restructuring and Regulation of Network Utilities*, already referred to several times and, sadly, out of print, though several chapters are available online in Google books. Let us just compare the conclusions reached above with page 1 Chapter 1 of Newbery's text (written in the last year of the twentieth century):

> *Network utilities are public utilities that require a fixed network to deliver their services, and include gas, electricity, water, rail and fixed link telephony. They are economically of high importance ...The networks of these utilities are classic natural monopolies; they create rents that are fought over. The networks are durable and fixed, so the rents persist. The capital of the network is large and sunk, so once created the balance of bargaining advantage shifts from investor to consumer. Finally the networks of gas, water, electricity and telecoms are directly linked to the consumer, giving their owner potentially large exploitative power. These consumers are numerous, are politically important, and have no choice of network. In the telling phrase of Alfred Hirschman, they cannot exit and so will use their voice.*
>
> *The problem facing investors and consumers is to devise an institution that will balance these interests and powers. The tension between the investor and consumer can be side-stepped by state ownership, which has the coercive power to finance the sunk capital without requiring the assurance of a future return from the utility. Alternatively, it can attempt to reconcile private ownership with consumers' political power through regulation. Either way, network utilities operate under terms set by the state.*

After reading this book I hope you join me in supporting every word of that. Newbery goes on to say that normally competition incentivises firms to minimise costs but this fails for natural monopolies. Conventional economic analysis of networks starts from this market failure and tries "to devise rules for setting prices and meeting demand that encourage efficiency." He continues

> *This book [i.e. his book] takes a rather different approach. It argues that designing price-setting rules is only a part of the policy agenda for network utilities. Network utilities pose special problems of ownership and regulation whose solution is constrained by the institutional endowment of the country. Public policy toward these utilities will inevitably reflect deeper political and cultural features of society, as will the institutions that evolve in response to these factors. How these utilities should be regulated, structured, and even owned, may vary over time in response to changing circumstances....*

So Newbery's book is a fully rounded work, written by a seasoned professional. If you want a mature text try to obtain a second hand copy of his book or persuade his publishers to issue a reprint. And if you find an alternative comprehensive yet well-written work please email the author, courtesy of the publishers, to let me know.

Restructurings in practice

In the 1980s the author, like many British people, did not agree with Mrs Thatcher's utility privatisations (opinion polls showed water privatisation was opposed by 70% of the public) and just continued with his private sector career. But, to the surprise of many economists, including the author, who returned to energy and utility economics in the 1990s, utility privatisation and restructuring has generally worked well *where it has been implemented well*. To achieve genuine competition in a potentially contestable segment of the value chain, or to obtain more efficient monopolies through yardstick comparative competition, requires years of work by dedicated teams of talented public sector officials.

The UK is sometimes viewed as a potential model for other countries to consider but policymakers should a) learn from the mistakes of the British, the Californians, the Chileans, and others, and b) listen to Newbery's wise words above about 'institutional endowments'. There really is no point in introducing privatisation and complicated systems of regulation to improve utility efficiency in countries where the proportion of people who receive core utilities is less than 80%, particularly if there is a dearth of talented, non-corrupt civil servants to form the core body of an independent regulator, and if the country has little tradition of strong independent institutions to bolster a durable form of accountable government. If the vast majority of a country – say 80-90% - are not actually receiving a designated utility service – net of all penetration rates and outages – the key priorities must be to *extend coverage*, and then to *improve service availability* to 95% of the time. Only then should policymakers even think about improving non-outage service levels or efficiency, since those who do not actually receive the services will almost always be the most needy in society, there will be large positive externalities from these people receiving the service, and public sector provision or private sector concessions that involve the community affected may well be the most effective way to do this.

Once a country has got beyond basic utility provision, and the service is actually available 95% of the time to 90% of the population, should one consider options to privatise utilities and then regulate them firmly. In contrast to California's electricity experiment, which was destroyed by greed and then reversed, electrical restructuring has generally worked well in Texas, Scandinavia, Argentina and the UK. Joskow's Top Ten Tips for successful electricity sector reform, as reviewed by other authors and this one, are summarised at the end of Chapter 9.

In the pipe monopolies gas and water restructuring and price-cap regulation have eventually worked well in the UK, and water trading seems to work very well in Australia. We examined the North American gas industry and found no obvious abuses of monopoly power in the contestable sectors, although the regulated sector may well suffer from the well-known problems of cost-of-service or rate-of-return regulation. For the obvious reasons that one can never ignore the political context we have not looked at the economic efficiency of the Russian gas industry.

In Chapter 12 we examined European attempts to restructure the rail industry and found some overall models that satisfyingly explain the main difficulties of the past two decades and a few decades to come. One area where de-regulation has worked astoundingly well is US rail freight; one of the root causes of this – and a possible root cause of the success of water reforms in Chile, in contrast to Chile's electricity reforms – was a past era of standardisation across the whole country, a hundred years ago in rail, that today ought to be emulated by the rest of the world's rail industry – whether freight or passenger.

The main results from successful utility reforms
In general most observers of those countries where utility reform has been properly thought-through and well implemented, would argue that
1. The lights have stayed on, the water and gas flowed etc.
2. There has been massive investment in electricity, gas, and water (and rail in the UK – though most was funded by the public sector)
3. Service levels (quantity and quality) have risen strongly to meet rising expectations, which will continue to rise in the 21st century
4. Monopolies subject to price-cap regulation do become more efficient
5. Comparative competition (peer pressure) has proved surprisingly effective in motivating managers
6. Where conditions (e.g. world energy prices) permit prices have fallen,
   - In water and wastewater there have been massive quality improvements over the last quarter century in most countries requiring significant cost increases for even the most efficient utility (the future trend of these is discussed in Chapter 6)
7. Rail is by far the most difficult sector to regulate:
   - On all but the shortest journeys the product is not a commodity but differentiable (service is personal)
   - It makes a loss in most countries
   - Yet rail is widely thought to have positive externalities of reducing congestion and pollution – if the alternative is road or air transport
   - Most (not all) taxpayers seem prepared to subsidise an option to travel on certain less-used rail routes
   - This equates to a subsidy for the infrastructure provider, and for Train Operating Companies' franchises
   - Motivating efficiency incentives for the TOC is easier than for the infrastructure provider

Thank you for your attention.

Appendix: suggestions for further reading
Professional texts

Alexander I and Harris C, 2005, *The regulation of investment in utilities: concepts and applications*, World Bank Washington DC, World Bank working paper no. 52, for a good exposition of general investment issues in utilities, and case studies of practical schemes used around the world

Coelli T, Prasada Rao D, O'Donnell C and Battese G, 2005, *An introduction to efficiency and productivity analysis*, (2nd edition), Springer New York. By far the most useful explanation of how to measure utilities' efficiency once you have absorbed the techniques in Chapter 7

Crew M and Parker D 2006 (eds), *International Handbook on Economic Regulation*, Edward Elgar, Cheltenham UK, cost £36 – focuses on economic regulation, as the title suggests; 28 authors

Finger F and Kunneke R 2011 (editors), *International Handbook of Network Industries: the liberalization of infrastructure*, Edward Elgar Cheltenham UK, cost approx. £130 – expensive but probably the most global text, focusses on experiences in more utilities than we have considered and in many countries, 40 authors

Henry C, Matheu M and Jeunemaitre A (editors) 2001 *Regulation of Network Utilities; the European experience*, Oxford University Press, £120 –a compilation of essays by 26 authors now out of print, and growing out of date as regulation inevitably moves on.

Newbery D 1999, *Privatization, restructuring, and regulation of network utilities*, MIT Cambridge MA, out of print but sections available on Google books; a classic – the best single-authored book, with a consistent theoretical interpretation of events, focuses heavily on electricity, now showing its age.

Textbooks

Lipczynski J, Wilson J and Goddard J, 2014 4th edition, *Industrial Organisation: competition, strategy, policy*, Financial Times Prentice Hall, Harlow England – a very good general textbook though with nothing new to say about utilities.

Grant R, 2013, *Contemporary Strategy Analysis*, Wiley 8th edition is just one of many excellent books on modern business strategy which should complement the student's choice of microeconomic textbook. As an economist, strategist and business person, the author's strong view is that if you are going to engage in business, or engage business people at all, strategy tools are generally far more effective than most economic tools, which tend to be of interest mostly to an academic audience. The one sector where economic tools do work is the network utilities – provided you use the right economic tools (the tools in this book!).

Appendix: the neoclassical theory of monopoly welfare losses
Demand curves and consumer surplus

In his 1890 book Principles of Economics the neoclassical economist Alfred Marshall popularised the demand curve by inviting students to imagine all the customers for a particular product being asked how much they would be prepared to pay for one extra unit of the good being studied, and then ranking customers in order, so that they were lined up, with those on the left prepared to pay the most, and those on the right the least. This downward-sloping-to-the-right Marginal Revenue curve is why demand or Average Revenue curves, whether convex, straight, or concave, always slope downwards to the right: they must do so, from the very definition of the term 'demand curve'[403]. If the curve slopes up at any point we do not have a demand curve, and must re-rank our customers until our curve does slope downwards to the right[404].

The supply curve was conceptually more tricky. Generally, the neo-classical economists made a good assumption that costs for different firms in the same industry differ, and then assumed that most firms would have a rough idea of their own cost base relative to others in the same industry. So, they argued, logically the first firms to enter an industry would be those which perceived their cost bases to be the lowest, followed by the average or typical firm, and lastly the highest cost producers. So, if we construct an industry supply curve by adding together all the firms' cost bases in a logical entry sequence, we will end up with a supply curve – a long run average or marginal cost curve for the whole industry – which slopes upwards to the right. If demand falls, those with the highest costs – the most marginal players – will be the first to leave, while if demand rises, new producers with still higher costs will enter the industry to balance supply and demand. European agricultural economics – where valley bottoms have the thickest topsoil and so are the most productive, valley sides have thinner topsoil, while the hilltops, where topsoil can be washed away, are the least productive – give us a clear example of farmers with different cost bases. As hilltop fields are the least productive they are the marginal production: hilltops are only cultivated for this crop when its price is very high.

Let us be clear about this: unlike the demand curve, the supply curve does not have to slope one way by definition, but will slope upwards provided firms have a generally correct perception of their relative costs (which is generally true in equilibrium[405]), and make logical entry or exit decisions (an assumption of rationality).

---

[403] Though the actual term Marshall used was 'Demand schedule'.

[404] Ignore Veblen and Giffen goods – they are generally irrelevant, particularly in utility products or services.

[405] If I incorrectly assess my competitive cost base, and enter too early – before others who actually have lower costs then me – the industry will be in disequilibrium until all those with lower costs than me have actually entered. After they have entered, the industry once again achieves equilibrium, and we can continue describing our supply curve.

Let us start by assuming no particular industry or cost structure and just a general, normally-price-sensitive, good. Then, applying the differential calculus to both the marginal and average versions of cost and revenue concepts, the familiar 'X' of supply and demand, illustrated in Figure 137, emerges with a unique, stable, solution at a quantity where marginal revenue equals marginal cost, and at a price where the marginal firm makes no super-normal profit. We will address some of the limitations of these assumptions in Chapter 3, but for the moment let us stroll down this main avenue of neo-classical micro-economics admiring the view.

Figure 137: Marshall's basic 'X' of neo-classical supply and demand

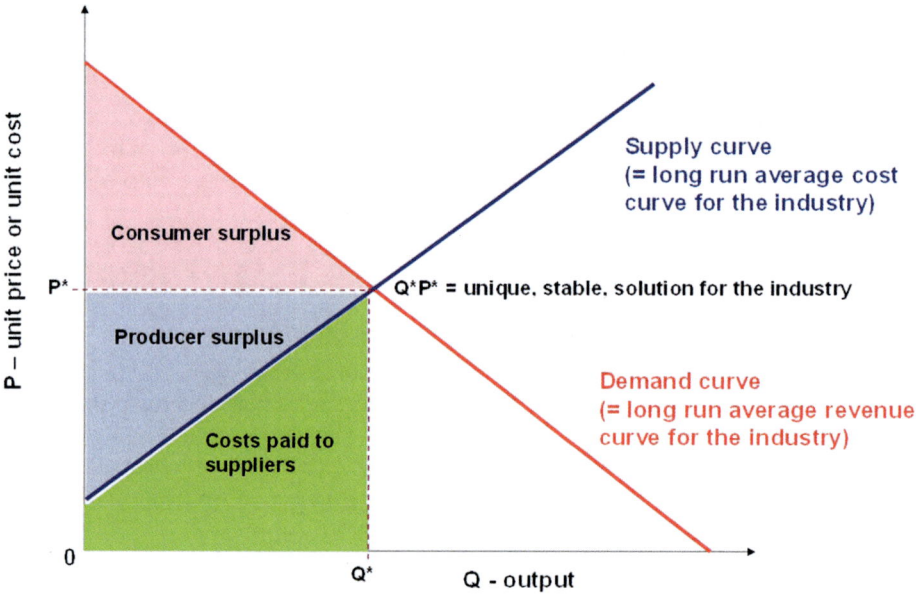

Being very mindful of the social implications of economic theories (the welfare effects, as we would call them today), Marshall noted from the definition of the demand curve that all customers to the left of the Q*P* solution would have been prepared to pay a higher price than P*[406], so these customers receive extra welfare which he called "consumer's rent" and we nowadays call consumer surplus. This is a clear gain to 'society'[407], which must occur whenever a good is sold commercially and its demand curve is not horizontally flat.

And, correspondingly on the production side, those firms with lower costs than the marginal players would have been prepared to produce quantities at a lower price than P*, so they are making super-normal profits which the neo-classicals assumed would eventually be absorbed by the 'creators' of this economic rent – landlords, risk-taking entrepreneurs, diligent managers, extra-skilled workers, and the like. So if it is the location of the business that yields better profits than

---

[406] Assuming no price discrimination.
[407] Let us define society as "all consumers", for want of a better definition, at this stage.

its rival can achieve, then the owner of the land will eventually reap a higher rent for the location. If it is better management then the manager will bid her wage or profit share up. And if it is the "girl in the pharmacy with a sweeter smile that makes you go there rather than to a rival, then she will, if she is smart, bid her wage up to her value in the market", as the author's first professor of economics used to say, when explaining how the providers of economic rent generally appropriate it.

Finally, the area below the supply curve represents the costs incurred by the suppliers in producing their outputs. "Suppliers" here means all economic agents who require payment to produce their contribution – raw materials and other bought-in costs, employees, managers, landlords, providers of capital etc. And gradually, if this unique Q*P* equilibrium were to continue for a significant time, the providers of the supernormal profits (the economic rent) would realise their worth in the market place, and inflate the supply curve up so that it would hit the horizontal P* line up to the point Q*P*.

This is a logical, internally-consistent, and widely-applicable story. It should be true in a static equilibrium sense – that is if conditions in this industry stay roughly constant and prevail for some time. It should also be locally stable: that is if demand or supply is disturbed by a single event such as a one-off fall in demand, or entry of a new low-cost producer, then the market will eventually find its way back to a new equilibrium Q and P, which will hold until the next disturbance arises. All in all, the neo-classical economists have come up with a neat, globally stable, theory – provided its assumptions are true.

Monopolies
Nothing in economics should be simpler than a monopoly. Some students try to quote various authors who say that an "effective monopoly" is any firm with a market share higher than 25%, or whatever[408]. Do not go down this route. It is not as though a 'monopoly' is some kind of abstract ideal which the real world never sees – as if, using the strict definition, there were no monopolies in the real world. The truth is that in every country in the world there are dozens of corporations (private firms or state-owned enterprises) whose market share, properly defined, really is 100%. So let's keep our theoretical concepts neat and clean. Do not listen to 'The Complicators': they are lost souls in a bewildering world trying to help, but actually only confusing themselves and you.

Definition
A monopolist is the only supplier in a market for a product with no close substitutes.

---

[408] For obscure legal reasons we will not go into here, in the UK a monopoly was legally defined in the 1973 Fair Trade Act for 25 years as a market share greater than 25%. This economic nonsense was comprehensively repealed by the Competition Act 1998. Sadly there are some economics textbooks (e.g. Begg and Ward, 2013, Economics for Business 4th edition, McGraw Hill, page 119) and ill-informed teachers that still repeat this outdated nonsense.

Measurement of the strength of the monopoly

As we have just noted, by definition a monopolist's market share must be 100%. Therefore, most interesting questions relate to the definition of the market and the strength of the product versus its substitutes. In theory, your Economics 101 course gave you a useful tool for measuring this: the cross-price elasticity of demand, which must be positive for substitutes[409].

A real example

Now let's consider a real world example. Eurotunnel has a legal monopoly, signed by two governments and valid until 2086[410], of all direct train journeys between England and France using the tunnel that it built and paid for under the English Channel. And a second company, Eurostar, having signed a contract with Eurotunnel to take trains through this tunnel, has a monopoly of all high speed trains between Paris and London, and between London and Brussels. This gives Eurotunnel a monopoly not just of the key stage of all direct rail travel between the UK and mainland Europe but also a monopoly of all road transport between the two that takes less than an hour for the crossing. But this does not mean Eurotunnel is a completely free "price maker". The British and French governments would never have signed away 'a licence to print money' like that. True, subject to any long term contracts it makes[411], Eurotunnel is free to set whatever tolls it likes for any vehicle travelling through the tunnel it built, but the commercial reality is that there are substitutes – ferries and aircraft – that constrain Eurotunnel's price-setting decisions.

Thus for a real monopoly – Eurotunnel – the interesting questions are all about the definition of the market. If we define the market very closely ("direct rail travel between the UK and mainland Europe") then Eurotunnel has a 100% market share of the key stage in the value chain: the 35 kilometres of undersea crossing. But is this the real market? Most business travellers would say "I don't care much how I cross the Channel. I could travel by train or plane. But from central London to central Paris or Brussels the high-speed train is faster and more comfortable than air[412]". And this is generally reflected in prices: the price of a Eurostar ticket relative to a flight is often slightly higher. But this is a keenly-fought commercial war, many customers are price-sensitive, and prices for air and rail travel are

---

[409] In practice this could be measured two ways: the effect on the substitute's demand of an increase in our product's price, and the effect on our product's demand of an increase in the substitute's price. There is no general reason the two should be equal.

[410] The 1987 Treaty of Canterbury was signed and ratified by Margaret Thatcher and President Mitterand. Eurotunnel was initially granted a monopoly in 1986 for 55 years, which was extended in 1997 to 89 years. At Mrs Thatcher's insistence the tunnel was built entirely with private sector funds.

[411] E.g. with Eurostar, or with large haulage companies who regularly put dozens of trucks a day through the tunnel.

[412] For non-Europeans I should explain that the airports are some distance out of town, which, combined with air security measures, mean the total travel time from city centre to city centre is usually quicker by train.

both volatile, so price-sensitive customers know they must compare prices frequently for the particular journey they wish to make.

Thus inter-city travel between London, Paris and Brussels is one market in which Eurotunnel competes vigorously through another monopoly – Eurostar. But there are two other large markets where Eurotunnel competes directly for customers: cross-Channel pedestrians, cars, and motorbikes, and the cross-Channel freight market (which is very price-sensitive), as well as niche markets such as people with a fear of air and sea travel (100% market share) and people with a fear of under-sea tunnels (0% market share)[413].

From this real world example we can immediately draw a number of conclusions:
1. the notion that monopolies rarely exist, and are complete price-makers, is wrong
2. real monopolies are surprisingly common at key stages in our modern economies
3. we need to break apart the stages in a commercial value chain to see how much market power monopolies actually have
4. much of the discussion about a monopolist's market power is really a discussion about the definition of the market, and the closeness of the substitutes.

Before we pass on you should consider whether there are any similar monopolies (or potential monopolies) in your home town. You might also ask yourself whether Eurotunnel would really pay a firm of professional economists much money for a set of properly worked out cross-price elasticities, as Economics 101 tells us they should.

Origins of monopolies:
Textbooks say that in general monopolies come about in three ways:
- By law
- By having unique production features
- By market control

Legally – by law
- The first monopolies arose when monarchs or governments (with ultimate executive powers) gave sole control of certain markets to certain people or organisations. Historically, the monarch obtained tax revenues from this, the company got the profits from its operations, *and* protection by the monarch's security forces.
- Governments can give the same powers to certain companies in return for control over prices. In many countries certain types of company are state-owned monopolies. As a mental exercise think of five examples.

---

[413] Eurotunnel 'competes' for this market by trying to persuade potential customers that their tunnel is safe and easy to use – i.e. by trying to shrink this segment of the market to zero.

- Patents and copyrights can give companies the sole rights to use their inventions *for a limited period of time* e.g. in pharmaceuticals: Glaxo and its predecessor companies had a legal monopoly of the anti-AIDs drug AZT for twenty years in the USA and Europe from the date of filing their invention[414].

So monopolies can be deliberately created, either permanently or temporarily, by governments passing laws which not only allow a firm to establish and sustain a monopoly, but also forbid anyone else from entering this market. Clearly, if you can get the government behind you, making it illegal for anyone to compete with you, this is an unbeatable "sustainable competitive advantage", to use a core business strategy concept. And your most important business asset or resource is your licence from the government – which in turn, of course, means that anything that threatens your licence is a potentially fatal threat to your firm.

Note that governments nowadays do not give these sorts of rights away cheaply – unless corruption is involved between the firm and the politicians. So legal monopolies often entail obligations as well as the opportunity to make monopoly profits. For instance in normal competitive industries, firms have the right to choose to produce at any level of output they wish, including the right to produce at zero output and zero inputs – i.e. to close production completely and 'exit the industry'. Many legal monopolies are either effectively required to produce at non-zero output by political and social forces, or are legally obliged to maintain a given service level. The first type of obligation effectively makes the company an arm of the state. For instance Air France has an effective monopoly on many flights to and from France. In the months after 9/11/2001, the demand for world air travel collapsed, so most commercial airlines cancelled many of their scheduled flights. But Air France was obliged by the French government to continue flying empty planes around the sky. The French government subsequently gave Air France hundreds of millions of euros to subsidise these (and other) loss-making flights.

The second type of obligation – to maintain a certain level of service across all customer segments, even if this is strongly unprofitable – is known as a Universal Service Obligation (USO): the monopolist must legally supply all customers in its designated areas to a given service level, no matter if this requires cross-subsidies from other customers, or even general subsidies from the government. The original example of this was the 1840 introduction of the penny postage stamp in the United Kingdom. In contrast to the various expensive, complicated, and corrupt private schemes which had operated before, in return for being established as a monopolist, the British Post Office was obliged to offer a simple single tariff which said that writers could post a half-ounce letter anywhere in the UK to anywhere else in the UK for one penny, regardless of the distance (transport cost) between sender and recipient. The Post Office could not refuse

---

[414] This patent expired in 2005. The World Trade Organization's (WTO) Agreement on Trade-Related Aspects of Intellectual Property Rights, states that patent protection should be available in WTO member states for a minimum of twenty years.

to serve a town, region or island, just because it was loss-making, as a rational private monopolist would. Clearly close correspondents were cross-subsidising distant correspondents, and the whole scheme made a loss for thirty years, so it ended up being generally subsidised by the government, but it probably promoted education, commerce, and social cohesion within the UK, so the government may eventually have got a social return for its money, while the Post Office got its monopoly of all inland mail, customers got cheap letters, and corrupt postmasters lost a source of unofficial income. Indeed, in the twenty first century, most national Post Offices around the world still have the same Universal Service Obligation forbidding them from shutting services in unprofitable regions.

In modern economies Universal Service Obligations also affect the telecommunications industry, in that many governments require telecoms companies to pay subscriptions into a USO fund which is used, in theory at least, to subsidise the construction of infrastructure such as broadband connections in remote regions.

Through having a unique production feature
Sometimes there is only one of a key production asset.
- Individuals have a monopoly over their own talents: sports stars / movie stars / musicians and song writers are classic examples
    - 'Colonel' Tom Parker created the Elvis brand and he (and Elvis Presley) had a monopoly of it!

- A single mine, well, bridge, tunnel, port, concession, boat, railway or distribution network gives the owner a monopoly of that product
    - Eurotunnel originally had a 90-year legal monopoly of land links between England and France, but this has been strengthened by the fact that they have built, and are now the legal owners of, the only tunnel linking the UK to Europe. Even when their legal monopoly expires in 2086 any competitor will face huge sunk costs to mount a direct competitive challenge.

Through market control
Look at Microsoft's Windows or Office software: each has substitutes, but none is as widely accepted, so Microsoft's entirely legal monopoly of Windows (it created and marketed this software around the world) gives it many monopoly characteristics. With Apple, Microsoft has close to a duopoly of the markets for PC operating software (Mac OS and Windows/Vista) and something close to a monopoly of common office software applications (Office).

The neoclassical monopoly model
The neoclassical monopoly model assumes the monopolist is a commercial company that has become the only supplier in its industry and is trying to maximise its profits, while not being subject to any special legal protection or control. We start by graphing producer unit costs and revenues against the

market's demand for the product. Recall that because the firm is the only supplier in the industry then not only are its cost curves the industry supply curves, but the firm's demand curve is the industry's demand curve. Looking at the basic elements of this, let us start with a typical demand curve and make a simplifying assumption:

Figure 138: A linear demand curve means the MR curve's slope is twice the AR curve's slope

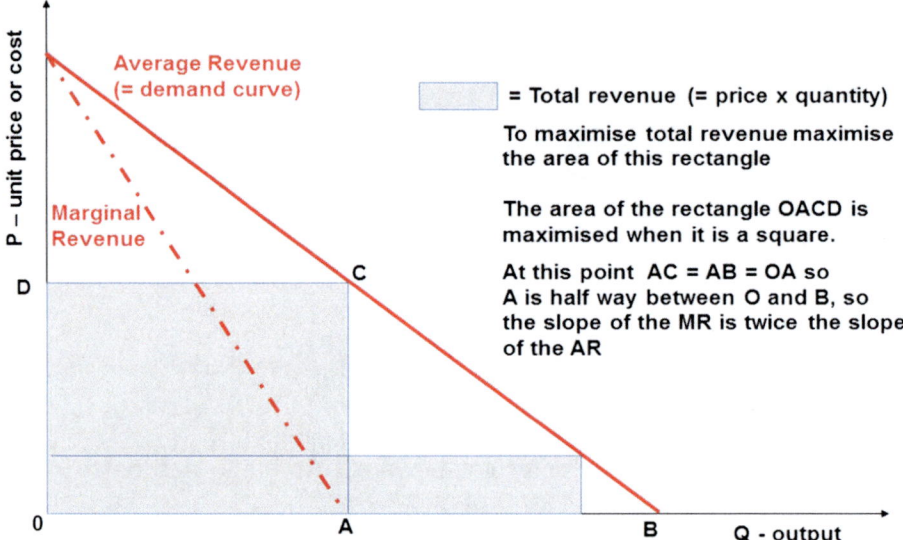

From Marshall's definitions we know that the demand curve must slope downwards. Neoclassical economics also shows us that if the demand (Average Revenue) curve happens to be straight, Total Revenue (the area of the grey rectangle in Figure 138 under any point on the Demand curve) will be maximised when the rectangle's sides are equal – i.e. when the rectangle is a square. At this point we cannot increase Total Revenue any more so the Marginal Revenue curve must be zero here, and cut the horizontal axis at point A in Figure 138. Because the rectangle's sides are equal (OA = AC) this distance (OA) will be half the distance to the point at which the Average Revenue itself cuts the horizontal axis (OB). So, neoclassical economics gives us the neat little theorem that if the Average Revenue curve is straight, rather than concave or convex, the Marginal Revenue curve must be twice as steep.

This might seem a pretty piece of geometry, but completely useless, as it is totally dependent on the convenient assumption of a straight demand curve. However we do not need to enter major consumer theory debates on the concavity or otherwise of demand curves, or be excessively purist about this: so long as the demand curve is continuous, fairly smooth, and roughly straight, the result holds *roughly* true, and in the absence of any prior knowledge about the shape of our demand curve, a straight line is a reasonable first approximation between a convex and a concave curve. So, we are not making strong (very restrictive) assumptions if we proceed with a roughly straight demand curve.

Now let's add some cost curves. First a set that means our monopoly makes losses no matter what level of output it produces at, and secondly a set that makes profits possible:

Figure 139: (a) Unprofitable and (b) profitable monopolies

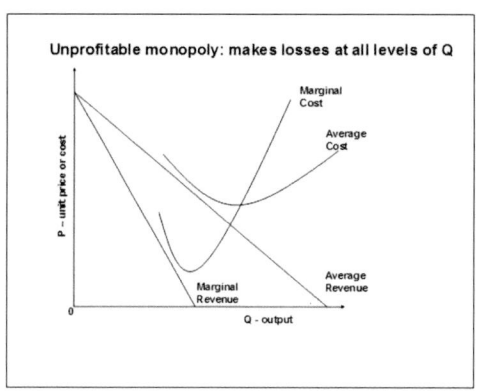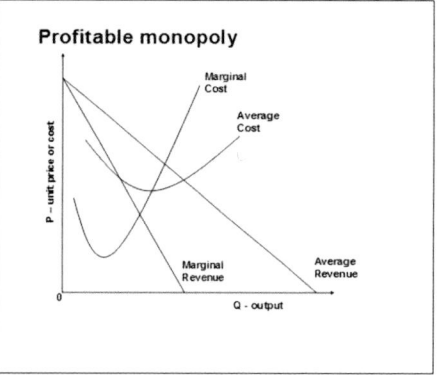

How might the lossmaker in Figure 139 have come about? Yes, demand may have fallen from some previous level – e.g. canals and railways are industries that once were profitable (or projected to be profitable) but substitutes have emerged. Nevertheless governments want them to continue operating, so the state subsidises them.

Now let's focus on the potentially profitable monopoly (Figure 140). At what output should it produce?
At the level of output QM where MR= MC. Fine, this gives us our Quantity of output – but not our Costs or Price, which must be read off the vertical line above QM on the relevant Average Cost or Revenue curves (ACM and PM).

So let's mark it on and compare how a profitable monopolist produces compared to a perfectly competitive industry comprised of exactly the same revenue and cost curves:

Figure 140: (a) Monopoly and (b) perfect competition in equilibrium

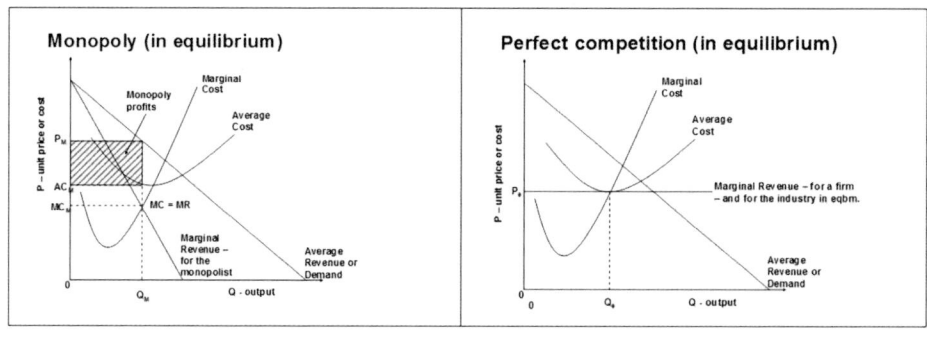

In perfect competition the Marginal Revenue curve *for a firm* is flat – each firm is small and a pure price-taker; if the firm tried to charge anything other than the market-clearing price it would get all or none of the entire market's demand, neither of which does it any good. This gives us the two extreme ends of the spectrum of industry competitiveness: an unconstrained profit-maximising monopolist, and a perfectly competitive industry structure in which almost no-one makes any supernormal profits. The practical inference is obviously that most real world industries will lie somewhere between the two.

Q: In Figure 140 (a) why doesn't some outside firm, attracted by the profits, enter, and compete them away?
A: They *are* attracted, but that's the significance of entry barriers: they stop or slow entrants.

To compare the two industry structures' effects on prices, profits and volumes examine Figure 141:

Figure 141: Comparison of monopoly with perfect competition (in equilibrium)

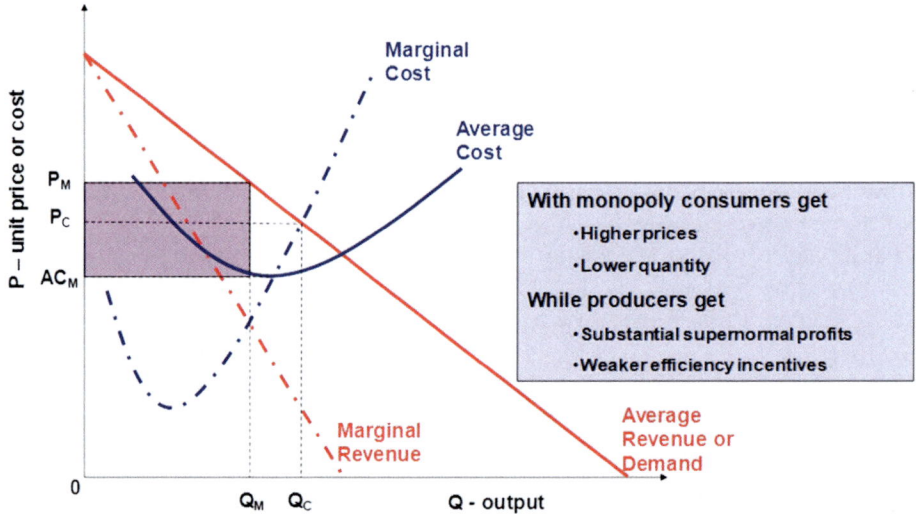

In brief, perfect competition produces lower prices, lower profits, and higher volumes. The key welfare consequences of the neoclassical monopoly model are summarised later in this chapter, but one does not need a degree in economics to see that monopolies can be bad for consumers. Actions or laws against private monopolies, or any producers with high market share, can be traced back thousands of years[415] – well before economics was invented – and can be seen as a prime example of JK Galbraith's general concept of countervailing power in societies.

---

[415] We know Royal monopolies were ruthlessly exploited by Ptolemaic Egyptian kings in 259 BC (using a combination of licences, control of strategic resources, and monopsony power; see "A social & economic history of the Hellenistic World" by M Rostovtzeff, 1941, Oxford University Press, Volume 1, pages 302-314) but Finley concludes ("The Ancient

Monopolistic ('imperfect') competition due to product differentiation

Monopolistic competition must not be confused with *monopoly*. Monopolistic or imperfect competition is *an industry structure that assumes many firms produce differentiated goods* or services (this is the absolutely critical difference between perfect and imperfect competition). This means each producer has a monopoly over its own *brand, which has some value in the market*, but the firm does not have a true monopoly because other firms' products can be close substitutes for its products (check the definition of monopoly a few pages back). The classic example would be restaurant meals: in any sizeable town it is quite possible to find dozens of restaurants. From a nutritional point of view all the meals may be equally healthy, but prices can easily range by a factor of ten between the cheapest and the most expensive restaurant in town. In theory, therefore, all the meals are to some degree substitutes for each other; indeed, customers might well use the cheapest restaurant one evening and an expensive one the next evening. So, few consumers would say that these restaurants have no "close substitutes". They are not monopolies, the language of monopolies is not appropriate, and a new theory is needed: the theory of monopolistic or imperfect competition.

The key difference lies not in the number of players in the industry – the number of restaurants in town is fairly irrelevant[416] – but in the product itself. If we were competing gas companies I could not differentiate a unit of my natural gas from a unit of your product, but if I am a chef I can certainly differentiate my meals from your meals[417]. In general for a market to be monopolistic consumers must acknowledge that a firm can *differentiate* its good from others in the market – *customers do not view the good as 'homogenous' (in economists' terms) or a 'commodity' (in marketing terms)* – but there is a limit to customers' willingness to allow each firm to raise its prices. The best description of how goods can be differentiated, and the difference between differentiation *in* a market and segmentation *of* a market, is to be found in the opening pages of Chapter 10 of Grant's "Contemporary Strategy Analysis"[418]. Grant understands differentiation deeply, in a way that many economists do not, and having taught many students who had actually been taught differentiation wrongly, by poor economists, I urge everyone to go the best source.

So the firm's demand curve is not completely flat, as in perfect competition (where it must take the market price or not trade), nor as steep as the entire industry's demand curve – the monopolist's AR curve. Instead it lies somewhere

---

Economy", MI Finley, 1999, University of California Press, Berkeley, pages 165-166) that "...monopolies in Greek city states were rare emergency measures" – until corrupt later Hellenistic kings and Roman emperors learned to abuse monopoly powers royally. So, in Finley's view, the much purer, citizen-friendly, Greek city states were well aware of the dangers of monopolies and took action to minimise them in normal times.

[416] So long as it is more than one.
[417] Indeed, in my family when I cook there is no doubt about who did the cooking.
[418] Grant RM "Contemporary Strategy Analysis" 7th edition, pages 247-249, John Wiley & Sons, Chichester.

in between, reflecting a degree of customer "loyalty", or conversely, customer "inertia" or "laziness".

Brand example:
A company always has a monopoly over its own registered brand names. So The Coca-Cola Company of Atlanta has a legal monopoly (a registered trademark) over the name "Coca-Cola" but no monopoly over Pepsi-Cola or other colas, which, most people would agree, are substitutes – some would say very close substitutes. The strength of Coca-Cola's 'monopoly' is entirely the strength of customers' belief that other colas are not as good substitutes as the original. This is the strength – and value – of Coca-Cola's brand. A company which completely fails to differentiate itself in the market has a flat marginal revenue curve and is a pure price taker. The most successful differentiators have the steepest MR curves.

Figure 142 illustrates the monopolistic firm's position graphically: the equilibrium quantity for the firm's output is lower than in perfect competition, and sold at price Z not Y, transferring consumer surplus of the shaded rectangular area to producer surplus ('profits'):

Figure 142: Monopolistic competition

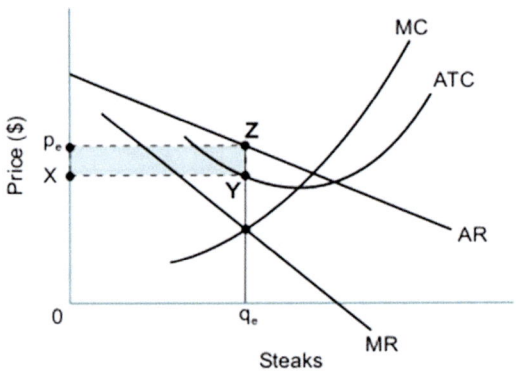

Comparison of monopolistic competition with monopoly
In passing we should ask just how does Figure 142 differ from the monopoly diagram (Figure 140a) three pages back?

The answer is that it doesn't at all, *conceptually*, though in practice a monopolistic company's AR and MR curves are flatter than a pure monopolist's cost curves, reflecting the firm's weakness compared to a true monopolist in differentiating their product from its closest substitutes.

The presence of these supernormal profits should attract competitors to enter the industry or to focus on this firm's customers, location, or whatever else it is doing right to create these profits. The firm's competitors may try to raise the slope of their own AR curve from a flat position to a steep one – at this firm's expense – or they may try to influence their rival's demand curve (AR) so that it is flatter[419]. However, if many competitors succeed in doing this they will, ironically, have created perfect competition. Also, to maintain some slope on its demand curve the firm may periodically have to maintain its industry-leading position by spending some of its producer surplus on functions such as firm-specific marketing (raising brand value) or product R&D. Classic examples include almost any branded or differentiated manufactured good such as clothes, food or drink.

To summarise, the key difference between a monopoly and monopolistic competition is that a monopoly means only one supplier of a product which may be a commodity or a differentiated product, while monopolistic competition arises only if the product or service is capable of being significantly differentiated. Proof that an industry is monopolistic should be provided by significant differences in price for a product that is notionally the same. Conceptually, however, there is no difference between the supply-demand positions – and hence welfare losses – of a monopolist and a successful differentiator in monopolistic competition, since *both* firms face downward-sloping marginal revenue curves.

So if you are in business to make money, in many ways achieving a monopoly is your strategic goal. Take note, though of the wise old saying "Beware of what you wish for: it may come true." Monopolists have their own problems – typically an apparently meek person called *the regulator* or external decision-makers called politicians.

Welfare losses from monopoly
Neo-classical comparative statics – the sorts of revenue and cost diagrams we have just been looking at – formed the starting point for some of the first rigorous attempts to formalise welfare economics in the twentieth century. Let's briefly recapitulate what this sort of analysis concludes about some of the less desirable consequences of private unregulated monopolies, starting with a monopoly facing the typical situation in neoclassical economics of rising costs:

A general monopoly with conventional rising costs

---

[419] For example by denigrating their rival's claims of superiority, or matching their points of differentiation one by one.

Figure 143: Welfare losses from a monopoly with rising costs

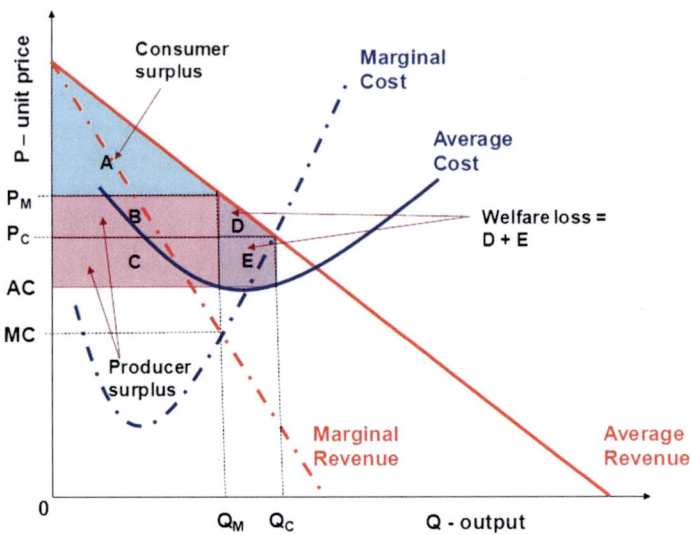

Figure 143 expands Figure 141. If we imagine a perfectly competitive privately-owned profit maximising industry facing the above revenue and cost curves then it will produce quantity QC at a price of PC, and at an average cost of AC, and a marginal cost of PC. This is a stable equilibrium because if the market price is lower than PC price-taking marginal firms will not earn a full rate of return and will (eventually) have to leave the industry, while if it is higher than PC firms that are ultimately non-viable will enter the industry. Prices are higher than *the industry's* average costs (the AC curve) – and so producer surplus of C + E is generated – because the non-marginal firms have lower costs than the marginal firms.

Facing a price PC for the quantity they buy, consumers reap a consumer surplus of the triangle above the PC line, A + B + D. The total amount they spend is the area of the rectangle below, OPC QC. Producers collectively receive all this block of revenue OPC QC, but since their total costs are the rectangle OACQC the two rectangles C and E are the supernormal profits for the industry.

Alternative illustration using areas under the marginal cost curve
Readers unfamiliar with diagrams where total costs are represented by rectangles under *average* cost curves, but who are familiar with total cost being the area under a *marginal* cost curve, should consider the alternative formulation, Figure 144:

Figure 144: Welfare losses from a monopoly with rising costs (MC version)

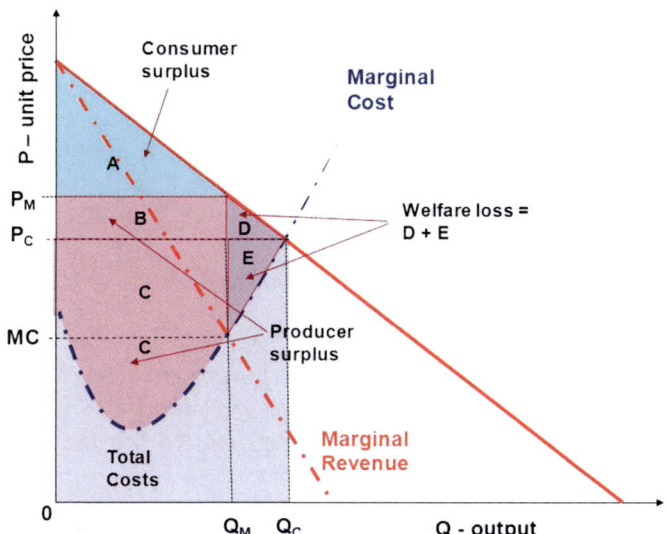

In this diagram total costs for the competitive solution are the light grey area under the curve, out to Q_C, and the producer surplus for the competitive solution is the area C + E.

Whichever diagram you prefer, Figure 143 or Figure 144, we can calculate the same welfare losses arising from monopoly, because although the shapes of C and E may be different, their areas should be the same. If the producers could collectively act as a private profit maximising monopoly they would earn more supernormal profit at QM than at QC: they would lose surplus E but gain B, which is clearly bigger. Incidentally, it is pure drawing convenience and a desire for simple clarity that the two ACs in Figure 143 are the same; in general they should be slightly different but fairly close. So the private monopoly equilibrium would be $P_M Q_M$ with higher prices and lower quantity.

Comparing the monopoly position to the competitive position, the welfare economists noticed that consumer surplus had shrunk from the areas A + B + D to just A, but while B has been transferred to the producers, the triangle D is an absolute or deadweight loss. In addition, the area E has been lost – to no-one. It is the second deadweight loss. So the welfare loss arising from a private unregulated monopoly setting a profit-maximising price over a competitive industry's solution at $P_C Q_C$ in either diagram is D + E. This is the formalisation of the simple truth suspected thousands of years ago, that monopolies are bad for society – unless 'I', the King or ruler, happen to be running them, in which case I'll put forward a 'Royal Prerogative' case for me to run them "in the interests of the State".

More relevant, though, is to consider the position the other way round. Suppose a democratic 'society' found itself starting with a monopoly industry producing at P_M Q_M, and the industry had rising costs as in Figure 143 or Figure 144. Consumers could collectively pay the monopolist a block of money B to lower the price from P_M to P_C, and there would be a net gain – a Pareto improvement – to consumers' welfare of the triangle D due to the elasticity of the *demand* curve. But the elasticity of the *supply* curve means that the monopolist would make a second supernormal profit equal to the area E from charging a competitive price PC above its average or marginal costs for much of the extra volume. So the overall welfare gain from this rather odd arrangement with a private monopolist is that society (producers and consumers) is better off to the tune of D + E.

In passing, note that the welfare losses or gains depend crucially on the supply and demand price elasticities of the product.

Natural monopolies with never-ending economies of scale

So far, so unlikely. Look at this realistically, and the chances that a real democratic government would strike the above Faustian pact with a monopolist seem as slim as a chive in a cheese omelette, unless there is corruption between the monopolist and the government, or the monopolist *is* the public sector. Indeed, for dictators there is little difference between any of these concepts: "The State? That's me" King Louis the Fourteenth[420] is said to have said, and most absolute dictators since have agreed with him, so taking the opportunity to line their pockets by awarding themselves state subsidies or profitable exclusive monopolies.

From our point of view, though, we are more likely to find a monopoly, and its associated welfare gains or losses, not in an industry where the cost curve rises, but in an industry where unit costs are always flat or falling.

Economies of scale – flat cost curves

Consider the case where the entire industry's long run unit costs appear to be roughly constant. Here average and marginal costs are conveniently the same, which leads to a classically simple welfare loss diagram:

---

[420] Actually it was attributed to him by a courtier who was attempting to summarise the King's position. The young Louis XIV was seeking to transfer powers from Cardinal Mazarin to himself in the Paris Parlement of April 1655.

Figure 145: Welfare losses with constant long run costs

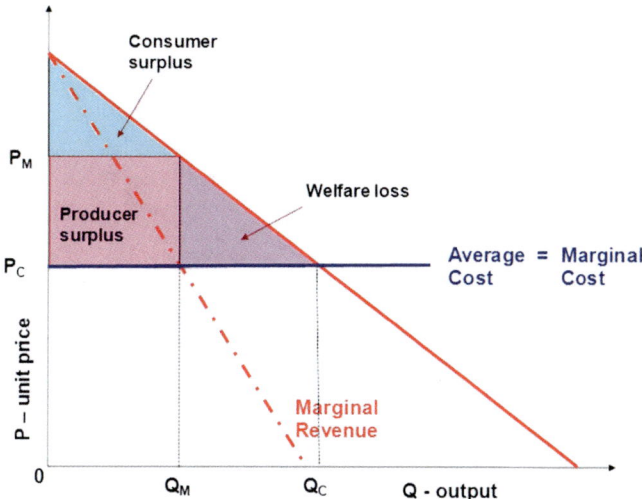

There is little more to say, really. The welfare losses in Figure 145 are smaller than in the rising costs case because of the absence of the supply elasticity area E in Figure 143 or Figure 144, and depend simply on the demand elasticity of the product (triangle D). In the absence of managerial dis-economies of scale we know this cost structure must lead to something other than perfect competition, quite possibly monopoly.

Economies of scale: falling costs

But what about the case where unit costs are not just flat, but actually falling? Isn't this very likely to lead to a monopoly, as the only way to exploit the economies of scale offered by the technology available? Consider this position in Figure 146:

Figure 146: Welfare losses from a monopoly with ever-falling unit costs

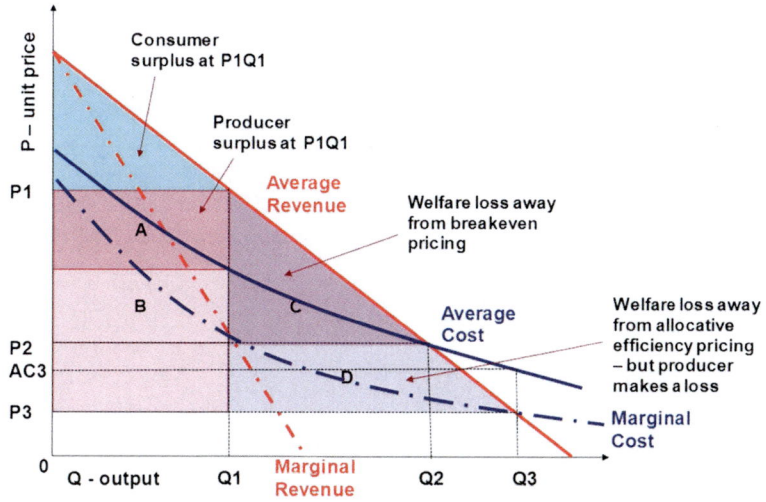

Starting with the private monopoly position, a private unregulated monopolist would choose to produce at volume Q1, where MR = MC, and charge price P1, maximising profit to achieve a producer surplus of rectangle A. Faced with this situation, however, and wishing to exploit potential scale economies for the benefit of the whole of society, a government could guarantee to pay the monopolist rectangle A provided he also lowered his price to P2 and produced at a market clearing volume of Q2, where he would break even on his operations (revenue equals long run costs, including a normal cost of capital for the risks involved). Consumers would then make the large welfare gain of triangle C, while the monopolist makes A as supernormal profit.

More radically, some economists advocate lowering the price to P3, the level of long run marginal costs, in order to gain the areas C+ D for consumers, and so achieve allocative efficiency of resources across the economy. This might be termed the "marginal-cost-pricing-no-matter-what" rule. The obvious problem with producing volume Q3 and selling at price P3 is that the monopolist makes a loss here and will therefore need to be subsidised. Of course there could be a case for doing this if there were positive externalities in the consumption of the good, but that is quite a different argument to saying that ordinary consumer surplus on this good is so important that we should subsidise its production.

Again, viewed the other way round, the welfare losses from private monopoly over the breakeven Q2 volume is the triangle C, but the welfare loss over the allocative efficiency volume Q3 is C + D.

The practicality of achieving these welfare gains
How likely is it that a society's government would actually pay a private firm to lower the price of its good in order to gain significant economies of scale and remedy the welfare loss? This pact might not seem so Faustian to voters who, although not generally acknowledging the concept of consumer surplus, might agree that society could be far better off at volume Q2 than volume Q1. However, this argument 'feels distinctly odd' because governments in market economies do not generally get involved in encouraging industries to produce more[421] *unless there is a clear positive externality* in consuming the good.

So, in reality, and in the absence of corruption or clear externalities, voters and policymakers in political parties would be deeply sceptical of such an arrangement with a private monopolist. The scepticism probably arises from
1. voters' scepticism that this industry's cost curve really does have such strong economies of scale – "Any industry could say this, and then we'd have to subsidise them all", and
2. how do we actually determine the size of sum A?

---

[421] Particularly in a century in which governments and society are acutely conscious of mankind's need to minimise our consumption of the planet's resources unless there is an overwhelming gain in consumers' satisfaction.

On point 2, text book writers assume that demand and cost curves are easily determined but the reality is that we typically know only a few points of observation along each curve before 'conditions change', as we see in Chapter 1. Of course if a private monopolist had already established Q1 production of some product at a price P1 and a supernormal profit of sum A, we would have to believe sum A is possible, but voters might still be sceptical of subsidising a lowering of price and an increase in production to long run break even because

    a) conditions might change, and another firm might emerge with another product demanding that we subsidise them. We would be back to point 1) above for both firms, that voters doubt the cost curves really slope down for either firm as steeply as alleged, and have little idea at all of the elasticity of the demand curves, and therefore the extra consumer surplus generated (in the absence of externalities);

    b) our general distrust of monopolies, and the idea of reinforcing a private monopoly position seems bizarre or downright wrong – unless the monopolist is publicly owned; but even then we have a wider worry:

    c) we doubt that any subsidised firm will remain efficient.

Neo-classical comparative statics does try to address the welfare effects of inefficiency.

Where monopoly creates inefficiency

It is widely believed by voters, businesspeople, and economists alike that the absence of competition leads the managers and employees of a monopoly to lead a quiet, comfortable, but inefficient, life, with costs higher than they could be. Figure 147 shows this for the simplest case, when long run unit costs are flat:

Figure 147: Welfare losses when monopoly leads to inefficiency

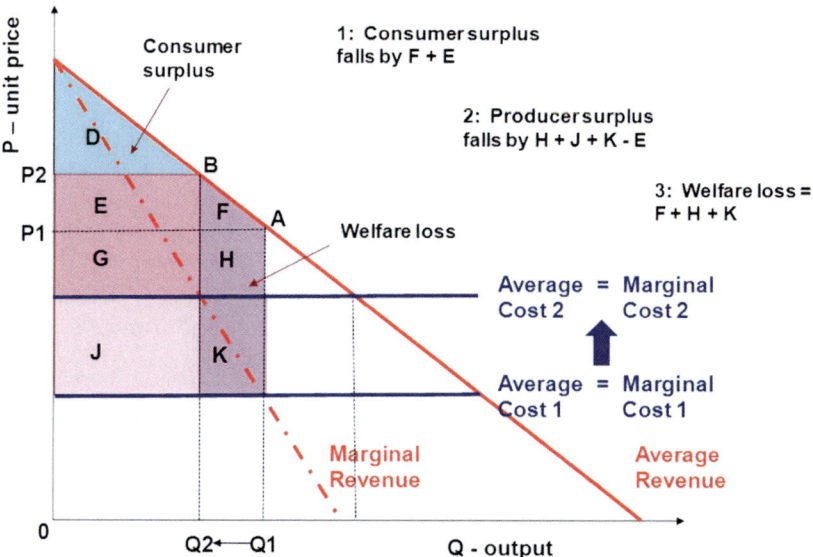

The hypothesis is that a firm in a competitive industry has to produce efficiently at point A, with a consumer surplus equal to the areas D + E + F, and a producer surplus of G + H + J + K, but if the firm achieves a monopoly it becomes sclerotic and inefficient, so its costs rise from AC1 to AC2. This means the optimal production volume falls from Q1 to Q2, production moves from A to B, price rises from P1 to P2, consumer surplus falls to just the triangle D, and producer surplus falls to the rectangles E + G.

So consumer surplus has fallen by E + F, producer surplus has fallen by H + J + K − E, the sum J goes to inefficient factors of production, including management and employees, while the welfare loss is the familiar trapezoid-shaped shaded area, F + H + K.

Realism of theoretical welfare losses

The usual textbook answer
How realistic are these welfare losses when there are real world natural monopolies such as energy and water grids? Given that heavy network utilities consist of solid engineering grids held together by welds, steel bolts, nuts, and concrete, with real engineers to maintain them, and that this is an applied economics textbook, we may ask if these theoretical welfare losses are ever actually applied in the real world.

One textbook answer is that this kind of thinking is fundamental to the establishment of mainstream competition regulators across the rich world. For instance, if you examine the websites of the US Department of Justice's Antitrust Division or the UK's Competition and Markets Authority you will find hundreds of references to welfare losses and attempts to model or remedy them. Clearly the concepts permeate professional competition thinking. But do the professionals really use pure neoclassical economic thinking?

An alternative view
I have already argued that monopolies are surprisingly common, and if they were privately owned but un-regulated they would almost certainly be in a position to set prices a long way from long run marginal cost. Provided the demand curve is above the cost curve, it could well be realistic for a private monopolist to produce at a quantity where marginal cost roughly equals marginal revenue, so maximising profits, depending, of course, on the height of entry barriers and the cross-price elasticities of the closest substitutes. Thus, the monopoly position looks realistic.

So if we grant that the monopoly position is realistic, and assume that a government with a general hands-off approach to business will encounter some industries like this, we should ask "Do real democratic societies aim to win neoclassical welfare gains from the competitive position?" Do societies *attempt* to achieve these Pareto improvements in welfare, and do they actually achieve them? Let us consider three real examples.

The global monopoly
Consider a real non-utility monopoly, like Microsoft's monopoly of its Office suite of applications. Let us also assume, quite reasonably, that no corruption and no externalities are involved. Microsoft has a monopoly of something it invented or legally acquired, periodically re-invents its product to prevent technological obsolescence and renew its intellectual copyright, and can charge what it likes. The product has a few rivals, but none is nearly so well known or widely used. Why should Microsoft not be in the PMQM position of Figure 145 or the P1Q1 position of Figure 146, depending on whether its costs are flat or falling? There may be an element of entry-deterring (lowering) in Microsoft's pricing strategy, but if so this would be a consumer surplus gain, and overall each year's financial numbers tell us the company makes a vast profit on Office. Indeed, why should it not? It's a huge commercial success story.

The relevant question, then, is how realistic would it be for the world's governments to pay Microsoft a huge sum, A, to lower its prices to equal Microsoft's long run average cost of producing, distributing and supporting Office? Well we did not see that happening on planet Earth in the twentieth century, and there are no signs of it in the twenty first. And, as for lowering costs even further, to P3Q3 in Figure 146, that is just a complete fantasy.

Global economies of scale
Alternatively, supporters of welfare loss theory might argue that in the last decade world governments have managed to persuade global drug companies to sell patented drugs to poorer countries at prices well below profit-maximising levels, and that this is a demonstration of society achieving such a welfare gain. However, there are major externalities to improving the health of poor people with pharmaceutical drugs, and the issue was presented to the global public as an issue of charity to the world's poorest countries (a distinctly non-economic sentiment), rather than greater consumer surplus. We also note that there was no massive payment (or tax break) to the drug companies of the forgone producer surplus, rectangle A. The drug companies simply had to swallow the loss of profit – i.e. it all went to consumer surplus – albeit to some of the least well-off people on the planet, who needed it most. So, in sum, it was a fine act of global charity, or global externality internalisation, but not a consumer-surplus-based welfare gain.

Local economies of scale
As a final example of a routine good with continual economies of scale, *consider the economics of printing the hard copy of this textbook.* My publisher has a monopoly of publishing this book and there do not seem to be many close substitutes in the market at present. Having run a large book printing company, I can tell you what any printer or publisher in the world knows, namely that average printing costs decrease continually the longer the print run (the more books you print in one go), and since the other costs of writing, editing, publishing, and marketing a textbook are largely fixed, we can be certain that average and marginal book publishing costs decrease almost without limit. This

is widely known in the publishing industry. It also seems likely that there is some price elasticity in the demand curve for textbooks of this type: cutting the price will almost definitely increase the quantity sold.

Figure 146 therefore, should accurately reflect the economics of publishing a profitable textbook. Now assume no significant externalities from this textbook: people read it for their own enjoyment (Ha!) or material advancement (let's hope so, or you and I have been wasting our time) and there is at most only an insignificant gain to society at large from you reading this book (sorry to be brutally honest). Seems reasonable, doesn't it? Neo-classical economists are saying that to achieve efficiency of resource allocation across the global economy, this textbook should be subsidised by global governments first to the break-even point P2Q2, and then beyond to P3Q3, when the wholesale price has fallen to the long run marginal cost of printing this book, which is basically the unit cost of a reprint in a reasonable-sized batch. In other words, first the publisher should be paid a block of supernormal profit, sum A, to lower the price to the break-even price P2, and then he should receive a significant subsidy per book to lower the wholesale price to the reprint unit cost.

"Dream on, you ivory-towered economists!" my publisher would say. And he's quite right. You, I, and the publisher all know there is something major missing from this analysis.

Index

A

Access pricing 30
Active customers 90, 91, 95, 96, 97, 101, 112, 131, 325,
Aigner 205, 206, 207
Aliens 115
Allocative efficiency 169, 171, 172, 173, 174, 255, 391, 415
Amtrack 372
Argentina 274, 278, 279, 280, 304, 348, 394
Ayer, AJ 197

B

Battle for reach 102, 131
Battle for market share 102, 131
Bayesian approaches 198
Beesley, Michael iv, 264
British Gas 50, 51, 259, 260, 289, 290, 318, 319, 320, 321, 322, 323, 324, 325
Business dynamics model 94, 95
Byatt, Ian iv, 264, 270, 271, 272, 273, 338, 339, 340

C

California 49, 152, 228, 243, 274, 286, 291-301, 312, 313, 318, 346, 394, 408
Canals vi, vii, 16, 30, 79, 84, 85, 95, 104, 105, 117, 227, 356, 362, 406
Capex 262
Cave, Martin 353
Caves, Christensen and Diewert 222
CEGB 52, 53, 285, 286
Chile 256, 274, 275, 278, 279, 280, 318, 343-345, 350, 355, 356, 359-362, 373, 392, 394, 395
City Gates 11, 143, 149
Coca-Cola 40, 43, 409
Coelli xxviii, 53, 166, 211, 219, 396
Colonel Stephens 79, 80, 81, 85
COLS, Corrected Ordinary Least Squares 178, 182
Commodity [good] 24, 25, 27, 29, 100, 105, 106, 113, 120, 142, 288, 290, 310, 313, 350, 352, 360, 366, 395, 408, 410
Common carriage 92
Cost drivers 38, 39, 42, 58, 147, 179, 203, 262, 391
Cost leadership 114
Cost of Service regulation 247, 256, 318

D

DEA 171, 182-187, 191, 193, 200, 202-205, 213, 214, 218, 219, 222, 223
Differentiated good 408
Differentiation strategy 106, 114
Dolly Parton vi
Duopoly 1, 87, 91, 93, 101, 102, 107, 111, 123, 124, 126, 288, 305, 314, 404
Dynamic pricing 75

E

Economies of scale vii, 6, 34, 36, 40, 47-52, 54-57, 74, 118, 127-129, 137, 139, 145, 146, 179, 218, 219, 227, 232, 288, 304, 325, 332, 340, 350, 413-415, 418
Economies of scope 39-42, 44, 46, 48, 52, 53, 218
Electricity distribution 9, 46, 48-50, 138, 245, 260, 273, 281, 287
Electricity transmission 1, 41, 45, 49, 61, 219, 220, 255, 269, 326
ENDESA 279
Entry barriers 1, 60, 74, 106, 113, 132, 173, 193, 284, 288, 302, 407, 417
Enron 286, 292, 294-299
ERCOT 291-293, 304
Exogenous cost drivers 39, 58, 147, 179, 203, 206

F

Fare 213, 222, 379, 382-385
Farrell iv, 184-187, 222
First Mover Advantage 103, 107, 114, 117, 129, 232, 233
Friedman, Milton 122, 197
Frontier Economics xxviii, 127

G

Gas mains 11
General Pinochet 279, 318
Geographical differentiation 106
Gold plating 246, 256, 265
Grant 48, 66, 70, 71, 94, 106, 112, 227, 243, 397, 408, 417

I

IBM xxvii, 240, 242
Ideal index 221
ISO, Independent System Operator 277, 291, 295-298, 301-304
Istanbul 163, 270, 271
Investment bubble 109-111

J

Joskow, Paul 301

K

Kant, Immanuel 196
Kay, John xxvii, 39, 242,
Kuiper belt 190

L

Laffont and Tirole 248, 267
Liebenstein, Harvey iv, 172, 173
Littlechild, Stephen iv, x, xxviii, 256-266, 273, 287, 288, 291, 301, 303, 304, 340
Logical positivism 197
Lumpy investment 76, 111

M

Maintenance 36, 38, 42, 44-46, 60, 68, 113, 119, 137, 139, 148, 154, 167-169, 190, 234, 235, 237, 239, 297, 317, 336, 345, 366, 367, 373, 374, 376, 378, 382-384, 387
Malmquist 213-219, 221-223, 391
Marshall, Alfred 140, 172, 190, 242, 397, 398, 404
Meeusen 205-207
MFP, Multilateral Factor Productivity 211
Millau viaduct 64, 66
Mill, JS 35, 127, 136, 139, 330
Mining 26, 63, 106, 356
Monopsony 143, 260, 319, 406
Moorsteen 211, 221, 222

N

National Grid xxviii, 8, 43, 51, 260, 283, 285, 325,
National Power 284-286, 288, 305
Natural monopoly 18, 36, 51, 127-129, 131, 132, 290, 330
NERA 289,
NETA 283, 285, 291
Nord Pool 274-277
Normative economics 194, 197, 198

O

Ofcom 90-101, 115-118
Ofgem (Office of Gas and Electricity Markets) 289-291
Ofwat xxviii, 82, 83, 135, 161, 178, 204, 220, 334, 337-342
Oort cloud 190
Opex 262, 263, 336
ORR (Office of Rail and Road) 377, 379-384
Oxera 51

P

Penetration rate 91, 394,
Pepsi 40, 43, 408
Pinochet, General 279, 318
PJM 277, 304,
Plant economies 52, 54, 145, 146, 179, 332
Pogo stick 67
Pont du Gard 65, 66, 270, 271
Popper, Karl 197
Positive economics 197, 198, 202
Positively skewed [distribution] 109, 207, 218
Powergen 285, 286, 288, 305
Pressure Reduction Station 11
Pretend to provide a service 13
Principal Agent theory 241 - 243
Proactive maintenance 137, 336
Productive efficiency 169, 173, 185, 211

R

Rate of return regulation 251, 256, 261, 264, 265, 318, 370, 394
Reached customers 102
Reactive maintenance 38, 44-46, 137, 139, 336
Reagan, Ronald 317, 318
Regulatory capture 251
Resources and Capabilities 71, 94, 95, 251
Resource Based View 39, 74, 94, 96
River Thames 18, 159, 165
RPI-X 257, 258, 261, 263-266, 340

S

Samuelson, Paul 197
Scooping the market 98, 100
Sequence model 73, 84, 117, 120, 121, 127, 129, 131, 132, 174
Sequential entry 87, 88, 111, 114
Sequential model vi, x, 59, 67, 68, 73, 240, 265, 391, 392
Severn, Trent xxvii, 333
Sewage treatment 13, 14, 28, 29, 143-145, 153-155, 157-159, 161-165, 219, 232, 234, 260, 332, 333, 338, 345, 348, 354, 392
Sewerage 27-29, 43, 46, 51, 53, 84, 95, 117, 149, 157, 160-162, 164, 165, 219, 245, 333, 336, 339, 345, 348
Sewers vii, 13, 14, 46, 64, 91, 120, 153-155, 157, 161-164, 232, 332, 338
Shleifer, Andrei 252-254, 256, 258, 261, 265, 267, 273, 344, 392
Simultaneous entry 85, 87, 101, 111-113
SOTA (State Of The Art) frontier 189-191, 193, 266
Stochastic frontiers 205-210, 218, 219, 391

Strategy Dynamics xxviii, 94, 101
Stuck in the middle 114
Sub-station 8, 11, 143, 149
Sunk costs 14, 16, 34, 59, 60, 62-64, 66, 71-75, 77-80, 84-86, 90, 97, 102, 103, 106-109, 111-121, 126-132, 231, 232, 245, 254, 266, 270, 301, 319, 328, 330, 331, 355, 362, 380, 384, 387, 391, 403
Sunshine regulation 78, 369, 370
Switching cost 85, 97, 99, 102, 103, 107, 108, 112, 131, 385
Sysdea 97, 100
Systems model x, 94, 96, 97, 100, 101, 131

T

Technical efficiency – see productive efficiency 169, 173, 185, 211
Texas 291-293, 300, 304, 309, 394
Thames Water xxvii
Thatcher, Margaret 256, 259, 260, 274, 278, 318, 320, 334, 345, 377, 378, 389, 394, 400
Tornqvist 221
Turvey, Ralph iv, 132, 133, 330
Twin-investor model [or theory] 111

U

United Utilities (see North West Water) 161
Unreached customers 102

W

Wastewater vii, 8, 13, 14, 18, 27, 28, 41, 42, 83, 91, 100, 121, 135, 143-143, 152-155, 157, 159, 161, 164, 165, 175, 179, 232, 260, 261, 269, 331-334, 336, 338, 340, 342, 343, 344, 348-350, 353, 354, 392, 395
Water mains 12, 149-151
Water treatment 12, 15, 63, 143-146, 156, 157, 175-177, 179, 232, 234, 270, 332, 338, 392

X

X-efficiency = see productive efficiency 169, 173, 185, 211

Y

Yardstick regulation 252, 254, 268, 325, 339, 341, 392

Z

Zero-based budget 254